# AGING

# AGING

## Volume II

### Internet — *You're Only Old Once!*
### Index

*Editor*
**Pamela Roberts, Ph.D.**
California State University, Long Beach

*Project Editor*
**Tracy Irons-Georges**

SALEM PRESS, INC.
Pasadena, California     Hackensack, New Jersey

*Editor in Chief:* Dawn P. Dawson
*Copy Editor:* Douglas Long
*Research Supervisor:* Jeffry Jensen
*Acquisitions/Photograph Editor:* Mark Rehn
*Production Editor:* Joyce I. Buchea

*Project Editor:* Tracy Irons-Georges
*Assistant Editor:* Andrea E. Miller
*Research Assistant:* Jun Ohnuki
*Assistant Photograph Editor:* Philip Bader
*Layout:* William Zimmerman

### Note to Readers

The medical material presented in *Aging* is intended for broad informational and educational purposes. Readers who suspect that they suffer from any of the physical or psychological disorders, diseases, or conditions described in this set should contact a physician without delay; this work should not be used as a substitute for professional diagnosis or treatment. This set is not to be considered definitive on the medical topics covered, and readers should remember that the field of health care is characterized by a diversity of opinions and constant expansion in knowledge and understanding.

### Library of Congress Cataloging-in-Publication Data

Aging / editor, Pamela Roberts.
    p. cm.
    Includes bibliographical references and index.
    ISBN 0-89356-265-3 (set : alk. paper) — ISBN 0-89356-266-1 (v. 1 : alk. paper) —
    ISBN 0-89356-267-x (v. 2 : alk. paper)
    1. Aged—Encyclopedias. 2. Aging—Encyclopedias. I. Roberts, Pamela, 1952-

HQ1061 .A42453 2000
305.26'03—dc21
                                                99-088984

First Printing

PRINTED IN THE UNITED STATES OF AMERICA

# CONTENTS

# ALPHABETICAL LIST OF ENTRIES

# AGING

# INTERNET

**RELEVANT ISSUES:** Culture

**SIGNIFICANCE:** With the advent of the Internet, the general public has gained greater access to information on aging and age-related services, as well as to increased opportunities for communication

As the Internet has become more accessible and on-line information more comprehensive, the value of computers to midlife and older adults has increased dramatically. Although the Internet includes services and communication networks for all age groups, it may be most beneficial to the aged, particularly when declines in physical health and shrinking social networks diminish opportunities for intellectual stimulation and communication with others. However, surveys in early 1999 indicated that only 5 percent of Internet users were aged sixty-five or older. Consequently, such organizations as SeniorNet have established special computer literacy courses for older adults. In addition, the American Association of Retired Persons (AARP) regularly sponsors Internet workshops, provides Internet discounts, and hosts on-line chat groups about computer technology for its members.

Internet resources on aging can be categorized into four basic types: research and education; government programs and information; other information, goods, and services; and communication and support networks.

## RESEARCH, EDUCATION, AND GOVERNMENT SITES

Most funding agencies, research institutes, educational institutions, and professional societies have Web sites displaying their programs on aging.

*Members of the Silver Stringers computer group bring up their Web site at the Milano Senior Center in Melrose, Massachusetts.* (AP Photo/Lisa Poole)

Information on current aging research can be easily accessed through the Web sites of professional organizations, such as the Gerontological Society of America and the American Society on Aging, or through government sites, such as the National Institute on Aging. Medical research reports can be found on the National Library of Medicine's Web site. Research on aging can also be explored through on-line libraries, such as the GeroWeb Virtual Library on Aging (sponsored by Wayne State University), or on-line catalogs of existing libraries, such as the Andrus Gerontology Library at the University of Southern California.

The most extensive and reliable Web sites are maintained by the American government; the most comprehensive is that of the Administration on Aging (AoA). The AoA regularly updates fact sheets on aging legislation and on programs that cover age discrimination, Alzheimer's disease, elder abuse, senior centers, nutrition programs, and other issues. Divisions of the AoA also produce Web pages on more specific topics, including moving and retirement decisions, guides for home safety and home modification, and various pages on exercise, nutrition, and health. Typically, AoA Web pages are thorough and easy to read. For example, one publication discusses the potential for memory loss with age, provides specific exercises to combat memory loss, and attempts to reduce the fear that normal memory changes can bring. In addition to providing access to AoA publications, the AoA Web site is linked to most government Web pages on aging. Thus, one can access Social Security, Medicare, and national volunteer programs through links on the AoA Web site.

## INFORMATION, GOODS, AND SERVICES

Other than the AoA, the Web site with the most comprehensive links to aging information, goods, and services is run by the AARP. Web pages on health, housing, finances, law, leisure, education, government programs, and research on aging are linked to the AARP Web site. In addition, AARP publications and programs (including monthly computer articles and on-line chat rooms) can be accessed through the AARP Web site.

Most large health organizations are on-line; Web sites are sponsored by the American Heart Association, the American Cancer Society, the National Parkinson Foundation, the Arthritis Foundation, the Alzheimer's Association, and other groups. The Alzheimer's Association Web site is typical, presenting facts about Alzheimer's disease and providing Web pages for patients about their diagnoses, what they might be feeling, and planning for the future. In addition, information on frequently needed services and updates on treatment and research (including how to volunteer for research trials) are posted. Finally, links to support groups for Alzheimer's patients and their caretakers are provided.

Web sites that contain general health information are maintained by universities, aging organizations, and the government. For example, Tufts University sponsors Nutrition Navigator, a guide to nutrition Web sites with a monthly newsletter on nutrition and health. Although the Web page is not age-specific, many links are for seniors, and the newsletter frequently focuses on senior health. The American Council on Exercise maintains a series of Web pages called Fit Facts, which discusses the relationship of exercise to such conditions as arthritis, heart disease, and diabetes. Health information of specific concern to middle-aged and older adults is published by the AoA, including Web pages on foot care, changes in eyesight, hearing problems, hormone replacement therapy, high blood pressure, and prescription medications. More information on health issues is provided by activist organizations, such as the National Council on the Aging and the National Council of Senior Citizens, which provide updates on legislation affecting senior health and promote senior input in the legislative process. Finally, the Internet hosts senior health clubs, which specialize in general fitness as well as specific sports and hobbies.

Housing is another topic for which there are many aging-related Web sites. One such site, sponsored by the American Association of Homes and Services for the Aging, provides guidelines for choosing various housing options (including roommate programs, senior housing facilities, continuing care communities, assisted living, and nursing homes) and links to housing programs listed by location. In addition, services that allow the elderly to remain in their homes longer, such as adult day care and home modification programs, have Web sites managed by the National

Adult Day Services Association and the Consumer Product Safety Commission.

A broad array of Web sites are devoted to aging information and services, which include everything from senior joke pages to sites on retirement planning and senior law. One education site is run by Elderhostel, whose on-line catalogs describe varied senior education opportunities, including programs to study Emily Dickinson's poetry in the New Hampshire mountains and to conduct field research on endangered dolphins in Belize. National volunteer organizations, such as the Service Corps of Retired Executives (SCORE), the Foster Grandparents Program, and America Reads, have their own Web sites, as do many local volunteer programs.

While there are a plethora of Web sites on aging-related topics, midlife and older adults use the Internet most often for functions that are not age-specific; for example, adults of all ages listen to radio programs, read commentaries, and plan vacations with Internet services. Similarly, as on-line monetary transactions become safer and more accessible, adults of all ages have begun shopping, banking, and paying their bills on the Internet. As this trend continues, Internet services may become essential to individuals with health problems and limited mobility.

### COMMUNICATION AND SUPPORT NETWORKS

Like the telephone, electronic mail (e-mail) allows for quick communication without leaving home, enhancing the ties of those who cannot visit regularly because of distance or disability. However, e-mail has several advantages over telephone communication: Charges are not related to the distance between the sender and recipient, the number of messages, message length, or the time of day messages are sent. In addition, e-mail communication is available to the hard of hearing, who often avoid telephone conversations. Thus, e-mail access may increase communication between the low-income elderly and their distant loved ones and provide better opportunities for communication to the hearing impaired.

Apart from e-mail, there are a variety of opportunities for communication on the Internet. On-line senior clubs are plentiful and cover a wide variety of topics, including gardening, skiing, bridge, gay and lesbian issues, and genealogy. Many Internet clubs have on-line chat rooms (in which messages are sent back and forth during the same time period), as well as message boards (where one leaves a message and others can respond at any time). Message boards also are hosted by multipurpose aging Web sites; for example, the message board topics at Seniors-site include grandparenting, genealogy, caregiving, medical insurance, housing, legal issues, prescription drugs, pets, widowhood, and Alzheimer's disease.

There are many support organizations on-line; for example, WidowNet is a service for bereaved spouses that includes advice, message boards, discussion forums, book recommendations, and links to services needed by the widowed, such as grief sites, memorial sites, financial services, and support groups. At the Worldwide Sharing Web site, stories of caring for Alzheimer's patients are posted by caregivers who encourage those in similar circumstances to contact them for support and dialogue. Other support groups are run by health organizations, many of which sponsor both on-line support and support group meetings through their various chapters.

Despite its promise, the Internet also has its drawbacks. Because the Internet is unregulated, it is often difficult to evaluate the accuracy of information found on Web pages. Those who use the Internet should be mindful of the source of any information they have attained there. The best Web sites are signed and note the goals and credentials of the sponsors. Generally, Web pages sponsored by government agencies (which contain the letters "gov"), educational institutions (ending with the letters "edu"), and well-known organizations are considered the most reliable. In addition to providing misinformation, the Internet is also a potential site for fraud. In 1996, the National Consumers League launched the Internet Fraud Watch, a Web site that provides tips for using the Internet, fraud alerts, and methods for reporting suspected fraud.

*—Pamela Roberts*

*See also* Advocacy; Alzheimer's Association; American Association of Retired Persons (AARP); American Society on Aging; Communication; Fraud against the elderly; Health care; Housing; National Council of Senior Citizens; National Council on the Aging; National Institute on Aging; Nutrition; Social ties; Volunteering.

**FOR FURTHER INFORMATION:**

Administration on Aging. http://www.aoa.dhhs.gov:80/.

American Association of Retired Persons. http://www.aarp.org.

Berger, Sandy. *How to Have a Meaningful Relationship with Your Computer.* Fairfield, Iowa: Sunstar, 1997.

Guide to Internet Resources Related to Aging. http://www.aarp.org/cyber/guide1.htm/.

Hegle, Kris Ann. "What Is Your User Type?" *Modern Maturity* 41, no. 6 (November/December, 1998).

National Institute on Aging. http://www.nih.gov/nia/.

National Library of Medicine. http://www.nlm.nih.gov/databases/freemedl.html.

Post, Joyce A. "Internet Resources on Aging." *Generations* 21, no. 3 (Fall, 1997).

_____. "Internet Resources on Aging: Geriatrics, Gerontological Nursing, and Related Topics." *Gerontologist* 37, no. 2 (April, 1997).

_____. "Internet Resources on Aging: Increasing Options and Human Factors." *Gerontologist* 37, no. 1 (February, 1997).

_____. "Internet Resources on Aging: Parts of the Internet." *Gerontologist* 36, no. 2 (April, 1996).

_____. "Internet Resources on Aging: Research." *Gerontologist* 36, no. 3 (June, 1996).

_____. "Internet Resources on Aging: Seniors on the Net." *Gerontologist* 36, no. 5 (October, 1996).

_____. "Internet Resources on Aging: Ten Top Web Sites." *Gerontologist* 36, no. 6 (December, 1996).

Stanek, William R. *Learn the Internet in a Weekend.* Rocklin, Calif.: Prima, 1997.

Williams, Robin. *The Little iMac Book.* Berkeley, Calif.: Peachpit Press, 1998.

**IRAs.** *See* **INDIVIDUAL RETIREMENT ACCOUNTS (IRAs).**

## JEWISH SERVICES FOR THE ELDERLY

**RELEVANT ISSUES:** Culture, demographics, religion

**SIGNIFICANCE:** Providing support and service for the elderly within the context of the Jewish religion has become an increasingly important component in the care of an aging population

Caring for the elderly is considered among the most important components of *tzedakah*, in literal context meaning an obligation within the Jewish religion. Services are provided not only to help the elderly survive but also to promote independence and maintenance of health in their senior years. There are few formal national organizations whose sole purpose is providing service for the elderly. Instead, most regions with a significant Jewish population provide programs under one of two umbrella organizations: the Jewish Community Center (JCC), providing mainly social programs, and Jewish Family Services, which provides a wide variety of counseling, care, and management programs.

The JCC generally provides a means for seniors to interact. It is often the site of lectures, informal academic courses, free films, and social gatherings. Jewish Family Services generally offers more comprehensive programming to aid the elderly in facing the challenges of aging. It provides support groups, advice in long-term care or planning, and outreach and elderlink programs. If necessary, the organization may provide home-care management, such as help with cleaning or shopping. Programs may include emergency assistance, emergency or periodic transportation, and day-to-day management, such as paying bills, depositing checks, or helping to decipher medical claims or solve problems. Help in contacting physicians if illness develops is also provided.

The JCC is often associated with the local synagogues, providing programs for a range of demographic categories, such as teenagers, local college students, and even infants. Officers are either elected or appointed by a governing board. In contrast, Jewish Family Services is generally overseen by geriatric professionals, whose purpose and training is in the care of the aged.

—*Richard Adler*

**See also** Cultural views of aging; Home services; Religion; Social ties.

## "JILTING OF GRANNY WEATHERALL, THE"

**AUTHOR:** Katherine Anne Porter

**DATE:** Published in 1930 in the collection *Flowering Judas*

**RELEVANT ISSUES:** Death, family, marriage and dating, religion

**SIGNIFICANCE:** This short story presents the universal themes that all people consider as they face death

At the age of eighty, Granny Weatherall, the central character of Katherine Anne Porter's short story "The Jilting of Granny Weatherall," had faced all of life's challenges except one, death. As she lay in her bed, on the eve of this final challenge, she considered all the things that her life had meant and what the costs has been. Throughout her life, she had served God; at the moment of death, she hoped for a sign from Him of what was to be, but no sign came.

God's failure to offer a sign was especially bitter to Granny Weatherall because by her bed stood God's emissary, her own priest. For the second time in her life, Granny Weatherall found herself in the presence of a priest without a bridegroom. As a young woman, she had been jilted by George, whom she had refused to think about for years. Now, at the moment of her death, the thought of George returned to her; she would have liked to have made him believe his betrayal had not mattered. She wanted George to know that although he had left her at the altar, she still had a good husband, a family, and a nice house. Unfortunately, at that moment, she also had to admit that George's betrayal had cost her a part of her soul. God offered no sign that that part of her soul would be returned to her; for this reason, Granny Weatherall felt a final betrayal. She was twice jilted.

The story shows the aged that it is normal to tally up one's triumphs and tragedies when contemplating the end of life. It also reveals that it is human to doubt God and to blame Him for failing to provide an easy answer to prayers, requests, and hopes.

—*Annita Marie Ward*

**See also** Death and dying; Literature; Religion.

## JOB LOSS

**RELEVANT ISSUES:** Economics, work

**SIGNIFICANCE:** During the final decades of the

twentieth century, increasing numbers of older workers found themselves experiencing job loss as a result of corporate downsizing, technological displacement, and occasional blatant age discrimination

Americans once believed that hard work and loyalty to a company would be rewarded with job security. By the 1990's, however, the volatility of a global economy caused many workers in their forties and fifties to become painfully aware that job loss can happen to anyone, regardless of personal effort. Technological displacement, corporate downsizing, and factory closings can all be factors in job loss, particularly for the older worker.

### AGE DISCRIMINATION AS A FACTOR IN JOB LOSS

Age discrimination in employment has been illegal in the United States since 1967, when Congress passed the Age Discrimination in Employment Act. With a few exceptions, such as airline pilots, the act forbids employers to refuse to hire, pass over for promotion, or elect to terminate a worker based solely on age if that person is over the age of forty. The fact that age discrimination is illegal does not mean, however, that it rarely occurs. Although attorneys specializing in employment law have long counseled firms to proceed cautiously when implementing plans for a "reduction in force" (RIF) as the expense of fighting an age discrimination lawsuit in court can negate any savings realized in the original reduction of the labor force, the 1980's and 1990's witnessed increasing numbers of complaints from alleged victims. By 1998, in fact, a poll conducted jointly by the Society for Human Resource Management and the American Association of Retired Persons (AARP) indicated that one out of every five employers surveyed had been subjected to age discrimination complaints filed by current or former employees.

If this is true, then age discrimination in employment presents a larger problem for American workers than the average person realizes. While sexual harassment and affirmative action cases have garnered headlines, job loss resulting from age discrimination appears to have been quietly growing. Despite the overall robust economy in the 1990's, long-term job security for individual workers became harder to attain. In a time of rapid technological change and numerous corporate

mergers, job loss became common. Younger workers are warned not to expect to remain with a single employer until they reach retirement age, as the twenty-, thirty-, or even forty-year sinecures their parents enjoyed no longer exist. Even corporations such as International Business Machines (IBM) and American Telephone and Telegraph Company (AT&T), both once famed for providing lifetime employment, downsized in the 1980's and 1990's.

For younger workers, the insecurities of the labor market may be disconcerting, but for older workers the uncertainties can be devastating. Older workers may find themselves in an untenable situation: vulnerable to RIFs because of their age, unable to find new employment that pays wages comparable to their old jobs, and psychologically traumatized by the loss of careers in which they had invested many years of their lives and had expected to remain until retirement.

Analysts have noted the effects of an increasingly globalized, high-tech economy on workers in industrialized nations. Technological displacement and RIFs, or downsizing, are generally cited as the inevitable price of remaining competitive in a fast-paced economic climate. Businesses have automated their production processes and thinned levels of management in attempts to reduce labor costs as much as possible. Technological displacement refers to jobs being lost when machinery or processes that reduce labor requirements are introduced into the workplace, or when new equipment requires skills that existing workers do not possess or are unable to master. Welding robots on automobile assembly lines, for example, eliminated numerous jobs while at the same time increasing the pace of work for the remaining workers. In an office setting, clerical workers in the 1980's who were unable to learn computer skills experienced technological displacement as typists became word-processing operators. By the 1990's in the United States, technological displacement of existing employees had become less of an issue than the mismatch between unemployed workers and the availability of technical training.

In addition, factories that are traditionally labor-intensive and thus not easily automated nor downsized, such as the garment trades, closed production facilities in the United States and Europe and moved to less-industrialized nations. Traditional minimal-skill, entry-level positions disappeared as corporations relocated factories to developing nations, where labor costs are low and government oversight and regulations are loose or nonexistent.

A common assumption is that the workers most affected by globalization are the young. Not only are the numbers of available entry-level positions reduced, but traditionally younger workers have been the first to be let go when a business thins its workforce. Younger workers are generally the most recent hires, and, as an old saying puts it, "Last hired, first fired." Older workers, the workers who presumably had years of experience within an occupation, perceived their positions as protected both by their seniority and by their expertise. Unfortunately for the older worker, this no longer holds true. Instead of perceiving expertise, too many employers may look at older workers and see stale ideas and obsolete skills.

### DOWNSIZING

In a competitive economy, corporations hoping to improve their bottom line often resort to "downsizing," or terminating significant numbers of employees. In addition to being perceived as being out of date in their thinking or job skills, older employees are often disproportionately represented among downsized workers because they are more likely to have been in the higher-salary brackets at a firm. The longer a person works at a job, whether it is as a janitor or as a systems analyst, the higher that worker's wages will be in comparison to other workers within the firm. Occasional merit raises, cost-of-living adjustments, and annual step raises all will have combined to boost the older worker with years of longevity with an employer well above the wages paid to entry-level employees.

Corporations once prized these older workers and viewed junior employees as expendable. Older workers were seen as more productive because of their years of experience. Some recent productivity studies, however, suggest that differences in productivity are negligible between a worker with twenty years of experience at a task and one with five years of experience. Thus, from the viewpoint of management, it seems logical to let go midlevel personnel at the higher end of the pay scale than to terminate younger workers still

earning entry-level wages. Productivity will not suffer significantly, and considerable savings in labor costs may be realized. This rationalization assumes, however, that terminating older, more senior workers will not have an impact on productivity in other ways, such as through diminished workplace morale or loss of employee loyalty.

In the early 1990's, downsizing on a dramatic scale became a popular tool employed by corporations hoping to convince investors that a firm was about to improve its profit margins. In a widely publicized example, AT&T terminated forty thousand employees in one year. Many of the furloughed employees had been with the company for their entire working lives. By the late 1990's, economists began to recognize that corporate downsizing was not the universal panacea they had hailed it as being only a few years before. Cutting labor force costs might provide a brief boost in profits, but the effect often proved short term as productivity suffered from the sudden shortage of experienced workers. The news media paid less attention to the fact that AT&T later rehired many of its terminated workers, so that the overall net job loss for the corporation proved to be considerably less than the well-publicized forty thousand initially reported. For the rehired workers, however, being rehired often meant accepting lower wages and a loss of all previously accrued seniority with the corporation. This is a common tactic in downsizing: Workers in high-wage categories are terminated, jobs are reclassified, and new workers are hired to perform the same tasks but at lower wages.

The point at which a worker begins to be seen as "too old" can vary considerably from industry to industry. There have always been occupations in which the conditions of work tended to push workers out at a comparatively young age. Work that is extremely physical or hazardous, such as some construction jobs or fire fighting, often results in workers being forced to retire or change careers in their thirties or forties as a result of work-related physical disabilities. While job loss because of age discrimination is usually associated with workers in their forties or fifties, in some high-tech industries the age at which one becomes unacceptably old has been creeping steadily downward. Software engineers and computer programmers, for example, may discover that employers consider their skills obsolete less than a decade after they enter the field.

Ironically, in the late 1990's, even as employers in high-tech firms complained that the lack of skilled workers to deal with the so-called millennium bug or Y2K problem threatened productivity, former computer programmers who had been terminated years before when their skills were declared obsolete found themselves back in demand and in a position to command lucrative consulting fees. This was a rare exception to the general rule within the computer industry that age is a handicap.

## THE EFFECTS OF JOB LOSS

Prospects often are bleak for older workers who have been downsized. It is unlikely that these workers will find new employment at wages comparable to their previous positions, and they may indeed discover that it is impossible to find meaningful work at all. It is not uncommon to find classrooms at vocational or technical colleges filled with former employees of high-tech industries. Having lost their jobs as systems analysts or mechanical engineers, these workers find themselves in their forties or fifties training for service industry occupations such as automobile mechanic or plumber. Although these blue-collar occupations may pay almost as well as the professional careers the workers left behind, when a midlife career change is involuntary and dictated by job loss, the shift in perceived status can be psychologically devastating.

Psychologists have long recognized that job loss can exact a heavy toll from its victims. For most workers, a sense of identity is inextricably linked with what they do to earn a living. Even in its most benign forms, such as when an employee enjoys a "golden parachute" and is provided with a generous severance package while agreeing to take an early retirement, the affected employee may experience depression severe enough to require professional counseling. Workers experiencing job loss often turn to alcohol or drugs, or lash out at friends and family members. It is not surprising that numerous studies of the effects of joblessness have found higher rates of mental illness, suicide, alcoholism, and domestic violence among the unemployed than in the general population. In a few extreme cases, workers who lost their jobs have become mentally unstable to the point of engaging in violent acts either against the employer they believe wronged them or against society as a whole.

## LEGAL REDRESS

Some workers seeking redress through litigation have met with success in the courts. Other displaced workers have been less fortunate. Federal appeals courts in Denver, Chicago, and Philadelphia rejected age discrimination claims based on employers' tendencies to terminate higher-salaried employees while downsizing.

The prevalence of age discrimination can vary from occupation to occupation, in addition to being affected by factors such as gender and ethnicity. Several well-publicized age discrimination in employment lawsuits, for example, were filed by women who alleged that they lost their jobs as television news anchorpersons because they no longer projected a youthful image while older men in similar positions were allowed to age naturally. Age discrimination in the mass media is not limited to women, however, as at least one male television reporter sued successfully for compensatory damages after being unlawfully terminated. In July, 1996, an appeals court upheld a California jury's ruling that Steve Davis, a veteran television reporter, had been unlawfully terminated as a result of his age.

Workers in less glamorous industries may have a much more difficult time convincing a court their terminations violated the provision of the Age Discrimination in Employment Act. In 1993, the U.S. Supreme Court found in *Hazen Paper Co. v. Biggins* that management decisions can have a more adverse impact on older employees than on younger ones without constituting illegal age discrimination. In other words, if a company decides to eliminate all workers in certain wage categories and it happens that all the workers in those categories are older than forty, the employer can legitimately argue that the terminations were based on economic factors, not age. A corporation can claim, for example, that the intent was to eliminate all midlevel managers earning over $100,000 per year and that the correlation with particular age ranges was an unfortunate coincidence. In order to sue successfully on the basis of age discrimination, terminated workers must be able to demonstrate that they were singled out based on their age. Therefore, if a corporation claimed to be terminating all employees in a certain category but in fact retained younger workers within that category while firing older ones, then the terminated workers might have a strong case against their former employer. Unfortunately for the wronged workers, in many cases the employee may recognize intuitively that he or she is a victim of age discrimination but find it is impossible to prove.

### LONG-TERM PROSPECTS

Long-term demographic trends suggest that employment discrimination based on age may become less of a problem by the mid-twenty-first century. The birthrate in industrialized nations has been declining steadily for decades. Already, some regions of the world are experiencing negative population growth. With fewer replacement workers entering the labor force, employers will become less inclined to push current employees out the door early. Rather than forcing workers out the door in their forties or fifties, many industries may be compelled to develop incentive programs to retain employees well beyond traditional retirement ages. Many service industries that once relied heavily on youthful workers, people in their teens and early twenties, already are recruiting increasing numbers of older workers. Some of these industries, such as fast food, have been notorious for offering only minimum-wage jobs, but as the pool of potential available employees has shrunk, market forces have pushed wage scales upward. The fact that long-term demographic trends may improve the employment outlook for older workers in the labor market by 2050 provides little comfort to aging workers experiencing job loss today.

—*Nancy Farm Mannikko*

*See also* Age discrimination; Age Discrimination Act of 1975; Age Discrimination in Employment Act of 1967; Ageism; Early retirement; Employment; Executive Order 11141; Forced retirement; Income sources; *Johnson v. Mayor and City Council of Baltimore*; *Massachusetts Board of Retirement v. Murgia*; Older Workers Benefit Protection Act; Retirement; *Vance v. Bradley*.

### FOR FURTHER INFORMATION:

Bytheway, Bill. *Ageism.* New York: Taylor & Francis, 1995. Serves up a scathing indictment of discrimination against the elderly in employment and elsewhere.

Falk, Ursula A., and Gerhard Falk. *Ageism, the Aged, and Aging in America: On Being Old in an Alienated Society.* New York: Charles C Thomas, 1997. Looks at ageism and age discrimination in employment within the cultural context of a modern industrialized society.

McEwen, Evelyn, ed. *Age: The Unrecognized Discrimination.* New York: State Mutual Book, 1989. Provides a general discussion of ageism both in society and on the job.

Mowsesian, Richard. *Golden Goals, Rusted Dreams.* New York: New Horizon Press, 1986. Looks at the growing mismatch between people's expectations of economic security and societal realities.

Pellicciotti, Joseph M. *An Analysis of the Age Discrimination in Employment Act.* New York: International Personnel Management Association, 1989. Examines specific provisions of federal legislation.

Strasser, Kristofer K. *Protecting the Growing Numbers of Older Workers.* New York: J. M. Olin, 1998. A discussion of problems that older workers may encounter on the job.

## JOBS. *See* EMPLOYMENT.

## JOHNSON V. MAYOR AND CITY COUNCIL OF BALTIMORE

**DATE:** Decided on June 17, 1985

**RELEVANT ISSUES:** Economics, law, work

**SIGNIFICANCE:** This United States Supreme Court decision established that state governments may not violate the Age Discrimination in Employment Act of of 1967 even when federal government employment practices differ

Under the Age Discrimination in Employment Act (ADEA) of 1967, employers are prohibited from discriminating on the basis of age against employees who are between the ages of forty and seventy. Thus, employers may not establish a mandatory retirement age of less than seventy, except when they can show that age is a "bona fide occupational qualification" (BFOQ) for for the work. A BFOQ is granted only if the employer can show that age as such is relevant to the duties of the employee and that testable health and fitness standards are impractical. The ADEA was amended in 1974 and 1978 to bring federal employees under its coverage, but the amendments excluded federal fire-fighters, for whom the mandatory retirement age was fifty-five. The city of Baltimore attempted to establish a mandatory retirement age of less than seventy for its own firefighters. Baltimore argued that the federal mandatory retirement practices had established a general BFOQ for firefighters. The petitioners, six Baltimore firefighters who were being involuntarily retired under the Baltimore law, sued under the provisions of the ADEA. The United States District Court held against the firefighters, but the Court of Appeals reversed the decision, and the firefighters appealed to the Supreme Court.

The Supreme Court held unanimously for the firefighters. The opinion, which was written by Justice Thurgood Marshall, argued that neither the ADEA nor the federal civil service law that determined the mandatory retirement age for federal firefighters showed congressional intent to establish a BFOQ of fifty-five years. In fact, Marshall argued, there was evidence in the legislative history of the civil service law suggesting that Congress's motive was to make employment as a federal

firefighter more attractive by making early retirement attractive and maintaining the image of a youthful workforce. According to the Court, neither of these justifications allowed Baltimore to override the provisions of the ADEA. If Baltimore wished to retire its firefighters automatically at age fifty-five, it would have to show evidence that age as such is relevant to the performance of the firefighter's duties and that physical examinations and fitness testing would not serve the city's interest in having competent firefighters.

Although the Supreme Court's ruling in this case is technically narrow, the case stands for a more significant proposition, which is that federal rules doing away with mandatory retirement before age seventy for all employers may be constitutionally applied not just to private employers but also to state and local governmental employers such as the city of Baltimore.          —*Robert Jacobs*

***See also*** Age discrimination; Age Discrimination Act of 1975; Age Discrimination in Employment Act of 1967; Employment; Forced retirement; *Massachusetts Board of Retirement v. Murgia*; Retirement; *Vance v. Bradley.*

## KING LEAR

**AUTHOR:** William Shakespeare

**DATE:** Produced c. 1605-1606, published 1608

**RELEVANT ISSUES:** Death, family, values, violence

**SIGNIFICANCE:** Shakespeare's only tragedy of old age dramatizes its dangers and humiliations; the play warns that love must replace any loss of dignity and authority

In William Shakespeare's tragic play of old age and its indignities, *King Lear*, an aged king in pre-Christian Britain rashly announces his plan to divide the kingdom into three parts. Under his foolish scheme, each of his three daughters is to receive her share in exchange for a proclamation of love for the old king. Lear is enraged when his youngest and most faithful daughter, Cordelia, refuses to conform to this charade.

When the two professedly loyal daughters soon humiliate him, Lear vows revenge and wanders off onto the bare heath. There, he grasps a basic truth: A human is only a "poor, bare, fork'd animal." Lear is last seen embracing the body of Cordelia, who has been hanged, and he dies pitifully, tormented by a false hope that his daughter might still be breathing. The play's subplot, involving Lear's loyal supporter, the duke of Gloucester, confirms the universality of Lear's painful situation. Gloucester is deceived into disinheriting his loyal son, Edgar, and he is viciously punished for aiding Lear by having his eyes plucked out. He grimly concludes, "As flies to wanton boys are we to th' gods./ They kill us for their sport."

A self-confessed "foolish fond old man," Lear dies with a glimmer of hope that Cordelia still lives, while Gloucester dies of a broken heart, despite the comfort of Edgar. The play seems to endorse Edgar's insistence that people must endure the harshness of life with fortitude: "Ripeness is all." *King Lear* is Shakespeare's only mature tragedy to focus on the decline of self-awareness that can accompany old age. —*Byron Nelson*

*See also* Death and dying; Family relationships; Fraud against the elderly; Literature; Old age.

*A scene from a 1916 production of William Shakespeare's play* King Lear. (The Museum of Modern Art, Film Stills Archive)

## KÜBLER-ROSS, ELISABETH

**BORN:** July 8, 1926; Zurich, Switzerland

**RELEVANT ISSUES:** Death, health and medicine, psychology, sociology

**SIGNIFICANCE:** Elisabeth Kübler-Ross pioneered the understanding of the terminally ill and conceptualized five psychological stages persons experience in facing their own deaths

Educated in Switzerland, Kübler-Ross won recognition while serving as a professor of psychiatry at the University of Chicago's Billings Memorial Hospital. Her innovative questioning of schizophrenic patients about what would help them in their own treatment led a group of theology students to ask her for help in counseling terminally ill patients.

In response, Kübler-Ross developed a series of seminars in which dying patients agreed to talk with her about their feelings and needs while audiences observed and listened behind a one-way window. The enormous impact of these sessions on health care providers, social workers, and theology students focused attention on the unmet needs of the terminally ill.

In 1969, Kübler-Ross published *On Death and Dying,* and later that year *Life* magazine featured an article about her. As a national best-seller, *On Death and Dying* popularized her theory of the five stages experienced by the terminally ill or those suffering from significant loss: denial, anger, bargaining, grieving, and acceptance. Blunt, compelling, and compassionate as a writer and lecturer, Kübler-Ross became an inspiring champion of the hospice care movement with its program of psychological, social, and spiritual support along with symptom and pain control. Public approval of Kübler-Ross's philosophy of terminal care and the five-stage theory remained high at the end of the twentieth century, but controversy surrounded her later research into the question of life after death.                    —*Irene N. Gillum*

**See also** Caregiving; Death and dying; Death anxiety; Death of a child; Death of parents; Family relationships; Grief; Hospice; Psychiatry, geriatric; Religion; Terminal illness; Widows and widowers.

## KUHN, MAGGIE

**BORN:** August 3, 1905; Buffalo, N.Y.
**DIED:** April 22, 1995; Philadelphia, Pa.
**RELEVANT ISSUES:** Law, media, sociology
**SIGNIFICANCE:** Kuhn founded the Gray Panthers, an advocacy and educational organization that works for social change for aging people

Maggie Kuhn was one of the leading opponents of discrimination based on age. After graduating from Case Western Reserve University in 1926, she worked for the General Alliance of Unitarian Women and the United Presbyterian Church of the United States, serving as editor of *Social Progress* magazine and as an alternative observer at the United Nations. In 1970, forced to retire from her career with the Presbyterian Church at age sixty-five, Kuhn and a group of her friends founded the Gray Panthers.

Kuhn's primary goal in creating the Gray Panthers was to establish an organization that worked on the issues that concern the elderly, including pension rights and age discrimination, and that also concerned itself with broader public issues, such as the Vietnam War and a variety of social problems. The core of Kuhn's message was that older people need to be in control of their lives and should be active in working for issues that they support. Her candor, charisma, and lively approach to the needs and problems of the aging drew major media attention and painted an image in the public mind that the elderly can make a difference in society.

Kuhn, who remained active in the Gray Panthers until her death at age eighty-nine, redefined the meaning of age and the importance of young and old working together to produce a better society. She and the Gray Panthers were directly instrumental in nursing home reforms, ending forced retirement provisions, and fighting fraud against the elderly in health care. She wrote several books, including *Get Out There and Do Something About Justice* (1972), *Maggie Kuhn on Aging* (1977), and *No Stone Unturned: The Life and Times of Maggie Kuhn* (1991).                    —*Alvin K. Benson*

**See also** Advocacy; Gray Panthers; *No Stone Unturned: The Life and Times of Maggie Kuhn;* Politics.

## KYPHOSIS

**RELEVANT ISSUES:** Biology, health and medicine
**SIGNIFICANCE:** Kyphosis, a marked increase of the normal curvature of the thoracic vertebrae or upper back, is sometimes referred to as dowager's hump because of its prevalence in elderly women

Patients with kyphosis appear to be looking down with their shoulders markedly bent forward. They are unable to straighten their backs, their body height is reduced, and their arms therefore appear to be disproportionately long. The increased curvature of the thoracic vertebrae tilts the head forward, and the patient has to raise her head and hyperextend her neck in order to look forward. This posture increases the strain on the neck muscles and leads to discomfort in the neck, shoulders, and upper back. It limits the field of vision and increases the patient's chances of tripping over an object not directly in the line of vision. It also shifts forward the body's center of gravity and increases the chances of falling.

In severe cases, kyphosis limits chest expansion during breathing. As a result, less air gets into the lungs, which become underventilated and prone to infections. Pneumonia is a common cause of death in these patients. In very severe cases, the curvature of the thoracic vertebrae is so pronounced that the lower ribs lie over the pelvic cavity. Patients with severe kyphosis are not able to lie flat on their backs, and many spend most of their time sitting up in a chair or in bed, propped by a number of pillows. Unless the patient changes positions frequently, the pressure exerted by the vertebrae on the skin and subcutaneous tissue may precipitate pressure sores (bed sores) on the upper back. Pressure sores may also develop on the buttocks. The sores often become infected, and the infection may spread to the blood, leading to septicemia and death.

The most common cause of kyphosis is osteoporosis, a disease in which the bone mass is reduced. As a result, the bones become mechanically weak and are unable to sustain the pressure of the body weight. The vertebrae gradually become wedged and partially collapsed, more so in the front (ante-riorly) than in the back (posteriorly), thus increasing the forward curvature of the thoracic vertebrae. Sometimes, the compression of a vertebra is associated with sudden, very severe, and incapacitating pain that is usually relieved spontaneously after about four weeks. In most cases, however, the compression is a gradual process associated with slowly worsening back discomfort. The discomfort is caused by the strain imposed on the muscles on either side of the vertebrae. In rare instances, the nerves exiting the spinal cord become trapped by the wedged or collapsed vertebrae, and the patient experiences severe pain that tends to radiate to the area supplied by the entrapped nerve. The availability of medications to treat and prevent osteoporosis should significantly reduce the prevalence of both that disease and kyphosis.

Less common causes of kyphosis include the compression of a vertebra as a result of tumors or infections. In these cases, the angulation of the thoracic curvature is very prominent.

*—Ronald C. Hamdy*

**See also** Back disorders; Bone changes and disorders; Mobility problems; Osteoporosis; Pneumonia; Safety issues; Women and aging.

# LAGUNA WOODS, CALIFORNIA

**DATE:** Leisure World built in 1964; Laguna Woods incorporated on March 2, 1999

**RELEVANT ISSUES:** Culture, recreation, sociology, values

**SIGNIFICANCE:** Laguna Woods is a community conceived and built to serve the needs, desires, and interests of active elderly people

In the late 1950's, Ross Cortese, a nationally recognized builder and developer in Southern California, conceived the idea of building a community for the elderly. Because of advances in health care and better living conditions, more people were surviving to old age. Observing the rapid growth in the elderly population, Cortese thought that major housing programs should be undertaken for this group; when no one else launched a program, he decided that he would. Cortese felt that elderly people would like to have their own housing, to live independently, to be near people of their own age group, to have nice recreational and religious facilities, and to be spared the details of maintenance of their homes and yards.

Early in 1961, Cortese built an adult community project in Seal Beach, California, that contained 3,472 dwellings for the elderly on 1,200 acres. It became the prototype for Leisure World (now Laguna Woods). In order to determine exactly what mature, elderly people needed and wanted, Cortese collaborated with the University of Southern California to obtain research results on what the elderly looked for in environmental conditions, social and recreational activities, and health and medical requirements. Based upon this information, Cortese purchased several sites across the United States, including 3,500 rural acres of the Moulton Ranch, located in the Saddleback Valley of southern Orange County, California. This site, which became his primary retirement housing development, was initially named Leisure World.

The goal of the Leisure World project was to provide the basic needs of life for people fifty-five years of age and older by creating a place of serene beauty, security, and recreation, with religious facilities. Following negotiations with city, county, and federal agencies, as well as the military administration of the nearby El Toro Marine Corps Air Force Base, construction of Leisure World began in the spring of 1963, with an initial phase of 530 dwelling units. On September 10, 1964, the first ten homeowners moved into Leisure World. In 1982, the final phase of Leisure World was completed, providing 12,500 dwellings on 2,100 acres.

One of the landmarks of the city is the clock tower at Clubhouse One that bears the crest of its founder, Ross Cortese. By 1999, there were eighteen thousand residents living in the gated community. Management and maintenance became the task of Professional Community Management, one of the nation's most respected community management organizations.

On March 2, 1999, the residents of Leisure World voted to change the name of their community to Laguna Woods and incorporate it as the thirty-second city of Orange County, California. Nearly 67 percent of the 15,498 registered voters cast ballots in the special election, and incorporation passed by a slim margin of 342 votes. The voters also elected five city council members from a field of sixteen candidates. Laguna Woods became the only municipality whose entire population was made up of elderly people. —*Alvin K. Benson*

**See also** Advocacy; Housing; Leisure activities; Politics; Relocation; Retirement communities; Social ties.

# LATINOS

**RELEVANT ISSUES:** Culture, family, race and ethnicity

**SIGNIFICANCE:** At the end of the twentieth century, Latino elders were one of the fastest growing groups in the United States

In 1999, Latino elders made up about 6 percent of the Latino population, or 1.8 million people. It was estimated that by 2050, this sixty-five and older group would represent 10.4 percent of the Latino population. This growth will bring with it much diversity because of the variety of countries from which these elders came and their different cultures. At the end of the twentieth century, 49 percent of Latino elders were of Mexican origin, 15 percent were Cuban, 12 percent were Puerto Rican, and 24 percent were from other Hispanic subgroups. There were seventy-one men for every one hundred women in this population, and nearly twice as many Latino men as women aged sixty-five and older were married and living with their spouses. Only 58 percent of this population had been born in the United States.

## WHO ARE LATINOS?

The Census Bureau identifies the Hispanic community as persons of Mexican, Puerto Rican, Cuban, Caribbean, Latin/Central American, or other Spanish origin. This definition looks at the spoken language to define "Hispanics." Some people find the Hispanic label uncomfortable and prefer to be called Latinos. "Latino" implies a connection with cultural similarities in addition to language. This overarching term also includes Chicanos and Mexican Americans, Cuban Americans, and so on. "Chicanos" is a term used by some Latinos (usually Mexican Americans) who are activists from the 1960's. Use of the term "American" after another nationality, as in "Cuban American," denotes that the person was born in the United States. Many Latinos prefer this method of self-identification, as it provides the country of origin of their ancestors and distinguishes them from other Latinos.

Older Latinos vary both within and between specific groups. The differences within a group are evident if one looks at the number of generations that a given family has been in the United States, as well as the reasons for immigrating and where the members live. A Mexican American elder may have a long family history of life in the United States and therefore be more acculturated. Recent Mexican American immigrants, on the other hand, are less acculturated. They often depend on their children to translate information for them and are more fearful of dealing with mainstream service providers and government agencies. There are also differences stemming from the reason for coming to the United States. For example, Latinos from El Salvador may have left to escape a regime of terror. They may have come as illegal immigrants and now shy away from being noticed by "outsiders" and government agencies. This fear and the need to go unnoticed permeates how they live from day to day and how they teach their children to survive. There may be a mistrust of any person or agent who represents the majority culture. Their interactions with almost everyone are guarded.

The differences between groups are based on cultural differences, history, and the reason for coming to the United States. For example, Cuban American elders are extremely different from other immigrants. The first group of Cubans fleeing the communist government were enthusiastically welcomed into the United States. This was the only Latino group to have this experience, which also differed from that of later Cuban refugees. This first group of Cuban refugees were, for the most part, well-educated, wealthy, and eager to learn about being Americans. This is in sharp contrast to Latinos who come from other countries and hope not to be discovered. These early Cuban refugees, who currently are the elders, were provided information about how to access services and no-interest loans to begin their businesses. They were welcomed as a political statement to demonstrate the superiority of a capitalist system over a communist one.

*As a group, older Latinos have less education, usually as a result of economic pressures and language barriers. Some are able to return to school later in life.* (James L. Shaffer)

Therefore, the degree of willingness to assimilate varies among Latino elders. Many of the differences between groups are also due to their geographic area of origin, the cultural norms that they bring with them, and how they view the government system both in the country of origin and in the United States.

In the late 1990's, the majority of Latino elders lived in metropolitan areas, with only 11 percent living in other areas. Also, the vast majority of Latino elderly lived in four states, each with different concentrations of Latino groups: The majority of the Latino population in California and Texas were from Mexico and Central America, Florida attracted the Cuban population, and New York received a large number of immigrants from Puerto Rico and Caribbean islands.

### EDUCATION

Of all minority elderly, those of Latino background are the least educated. This is particularly significant because education greatly influences other aspects of people's lives. In the United States, a higher educational level also allows individuals to have access to resources provided within their communities.

The proportion of Latino elders with no formal schooling is nine times as great as for whites. Of Latinos sixty-five and older in 1999, 10 percent had no education and only 20 percent had been graduated from high school. In addition, 33 percent had less than five years of education.

In comparing the three largest Latino groups (Mexican American, Cuban American, and Puerto Rican), Cubans have the highest educational levels of the three and Mexican Americans have the lowest. More specifically, in 1999, Cuban Americans had a mean of 8.11 years of education, Puerto Ricans had a mean of 5.23 years, and Mexican Americans had a mean of 5.21 years of formal education. There is also some variance by gender, with the men in all three groups having more years of formal education in comparison to the women.

### SOCIOECONOMIC STATUS

At the end of the twentieth century, the percentage of Latino elders with incomes below the poverty level was twice as large (22.5 percent) as among elderly non-Hispanic whites (10 percent). Poverty rates were higher in nonmetropolitan than in urban areas and higher among women than among men. Thus, nonmetropolitan women were the most impoverished group of all. For example, among the Latino elderly, 22.7 percent of nonmetropolitan women had a below-poverty income, as compared to 15.7 percent of white nonmetropolitan women. Generally, elderly Latinos have lower incomes than their white counterparts. For example, in 1995 the median personal income for elderly Latinos was $6,411 while the median income for white elders was $10,767. In addition, in many cases, elderly Latinos may retire from work earlier than the retirement age. These elders are more likely to become impoverished because of lower benefit levels throughout the rest of their lives.

In comparing late 1990's income levels among the three largest groups of Latinos, Cuban Americans had the highest annual income ($11,950), followed by Mexican Americans ($10,650) and then Puerto Ricans ($9,649). Again, in all three groups, the men earned higher incomes than the women, which meant that Puerto Rican women were the most likely to be poor.

Private pensions and incomes from interest-bearing accounts are uncommon among elderly Latinos because the majority of them worked in jobs with little access to retirement benefits. Another issue that contributes to low socioeconomic status is that Latinos do not access Social Security at the same rates as their white counterparts. In 1988, a mere 77 percent of Latino elders received Social Security, compared to 93 percent of white elders. Those who do receive Social Security are more likely to receive lower benefits as a result of their history of working in low-paying jobs such as laborers, farm or migrant workers, and in the service industry. The combination of these facts makes Latino elders more impoverished as well as more likely to depend on family for financial support. Those who do receive Social Security are more likely to depend on it for a greater amount of their subsistence.

Another resource that is not used to the extent that it could be is Supplemental Security Income (SSI). It has been estimated that only 44 percent of eligible Latino elders receive this benefit. This benefit is for those who are near poverty even after receiving Social Security. This statistic illustrates the low rate of benefit utilization among Latinos even though these elders may be very poor.

*Latino families are often multigenerational and close-knit.* (James L. Shaffer)

### HEALTH

Many individuals in all groups who are sixty-five and older and who do not live in nursing homes report at least one chronic ailment and some limitation in performing day-to-day activities. Latino elderly have somewhat higher rates of activity limitation and have more days per year in bed because of illness. Latinos suffer from high rates of hypertension, and additional health concerns include high cholesterol, diabetes, and arthritis. Latinos have a higher incidence of cardiovascular disease, which is the leading cause of mortality in this group. Cancer is the second-highest cause of mortality; while Latinos have lower rates of cancer than their white counterparts, the incidence is increasing. Noninsulin-dependent (type II) diabetes mellitus is a significant cause of morbidity and mortality that affects 25 percent of adult Puerto Ricans and Mexican Americans.

Health is an area that sometimes may be perceived differently by different people. Among elderly Mexican Americans, Cuban Americans, and Puerto Ricans, only 11.4 percent said that their

health was poor. However, 41.9 percent said that their health status was fair. In looking at how these same elders perceived their limitations by activities of daily living (ADLs), 16.3 percent had three or more ADLs. Similarly, 17.7 percent said that they had three or more limitations in instrumental activities of daily living (IADLs). ADLs and IADLs are a prevalent evaluation tool for assessing an individual's ability to remain independent and out of nursing homes or other care facilities. Usually, the assessment is based on a combination of limitations, with a final decision based on the overall health of the individual as well as the ability to remain at home with informal and formal support systems playing a significant role. One of the ADLs that is highly correlated with one's ability to remain independent and in one's own home is mobility. This activity is usually assessed by the ability of an elder to walk and to get in and out of bed or chairs. In looking at the three groups of Latino elders in 1999, 27.3 percent had problems with walking and 21 percent had problems with getting in and out of bed or chairs. Therefore, although only

11.4 percent said that their health was poor, it is likely that the family or informal support system is keeping them out of long-term care facilities.

In spite of higher activity limitations, in 1989, 33 percent of all Latinos had no health insurance. Much of the lack of insurance is attributable to the fact that in their working years, many elderly Latinos held jobs that simply did not offer health or retirement benefits. The impact of this situation is far-reaching in the older years. With a history of lacking insurance, there has been little preventive care. As a result, when Latino elders do go in for health care, they usually need more intense levels of care and their diseases are more complicated and therefore more costly to treat. As in other arenas, there are differences among the Latino groups on rates of health care insurance. In the late 1990's, it was estimated that 38 percent of Mexican American elders, 16 percent of Puerto Rican elders, and 24 percent of Cuban American elders were not insured. Puerto Rican elders were more likely to have Medicaid coverage, which plays a role in decreasing the numbers of these elders who are not insured.

Mental health issues in old age are exacerbated by years of poverty or near poverty, low educational levels, substandard housing, and a lack of opportunity. Generally, Latinos have larger families, which is a resource for them in their old age. As more and more families are influenced by mainstream society, however, more adult children move away to seek jobs or to improve their economic status. In these situations, elders are left to deal with health and mental health issues with the help of established community resources such as priests, friends, and extended family members. In many cases, this amounts to few formal services being accessed by these elders. Studies that looked at psychological distress in Mexican American populations found a lower incidence of psychological distress than in the White non-Hispanic population that was studied.

Puerto Rican-born and Cuban-born older men have higher rates of suicide than other groups. In contrast, all Latino women have a lower rate of suicide. At issue is the ability to discern when a Latino elder is depressed or experiencing psychological problems. An important variable is whether psychometric tests are applicable to these populations. Another variable that has to be considered is whether the language and interpretation of the test are valid. There is a high probability that with these variables, there may be an underdiagnosis of psychological distress in this population.

## EXTENDED FAMILY SYSTEMS

Latino families are noted for being tightly connected and supportive of their family members. Generally, among the elders, the family and not the individuals make decisions. Functionally, this implies that decisions are a result of familial cooperation, interdependence, and affiliation. While this process may be on the decline due to the relocation of younger families away from their parents, this is still a common occurrence. Mexican American families tend to be larger, with a mean of 4.15 persons per family in the late 1990's. Next were Puerto Rican families, with a mean number of 3.62 persons per family. Cuban Americans had the smallest mean number of persons per family, with 3.13.

In essence, these family members and their children become the most important informal support for these elders. In many cases, the family support system works so well that agencies tend to forget to plan services for Latino elders. Yet, given that even the younger family members are also likely to be in poverty or have limited resources, caring for elderly family members becomes a serious burden to families. Outreach services to provide information about services and about eligibility guidelines need to be aggressive in Latino communities. Otherwise, Latino elders and their adult children will carry an inordinate portion of the care and responsibility of these elders.

Another component is that by the time Latino elders receive services, be they health or other, they are more frail and their needs are more complicated. By this time, they have exhausted all or most of the family's resources, both financial and emotional. This family dynamic is responsible for lower utilization rates of all services among Latinos. —*Sara Alemán*

**See also** *Bless Me, Ultima*; Cultural views of aging; Family relationships; Health care; Multigenerational households; National Hispanic Council on Aging; *Old Man and the Sea, The*; Poverty.

## FOR FURTHER INFORMATION:

AARP Minority Affairs Initiative. *A Portrait of Older Minorities.* Washington, D.C.: AARP, 1995.

Alemán, Sara. *Hispanic Elders and Human Services.* New York: Garland, 1997.

Bassford, Tamsen L. "Health Status of Hispanic Elders." *Clinics in Geriatric Medicine* 11, no. 1 (February, 1995).

Chelimsky, Eleanor. *Hispanic Access to Health Care: Significant Gaps Exist.* Washington, D.C.: U.S. General Accounting Office, 1992.

Lopez, Cristina, with Esther Aguilera. *On the Sidelines: Hispanic Elderly and the Continuum of Care.* Washington, D.C.: Policy Analysis Center and Office of Institutional Development, National Council of La Raza, 1991.

Pousada, Lidia. "Hispanic-American Elders: Implications for Health-Care Providers." *Clinics in Geriatric Medicine* 11, no. 1 (February, 1995).

U.S. Bureau of the Census. *Statistical Abstract of the United States: 1997.* 117th ed. Washington, D.C.: U.S. Department of Commerce, Economics and Statistics Administration, Bureau of the Census, 1997.

## Leisure activities

**Relevant issues:** Culture, recreation, values

**Significance:** Leisure roles may be undertaken on the initiative of the older individual, who has complete latitude as to when, where, how much, and whether such roles will actually be performed

Aging is the outcome of living. Longevity is a matter of genetics and other environmental factors that permit long life, but whether an individual merely survives or has a quality of life that is satisfying and enjoyable depends on many variables, not the least of which is the positive use of leisure. If one is to hold off the vicissitudes of life and the vulnerabilities that the normal aging process brings, it appears that that life is best which contributes to the common good and fosters participation, in the sense of focus, involvement, and enjoyment. These values can be obtained when two fundamental needs are met. The first is interpersonal behavior or social contact, and the second is physical capacity to perform. The commingling of these experiences leads to the good life.

The older adult has many needs, in which the impingements to which the human organism is vulnerable as it ages is a prime factor. If a person has an educational preparation suitable for all aspects of life, then it is probable that leisure used in a variety of activities will have been acquired. Where this assumption is invalid, the individual may have a lack of interests and be forced to be passive or vegetate. While a number of agencies may be able to stimulate the learning of leisure skills and other socializing experiences, too frequently the older adult does not know about the opportunities at his or her disposal or the agencies that should be concerned are not aware of the older person's existence. When this occurs, no service is given or received.

For the most part, recreational activity is defined as enjoyable, voluntary, socially acceptable, and occurring in leisure. All four aspects must be operational at the same time. The physical activity or motor skill and interpersonal relationships justify each other and contribute to the overall pleasure and satisfaction that a person needs throughout life generally and intensely during later life.

Financial status, condition of health, cognitive ability, sensory acuity, personal loss, residence, transportation availability, and other factors are involved to an increasingly significant extent in an older person's leisure. Leisure in abundance is the experience of the older adult, especially for the retired person, and may be viewed as either a reward or a punishment. Depending upon the perception of the individual and the preparation that has been garnered in preceding years, leisure may be the enrichment of old age or it can be poor, drab, and a time of boredom.

### Recreational Services for the Aging

The aging process and its implications for the recreational service field (primarily leisure-based) and other related services may be analyzed in terms of the responsibilities of social agencies that sponsor programs for older adults (public recreational service departments, age-oriented agencies, sectarian agencies, and other voluntary organizations), treatment centers (convalescent homes, rehabilitation centers, skilled nursing facilities, and other such organizations), and opportunities for private marketing enterprise. Increasingly, older adults who are able want to be involved and active during their leisure. The varied experiences available to aging individuals present challenges and opportunities to use cognitive ability, knowledge, appreciation, proficiency, and physical capacity to perform. The spectrum of opportunities available during leisure includes a surprising variety of organizations and individual initiatives to which the older person may apply insofar as recreational engagement is concerned.

Recreational programs for the elderly sponsored by social agencies (public, quasi-public, or private) need to combine enjoyable activities with emphasis on social service programming to meet the entire range of needs of the aging person. Whenever feasible, recreational programs should incorporate the possibility of having older persons provide meaningful service for others. This strengthens the volunteer's sense of self-esteem, maintains his or her interest, and furthers involvement.

It is worthwhile to promote intergenerational activities and break down the barriers of age segregation. The recruitment of elderly people as volunteers to work with children or adolescents is one of the effective means to increase personal growth, development, and satisfaction.

An important area of leisure opportunity is touring for older adults. There is growing commercial interest in providing travel experiences for elderly people, and it is obvious that many older adults (even those with disabilities) are interested. Different approaches in terms of accommodations, arrangements, security, comfort, and destinations may be required, but this seems to be a significant sector of growth for tour operators and other organizations in the travel industry.

Only about 6 percent of persons over the age of sixty-five are institutionalized in any one year. This means that 94 percent continue to reside in the community. While not all within the community are able to participate in leisure experiences outside the home, for any number of health or disability reasons, the greater proportion of

*Two residents of the Redwoods Retirement Center demonstrate how to do the Charleston at the "Senior Prom." Dancing can fulfill both social and physical needs for the elderly.* (AP Photo/Lacy Atkins)

older persons are not dependent and have the capacity to do whatever they want to do, if they have the means and the information, concerning leisure use.

Even when the older adult is disabled, to the extent that institutionalization is necessary, leisure experiences can be extended through a variety of recreational experiences that can assist the dependent adult in reclaiming a sense of purpose and control in an environment that tends to undermine individuality and choice. Special care facilities can arrange for a comprehensive series of recreational activities that will accommodate whatever limitation the older person has due to a pathological condition or other debilitation which accrues as a result of advanced age. Many older adults confined to treatment centers of various types have much free time on their hands. Adroit programming dedicated to the psychosocial needs of these residents can do much to overcome the tendency to withdraw from social contact and become isolated. It is particularly important to assess individual needs and thereby determine the interests, based upon past performance, that might stimulate participation on the part of these confined and sometimes nonambulatory persons.

Many elderly persons are in good health, vigorous, extroverted, financially secure, and actively involved in a variety of activities. Some of these individuals are still fully employed because they receive a sense of identity and purpose from their position. Others work on a part-time basis in order to obtain additional money for discretionary use or for the social contact that such employment offers. In many instances, volunteering in service organizations does much to satisfy the need for socialization as well as to provide personal enjoyment and satisfaction when assistance is given to others. Older persons continue to be active in sports and fitness activities, engage in sexual relationships, are active within their communities, and continue to be creative and innovative and to seek satisfactions in ways that are a natural outgrowth of typical life experiences. Moreover, these people tend to be independent.

The number of agencies devoted to the provision of recreational activities for elderly people runs the gamut from senior centers and "golden age" clubs to retirement communities and age-oriented organizations that operate travel and study opportunities. Intergenerational experiences and other leisure-based activities designed to take advantage of the individual's talents, skills, interests, and vital capacities are also served by these kinds of organizations.

## LEISURE ACTIVITIES AND SERVICES

Vigorous physical activity is important for life maintenance as well as personal enjoyment and high-quality living. It would be extremely beneficial if everyone developed the habit of exercise at a young age and engaged in it throughout their lives, but there are individuals to whom any physical activity is anathema. They must be convinced of the enjoyment and health benefits that can accrue during such participation. These persons need to be persuaded to participate in vigorous physical activity not only for the beneficial outcomes that are gained but also for the pure pleasure of putting one's body through its paces. Maintaining strength is a fundamental factor for staying active into the later years. It is tremendously important for older adults, so that they can sustain their daily-living activities as well as their recreational activities. Essential skills, such as getting up from chairs, beds, and toilets, depend on muscle strength. The core of strength training is that one obtains high functional capacity so as to be better able to carry out activities of daily living. By keeping muscles stronger, one can postpone and, to some degree, prevent the inevitable muscle weakness that usually accompanies old age.

Strength is a benefit at any age and at any level of fitness. People who participate in some physical activity that requires skill, flexibility, or stamina will only improve their performance if they become stronger. In order to become stronger, people need to engage in strength-building activities. These activities do not have to be daunting, nor do they have to be competitive. The range of physical experiences can include everything from simply walking to cross-country skiing. Most experts indicate that at least twenty minutes of walking (or any activity that uses large muscles of the lower body), at least three times a week, will dramatically increase fitness with that first step from nonactivity to activity. The keyword is moderation. People can be accommodated for participation in physical activity of almost any kind that requires a modicum of regular time investment and moderate energy output.

The entire orientation of physical activity in successful aging should be in terms of fun or enjoyment. Integrating enjoyable recreational activity into a person's life can stimulate participation for fitness. Although some older adults may be attracted to competitive experiences, for the majority a variety of activities, moderately undertaken and balanced between aerobics and resistance activities, helps to develop strength and flexibility. Such activity should become an integral part of life. Positive leisure experiences are typically performed because the individual anticipates enjoyment in the performance. There usually is no ulterior motive. It is fortuitous that this kind of activity can also contribute to a healthy and attractive life condition.

### SOCIAL EXPERIENCES

Recreational activities performed during leisure provide the individual participant with a sense of purpose and an augmented physical capacity to perform. There is a concomitant upgrade in self-esteem, a feeling of mastery or being in control of one's self, and the ability to achieve whatever objectives have been set. Yet these activities are not done in isolation. Older people realize and appreciate the need for social interaction. There is much to be said for single-participant activity. However, it is much more enjoyable to be with others and to contribute to some cooperative enterprise or to take part in an activity that requires coordination and teamwork in order to achieve satisfaction. For this reason, most older adults choose activities that require the presence of one or more others for the experience to be successful. Walking by oneself may be pleasurable, but walking within a group is much more enjoyable because of the opportunity for commentary and conversation while walking. The same holds true for exercise classes, dance, cross-country skiing, craft activities, and nature oriented activities such as camping, rock climbing, fishing, or bird watching. The social aspect of being within a group enhances the activity. Therefore, older people enjoy participating in a wide variety of group activities—some with a physical orientation.

Essentially, physical recreational activity within the social context stimulates a desire for further similar experiences and provides the motivation for continued participation. The result is an exhilarating feeling of well-being and personal fulfillment. Whether the activity is racquet sports, softball, marathon running, bowling, dancing, or volleyball, the give and take of social intercourse, as much as the activity itself, creates an atmosphere of satisfaction and high morale.

Older adults tend to be retired from active employment and, therefore, have free time, which offers opportunity to reinvest themselves in a personally profitable and valuable experience. Moreover, the loss at retirement of social contact that the work life provides can be compensated for through the highly social context of recreational activity. Coupling these two elements, free time or leisure and social interaction, with the third facet of physical activity brings the disparate pieces of existence into an integrated whole. This mosaic represents a situation of voluntary, wholesome participation during leisure in a totally enjoyable setting. A salubrious outcome encourages further experimentation so that the participants become more enthusiastic about their potential. In this way, attention is future focused and there is a tendency to look ahead to the next possibility.

Midlife preparation for the inevitable process of aging as well as retirement from the workforce should be emphasized by employing organizations and other agencies that operate preretirement seminars or other educational programs. These workshops need to stress that leisure will loom large in the later years and that recreational activity is an integral element of the entire process. In fact, public agencies whose responsibility it is to serve the needs of all citizens should be closely involved with the development of comprehensive planning for the aging.

### SUMMARY

Recreational activity, set in leisure, creates an environment in which the individual can take pleasure in the fact that he or she has lived to the fullest. The twin requisites for the aging person, fitness and socialization, need to be founded early on, but they can be embarked upon profitably at any age. If individuals can be persuaded to perform, they will soon find such activity is an antidote to the average problems that typically confront the older person.

Positive leisure activity is not an elixir, and it may not add years to life, but it does make a difference in the kind of lives led by those who participate. From the interconnection between group-supported recreational activity comes integration of character and the certainty of function. Whether or not an individual who is fit will live longer is not the question. Rather, the question is concerned with the condition of the individual when the aging process really begins and the period between that onset and death. Those years, whether few or many, can be successful in terms of high-quality living. To be able, to be involved, and to extend oneself to the maximum offers the performer the actuality of achievement and a heightened sense of contentment. —*Jay S. Shivers*

*See also* Creativity; Disabilities; Exercise and fitness; Friendship; Retirement communities; Retirement planning; Senior citizen centers; Social ties; Sports participation; Successful aging; Vacations and travel; Volunteering.

## FOR FURTHER INFORMATION:

Greenblatt, Fred S. *Therapeutic Recreation for Long-Term Care Facilities.* New York: Human Sciences Press, 1988. This book provides a basic overview of therapeutic recreational service. The elements discussed follow closely the components of the leisure ability model. The majority of the information provided pertains to program development and implementation of activities in a long-term care facility.

Hoffman, Adeline M. *The Daily Needs and Interests of Older People.* 2d ed. Springfield, Ill.: Charles C Thomas, 1976. This book addresses numerous issues related to growing older. The author of this book provides general characteristics of older adults as well as specific problems these persons face during the late stage of life. Different perspectives offer the readers several ways to analyze the physical, psychosocial, and economic needs of older adults.

Leitner, Michael J., and Sara F. Leitner. *Leisure in Later Life: A Source Book for the Provision of Recreational Services for Elders.* New York: Hawthorne Press, 1985. This book discusses the provision of recreational activities for older adults. A basic review of program components includes planning, implementation, and evaluation of recreational programs in institutional and community settings. Recreational activity suggestions incorporate therapeutic modalities and diversionary activities into a number of comprehensive programs, designed to address a variety of physical and psychosocial needs of older adults.

Teaff, Joseph D. *Leisure Services with the Elderly.* St. Louis: Times Mirror/Mosby College, 1985. This book reviews the recreational needs of older adults. Several chapters highlight general characteristics and needs of elderly persons. Recreational program components and considerations are discussed as they relate to a variety of residential settings.

Weisberg, Naida, and Rosilyn Wilder. *Creative Arts with Older Adults: A Sourcebook.* New York: Human Sciences Press, 1985. This book discusses the potential benefits of incorporating creative arts into recreational activity programs for older adults. Many chapters highlight specific programs including dance, movement, art, photography, and creative writing in a number of diverse settings. Methods of program implementation address goal dedication and leadership techniques.

## LESBIANS. *See* GAY MEN AND LESBIANS.

## LIFE EXPECTANCY

**RELEVANT ISSUES:** Death, demographics, health and medicine, race and ethnicity

**SIGNIFICANCE:** Life expectancy at birth is a measure of longevity that has been increasing steadily, though disparities remain between males and females and among people of different ethnic and socioeconomic backgrounds

In an attempt to maximize profits, life insurance companies devised a method for estimating the amount of time a person will live, given his or her current age. This demographic measure, known as life expectancy ($e_x$), is based on prevailing death rates and is expressed as the average number of additional years a person of age $x$ can expect to live. By collecting statistics on the age at death in a particular population (compiling what is known as a static life table), it is possible to determine the current probability of surviving infancy, childhood, young adulthood, middle age, and old age. Using these patterns of survival, one can project how much longer a given person is likely to live (an actuarial prediction of the mean expectation of life for someone alive at beginning of age $x$

## Increasing U.S. Life Expectancy, 1940-1995

*Source:* U.S. Bureau of the Census, *Statistical Abstract of the United States: 1997.* Washington, D.C.: GPO, 1997.

based on a hazard model applied to each age and sex group).

Because some age groups experience lower survival rates than others, life expectancy changes with age. For example, once a person has made it past a particularly difficult stage of life (such as surviving infancy in the early twentieth century), the chances of living a long life actually increase. While life expectancy at birth may be seventy, it can easily jump to seventy-six years when the person reaches age one. Populations with high infant mortality have a smaller proportion of the population living to old age, but the population will still comprise the entire range of ages.

Although the demographic measure "life expectancy" is formally calculated for a specific age class, the term is commonly used to refer to $e_0$, or "life expectancy at birth." This figure estimates the average length of time a baby born that year is ex-

pected to live (based on the death rates of the population). It serves as an important summary measure of longevity and an indicator of the health of a population.

### INCREASES IN LIFE EXPECTANCY

Among wealthier populations, life expectancy has shown extraordinary increases. For example, in 1900, the average American could not expect to live more than fifty years. By 1999, however, U.S. life expectancy at birth had climbed to seventy-six years. This increase in life span can be attributed to increases in the survivorship of infants and to decreases in both death during childbirth and the spread of infectious childhood diseases. Slowing of the onset of and decreasing of the mortality associated with a variety of diseases has further extended longevity. In North America and elsewhere, gains have been made through immunization programs, decreases in teenage motherhood, declines in the incidence of smoking, and improved medicines and technologies for combating heart disease and cancer (the two largest killers in the United States).

Gains in life expectancy have spawned a debate as to the upper limit of the human life span. Some project a practical upper limit of eighty-five years, pointing to the slowing decrease in mortality in the 1980's as evidence that most of the "easy" gains in longevity have already been made. Studies of the influence of genetic makeup on longevity, and the observation that the number of people in the oldest age groups is increasing rapidly, lead others to speculate that the natural human life span may be in excess of 120 years. In fact, in 1997, people one hundred and older were the fastest-growing age class in the U.S. population.

### The Consequences of Longer Life

The combination of longer life span and lower birthrates means that the U.S. population is aging. This changing demographic makeup raises some difficult social and political issues. Some fear that aging baby boomers (those people born between 1945 and 1964) will create a financial burden on society, as the ratio of workers to retirees (the dependency ratio) was projected to shift from sixteen to one in 1950 to two to one in 2030. The "graying of America" means that the wealth span of the population is also increasing, with less years being spent in the (preretirement) accumulation stage of life and more years spent in the (postretirement) expenditure stage. Questions were raised as to whether various assistance programs (Social Security, Medicare, and Medicaid) could remain viable, since the "pay-as-you-go" (rather than investment) structure of these programs requires that the number of people working be larger than the number collecting benefits. Socially, increased longevity also means that most families now include three generations. This situation has the potential to "sandwich" the middle aged between financially dependent teenagers and older parents. Financial gerontologists predict a shift in financial burden away from children (since families are increasingly smaller) toward longer-lived elder parents, with a growing need for intergenerational transfers of finances.

Not everyone has predicted economic stagnation as a result of the graying of the U.S. popula-

tion. Some see the potential for growth in "silver industries" (those geared toward the senior or "mature" market). They also point to the large investment capital created by the pension funds of this swelling age group. It is also clear that retirement need no longer be age-dependent, as improved health in later life means improved ability for people to work into their sixties, reducing the strain on the retirement system.

### The Quality of Longer Life

Another concern associated with longer life is the question of adding quality as well as quantity to the extension of life. While the concept of quality is elusive, most agree that an increase in disability-free years (years in which the individual is still able to perform routine activities) is desirable. Fears associated with a longer life include concerns about failing health, insufficient funds, loss of mental acuity, and loss of independence. Fortunately, advances in health care and an increased awareness of the role of lifestyle in preventing disability mean that old age has become less unpleasant and expensive. For women, moderate hormone replacement (estrogen) therapy, taken for less than ten years or in a "designer estrogen" form, increases life span by adding bone density and protecting against heart disease. A diet high in fruits and vegetables and low in meat also adds years, as does having a physically and mentally active lifestyle. Companionship and an optimistic view of life also appear to increase the human life span.

Almost all the years added to the life span between 1980 and 1990 were disability-free years, with the average age of nursing home residents increasing from sixty-five in 1950 to eighty-one in 1999. The increase in the proportion of life spent free of disability is known as the compression of morbidity. The prevention of chronic health problems means that people are able either to "live longer and die faster" or to "die young at an old age."

### Disparities in Life Expectancy

Despite improved public heath practices and advances in technology, not everyone has benefited equally from increases in life expectancy at birth. By the late 1990's, the continuing acquired immunodeficiency syndrome (AIDS) epidemic prompted some researchers to project that longevity in Central and South Africa would decrease by as much as sixteen years from 1990 to 2015. Life expectancies had also dropped to 1980 levels in former Soviet bloc nations of Eastern Europe as a result of economic and social changes that accompanied the breakup of the Soviet Union.

While those born in the most-industrialized nations in 2000 could expect to live to seventy-nine, those in the least-developed countries could expect to live only to the age of forty-two. Life expectancy at age sixty-five is much more similar from one country to another, yet inferior public health conditions in poorer nations may mean poor quality of life for the elderly.

Probably most striking are the disparities within the U.S. population itself. The United States has a bigger spread in longevity than any other high-income nation. A 1997 study by Christopher Murray of Harvard University revealed that some residents of inner cities, American Indian reservations, and the South had life spans comparable to those in less-developed countries. He reported that an American Indian male in South Dakota could expect to live only 56.5 years and that an African American male in Washington, D.C., could expect to live just 57.6 years—the same life expectancy as a male in Bangladesh or Senegal. Even within the city of Chicago, longevity varies up to twenty years from one neighborhood to another, a gap that doubled between 1980 and 1999. These disparities are based on sex, race, ethnicity, income, and educational differences. In general, the poor and less-educated die younger, with increased mortality at all ages and from all causes. Those with less than a high school education have a shorter overall life span as well as a decrease in active life.

Women in the United States outlive men by an average of six to eight years, although this gap appears to be narrowing with time. While women live more years, they also have a higher proportion of disabled years than their male counterparts. Similarly, African Americans and American Indians are more likely to have chronic health problems, leading to racial inequalities in the active life span. These differences may be attributable to lower socioeconomic status. As a group, African Americans and young Latinos experience more risk of death from homicide and human immunodeficiency virus (HIV) infection than the population at large, and American Indians experience increased risk from suicide. Because of their mixed European, African, and American Indian ancestry, however, Latinos (or Hispanics) have been inconsistently reported in mortality reports, with many vital statistics for Latinos available only after 1989. In general, factors other than ethnicity, per se, are the main determinants of longevity. Differences in risk factors (smoking and obesity), genetic predisposition for certain diseases, access to health care (as a result of insurance, financial, or immigrant status), preventive care, nutrition, and health consciousness (which is tied to educational and cultural differences) all contribute to differences in life span.                              —*Lee Anne Martínez*

*See also* African Americans; Aging: Historical perspective; American Indians; Antiaging treatments; Asian Americans; Baby boomers; Centenarians; Death and dying; Demographics; Graying of America; Latinos; Longevity research; Middle age; Old age.

FOR FURTHER INFORMATION:

Bosworth, Barry, and Gary Burtless, eds. *Aging Societies: The Global Dimension.* Washington, D.C.: Brookings Institution, 1998.

Council of Economic Advisors for the President's Initiative on Race. *Changing America: Indicators of Social and Economic Well-Being by Race and Hispanic Origin.* Washington, D.C.: Author, 1998.

Cowley, Geoffrey. "How to Live to One Hundred." *Newsweek* 129, no. 26 (June 30, 1997).

Pardo, Natalie. "Health Watch: Life Cut Short for City's Minorities." *The Chicago Reporter* 28 (April, 1999).

Stiling, Peter. "Population Growth." In *Ecology: Theories and Applications.* 3d ed. Upper Saddle River, N.J.: Prentice Hall, 1999.

## LIFE INSURANCE

**RELEVANT ISSUES:** Death, economics, family

**SIGNIFICANCE:** People purchase life insurance so that their beneficiaries can receive money to pay off debts and final expenses and to create an estate for survivors, but many people also think of life insurance as an investment for their retirement years

People have been purchasing life insurance policies since the colonial period in America. Until relatively recently, almost all policies sold were whole-life policies, which included level premiums for the life of the policy, guaranteed death benefits, and cash values that accumulated gradually in older policies. Many insurance companies have also begun to offer term-life policies that provide less expensive pure life insurance coverage but do not contain cash values.

Agents selling term policies normally encourage their customers to invest the difference in price between less expensive term policies and more expensive whole-life policies. Customers who are averse to risk prefer whole-life policies that contain guaranteed cash values, whereas those who believe that they can do better by investing in mutual funds or stocks tend to prefer term policies. There are also combinations of whole-life and term policies such as universal life policies, which contain a guaranteed death benefits with cash values and death benefits that can vary depending on the performance of the investments selected by customers for their individual investments.

### REASONS FOR PURCHASING LIFE INSURANCE

Life insurance companies rely on actuarial tables to determine premium rates for customers. Premiums are more expensive for older people than for younger customers because companies assume that younger customers will live longer. Health factors also influence premium rates. Smokers pay more than nonsmokers of the same age, and people with certain health problems or those who work in dangerous professions may either be denied coverage or be rated and offered life insurance coverage only at higher premiums. Since the premiums for life insurance policies are determined largely by the customer's age when he or she purchases a policy, life insurance agents frequently encourage clients to purchase as much insurance as they can afford when they are young and healthy because similar policies will definitely cost more in the future and may be unavailable if the customer develops health problems.

Licensed life insurance agents and financial planners need to explain carefully to customers that life insurance needs will vary greatly for people as they age. Parents with young children clearly need a large amount of life insurance because the surviving spouse requires a significant immediate estate to replace the deceased person's income so that there will be enough money to raise and edu-

cate the children. Parents of young children have not yet had enough time to accumulate sufficient assets by investing in mutual funds or the stock market, and they need to purchase life insurance policies in amounts equal to between six and ten times their annual income. An insurance agent also needs to take into account the specific needs of individual clients. A single person with no children will need less insurance than married people with young children, but an experienced agent must not lose contact with his or her client because the client's insurance needs may change if there are new children or if there is a marriage or divorce. The owner of an insurance policy has a right to designate and change beneficiaries. Following a divorce, for example, the owner of a policy may very well want to change his or her beneficiary.

Financial planners agree that life insurance plays an essential role in financial planning, but there is serious disagreement about the type of life insurance policy that people should purchase. Traditionally, life insurance policies were presented to customers as ideal investments that combined income replacement protection with retirement planning. Life insurance agents who sell whole-life policies explain to their clients that such policies can provide them with income protection while they are working and can also be used for retirement income if they choose to turn in their policies for the cash values once they retire. Owners of whole-life policies can also borrow from their cash values and pay back these loans at either guaranteed or variable rates.

The problem with whole-life policies is that the return on cash values is often quite low, perhaps as low as 1 to 3 percent. Whole-life policies are very profitable for insurance companies because they can invest these cash values in the stock market or mutual funds and receive a return on this money that is much greater than that given to policyholders. Many retired people who purchased whole-life policies when they were much younger discover to their displeasure that the cash values in these policies are insufficient to meet their present needs. The life insurance company will pay life insurance benefits once it receives a death certificate for the person insured under a life insurance policy, but the money invested in whole-life insurance policies does not produce returns comparable to what people could have earned by investing similar amounts in mutual funds or the stock market.

Many senior citizens find themselves with much more insurance coverage than they need, but if they turn in their policies, they will receive a very poor return on their premium investments. They find themselves in a difficult situation. They may want their children or the surviving spouse to receive the life insurance benefits, but they need the money now, and the cash values are not sufficient to meet their present needs.

### TYPES OF LIFE INSURANCE POLICIES

There are advantages and disadvantages to both whole-life and term policies. Clients who believe that they lack the discipline to invest regularly for their retirement may conclude that it is wiser for them to purchase whole-life policies so that they will at least have something for their retirement years. Some whole-life policies can be fully paid after twenty years or at a certain age, normally sixty-five. Whenever the annual interest paid exceeds the annual premium, the premium will be paid from this interest. The client will then have a paid policy. Many clients like the absolute guarantee provided by whole-life policies, but they should not think of life insurance policies as investments that will produce enough money for them to live on during their retirement years.

Life insurance agents from whole-life insurance companies continue, however, to present such policies not only for income protection but also as investment vehicles. They are correct in stressing both aspects of whole-life policies, but they also should explain to their clients that they need to have investments separate from their whole-life policies so that they can afford to send their children to college and to maintain the lifestyle to which they have become accustomed during their retirement years. Whole-life agents tend not to educate clients on the poor return on cash values because such information would discourage people from purchasing whole-life policies. During the last two decades of the twentieth century, however, more and more people learned about the differences between whole-life and term-life policies. As a result, the percentage of whole-life policies purchased decreased significantly as the percentage of term-life policies purchased increased.

Term-life policies have become more popular in recent years largely because they enable people to purchase for the same monthly or annual premium significantly more coverage than they could obtain with whole-life policies, but many clients do not fully understand how term policies work. As the very expression "term life" indicates, benefits for a term-life policy will be paid only if the person covered by this policy dies while the coverage is in effect. Such policies build no cash values, and therefore people cannot borrow from them. Many different types of term-life policies exist, including annual renewal policies, in which the policies increase every year, and level-term policies, in which the same premium is paid each year for a guaranteed numbers of years (normally ten, twenty, or twenty-five years). Some term policies can be converted to whole-life policies at certain times during the life of the policy, if the client chooses to do so. Many clients combine relatively inexpensive term-life coverage with regular investments in mutual funds that generally produce a better return than whole-life policies. Many clients, however, simply purchase term policies and do not commit themselves to a regular investment plan by contributing a set amount of money each month for their retirement. Then they are left with neither life insurance coverage nor significant investments to live on during their retirement years.

Several term-life insurance companies have developed a marketing strategy to encourage people to buy term policies and to invest the difference between the less expensive term policy premiums and more expensive whole-life policy premiums. Frequently such a strategy is referred to as "buy term and invest the difference." Some clients choose to purchase both whole-life and term policies. They may purchase a relatively small whole-life policy of perhaps $25,000, to cover final expenses and to pay certain debts, and a large term policy for income replacement during their working years when their responsibilities to their children are the highest. They also begin to make regular investments during their working years so that they can accumulate enough money for their retirement years.

Many senior citizens find themselves in difficult circumstances during their retirement years largely because they did not receive effective financial planning while they were much younger. Until the 1980's, most people thought that only wealthy people needed financial planning. This was not the case, but financial planning was relatively expensive and people believed that they did not need to plan for their retirements because they could rely on Social Security and employee pensions. People trusted their local life insurance agents who sold them reliable whole-life policies and gave them some financial advice. Life insurance agents were often licensed securities agents as well, and they would often offer their clients one or two mutual funds sold by their companies, but the choices of mutual funds were often severely limited. When the high inflation of the 1970's and the early 1980's began to significantly decrease the actual value of pensions and the cash values in whole-life policies, people suddenly began to realize that they could no longer rely on Social Security and company pensions for their retirements. Throughout the 1980's, many companies made it more and more difficult for people to qualify for meaningful pensions. Since most employees now change jobs at least seven times during their working years, they never accumulate enough years with a single company to receive a meaningful pension.

## THE ROLE OF LIFE INSURANCE FOR RETIRED PEOPLE

Senior citizens do not want to be a burden to their children. For this reason, many retired people set aside enough money to pay for their funerals or prepay their final expenses by means of a life insurance policy paid for in full through just one payment at a funeral home. Such "single-pay" policies were marketed very successfully by funeral home directors starting in the 1980's because they met a definite need. People who purchase such policies normally designate the funeral home as the beneficiary. In most states, funeral home directors commit themselves to accepting the benefits paid from such policies as full payment for funeral expenses, as long as the survivors do not change the original funeral arrangement by choosing, for example, a more expensive coffin.

Senior citizens who received effective financial planning during their working years do not need much life insurance during their retirement years because their responsibilities are then much lower. For example, they no longer have to pay for the education of their children. If they began investing

regularly when they were younger, they now have enough money on which to live. Their insurance needs are now very different. As people age, nursing home insurance becomes more important for their financial planning than life insurance. Such policies normally cover the first two or three years of residence in a nursing home, after a specified waiting period. By their very nature, nursing homes are labor-intensive and very expensive to live in. Many elderly people each year have debilitating strokes or are diagnosed with illnesses such as Alzheimer's disease, which may make it necessary for the spouse or the adult children to place the person in a nursing home, largely because no other choices remain. Life insurance plays an important role in people's lives during their working years, but other forms of insurance become more important for people during their retirement years.

—*Edmund J. Campion*

**See also** Death and dying; Fraud against the elderly; Funerals; Income sources; Life expectancy; Nursing and convalescent homes; Pensions; Retirement; Retirement planning; Smoking.

**FOR FURTHER INFORMATION:**

Bishop, George A. *Capital Formation Through Life Insurance: A Study in the Growth of Life Insurance Services and Investment Activities.* Homewood, Ill.: Richard D. Irwin, 1976. Explains clearly how cash values and insurance premiums are calculated and indicates how life insurance companies invest cash values in the stock market.

Black, Kenneth, Jr., and Harold D. Skipper, Jr. *Life Insurance.* 12th ed. Englewood Cliffs, N.J.: Prentice Hall, 1994. A college textbook that explains clearly the nature of life insurance policies and the investment strategies of life insurance companies.

Cummins, J. David, and Joan Lamm-Tennant, eds. *Financial Management of Life Insurance Companies.* Boston: Kluwer, 1993. Explains clearly why certain life insurance companies have prospered while others went bankrupt. Also describes how states regulate life insurance companies.

Gollin, James. *Pay Now, Die Later.* New York: Random House, 1966. Albeit somewhat old, this book explains well how agents persuade people to buy whole-life and not term policies.

Pedoe, Arthur. *Life Insurance, Annuities, and Pen-*

*sions.* Toronto: University of Toronto Press, 1970. Describes very clearly how life insurance policies, annuities, and pensions are calculated and paid.

## LITERATURE

**RELEVANT ISSUES:** Culture, media, values

**SIGNIFICANCE:** Literature about growing old may have themes of unresolved conflicts, stereotypical attitudes, family relationships, and physical limitations

Identities of aging in literature reflect the delicate balancing acts faced in old age. Older adults strive to remain active, healthy, and engaged in life. At the same time they draw upon a rich storehouse of memories, continue to face unresolved conflicts relating to families and other relationships, and are constantly challenged by loss, grief, and death.

### AUTOBIOGRAPHY

The unfolding of one's identity through time is often expressed in old age in the form of autobiography. May Sarton's poetry and extensive journals exemplify the qualities of introspection, creativity, and self-awareness available in old age. In her poem "Gestalt at Sixty," she charts the patterns of her existence that have contributed to her development. In "On a Winter Night," she meditates on the aging process and finds images of clarity, growth, seasoning, and regeneration to overcome the anxieties and tensions of old age. Sarton's journals are a record of her aging and her struggle to resolve tensions between her need for solitude and her obligations to society as a writer. Representative works include *Journal of a Solitude* (1973), *At Seventy* (1984), and *After the Stroke* (1988). *Endgame: A Journal of the Seventy-ninth Year* (1992) summarizes the indignities of chronic illness, frailty, loneliness, loss, and recurring bouts of depression that dominate her old age. She feels a loss of identity—she feels that the Sarton people have known has become a stranger, someone who is ill and frail. Her next journal, *Encore* (1993), shows her rejuvenated and restored to her former strength as she engages life.

Other significant autobiographical works include Alan Olmstead's *Threshold: The First Days of Retirement* (1975), Elizabeth Gray Vining's *Being Seventy: The Measure of a Year* (1978), and Florida Scott-Maxwell's *The Measure of My Days* (1968). The former texts emphasize the pitfalls, pleasures, and eventual fulfillment experienced in retirement. Scott-Maxwell explores issues of aging and identity with subtlety and depth. She maintains that the task of old age is to add to and clarify one's sense of self, whatever the cost.

### LIFE REVIEW

Older adults find meaning in their lives and gain insights into their identities through the processes of reminiscence and life review. Identity in old age is forged through self-reflection, memory, and integration. Such concerns may be addressed by older adults in autobiographical works, as noted above. Similar concerns may be addressed as well in fictional works. In some cases elderly characters fail to complete a life review that provides a sense of perspective. For example, the old woman in Katherine Anne Porter's story "The Jilting of Granny Weatherall" rehashes on her deathbed the awful events that led to her life of isolation and loneliness. She dies with the effects of her early loss unresolved in her memory. Willy Loman's life review, in Arthur Miller's play *Death of a Salesman* (1949), leads to a stripping away of the lies that have been the basis of his character and identity. He is exposed as lonely, vulnerable, and a dreamer. He dies without resolving important personal and family conflicts.

Other characters in fiction use life review to gain insights into their identities. The retired literary agent in Wallace Stegner's novel *The Spectator Bird* (1976) faces feelings of guilt over the death of his adult son and uncertainties over an unresolved relationship with a woman he met on a trip twenty years earlier. He exorcises these demons from the past only by confronting his memories and remaining receptive to his supportive and loving wife. Similar ghosts from the past haunt Hagar Shipley, in Margaret Laurence's *The Stone Angel* (1964). At ninety, Hagar maintains a grudge against God because her favorite son died in a tragic accident. By confronting her past, Hagar begins to learn that her unforgiving character, and her inability to acknowledge the love of key people in her life, have kept her alienated and isolated. A similar movement toward integration through life review is experienced by Eva, the main character in Tillie Olsen's novella *Tell Me a Riddle* (1976). Eva has lived for others her entire married life. When her husband wishes to move to an old folks' home, she rebels. As the conflict between husband and wife emerges in the story, Eva begins to reminisce and relive her turbulent childhood in Russia and her mentoring by a woman who was a political activist.

### MENTORING

Old people often are portrayed as mentors in literary works. The basis of their identity is their capacity to pass on truths and inspire the young. Examples include the novels *Set for Life* (1991), by Judith Freeman, and *Balancing Acts* (1981), by Lynn Sharon Schwartz. In Lisa Koger's story "Ollie's Gate," a young woman finds love and wisdom in a neighbor woman once disgraced for having an illegitimate child.

The tensions inherent in intergenerational relationships are vividly re-created in many works. Two examples are Daniel Menaker's collection of stories *Old Left* (1987) and Ernest Thompson's play *On Golden Pond* (1979). In the first example a young man spends years resisting the influence of his uncle, an irascible old man who has never lost his appetite for radicalism. After years of caregiving the nephew begins to yield to the old man's influence over his life. In Thompson's play an old man works out a lifelong tension with his adult daughter when she arrives for a visit to her parents' New Hampshire cabin.

The identity of African American elders is often based on relationships within the family. Commitment to family and to traditions is a recurring role in fictional portrayals. For example, Peter Taylor's story "What You Hear from 'Em?" is about an illiterate old woman, Aunt Munsie, who lives in a small Tennessee town and raises two white children after their mother dies. Aunt Munsie lives in hope that the boys she has raised, successful businessmen in Nashville, will return to live in the small town. Her loss of a well-defined role represents the tragedy of being cast aside for the sake of progress and social conformity.

Alice Walker's story "To Hell with Dying" portrays a town's response to a similar character, a man named Mr. Sweet, who relies on neighbor children to rejuvenate him when he seems near death. The narrator recalls the importance of this man to her personal development. The central

role of spiritual life to the identity of African American elders is expressed in the Allan Gurganus novella *Blessed Assurance* (1990). In this story an African American woman becomes an unlikely mentor to a white teenager, who sells funeral insurance one summer to poor black people in rural North Carolina. The old woman is ninety-four, nearly blind, and a devoted Christian. Her goodness and spirituality overwhelm the young man and provide him with new perspectives on wisdom and old age.

Ernest J. Gaines's novel *The Autobiography of Miss Jane Pittman* (1971) is structured as an oral history of a former slave who has lived more than one hundred years and has witnessed the beginnings of the Civil Rights movement in the South. Miss Jane's tenacity of character, her faith in the land, and her dedication to her loved ones are the essential traits of her identity. Her story offers painful testimony to the injustices inflicted upon African American people throughout American history. This story illustrates the importance of African American family life and reveals the quality of perseverance that

*Ernest J. Gaines, the author of* The Autobiography of Miss Jane Pittman. (Jerry Bauer)

is essential to Miss Jane's character.

African American culture and Jewish ethnicity collide in the play *Driving Miss Daisy* (1988) by Alfred Uhry. In this play Daisy Werthan, in her seventies, gradually mellows under the firm and loving hand of Hoke Coleburn, twenty years her junior, an itinerant laborer hired as a chauffeur. The two grow old together and become the closest of friends, despite the differences in race and class. A devout Jew is the focus of Max Apple's novel *Roommates: My Grandfather's Story* (1994). In his memoir, *Patrimony: A True Story* (1991), Philip Roth gains insights into his inheritance of the familial, cultural, and religious qualities that characterized his father. In doing so, he realizes how much his father's Jewish heritage means to his own identity and values.

### FRAILTY

Sometimes old people are stereotyped as always being frail, ill, or disabled. These physical conditions do have a serious impact on how the elderly regard themselves. They are not, however, the final determinant of one's identity in old age. For instance, Tracy Kidder's *Old Friends* (1993) is a study of life in a nursing home. The two men Kidder profiles continue to sustain meaningful lives despite the limitations of blindness and the effects of a stroke. Mark Van Doren's poem "The First Snow of the Year" tells of an elderly couple maintaining their affection for each other and recovering memories of their youthful love, despite the husband's increasing frailty.

Sometimes the effects of a particular disease seem to overwhelm one's identity and hope for a normal life in old age. Memoirs are often the chosen medium for depicting the ravaging effects of Alzheimer's disease on the victim as well as on the family. Rosalie Walsh Honel's *Journey with Grandpa: Our Family's Struggle with Alzheimer's Disease* (1988) and Carol Wolfe Konek's *Daddyboy* (1991) are two examples. Richard Stern's story "Dr. Cahn's Visit" illustrates a son's dedication to affirm the identities of his parents despite his mother's wasting away from cancer and his father's dementia.

### LOSS, GRIEF, DEATH

Understanding the complexity of identity in old age requires an examination of literary works about the end of life. Key works include Linda

Pastan's poems in *The Five Stages of Grief* (1978) and Mary Jane Moffat's anthology of stories and poems, *In the Midst of Winter: Selections from the Literature of Mourning* (1982).

Robert Anderson's play *I Never Sang for My Father* (1968) portrays a middle-aged son's fruitless attempts to find the perfect image or ideal of father. Eventually he acknowledges his father's identity as a bitter, unforgiving old man. Two poems, William Carlos Williams's "The Last Words of My English Grandmother" and Robert Frost's "An Old Man's Winter Night," portray contrasting contrasting responses to the end of life. In the first poem an irascible old woman ends life raging against what she considers to be life's inequities. In the second poem an old man, living alone in a remote farmhouse, acknowledges the uneasy balance that must be struck so that the old can sustain themselves in their own homes.                   —*Robert E. Yahnke*

*See also* Ageism; Aging: Biological, psychological, and sociocultural perspectives; Aging: Historical perspective; *Autobiography of Miss Jane Pittman, The; Bless Me, Ultima*; Creativity; Cultural views of aging; "Dr. Heidegger's Experiment"; *Driving Miss Daisy; Full Measure: Modern Short Stories on Aging; Gin Game, The; Having Our Say: The Delany Sisters' First One Hundred Years; I Never Sang for My Father;* "Jilting of Granny Weatherall, The"; *King Lear; Measure of My Days, The; Memento Mori; No Stone Unturned: The Life and Times of Maggie Kuhn; Old Man and the Sea, The; On Golden Pond;* "Roman Fever"; Sarton, May; Stereotypes; *Tell Me a Riddle; When I Am an Old Woman I Shall Wear Purple;* "Worn Path, A"; *You're Only Old Once!*

### FOR FURTHER INFORMATION:

Cole, Tom. *The Journey of Life: A Cultural History of Aging in America.* Cambridge, England: Cambridge University Press, 1992. An important contribution to social history, literature, and religious life as they apply to aging.

Rubin, Rhea Joyce. *Of a Certain Age: A Guide to Contemporary Fiction Featuring Older Adults.* Santa Barbara, Calif.: ABC-Clio, 1990. More than three hundred novels and stories written after 1980 are annotated and indexed according to a variety of subjects.

Shenk, Dena, and W. Andrew Achenbaum. *Changing Perceptions of Aging and the Aged.* New York: Springer-Verlag, 1994. Essays reflecting upon personal impressions of aging, aging in various cultures, images of women, and images of aging in literary works.

Yahnke, Robert E., and Richard M. Eastman. *Literature and Gerontology: A Research Guide.* Westport, Conn.: Greenwood Press, 1995. More than 340 annotated entries on novels, plays, poems, stories, and autobiographical works. Each entry is cross-referenced to one of forty-four topics in gerontology.

## LITTLE BROTHERS-FRIENDS OF THE ELDERLY

**DATE:** Founded in 1946

**RELEVANT ISSUES:** Economics, sociology

**SIGNIFICANCE:** This organization provides food and attention to isolated elderly people; volunteers provide medical transportation, advocacy skills, entertainment outings, and regular visits that promote mutual friendships

After World War II in Paris, nobleman Armand Marquiset began a Catholic lay brotherhood whose mission was to deliver hot meals, accompanied by a bouquet of flowers, to the elderly poor. Called Les Petits Frères des Pauvres (Little Brothers of the Poor), Marquiset's organization spread to the United States in 1959 when he sent Michael Salmon to Chicago, where he founded a branch of the Little Brothers.

In 1967, Salmon married, and Little Brothers opened its volunteer opportunities to men and women of all faiths and ages. In 1983, the United States branch of the Little Brothers of the Poor was renamed Little Brothers-Friends of the Elderly. By the late 1990's, Little Brothers had eight member countries: Canada, France, Germany, Ireland, Mexico, Morocco, Spain, and the United States. Offices in the United States exist in Boston, Chicago, Cincinnati, Hancock (Michigan), Minneapolis, Philadelphia, and San Francisco. Smaller affiliates, called Friends of Little Brothers, consist of groups of volunteers in other cities who provide services to the elderly under the auspices of the national organization.

Volunteers are usually matched with an elderly friend to provide companionship and any services that are needed, such as providing transportation to a doctor, delivering hot meals, writing letters, reading, shopping for food, and running other errands. Little Brothers also provides group outings, such as holiday parties, summer picnics, and travel to tourist attractions, thus supporting the Little Brothers' credo, Flowers Before Bread. In the United States during the 1990's, this small organization boasted a staff of 6,500 volunteers, with 78 percent of its funds going directly to programs.

—*Rose Secrest*

*See also* Friendship; Home services; Leisure activities; Loneliness; Social ties.

## LIVING TOGETHER. *See* COHABITATION.

## LIVING WILLS

**RELEVANT ISSUES:** Family, health and medicine, law

**SIGNIFICANCE:** A living will is a directive to physicians giving directions as to what methods of life-prolonging medical treatment should or should not be used when individuals have a terminal condition and become unable to make their wishes known

Living wills are not wills in the traditional sense. Traditional wills do not take effect until after persons die. Living wills come into effect while individuals are still alive but are unable to make their wishes known (for example, if they are in a coma) or when they do not have the mental ability to legally make their wishes known (for example, if they have Alzheimer's disease or dementia). Living wills are also known as medical directives, advance directives, or directives to physicians. Living wills are directives to physicians and other health care personnel to perform or not to perform certain life-sustaining medical treatments that artificially prolong life, such as resuscitation, force feeding, or breathing assistance. Persons may also say that they want drug therapy to alleviate pain. Living wills are valid only in the case of terminal illnesses in most states, and in some states doctors are permitted only to withhold treatment.

Over the years the right to die with dignity and without the expense of large medical bills has been discussed by federal and state legislators. The U.S. Supreme Court in *Cruzan v. Director, Missouri Department of Health* (1990) decided that individuals have the right to control their medical treatment. Individuals' desires come first, even if they choose to forgo life-prolonging medical treatment while family members or physicians want to prolong life. Sometimes individuals can make such decisions themselves. For example, they can ask to be discharged from the hospital and return home. However, when persons are near the end of an illness or are involved in severe accidents, they are often no longer capable of making their wishes known. It is in such circumstances that living wills take effect, directing physicians to take or not to take action. Physicians who are not willing to abide by individuals' wishes must turn such cases over to other physicians.

Because accidents can happen to persons of all ages, living wills are not just for the elderly. It is easy to make a living will. Most hospitals and physicians have standard forms that have been approved by the state. When people are admitted to the hospital, they are usually asked if they have a living will. If not, they will be given the opportunity to make one. If they have specific wishes, they may decide to have attorneys draw up a living will.

One of the problems with living wills is that persons must decide in advance, without taking future circumstances into account. Another problem with them is that they only take effect when a patient's condition is terminal. Persons in the early stages of Alzheimer's disease, although not terminally ill, may not be mentally fit to make health care decisions. A durable power of attorney for health care or health care proxies allows individuals to deal with all these problems.                    —*Celia Ray Hayhoe*

**See also** Alzheimer's disease; Caregiving; Death and dying; Durable power of attorney; Health care; Hospice; Hospitalization; Mental impairment; Nursing and convalescent homes; Terminal illness; Wills and bequests.

# LONELINESS

**RELEVANT ISSUES:** Death, health and medicine, psychology

**SIGNIFICANCE:** Loneliness has profound effects on physical and mental health in all age groups; however, elderly people may be particularly susceptible to its effects

Human beings are social animals. Most people are raised in families, and most develop significant and important relationships during the course of their lifetimes in their many different roles: spouse, significant other, parent, child, friend, col-

league, or fellow member of religious or civic group. Interpersonal relationships are central to people's sense of self and to their lives. In later life, virtually all people experience changes in their personal relationships because of retirement from paid employment, divorce, illness, death of friends and loved ones, relocation to a new community, or the move of children to their own homes. These changes can lead to a sense of isolation and loneliness or, after a period of grieving for the loss of the original relationships, to new and different, but equally rewarding, relationships.

### DEFINING LONELINESS

Loneliness is largely a matter of perception. Some people are not lonely when they are by themselves, while others experience loneliness even when they are with other people. Loneliness can be defined as an uncomfortable sense of being isolated from others. It is a sense of not having anyone to rely on, even if living with others. Some researchers divide loneliness into two categories: external and internal. External loneliness occurs because of life circumstances, such as loss of a spouse; internal loneliness, on the other hand, is more a product of the personality of the person who feels alone.

Researchers who have examined loneliness in the elderly have found that about two-thirds of older people describe themselves as rarely or never lonely, about one-fifth as sometimes lonely, and one-tenth as frequently lonely. Elderly people who are chronically ill or homebound because of disability are particularly susceptible to loneliness. Others who are more likely to describe themselves as lonely include the oldest seniors, people who have lost a spouse, and those who care for a chronically ill person. Poverty, inadequate financial resources, and city dwelling are also associated with loneliness. People least likely to describe themselves as lonely are those who have a strong sense of community and a good social support system. Good health and adequate financial support are other important factors.

### EFFECTS OF LONELINESS ON HEALTH

Studies of heart health have demonstrated that people with strong social support systems have lower blood pressure and other evidence of good cardiac functioning. In addition, people undergoing stressful situations have lower heart rates in the presence of a familiar person than in the presence of a stranger. In addition, people who live alone are more likely to die following a heart attack. One study showed that a far greater proportion of people with good social support who had a heart attack were still alive five years later than those who were socially isolated. The death rate from all causes is two to four times higher in people who are socially isolated.

Some cardiac changes in socially isolated people may be caused by poor health habits. Lonely people may have increased difficulty buying or preparing food for themselves or even feeling like eating. They may also have difficulty getting sufficient exercise. They have no one to remind them to take their medications. These lifestyle factors may, in turn, contribute to heart disease and other health problems, such as osteoporosis. Most researchers feel, however, that the explanation for the effects of social support or isolation on the heart are more complex than changes in health habits that come with isolation. Social support and isolation seem to affect the complex interactions of the nervous system, hormones, cells, and tissues.

The hypothalamus and pituitary gland regulate body functions by releasing stimulating hormones that cause responses in target organs elsewhere in the body. These target organs in turn release hormones that provide feedback to the hypothalamus and pituitary, telling them when to shut off the flow of stimulating hormones. When a person is under stress (including the stress of loneliness), the hypothalamus and pituitary activate the adrenal glands. The adrenals then produce a number of hormones, including norepinephrine, which stimulates the sympathetic nervous system. The sympathetic nervous system in turn causes the blood flow and heart rate to increase and breathing to be more rapid. While these changes are valuable in an emergency, they are detrimental when they continue for long periods of time, as in the chronic stress of loneliness, and may ultimately lead to heart attack or other cardiac problems.

Other studies have shown that the immune systems of older people with good social support function better than those of lonely people. People with close personal relationships have a better response to immunizations, for example. People who are lonely have fewer antibodies against

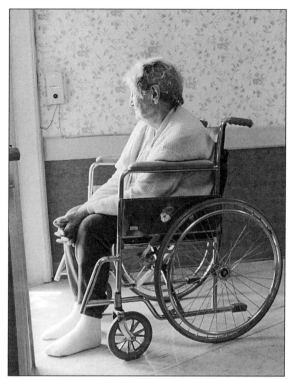

*Some elderly women find their social network shrinking as loved ones die or move away and opportunities for new relationships become more limited.* (James L. Shaffer)

pneumococcal disease, a common cause of pneumonia in older people. Levels of natural killer cells that fight infection are lower in lonely people, and white blood cells respond more slowly.

Loneliness is thought to be at the root of much of the anxiety and depression seen in older people. In addition, some people may increase their alcohol or other drug intake to deal with the psychological pain associated with loneliness, leading to alcoholism or addiction. Loneliness also contributes to suicide. Factors strongly associated with suicide include widowed or divorced states, retirement or unemployment, solitary living conditions, isolation, recent moves, poor health, depression, alcoholism, loneliness, and feelings of rejection or of being unloved.

### RECOGNIZING AND OVERCOMING LONELINESS

Older people often do not reveal their feeling of loneliness to others. Health care workers, friends, and family may have to recognize loneliness through other clues. Psychologists have identified many behaviors that may indicate loneliness, including clutching at a visitor's arm or hand, talking excessively, sitting with tightly crossed arms or legs, or wearing drab clothing. People who are deaf or depressed or who have urinary incontinence may be reluctant to interact with others, increasing their isolation and loneliness.

The key to overcoming loneliness is often as simple as increasing contact with other people. Senior centers serve group meals, offer classes, facilitate "foster grandparent" programs, and provide transportation to various places. Volunteering at a hospital, child care center, library, church, or school is another way of making contact with people. Pets may also provide needed companionship. Moving out of a house and into a retirement center is a solution for some. These centers allow people to live in the privacy of their own apartments but give them access to communal dining, group activities, opportunities for social and cultural events, and medical care.

Friends and relatives can visit or otherwise communicate with the homebound on a regular basis. In addition to the more traditional telephone call or letter, newer technologies, such as interactive television and the Internet, offer interesting possibilities for maintaining contact with loved ones who are far away. Some city planners have designed neighborhoods and buildings that make it more likely for people to interact formally and informally with others. Local, state, and federal governments can assist with appropriate housing and safety policies that support the elderly.

Psychotherapy may also be useful in helping people deal with loneliness. One study indicated that blood pressure improved among elderly people who described themselves as lonely after small-group discussions. Support groups may be helpful both for individuals with chronic illness and for their caregivers. Individual counseling to guide and encourage lonely people in their interactions with others, as well as antidepressant medications, may also be useful.

*—Rebecca Lovell Scott*

**See also** Alcoholism; Communication; Depression; Family relationships; Friendship; Heart attacks; Heart changes and disorders; Illnesses among the elderly; Internet; Pets; Psychiatry, geriatric; Senior citizen centers; Social ties; Stress and coping skills; Suicide; Volunteering.

**FOR FURTHER INFORMATION:**
Boyd, Malcolm. "It Comes Down to Hope." *Modern Maturity* 38, no. 6 (November/December, 1995).
Dykstra, Pearl. "Loneliness Among the Never and Formerly Married: The Importance of Supportive Friendships and a Desire for Independence." *The Journals of Gerontology, Series B* 50, no. 5 (September, 1995).
Forbes, Anne. "Loneliness: Caring for Older People, Part 5." *British Medical Journal* 313, no. 7,053 (August 10, 1996).
Frauenhofer, Dorothy, et al. "Relationships in Middle and Later Life." In *The New Ourselves, Growing Older: Women Aging with Knowledge and Power,* edited by Paula Doress-Worters and Diana Laskin Siegal. New York: Touchstone, 1994.
Friedan, Betty. *The Fountain of Age.* New York: Simon & Schuster, 1993.
"Hearts and Minds, Part 2." *Harvard Mental Health Letter* 14, no. 2 (August, 1997).
Koropeckyj-Cox, Tanya. "Loneliness and Depression in Middle and Old Age: Are the Childless More Vulnerable?" *The Journals of Gerontology, Series B* 53, no. 6 (November, 1998).
Seid, Roberta Pollack. "Only the Lonely . . ." *Shape* 17, no. 6 (February, 1998).
Thone, Ruth Raymond. *Women and Aging: Celebrating Ourselves.* New York: Hayworth Press, 1992.

## LONG-TERM CARE FOR THE ELDERLY

**RELEVANT ISSUES:** Biology, family, health and medicine, psychology

**SIGNIFICANCE:** The management of the health, personal care, and social needs of elderly people is crucial as they experience decreases in physical, mental, and/or emotional abilities

The process of aging is inevitable. In the earlier stages of life, aging involves the acquisition and development of new skills and abilities, facilitated by the guidance and assistance of others. Later, the middle stages involve the challenges of maintaining and applying those skills and abilities in a manner that is primarily self-sufficient. Finally, in the end stages of life, aging involves the deterioration and loss of skills and abilities, with adequate functioning again being somewhat dependent on the assistance of others.

*Many different types of residential housing are available for the extended care of seniors, ranging from retirement communities to nursing homes.* (James L. Shaffer)

For many individuals, the final stages are brief, allowing them to live independently right up to their time of death. Thus, many experience little loss of their abilities to function independently. Others, however, endure more extended stages of later life and require greater care. For these individuals, losses in physical, emotional, and/or cognitive functioning (mental processes such as awareness, knowing, reasoning, problem-solving, judging, and imagining) frequently result in a need for specialized care. Such care involves whatever is necessary so that these individuals may live as comfortably, productively, and independently as possible.

### THE NEEDS OF ELDERS

The conditions leading to a need for long-term care are as varied as the elderly are themselves. Special needs for elders requiring extended care often include the management of physical, health,

emotional, and cognitive problems. Physical problems dictating lifestyle adjustments include decreased speed, dexterity, and strength, as well as increased fragility.

Changes to the five senses are also common. Visual changes include the development of hyperopia (farsightedness) and sometimes decreased visual acuity. Hearing loss is also common, such that softer sounds cannot be heard when background noise is present or sounds need to be louder in order to be perceived. Particularly noteworthy is that paranoia, depression, and social isolation often result as side effects of visual and hearing impairments in elders; they are not always signs of mental deterioration. Similarly, one's sense of touch may also be affected, such that the nerves are either more or less sensitive to changes in temperatures or textures. Consequently, injuries attributable to a lack of awareness of potential hazards or supersensitivities to temperature or texture may result. One example would be an elderly woman overdressing or underdressing for the weather because of an inability to judge the outside temperature properly. Another would be an elderly man cutting or wounding himself out of a lack of awareness of the sharpness of an object. Finally, both taste and smell may change, creating a situation in which subtle tastes and odors become imperceptible or in which tastes and smells that were once pleasant become either bland or unpleasant.

Health problems among the aged often demand increased management as well. Case management is an interdisciplinary approach to medical care characterized by the inclusion of physical, psychological, social, emotional, familial, financial, and historical data in patient treatment. Coordination of drug therapies and other medical interventions by a case manager is critical, as a result of increasing sensitivities in elders to physical interventions. Typical health conditions bringing elderly people into long-term care settings may include heart disease and strokes, hypertension, diabetes mellitus, arthritis, osteoporosis, chronic pain, prostate disease, and cancers of the digestive tract and other vital organs. Estimates are that approximately 86 percent of the aged are affected by chronic illnesses. Long-term care addresses both the medical management of these chronic illnesses and their impact on the individual.

An issue related to health and physical problems in the aged is malnutrition, a physical state characterized by an imbalance of dietary proteins, carbohydrates, fats, vitamins, and minerals, given an individual's physical activity and health needs. For a variety of reasons, elders often fall victim to malnutrition, which can contribute to additional health problems. For example, calcium deficiency can increase the severity of heart disease and increase the likelihood of osteoporosis and tooth loss. Thus, a vicious cycle of medical problems can be put into motion. Factors contributing to malnutrition are multifaceted. Poverty, social isolation, decreased taste sensitivity, and tooth loss combine with lifelong dietary habits that can sometimes predispose certain elders to malnutrition. As such, attention toward the maintenance of healthy dietary habits in the elderly is critical to successful long-term care, regardless of the type of setting in which the care is being given.

Along with these physical aspects of aging come emotional and cognitive changes. Depression, anxiety, and paranoia over health concerns, for example, are not uncommon. Additionally, concerns about the threat of losing one's independence, friends, and former lifestyle may also contribute to acute or chronic mood disorders. Suicide is a particular danger with the elderly when mood disorders such as depression are present. Elderly people are one of the fastest growing groups among those who commit suicide. The stresses accompanying losing a spouse or enduring a chronic health problem can often be triggers to suicide for depressed elders. One should note, however, that elders are not particularly prone to depression or suicide because of their age but that they are more likely to experience significant stressors that lead to depression.

More common, less lethal problems associated with conditions such as depression, anxiety, and paranoia are weight change, insomnia, and other sleep problems. Distractibility, decreased ability to maintain attention and concentration, and rumination over distressing concerns are also common. Finally, some elders may be observed as socially isolated and prone to avoidance behavior. As a result, some become functionally incapacitated because of distressing emotions.

What is critical to remember, in addition to these signs, is that some elders may not describe their problems as emotional at all, even though that is the primary cause of their discomfort. Individual differences in how people express themselves must be taken into account. Thus, while some elders may report being depressed or anxious, others may instead report feeling tired. Reports of low-level health problems that are vague in nature, such as aches and pains, are also common in elders who are depressed. It is not uncommon for emotional problems to be expressed or described indirectly as physical complaints.

Decreased cognitive functioning may result from more serious problems than depression, such as organic brain syndromes, which are clusters of behavioral and psychological symptoms involving impaired brain function (including delirium, delusions, amnesia, intoxication, and dementias) where etiology is unknown. These typically include problems such as dementias from Alzheimer's disease, Pick's disease, Huntington's chorea, alcohol-related deterioration, or stroke-related problems. Other causes may be brain tumors or thyroid dysfunction. With all dementias, however, the hallmark signs are a deterioration of intellectual function and emotional response. Memory, judgment, understanding, and the experience and control of emotional responses are affected. Functionally, these conditions reveal themselves as a combination of symptoms, including increased forgetfulness, decreased ability to plan and complete tasks, difficulties finding names or words, decreased abilities for abstract thinking, impaired judgment, inappropriate sexual behavior, and sometimes severe personality changes. In some cases, affected individuals are aware of these difficulties, usually in the earlier stages of the disease processes. Later, however, even though their behavior and abilities

may be quite disturbed, they may be completely unaware of the severity of their problems. In these cases, long-term care often begins as a result of outside intervention by concerned friends and family members.

### OPTIONS FOR LONG-TERM CARE

Extended care for the aged requires an interdisciplinary effort that usually involves a team of physicians, psychologists, nurses, social workers, and other rehabilitative specialists. Depending on the nature of the problems requiring care and management, any of these professionals may take part in the care process. Additionally, the involvement of concerned individuals who are close to the elder needing care is critical. Family members (including the spouse, children, and extended fam-

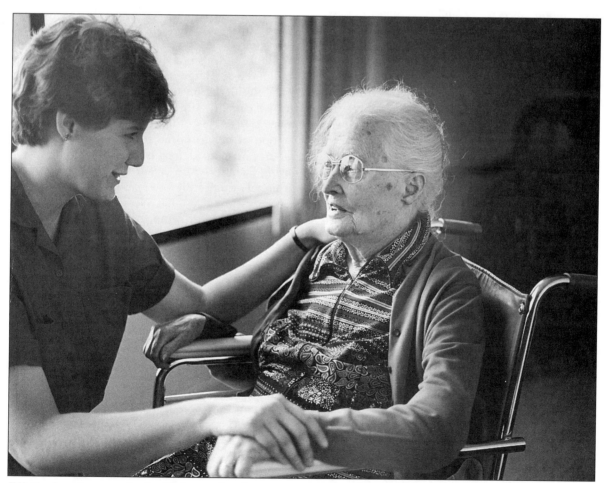

*Effective long-term care for the elderly must involve social interaction as well as medical or custodial attention.* (James L. Shaffer)

ily) and close friends are invaluable sources of information and of emotional and instrumental support. Their ability to assist an elder with instrumental tasks such as cooking, house cleaning, shopping, and money and medication management is crucial to the successful implementation of a long-term care plan.

In all cases, long-term care for the aged involves the design of a comprehensive plan to address the multifaceted needs of the elder. Just as younger persons have psychological, social, intellectual, and physical needs, so do elders. As such, thorough assessment of an elder's abilities, goals, expectations, and functioning in each of these areas is required. The primary methods of evaluation are usually a thorough physical examination and a mental status examination, which is a comprehensive evaluation assessing general health, appearance, mood, speech, sociability, cooperativeness, motor activity, orientation to time and reality, memory, general intelligence, and other cognitive functioning. Once needs are identified, a plan can then be designed by the team of health care professionals, family and friends assisting with care, and, whenever possible, the elder. In general, the overarching goal is to design a case management plan that maximizes the independent functioning of the aged person, given certain physical, psychiatric, social, and other needs.

Specific management strategies are designed for the problems that need to be addressed. Physical, health, nutritional, emotional, and cognitive problems all demand different management settings and strategies. Additionally, care settings may vary depending on the severity of the problems that are identified. In general, the more severe the problems, the more structured the long-term care setting and the more intense the psychosocial interventions, or treatments that enhance individual psychological and social functioning by assisting with the development of the skills, attitudes, or behaviors necessary to function as independently as possible.

For less severe problems, adequate management settings may include the elder's own home, the home of a family member or friend, a shared housing setting, or a seniors' apartment complex. Shared housing is sometimes called group-shared, supportive, or matched housing. Typically, it refers to residences organized by agencies where up to twenty people share a house and its expenses, chores, and management. Ideal candidates for this type of setting include elders who want some daily assistance or companionship but who are still basically independent. Senior apartments, also called retirement housing, are usually "elderly only" complexes that range from garden-style apartments to high-rises. Ideal candidates for this type of setting include nearly independent elders who want privacy, but who no longer desire or can manage a single-family home. In either of these types of settings, the use of periodic or regular at-home nursing assistance for medical problems, or "home helpers" for more instrumental tasks, might be a successful adjunct to regular consultation with a case manager or physician.

Problems of moderate severity may demand a more structured setting or a setting in which help is more readily available. Such settings might include continuing care retirement communities or assisted-living facilities. Continuing care retirement communities, also called life care facilities or communities, are large complexes offering lifelong care. Residents are healthy, live independently in an apartment, and are able to use cafeteria services as necessary. Additionally, residents have the option of being moved to an assisted-living unit or an infirmary as health needs dictate. Assisted-living facilities—also called board-and-care, institutional living, adult foster care, and personal care settings—offer care that is less intense than that received in a medical setting or nursing home. These facilities may be as small as a home where one person cares for a small group of elders or as large as a converted hotel with several caregivers, a nurse, and shared dining facilities. Such settings are ideal for persons needing instrumental care but not round-the-clock skilled medical or nursing care.

When more severe conditions such as incontinence, dementia, or an inability to move independently are present, nursing, convalescent, or extended care homes homes are more appropriate settings. Intense attention is delivered in a hospital-like setting where all medical and instrumental needs are addressed. Typical nursing homes serve a hundred clients at a time, utilizing semiprivate rooms for personal living space and providing community areas for social, community, and family activities. Often, the decision to place an elder in this type of facility is difficult to make. The decision, however, is frequently based on the knowledge that these types of facilities provide the best possible setting for the overall care of the elder's medical, health, and social needs. In fact, appropriate use of these facilities discourages the overtaxing of the elder's emotional and familial resources, allowing the elder to gain maximum benefit. An elder's placement into this type of facility does not mean that the family's job is over; rather, it simply changes shape. Incorporation of family resources into long-term care in a nursing home setting is critical to the adjustment of the elder and family members to the elder's increased need for care and attention. Visits and other family involvement in the elder's daily activities remain quite valuable.

Regardless of the management setting, some basic caveats exist with regard to determining management strategies. First and foremost is that the aged individuals should, whenever possible, be encouraged to maintain independent functioning. For example, even though physical deterioration such as decreased visual or hearing abilities may be present, there is no need to take decision-making authority away from the elder. Decreased abilities to hear or see do not necessarily mean a decreased ability to make decisions or think. Second, it is crucial to ask elders to identify their needs and how they might desire assistance. Some elders may wish for help with acquiring basic living supplies from outside the home, such as foods and toiletries, but desire privacy and no assistance within the home. In contrast, others may desire independence outside the home with regard to social matters but need more instrumental assistance within the home.

Finally, it is important to recognize that even the smallest amount of assistance can make a significant difference in the lifestyle of the elder. A prime example is availability of transportation. The loss of a driver's license or independent transportation signifies a major loss of independence for any elder. Similarly, the challenges posed by public transit may seem insurmountable because of a lack of familiarity or experience. As such, simple and small interventions such as a ride to a store or a doctor's office may provide great relief for elders by assisting their efforts to meet their own needs.

Special management strategies may be required for specific problem areas. For physical deterioration, adequate assessment of strengths and weaknesses is important, as are referrals to medical, re-

habilitative, and home-help professionals. Hearing and visual or other devices to make lifting, mobility, and day-to-day tasks easier are helpful. Similarly, assisting the aged with developing alternative strategies for dealing with diminished sensory abilities can be valuable. Examples would be checking a thermometer for outdoor temperature to determine proper dress, rather than relying purely on sensory information, or having a phone that lights up when it rings. Health conditions also demand particular management strategies, varying greatly with the type of problem experienced. In all cases, however, medical intervention, drug therapies, and behavior modification therapies are commonly employed. Dietary problems (such as malnutrition or diabetes), cardiovascular problems (such as heart attacks), and emotional problems (such as depression) often require all three approaches. Finally, cognitive problems, particularly those related to depression, are sometimes alleviated with drug therapies. Others related to organic brain syndromes or organic mental disorders, which are mental and emotional disturbances from transient or permanent brain dysfunction (including drugs or alcohol ingestion, infection, trauma, and cardiovascular disease) with known organic etiology, require both medical interventions and significant behavior modification therapies and/or psychosocial interventions for elders and their families.

## PERSPECTIVE AND PROSPECTS

Advances in modern medicine are continually extending the human life span. Cures for dread diseases, improved management of chronic health problems, and new technologies to replace diseased organs are facilitating this evolution. For many, these advances translate into greater longevity, the maintenance of a high quality of life, and fewer obstacles related to ageism, or discrimination against individuals based on their age or the overlooking of individuals' abilities to make positive contributions to society because of their age. For others, however, the trade-off for longevity is some loss of independence and a need for extended care and management. Thus, the medical field is also affected by the trade-off of extending life, while experiencing an increasing need to improve strategies for long-term care for those who are able to live longer and longer despite health conditions.

As a result of this evolution, long-term care for the aged presents special challenges to the medical field. Over time, medicine has been a field specializing in the understanding of particular organ systems and the treatment of related diseases. While an understanding of how each system impacts the functioning of the whole body is necessary, health care providers must struggle to understand the complexities in the case management required for high-quality long-term care for the aged. Care must be interdisciplinary, addressing the physical, mental, emotional, social, and family needs of the aged individual. Failure to address any of these areas may ultimately sabotage the successful long-term management of elderly individuals and of their problems. In this way, medical, psychiatric, social work, and rehabilitative specialists need to work together with elders and their families for the best possible results.

Integrated case management with a team leader is increasingly the trend so that a variety of services can be provided in an orchestrated manner. While specialty providers still play a role, managers, usually a primary care physician, ensure that complementary drug therapies, psychiatric, and other medical treatments are administered. Additionally, they are key in bringing forth family resources for emotional and instrumental support whenever possible, as well as community and social services when needed.

What was once viewed as helping a person to die with dignity is now viewed as helping a person to live as long and as productive a life as possible. Increasing awareness that old age is not simply a dying time has facilitated an integrated approach to long-term care. The news that elders can be as social, physical, sexual, intellectual, and productive as their younger counterparts has greatly stimulated improved long-term care strategies. No longer is old age seen as a time for casting elders aside or as a time when a nursing home is an inescapable solution in the face of health problems affecting the aged. Alternatives to care exist and are proliferating, with improved outcomes for both patients and care providers.                 —*Nancy A. Piotrowski*

***See also*** Abandonment; Adult Protective Services; Aging: Biological, psychological, and sociocultural perspectives; Aging process; Alzheimer's disease; Arthritis; Bone changes and disorders; Brain changes and disorders; Cancer; Canes and walkers; Caregiving; Children of Aging Parents; Death and dying; Dementia; Depression; Diabetes; Disabilities; Euthanasia; Family relationships; Filial responsibility; Forgetfulness; Geriatrics and gerontology; Glaucoma; Health care; Hearing aids; Hearing loss; Heart disease; Home ownership; Home services; Hospice; Hospitalization; Housing; Hypertension; Illnesses among the elderly; Incontinence; Independent living; Injuries among the elderly; Malnutrition; Meals-on-wheels programs; Medications; Memory changes and loss; Mental impairment; Mobility problems; Neglect; Nursing and convalescent homes; Nutrition; Osteoporosis; Overmedication; Prostate cancer; Psychiatry, geriatric; Reading glasses; Retirement communities; Safety issues; Sensory changes; Stress and coping skills; Strokes; Terminal illness; Transportation issues; Vision changes and disorders; Wheelchair use.

**FOR FURTHER INFORMATION:**

*Diagnostic and Statistical Manual of Mental Disorders: DSM-IV.* 4th ed. Washington, D.C.: American Psychiatric Association, 1994. This manual provides detailed descriptions of the behavior symptoms used to diagnose psychiatric disorders, such as organic brain syndromes and affective disorders. Written by mental health professionals, this manual covers issues related to psychiatry, psychology, and social work.

Gerike, Ann E. *Old Is Not a Four-Letter Word: A Midlife Guide.* Watsonville, Calif.: Papier-Mache Press, 1997. This lighthearted book describes an alternative approach to aging that is focused on the positives.

Kane, Robert L., and Rosalie A. Kane. "Long-Term Care." In *Geriatric Medicine,* edited by Christine K. Cassel, Donald E. Riesenberg, Leif B. Sorensen, and John R. Walsh. 2d ed. New York: Springer-Verlag, 1990. This article describes trends in long-term care in the United States. Target populations, special risk factors, alternatives to long-term care, and case management issues are discussed.

Katz, Paul R., Robert L. Kane, and Mathy D. Mezey. *Advances in Long-Term Care.* Vol. 1. New York: Springer, 1991. One volume in an ongoing series covering issues related to the long-term care of elders by caregivers, both professional and nonprofessional. Written by medical, psychiatric, and nursing professionals, and discusses issues ranging from problem prevention to problem management.

Kübler-Ross, Elisabeth. *On Death and Dying*. New York: Collier Books, 1970. A classic in the study of grief. The nature of the grief process is outlined, and common emotional experiences related to grief and loss are described. Highly recommended for persons wanting to understand their own grief processes or the perspective of others who are experiencing loss.

Levin, Mora Jean. *How to Care for Your Parents: A Practical Guide to Eldercare*. New York: W. W. Norton, 1997. This book may be of practical use to individuals anticipating a need to care for disabled elders.

Mace, Nancy L., and Peter V. Rabins. *The Thirty-Six-Hour Day: A Family Guide to Caring for Persons with Alzheimer's Disease, Related Dementing Illnesses, and Memory Loss in Later Life*. Rev. ed. Baltimore: The Johns Hopkins University Press, 1991. An excellent reference for anyone dealing with dementia. It is appropriate both for individuals who are interested in learning about dementia because of personal concerns and for individuals who are concerned about managing a friend or relative. Symptoms, accompanying problems, management issues, and strategies for solutions are outlined.

Viorst, Judith. *Necessary Losses*. New York: Simon & Schuster, 1986. This book, written by a mental health specialist, focuses on clarifying losses that are common to all people at different times in the life cycle. An excellent and easy-to-read general resource for individuals experiencing losses caused by age and other factors or for those concerned about elders who are experiencing losses.

## LONGEVITY RESEARCH

**RELEVANT ISSUES:** Biology, demographics, economics, health and medicine

**SIGNIFICANCE:** Life expectancy improved dramatically in industrialized countries throughout the world in the twentieth century as a result of advances in nutrition and medicine

With many of the declines associated with aging having been eliminated or their onsets delayed, humans now live longer, more healthy lives. Never-theless, the search for better understanding and control over the aging process continues. Although most aging factors are unknown, many medical treatments have been explored to prevent the process. Dietary modification, exercise, antioxidants, and hormone treatments have all been suggested as avenues to slow aging. Unfortunately, due to the close interrelationship between disease and aging, there are practical limitations in life extension research. It is often impossible to ascertain which developmental phenomena are caused by natural aging and which are disease-related. More research is necessary to assess the ethics, safety, and effectiveness of many life extension strategies.

### THEORIES OF AGING

Why do humans age? Evolutionary biologist Richard Dawkins has suggested aging is part of humanity's natural evolution. Successful evolution is dependent on reproductive fitness, literally the efficiency of a species to reproduce. Yet, reproductive fitness has little to do with longevity. Humans do not need to live past the age of thirty (two human generations); in terms of evolution, any extra time alive after reproduction is superfluous. Humans need only to live long enough to pass on their genes to the next generation and ensure that generation's survival. Because long life is not important in engendering the next generation, some researchers believe that a trait for longevity is not something that can evolve.

Aging appears to be programmed into human cells from birth. Two pieces of data support this statement. First, it was once thought that human cells grown in tissue culture were immortal and could be grown indefinitely. Stanford University researcher Leonard Hayflick demonstrated that animal cells in culture could only be grown for a limited time as they were passed from one petri dish to the next. Eventually the cells died. The number of times the cells could be passed between petri dishes in the laboratory was called the Hayflick limit. This strongly supports the idea that death is programmed into the cells themselves. The second piece of data supporting this hypothesis is that telomeres, the deoxyribonucleic acid (DNA) sequences at the ends of chromosomes, seem to act like molecular clocks in aging. As cells age, telomeres shorten with each division, like tiny timekeepers keeping track of each cell multiplication.

*Florence Poston, 103, works on a sculpture at a senior citizen center in 1999. The goal of longevity research is to find ways to expand the human life span while maintaining as many quality years as possible.* (AP Photo/Chris Kasson)

Cancer cells do not have shortening telomeres, nor do they have Hayflick limits. These virtually immortal cells may be the key to understanding aging. Woodring Wright, a University of Texas researcher, took the enzyme telomerase, which lengthens telomeres in cancerous cells, and introduced the gene into normal cells. He examined the possibility that normal cells with telomerase can be made immortal without becoming cancerous. He hoped that if telomere shortening acts as the biological clock, he could bypass its effects.

Another theory suggests that aging occurs due to accumulated errors in DNA. Many factors damage cells and DNA. The buildup of errors over time may lead to aging as the enzymatic systems that repair DNA can no longer cope. Although ultraviolet and gamma radiation contribute to combined genetic errors, researchers suggest that cells and DNA are primarily damaged by dangerously modified molecules of oxygen. When oxygen becomes a charged, "free radical" molecule, it can easily damage DNA and proteins. Over the long term, this increasing damage presumably becomes irreparable. Substances that tend to inhibit this oxidative damage are known as antioxidants. It has been proposed that antioxidants may extend life by inhibiting the accumulation of DNA damage.

Related hypotheses suggest other ways aging damage might occur. Researcher Donald Morse proposed that cellular damage is caused by a buildup of "age pigments" that choke off and inhibit metabolic activity. Another theory suggests that thermal damage over a lifetime of heat exposure causes loss of enzymatic functions. Some researchers have suggested that lysosomal enzymes, used in cells to degrade waste, are released as bodies age and produce cellular corruption. A fourth theory states that errors accumulate in DNA as the damage repair systems decay over time. Researcher Harold Rabinowitz proposed that aging may be the result of lowered oxygen levels in critical areas of the body. One final speculation submits that aging is a result of the immune system self-destructing and attacking the body's cells. These hypotheses have little or no experimental support.

Cynthia Kenyon, a University of California researcher, believed that aging may be dependent on the activity of just a few genes. She isolated a flatworm longevity gene, called daf-16. Kenyon demonstrated that when the gene is activated, the life span of a normal adult flatworm is doubled. The gene acts through a central signaling mechanism and may function analogously to a system in human beings.

Related to Kenyon's work is that of researcher Huber Werner. Werner isolated the human mutant gene "wrn." A mutation in the single wrn gene causes Werner's syndrome, a disease characterized by rapid, premature aging in youngsters. The existence of this disease supports the hypothesis that human aging may be precipitated by just a few genes. Although it is not known how a single gene could cause premature aging, studies continue.

### Physical Approaches to Life Extension

Body weight was once thought the most important factor in longevity. Much of this evidence came from the Framingham Heart Study performed over several decades in Massachusetts with a group of 5,209 men and women. The Framingham study suggested that men overweight by as little as 20 percent had significantly higher mortality—but surprisingly, the mortality of underweight men was also greatly increased. Other studies by Harvard researchers I-Min Lee and Ralph Paffenbarger suggested that body weight, within 15 percent of optimal, is unrelated to mortality and that weight fluctuations contribute more to mortality by enhancing coronary stress. The Framingham data were reanalyzed by Yale researcher Kelly Brownell to examine fluctuations of body mass over time, and results were found to support the conclusions of Lee and Paffenbarger; changes in the body mass of both men and women were positively associated with increases in mortality. The data do not advise staying obese or under-weight to avoid changes in body mass, but suggest that the link between weight and longevity is complex.

Evidence from the classic work of Granville Nolen suggests that body mass is less important than caloric intake in increasing life span. In Nolen's study, one group of rats was allowed to eat freely while a second group was limited from an early age (thirty-five days) in their caloric intake to 60 to 80 percent of the control group. The life span of the restricted-diet group increased on average from about seven hundred days (in controls) to about nine hundred days. Also, caloric restriction extended life when mice started their restrictive diets at an older age of one hundred eighty days. It is still unclear whether caloric intake can be used to extend human life. The magnitude of the caloric restriction as well as the timing of it in humans is still being explored.

The amount and calories of the food eaten are not the only factors that affect longevity. Since early times one's diet has been said to contribute to longevity. The Romans and Greeks believed eating ambrosia, the "food of the gods," could grant immortality. Ambrosia is believed by ethnologist James Arthur to be a species of mushroom. In the 1800's, cod-liver oil was believed to be a life-extending agent. In the 1960's, eating oysters was said to increase virility and male potency in the elderly. In the 1970's, marketers insinuated that villages of Russian centenarians existed whose yogurt eating had brought them well into their second century of life. In the 1980's, bran, garlic, and olive oil were all proposed to lengthen life. In the 1990's, ginseng and tomatoes were touted as life extenders.

The negative aspects of foods have been stressed as well. "Age gurus" such as Karlis Ullis exhort that consuming white sugar and bleached flour may increase mortality, though this belief has little scientific support. Eating red meat is believed by many to contribute to the aging process; some even believe all meat introduces age-inducing "poisons" into the human body.

Although it seems likely that in balanced diets specific foods do not have an adverse effect upon life duration, specific nutrients of those foods may have a great impact upon mortality. Researchers Mary DeMarte and Hildegard Enesco gave one group of mice a balanced diet and another a diet without the amino acid tryptophan. Both groups received the same number of calories. The tryptophan-deficient group lived seventy days longer on average than the control. The mechanism by which this dietary restriction extends life is unknown; it may be by encouraging weight loss or caloric restriction or by reducing protein levels.

The least-understood strategy to increased longevity is physical exercise. In the 1800's, extreme physical exercise was said to damage the body, although this belief is no longer credited. Long-term studies of professional athletes suggest no adverse associations between athletic competition and longevity. However, it is still not clear whether physical exercise increases human life span. John Hollozsy of Washington University studied the effects of exercise on laboratory rats and found they have a longer life expectancy on average than the sedentary controls (approximately one thousand days versus approximately nine hundred days). Both groups were given as much food as they desired, but the active mice ate less food. This makes interpretation of the data complex. Did the experimental group have a longer life expectancy due to increased exercise, decreased caloric intake, other metabolic effects of the physical stress, or a combination of the three? It is not clear whether physical activity acts as a disease modifier or a true life extender.

## PHARMACOLOGIC APPROACHES TO LIFE EXTENSION

Many strategies using hormones or medications to produce life extension have been tested successfully in animal systems, but these treatments have not been appraised with humans. Care must be taken in applying the results of animal testing to humans.

Antioxidant treatments may be one path to life extension. Antioxidants are dietary supplements that destroy free radicals or prevent their production in the body. Several antioxidants have been administered to rats and humans in an attempt to lengthen life. Researchers Marc Bernarducci and Norma Owens reported that vitamin E treatments increased longevity in rats and flatworms by 10 to 15 percent. This seems promising for humans, but studies by Linus Pauling suggest that "megadosing" vitamin E may actually reduce life expectancy in men and women. Animal studies have also

been performed with vitamin C, but Bernarducci and Owens reported that vitamin C treatments alone had no significant effect on life span. It may be that antioxidant chemicals such as vitamins A, E, and C do not lengthen life by themselves but prevent the onset of cardiovascular and neoplastic diseases.

Spanish researcher Gustavo Barja suggested that enhanced production of antioxidant enzymes may be more effective than antioxidant dietary supplements. Barja treated frogs with amino-thiazole known to induce the synthesis of an antioxidant enzyme called superoxide dismutase (SOD). The enzyme is able to degrade and nullify free radicals. Frogs receiving aminothiazole demonstrated increased longevity over untreated frogs. Clinical applicability in humans is being examined; long-term effects of chemicals like aminothiazole in humans has not yet been determined.

In addition to experiments with chemicals or dietary supplements, longevity studies have been performed using various human hormones. There may be a connection between aging and the levels of many hormones that decline during aging. It is believed by many that hormone replacement therapy may be a route to extending human life. Human growth hormone (HGH), made in the adrenal glands, is important in maintaining skeletal and muscle strength. University of Florida researcher David Lowenthal observed that as humans age, HGH levels are reduced and in the elderly become deficient. Lowenthal administered HGH to elderly men and found benefits such as reduced body fat and increased muscle mass. There are several drawbacks with HGH, such as high cost, repeated need for injections, adverse physical effects such as carpal tunnel syndrome, and no evidence that it extends life.

Use of male hormones (androgens) in hormone replacement therapy have been documented since 1889 when Charles Edouard Brown-Sequard, the founder of modern endocrinology, self-administered canine testicular extract. The elderly Brown-Sequard claimed that the treatment increased his strength and mental clarity and gave him more energy. Although use of androgens as longevity agents has not been actively pursued, chemical precursors of androgens have been used to treat the aged.

In elderly men, there is a reduction in testosterone levels associated with a decline in its chemical precursor dehydroepiandrosterone (DHEA) made in the pituitary. Blood levels of DHEA are quite high in infancy but diminish as an individual ages. Researchers Pertti Ebeling and Veikko Koivisto found that in individuals over seventy, DHEA is virtually not detectable. Long-term DHEA treatment in mice reduces weight, lengthens life, and delays the onset of immune dysfunction. The DHEA hormone may act to increase life span through a mechanism similar to caloric restriction. According to studies by University of California researcher Samuel Yen, humans do benefit from DHEA treatment. Men and women taking fifty milligrams of DHEA a day for three months felt significant increases in physical and psychological well-being. Long-term effects of DHEA treatment are still being analyzed. There are concerns that, with extended use, DHEA may increase risks for cancer and other diseases.

Melatonin is a hormone produced by the pineal gland. It has been implicated in a range of activities including modulation of aging, sleep, sexual maturation, and fertility. Melatonin production is circadian with maximal synthesis occurring at night. Like HGH and DHEA, melatonin production decreases with advancing age. Bernarducci and Owens report that reduced melatonin levels in adult humans have been associated with cancer and chronic insomnia. Experiments have examined whether melatonin treatments can extend life. Swiss researcher Walter Pierpaoli gave mice drinking water treated with ten milligrams of melatonin per milliliter. Mean survival was increased significantly in the melatonin-treated versus control group (930 days versus 752 days). Treated mice were more vigorous and active and had better posture.

There is evidence that part of the life-extending mechanism of melatonin may be its activity as an antioxidant. Finnish researcher Seppo Saarela suggested that melatonin is a free radical scavenger and the most powerful antioxidant known. The hormone can significantly reduce tissue damage caused by free radical generation in sunlight. Additionally, melatonin appears to be nontoxic in high, prolonged dosages. Humans who take megadoses of melatonin (300 milligrams per day) for up to five years have demonstrated few ill effects.

Despite how benign and promising melatonin appears, questions have been raised about the hormone's physiological effects. It is still not clear if melatonin functions in the same way in humans as in mice. Since the hormone is normally produced in a well-defined cycle, it is not clear what administration schedules and dosages may be best for humans. Bernarducci and Owens also report worries that artificially high levels of melatonin in humans may alter levels of other hormones, such as thyroid hormone or testosterone. As with many of the treatments described, more study is required before all the risks of melatonin are understood.

*—James J. Campanella*

**See also** Aging process; Antiaging treatments; Antioxidants; Caloric restriction; Cancer; Cross-linkage theory of aging; Estrogen replacement therapy; Free radical theory of aging; Life expectancy; Nutrition; Vitamins and minerals; Weight loss and gain.

**FOR FURTHER INFORMATION:**

Bernarducci, Marc P., and Norma J. Owens. "Is There a Fountain of Youth?: A Review of Current Life Extension Strategies." *Pharmacotherapy* 16, no. 2 (March/April, 1996). Review covering the major paths of longevity research.

Heinerman, John. *Dr. Heinerman's Encyclopedia of Anti-Aging Remedies.* New York: Prentice Hall, 1997. Compilation of antiaging remedies from around the world.

Lee, I-Min, and Ralph Paffenbarger. "Change in Body Weight and Longevity." *JAMA: The Journal of the American Medical Association* 268, no. 15 (October 21, 1992). Study examining the importance of weight fluctuation in longevity.

Morse, Donald, and Harold Rabinowitz. "A Unified Theory of Aging." *International Journal of Psychosomatics* 37, nos. 1-4 (1990). Review of aging theories and their validity.

Nolen, Granville. "Effect of Various Restricted Dietary Regimens on the Growth, Health, and Longevity of Albino Rats." *The Journal of Nutrition* 102, no. 11 (November, 1972). Study examining the effects of restricting the caloric intake on longevity of rats.

Ullis, Karlis, with Greg Ptacek. *Age Right: Turn Back the Clock with a Proven, Personalized Antiaging Program.* New York: Simon & Schuster, 1999. Discusses the theories of mind and body aging and suggests how to build a personal antiaging program.

Weindruch, Richard. "Caloric Restriction and Aging." *Scientific American* 274, no. 1 (January, 1996). Review of recent research into caloric restriction and aging.

## LOOK ME IN THE EYE: OLD WOMEN, AGING, AND AGEISM

**AUTHOR:** Barbara Macdonald, with Cynthia Rich
**DATE:** Published in 1983
**RELEVANT ISSUES:** Culture, psychology, sociology
**SIGNIFICANCE:** Macdonald's collection of essays addresses the impact of both internalized and externalized biases against aging and the aged on older women

Over a five-year period, Barbara Macdonald wrote a series of essays concerning her experience with aging and ageism—the bias against older adults. Together with two articles written by her lesbian partner, Cynthia Rich, these writings were published as *Look Me in the Eye: Old Women, Aging, and Ageism.*

Macdonald begins by writing about her life as a lesbian and her early experiences with prejudice and discrimination. She quickly shifts, however, to her new struggles with the experience and stigma of aging. She begins describing her own sense of disconnection with her aging body and ends the book by discussing the realities of dying. Between the two, the reader is provided an intimate glimpse into the emotional and physical realities of age and the impact of ageism on an older woman.

Macdonald's essays reflect her personal experiences with ageism. She describes the emotional impact of people's failure to look her in the eye simply because of her gray hair and wrinkles. Often her essays reveal great personal anger, pain, and frustration in the face of diminishment caused by age. In one essay, Macdonald describes her treatment during a women's march. Event organizers were afraid that she would not be able to keep pace with the march. They based this concern simply on her appearance as an older woman. To compound the problem, organizers pulled her younger lover aside to ask if she thought Macdonald's age would be a problem. Macdonald's intimate essay chronicles her emotions, from the initial exhilaration at being part of the crowd to helplessness and fury.

Macdonald highlights the presence of ageism in the women's community. She describes a community that prides itself on inclusiveness and openness to diversity. Yet she attends women's events and sees few older women. She refers to this bias as the "invisibility of age." Additionally, Macdonald challenges the stereotypic view of older women as isolated, lonely, depressed, and ill. This is most notable in a letter Macdonald addresses to the women's community in response to a program questionnaire she received. The new program being developed was based on the stereotypic assumptions already described. As part of this letter, Macdonald outlines suggestions for combating ageism within the women's community.

Throughout her work, Macdonald provides a window into the private world of physical aging. Whether she is discussing thinning hair, wrinkles, or cataracts, the description is frank and personal. She exhorts older women to break the silence imposed on them to not talk about physical aging and the process of dying. She views this form of silencing as innately political and, like much of ageism, the result of patriarchy.

Rich's articles are written for a professional audience and provide a nice complement to Macdonald's essays. Rich's contributions include a book review and newspaper article analysis. The latter provides an excellent example and commentary on ageist language in the media.

—*Linda M. Woolf*

*See also* Ageism; Gay men and lesbians; Women and aging.

## LUNG DISEASE. *See* RESPIRATORY CHANGES AND DISORDERS.

# MACULAR DEGENERATION

RELEVANT ISSUES: Health and medicine

SIGNIFICANCE: Age-related macular degeneration (ARMD), a degenerative condition of the macula or central retina, affects about 15 percent of the U.S. population by age fifty-five and over 30 percent by age seventy-five. It is the leading cause of legal blindness in people over the age of sixty-five.

The macula is the tiny central region of the retina in the eye. It is made up of millions of light-sensing cells that help to produce central vision and provide maximum visual acuity. When the macula is damaged, a blind spot called drusen, made up of tiny yellow drops, develops in the central field of vision, and central vision becomes blurred or distorted. Central vision is needed to see clearly and to perform everyday activities such as reading, writing, driving, and recognizing people and things. Macular degeneration does not cause complete blindness since peripheral (side) vision is not affected.

There are two forms of ARMD: dry and wet. The dry form involves thinning of the macular tissues and disturbances in its pigmentation. About 70 percent of patients have the dry form. The remaining 30 percent have the wet form, which can involve bleeding within and beneath the retina, opaque deposits, and eventually scar tissue. The wet form accounts for 90 percent of all cases of legal blindness in macular degeneration patients.

## SYMPTOMS AND CAUSES

Neither dry nor wet macular degeneration causes pain. The most common early sign of dry macular degeneration is blurring vision that prevents people from seeing details less clearly in front of them, such as faces or words in a book. In the early stages of wet macular degeneration, straight lines appear wavy or crooked. This is the result of fluid leaking from blood vessels and lifting the macula, distorting vision.

The root causes of macular degeneration are still unknown, but medical authorities consider a number of factors as probable factors. Aging is the leading cause, with genetics, nutrition, smoking, and sunlight exposure all playing a role.

Age is the most important risk factor for macular degeneration. The older the patient, the higher the risk. Studies have shown that having a family with a history of macular degeneration raises the risk factor. Because macular degeneration affects most patients later in life, however, it has proven difficult to study cases in successive generations of a family.

Heavy smoking, at least a pack of cigarettes a day, can double a person's risk of developing ARMD. The more a person smokes, the higher the risk of macular degeneration. Moreover, the adverse effects of smoking persist, even fifteen to twenty years after quitting.

Poor dietary habits contribute as well. A diet high in saturated fats may clog the vessels leading to the eyes, thus reducing the flow of nutrient-rich blood. Excess fat may deposit itself directly in the membrane behind the retina. In this case, nutrients might not be able to pass through the "fat wall" to reach the cells that nourish the retina. There is evidence that eating fresh fruits and dark green leafy vegetables (such as spinach and collard greens) may delay or reduce the severity of age-related macular degeneration.

Some studies indicate that the mineral zinc might affect the development of macular degeneration. Zinc is important to chemical reactions in the retina. It is highly concentrated in the eye, particularly in the retina and the tissues surrounding the macula. Older people may have low levels of zinc because of poor diet or poor absorption from food. Some doctors believe that zinc supplements may slow down the progress of macular degeneration. Studies are not complete, however, and there are some adverse side effects of zinc supplements. They might interfere with other important trace metals such as copper, and in some people, the long-term use of zinc can cause digestive problems and anemia.

Strong sunlight seems to accelerate macular degeneration. Wearing special sunglasses may decrease the progress of the disease.

## TESTS AND ADJUSTMENTS

An effective test to determine if a person has wet macular degeneration is fluorescent angiography. A special dye is injected into a vein in the patient's arm and then flows to the blood vessels in the eye. Photographs are taken of the retina. The dye highlights any problems in the blood vessels and allows the doctor to determine if they can be treated. Annual eye examinations that include dilation of the pupils are also useful in early detection. Early detection is important because a person destined to develop macular degeneration can sometimes be treated before symptoms appear, which may delay or reduce the severity of the disease. Anyone who notices a change in vision should contact an ophthalmologist immediately.

People with macular degeneration learn to make use of the areas just outside the macula to see details. This ability to look slightly off center usually improves with time, though vision is never as good as it was before the macula was damaged.

A number of aids can help people with ARMD make the most of their remaining vision. Some low-vision aids include magnifying glasses, special lenses, electronic systems, and large-print books and newspapers. Sound aids include books on audiotape and products equipped with voice synthesizers such as calculators and computers. Using lamps that provide direct lighting for reading or tasks that require close vision, keeping curtains open, and painting walls and ceilings white make it easier for macular degeneration patients to see in the home.

### Treatment

There is no proven medical treatment for dry macular degeneration. In some cases of wet macular degeneration, laser photocoagulation is effective in sealing leaking or bleeding vessels. Laser photocoagulation usually does not restore vision but does prevent further loss. The surgery can be performed in a doctor's office or in an eye clinic on an outpatient basis.

Three other treatments have shown promise. One is surgery to reposition the retina. The doctor cuts through the outer layer of the eye to gain access to the retina, which can then be detached and repositioned without cutting. This technique enables the surgeon to maneuver the center of the macula away from the leaking blood vessels and place it next to healthier eye tissue.

Low-level radiation can also be used to stop blood vessel proliferation. The radiation is carefully measured to be high enough to stop the growth but low enough so that the retina is not damaged.

The third treatment is to inject photosensitive chemicals into the bloodstream of people with macular degeneration and to use lasers to stimulate those chemicals in the eye. When activated, the substances halt the proliferation of blood vessels. If blood vessels begin to grow again, repeat doses can be administered without adverse side effects.

A radical and controversial treatment was made by a team of doctors from the University of Chicago Medcial Center in 1997. They took cells from the retina of an aborted fetus and surgically transplanted them into the severely impaired left eye of an eighty-four-year-old patient. The transplanted cells proliferated, forming minute projections that stretched toward the patient's macula.

Fetal cells can divide and thus increase in number. Also they are likely to continue functioning for a number of years. Because the fetal cells are immature, they provoke little or no response from a transplant recipient's immune system. In the short term, the transplant appeared successful, but long-term results were not yet available. Because of the radical nature of the operation, the patient selected was severely impaired and had no other hope for improvement. Moreover, some people protested the use of cells from an aborted fetus. The need for severely impaired patients and ethical concerns virtually stopped research into this surgical procedure. —*Billie M. Taylor*

***See also*** Aging process; Cataracts; Disabilities; Health care; Nearsightedness; Reading glasses; Smoking; Vision changes and disorders.

**For Further Information:**

Munson, Marty, and Yun Lee. "See Better Days?: Veggies Make Help Hold Sight Steady." *Prevention* 48, no. 9 (September, 1996): 32-34.

Munson, Marty, Therese Walsh, and Yun Lee. "Please Pass the Butter: Skipping the Fat May Save Your Sight." *Prevention* 448, no. 1 (January, 1996).

Nash, J. Madeleine. "In Search of Sight." *Time* 150, no. 19 (Fall, 1997).

Pennisi, Elizabeth. "Gene Found for the Fading Eyesight of Old Age." *Science* 277, no. 5333 (September 19, 1997).

Ross, Linda M., ed. *Ophthalmic Disorders Sourcebook.* Detroit: Omnigraphics, 1997.

Seppa, Nathan. "New Treatments for Macular Degeneration." *Science News* 152, no. 13 (September 27, 1997).

Shapiro, Sara. "Tests and Treatments for Old-Age Eye Conditions." *Eye Q,* Spring, 1997.

Wolfe, Yun Lee. "'Rays' Your Eyesight: Radiation May Stabilize Age-Related Blindness." *Prevention* 49, no. 4 (April, 1997).

# MALNUTRITION

**RELEVANT ISSUES:** Health and medicine

**SIGNIFICANCE:** Malnutrition refers to both excess and deficient intakes of calories or nutrients; physical, psychological, and social factors all contribute to malnutrition in the aging population

Malnutrition literally means "bad nutrition"—that is, impaired health caused by an imbalance of specific nutrients or a deficiency or excess of energy (calories). However, malnutrition is most commonly thought to denote undernutrition or deficient intake, meaning consumption of inadequate amounts of nutrients to promote health.

Malnutrition in the elderly is a complex phenomenon. Contributing factors include poor physical health, functional disability, psychological problems, and socioenvironmental factors. The frail elderly, who are typically underweight and may suffer from a chronic illness, may require higher nutrient and caloric levels just to sustain health. Some of the illnesses associated with such malnutrition are emphysema, cancer, stroke, and end-stage Alzheimer's disease. Without adequate amounts of such nutrients as protein, vitamin $B_6$, iron, and zinc, the immune system is compromised, leaving the elderly susceptible to infections and further deterioration. For example, bedridden elderly are prone to bed sores, which are aggravated by malnutrition.

Undernutrition among the elderly frequently results from other conditions, such as a chronic disease, poverty, isolation, depression, or poor dental health. The most severe form of undernutrition is called protein energy malnutrition (PEM). In PEM, body fat stores are used up to provide energy, and eventually muscle tissue is broken down for body fuel. This type of wasting away is frequently associated with diseases such as cancer, end-stage Alzheimer's disease, emphysema, and other chronic degenerative diseases. PEM is sometimes identified among the elderly living in long-term care facilities and among those who are hospitalized. PEM is accompanied by multiple nutrient deficiencies.

## MALNUTRITION AND VITAMINS

Classic vitamin deficiency diseases, such as scurvy (vitamin C deficiency) and pellagra (niacin deficiency), are not as common among the elderly as conditions related to long-term inadequate nutrient intakes. Years may pass before the symptoms of long-term nutrient inadequacies surface.

Heart disease is thought to be associated with overnutrition: excess dietary fat, saturated fat, and cholesterol. However, low intakes, and consequently low blood levels, of certain B vitamins have been linked to heart disease. High levels of an amino acid derivative called homocysteine are associated with heart disease. Vitamins $B_6$, $B_{12}$, and folate are involved in clearing this from the blood. High levels of homocysteine are not always a result of a poor diet. Many elderly, especially those over sixty, develop a common stomach condition in which damaged stomach cells produce less stomach acid. Stomach acid is needed for the absorption of those B vitamins. Thus, inadequate absorption causes higher homocysteine levels in the blood and places one at risk for heart disease.

Absorption of vitamin $B_{12}$ requires a special protein called intrinsic factor. Some aging people produce less of this factor. As with other B vitamins, stomach acid is required for vitamin $B_{12}$ absorption. Without intrinsic factor or stomach acid, a deficiency disease known as pernicious anemia develops. Since vitamin $B_{12}$ is responsible for the maintenance and growth of nerve cells, its absence may lead to paralysis of the nerves and muscles; if not identified and treated with an injection of vitamin $B_{12}$, this condition may cause permanent damage to the spinal cord.

Researchers continue to investigate the role of antioxidant nutrients in retarding aging. Inadequate intakes of antioxidant nutrients such as beta carotene and vitamins C and E may be related to increased risk of several diseases, such as cardiovascular disease, cancer, cataracts, and even immune dysfunction.

## MALNUTRITION AND MINERALS

Osteoporosis is one of the best-known mineral deficiency diseases of aging. During adolescence and into early adulthood, bones become thicker and denser as calcium is deposited. Between ages thirty and forty, bone loss begins to exceed bone formation. If calcium intake has historically been poor, an inadequate amount of calcium has been deposited to compensate for bone loss during aging. Bones become brittle and susceptible to fracture. Osteoporosis is a major cause of disability and death for the elderly and places a heavy financial burden on society.

Research has revealed that osteoporosis is not exclusively a calcium-deficiency disease. Calcium is only one of several known osteoporosis risk factors; other factors include hormone status, body weight, physical activity, and vitamin D. Vitamin D works more like a hormone in the body and is responsible for enhancing calcium absorption. For several reasons, vitamin D levels in the blood are often lower as one ages. The primary source of vitamin D in the diet is milk, but many elderly people tend to decrease the amount of milk in their diet for various reasons. Even though the body can make vitamin D if the skin is exposed to sunlight, the elderly often avoid sun exposure, use sunscreens, or are homebound, making sunlight a less reliable source of vitamin D. In addition, the body must activate functional vitamin D, and activation declines with age.

Aging individuals may suffer from iron-deficiency anemia. The cause may be blood loss rather that dietary inadequacy. The most likely causes of anemia are gastrointestinal blood loss caused by chronic use of drugs such as aspirin, or blood loss from tumors. Low intake of zinc in the aging population can cause problems such as poor immune response and reduced taste perception for salt. One of the best sources of zinc is meat, but because some elderly people may not be able to afford meat or chew it, zinc intake may be inadequate.

### OVERNUTRITION

As people grow older, many suffer from diseases caused by overnutrition such as heart disease, diabetes (type II), osteoarthritis, some cancers, and gout. The prevalence of obesity increases with aging and often contributes to such diseases. The most important risk factor for heart disease is a high intake of saturated fat. Other contributing nutrients are dietary fat and cholesterol. Although overconsumption of dietary sodium is blamed for high blood pressure (hypertension), obesity is more often the cause. Obesity is also associated with endometrial and breast cancers and osteoarthritis.

Type II diabetes, also known as noninsulin-dependent diabetes mellitus, typically has its onset in adulthood and is characterized by the inability of body cells to use insulin. Many elderly people with diabetes suffer severe complications such as kidney disease, loss of vision, heart disease, and destruction of sensory function.

### MALNUTRITION AND BRAIN FUNCTION

Proper nutrition is important for normal brain function. Dietary inadequacy of vitamins $B_{12}$ and C have been associated with short-term memory loss; low intakes of riboflavin, folate, vitamin $B_{12}$, and vitamin C have been associated with poor performance in problem-solving tests; and inadequate intakes of thiamine, niacin, zinc, and iron have been associated with diminished cognition, degeneration of brain tissue, and dementia. Brain communication chemicals called neurotransmitters are synthesized from components of protein. One example is serotonin, which the body makes from an amino acid (protein building block) called tryptophan. Senile dementia is loss of brain function beyond that which is considered the normal memory loss of aging. There is evidence that people with senile dementia of the Alzheimer's type require more calories to maintain weight, perhaps because of the fidgeting and pacing behaviors that accompany the disease. Further complications include the inability to remember to eat or how to use utensils. Because it is important that these people maintain adequate body weight, they must be provided with nutritious meals and snacks that are easy to eat.

### TREATING MALNUTRITION

The biggest challenge faced by nutritionists is matching the type of nutritional support to the aging individual to best promote health. Special screening initiatives have been promoted to help increase the public awareness of malnutrition in the elderly population so that needy individuals can be identified. Special attention must be given to drug and nutrient interactions. Medications may compromise nutrition status by altering absorption or increasing excretion of nutrients. Attention must be given to physiological declines in the senses of smell and taste. Poor dentition and improperly fitting dentures can affect food consumption. Elderly people who have suffered from strokes may have difficulty swallowing, causing inadequate food intake. Poverty, depression, alcoholism, and social isolation are important contributing factors to malnutrition.

Special attention must be given to frail aging people who are recovering from illness to ensure that they are receiving enough calories as well as adequate amounts of other nutrients. Without both caloric and nutrient adequacy, the frail person can deteriorate rapidly. Therefore, nutritional supplementation in the form of liquid meal replacement or other fortified products may be necessary. For the overnourished and obese individual, nutritional support must provide high-quality, nutritious foods within a reasonable caloric intake to prevent further weight gain. Malnutrition as a result of poverty is exacerbated by lack of nutritional knowledge and poor food choices. Therefore, overall treatment of malnutrition involves addressing numerous psychosocial issues as well as the diet.                                          —*Wendy L. Stuhldreher*

*See also* Alzheimer's disease; Antioxidants; Caloric restriction; Cancer; Diabetes; Heart disease; Nutrition; Obesity; Osteoporosis; Sensory changes; Vitamins and minerals; Weight loss and gain.

## FOR FURTHER INFORMATION:

Rolfes, Sharon, Linda K. DeBruyne, and Eleanor Whitney. *Life Span Nutrition: Conception Through Life.* 2d ed. Belmont, Calif.: West/Wadsworth, 1998.

Schlenker, Eleanor D. *Nutrition in Aging.* 3d ed. Boston: McGraw-Hill, 1998.

Wardlaw, Gordon M. *Perspectives in Nutrition.* Boston: McGraw-Hill, 1999.

Whitney, Eleanor N., and Sharon R. Rolfes. *Understanding Nutrition.* 8th ed. Belmont, Calif.: West/Wadsworth, 1999.

## MANDATORY RETIREMENT. *See* FORCED RETIREMENT.

## MARRIAGE

**RELEVANT ISSUES:** Family, psychology

**SIGNIFICANCE:** Longer life expectancies now allow seniors to spend more than one-third of their married years together after their children have left home; for most, these years are characterized by happiness, intimacy, and social support

*The divorce rate is relatively low among the elderly—most unhappy couples split up before they reach later life, and for other couples shared memories and experiences create strong bonds of friendship as well as love. (James L. Shaffer)*

Individuals change over time, and so do their relationships. Marriage is no exception. As couples get older, they move into the stage that gerontologists call postparental marriages, referring to the time of life after the children have grown up and left home. This stage of marriage has been extended significantly as elders live longer and have fewer children. At the beginning of the twentieth century, it was typical for at least one of the parents to die before the last child had left home. By the end of the same century, parents were spending an average of thirteen years, or about one-third of their married life, together after their last child had left the house.

## BENEFITS OF MARRIAGE IN LATER LIFE

Many demographic studies of technological societies during the second half of the twentieth century showed that married men and women live longer and enjoy better physical and mental health than unmarried men and women. Although it can be argued that healthier people are more apt to marry than those in poor health, there is a lot of evidence that close relationships contribute to better mental and physical health. Other research shows that happily married people are healthier and better adjusted than either unmarried people or unhappily married people and that suicide rates for men are higher for those who are divorced, separated, or widowed than for those who are married.

Marriage also has economic benefits, especially for women. On average, both divorced and widowed women have lower incomes and fewer assets than all men and married women their age. Each year, a greater proportion of older women fall below the poverty line, a situation called the feminization of poverty. This occurs because of the combined facts that women generally spend fewer years in the workforce, have lower salaries and fewer benefits, take more financial and physical responsibility for their children, have more chronic illnesses and medical expenses in later years, and have longer life expectancies than their spouses.

The benefits of marriage also include social relations. Regardless of the increasing number of divorced and widowed individuals among older adults, the social world is still one of couples. Widows and widowers report being excluded from their long-term social groups and activities once they are no longer one-half of a couple. However, women seem to be able to form new social groups with other women, while men seem to become isolated without a spouse.

Although marriage vows traditionally include "in sickness and in health," young couples do not often consider that their role may include caregiver to an aging spouse. However, as life expectancy gets longer, there is a good chance that one or another spouse may spend the last years of their marriage in this role. A large number of Alzheimer's disease patients are cared for at home by their spouses, and the major caregivers for married people with other lingering illnesses are also usually spouses.

## THE QUALITY OF POSTPARENTAL MARRIAGES

Research on long-term marriages shows that older husbands and wives tend to be very much alike. They not only agree with each other when making plans or solving problems, but they also tend to give similar answers when asked individually about goals and favorite activities. Part of this may be because of the tendency for people to marry others who are similar to themselves, but part of this similarity between couples in late life comes from learning from each other and sharing a lifetime of experiences on which they base their opinions.

When discussions between middle-aged and elderly married couples have been compared, researchers have found that the older husbands and wives, regardless of the topic, show more positive and caring communication styles. They are more approving and respectful of each other, and they express less anger and aggression than the middle-aged couples. Several interpretations of these findings have been suggested. One is that age itself brings more tranquility and that couples no longer experience the same levels of intensity in their emotions. Another interpretation is that, as the years ahead become fewer, the motivation to change one's spouse decreases. Still another explanation is that married couples continually become closer and closer and that by late adulthood they approve of and respect each other more than ever before.

Divorce is rare in older adults. In the late 1990's, only about 5 percent of people over sixty-five were divorced, while 33 percent were widowed. However, this low divorce rate is not necessarily a reliable indicator of marital harmony. It is estimated by several researchers that about one-third of older marriages show some deterioration. One of the major reasons for a drop in marital quality is disequilibrium caused by the illness of one of the partners. Alzheimer's disease, for example, causes profound and chronic changes in the patient, and the emotional and physical stress of caregiving on an older husband or wife can take its toll in anger and depression.

Another cause of marital distress in older couples is a shift in dominance patterns, with women who were traditionally subordinate to their husbands becoming more dominant as they age. This happens for a variety of reasons. One is simply the

# Married and Unmarried Americans, 1950-1995

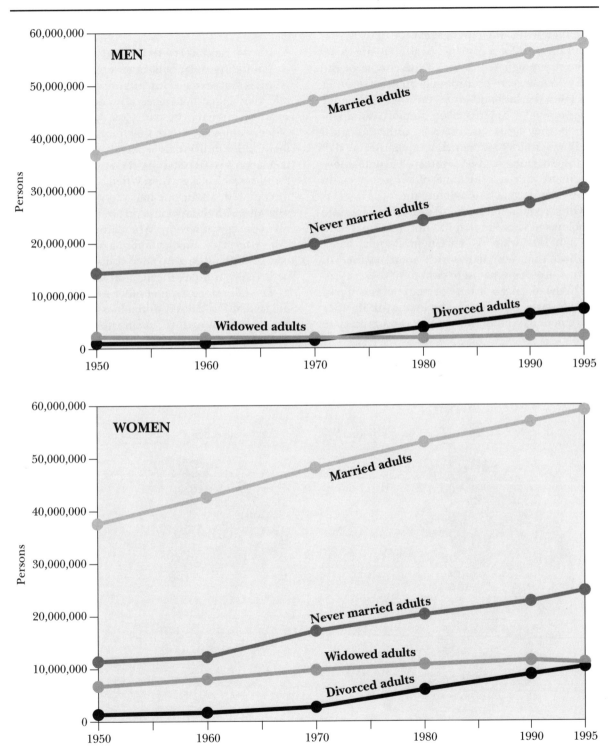

*Source: The Time Almanac 1998.* New York: Information Please, 1997.

trend of women's progress in many arenas. Older women are now more likely to have worked for a time outside the home. Also, men are usually older than their wives and tend to age more quickly, so it is not unusual for a younger, healthier wife to become the designated driver of the couple or the one who takes care of the family finances or other tasks that the husband once controlled. Evidence that women have always taken on more dominant roles as they age is supported by anthropological studies in a variety of societies. In almost one-half of the societies studied, women become more dominant with age; in none of the societies do older men become more dominant.

One frequently discussed cause for marriage problems in later life that has not held up well to the light of research is retirement. Popular belief has been that retirement brings about a variety of marital problems that were either not present earlier in the marriage or were present but not apparent. However, research on the quality of life after retirement has shown that couples report the same level of marital happiness that they did before retirement. The only problems that retirement seems to bring are those associated with lowered income.

### SEXUALITY IN LATER YEARS

Another popular belief about marriage in older adults is that sexuality loses its importance with age and that older marriages are companionate instead of intimate. Research on sexual activity in older couples has shown that this is not true. While many older individuals report that they no longer engage in sexual relations, the major reason cited for this is lack of a partner. When older couples are interviewed, about one-half report having sexual relations with their spouse on a regular basis, even up to the age of seventy. When illness, disability, or side effects of medication makes sexual intercourse difficult, many older couples find ways to be sexually intimate throughout their marriages.

The false stereotype of older marriages not being sexual has caused difficulties for many older couples who move into nursing homes. Before pas-

## Marital Status of Men and Women in the U.S. over the Age of 65

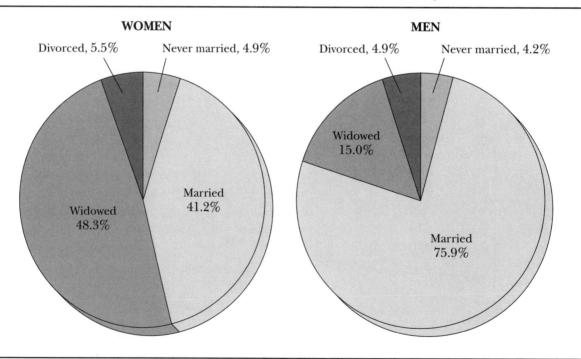

WOMEN

Divorced, 5.5%  Never married, 4.9%

Widowed 48.3%

Married 41.2%

MEN

Divorced, 4.9%  Never married, 4.2%

Widowed 15.0%

Married 75.9%

*Note:* Percentages are rounded to the nearest 0.1%.
*Source:* Bureau of the Census (1992).

*Higher divorce rates in middle age and longer life expectancies have resulted in an increasing number of remarriages in the older years. Such marriages often present unique challenges pertaining to finances and family members.* (James L. Shaffer)

sage of the Patients' Rights Act of 1980, it was not uncommon for spouses to be separated at night into male and female wings of the facility and to be denied the private atmosphere conducive to intimate relations. However, some older couples living with their children complain about the lack of privacy and time alone together.

### HIS AND HER MARRIAGES IN OLD AGE

According to many sociologists, there are two views of all marriages: his and hers. This seems to be especially true in late adulthood. For most couples in this stage of life, marriage is more central for the husband than it is for the wife. Several reasons for this have been suggested. First is that women have traditionally found other facets of life to attend to while their husbands were absorbed in their careers. If they did not work outside the home, women forged close bonds with their children and with other family members. They developed hobbies and were involved in volunteer

work. They formed close relationships with other women. Those who had jobs were more apt to form social relationships with their coworkers than their spouses did. When men retire, they depend heavily on their wives to be spouse, friend, confidante, and social partner. When retired, married men are asked to name their best friend, they typically respond, "my wife." Wives, in contrast, typically name a female friend or relative. Another reason that men are invested so heavily in their marriages in old age is that other men become scarcer and scarcer as the years go by. It is not unusual for a man in his seventies to have outlived all of his friends, coworkers, and brothers, and to find himself in a society of women.

This difference in viewpoint of marriage between partners is especially apparent when a spouse dies. Although men and women react similarly to the death of a spouse, women are surrounded by the social support of their children, their relatives, and their friends. Men, in contrast, have often lost their entire social group by the death of their spouse. It is suggested that this is one of the factors behind the high suicide rate for older men.

### CHILDLESS MARRIAGES IN OLD AGE

About 90 percent of married couples are also parents. The remaining 10 percent of couples with no children often experience a more stable relationship over the years. Couples who do not have children start out happy and do not experience the middle-aged dip in marital satisfaction that seems to be caused by the presence of children.

Whether childless couples are happier in old age than those with children has not been firmly established. Elderly parents report that a major cause of concern and anxiety for them is the problems of their adult children; examples include financial problems, divorce, business failures, and health problems. Couples with no children are spared that distress in their later years. However, elderly parents also report that a major source of happiness and pride is the achievements of their adult children, listing such examples as grandchildren, affluence, professional attainment, and concern for parents.

Childless couples tend to have higher incomes in later years, not simply because of the lack of college tuition, weddings, and other direct costs of having children but also because both spouses have been able to work and pursue careers full time without taking time out for parenting responsibilities. Similar to women who never marry, working women who marry and have no children have more education, higher incomes, and better retirement benefits.

In middle adulthood, childless couples are more apt to be caregivers for aging parents than their siblings who have children. However, since they have only one generation to care for, they are not caught in the generational squeeze familiar to those who have both children and aging parents making demands on their time and resources.

One stereotype of childless couples in the later years is that of being lonely and having no one to care for them. Research has shown that this is not an accurate portrayal of this group. Childless couples have levels of social support in old age that are similar to those of couples with children. The difference is that their social support comes from friends and other relatives instead of children and grandchildren. In fact, several studies have shown that happiness, life satisfaction, self-esteem, and satisfaction with social support are all unrelated to the amount of contact older people have with children and grandchildren.

### REMARRIAGE IN LATE LIFE

A number of older adults who have been divorced or widowed marry again. More older men remarry than older women, partly because there are a greater number of women in older age groups than there are men and partly because marriage is more central to the lives of men at this age. Remarriage often includes differences in the wife's and the husband's experiences. For remarried men, the relationship with the wife takes precedence to the relationships he might have with his children, other relatives, and friends. For the woman, the opposite is true: The relationship with the new husband becomes a marginal relationship compared to that with her children, other relatives, and friends.

Remarriage in the later years tends to be happier than remarriage in young adulthood or midlife and happier if the participants have been widowed rather than divorced. The biggest problems for remarried couples of any age are stepchildren, and it can be argued that this is especially true in later life. The adult children of both spouses often view the new spouse as an intruder in the family, and they may worry about sharing their inheritance and about having the responsibility of caring for another aging family member.

*—Barbara R. Bjorklund*

***See also*** Alzheimer's disease; Caregiving; Childlessness; Communication; Divorce; Friendship; Men and aging; Nursing and convalescent homes; Parenthood; Poverty; Remarriage; Retirement; Sexuality; Social ties; Stepfamilies; Suicide; Widows and widowers; Women and aging.

### FOR FURTHER INFORMATION:

Bee, Helen L., and Barbara R. Bjorklund. *The Journey of Adulthood.* 4th ed. Upper Saddle River, N.J.: Prentice Hall, 1999. This textbook on adulthood and aging provides scientific information presented in a warm, readable style. It is written for undergraduate students in a variety of fields.

Gottman, J. M. *The Seven Principles for Making Marriage Work.* New York: Crown, 1999. The author is a research psychologist who studies married couples and is often able to predict problems and intervene. Much of his work is based on studies of long-term successful marriages.

Houseknecht, S. K. "Voluntary Childlessness." In *Handbook of Marriage and the Family,* edited by M. B. Sussman and S. K. Steinmetz. New York: Plenum Press, 1987. This chapter describes research that compares couples who choose not to have children with couples who choose to have children and those who are childless but wanted to have children.

Levy, J. "Sex and Sexuality in Later Life Stages." In *Sexuality Across the Life Course,* edited by A. S. Rossi. Chicago: University of Chicago Press, 1994. Levy has compiled four factors that determine whether an older person will be sexually active.

Rowe, J. W., and R. L. Kahn. *Successful Aging.* New York: Pantheon Books, 1998. Rowe and Kahn are experts on the biology and psychology of aging. They have taken a different approach than other gerontologists by studying what healthy, happy elders are doing right. They have published their findings in many medical journals, but this book is written for the general public. They stress the importance of "connectedness" through marriage or friendship, especially in late adulthood.

## MASSACHUSETTS BOARD OF RETIREMENT V. MURGIA

**DATE:** Decided on June 25, 1976

**RELEVANT ISSUES:** Law, values, work

**SIGNIFICANCE:** In this case, the Supreme Court determined that mandatory retirement of uniformed officers in the Massachusetts State Police does not violate equal protection under the law

*Massachusetts Board of Retirement v. Murgia* involved Robert Murgia, a uniformed officer in the Massachusetts State Police who was forced to retire against his wishes at age fifty by the Massachusetts Board of Retirement. Four months before his compulsory retirement, Murgia passed an annual physical and mental test that strongly implied that he was still capable of satisfactorily performing the duties of a uniformed state police officer. Murgia sued the Massachusetts Retirement Board, claiming age discrimination and a denial of equal protection of the laws by virtue of this "arbitrary" retirement age set by Massachusetts law. A district judge dismissed Murgia's complaint, saying no constitutional question was involved. However, the U.S. Court of Appeals upheld Murgia's claim and ruled that compulsory retirement at age fifty by itself does not further any substantial or rational state interest. The U.S. Supreme Court reversed the federal appeals court.

The majority opinion of seven members of the U.S. Supreme Court held that a Massachusetts state law that makes it mandatory for state patrol officers to retire at age fifty does not deny equal protection of the laws. Maintaining a government job is not a fundamental right, and the law in question protects the public by assuring the physical and mental preparedness of its state police. People over the age of fifty are in middle life; thus, the Massachusetts Retirement Board and the state law do not discriminate only against its senior citizens. Furthermore, it is a legislative and not a judicial task to make distinctions about fitness for uniformed police work.

The Massachusetts legislature, said the Court, sought to protect the public's safety and welfare by reminding citizens that the arduous duties of controlling prison and civil disorders, patrolling highways in marked cars, and apprehending criminals are hard work. Clearly, men above middle age are not usually physically able to perform such strenuous duties all the time. The court noted the substantial economic and psychological effects that mandatory, premature retirement can have on people but said that these individuals can continue to contribute to society in some other way.

Justice Thurgood Marshall dissented, saying that the right to work is the very essence of personal freedom and opportunity, and it is the purpose of the Fourteenth Amendment to secure that important right for citizens discriminated against and deprived of governmental employment simply because they reach a certain age. Once terminated, middle-aged and elderly citizens cannot easily find alternate work, and mandatory, arbitrary retirement of physically capable people such as Murgia is economically and emotionally damaging. Retiring state police officers for no other reason than they are fifty years old, said Marshall, is the height of a state's irrationality and thus violates the equal protection of the laws.

—*Steve J. Mazurana*

**See also** Age discrimination; Age Discrimination Act of 1975; Age Discrimination in Employment Act of 1967; Employment; Forced retirement; *Johnson v. Mayor and City Council of Baltimore*; Retirement; *Vance v. Bradley*.

## MATLOCK

**CAST:** Andy Griffith, Don Knotts
**DATE:** Aired from 1986 to 1995
**RELEVANT ISSUES:** Culture, law, media, work
**SIGNIFICANCE:** This television series depicted an older attorney and amateur sleuth who capably solved mysteries and vindicated clients in the courtroom, appealing demographically to older viewers

First aired by the National Broadcasting Company (NBC) on September 20, 1986, the *Matlock* televi-

*Star Andy Griffith (second from right) with other cast members from the television series* Matlock. *(Archive Photos)*

sion series starred sixty-year-old Andy Griffith as Ben Matlock, an amiable Atlanta attorney who was famous nationwide. Seeking justice, Matlock questioned witnesses, visited crime scenes, and cleverly exposed liars in dramatic courtroom scenes. Characterized as a country lawyer in the big city, Matlock defended underdog protagonists against greedy, corrupt villains in murder cases about stolen inheritances, mistaken identities, spurned lovers, art thefts, and blackmail. Violence was minimized in episodes. The predominantly wealthy suspects often arrogantly underestimated Matlock's intelligence to unravel their ruses, yet Matlock consistently and competently exposed wrongdoing. "Matlock is a good man, but he wants to win. He's very shrewd," Griffith noted. Plots also involved Matlock's daughter, also an attorney, and his interactions with younger colleagues. Don Knotts later joined the cast as Les Calhoun, Matlock's meddling retired neighbor.

*Matlock* quickly gained fans and was ranked among the top twenty television shows every week. Television movies featuring Matlock won ratings sweeps. Griffith credited viewer interest to the show's humor and Matlock's eccentricities, such as always wearing a gray suit, eating hot dogs, and playing a ukelele. In 1992, NBC canceled *Matlock*, hoping to attract a younger audience to gain more advertising dollars. Although ranked third with adults over fifty, *Matlock* was eighty-third with viewers under fifty. At that time, 44 percent of NBC viewers were over fifty. The American Broadcasting Company (ABC) added *Matlock* to its schedule, airing shows through 1995. Syndicated *Matlock* reruns were broadcast on cable networks.

—*Elizabeth D. Schafer*

**See also** Advertising; Communication; *Murder, She Wrote*; Television.

## MATURITY

**RELEVANT ISSUES:** Psychology, sociology, values
**SIGNIFICANCE:** The achievement of maturity in middle and late life enriches the individual's ability to make decisions and enjoy the rewards of a lifetime

The mature adult of any age is often defined as one who has made personal choices and has committed to them. Choices relate to life partners, work, religion, friends, interests, and hobbies. Mature adults are balanced in terms of attention to and understanding of self and others. They have a set of inner principles that guide their lives. Although these attributes are basic for all mature adults, there are aspects of maturity that change with age.

There is no single way to achieve maturity in middle and late life. Sociologists and psychologists have not been able to define one pattern of living or one personality type that leads to maturity in aging. They find so-called successful aging among people who are actively involved in life and among those who are disengaged or withdrawn from social life; they find contented, fulfilled older people with many different lifestyles and personality types.

Early psychologist Erik Erikson described the course of life as a group of stages and suggested that there are tasks in every stage that must be accomplished for successful development. In midlife, the task is to be productive, what Erikson termed "generativity." Mature, middle-aged adults use their skills to be productive in areas that represent their commitments. For example, mature, middle-aged people may contribute a great deal to their chosen field of work or may share in satisfying marriages or friendships. One who is active in church may be given a responsible position because of experience, while one who has coached soccer for years may be asked to manage a soccer league. Thus, maturity at midlife often relates to the individual's use of accumulated skills to enhance humankind.

During midlife, most people begin to gain a different perspective on life. With the realization of mortality, individuals begin a process of introspection that continues into late life. Midlifers often think about what they still want to accomplish. This examination of goals sometimes leads to significant changes, such as divorce or career switches. The world generally views these as midlife crises.

In late life, this introspection turns toward finding meaning in one's life. Erikson's task for late life is finding integrity. Young people may be considered egotistical if they focus too much on themselves, but many psychologists claim that older people need to be introspective. To mature in late life is to find the meaning of one's life and to be able to see oneself in the context of all humanity. Family members are sometimes able to help older relatives during the life review process by support-

ing them with positive memories. Older people working on this process often forgive themselves and others for the inevitable "wrongs" of life and think about positive influences they have had on family, friends, and their work.

The components or personal attributes of maturity remain the same throughout adulthood. However, the tasks of midlife and old age differ in that the focus of the first is on fulfillment of goals, while the focus of the second is on feeling satisfied with the accomplishment of some, if not all, of these goals. —*Virginia L. Smerglia*

*See also* Creativity; Erikson, Erik H.; Middle age; Midlife crisis; Old age; Successful aging; Wisdom.

## MEALS-ON-WHEELS PROGRAMS

RELEVANT ISSUES: Economics, health and medicine, sociology

SIGNIFICANCE: Meals-on-wheels food programs provide nutritionally balanced, home-delivered meals to an elderly population that is at increased risk for malnutrition

Good nutrition is an important part of the quality of life as people age. Good nutrition means not only eating a balanced diet but also eating enough to maintain a healthy lifestyle. Older adults are at much greater risk for malnutrition than the general population because of both normal and disease-related changes that occur with aging. These changes are many and varied. For example, physiological changes can impair food absorption, or a decline in functional ability may limit an older person's capacity to go to the store and shop for food or to prepare food. Declining functional status may also make it difficult to eat a meal once it has been prepared. Most elderly people are on fixed incomes, so the cost of food must be balanced against other demands, such as rent and utilities. Finally, eating is a social experience—most people do not choose to eat alone, although the homebound elderly are often forced to do so by the death of a spouse or by their own limitations.

Meals-on-wheels programs are designed to help meet these challenges. In 1999, there were more than eight hundred nonprofit meals-on-wheels programs in the United States. Many of them received funding from the Older Americans Act Program and the Department of Agriculture. These programs deliver one nutritious midday meal on a

*A volunteer prepares dinner as part of a meals-on-wheels program for the elderly. Such daily deliveries may constitute the only nourishment and social interaction for some seniors.* (Bob Daemmrich Photography)

daily basis to the disabled and the elderly who are homebound and unable to prepare their own meals. Individual programs differ; many deliver different kinds of meals, including regular, low-salt (2 to 3 grams of sodium), and diabetic meals. Costs vary from program to program. Meals-on-wheels programs are set up to serve specific geographic areas. Each program is responsible for client intake, client assessment, and the day-to-day activities required to provide the meals to the elderly at their homes. Many rely on volunteers and recruit them from the community.

Meals-on-wheels programs do not deliver only food. They provide daily social contact with a trained volunteer for homebound elderly. Sometimes this is the only person these people see during the day. Meals-on-wheels volunteers also provide important referral information about other appropriate community resources.

Among meals-on-wheels participants, 59 percent reported having three or more diagnosed, chronic illnesses or conditions. Only 46 percent of participants reported getting out of their homes at least once during the week. When poor health is compounded by low income, elders are at risk. Although means testing is prohibited, surveys estimate nearly 50 percent of the participants have family incomes below the established poverty level. Many program participants divide their midday meals in order to have something for dinner. For these elderly in particular, meals-on-wheels programs promote a better quality of life.

Two major aging trends ensure that the demand for meals-on-wheels services will continue to increase. It has been estimated that the elderly population in the United States will reach 80 million people by 2050. Within this aging population, the oldest-old—those eighty-five or older—are the fastest growing group. The number of people within the oldest-old category is expected to reach 19 million by 2050. This population requires more services, such as meals-on-wheels programs, to remain independent in the community.

—*George F. Shuster*

**See also** Disabilities; Home services; Malnutrition; Mobility problems; Nutrition; Older Americans Act of 1965; Poverty; Social ties.

## MEASURE OF MY DAYS, THE

**AUTHOR:** Florida Scott-Maxwell
**DATE:** Published in 1968
**RELEVANT ISSUES:** Death, family, health and medicine, religion
**SIGNIFICANCE:** Scott-Maxwell reflects upon love, death, and wonder in her eighties, thus providing a model for the struggle to gain identity and meaning in later life

Disengaged from careers in fiction writing and Jungian psychology, Florida Scott-Maxwell entered her eighties armed with a newly found passion for reflection on humanity and on her own rich life. Not one to romanticize old age, Scott-Maxwell, in her book *The Measure of My Days,* rages against disappointment, illness, uncertainty, and most of all, the threat of becoming a burden. Yet her awareness that life's crucial task is the achievement of balance leaves her little room for self-pity. She finds that pain gives rise to energy, and energy stimulates vitality and love.

Scott-Maxwell declares that the chief aim of old age is the protection of one's identity, a sacred self that vacillates between differentiation from others, on one hand, and assimilation to the masses, on the other. The temptation to hide from the struggle for identity competes with the need to assume responsibility for one's existence. Responsibility derives from openness to personal experience; even immortality, as experienced here and now, is a real part of one's self.

Scott-Maxwell asserts that in old age, one's soul serves as one's best companion. The soul cries, exults, and remains silent, but, in the main, waits. At times, the elderly are too full of life inside to die; at other times, they feel too full of illness not to die. In neither state of mind does Scott-Maxwell mourn for herself or for her losses; rather, she mourns for the incomprehensibility of life and for what she deems confused and arid times. Scott-Maxwell concludes, though, that all people possess a reservoir of "unlived life" that passes to the next generation.                    —*Gregory D. Gross*

*See also* Literature; Old age.

## MEDICAL CARE. *See* HEALTH CARE.

## MEDICAL INSURANCE

RELEVANT ISSUES: Death, demographics, economics, health and medicine, work

SIGNIFICANCE: Affordable medical insurance is important in obtaining the quality health care needed to address both the normal changes and the abnormal disease states that accompany aging; the middle aged and elderly usually have several options available

Medical insurance in the United States began in the 1850's when insurance companies began offering policies protecting railroad passengers against injury. Health maintenance organizations (HMOs) were first implemented in the 1930's, with the 1970's seeing increased HMO proliferation due to higher health care costs and increased competition between growing numbers of physicians. The Health Maintenance Organizations Act of 1973 provided federal grants and loans for HMOs and required many employers to offer HMO membership to employees as a health insurance alternative.

The HMO concept served as a means to control costs by discouraging physicians from performing unnecessary and costly procedures, meet the increased demand for health insurance particularly in medically underserved areas, and foster preventive medicine. Financial incentives are, in theory, the major force behind personal freedom of choice, containment of costs, and assurance of quality. Preferred provider organizations (PPOs) appeared in the 1980's as a flexible alternative to standard HMOs, with many health insurers such as Blue Cross and Blue Shield exerting control over their daily operations.

Medicare and its companion program Medicaid are federally administered programs begun in the 1960's that guarantee medical insurance coverage for elderly and low-income American citizens. Other government medical insurance plans cover armed forces personnel, veterans, American Indians, and federal employees. Social Security pays disability benefits to covered persons and their dependents, whereas workers' compensation pays medical expenses and covers income losses for workers injured on the job. Medical insurance plans can be generally divided into medical expense insurance, income loss insurance, and accidental death and dismemberment coverage.

### PRIVATE MEDICAL INSURANCE PROGRAMS

Private insurance companies provide a majority of the medical insurance plans in the United States. Some are for-profit stock companies or mutual companies owned by their policyholders. Nonprofit hospital associations such as Blue Cross and medical associations such as Blue Shield also provide insurance for hospitalization and surgical expenses, respectively.

Hospitalization insurance generally covers the cost of hospital room and board and expenses such as X rays, blood tests, and medications required as an inpatient. A deductible often applies before the insurer begins to pay benefits, with coverage often also limited to a specified number of days per illness. Hospitalization insurance generally does not cover general physician or surgeon fees, with many policies dictating a specified amount per clinic visit or surgical procedure. Prescription drugs, rehabilitation costs, and items such as prostheses are also often covered as stated in the policy.

Major medical insurance has a much higher maximum benefit limit, often over one million dollars and sometimes unlimited. A larger deductible generally applies, with the insurer often paying 80 percent of the expenses over the deductible. Comprehensive major medical policies often do not have an initial deductible and require the insurer to pay all expenses up to a stated amount, with the insurer paying 80 percent of all expenses over that amount.

Disability insurance protects against loss of income resulting from accidental injury or illness, with benefits often structured to pay approximately 40 to 60 percent of earnings up to the maximum total amount. Accidental injury cases may receive payments beginning with the day of injury, whereas illness benefits may not be paid until the insured person has been unable to work for a specified period of time.

Accidental death or dismemberment insurance, commonly advertised in vending machines at transportation centers such as airports, provides benefits in the event of death or loss of organs or limbs as a result of travel.

### Health Maintenance Organizations (HMOs)

HMOs provide medical insurance to groups and individuals for an established, prepaid monthly premium. Generally, an HMO attempts to provide care at a lower cost than traditional fee-for-service insurance programs by transferring financial risk to physicians through capitation and other incentives. The result is that patients often have to accept fewer choices in treatment options and specialist providers. Preferred providers are physicians and other health care providers and hospitals who choose to provide health care on a reduced-cost basis to subscribers of an HMO. HMOs function in a dual role as both a health insurance company and a provider of health services, roles that were previously separated within American health care.

HMOs are often organized by employers, physician groups, unions, consumer groups, insurance companies, or for-profit health care agencies. They were originally formed from one, or a mixture of, the following practice models: point of service, staff, group, and independent practice association. A point-of-service model HMO, also called an open-ended HMO, includes an option that allows subscribers to seek medical care outside the established network and receive partial reimbursement, with all remaining expenses paid out of pocket. A staff model HMO is directly controlled at its headquarters locations, with all physicians and other health care workers being direct, full-time salaried employees. A group model HMO is organized by physicians whereby a private professional corporation is established that then individually contracts with an HMO to provide services exclusively for its subscribers. An independent practice association model HMO provides a flexible arrangement created by office physicians and administrators designed to compete with the classic HMOs; several office physicians in a community form a networked professional corporation that seeks group contracts among local employers and provides all medical care for a capitated rate per client per month to subscribers who often choose a personal primary care physician.

The term "managed care" describes the techniques by which an HMO, a health insurance carrier, or a self-insuring employer makes certain that the health care services it endorses are high quality and cost effective. An HMO will also furnish services from other health care providers, such as physical and occupational therapists, pharmacists, and mental health professionals.

HMOs are attractive to employers because the annual medical bill for the average subscriber-patient has consistently proven to be approximately 30 percent less than that of conventional insurers. Advantages of HMO membership include that all medical expenses, from routine and emergency care to hospitalization, are covered within a single, fixed monthly premium and that presenting an HMO membership card at the time of services with a small copayment requires no forms to fill out, deductibles to pay, or bills to submit. Disadvantages include that subscribers often cannot keep a trusted physician that they have had for years, providers become extremely busy when they are assigned five hundred or more patients in exchange for a fixed fee, and subscribers often have to accept fewer choices in treatment options.

Each client is assigned to a "primary care gatekeeper," a physician who is expected to provide most care in his or her private office for limited fees. When a referral to a specialist, laboratory, or hospital is necessary, authorization is required from the headquarters of the managed care organization. Hospitals contract with these organizations to limit their charges and follow established rules about economical care and prompt discharge. The managed care organization reviews utilization by physicians and hospitals, attempts to correct wasteful practices, and subsequently drops health care providers with expensive and/or poor practice styles.

In contrast to more traditional HMOs, point-of-service plans have emerged that enable clients to have freedom of choice with respect to providers and some treatment options but that require them personally to pay the balance for their chosen higher-priced services. If a patient goes to physicians, hospitals, and other providers within the network and follows rules about utilization and authorization, the out-of-pocket financial costs are minimal. The patient retains the option to go to an out-of-plan provider, pay the bill in full, and then be reimbursed for the limited amount established in the individual plan. The employer's group contract with the managed care organization provides for limited and predictable premiums. The considerable costs of out-of-plan services thus are shifted from the group contract to the individual patient.

Managed care plans will continue to monitor closely the treatment patterns of physicians and encourage them to prescribe cheaper medications, develop standards that physicians are expected to follow in the treatment of various diseases, and have utilization review panels that examine patient records and decide which treatments a patient's health plan will cover and which it will not. Many states have passed comprehensive managed care laws as a result of numerous consumer complaints about the decisions of case managers who often have no medical training. Legislation has focused on issues such as adopting measures to ban physician gag clauses, establish consumer grievance procedures, require disclosure of financial incentives for physicians to withhold care, conduct external reviews of an HMO's internal decision to deny care, and grant the ability to sue an HMO for malpractice.

The largest looming question regarding the future of HMOs is whether physicians and other health care workers and client subscribers will continue to enroll in and thus support the system. Managed care necessarily adds substantial administrative overhead, with the ongoing question of whether the final result is greater efficiency for the entire system or just for the subscribing employers. An organization that will exert considerable influence on future HMO developments is the American Association of Retired Persons (AARP), a large nonprofit advocacy group for Americans over the age of fifty with more than thirty million members. AARP has begun giving endorsements to HMOs that meet its standards of quality and price.

## MEDICARE AND MEDICAID

In 1965, amendments to the Social Security Act of 1935 that established Medicare and Medicaid were enacted. Medicare went into effect in 1966 and authorized compulsory health insurance for American citizens aged sixty-five and older who were entitled to receive Social Security or railroad retirement benefits. Medicaid was established by the 1965 amendments as a means-tested entitlement program to provide medical assistance to low-income persons who were aged, blind, disabled, pregnant, or members of families with dependent children, as well as other groups of needy children.

The establishment of Medicare and Medicaid followed considerable heated political debate over the feasibility of a national health care program, stimulated by a 1963 government survey that revealed only about 50 percent of elderly American citizens had health insurance. Many older Americans could not afford private coverage, and the elderly who attempted to pursue coverage were often denied on the basis of age or preexisting conditions. Passage of Medicare and Medicaid guaranteed insurance coverage for elderly and low-income Americans and initiated numerous major changes involving private financing relationships between physician and patient, physician training, insurance industry growth, and expansion of hospital-only coverage to extended care. The late 1960's saw these programs become substantially more expensive than originally anticipated, with amendments in 1972 being the first major attempts to limit expenditures.

Medicare's basic benefits package, which includes part A (hospital insurance) and part B (supplemental medical insurance), has changed little since its inception, with the only major variation being that many services are now delivered beyond traditional acute care settings. Part A is an earned benefit for most Americans and requires no premium upon eligibility, whereas part B is voluntary for a monthly premium. Nearly all older and disabled beneficiaries elect to participate in part B. Part A benefits include inpatient hospital care coverage for the first sixty days, less a deductible for each period of acute illness; inpatient psychiatric care; skilled nursing care or rehabilitation associated with recuperation for up to one hundred days following hospitalization; home health care as prescribed by a physician; and hospice care for the terminally ill. Not covered are outpatient prescription drugs, routine physical examinations, nonsurgical dental services, hearing aids and eyeglasses, and most long-term care in nursing facilities, in the community, or at home. In 1972, Medicare coverage was extended to persons of any age with end-stage renal (kidney) disease, those receiving Social Security Disability Insurance for at least two years, and persons aged sixty-five and older who are otherwise not eligible but elect to enroll by paying a monthly premium.

In the late 1990's, Medicare accounted for 28 percent of all hospital payments in the U.S. health care system and 20 percent of all physician payments. Medicare covered 45 percent of overall health care spending for the elderly but a lower percentage for the very elderly, particularly those requiring full-time nursing home care.

The Medicare Catastrophic Coverage Act of 1988 attempted to require Medicare beneficiaries to pay the full cost of expanded benefits through an income-related tax surcharge and a flat premium. Elderly citizens organized groups in intense opposition to premium funding, leading to the repeal of the act one year later. Beginning in 1984, Congress made amendments to Medicaid to require individual states to cover all infants and pregnant women below the poverty level, with their eligibility determined by an index based on income level and family size. The Catastrophic Coverage Act gave states the option of covering those below 185 percent of the poverty line and required the states to pay Medicare cost sharing for all poor elderly and disabled Medicare beneficiaries. These provisions were retained when the act was repealed.

## OTHER GOVERNMENT MEDICAL INSURANCE PROGRAMS

Numerous other programs exist at various levels of government to help Americans pay medical expenses and meet income losses. The federal government provides medical insurance for armed forces personnel and their dependents, veterans, American Indians, and federal employees. Social Security pays disability benefits to covered workers and their dependents until the individual recovers and returns to work, dies, or reaches age sixty-five, when retirement benefits are received. Workers' compensation pays medical expenses and covers income losses for workers injured on the job.

*—Daniel G. Graetzer*

**See also** Health care; Hospice; Hospitalization; Life insurance; Medicare; Politics; Social Security.

### FOR FURTHER INFORMATION:

Brink, Susan, and Nancy Shute. "Are HMOs the Right Prescription?" *U.S. News and World Report* 123, no. 4 (October 13, 1997): 60-65. Covered in this well-researched article is the growing dissatisfaction of subscribers with the quality of health care received, with a rating of the best HMOs in the United States.

Gold, M. "Health Maintenance Organizations: Structure, Performance, and Current Issues for Employee Health Benefits Design." *Journal of Occupational Medicine* 33, no. 3 (1991): 288-296. From an occupational medicine viewpoint, this manuscript reviews numerous health benefit plans designed for large and small company employees by examining consumer satisfaction, quality of health care, and analysis of the cost-benefit ratio.

National Academy on Aging. *Facts on Medicare: Hospital Insurance and Supplemental Medical Insurance.* Washington, D.C.: Author, 1995. Contains current information and answers to frequently asked questions about Medicare. Current information can also be obtained from Medicare's Web site: http://epn.org/aging/agmedi.html.

## MEDICARE

**RELEVANT ISSUES:** Economics, health and medicine

**SIGNIFICANCE:** Medicare is a national health insurance program for people aged sixty-five years and older, for people with permanent kidney failure, and for people with specified disabilities

Medicare is designed primarily as a health insurance supplement for older Americans receiving Social Security. The program consists of two components: Part A, or hospital insurance (HI), helps pay for hospital and related costs, while part B, or supplementary medical insurance (SMI), helps pay for physician services, medical equipment, and other health care expenses. Part A is financed by a payroll tax, with the employer and employee each paying 1.45 percent of the employee's total wage. To participate in part B, beneficiaries are required to pay a monthly premium ($43.80 per month in 1998). Medicare, in contrast to Medicaid, is not considered a form of public assistance, and benefits are not dependent upon financial need.

### BENEFITS

On the average, Medicare covers less than 60 percent of the health care costs of its noninstitutionalized elderly enrollees. Under part A, or HI, beneficiaries must pay a deductible for hospital care, which is equivalent to the approximate cost of one day of hospital care ($764 in 1998). Medicare then pays the full cost for the first two months in the hospital, about 75 percent of the costs for the third month, and approximately one-half of the cost of stays beyond three months. Medicare also covers part of the costs of posthospital care in a nursing home for a maximum period of one hundred days. Although Medicare does not pay for long-term nursing home care, it does pay most of the costs of hospice care for terminally ill patients. Because late-stage care is especially labor-intensive, approximately 30 percent of Medicare funds are spent on patients who are in the last year of life.

Since the premiums of part B, or SMI, are much less expensive than those of private insurance policies, about 98 percent of the elderly participate in the SMI program. In 1998, in addition to premiums, beneficiaries were required to pay a deductible of $100 per year, and they were also responsible for coinsurance payments of 20 percent of allowable physicians' charges. Physicians may bill the government directly, or the patients may pay the physician and obtain reimbursement from Medicare. Medicare generally does not pay for

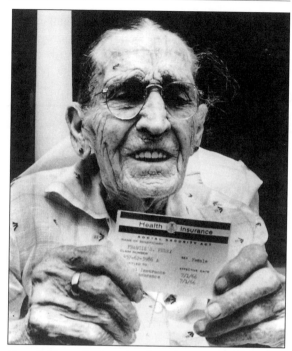

*Francis Perry, 100, receives her Medicare card on July 1, 1966, the first day that the health insurance plan started operation.* (Library of Congress)

prescription drugs, a source of real hardship for many seniors with chronic health conditions. Some private companies provide managed care options that combine parts A and B under one contract for all covered services.

Many elderly people purchase private health insurance policies to pay for services not provided in parts A and B. These so-called Medigap policies are regulated by law. Medicare recipients who are poor may qualify for Medicaid assistance to help pay for coinsurance, medication, and other medical expenses. In addition, when poor people under Medicaid do not qualify for Medicare coverage, the states are able to "buy into" the Medicare program on their behalf.

The most significant limitation on Medicare's coverage is that it does not provide for most of the costs of long-term nursing home care. Because of the great expense (usually $40,000 per year or more in 1999), long-term care places a substantial burden on many of the nation's elderly and their families. Of the 7.3 million elderly people in 1994, about 22 percent, or 1.6 million, lived in nursing homes, and another 1 million individuals lived in assisted-living facilities. Although one-half of direct payments for long-term care are paid by public funds, about 80 percent of these funds come from Medicaid, and individuals can participate in Medicaid only after they "spend down" their assets and become indigent. In view of the potential impact on the budget, it is unlikely that Congress will expand Medicare coverage to include long-term

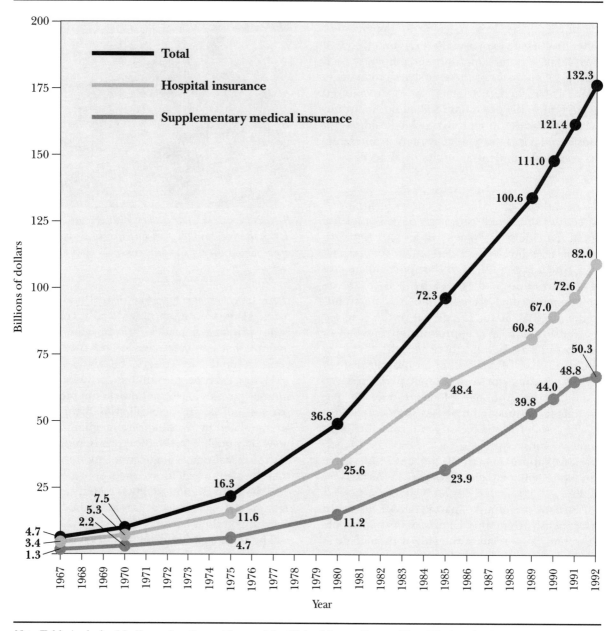

**Medicare Expenditures by Type of Insurance**

*Note:* Table includes Medicare data for residents of the United States, Puerto Rico, Virgin Islands, Guam, other outlying areas, foreign countries, and unknown residence.

*Source:* Health Care Financing Administration.

care. For a short period in the 1980's, an attempt was made to fund long-term care through Medicare premiums, but the strong protests caused Congress to terminate the program.

## BEGINNINGS

The evolution of the 1965 Medicare Act really began during the New Deal period. In 1934, President Franklin Roosevelt's Committee on Economic Security announced that it was considering a national health insurance program; this provoked such a public outcry that the idea was dropped in order to promote the passage of the Social Security Act. President Harry S Truman resurrected the proposal as part of his Fair Deal, and, in 1949, Congress gave some consideration to the Murray-Wagner-Dingell Bill, which would have provided comprehensive medical services to all citizens. A coalition of Republicans and southern Democrats, however, killed the bill.

In 1951, Wilbur Cohen and other advisers of the Federal Security Agency drafted a more modest proposal that limited coverage to the beneficiaries of the Old Age and Survivors Insurance program. The public was especially sympathetic to the special health needs of the aged, who were widely perceived as more deserving than other groups. Congress, nevertheless, held no hearings on the proposal until 1958, when the Forand Bill was introduced and debated. Labor unions were the strongest supporters of the bill, while the American Medical Association (AMA) led the opposition. In 1960, Congress passed a conservative alternative, the Kerr-Mills Bill, which provided federal grants to the states for assisting those in severe financial need.

President John F. Kennedy's New Frontier platform included a proposal for a compulsory health insurance law for aged Social Security beneficiaries, and he appointed Cohen as head of a task force to draft such a bill. Supported by about 60 percent of the public, the Medicare bill was finally passed by Congress after the overwhelming Democratic victory in the elections that followed Kennedy's assassination in 1964. President Lyndon B. Johnson's initial proposal, a key element of his Great Society, was limited to hospital insurance, but the House Ways and Means Committee, led by Representative Wilbur Mills, expanded the bill to include both an SMI component and a Medicaid

program for the indigent. After Congress passed the bill, President Johnson flew to Missouri, where he signed the legislation in the presence of former president Truman on July 30, 1965.

## GROWTH OF THE PROGRAM

When Medicare began, the nation's economy was very strong, and medical technology was much less advanced, and must less expensive, than it became two decades later. Also, because the large baby-boom generation was just beginning to enter the workforce, the percentage of the population relying on Medicare was relatively small. As a result, the financing of the program was not especially difficult for the first few years. In order to minimize the AMA's opposition to Medicare, the early administration policies were designed to encourage hospitals and physicians to participate in the program, and there were almost no limits to the charges allowed.

In 1972, Congress tried to contain runaway costs by enacting maximum limits on payments, by allowing an option for enrollment in health maintenance organizations (HMOs), and by establishing professional review organizations (PROs) to determine reasonable rates. In 1974, Congress expanded Medicare to include chronic renal disease patients and the disabled. In 1977, the Health Care Financing Agency (HCFA) was established to administer Medicare under the Department of Health and Human Services. As costs continued to rise more rapidly than inflation, Congress, in 1983, passed Social Security amendments to increase the tax rate. About the same time, President Ronald Reagan convinced Congress to establish the prospective payment system (PPS), which pays hospitals according to fixed scales for about five hundred conditions. As a result, hospitals began to "cost shift" Medicare losses to private patients, and they tended to put pressure on physicians to discharge patients as early as possible.

Growth in Medicare costs has reflected the general increase in health care expenditures in the United States. While national health expenses were only $247 per person in 1967, by 1994 they had grown to $3,510. The aging of the population was one of the major reasons for the growth of Medicare. In 1967, 19.5 million people were enrolled for Medicare coverage; by 1996, the number had grown to 38.1 million. Medicaid expanded

## Public Opinion on Medicare Premiums

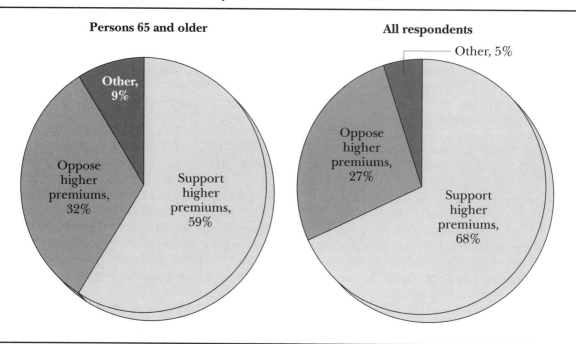

**Persons 65 and older**

Other, 9%

Oppose higher premiums, 32%

Support higher premiums, 59%

**All respondents**

Other, 5%

Oppose higher premiums, 27%

Support higher premiums, 68%

*Note:* In September, 1997, the *Los Angeles Times* asked more than 1,250 adults nationwide whether they would support raising Medicare premiums for the more affluent as a way to keep Medicare solvent in the future. These charts summarize the responses.

*Source: Los Angeles Times* (Sept., 1997).

even more rapidly—from 10 million people in 1967 to 37.5 million in 1996. As medical technology became more efficacious, the level of usage increased accordingly. The ratio of aged Medicare users of any type of covered service was 367 per 1,000 enrollees in 1967, while it was 821 per 1,000 enrollees in 1994. Likewise, Medicare enrollees with end-stage renal disease grew from 66,700 recipients in 1980 to more than 250,000 in 1995, an increase of 285 percent.

By the 1990's, there were almost constant political battles about how to finance the ballooning costs of Medicare. The public has strongly supported the Medicare program, and few politicians have been willing to support any decrease in its funding. In 1994, Republicans and President Bill Clinton had a major confrontation about limiting the program's growth. The Republicans proposed reducing the growth of Medicare by $270 billion over seven years, much more than the Clinton administration favored. After heated debates, the

two sides eventually agreed on a compromise of $137 billion in reductions. Informed observers generally agreed that the dispute helped boost the popularity of President Clinton and the Democrats.

As part of the Balanced Budget Act of 1997, Congress created the Medical Payment Advisory Commission (MedPAC). The purpose of the sixteen-member nonpartisan commission was to collect data and to make recommendations to Congress about possible ways to solve the long-term financial problems of the program. At the same time, Congress expanded the options for the delivery of services. Seniors were given two more expensive options: government-subsidized private insurance and Medicare medical savings accounts (MMSAs). In 1998, the Clinton administration advocated expanding Medicare to include the cost of prescription drugs and to allow early retirees to purchase coverage in the system. Conservatives replied that the additional costs would be prohibitive.

## CONCERNS FOR FUTURE FINANCING

With technological advances and rising life expectancy, the costs of Medicare have consistently grown much more rapidly than the inflation rate. At the end of the twentieth century, the program was in deep trouble, and there were many pessimistic projections about the possibility of bankruptcy early in the twenty-first century. In 1999, experts predicted that the Trust Fund would run out of money in 2008 unless changes were made. Between 1990 and 1995, the hospital fund had increased by 73 percent, while the payroll taxes that financed the fund had grown by only 40 percent. By 1997, Medicare expenditures, about $200 billion, represented about 11 percent of the federal budget, and they were projected to grow to 14 percent of the budget by 2002.

The percentage of the elderly population was increasing rapidly, and it was expected to explode when the baby-boom generation—about 76 million people born between 1946 and 1964—would begin to retire in 2010. While the elderly made up about 13 percent of the population in 1999, they were expected to represent about 20 percent of the total population in 2030, when the first baby boomers would become eighty-five years old. The greatest growth was expected to occur within the percentage of the very old, those over eighty-five. Members of this group tend to be frail, with the most expensive medical needs. Such people numbered 3.9 million in 1999, and it was predicted that they would swell to 8.5 million in 2030 and to 18 million in 2050.

There have been numerous proposals for reforming Medicare to alleviate the impending financial crisis, but few politicians have advocated the unpopular idea of restraining medical expenditures. Some have suggested that coverage should begin at the age of sixty-seven or older. Working to a more advanced age, however, is difficult for people in physically demanding jobs, and such a policy would increase the numbers of retired people whose nonworking spouses are too young to qualify for Medicare. Another controversial idea is to increase Medicare payroll taxes from the 2.4 percent paid in 1999, but many economists fear that higher taxes on workers would have a negative impact on economic growth. For the SMI portion of Medicare, it is generally agreed that in the future beneficiaries will have to pay higher premiums. In 1999, Democratic proposals suggested that monthly fees should be set at $77 in 2002, while Republicans wanted the fees to be raised to $89.

The favorite solution of many conservatives is some form of privatization. One proposal is to allow the Medicare Trust Fund to invest a portion of its reserves in the stock market. A similar idea is to allow individual workers to invest a portion of their Medicare taxes in individual savings accounts. Critics of these proposals argue that stocks have the risk of decreasing dramatically in value and that many workers do not have the necessary knowledge about making wise investments.

The most radical suggestion for containing Medicare costs is to ration care, a form of triage. It has been suggested, for example, that expensive surgeries should not be performed beyond a certain age. Because rationing would mean that some individuals would not receive health services that are beneficial, the entire idea is extremely controversial. Obviously, most taxpayers want the best possible treatment for their aging parents and grandparents. Contrary to what many people think, the bulk of Medicare dollars do not go for heroic or unusual treatments. Rather, most dollars go for standard treatments considered medically necessary. For example, it is fairly common for an elderly person to break a hip, which usually requires surgery and extensive hospital care.

The experts do not agree in their projections about the future financing of Medicare. Some optimists expect that medical science will make it possible for the elderly to become more healthy and have less expensive medical needs, while others predict that people will continue to live longer but with increasingly expensive medical needs, resulting in a true financial crisis. Unfortunately, there is no truly accurate way of anticipating the costs of future medical technologies, just as there is no dependable way for determining how much workers will be willing to spend on the health needs of elderly baby boomers.
—*Thomas T. Lewis*

**See also** Baby boomers; Hospice; Hospitalization; Long-term care for the elderly; Medical insurance; Medications; Nursing and convalescent homes; Politics; Terminal illness.

## FOR FURTHER INFORMATION:

Cash, Connacht. *The Medicare Answer Book: What You and Your Family Need to Know.* Provincetown,

Mass.: Race Point Press, 1997. A user-friendly guide for helping consumers understand the complexities of Medicare; includes a glossary and information about agencies.

Davis, Karen, and Diane Rowland. *Medicare Policy: New Directions for Health and Long-Term Care.* Baltimore: The Johns Hopkins University Press, 1986. Although somewhat dated, this work is filled with helpful information.

Knaus, Denise. *Medicare Made Simple: A Consumer's Guide to the Medicare Program.* Los Angeles: Health Information Press, 1996. A comprehensive guide that answers practical questions about the program; includes a glossary and a list of peer-review organizations.

Marmor, Theodore. *The Politics of Medicare.* Rev. ed. Chicago: Aldine, 1973. A fascinating historical account that explains how the Medicare Act was passed in 1965.

Smeeding, Timothy, ed. *Should Medical Care Be Rationed by Age?* Totowa, N.J.: Rowman & Littlefield, 1987. Many of these stimulating articles deal with the funding of Medicare.

Wolfe, John. *The Coming Health Crisis: Who Will Pay for Care for the Aged in the Twenty-first Century?* Chicago: University of Chicago Press, 1993. Includes an interesting analysis of the problem of financing Medicare when baby boomers retire.

Young, Donald, Laura Dummit, and Stuart Guterman. *Medicare and the American Health Care System.* Burlington, Vt.: Diane, 1997. Examines trends in health care spending and the financing and delivery of Medicare.

# MEDICATIONS

**RELEVANT ISSUES:** Health and medicine

**SIGNIFICANCE:** Older people are the largest users of prescription medications; in fact, 50 percent of all drug consumption is attributed to them

### MISUSE OF DRUGS

Belief by the aged and the population at large that there is a "magic bullet" for every complaint is widespread. Elders living at home consume between three and seven drugs daily, whereas those living in nursing homes take, on average, four to seven different medications. In addition, when five or more drugs are ingested, the incidence of drug poisoning rises 50 percent; when eight or more are taken together, the incidence rises 100 percent.

Overuse, underuse, and erratic use of medications constitutes a major problem among older people. Between 12 and 17 percent of hospital admissions among elders involve adverse drug reactions. Of these, approximately 80 percent are reactions from commonly prescribed medications. Drugs for mental and nervous system disorders are among the ten most prescribed drugs, yet these disorders account for less than 7 percent of problems in older people. It is estimated that 40 percent of older people living in their own homes experience drug reactions. Overdoses involving barbiturates, sedatives, tranquilizers, and alcohol are common occurrences.

### PHYSICAL CHANGES OF AGING

It is well known that absorption, distribution, metabolism, and elimination of medications markedly differ in older persons. As a person ages, lean body mass, decreased functional tissue, and an increased number of fat deposits create differences in the ability of the body to use standard doses of drugs. Chemical changes in the body also affect how drugs act on the body. The type, the intensity, and the duration of drug action depends on these changes.

The time required for medication to enter the general circulation is termed absorption. In older people, change in gastric motility seems to be the one factor that influences absorption. Increase or decrease in movement of medications through the digestive tract may enhance or interfere with their purpose. For example, coated tablets may pass through the digestive tract slowly and be delayed too long. Because of the delay, their action may inadvertently begin in the stomach, causing nausea and irritation.

Distribution, or transport, depends on a healthy circulatory system. Some older people have decreased cardiac output and sluggish circulation that may delay delivery of medication to the target site, retard the release of a drug from storage tissue, and stall excretion of a drug. A drug like Coumadin (warfarin), a common blood thinner, attaches to protein in the blood. Some is available for use, and some stays bound to the protein. Older people have less protein in the blood, so more drug freely circulates, creating a climate of potential toxicity. As a result, the dose of a protein-bound drug like Coumadin may need to be ad-

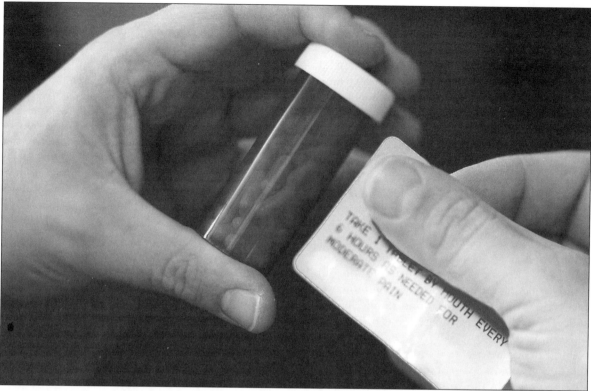

*Accurate labeling is the first step in ensuring the safety of elders taking medications; the patient must be able to read and understand the label, noting the proper dosage, expiration date, and any other important information.* (PhotoDisc)

justed downward to avoid too much circulating drug. Also, a person in a poor nutritional state, with poor protein reserves, would need close monitoring to derive benefit from or avoid an adverse reaction to a drug such as Coumadin.

The vehicle through which a medication is delivered is important. Medicines come in various forms, such as capsules, coated beads, layered tablets, or plastic matrix tablets. Drugs are prepared by manufacturers in a certain way to provide the most therapeutic effect—to make certain that an accurate dose reaches the target area. Altering the form in any way may change drug effects or destroy their effectiveness altogether. Medications are prepared with special coatings or substances to avoid destruction by stomach acid. Crushing or manipulating tablets meant for sustained release spills all of a drug in one location and destroys its intended long-acting effect.

In older people, the amount of fatty tissue increases in relation to a decrease in muscle mass. Vitamins such as A, D, E, and K are fat-soluble. Fat-

soluble medications are stored and not readily passed, leading the way to toxic accumulation. Generally these vitamins must be taken with food to ensure more efficient absorption and distribution in the body. Older people who take vitamin A, D, E, and K supplements freely subject themselves to serious consequences. Vitamins A, D, and E are sold in various forms over the counter. Elders should seek the advice of a physician, pharmacist, or nurse before taking fat-soluble supplements.

Relative body water declines in older people. When there is a decrease in relative body water, drug levels are elevated and sustained. This means that water-soluble drugs are not distributed evenly or adequately. Cimetadine (Tagamet), a drug sold over the counter and frequently taken by elders for gastric irritation, is water-soluble. Digoxin, a frequently prescribed heart medication, is also water-soluble and must be closely monitored in older adults. Elders must drink plenty of fluids and remain well hydrated to derive benefit from these drugs.

Each person metabolizes medications in a unique way. Genetic differences and ethnic variations explain why people react to drugs in different ways. Body composition, weight, and gender, as well as nutritional status and disease, determine how drugs are metabolized. Smokers metabolize drugs more rapidly and experience both adverse and toxic drug effects.

The liver is the organ that breaks down, detoxifies, and removes by-products of drugs metabolized by the body. Decreased blood flow through the liver decreases metabolism, which means that ingested drugs will stay in the body longer. Because common drugs such as acetaminophen (Tylenol) and ibuprofen (Advil or Motrin)—two widely used drugs for pain—are detoxified in the liver, they must be taken with caution and only when needed. Routine use of these common over-the-counter (OTC) medications should be discouraged as their excessive use can cause irreversible liver damage.

Most drugs are excreted in the urine, some in the bile. Antibiotics and some cardiac drugs are excreted solely by the kidneys. Kidney function is very important in older adults, as toxic accumulation of drug by-products, particularly antibiotics, can cause retention of substances that will damage kidneys. Diuretics are drugs that remove water from the body and decrease the amount of fluid circulating in the bloodstream. Many older people take diuretics as treatment for high blood pressure and other heart ailments. When taking these drugs, timing and hydration are two important factors.

"Water pills" should be taken in the morning and not in the evening to accommodate frequent trips to the bathroom and allow for undisturbed sleep. Drinking water, decaffeinated beverages, and citrus juices restores the chemical balance in the body, keeps the older adult well hydrated, and prevents kidney problems as well as erratic heartbeat.

Because of visual and perceptual changes associated with aging, older people often confuse pill colors or misinterpret shapes. Some elders cannot read the small print of drug labels. Impaired hearing and unclear instructions by health care providers preclude proper timing of medications. Lapses in memory interfere with routine dosing and aggravate existing symptoms. Stiff hands make opening bottles difficult. Some elders skip meals, especially when alone, and inadvertently skip medications ordinarily taken with meals. Some medications have embarrassing side effects that cause older people to eliminate doses when away from home or when at social gatherings.

## POLYPHARMACY

The use of multiple medications is common among older adults. Some older people see many doctors for a variety of ailments. In doing so, the risk of hoarding a variety of medications that interact and cause unfavorable results is likely. Elders take over-the-counter (OTC) medications as well as prescription drugs and are often unaware of potential toxic effects. Laxatives interfere with the action of blood pressure drugs, and calcium-based antacids and those containing aluminum and magnesium cut the absorption rate of tetracycline antibiotics by 90 percent. Use of OTC medications can also mask signs of serious infection or serious undiagnosed disorders. Some OTC medications, like inhaled sprays used to relieve temporary symptoms of asthma, are dangerous in diabetics and those with high blood pressure. The underlying airway disease remains undiagnosed, and the OTC medications can cause fatal reactions like cardiac arrest or diabetic coma.

## NECESSARY INFORMATION

For satisfactory treatment it is important to know how often a person sees a physician, what medications are prescribed from all sources, and what OTC medications the older person is taking. Equally important are questions about herbal remedies. Diverse populations of elders follow cultural preferences and do not consider herbs "medicines." In the same vein, most older adults do not include vitamin and mineral supplements in the category of medicines. Therefore, it is important to ask older people on a daily basis what drugs prescribed they take, how often they take them, and what vitamin and mineral supplements and OTC medications are in their arsenal of self-medication.

"Back-fence" is a term used to describe the common practice of sharing medications among friends and relatives. The "back-fence" idea refers to sharing medications among neighbors. Elders share information with neighbors who often have a prescribed remedy that seems to suit the symptom. Sharing medications follows among friends, neighbors, and family members. However well intended, this sharing can have dire consequences.

Some clinics that follow an older clientele have so-called brown bag days. Elders are asked to put all medicines they have at home in a brown paper bag and bring them to the clinic for review. Expired drugs, different doses of the same prescribed drugs, herbal remedies, and OTC drugs are commonly found by health care personnel. Elderly clients are advised to throw away expired medications, keep the most recently prescribed dose of the one-and-the-same drug, and dispose of all other multiple doses. They are also asked questions about their herbs and OTC medications. Because of vision changes and cultural differences, labels should be read and questions asked if information is unclear. Communication problems lead to drug problems.

Medication problems increase with the use of multiple pharmacies and physicians. Some pharmacies have a central repository of information that can locate all medications prescribed for one person. To some degree this controls duplication and provides the margin of safety needed. However, it does not record OTC medications or information on supplements.

A close relationship with a local pharmacist is wise. Printed information given to elders at the time of drug dispensing is helpful. At that time, the pharmacist should review side effects of the medication; discuss when and how to take it; alert the older person to prominent adverse effects; and advise the person to seek medical advice if any unusual changes in feeling, behavior, or function occur.

### PREVENTING PROBLEMS

Several strategies can be used to decrease adverse interactive effects of medications associated with the normal physical changes of aging and ensure a smooth therapeutic course. If an older person takes multiple medications, a pill box that holds a seven-day supply is a good idea. The box is labeled by day of the week, and the compartments of the box are loaded once a week. Each compartment can be opened only on the day of the week marked and at the preset time the medicine is to be taken. Another method to ensure accuracy is a check-off chart. Medicine bottles are color-coded with colors easily identified by the older person.

The chart lists the name of the medication in the same color as the medicine bottle. When the medicine is taken, the chart is checked off.

Elders should be advised to take medications on time. If a dose is missed, it is inadvisable to double up on the medicine. The dose should be taken as soon as remembered and the next dose rescheduled according to the time frame prescribed.

Medicines retain their potency when stored in cool, dry places, unless otherwise directed. The worst place to store medicines is in the bathroom medicine cabinet, where humidity will either decompose the drug or decrease its potency. Dark containers prevent light from entering and thus prevent medicines from decomposing. Elders should not change containers. In this same vein, it is inadvisable to mix old and new medicines. Elders are advised to use all pills contained in one bottle and to dispose of expired or hardly used medicines. Potency ensures therapeutic effect; expired drugs are not efficacious.

The best advice to elders is to be aware of what to do if feeling poorly after ingesting medications. Phone numbers of the pharmacist, physician, or nurse should be readily available for quick reference.
—*Maureen C. Creegan*

***See also*** Fat deposition; Gastrointestinal changes and disorders; Health care; Malnutrition; Nutrition; Overmedication; Vitamins and minerals.

### FOR FURTHER INFORMATION:

Graedon, Joe, and Teresa Graedon. *Fifty Plus: The Graedons' People's Pharmacy for Older Adults.* New York: Bantam Books, 1988. A comprehensive, easily readable source for middle-aged to older adults with chapters devoted to avoiding drug dangers, taking medicines wisely, balancing nutritional needs, and managing joint pain, among others.

_____. *The People's Pharmacy.* Rev. ed. New York: St. Martin's Press, 1996. Chapters provide information on OTC medications, drug and food allergies, self-medicating, and interactive effects of OTC drugs and prescribed drugs.

Hausman, Patricia. *The Right Dose: How to Take Vitamins and Minerals Safely.* Emmaus, Pa.: Rodale Press, 1987. Description of fat-soluble and water-soluble vitamins, and comprehensive discussion of what supplements can and cannot do. Issues of safety and efficacy are also covered.

Hussar, Daniel A. *Drug Interactions in the Elderly.* East Hanover, N.J.: Sandoz Pharmaceuticals, 1991. Booklet prepared by a pharmaceutical company on mechanisms of drug interaction in the elderly, with attention to OTC interactions. Multiple tables and charts of drug-to-drug interactions are provided.

Marsa, Linda, and Hillary Broome. "Hey, Who Needs a Prescription?" *Los Angeles Times* 115, Mag. 10 (September 29, 1996). A comprehensive discussion by physicians, pharmacists, and pharmacologists of over-the-counter medication misuse and abuse. Suggestions for proper use of OTC drugs and prevention of interactive effects as well as warnings are presented.

Pronsky, Zaneta M. *Powers and Moore's Food Medication Interactions.* 10th ed. Pottstown, Pa.: Food Medication Interactions, 1997. Spiral-bound pocket guide that offers information about specific drugs and how food and nutritional status can effect older people on multiple medications.

U.S. Department of Health and Human Services. *Using Your Medicines Wisely: A Guide for the Elderly.* Rockville, Md.: U.S. Government Printing Office, 1990. Free booklet of tips on "dos and don'ts" for older people. A handy pocket guide with helpful information on how to take medications and pitfalls to avoid.

# MEMENTO MORI

**AUTHOR:** Muriel Spark
**DATE:** Published in 1959
**RELEVANT ISSUES:** Death, family, religion, values
**SIGNIFICANCE:** This novel presents one of few serious examinations in fiction of attitudes among elderly toward death

Scottish-born novelist Muriel Spark takes the title of her tragicomic novel *Memento Mori* from jewelry and other tokens sometimes worn in the past to remind humans of the shortness and uncertainty of life; the Latin term *memento mori* means "remember you must die."

For Spark, a Roman Catholic convert, death is the central fact of life. Only three characters in her novel remember this fact. Most, however, receive anonymous calls, each in a different voice, warning the person that he or she must die. Their reactions range from the Christian to the paranoiac.

*Muriel Spark, the author of* Memento Mori. *(Jerry Bauer)*

Jean Taylor, dumped into a public geriatric ward when she is no longer of use as a companion/servant, needs no phone reminder; a Catholic convert, she turns the horrors of the ward into a Christian acceptance of suffering and death. Charmian Colston, a Catholic, is not alarmed; she moves out of her house to avoid her jealous husband and possibly homicidal servant and calmly awaits death. Retired policeman Henry Mortimer, a stoic searcher for truth, alone understands that the telephone voice is that of death itself. For him, death is the end of weariness and suffering.

Others cannot face their own mortality. Dame Lettie Colston, noted prison reformer, reveals the shallowness of her reforms when she regrets that harsh punishments, such as flogging, can no longer be used to punish the caller. Increasingly paranoid, she isolates herself and thus inadvertently causes her own violent death. Most characters, such as her brother Godfrey Colston, simply refuse to acknowledge time and change, tragically or comically reliving the emotions, problems, and views of the past. For example, Alec Warner, a former sociologist, can only collect useless statistics; in him, Spark satirizes the approaches of social sciences to this central fact of human life.

—*Betty Richardson*

*See also* Death and dying; Death anxiety; Literature; Religion.

## MEMORY CHANGES AND LOSS

**RELEVANT ISSUES:** Biology, health and medicine, psychology

**SIGNIFICANCE:** The past contributes to present self-identity and allows people to cope on a day-to-day basis in a changing world; without memory, life would be stripped of the ability to live independently

There are a number of myths regarding memory loss and aging. One myth concerns a widely held belief that memory decreases across the board as one ages. A faulty underlying assumption that helped promulgate this myth is the belief that memory is a unitary construct. However, cognitive scientists have learned that memory is really a collection of dozens of different memory processes with many of them being driven by different neurobiological mechanisms. As one ages from childhood to young adulthood to old age, one finds that some types of memory actually improve. It is true that older adults can experience a number of memory problems, but the deficits are not as global as the general public typically view them. A second myth is the belief that aging, particularly for individuals seventy years or older, can cause profound memory loss that in some instances results in the person becoming incapacitated. Aging is not the culprit; rather, this memory loss is most likely due to a neurological disease or some other risk factor that is associated with advanced years. It is important to understand which memory problems arise due to old age and which are brought on by age-related risk factors.

Scientists who study memory changes that occur across the life span have two basic approaches from which to choose: cross-sectional or longitudinal research designs. Cross-sectional research involves recruiting subjects from different age-cohort groups. For example, a typical study might involve three groups of subjects aged twenty years, forty-five years, and sixty-five years. Next, an assortment of memory tests would be administered and subsequently scored. Statistical comparisons would be made among the different cohort groups to see if one group scored significantly higher or lower than the others. An alternative research strategy—the longitudinal design—would seek out a group of twenty-year-olds and then study them repeatedly as they aged. Whereas this design requires a lot of patience, time, and expense, since the investigators must wait until the subjects grow older and then locate them for repeated testing, it has the advantage over the cross-sectional design of circumventing age-cohort effects.

These cohort effects refer to the problems introduced by using subjects who were born at different time periods. These different time periods can be associated with other factors that directly relate to the assessment of memory. One example of this is that a twenty-year-old born in the 1970's would be better educated and have had more practice taking timed tests than individuals who were twenty years old in the 1950's. The bottom line for the researcher interested in studying memory is to choose the design that will best test the specific hypotheses being put forth.

### MEMORY THAT DECLINES WITH AGE

Specific kinds of memory loss begin much earlier than middle age but become more noticeable once one reaches the mid-sixties. Generally, as one gets older, it is not the early memories that are forgotten but rather the recent past that is difficult to recall. Episodic memory refers to specific events and experiences in life. Recalling episodes from a family vacation, or a game of basketball that was played, or a first kiss, are considered episodic memories. They tend to fade as one ages.

Research shows that older adults have more difficulty on a free-recall test than young adults. In a free-recall test, subjects are shown a list of words or pictures and are then asked to recall as many of the stimuli as possible. If a delay exists between the presentation of the items and their recall, larger memory deficits are revealed for the older adults. Not only does free-recall ability decline, but another type of memory called cued recall begins to weaken as one gets older. Cued recall is similar to free recall except that during the test phase some kind of a cue is given to help facilitate the memory. In this kind of research it is common to use a cue such as a word that rhymes with the stimulus that needs to be recalled.

Cognitive psychologist Karl Haberlandt points out in his book *Human Memory: Exploration and Application* (1999) that age brings on deficits in a variety of areas. For example, younger people perform better than older adults at remembering medicine labels, the names and faces of people, songs they have heard on the radio, and television programs they have watched. Haberlandt mentions that spatial memory declines with age as shown by poorer memory for the location of specific buildings on familiar streets, or the layout of museums that have been visited.

Part of the difficulty for older adults can be explained by the greater difficulty they have in reinstating the circumstances under which they acquire information. Fergus I. M. Craik and colleagues in their article "Memory Changes in Normal Aging," found in Alan Baddeley's *Handbook of Memory Disorders* (1995), referred to this as source forgetting. If a person is not able to recall as many details that were a part of the original context in which the information was encoded, the probability that the item or event will be recalled is greatly diminished. However, source forgetting does not explain all the memory difficulties brought on by age. It has been found that cognitive processes that are necessary for efficient memory performance tend to change over time and ultimately reduce the likelihood of retaining information. One such process is the rate of rehearsal. Rehearsal is a specific kind of control process that is used to facilitate the transfer of information from short-term storage to a more permanent storage. If a problem develops with the rehearsal mechanism, subsequent memory transfer will be adversely affected. In the case of older adults, evidence suggests that the rate of rehearsal is slowed compared to younger adults.

As people age, they become more susceptible to risk factors that could lead to potentially devastating memory loss. These factors are not directly related to the aging process but arise due to some kind of injury to the brain. Once the brain is damaged, whether it be due to alcoholism, a closed head injury such as a stroke, or a poorly understood disease as in the case of Alzheimer's disease, the aged brain is not able to adapt and recover as well as a young brain.

## MEMORY THAT STAYS INTACT WHILE AGING

Tasks that are least likely to cause memory problems for older adults tend to be meaningful, highly practiced, and well learned. Fortunately, there are a handful of memory processes that are particularly resistant to injurious aging effects. One such process is the memory for motor skills—procedural memory. T. Salthouse in his 1984 article "Effects of Age and Skill in Typing," published in the *Journal of Experimental Psychology*, compared speeds of different typists of different ages. Although he found that on a simple reaction-time task, older subjects were slower than younger ones, no differences were found in typing speeds. Although this was somewhat puzzling at first, he later discovered that older adults were better able to adopt compensatory strategies—such as looking further ahead on the page and anticipating upcoming keystrokes better—than their younger counterparts.

One common test of short-term memory found on intelligence quotient (IQ) tests is the measure of digit span. This involves the test administrator calling out different sequences of numbers and then having the subject immediately repeat back as many of the digits in their correct order as possible. Some of the sequences must be repeated in the same order they were read, in other instances they must be recited in reverse order. Research has shown that the digit span stays relatively stable through the age of seventy years. However, memories that stay intact are not limited to those recently acquired. Recognition memory changes only slightly as one advances in age, even when the items to be recognized were encoded days before they were asked to be recalled. In addition, semantic memory processes—such as memory for words—tend to be robust toward any kind of decline associated with aging. Studies that do show some performance loss of semantic knowledge in aging individuals reveal that the decline is due to a slower speed at which older people can access their knowledge.

## THEORIES OF MEMORY LOSS

It is important to cognitive scientists who study memory loss to develop theoretical models that attempt to explain why it occurs as one grows older. Conducting research studies that merely describe the kinds of memory losses one might experience later in life is helpful; however, it does not explain what the underlying causes of memory loss might be. Data from studies conducted on memory need to be inductively organized into cohesive theoretical propositions. Once this has been done, the scientific community can begin to test the theories that have been constructed and gain a better understanding of which ones are receiving empirical support. Ultimately, this process will help get at the underlying causes of memory loss.

One theory that has received a lot of attention could be referred to as a cognitive slowing hypothesis. This is the proposition that some aspect of the ability to process information declines in speed and efficiency over time. As people reach middle and eventually late adulthood, the decline becomes noticeable enough that it might cause the normal aging adult to be concerned. Experts for the most part agree that the cognitive slowing hypothesis is a good candidate for understanding what causes memory deficits. At issue is whether the slowing mechanism is best understood as a general process or perhaps is due to a specific functional problem. Slower activation due to the central nervous system would be an example of the general process. One mechanism that could cause this slowing could be the proliferation of weakened or broken synaptic connections in the brain. Scientists who study brain waves—which happen to originate from nerve cell synaptic connections—have found evidence that the brain takes a little bit longer to react to a stimulus in older adults. This could lead to poorer encoding, slower retrieval, and less efficient organization of material. All of this could add up to poorer performance on memory recall tasks. It is known that the cognitive slowing down is integrally related to task complexity. If a task is particularly complex, de-

manding significant attentional resources, then an exaggerated decrease in performance is seen.

A competing theory, called the inhibition deficit hypothesis, attempts to explain the cause of memory loss as one gets older. This hypothesis has received wide support. The basic premise of the inhibition deficit hypothesis is that the information maintained in working memory—the information brought into conscious awareness—is not managed very well. Specifically, the theory states that irrelevant information is not discarded from working memory in a timely manner. Since working memory has a limited capacity, it would be most efficient for the brain to use the available resources for items of information that would be most germane to the problem that is being solved. If unnecessary information cannot be ignored or discarded, it could potentially interfere with cognitive processing. The term "inhibition" in this context refers to the ability to reduce or block out information that will ultimately interfere with proper mental functioning. Empirical support has been found that indicates that older adults tend to keep more of a sustained activation of irrelevant information than younger adults.

Some theorists believe that the central cause of age-related memory loss is an inefficiency in using attentional resources. An individual's working memory has a limited capacity. Thus, if one attends to a number of tasks simultaneously, there is a high probability that some of the tasks will suffer a performance loss, particularly if one task is complex. More complex tasks use up a larger portion of the attentional resources than less complex or more automated tasks. One example of this would be a person who has just learned how to drive a car. Initially, it might be too distracting for the person to have the radio blaring and a friend in the front

### Performance on Memory Tasks in Late Adulthood

| *Memory Declines* | *Memory Remains or Improves* |
| --- | --- |
| Free recall | Memory for motor skills |
| Cued recall | Digit span |
| Explicit memory | Semantic memory, particularly for vocabulary words |
| Episodic memory | Implicit memory tasks |
| Knowing where information was learned | |
| Spatial memory | |

seat trying to hold a conversation. This scenario could cause the person to exceed available attentional resources, since the skills and concentration needed to drive a car have not been practiced to a point where the skill has become automated. The resources needed when learning how to drive are significantly higher than when one does not have to think about driving. In the case of an older adult, it is believed that more attentional resources are needed to perform mental operations than what was needed at younger ages. Since more resources get used up faster, perhaps fewer resources can be devoted to encoding and retrieval strategies. The end result, if this were the case, would be memory performance loss.

—*Bryan C. Auday*

*See also* Alzheimer's Association; Alzheimer's disease; Brain changes and disorders; Dementia; Forgetfulness; Psychiatry, geriatric; Reaction time.

**FOR FURTHER INFORMATION:**

Craik, Fergus I. M., and J. M. Jennings. "Human Memory." In *The Handbook of Aging and Cognition*, edited by Craik and T. A. Salthouse. Hillsdale, N.J.: Lawrence Erlbaum, 1992. This is a comprehensive book that deals not only with memory loss and aging but other kinds of cognitive processes, such as reasoning and problem solving for the older adult.

Haberlandt, Karl. *Human Memory: Exploration and Application.* Boston: Allyn & Bacon, 1999. This book provides an overview of different aspects of human memory. Chapters can be found on memory for facts, skills, and autobiographical events.

Neath, Ian. *Human Memory: An Introduction to Research, Data, and Theory.* Pacific Grove, Calif.: Brooks/Cole, 1998. This book has excellent chapters on forgetting, sensory memory, implicit memory, and the controversial area of reconstructive processes in memory.

Parkin, Alan J. *Memory and Amnesia: An Introduction.* 2d ed. Malden, Mass.: Blackwell, 1997. Written by an author who has personally studied memory for the majority of his professional life, this is an excellent starting point for learning about different kinds of memory loss that can occur across the life span.

Searleman, Alan, and Douglas Herrmann. *Memory from a Broader Perspective.* New York: McGraw

Hill, 1994. This well-written volume on human memory is more comprehensive than a number of other published works. It includes chapters that are not typically found in this kind of text on the subject of the environment and memory as well as social interactions and memory.

Spear, Norman E., and David C. Riccio. *Memory: Phenomena and Principles.* Boston: Allyn & Bacon, 1994. This book discusses the topic of learning as related to memory processes. There is a good chapter of the structure of memory as well as on the topic of human amnesia.

## MEN AND AGING

**RELEVANT ISSUES:** Economics, family, health and medicine, recreation

**SIGNIFICANCE:** As life expectancy for men grew from about forty-eight years in 1900 to a projected eighty years by 2010, issues surrounding men and aging received considerable attention

The statistics of life expectancy have undergone considerable change over the centuries. In classical Greece and Rome, the average life expectancy was between twenty and thirty years, although this figure is perhaps misleading because factored into it is a high infant mortality rate. Certainly most of the classical writers and thinkers whose work has survived lived into what would today be considered old age. Socrates, for example, was about seventy when he drank the hemlock that ended his life.

By 1900, life expectancy for males in the United States was about twice what it had been in ancient Greece and Rome. Men born in 1900 lived on average just short of forty-eight years, women three years longer. A great demographic change occurred, however, in the next eight decades. Life expectancy for men born in 1984 was seventy-two years. It is estimated that by 2010 this figure will have advanced to a life expectancy for men of over eighty years.

### REASONS FOR INCREASES IN LONGEVITY

The increases in life expectancy for men have been directly related to several factors. As industry has become increasingly automated, fatal accidents in factories have declined substantially. In the United States, government agencies oversee the implementation of safety precautions in the workplace. The Occupational Safety and Health

Administration (OSHA) enforces strict regulations to ensure the safety of all workers, particularly in the heavy industries that employ large numbers of men.

A major factor affecting both men and women has been decreases in the rates for infant mortality. In 1915, one hundred out of every thousand infants died before their first birthdays. By 1991, that figure had decreased to just under nine deaths for every thousand infants.

As medical science has advanced, the spread of such devastating diseases as polio, diphtheria, influenza, and bubonic plague has been checked by immunization or by effective treatment with sophisticated medications. Preventive medicine is widely practiced throughout the industrialized world, with massive immunization programs offered free of charge or at affordable fees by various health agencies. The United States and Canada have been exemplary in their attempts to eliminate the kinds of air and water pollution that once led to illness and death among large populations. Such disabling and often-fatal illnesses as cholera, amoebic dysentery, typhoid fever, yellow fever, and malaria are well controlled in North America.

Even diseases that remain incurable, such as diabetes and acquired immunodeficiency syndrome (AIDS), have become manageable. Medical science has also made huge advances in the treatment of cancer and cardiovascular disease both by publicizing ways to avoid such diseases and by aggressively spearheading their treatment when they do occur. The media have worked to inform the public about health and longevity.

Most American men understand the relationship between diet and good health, the value of regular exercise, the advisability of limiting alcoholic intake, and the need to avoid tobacco. Antismoking campaigns have succeeded in driving smokers from public places and conveyances and have reduced substantially the numbers of smokers in American society. The use of alcoholic beverages among men past thirty has also been in steady decline.

Perhaps the most important factor resulting in increased longevity for men and women in much of the industrial world is the easy and virtually universal availability of medical treatment. In many countries, socialized medicine has put medical care within the reach of all citizens, regardless of their economic levels. In the United States, insur-

*Although American society is more critical of the physical changes that accompany aging in women, men must deal with such consequences as wrinkles, glasses, gray hair, and baldness.* (James L. Shaffer)

ance programs offered by many employers and the growth of health maintenance organizations (HMOs) have made medical care easily accessible to much of the population. Many of those who are not covered by insurance qualify for Medicaid. For those over sixty-five, Medicare pays a substantial portion of their medical expenses, although it still does not cover prescription drugs, which have become increasingly sophisticated and expensive.

All these factors have contributed to increases in life expectancy for men, although their life expectancy remains considerably lower than that of women. Many factors explain this disparity, although as more women enter the workforce and are subject to the same sorts of stresses as men, some demographers think that the gap between male and female life expectancy will be narrowed.

### WHY WOMEN LIVE LONGER THAN MEN
There is no clear answer to the question of why women outlive men. On the surface, it might seem

that men are subjected to more stress in the workplace than women are. Certainly more men have jobs that pose physical dangers than women do. With the increase in the numbers of working women, trends will soon be identified to test the hypothesis that stress in the workplace accounts for the shorter life expectancy of males.

Most biologists discount the role that stress plays in causing the disparity in life expectancy between the sexes. They point out that this disparity is not limited to humans but that in nearly all animal species, females outlive males, suggesting that the disparity is genetic or in some way biologically determined rather than environmental.

Some research has implied that women outlive men because of their sex hormones. When premenopausal women are producing estrogen, their incident of heart disease and high blood pressure is substantially less than it is after the menopause, when their production of estrogen diminishes or ceases. Thus, up to age forty-five or fifty, most women seem to have built-in protection against heart disease, although after the menopause the incidence of heart disease among women is comparable to that among men.

### The Aging Process

All organisms undergo the aging process, during which irreversible changes occur that ultimately lead to ill health, disability, and death. In humans, the aging process is usually so gradual as to be barely perceptible on a day-to-day or month-to-month basis, although serious illness, severe emotional stress and shock, and other such factors can accelerate the process so that it becomes noticeable. The hair of some people who have undergone a great emotional shock, for example, will turn white within a month or two.

The changes that take place in men are not only obvious changes such as wrinkling of the skin, increased brittleness of the bones, or increased fat deposits in the abdomen. Some changes are functional, making it difficult or impossible for people to perform tasks that they were once able to perform with ease. Sometimes, the aging process involves stooped posture, a shuffling gait, reduced muscular coordination, or lapses in memory. The effects of aging are different for everyone; they have little direct relationship to age. Some men are old at sixty, while others continue to be active

and functional into their nineties. Any generalizations one makes about aging are filled with exceptions and fraught with inconsistencies.

Aging is partly cultural and partly genetic. Men who have led hard lives, received little medical treatment, and had little mental stimulation tend to age more rapidly than those who have had easier lives, have had easy access to medical treatment, and have been stimulated mentally. In the United States, it has been observed that educational level has a correlation to life expectancy: On the whole, college graduates live three years longer than high school graduates. This disparity may exist because college graduates usually have less physically demanding jobs than high school graduates or because college graduates often have a broad range of interests to keep them alert and involved. Also, educated people probably demand more sophisticated medical assistance than those who are less educated.

The genes one inherits appear to have a direct relation to longevity. Men whose parents and grandparents lived to be eighty years old can expect to live six years longer on average than men whose parents and grandparents died before sixty. Apparently within the genes of all living organisms there is a mechanism that controls life span, that imposes a maximum upon how long the organism can live: three months for the common housefly, about twenty years for dogs, about forty-five years for horses, and about two hundred years for some tortoises. By the end of the twentieth century, the oldest documented human life was 123 years, although undocumented claims have been made of anywhere from 140 to 160 years. Some biologists see no reason that life expectancy among humans should not eventually exceed 100 years and that ages of 150 or more will be attainable by some people.

Research by Michael Rose, an American evolutionary biologist, suggests that maximum life spans can be extended through genetic engineering. Rose extended the lives of his selectively bred, experimental fruit flies by 100 percent, thereby doubling their life spans. Other researchers, by manipulating the gene that sets puberty in motion, were able to extend the average life spans of some platyfish by as much as ten months. Obviously, these experiments have little immediate relevance for humans, but they challenge the long-held belief that there are upper limits to the life spans of all organisms. The Human Genome Project, which is unraveling the intricacies of the human genome, offers the promise that one day the human life span and the years of healthy, productive living among humans will be extended substantially.

## DEFINING OLD AGE

Specific designations of old age vary from culture to culture and from person to person. To a ten-year-old, someone who is thirty seems old. In most cultures, men are considered old when they leave the workforce, when they cease to be economically productive. In male-dominated cultures, which still prevail in most parts of the world, women are often categorized in reference to their husbands, so that when a husband is considered old, his wife is also considered old, although she may continue to work strenuously at her household duties.

In contemporary American culture, many people, through early retirement, leave the workforce long before they are technically considered old. Because the Social Security Act of 1935 set sixty-five as the age when benefits began (increased to sixty-six in 2000 and to sixty-seven in 2003), in the eyes of many sixty-five has been considered the beginning of old age. This is the also age at which Chancellor Otto von Bismarck of Germany granted the first old-age pensions in a system established under his direction in the 1880's. At that time, few people lived much beyond sixty-five. Today, men and women receive equal benefits under Social Security, despite discrepancies in life expectancy.

In contemporary culture, one can identify at least four stages through which men normally pass as they make the transition from middle age to old age, from working full time to full-time retirement. In the first stage, many early retirees, who cannot really be viewed as old, continue to work but at less demanding, less remunerative jobs than they have held during most of their lives. Often they work only part-time. Many early retirees try to live solely on the income from this work because, if their children are now independent, they can live on less money and permit their savings to compound. This stage of retirement often lasts, for men, anywhere from five to ten years.

Most male retirees eventually begin to pursue one or more kinds of leisure activity, such as golf, tennis, swimming, or travel, gradually reducing their work schedules and devoting more time to such nonwork activities. During this stage, many men begin to feel a diminution in their physical strength brought about by the heart's reduced ability to supply blood to the muscles. In a twenty-year-old male, the heart typically pumps 6.5 liters of blood per minute, whereas in his eighty-five-year-old counterpart, only about 3.5 liters per minute are pumped through the circulatory system.

Older men can, however, substantially improve their heart action through moderate exercise. Many begin to pursue exercise programs to strengthen their bones and muscles and to improve their heart action and blood flow. Such programs usually involve light exercise, some weight lifting, and a commitment to devote at least twenty to thirty minutes a day to it. In time, however, many men find athletics and travel too strenuous and revert to less physically taxing activities, such as reading, gardening, or walking. Such people are still healthy and well able to cope with the daily routine of living and looking after themselves.

The final stage that affects those who live into old age is the period when health begins to fail and when the older person cannot easily live independently and look after himself. At this stage, some men need help in getting out of bed or up from chairs. They might not be able to dress and groom themselves. They may need to have someone feed them. Because women live longer than men, they are often available to look after husbands whose health declines to the point that they require some custodial care. Widows are more numerous in most cultures than widowers. Often widows who have attended their husbands through terminal illnesses have no one to look after them as they weaken, so they enter group-living facilities, retirement communities, or nursing homes. The populations of such facilities are disproportionately female.

## HOW MEN ADJUST TO OLD AGE

Most men work outside the home longer than women typically do, although various social changes have altered that situation. Before World War II, most wives were stay-at-home mothers, whereas most men went daily to a place of business and were away from home for five or six days a week during most of the daylight hours. If women worked outside the home, they usually had done so before marriage and/or after their children had been raised, so their work for pay was not continuous and their total number of years in the workforce was considerably less than that of the typical man.

When retirement comes to a married man who has been used to leaving the house five or six days a week to go to a job and to mingle with other people, a rude awakening often occurs for both husband and wife. The husband wakens in the morning and sees sprawled before him a long day with little to fill it. The wife, even the working wife, has usually grown used to having time to herself during the day after the husband goes to work or before he comes home. Wives of newly retired men often comment that they married their husbands for better or worse but not for lunch. The adjustment to retirement can be traumatic for both husbands and wives, particularly if, like 75 percent of new retirees, the initial withdrawal from the workplace is total. Sociologists note that retirement is generally more difficult for men than for women because married men are less likely to bond with other men than women are with other women. Often, a man's chief social outlet is the workplace. When this outlet is no longer available, many men feel abandoned and despondent.

Some companies and educational institutions have instituted graduated retirement systems under which men reduce their workloads slowly over a period of two or three years, thereby easing into retirement rather than plunging into it. Where it is possible for men to take a graduated retirement, it is usually desirable for them to leave the workforce in this way. Their reduced schedules will enable them to develop new interests, make new friends, and find activities with which to fill their days when their retirement becomes total. Also, a graduated retirement helps wives adjust to having their husbands around more than they have been accustomed to.

One cannot reasonably define old age as the point at which one retires. Most current retirees can look forward to two or more decades of not working full time. As life expectancy increases and early retirement becomes more usual, it is thought that many men retiring after 2010 will spend almost a third of their lives in retirement, which is almost as much as most of them will have spent in the workforce. Perhaps old age is best defined in terms of how well one functions physically and mentally. Active retirements keep men from deteriorating, and the availability of first-rate medical services makes debilitating diseases less of a problem for the elderly than they once were. While physical deterioration cannot be avoided altogether, it can, in most men, be forestalled by regular exercise, proper diet, and mental stimulation.

*Some men face a difficult period of adjustment following retirement when their primary means of social interaction comes to an end. Many older men must become more active in seeking companionship.* (James L. Shaffer)

## THE MALE SEX DRIVE

As men age, the level of testosterone that is secreted in the testes diminishes steadily. The endocrine glands, however, continue to produce sex hormones. Most people think that as testosterone levels in the blood decrease, the male sex drive diminishes and sexual activity becomes less frequent as well as less satisfactory. Research into this matter does not support popular opinions about declines in the sex drives of older men.

Actually, almost no correlation has been found between the level of testosterone in the blood and a man's sexual prowess. What seems to determine the sexual activity of older men is their general health and social customs. If they believe that sex is for the young, then they may suffer sexual dysfunction even in middle age. If they have had fulfilling sex lives, then their sexual activity is likely to continue well into old age.

Attitude has a great deal to do with human sexuality at all ages, but particularly in old age. Physical changes and disorders, however, can be a factor. Impotence, permanent or temporary, can result from some kinds of illnesses. Men whose prostate glands have been removed may be unable to perform sexually in the ways to which they have been accustomed. Prostate disorders are common in older men. It has been said that every man, if he lives long enough, will be afflicted by prostate cancer. In men over seventy, a malignancy in the prostate often goes untreated because it is a slow-growing type of cancer. Men in their seventies who have prostate cancer will probably die of something else rather than be killed by their cancers. In younger men who have prostate cancer, radiation and, more drastically, removal of the prostate gland may be indicated.

All men over the age of fifty should have annual prostate screenings, which involve both a digital examination of the prostate and a test that reveals prostate-specific antigen (PSA) levels in the blood. In many cases, the digital examination does not reveal cancer in its earliest, most manageable stages, but if PSA levels are elevated, cancer is usually present.

## THE ILLNESSES OF OLD AGE

Among American men over sixty-five, the most common illnesses are arthritis, hypertension, hearing impairment, heart disease, and cataracts.

Most of these illnesses are manageable, and treatment of one may cause decreases in others. For example, by controlling hypertension, which is easily done with a broad spectrum of readily available medications, a man's likelihood of developing heart disease is reduced substantially. Visual and hearing problems are easily dealt with in most cases through corrective lenses, laser surgery, or hearing aids. The removal of cataracts from the eyes has become a routine, outpatient procedure.

In old age, responses to stimuli are generally reduced. Many elderly men find it virtually impossible to deal with several stimuli simultaneously, which can make driving or the operation of machinery dangerous for them and for others. Men aware of their reduced response time can adjust by driving more slowly, avoiding crowded highways, and generally exercising considerable care on the road. As long as their vision is adequate, many men can continue driving well into their nineties.

The most common causes of death among elderly men are, in the following order, heart disease, cancer, cerebrovascular diseases (strokes), chronic obstructive pulmonary disease, and accidents, often drowning or falling. All these causes except for accidents can be managed well if they are detected early and treated aggressively and consistently.

As people age, they lose brain cells at a steady rate, although humans have so many brain cells that losing even a million a day should not quickly result in perceptible changes in the person. As brain cells are lost, the surviving cells in most people increase the number of connections that they make with other cells, thereby eliminating substantial neuronal loss. In some older people, however, the cells are unable to make the connections that in most people are made routinely. Two of the most frustrating illnesses of old age are Alzheimer's disease and Parkinson's disease, both diseases of the nervous system that can have devastating outcomes for their victims, who usually succumb to the disease.

To date, there is no cure and little palliative treatment for either of these two diseases in their advanced stages. Many men who have Parkinson's disease continue to function for many years, although tremors will affect their extremities. Alzheimer's disease in essence robs its victims of their personhood. Their memories are virtually wiped out. They do not recognize members of their families. They are constantly disoriented and cannot focus long enough to read or to follow what is going on in television shows or films. Of all the research on aging that is currently afoot, research on these two diseases is perhaps the most important.

—*R. Baird Shuman*

*See also* Aging process; Cancer; Cultural views of aging; Death and dying; Divorce; Early retirement; Employment; Genetics; Heart attacks; Heart changes and disorders; Heart disease; Home ownership; Hypertension; Impotence; Life expectancy; Longevity research; Marriage; Middle age; Midlife crisis; Old age; Pensions; Prostate cancer; Prostate enlargement; Remarriage; Reproductive changes, disabilities, and dysfunctions; Retirement; Rhinophyma; Sexuality; Smoking; Sports participation; Stress and coping skills; Strokes; Urinary disorders; Widows and widowers; Women and aging.

**FOR FURTHER INFORMATION:**

Aiken, Lewis R. *Aging: An Introduction to Gerontology.* Thousand Oaks, Calif.: Sage Publications, 1995. Useful chapters in this carefully documented study are "Economics and Aging" and "Living Arrangement and Activities." Although the emphasis is not specifically on men, the coverage is sufficiently broad to include worthwhile insights about aging problems specific to men.

Arber, Sara, and Jay Ginn. *Gender and Later Life: A Sociological Analysis of Resources and Constraints.* Thousand Oaks, Calif.: Sage Publications, 1991. Valuable for its comparative statistics relating to various aspects of later life in men and women. The emphasis is more on women than on men, as is true in most literature of this sort because women typically outlive men.

Berger, Raymond M. *Gay and Gray: The Older Homosexual Man.* Urbana: University of Illinois, 1982. Largely anecdotal, consisting of information gained from in-depth interviews with fifteen older gay men who represent a broad economic and educational spectrum. Although somewhat outdated, it remains an indispensable resource for those interested in this segment of the older male population.

Costa, Dora L. *The Evolution of Retirement: An American Economic History, 1880-1990.* Chicago: University of Chicago Press, 1998. The best book of its kind in showing how various concepts of retirement evolved. Most of the data relate to men because, as Costa states, until quite recently men were the dominant force in the workplace, unlike women generally having worked continuously until retirement.

Crewes, Douglas E., and Ralph M. Garruto. *Biological Anthropology and Aging: Perspectives on Human Variation over the Life Span.* New York: Oxford University Press, 1994. The chief value of this book is its cross-cultural consideration of aging. The broad view that the authors present provides insights unavailable in most sources. Because most of the book deals with male-dominated societies, it is relevant to those interested in men and aging.

McQuire, Francis A. *Leisure and Aging: Ulyssean Living in Later Life.* Champaign, Ill.: Sagamore Press, 1996. Focuses on the healthy aspects of life among the elderly. McQuire emphasizes the need for old people to keep physically and mentally active, placing considerable attention on the value of traveling.

Nichols, Barbara, and Peter Leonard, eds. *Gender, Aging, and the State.* New York: Black Rose Books, 1994. The chief thrust is on the disparities that exist between the treatment of men and women who need public assistance in retirement.

## MENOPAUSE

**RELEVANT ISSUES:** Biology, health and medicine

**SIGNIFICANCE:** The hormonal changes that take place with the menopause at midlife have long-term effects on the health and well-being of women

Once a secret passage dreaded by women as the final loss of youth, the menopause—the cessation of menstruation—is now being encountered by the baby boomers, and they are not going quietly into this next stage of life. Women in their forties and fifties have formed support groups with names such as the Red Hot Mamas and Crone Societies. Television programs, books, and articles in newspapers and magazines offer advice on recognizing and managing the changes that occur with the onset of the menopause. Increased numbers of studies on the physiology of the menopause, as well as the overall physiology of aging, have accompanied this popular trend.

Until a few hundred years ago, humans typically lived about twenty to forty years. The average life expectancy of an infant born in 1900 was forty-eight years. By the end of the twentieth century, the average female life expectancy in the United States was almost eighty years. It is clear that many more women live beyond the age of fifty these days than at any time in human history.

When a woman reaches fifty to fifty-two years of age, her ovaries run out of eggs. The depletion of eggs marks the end of the menstrual cycle and is accompanied by dramatic hormonal changes—the most obvious is a significant drop in estrogen production by the ovaries. The menopause is clinically defined as complete once a woman has gone one year without a menstrual period, although changes that ultimately lead to the menopause may begin as early as thirty-five years of age. The period preceding the menopause during which estrogen levels begin to decline is referred to as the perimenopause.

## THE MENSTRUAL CYCLE PRIOR TO THE MENOPAUSE

Each month, in response to hormones secreted by the pituitary gland, which is located in the brain, an ovarian follicle consisting of an oocyte (egg, or ovum) and surrounding cells is readied for ovulation. This process usually takes about two weeks. Although typically only one oocyte is released, many follicles actually begin to develop. Typically, all but one degenerate before reaching maturity. During the two-week period prior to ovulation, the follicular cells surrounding the oocyte secrete increasing amounts of estrogen. Peak estrogen secretion is reached just prior to ovulation. Estrogen plays many important roles; one of the most obvious is to stimulate the inner lining of the uterus, the endometrium, to grow in thickness.

At ovulation, the oocyte is released from the surface of the ovary and enters the oviduct. The remaining cells of the follicle collapse back into the ovary and form the corpus luteum, a structure that secretes both estrogen and progesterone. Estrogen and progesterone together act on the endometrium to make it a hospitable substrate in which an embryo may implant itself, should fertilization take place. The corpus luteum secretes

these hormones for about ten days. If fertilization does not occur, it ceases to function. Without the hormones secreted by the corpus luteum, the uterine lining is not maintained and is soon sloughed off in menstrual flow. If fertilization occurs, the corpus luteum does not degenerate, but instead persists almost to the end of pregnancy.

As a result of cyclic fluctuations in the levels of a finely orchestrated set of hormones, a woman's menstrual cycle repeatedly supplies ova for possible fertilization and readies the uterus (womb) for pregnancy. Near the age of fifty, this cycling usually becomes irregular and then stops. Many events lead to this change. Not all are understood, but it is clear that cycling stops with the end of available ovarian follicles.

## THE OVARIES FROM BIRTH TO THE MENOPAUSE

A female infant is born with all the follicles she will ever produce. Her reproductive potential is determined even before she emerges from the womb of her mother. It is estimated that, at birth, each ovary contains about one million immature follicles. After birth, many of these follicles degenerate, so that at menarche (the onset of menstruation) there are an estimated 250,000 to 500,000 follicles per ovary. Between menarche and the menopause, only about four hundred follicles reach maturity and are ovulated. Because many follicles begin to develop each month and then degenerate, the huge reservoir of follicles with which she began life is depleted as a woman approaches the menopause. Without the cyclic maturation of follicles, estrogen production drops significantly. Investigators have learned about the declining number of follicles that accompanies aging by studying ovaries surgically removed from living women or those taken from cadavers. They have learned about hormone levels by analyzing blood samples taken from women of different ages and varying menstrual stages.

Although the ovaries at the menopause no longer produce follicles for ovulation, it is important to point out that the ovarian tissues are not inert. For several years beyond the menopause, the remaining tissues secrete androgens ("male" hormones such as testosterone), which are converted to estrogen by fat cells in the body. The adrenal glands also secrete androgens that are converted to estrogen. "Estrogen" is a generic term that re-

*The executive director of the Florida Nurses Association holds a press conference in 1999 to educate older women about the health challenges that they encounter after the menopause.* (AP Photo/Mark Foley)

fers to a family of closely related molecules. For example, the estrogen secreted by ovarian follicles is estradiol, while the main estrogen formed in postmenopausal women is estrone.

### THE EFFECTS OF ESTROGEN

Estrogen circulates in the blood and interacts at specific sites called receptors in a variety of target tissues, including the endometrium, lining of the vagina, urinary tract, skin, bones, blood vessels, and brain. A decline in estrogen levels produces wide-ranging effects. The endometrium is not stimulated to increase in thickness, so cyclic menstrual bleeding stops. The vaginal lining tends to become thin and dry, which may lead to itching and discomfort during intercourse. The urinary tract and bladder lose muscle tone, leading to more frequent feelings of the need to urinate and possibly to urinary stress incontinence (leakage of urine with sneezing or coughing). The loss of flexible connective tissue beneath the skin leads to wrinkling. Thinning of the bones (osteoporosis) may result in fractures. Reduced levels of estrogen also appear to be correlated with development of atherosclerotic plaques (hardening of the arteries), which can lead to heart attacks or strokes. Decreased estrogen in many women leads to hot flashes, which may cause sleep disturbances and resulting fatigue and irritability. It is believed that hot flashes result from a disruption of signals in the hypothalamus, the part of the brain that regulates body temperature. Finally, emerging studies suggest that estrogen also plays an important role in memory and cognition.

Adult women of any age who have had a bilateral ovariectomy (both ovaries removed), which sometimes is done with a hysterectomy (removal of the uterus), immediately cease menstruation and often report having hot flashes and vaginal dryness. Estrogen replacement therapy, giving estrogen, reverses the effects of low estrogen.

## SYMPTOMS AND CONSEQUENCES OF ESTROGEN REDUCTION

Women who go through a natural (not surgically induced) perimenopause and menopause report a wide variety of symptoms related to fluctuating levels of estrogen and other hormones, such as follicle-stimulating hormone (FSH) secreted by the pituitary gland. As estrogen gradually declines during the perimenopause, women in their forties may experience menstrual irregularities, lighter or heavier menstrual flow, premenstrual syndrome (PMS), or menstrual cramps that they had not had before. While some women passing through this decade experience a gradual increase in the time between menstrual periods and gentle waning of menstrual flow, others have frequent and heavy bleeding with clots. Some women never have hot flashes; others report being incapacitated by frequent and intense hot flashes that interrupt their sleep or disrupt their work. Similarly, women report a spectrum of mild to severe problems with vaginal dryness and urinary tract problems. Decreases in muscle mass and increases in weight have also been reported.

Hot flashes and mood swings generally abate once a woman has her last menstrual period and her hormonal secretions settle into postmenopausal levels. (However, some women report hot flashes well into the postmenopausal years.) Vaginal dryness and urinary symptoms both result from low levels of estrogen and will continue in many women for the rest of their lives. Likewise, low estrogen levels can lead over time to osteoporosis and cardiovascular disease. Over their lifetimes, one in five women will develop osteoporosis. The dowager's hump (kyphosis) and broken hips, common signs of osteoporosis, manifest themselves at advanced ages, but they are the result of bone silently lost over a long period of time. Men and women alike begin to lose bone around thirty-five years of age. With the abrupt drop in estrogen levels at the menopause, however, women experience accelerated rates of bone loss. Cardiovascular disease is the number one killer of women over the age of fifty. By comparison with men, strokes and heart attacks occur relatively infrequently in women prior to the menopause. With the loss of the protective effects of estrogen, postmenopausal women become increasingly vulnerable to heart and blood vessel disease. Finally, researchers have found evidence suggesting an association between a lack of estrogen and the occurrence of Alzheimer's disease.

## TREATMENT OPTIONS

Women who live many years beyond the menopause will experience the long-term effects of low levels of estrogen. A vigorous debate is taking place between those who characterize the menopausal years as hormone-deficient and in need of treatment by means of hormone replacement therapy (HRT) and those who characterize those years as a normal part of the female life experience needing only sensible living habits to maintain good health. Proponents argue that osteoporosis and cardiovascular disease are critical public health issues. Opponents point out that the effects of long-term use of HRT are unknown and that women who take supplemental hormones are potentially at risk for equally devastating diseases.

As the debate continues, pharmaceutical companies are developing new "designer estrogens." These drugs are also called selective estrogen receptor modulators (SERMs). They act like estrogen only at certain estrogen receptor sites and therefore have more narrowly defined actions than estrogen itself. For example, raloxifene (Evista) is known to mimic estrogen at estrogen receptors in bone (therefore protecting against osteoporosis) but not at estrogen receptors in the breast and uterus (which means it protects against cancers of the breast and endometrium). Raloxifene may protect against heart disease, but it does not block hot flashes.

Women seeking natural ways to increase their levels of estrogen may include phytoestrogens (estrogens from plants such as soybeans) in their diets or in supplements. To treat vaginal and urinary symptoms, estrogen creams may be applied to the vagina.

Unlike earlier generations, today's women have a growing number of options available to treat the symptoms of the perimenopause and menopause. A woman and her doctor need to consider her individual health risks, estrogen levels, and symptoms to determine the most appropriate course of action to alleviate or prevent the consequences of low levels of estrogen.

Whether hormonal or other treatment is sought, a woman will improve her later years by eating a diet rich in calcium and vitamin D (to combat osteoporosis) and low in fat (to combat cardiovascular disease and weight gain). She is well advised to stop smoking if necessary. Smoking has been implicated in heart disease, osteoporosis, and earlier onset of the menopause, as well as in lung disease. She should exercise aerobically to stimulate the heart and maintain a healthy body weight and do load-bearing exercises (including walking) to facilitate strengthening the bones. She will find that Kegel exercises (squeezing the muscles at the floor of the pelvis) will improve bladder control and sexual pleasure.

### THE BIOLOGICAL SIGNIFICANCE OF THE MENOPAUSE

The overall process of aging involves a variety of physiological declines, but the human female reproductive system is shut down noticeably early. Is there a selective advantage to the human species to have women stop reproducing relatively early and then to live beyond their reproductive years? Two opposing hypotheses have been proposed to explain the menopause. One is the grandmother hypothesis based on studies of the Hadza people, contemporary hunter-gatherers in Tanzania. The Hadza grandmothers play an important role in providing adequate food for their grandchildren while their daughters are bearing and nursing new young. The argument is that the postmenopausal grandmothers are assured of their own genes being passed on through their daughters by contributing to the survival of their daughters' children.

The opposing hypothesis of reproductive senescence is based on studies of populations of baboons and Serengeti lions, both similar to humans because they live in social groups that involve female kin relationships. Because all mammals require considerable maternal care following birth, this hypothesis holds that a female becomes infertile early enough to ensure that her last offspring would be able to survive on its own after she died.

For early humans, assuming that maternal care was needed until the child reached about ten years of age, females entering the menopause between forty-eight to fifty-five would have lived to be fifty-eight to sixty-five years old.

Whatever investigators conclude is the evolutionary significance of the menopause, all agree that it is a significant feature of the reproductive life of human females. The future is expected to bring a more detailed understanding of the physiology of the perimenopause and menopause. With that understanding, better-tailored treatments can be devised to assure healthy, productive, and fulfilled lives to women during the decades beyond their reproductive years.         —*Margaret Anderson*

***See also*** Aging process; Alzheimer's disease; Arteriosclerosis; Beauty; Biological clock; Bone changes and disorders; Breast cancer; *Change: Women, Aging, and the Menopause, The*; Childlessness; Estrogen replacement therapy; Exercise and fitness; Fractures and broken bones; Heart attacks; Heart disease; Hip replacement; Infertility; Middle age; Midlife crisis; Osteoporosis; *Ourselves, Growing Older: A Book for Women over Forty*; Reproductive changes, disabilities, and dysfunctions; Sexuality; Strokes; Temperature regulation and sensitivity; Weight loss and gain; Women and aging; Wrinkles.

### FOR FURTHER INFORMATION:

Boston Women's Health Book Collective. *Our Bodies, Ourselves for the New Century.* New York: Simon & Schuster, 1998. The latest remake of a long-respected resource on women's health written by women devoted to promoting women's health.

Hawkes, K., et al. "Grandmothering, Menopause, and the Evolution of Human Life Histories." *Proceedings of the National Academy of Sciences of the U.S.* 95, no. 3 (February 3, 1998): 1336-1339. Data obtained from studies of contemporary hunter-gatherers in Tanzania.

Huston, James E., and L. Darlene Lanka. *Perimenopause: Changes in a Woman's Health After Thirty-five.* Oakland, Calif.: New Harbinger, 1997. A discussion of bodily changes leading up to the menopause and how women can prepare for healthy postmenopausal life.

Packer, Craig, et al. "Reproductive Cessation in Female Mammals." *Nature* 392, no. 667 (April 23,

1998): 807-811. Data obtained from studies of lions and baboons in Tanzania.

_____. "Why Menopause?" *Natural History* 107, no. 6 (July/August, 1998). An argument against the grandmother hypothesis and in favor of reproductive senescence, based on the more detailed studies published in *Nature.*

Shandler, Nina. *Estrogen: The Natural Way.* New York: Villard Books, 1997. Advice and recipes using foods rich in plant estrogens.

Sherwood, Lauralee. *Human Physiology: From Cells to Systems.* 3d ed. Belmont, Calif.: Wadsworth, 1997. A college-level textbook that provides excellent background on all aspects of human physiology, including reproductive physiology.

## MENTAL IMPAIRMENT

**RELEVANT ISSUES:** Health and medicine, psychology

**SIGNIFICANCE:** Although mental illness is common in elderly people, with approximately 25 percent of those over sixty-five having some type of mental health problem, impairment is not more prevalent in the older population and may even be less so

Mental impairment may be defined as a disturbance of cognition or affect characterized by one or more of the following: the inability to engage in orderly thought; a lack of power to distinguish, choose, or act decisively and/or rationally; loss of memory; and/or impaired reality testing. Mental disturbance may be accompanied by disordered speech and abnormal psychomotor behavior. The causes of mental disturbance may be reversible, irreversible, or a combination of the two conditions.

### THE RELATIONSHIP OF MENTAL IMPAIRMENT TO MENTAL ILLNESS

Mental impairment is not synonymous with mental illness and can be temporary or permanent. Delirium is an example of mental impairment that is usually reversible and temporary. According to the American Psychiatric Association's *Diagnostic and Statistical Manual of Mental Disorders: DSM-IV* (4th ed., 1994), the features of delirium include acute onset; confusion fluctuating with periods of lucidity; a duration of hours to weeks; reduced awareness of the environment; abnormally high or low alertness; impaired orientation to

time, place, and person; recent and immediate memory impairment; disorganized thinking; perceptual difficulties; impaired speech; and a disrupted sleep-wake cycle. Common causes of delirium include drug toxicity, infection, early signs of a stroke, fluid and electrolyte imbalances, alcohol withdrawal, untreated diabetes, respiratory disturbances, head trauma, physical isolation, and extreme emotional stress.

A common stereotype is that most older people are senile, and/or that senility is an inevitable and untreatable mental illness. In fact, "senile" and "senility" are outdated terms. This stereotype is extremely dangerous when health professionals believe it. It leads to lack of health promotion, prevention, and treatment, thus becoming a self-fulfilling prophecy. The fact is that mental impairment and mental illness are neither inevitable nor untreatable. Only about 2 percent of those sixty-five and older are institutionalized with a primary diagnosis of psychiatric illness. According to the *NGNA Core Curriculum for Gerontological Nursing* (1996), most community studies show that older people have fewer mental impairments than younger people.

### CULTURAL INFLUENCES

The cultural context influences how mental health and illness are defined by older people and their significant others. Culture may be defined as the collective behavior patterns, communication styles, beliefs, concepts, values, institutions, standards, and other factors unique to a community that are socially transmitted to individuals and to which individuals are expected to conform. According to the *NGNA Core Curriculum for Gerontological Nursing*, cultural variables include social institutions, belief systems, values and customs, religion, self-concept, behavior, and language.

Actions considered mental impairment in one culture may not be considered a deviation from the normal in another culture. C. Fong's CONFHER model, described in the 1985 article "Ethnicity and Nursing Practice," is excellent for obtaining a cultural profile. It is suggested that before completing an individual's profile, health practitioners complete their own. The letters of CONFHER represent communication style, orientation, nutrition, family relationships, health beliefs, education, and religion. To be culturally competent implies a sensitivity to diverse cultures.

## THE COMMUNITY MENTAL HEALTH MOVEMENT

Before 1960, the majority of mentally ill persons received treatment in isolation from their home communities. Having to travel great distances for treatment contributed to the difficulty of achieving mental health promotion and maintenance. The establishment of the Community Mental Health Centers Program of the National Institute of Mental Health (NIMH) was an attempt to alleviate some of these problems. A number of political forces contributed to the Community Mental Health Centers Construction Act of 1963. Together with the Community Mental Health Centers Amendments of 1975, it provided for the establishment of community-based therapeutic centers to replace custodial mental institutions.

The NIMH identified the essential elements of comprehensive community mental health services: inpatient services, partial hospitalization or at least day care service, outpatient services, emergency services provided on a twenty-four-hour-a-day basis and available within at least one of the three services listed, and consultation and educational services available to community agencies and professionals. The evaluation of community mental health program effectiveness is of great importance.

## MENTAL STATUS TESTING

No one assessment tool will provide all the information needed for a complete and comprehensive mental status examination. As listed by J. J. Gallo and colleagues in the *Handbook of Geriatric Assessment* (1988), instruments for evaluating cognitive loss designed to be short evaluations that indicate current status include the Short Portable Mental Status Questionnaire (SPMSQ), the Mental Status Questionnaire (MSQ), the Mini-Mental State Examination (MMSE), and the Set Test. Having to translate screening instruments to assess cognitive impairment adds to the complexity of establishing that the reverse translation actually asks the intended question. It is also important to remember that none of these screening instruments can be used to make a diagnosis; they are only indicators that a problem exists.

The Geriatric Depression Scale is an example of a tool used to assess the psychological dimension. It is a reliable, valid measure of depression that consists of thirty questions that are answered by "yes" or "no." A short version is also available. The Hamilton Rating Scale is often used to quantify depression. The CAGE model is an example of a screening tool for alcoholism. It consists of four questions, represented by the letters CAGE: "Have you ever felt you ought to *c*ut down?" "Have you ever been *a*nnoyed by criticism of your drinking?" "Have you ever felt *g*uilty about your drinking?" "Do you ever take a morning drink (*e*ye opener)?" Two affirmative answers are said to be suggestive of alcoholism. The Zarit Burden Interview is an example of a tool that attempts to identify feelings engendered in the caregiver that contribute to "burden" in caring for an impaired older adult. It has been commonly used in research.

## MENTAL IMPAIRMENT AND DEPRESSION

Mental impairment in the older adult may co-exist with any number of conditions, including depression. Depression may be defined as a clinical syndrome characterized by lowered mood tone, difficulty thinking, and sleep changes precipitated by feelings of loss and/or guilt. According to the DSM-IV, the essential feature of a major depressive episode is a period of at least two weeks during which there is either depressed mood or the loss of interest or pleasure in nearly all activities

Depression may be a result of psychodynamic, biochemical, genetic, or existential factors. The psychodynamic factor includes depressive tendency that begins early in life if a child's dependency needs are not met during first year of life; for example, if oral needs are not satisfied, longing for love and security may develop. The biochemical factor relates to alterations in mood involving complex biochemical changes, such as electrolyte imbalance, that alter functioning of the adrenal cortex and the autonomic nervous system. Neurotransmitter deficiency may be a factor. Norepinephrine deficiency could contribute to depression, while serotonin deficiency, dopamine, and excess norepinephrine levels could lead to manic episodes. Current research supports the theory of genetic factors in bipolar and possibly other affective disorders. Finally, according to the *NGNA Core Curriculum for Gerontological Nursing,* the existential view supports the notion that multiple life events contribute to affective disorders.

The professional assessment of the older individual in crisis includes a determination of homicidal or suicidal ideation and an identification of strengths and past coping skills. The precipitating event is clarified through reframing the event clearly from the elder's own words, determining the degree of disruption to the elder's life, and determining the effects of this disruption on others in the environment. In addition to being over age fifty-five and/or male, there are many risk factors for suicide: chronic and disabling physical illness or chronic pain, living alone, a history of attempted suicide at younger ages, a family history of suicide or mental illness, a history of drug or alcohol abuse, depression (especially with agitation), excessive guilt, insomnia, self-reproach, loss of income or indebtedness, bereavement or prolonged grief, preoccupation with suicide in conversation, definitive and well-defined plans for completed suicide, resolving depressive illness in the presence of increased energy, history of poor personal relationships or poor marital history, and poor work record.

Mental health professionals should take the following into consideration during the care management planning phase for the depressed older client: individual coping mechanisms, the degree of hopelessness, the degree of powerlessness, the degree of spiritual distress or distress of the human spirit, and the potential for self-directed violence. The *NGNA Core Curriculum for Gerontological Nursing* lists many possible interventions for the depressed elder: assisting the individual to meet self-care needs, seeking input for self-care decisions, offering positive feedback, establishing contact and rapport, creating diversionary activities, offering options for increasing social support, providing opportunities to express feelings, teaching effective communication techniques, assessing suicide risk, monitoring and reinforcing positive coping strengths, providing unconditional positive regard, encouraging positive self-statements, supporting independent behavior, encouraging decisions about activities of daily living (ADLs) and health care, teaching discrimination between controllable and uncontrollable events, assisting in the setting of realistic goals, pointing out alternative coping behaviors, teaching relevant information about illness and treatment, teaching stress-reduction techniques, and providing family and caregiver teaching. The evaluation of interventions for the depressed elder should include the degree of progression toward goals and decreased signs and symptoms of depression.

Interventions for suicide prevention should take several factors into consideration. No one should be afraid to ask the older adult at risk about suicidal thoughts or intentions; such questions do not "cause" people to commit suicide. Most people readily communicate their feelings when asked, even if they do not offer the information. Access to someone who cares about those feelings may result in a sense of relief in the older adult or an opportunity to share a topic considered taboo. People should listen to the content and emotions expressed by the elder. It is important to determine if there is a plan that consists of a method (gun, drugs, poison), what the availability of that method is, whether the plan has any specificity (time, place, dose), and what the virulence or degree of lethality of the plan is. All answers should be accepted, and negativity regarding the plan or suicidal ideation should be avoided. The *NGNA Core Curriculum for Gerontological Nursing* suggests the following questions or comments to pursue identified risks: "You seem 'down.' Have you thought about ending your life?" "Do you think about suicide?" "Do you have a plan for suicide? Tell me about it." "How do you see yourself dying?" The evaluation of interventions to prevent suicide may include determining referral contacts where appropriate, reviewing methods used to assess the potential for suicide, reviewing the elder's response to encouraging verbalization about suicide, and following up with a referral source to determine the elder's recovery.

## MENTAL IMPAIRMENT AND GRIEVING

Older individuals who have recently experienced the loss of a loved one or valued object may exhibit mental impairment as they engage in the grieving process. The assessment of grief and loss issues is also important. Grief and grieving are not synonymous with depression. Grief is considered a normal dynamic of the human experience. Physical losses may be of physical capacity, good health, or physical attractiveness. Psychosocial losses may be of a spouse or significant other, social activities, financial security, and roles. Identified phases of grief include shock, denial, anger, depression, and understanding or acceptance. An individual may not necessarily go through each phase, or the phases may change in order. The signs and symptoms of grief may include anorexia (appetite loss), insomnia, immobilization, fatigue, sadness, depression and/or anxiety, guilt, loneliness, isolation, failure to maintain personal appearance, and diminished sexual interest.

Pathological grief should be suspected if the signs and symptoms are of long duration. The intensification of the following signs and symptoms tend to be associated with pathology: deepening depression, suicidal ideation, significant weight loss, alcohol abuse, and mood disorders. Interventions for grief work support the grief process by identifying the importance of grieving the significant loss; supporting and/or increasing areas of strength such as religious affiliations, social networks, intellectual activity, exercise, and coping abilities; allowing some use of denial and other defense mechanisms as appropriate; and encouraging involvement in support groups with those experiencing a similar loss. Older adults coping with the loss of a loved one need to identify realistic good and bad memories of the deceased, to learn how to comfort others who are grieving, and to establish or revive social relationships.

### MENTAL IMPAIRMENT AND CRISIS

Mental impairment can precipitate a crisis and vice versa. A crisis occurs when a person is unable to use customary methods of problem solving to overcome obstacles to important life goals. It is usually a time-limited event characterized by upheaval in an older individual's steady state. Balancing factors that assist an individual in maintaining equilibrium include the perception of the event as realistic (versus distorted), adequate situational support (versus inadequate support based on significant others or the environment), and adequate coping mechanisms. Dominant characteristics of older people in crisis include increased receptivity to assistance; heightened sensitivity to suggestions, with interventions producing maximum results; and more dependency of a time-limited nature.

Professional assessment of an older individual in crisis includes a determination of homicidal or suicidal ideation and an identification of strengths and past coping skills. The precipitating event is clarified through reframing of the event clearly from the elder's own words, determining the degree of disruption to the elder's life, and judging the effects of this disruption on others in the environment. During the care management planning phase of a crisis, the following factors are taken into consideration: the individual's ability to implement coping techniques, the presence of other people in the individual's life from whom to seek involvement, and alternative methods of coping currently in use. Interventions address the need to cushion the impact of stress that has thrown the person off balance, to help mobilize the resources of those affected directly by the stress, and to prevent permanent disability.

### MANAGEMENT OF MENTAL IMPAIRMENT

Many measures can be taken in an effort to manage mental impairment in an older individual. Finding the cause of the impairment is of utmost importance. If an individual is taking numerous medications or has recently introduced a new one and behavioral change results, an examination of the array is drugs is important in order to determine if one or more drug interactions is the source of the mental impairment. A visit to a physician or other health care practitioner may be necessary to determine if a disease process is the source of the impairment.

For example, pneumonia is sometimes accompanied by mental confusion. Transient ischemic attacks (TIAs), or "mini-insults," to the brain cells can signal the early signs of a stroke, with accompanying mental impairment. Older individuals who are dehydrated or in body fluid overload may also experience changes in mental status; an assessment of the degree of fluid and electrolyte imbalance could reveal such conditions. Elders who are going through alcohol withdrawal in the form of delirium tremens often exhibit mental impairment, frequently in the form of poor reality testing. Hallucinations are often a sign of delirium tremens for the alcoholic in withdrawal. Head trauma can be a "hidden" entity if the victim is still conscious and the insult occurred when no one else was present. Physical and emotional isolation can contribute to mental impairment. For individuals at risk due to isolation, measures can be used to help strengthen social supports and increase social contacts, such as home companions, occupational or recreational therapy, or senior centers or adult day care centers. Finally, caregivers and friends need to be supportive rather than confrontational in order to decrease emotional stress.

—*Mary E. Allen*

*See also* Alcoholism; Alzheimer's disease; Brain changes and disorders; Cultural views of aging; Death and dying; Dementia; Depression; Grief; Medications; Pneumonia; Psychiatry, geriatric; Stress and coping skills; Strokes; Suicide.

## FOR FURTHER INFORMATION:

Collins, C., M. Liken, S. King, and C. Kokinakis. "Loss and Grief Among Family Caregivers of Relatives with Dementia." *Qualitative Health Research* 3, no. 2 (1993): 236-253. Implications for clinical practice and research are presented. Concludes that there is a need for further research regarding how specific illnesses and social support affect prebereavement reactions and postbereavement outcomes.

Fong, C. "Ethnicity and Nursing Practice." *Topics in Clinical Nursing* 7, no. 3 (October, 1985): 1-10. This article describes a model for the generation of a cultural profile. Specific questions are designed to elicit information about the parameters of communication style, cultural orientation, nutrition, family relationships, health beliefs, education, and religion.

Gallo, J. J., W. Reichel, and L. Andersen. *Handbook of Geriatric Assessment.* 3d ed. Gaithersburg, Md.: Aspen, 1999. This book focuses on multidimensional assessment in primary care geriatrics. Various assessment instruments are described that have been used to detect and monitor the course of mental impairment and the capacity to perform activities of daily living and to assess social and economic functioning.

Luggen, A. S., ed. *NGNA Core Curriculum for Gerontological Nursing.* St. Louis: C. V. Mosby, 1996. A comprehensive curriculum guide initiated by the National Gerontological Nursing Association (NGNA). The core curriculum is organized into nine units. Unit 1 deals with professional issues of gerontological nursing. Unit 2 focuses on trends and issues of interest to gerontological nurses. Unit 3 discusses legal and ethical issues. Unit 4 has four major administration areas: management principles, evaluation issues, regulatory and reimbursement mechanisms, and education issues. Unit 5 addresses nursing research. Unit 6 describes different care and service delivery areas. Unit 7 provides an outline of environment issues for older adults. Unit 8 discusses extensive nursing assessment and data collection methods. Unit 9 outlines the major health problems of older adults. Case studies are included to illustrate selected problems and the associated care.

# MENTORING

RELEVANT ISSUES: Economics, psychology, work

SIGNIFICANCE: Older individuals can either serve as mentors or be mentored by others, particularly in the workforce; this type of relationship, whether formal or informal, can occur at any point in an individual's career or life stage

Mentors are people who serve as close, trusted, and experienced counselors or guides. Additionally, mentors function as teachers, tutors, or coaches. Technical, interpersonal, and political skills can be conveyed in a relationship from the mentor to the person being mentored. Not only does the less experienced (often younger) person benefit from this type of relationship, but the more experienced (often older) individual may enjoy the opportunity to share previously acquired knowledge, skills, and abilities.

## OLDER WORKERS AND MENTORING

The concept of mentoring in the work environment has evolved over time from the formal arrangement of apprenticeship to an informal protégé situation involving advice and back to a more formal relationship. Mentoring seems to work well in many employment situations. For example, women with mentors advance in a career more quickly than those without them. Further, it is more likely that a person who has been mentored will, in turn, mentor others. Mentoring is a useful tool that can be used to establish and enhance networks and references.

Older workers may act as mentors for younger colleagues. People anticipating a transition to retirement enjoy the role of mentor and look forward to having an opportunity to share acquired history, culture, and informal dealings in work situations. These workers are often skilled in the oral tradition of passing information from person to person. Older workers hired at a new company or in a new field or returning to work after an absence may also appreciate the guidance provided by having a mentor.

Older workers often face prejudice and discrimination in the workplace. This situation, sometimes called the gray barrier, describes a situation in which an older worker is not hired or does not get promoted as quickly as other workers. When knowledge, skills, and abilities are equal among employees, the gray barrier can be one explanation for the older employee's lack of employment progress. Although little real research exists on this issue, numerous personal narratives and anecdotes confirm that such a barrier exists. Additionally, it is clear that hiring and promotion activities occur to the detriment of older workers. Age discrimination exists in government, profit, and nonprofit fields.

While the situation may be changing in the government sector as a result of the influence of organizations like the American Association of Retired Persons (AARP), mandated employment practices, and numerous labor union activities, the pace of change is relatively slow. Having a mentor can often ameliorate this situation. Successful older workers also report pushing through the gray barrier by using political savvy, establishing credibility, fitting in with the current management style, and understanding the nature of the customer base.

## STAGES OF FORMAL MENTORING RELATIONSHIPS

Formal arrangements for mentoring in the workplace can be established through meetings, instruction manuals, and regular appraisal sessions. During the initiation phase, which typically lasts between six months and one year, the mentor's knowledge, skills, and abilities are acknowledged without question. The mentor serves as a source of support and guidance. Mentors begin to recognize the potential of others requesting mentoring. A time period of two to five years typically outlines the cultivation stage. Mentoring relationships gain self-confidence and mutual respect. Differences of values and styles of operation are explored. Mentors begin to provide challenging work, actively coach individuals, and sponsor individuals in new work situations.

Mentoring relationships should not last indefinitely; a separation phase typically takes six months to a year. Just as it is not advisable to begin mentoring relationships precipitously, neither should they be terminated without care. One reason is the experience of simultaneous freedom in decision making coupled with anxiety of evolving away from the mentor relationship. Most successful mentoring relationships, however, are measured by the success in moving away from the closeness of this type of work situation. As is true of other work systems, successful mentoring should include ongoing information gathering to redefine and inform the mentoring process. Both the mentor and the person being mentored are excellent resources of information for change during the process.

## ENTRY-STAGE ISSUES

Older workers are often presented with unfamiliar work environments and cultures when returning to the world of work. A mentor can exert a strong influence in determining how to adjust to culture differentials. The initial weeks at any job are often the most critical. Mentors can smooth over many of the usual problems in the workplace while at the same time establishing boundaries for untoward circumstances at work. Many times, there appears to be no place to turn when attempting to understand a new workplace. Early stages of work, for both older and younger workers, are the times when aspirations and ideas meet reality. This matching of culture and individual can be as important for the older worker as the skill, knowledge, and ability level brought to the job.

Mentors can ensure the appropriate level of challenge for an older worker to avoid unpleasant situations during the initial period of adjustment. At the same time, when high expectations do not match the nature of the job requirements or settings, a mentor can provide a different perspective for the older worker. Many work situations provide initial job assignments that may be more challenging than usual. This type of increased responsibility for the older worker can be especially perplexing if not mediated by a mentor arrangement.

Early in the career development of an older worker, a clear set of goals and objectives should be mutually agreed on. These goals emphasize vocational or educational work outcomes as well as social outcomes in the workplace. An orientation that discusses roles, responsibilities, and expectations should follow. Frank and open discussion of personal characteristics, skills, and specific objectives of the mentor relationship is important. A period of training for overcoming shortcomings and deficits should follow. Equally important is a trial period or a preparatory time for testing the relationship before any long-term commitments are made by the mentor or the older worker. Following the trial period, an extensive review of expectations and applications should take place.

The concept of group mentoring should be explored as an alternative. Small businesses or self-employed individuals may not be able to take advantage of the formal mentor relationship often found in larger organizations. These group mentoring relationships often take the form of membership in professional organizations and trade associations. In addition to the provision of an effective career development tool, important networking opportunities are established and enhanced.

### BENEFITS AND DRAWBACKS

Mentors can provide a broader overview of the work environment and the relationship of functional areas. Communication on work activities maintains a dynamic perspective of work functions. Job description changes, salary modifications, and work assignment evolution are important parts of the communication base. This type of mentor relationship helps alleviate the initial feelings of being overwhelmed and the ongoing feelings of being lost in a large, faceless workplace. In addition to the career or work function mentors often perform, an additional psychosocial function also exists. Aspects of the workplace such as competence, self-esteem, and perception by others can be better observed through the eyes of a mentor.

Mentoring is not a panacea without problems. Older workers often find it difficult to find a mentor willing to work with them. Often, the willingness to work with older workers is undermined by the same prejudice and discrimination originally present in the hiring process. Mentors who are not satisfied with a work situation may use a mentoring opportunity to sabotage the potential successful work situation of someone else. This can be avoided by developing several mentoring relationships, either concurrently or sequentially. The pejorative notion of mentors manipulating workers has gained some acceptance. This stereotype is usually overstated; a cooperative working relationship is more indicative of the mentor's role.

Older workers sometimes resist entering into a mentoring relationship because the formal definition of mentoring is a relatively new workforce concept. Workers who were trained in another era and have not been introduced to the benefits of a mentoring relationship may be reluctant to embrace such a practice. Workers trained without mentors find that they may understand the informal nature of mentoring but do not see the value of formalizing the relationship. Additionally, work attributes of power and achievement are emphasized through formal mentoring relationships. Older workers often have been trained in a more passive work setting.       *—Daniel L. Yazak*

***See also*** Age discrimination; Ageism; Communication; Employment; Retirement; Wisdom.

### FOR FURTHER INFORMATION:

Dessler, Gary. *Human Resource Management.* 8th ed. Upper Saddle River, N.J.: Prentice Hall, 1999.

Goethals, George R., Stephen Worchel, and Laurie Heatherington. *Pathways to Personal Growth: Adjustment in Today's World.* Boston: Allyn & Bacon, 1999.

Gomez-Mejia, Luis R., David B. Balkin, and Robert L. Cardy. *Managing Human Resources.* 2d ed. Upper Saddle River, N.J.: Prentice Hall, 1998.

Herr, Edwin L., and Stanley H. Cramer. *Career Guidance and Counseling Through the Life Span.* 5th ed. New York: HarperCollins, 1996.

Mathis, Robert L., and John H. Jackson. *Human Resource Management.* 8th ed. Minneapolis/St. Paul, Minn.: West, 1997.

## MIDDLE AGE

**RELEVANT ISSUES:** Biology, demographics, family, health and medicine, psychology, sociology

**SIGNIFICANCE:** Middle age is a period in life filled with change and requiring major adaptations on the part of the individual and society

Middle age is broadly defined as the period between young adulthood and senescence. While there are no precise age limits associated with this period, it is usually defined as the period from forty to sixty-five. During this period, development continues to occur at a steady pace, but changes become more readily apparent than they were in the past. As a result, this is a period that often has many negative stereotypes associated with it. In spite of these stereotypes, most elderly adults report that middle age is the period that they would prefer to return to given the chance.

## PHYSICAL CHANGES

Changes in skin integrity, pigmentation, muscle mass, distribution of body fat, vision, and joints do not begin during middle age but rather reach a level where alterations become noticeable. For this reason, middle age is often viewed as a period of physical decline.

Among the changes that commonly become noticeable in middle age are graying of hair, wrinkling of skin, development of "middle-age spread," decrease in metabolic rate leading to more rapid weight gain, and development of some signs of a arthritis in many individuals. Vision changes abound: Farsightedness develops with the ability to accommodate decreasing; the retina becomes less sensitive to low levels of illumination, so that middle-aged adults require brighter illumination to see as well as they had in the past; and the size of the blind spot typically enlarges as a result of decreased blood supply to the eye.

Changes in the functioning of the sex organs and related endocrine changes are most readily apparent in women in the case of the menopause. The cessation of menstruation, and the signs and symptoms associated with it, is the single most common physical change in middle-aged women. While the hormonal and sex-related changes in middle-aged men are less obvious, there is a comparable decline in testosterone level.

A less well known but definitely important physical change in middle age takes place within the nervous system itself. Demyelination (breakdown of the myelin sheath) of the axon of the neurons results in slower transmission of the neural impulse. This is one factor that results in increased reaction time with age. Therefore, as one gets older, it takes a longer time to respond completely to a stimulus.

*According to psychologist Erik Erikson, the task of middle age is generativity, the need to contribute to the world and the well-being of future generations. For many, this need is met through parenthood. (James L. Shaffer)*

## HEALTH AND SEX

Middle age is a time when many adults begin to complain about their health and health-related issues. The "aches and pains" of arthritis (inflammation of the joints) usually become apparent during middle age. The decrease in metabolic rate makes the middle-aged adult more easily prone to weight gain, increasing concern with proper diet and exercise. Hypertension (high blood pressure) typically appears for the first time in middle age, requiring more diligent health screenings to allow early detection and treatment. Similarly, cancer screenings and cholesterol checks are more routinely done in midlife in an attempt to promote wellness. Despite these concerns, more than 70 percent of middle-aged adults in a nationwide survey indicated that they viewed their health as excellent.

There is little change in the ability of men and women to function sexually in middle age (although women normally do lose their ability to reproduce by their mid-fifties). In spite of this, sexual activity tends to occur less frequently than it did in young adulthood. This decline in sexual activity may occur in part because of job-related stress, family matters, changing energy levels, or routine. Research indicates that sexual activity is greatest in twenty-five- to twenty-nine-year-olds and drops off considerably by the time individuals reach middle age. In a national survey, fewer than 25 percent of adults in their forties to fifties reported engaging in sexual intercourse at least twice a week, while 40 percent reported having intercourse only a few times per month. While participation in sexual activity in middle age shows a decline, most middle-aged adults remain sexually active and report continued enjoyment of intercourse and sex-related behaviors.

## FAMILY

Marital satisfaction appears to increase in middle age. Nearly three-fourths of married couples in a nationwide survey by the MacArthur Foundation indicated that they had very good relationships with their spouse. This increase in marital satisfaction may be related to changes within the family (resulting in more time and energy for each other), lessening of stressors and responsibilities as children develop and work roles change, or the fact that dissatisfied couples have separated by

middle age, resulting in fewer marriages but more happy marriages.

Middle age is typically viewed as a time of changing family roles. While (nuclear) family size tends to have stabilized, three major family changes usually occur during the middle years that require relatively major adaptation on the part of the individual. This is a period in which offspring develop independence. Middle-aged adults report having a difficult time adapting to the independent functioning of their children. As a result, many middle-aged parents with adolescents experience a generation gap before the children leave home. Once the grown children have moved out of the house, and on with their lives, the middle-aged parents may experience the empty nest syndrome. If all the offspring leave home (the nest), the parents are faced with adaptation as they return to the original dyad. In some households, these changes are greeted tearfully, while in other households they are viewed very positively. In still other households, the nest does not remain empty as grown children take turns returning to the home and leaving again because of school situations, social and family relationships, or financial and job-related matters. Rather than the empty nest, these middle-aged parents experience the revolving door syndrome.

As these offspring go off on their own, a second major change is likely to occur within the family with the birth of grandchildren. Adapting to grandparenthood is the single most positive change that middle-aged adults report. The majority of grandparents report that the birth of grandchildren gives them a sense of renewal as well as a sense of continuity. They enjoy experiencing developmental mile stones that they missed in their own children's lives or that they barely had time to enjoy. Traditional middle-aged grandparents also report enjoying the fact that they can spend time with their grandchildren without having to be fully responsible for them.

The third major change in family roles involves the fact that elderly parents often develop dependence on their middle-aged children. This is the change to which middle-aged adults have the hardest time adapting. Viewing one's parents (who have always been there for one to count on) as suddenly frail or in need of help requires major adjustments in life. If the development of this dependence occurs prior to the complete independence of all offspring, the middle-aged parents enter the sandwich generation. Most members of the sandwich generation report having a difficult time juggling their responsibilities related to their now-dependent parents and still-dependent children. Often, this conflict comes to an end with the death of one's parents. This loss not only requires major adaptation but also leaves individuals with a heightened sense of their own mortality, as they begin to think more about their own death.

### PLANNING FOR THE FUTURE

With middle age comes the realization that life is finite, that there is less time ahead than in the past. Along with this notion comes psychologist Erik Erikson's notion of generativity. This concern for the future spurs many middle-aged adults to do what they can to make the world a better place through mentoring, volunteering, charitable contributions, or political involvement. At the same time that they are thinking about the future of the world, they are planning for their own futures. Major concerns usually include planning for retirement and planning for health-related issues and death.

Middle-aged adults have typically begun planning financially for their retirement and begin to think about how and where they would like to spend their time. Studies indicate that better planning leads to a happier future. Access to health care is a major issue for all age levels. Concerns about health insurance (including long-term care and catastrophic coverage) are common. Often of greatest importance is concern with end-of-life issues. All adults have the option of creating an advance directive: a living will or durable power of attorney for health care. By so doing, they can make their medical wishes known for the future, as well as appoint an individual to make sure that these wishes are carried out.

### CONCLUSION

Clearly, the time from forty to sixty-five is a period filled with change. The majority of these changes are dealt with in a positive manner. As a result, middle age is often considered (by the elderly) to be the best years of life.

—*Robin Kamienny Montvilo*
*See also* Absenteeism; Aging: Biological, psycho-

logical, and sociocultural perspectives; Aging process; American Association of Retired Persons (AARP); Arthritis; Baby boomers; Beauty; Biological clock; Breast cancer; Breast changes and disorders; Caregiving; *Change: Women, Aging, and the Menopause, The*; Childlessness; Children of Aging Parents; Cosmetic surgery; Death anxiety; Death of a child; Death of parents; Demographics; Divorce; Dual-income couples; Early retirement; Employment; Empty nest syndrome; Erikson, Erik H.; Estrogen replacement therapy; Face lifts; Family relationships; Fat deposition; Filial responsibility; 401K plans; Full nest; Grandparenthood; Gray hair; Hair loss and baldness; Hypertension; Individual retirement accounts (IRAs); Marriage; Maturity; Men and aging; Menopause; Midlife crisis; Multigenerational households; Nearsightedness; Old age; Over the hill; Parenthood; Premature aging; Reaction time; Reading glasses; Remarriage; Reproductive changes, disabilities, and dysfunctions; Retirement; Retirement planning; Sandwich generation; Sensory changes; Single parenthood; Stepfamilies; Successful aging; Vision changes and disorders; Weight loss and gain; Women and aging; Wrinkles.

### FOR FURTHER INFORMATION:

Belsky, J. *The Adult Experience*. St. Paul, Minn.: West, 1997.

Birren, J. E., and K. W. Schaie. *Handbook of the Psychology of Aging*. 4th ed. San Diego: Academic Press, 1996.

Brim, O. G. Midmac. *Midlife Research: The John D. and Catherine T. MacArthur Foundation Research Network on Successful Midlife Development*. http://midmac.med.harvard.edu.

Hoyer, W. J., J. M. Rybash, and P. A. Roodin. *Adult Development and Aging*. Boston: McGraw-Hill, 1999.

Santrock, J. W. *Life-Span Development*. 7th ed. Boston: McGraw-Hill, 1999.

# MIDLIFE CRISIS

**RELEVANT ISSUES:** Biology, death, family, psychology

**SIGNIFICANCE:** Midlife crisis, once thought to be a common, traumatic reaction to the realization of one's own aging and mortality, was found by the late 1990's to be relatively infrequent and atypical

The concept of midlife crisis, which has been called the most celebrated feature of adult development, originated with psychoanalyst Elliott Jacques, who, in 1965, wrote about the fact that most artists undergo a crisis in their late thirties propelled by their awareness of time left to live rather than time since birth. Jacques believed that everyone experiences midlife crisis in some form, as death ceases to be a general concept and becomes a personal matter. People who reach middle age without becoming successfully established in work and family life, or who neglect emotional issues to engage in frantic levels of activity, may experience pronounced psychological disturbance. Jacques noted that midlife crisis for these individuals can include preoccupation with appearing young, overconcern with health, sexual promiscuity, a search for solace in religion, and a tendency to stop enjoying life. Many of these symptoms made their way into the stereotype of midlife crisis. Healthier people, Jacques stated in his article "The Midlife Crisis," enter into awareness of their own death "with the sense of grief appropriate to it"; but even for them, midlife crisis is "a period of purgatory—of anguish and depression."

### DEFINITION AND CHARACTERISTICS

When Jacques first wrote about midlife crisis, the idea of developmental stages in adulthood was fairly new. In 1980, Solomon Cytrynbaum defined the phenomenon, in his article "Midlife Development: A Personality and Social Systems Perspective," as a "perceived state of physical and psychological distress that results when internal resources and external social support systems threaten to be overwhelmed by developmental tasks that require new adaptive resources."

Whether people experience a crisis or a transition at midlife, certain characteristics can be observed. The process may take a short time, or it may last five to twenty years. The individual's reaction to the process may be open, adaptive, conscious, and masterful, or it may be passive, defensive, and unconscious—or the person may vacillate between the two. The process can be seen as a series of tasks that must be mastered: accepting one's mortality, coping with biological changes and health limitations, reassessing career and marriage, and reevaluating sexuality and self-concept. If the tasks are not mastered successfully, subse-

*Although the concept of a midlife crisis has probably been exaggerated, some people go through a reevaluation of their goals that results in significant changes in occupation, relationships, and lifestyle.* (Marilyn Nolt)

quent stages of life can be unhappy. The process can bring about personality changes, such as increasingly inward focus and greater attention to previously neglected parts of the personality (particularly those associated with the opposite gender). Women grow more in touch with their independent, competitive, and aggressive aspects, while men become more willing to be expressive, dependent, and sensuous. Some researchers contend that the characteristics that reemerge after midlife transition are any that were previously rejected or unrealized, not just those that are gender related.

Several studies report that development occurs in stages during midlife transition. One model refers to the stages as "progress" and "regression." Another proposes the stages of destructuring, reassessment, reintegration or restructuring, and behavioral or role change. Destructuring, provoked by awareness of mortality, biological changes, or a variety of life events, can cause alternating euphoria and depression. Reassessment, which consists of reactions to these precipitators, might involve mourning the loss of goals, denial, transitional partners, and reassessment of one's primary relationship. Reintegration or restructuring involves testing new ways of relating to the important people in one's life, integrating the previously neglected personality characteristics, and finding and exploring new aspirations. Behavioral and role changes solidify the new dreams and new ways of relating to others.

### CONFLICTING ESTIMATES OF PREVALENCE

In 1977, Paul T. Costa created a "midlife crisis scale" with questions pertaining to the feelings usually mentioned in studies of midlife crisis: inner conflict and confusion, preoccupation with death and decline, a sense of meaninglessness, and unhappiness with family and work. In a study of 350 men aged thirty to sixty, there was no increase in these feelings at the middle of the age range. Only 2 percent of respondents met the scale's definition of midlife crisis. A replication with three hundred men found similar results. By 1985, some scholars were writing about the "myths" connected with midlife crisis, partly because of disparities in reports of its frequency. Some studies called midlife crisis a rare occurrence; others said 10 percent of people experience it; still others, 70 to 80 percent. A 1994 review of the literature concluded that most studies disconfirm the statement that the majority of people experience a midlife crisis.

Several researchers have noted that people who meet the definitions of midlife crisis have predictors of this painful transition earlier in life—in poor life choices or in high scores on neuroticism scales. Narcissistic people are also susceptible to traumatic midlife transitions. People with enduring personality characteristics such as these experience crises throughout adulthood.

Undoubtedly, people undergo a change in perspective at midlife—a realization that there is no longer time for everything, so new goals must be formed and complex choices made. For most, the experience may not properly be termed a "crisis." Some scholars believe most people experience a midlife "transition," as described by Daniel Levinson in *The Seasons of a Man's Life* (1978)—a deeply affecting, sometimes painful reassessment.

People in crisis respond with abrupt action in order to avoid their past choices, current responsibilities, and the future's seemingly limited possibilities. Those in transition respond with careful thought, making changes only after assessing the possible consequences.

Another view of what happens at midlife is inspired by psychoanalyst and human development theorist Erik Erikson. He believes that in the matured adulthood stage, the primary developmental task is to resolve the tension between "generativity" and "stagnation." Generativity is the process of identifying something that is vitally important and taking action so that it is maintained and cared for. Generativity is a way of moving forward, rather than regressing to past patterns by trying to regain lost youth. Stagnation is a refusal to grow, an acquiescence to old methods and perspectives, perhaps because of the belief that it is too late to accomplish new goals, or perhaps because of a fear of change. For some people, the search for generativity may lead to excess—doing so much for others that one is worn out and family relationships are stressed. Other people may stagnate rather than changing and growing because of the structure of their lives prior to midlife. People who experienced premature career, creative, or artistic success (perhaps in their twenties), or who enjoyed a career pinnacle in their early forties, may view the remainder of life as anticlimactic and have trouble imagining what is left to do. Those who have relied too heavily on their spouse's or children's successes rather than developing their own sense of identity may also struggle with forming goals for the next life stage. Generativity may find outlets through a new approach to one's existing job, a job change, volunteer work, or political activity.

### THE MIDUS SURVEY

In 1999, initial results were released from the Midlife Development in the United States (MIDUS) survey, at that time the most comprehensive examination of midlife ever undertaken. The study was funded by the John D. and Catherine T. MacArthur Foundation's Research Network on Successful Midlife Development. The team of twenty-eight researchers was led by Orville Gilbert Brim. The study encompassed 7,861 people aged twenty-five to seventy-four (to give data for comparisons of other life stages with midlife) but focused on ages forty to sixty. Three thousand of the participants completed a thirty-minute telephone interview as well as a two-part self-administered questionnaire. The remaining five thousand people were involved in eleven other studies. The study's one thousand questions addressed twenty-seven different areas of life, with the intention of developing a concrete picture of what actually happens to people during midlife. The study looked at factors that spur midlife development—including life events, work, family, illness, and culture—and also examined the strategies people use to cope with these issues.

The majority of respondents found midlife a period of greater control over many areas of life, including work and finances; great satisfaction with marriage and family; extremely busy lives; increased autonomy and environmental mastery (handling of daily responsibilities); excellent health; and optimism about health in the future. Although both women and men improved in personal autonomy during midlife, women gained in greater increments. Brim reported that 95 percent of Americans could define the term "midlife crisis" and knew someone who had experienced it. Among MIDUS survey participants, however, only 23 percent reported having had a midlife crisis. Only one-third of this group linked their crisis to awareness that they were aging. For the rest, midlife crisis was provoked by particular life events, some of which had no connection to aging. The survey's researchers concluded, therefore, that only 10 percent of participants had undergone a "classic" midlife crisis (as originally defined by Jacques). These people were likely to have high scores on neuroticism scales (a finding that was in keeping with earlier studies) and were highly educated. The researchers noted that because many previous studies of midlife crisis had been based on clinical populations, the frequencies those studies reported may not have paralleled the incidence among the general population. They also surmised that the midlife crisis myth persists because nearly everyone knows someone who seems to have experienced it and retains vivid memories of its tumultuous impact on that person.

The MIDUS survey results also addressed other factors that studies have named as contributors to midlife crisis. Most of the postmenopausal women said they felt "only relief" when their menstrual periods ended, and 50 percent went through the menopause with no hot flashes at all. Rather than being concerned about future health and about biological changes associated with aging, participants surprised and concerned researchers with their optimism about their health. However, 70 percent reported being overweight, while 42 percent of women and 24 percent of men said that hurrying on level or slightly sloping ground made them short of breath. Only 23 percent strongly agreed that they worked hard to stay in good health, and most of the smokers did not believe they had an above-average risk of contracting heart disease or cancer.

In addition, 72 percent of participants rated their marriage excellent or very good, and 90 percent said it was unlikely that their marriage would ever end. Of those surveyed, 21 percent were experiencing anxiety or depression—a lower rate than was found in younger adults. Survey participants in their forties said they were dealing with high numbers of negative life events involving children and other family members, but many were showing great resiliency. Only 5 percent of all respondents had consulted a psychiatrist in the past year; 9 percent had talked to a counselor, 20 percent had consulted a family physician about emotional problems, and 19 percent had attended a self-help group during some period in their lives.

—*Glenn Ellen Starr Stilling*

***See also*** Alcoholism; Death anxiety; Divorce; Erikson, Erik H.; Marriage; Menopause; Middle age; Personality changes; Suicide.

**FOR FURTHER INFORMATION:**

Bergquist, William H. *In Our Fifties: Voices of Men and Women Reinventing Their Lives*. San Francisco: Jossey-Bass, 1993. Using the theories of Erik Erikson, Bergquist claims that the fundamental task of people in their fifties is resolving the tension between stagnation and generativity.

Cierna, James R. "Myths About Male Midlife Crisis." *Psychological Reports* 56 (1985). Focuses on three symptoms of personal disorganization—alcoholism, divorce rate, and suicide rate—that studies often use to detect the presence of midlife crisis. Cierna finds that available research data do not indicate increases in these behaviors at midlife.

Colarusso, Calvin A. *Fulfillment in Adulthood: Paths to the Pinnacle of Life.* New York: Plenum Press, 1994. Colarusso provides an extensive discussion of the myth that artist Paul Gauguin, at midlife, deserted family and career to bask in the tropics with beautiful, bare-breasted native women. This myth, along with media reports and popular press accounts, have oversimplified midlife crisis, which Colarusso considers a relatively uncommon disorder. He contrasts midlife crisis to Daniel Levinson's concept of midlife transition.

Cytrynbaum, Solomon, et al. "Midlife Development: A Personality and Social Systems Perspective." In *Aging in the 1980's: Psychological Issues,* edited by Leonard W. Poon. Washington, D.C.: American Psychological Association, 1980. A thorough review of studies on midlife crisis prior to 1980, noting the studies' contradictory results and commenting on problems with methodology among some of them.

Elias, Marilyn. "What Midlife Crisis? Forget the Age-Old Myths: 'Midlife Is the Place to Be.'" *USA Today* 16 (February, 1999). Elias provides highlights from a major study of midlife development in the United States funded by the MacArthur Foundation. A nationally representative sample of adults aged twenty-five to seventy-four was questioned by a team of twenty-eight researchers. Most midlife people find life overfull but rewarding. They feel less anxious and more financially secure than people under forty. Only 10 percent report having had a genuine midlife crisis.

Jacques, Elliott. "The Midlife Crisis." In *Early Adulthood.* Vol. 5 in *The Course of Life.* 1980. Revised and expanded ed. Madison, Wis.: International Universities Press, 1993. Jacques concludes that midlife crisis is experienced by everyone and is signified by the realization that one's own death is inevitable. Its results are greater self-awareness and capacity for love, acceptance of personal shortcomings, and resignation. He accompanies these conclusions with discussions of midlife crisis among artistic geniuses and with some detailed psychoanalytic case studies.

Kruger, Arnold. "The Midlife Transition: Crisis or Chimera?" *Psychological Reports* 75 (1994). After studying the literature, Kruger concludes that the idea that most people undergo a midlife crisis is disconfirmed by most studies. Kruger proposes that midlife crisis be classified, according to the *Diagnostic and Statistical Manual of Mental Disorders: DSM-IV* (American Psychiatric Association, 1994), as an adjustment disorder that will subside when the stressing event ceases or when the individual achieves a new level of adjustment.

McCrae, Robert R., and Paul T. Costa, Jr. *Personality in Adulthood.* New York: Guilford Press, 1990. See especially chapter 8 and pages 165 to 166. Reviews theories of life stages that include midlife and midlife crisis, particularly those of Daniel Levinson and R. L. Gould. Discusses problems of collecting data through surveys and interviews, findings of studies using midlife crisis scales, and the influence of personality problems such as neuroticism on midlife crisis.

Sheehy, Gail. *Passages: Predictable Crises of Adult Life.* New York: E. P. Dutton, 1976. See part 6, "Deadline Decade," pages 242 to 340. These chapters discuss the "sense of deadline" and feelings ranging from vulnerability to upheaval that can accompany the midlife passage. Sheehy reviews the theories of psychologists Elliott Jacques, Carl Jung, and Erik Erikson, along with the thoughts of writers in a variety of other fields. She treats working men, both working and nonworking women, and public figures. She deals with the impact of midlife on both individuals and couples in terms of their relationships and their sexual needs, and also presents a variety of case studies, both brief and lengthy, to illustrate issues and reactions involved in the midlife passage.

## MOBILITY PROBLEMS

**RELEVANT ISSUES:** Demographics, economics, family, health and medicine

**SIGNIFICANCE:** The aging of the society posits important questions about mobility problems and mobility needs in the elderly, as mobility strongly influences the ability to maintain independence and to access various resources

Mobility is one of the essentials of human well-being. Especially for an older adult, daily activities are impacted and determined by mobility. Thus, an inability to meet the needs of mobility could lead to changes in the physical, social, and psychological health of the elderly. As the population is aging, mobility problems will become more severe in the near future.

The physical measurements of mobility include gait and balance. Gait and balance can be assessed by a simple test called "Get Up and Go." The procedure of the test is to begin sitting in a chair with standard height and straight back, then get up from the chair without use of armrests, stand still momentarily, walk forward 10 feet, turn around and walk back to the chair, turn, and be seated. Mobility problems associated with gait include difficulties in sitting balance, transferring from sitting to standing, walking (pace and stability), and turning (such as staggering). Some self-reported information is also helpful to determine physical mobility. The information could include feeling unsteady when walking or needing help when walking. Mobility is often closely related to a history of falls. People with poor mobility are more likely to have falls and to be institutionalized in a hospital or a nursing home.

### PREVALENCE OF MOBILITY LIMITATIONS IN THE UNITED STATES

Mobility limitations are defined as health conditions lasting six months or longer that make it difficult for individuals to go outside the home alone without help. In the U.S. census of 1990, data on civilian and non-institutionalized persons sixty years and older indicated that mobility limitations increase with age: 3.4 percent for people aged sixty to sixty-four, 4.9 percent for people aged sixty-five to seventy-four, 11.1 percent for people aged seventy-five to eighty-four, and 21.9 percent for people aged eighty-five years or older.

Indoor mobility is often measured as part of self-care limitations. Self-care limitations are health conditions lasting six or more months that make it difficult for individuals to take care of their personal needs, including getting around inside the home. The 1990 census data showed that in the United States 17.3 percent of civilian and non-institutionalized persons aged sixty years or older suffered from either or both mobility limitations and self-care limitations, with states ranging from a high of 24.3 percent (Mississippi) to a low of 11.5 percent (North Dakota). The national patterns showed that

the six states with the highest percentages of such limitations were Mississippi, Alabama, West Virginia, Kentucky, Louisiana, and Georgia. The variation among states was even greater for persons aged eighty-five years and older who had mobility limitations or self-care limitations, such as 57.9 percent in Kentucky and 33.6 percent in North Dakota.

### CAUSES AND CONSEQUENCES OF DECREASE IN MOBILITY

Any health conditions that result in movement restrictions could decrease an individual's mobility. These medical conditions include stroke, Parkinson's disease, hip fractures, severe arthritis, and other neuromuscular diseases. One of the common causes of decreasing mobility in older people is fear of falling, caused by experiencing a fall. Such fear may lead the elderly to restrict their own activity, especially mobility. Regardless of physical trauma, the response to a fall and decreased mo-

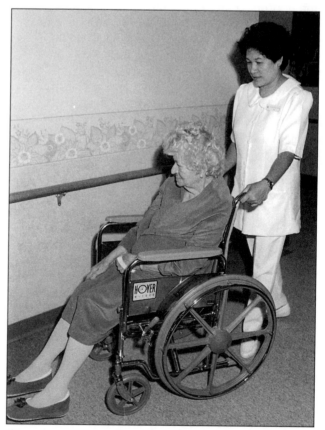

*The aging process can result in a loss in mobility that necessitates greater reliance on other people.* (Ben Klaffke)

bility consequently determines emotional, psychological, or social changes. Thus, these changes affect older people's quality of life significantly.

In 1997, the journal *Age and Ageing* published an article titled "Fear of Falling and Restriction of Mobility in Elderly Fallers" by Bruno J. Vellas and associates. The article reported the results of a study on 487 people over sixty years old who lived independently in the community. During a two-year study period, 219 study participants (45 percent) experienced a fall. Among those who had a fall, 70 (32 percent) reported a fear of falling afterward. As a result of the fear, mobility level decreased among these older people. Compared to men, women were more than twice as likely to develop fear of falling (74 percent in women versus 26 percent in men). The same study also showed that those who were afraid of falling again after a fall had poor balance and gait disorders at the beginning of the study, which indicates that older individuals appear to have quite an accurate perception of problems with their own balance and gait. Thus, if any balance and gait disorder can be prevented or treated, it could decrease older people's subsequent fear of falling and self-imposed reduction in mobility.

*Age and Ageing* also published another article that addressed the consequences of a decrease in mobility. The article's title is "Muscle Strength and Mobility as Predictors of Survival in 75-84-Year-Old People" by Pia Laukkanen and associates. This article reported a study conducted in Finland to determine if physical capacity, as measured by mobility and muscle strength (such as walking speed, hand grip strength, and knee extension strength, which are all related to indoor or outdoor mobility), could be used as an indicator of survival in older people. Among 1,142 people who participated in this mobility study, the risk of death in those aged seventy-five to eighty-four was very closely related to mobility and other muscle functioning. Those who had difficulties in indoor mobility experienced a death rate twice as high as individuals without such difficulties during a study period of four to five years. The risk of death was even higher for those who had difficulties in outdoor mobility. Similar study findings were also observed from other research. These study results suggest that reduced mobility is a significant mortality risk.

## PRESERVING MOBILITY IN OLDER PEOPLE

There is a cycle in older people of age-related loss of muscle strength, falls, fear of falling, decrease of mobility, and further loss of muscle strength. To preserve mobility in older people, this negative cycle needs to be broken. Two common ways to prevent or delay this cycle and maintain mobility are exercise and trophic factors.

Exercise, particularly strength training (such as weight lifting), preserves muscular performance and mobility. Many research studies have confirmed that higher levels of physical activity are associated with greater muscular performance, better mobility, and a lower risk of falls. Although there is some concern that high levels of physical activity may increase the risk of falls and injuries, physically active older people appear to have less disability even after accounting for the illness due to exercise. In the 1970's, it was questioned whether muscles in older people could even respond to exercise training. However, more recent research shows that strength training increases skeletal muscle strength even in older people, as studies conducted with eighty- and ninety-year-old individuals report increases in strength with resistance training. Strength training affects muscle physiology as well as function in older people. When older and younger individuals are trained in the same program at the same relative intensity, their increments in maximum oxygen consumption are similar. Thus, the fitness response to an endurance training program in previously sedentary but healthy older people is comparable to that of younger people. Study results are also available to evaluate the effects of strength and endurance training on mobility measured by gait speed and balance. Several randomized clinical trials reported that strength and endurance training improves gait speed by a modest amount, although there are some other trials that have failed to find such an effect. The controversy between findings could be explained partially by the variation in frequency, duration, and intensity of training. Whether or not strength training improves mobility by improving balance in healthy older people is still unclear; however, strength training has been shown to improve balance in weak individuals in nursing homes.

Trophic factors are related to hormones that can enhance muscular performance. The idea of using hormones to improve muscular performance was initiated in the 1980's when it became possible to produce large quantities of hormones with new technologies. The hormones that can enhance muscular performance include growth hormone, estrogen, and testosterone. Growth hormone can increase muscle mass; however, there are side effects from using growth hormones, including glucose intolerance (early stage of diabetes). Also, one study reported that growth hormone supplementation has no effect on mobility and functional limitations. Use of estrogen, also called hormone replacement therapy, is much more common in postmenopausal women. Research evidence indicates estrogen decreases the chance of developing heart disease and osteoporosis in older women. Evidence about the effect of estrogen on muscle strength and mobility is limited and inconsistent. An epidemiologic (population) study reported that estrogen use is correlated with the preservation of muscle strength in postmenopausal women. Testosterone can increase muscle strength in young men, but less information is available on older men, and the effects of testosterone on mobility and functional limitation in older people remains unclear.

In conclusion, regular physical activities, especially strength training, are recommended for older people to preserve their muscular performance and mobility. However, studies show that only 5 to 6 percent of older men and 1 to 3 percent of older women report doing activities like weight lifting to increase muscle strength. A recent U.S. Surgeon General's report affirmed the accumulating evidence favoring the health benefits of strength training in older people. It recommends that cardiorespiratory endurance activity should be supplemented with strength-developing exercises at least twice per week for adults in order to improve musculoskeletal health, maintain independence in performing the activities of daily life, and reduce the risk of falls.

## DRIVING AND MOBILITY

Besides the physical factors related to mobility in older people, some other factors also contribute to mobility, particularly outdoor mobility. In the United States, mobility outside the home has mainly relied on the automobile since the time that private vehicles became popular. Changes in housing patterns, such as moving from central urban areas to the suburbs, further the dependence on automobiles. Availability of an automobile and capability of driving an automobile significantly influence one's outdoor mobility.

As the proportion of elderly people rises, the number of older drivers is increasing rapidly. The percentage of licensed drivers in people aged sixty-five years or older increased from 60 percent in 1980 to 70 percent in 1989. In the late 1990's, over 13 percent of all drivers were sixty-five years of age or older. Although older people travel less and drive fewer miles than do the rest of the population, they still depend on the car for most trips. In the 1990's, the number of trips made by private automobiles increased in people age sixty-five years or older, and the trends show that the mileage will continue to increase in the future. National survey data show that for people aged sixty-five years or older, more than three-fourths of the trips were made by private vehicles. Particularly for people sixty-five to seventy-four years old, private vehicles accounted for more than 84 percent of their trips. Public transportation accounts for less than 4 percent of trips made by older people. Taxis were rarely used by older people, who considered them either too expensive or not convenient. Walking as a mode of transportation was more often seen in older people than in the younger population. About 10 percent of the trips by older people were done by walking, and the older the individual, the greater was the proportion of walking for transportation. Community-provided transportation services for older people, such as senior citizen's vans, are seen more often.

Older people usually do not depend on automobiles for long trips but use them regularly for short trips, such as going to the doctor's office, grocery shopping, or visiting relatives or friends. Thus, in older people outdoor mobility and independent living are closely associated with the ability to drive an automobile. However, at some point in late life, one has to stop driving due to financial reasons or physical conditions. Some older people give up driving because of limited income and the increased cost of purchasing and maintaining a car, but most older people stop driving because of health problems. The common medical conditions resulting in driving cessation are vision impairment, muscle or joint weakness (or mobility limitations), and mental problems (such as dementia). Currently, the decision of the time to stop driving is mostly made by older people themselves or their family. Medical doctors or other health professionals may provide recommendations to stop driving for older people with certain medical conditions. Police departments may also be responsible for stopping some unsafe older drivers.

Whether it is safe to drive at an advanced age depends on the individual. Some healthy and fit older drivers may drive as safely as younger people, while others may have more difficulties driving in certain situations, such as at night, during rush hours, on snowy days, on highways, or at intersections. Every year about 10 percent of fatal car crashes occur in drivers sixty-five years or older. If car crash involvement rates are evaluated by the number of drivers in different age groups, drivers of sixteen to nineteen years old are four times as likely to be involved in a traffic accident than older drivers. The crash involvement rates decrease as age increases, and the absolute number of crashes is lowest in the oldest age group. However, when adjusting the number of crashes with the total mileage traveled by members of each age group, the older drivers and youngest drivers have the same high-risk levels to be involved in a car crash compared to middle-aged people. Thus, older people drive less and have a lower chance of being involved in a car crash, but for every driven mile, an older driver experiences an increased risk of being involved in a car crash.

To ensure the safety of older drivers and other drivers on the road, some states in the United States have legal restrictions regarding renewal of licensure in older drivers. Several states require vision testing as part of a driver's license renewal. Some states require written or road tests and shorter intervals between renewals for older drivers.

### SERVICES AVAILABLE TO MEET MOBILITY NEEDS

Society recognizes the value of older people meeting their own mobility and transportation needs and keeping older drivers on the road as long as possible. Many programs are available to help older drivers retain the skills necessary for safe driving, including the American Association of Retired Persons (AARP), 55 Alive, the Mature Driving Program, and the Safe Driving for Mature Operators by the American Automobile Associa-

tion (AAA). These courses are offered in many locations around the United States. Some insurance companies provide a reduction in auto insurance premiums for older drivers who have completed such a course. Physical or occupational therapists have developed driver retraining programs to treat individuals whose driving ability has been impaired by disease, injury, or the aging process. These programs can help people adapt to disability and train older drivers with functional limitations to drive. Also, these programs provide the use of special adaptive driving equipment, which compensates for many types of deficits in older drivers.

In general, older individuals who experience outdoor mobility problems are usually those who are unable to own and operate their own vehicles. Lack of such ability produces barriers to travel in older people, limits their independence, restricts their activities, and impairs their ability to take advantage of desirable services. People who have never driven or who stopped driving have significantly lower numbers of activities outside the home than those who are current drivers. Where they exist, adequate public transportation systems can help older people overcome their mobility problems.                          —*Kimberly Y. Z. Forrest*

***See also*** Arthritis; Balance disorders; Bone changes and disorders; Canes and walkers; Driving; Exercise and fitness; Fractures and broken bones; Hip replacement; Home services; Independent living; Multiple sclerosis; Osteoporosis; Parkinson's disease; Safety issues; Sarcopenia; Strokes; Transportation issues; Vision changes and disorders; Wheelchair use.

### FOR FURTHER INFORMATION:

Buchner, David. "Preserving Mobility in Older Adults." *The Western Journal of Medicine* 167, no. 4 (October, 1997). This article intensively reviews the study findings of the methods available for preserving mobility in older people.

Ray, Wayne. "Safety and Mobility of the Older Driver: A Research Challenge." *JAMA* 278, no. 1 (July, 1997). Discussion of safety and mobility problems in older drivers.

Schwarts, R. S. "Exercise in the Elderly: Physiologic and Functional Effects." In *Principles of Geriatric Medicine and Gerontology*, edited by W. R. Hazzard. New York: McGraw-Hill, 1993. Detailed discussion of effects of exercise on physical functioning in older people.

U.S. Department of Health and Human Services. *Physical Activity and Health: A Report of the Surgeon General*. Atlanta: Centers for Disease Control and Prevention, 1996. An overview of exercise and health, and guidelines of exercise for all ages.

Vellas, Bruno, et al. "Fear of Falling and Restriction of Mobility in Elderly Fallers." *Age and Ageing* 26, no. 3 (May, 1997). A report of a study on the relationship between falls, fear of falling, and mobility in older people.

**MOVIES.** *See* **FILMS.**

**MS.** *See* **MULTIPLE SCLEROSIS.**

## MULTIGENERATIONAL HOUSEHOLDS

**RELEVANT ISSUES:** Culture, demographics, economics, family, marriage and dating, psychology, race and ethnicity, values

**SIGNIFICANCE:** The study of multigenerational households is important because this living arrangement is an increasingly common form of informal caregiving for family members and provides a means for intergenerational communication

Multigenerational households consist of two or more adult generations residing in the same home, with or without minor children also living there. Only rarely are multigenerational living situations preplanned. Western values such as personal independence, economic factors such as social security benefits for older adults, and demographic trends including moving from rural to urban areas in search of jobs all work to promote the establishment of independent households among the generations. The majority of multigenerational households result from negative life and health events that necessitate the financial, emotional, and tangible everyday support (for example, child care) from family members to assist in day-to-day survival.

These types of living arrangements occur primarily in three forms. The first arrangement includes older individuals, frequently with dementia or some other physical ailment, being cared for by their adult children. The second arrangement includes middle-aged and older individuals supporting their adult children (often with minor grandchildren) because of economic necessity, single parenthood in the younger generation, recovery from substance abuse problems, or other factors that preclude adult children from establishing their own households. The third arrangement involves immigrant or American Indian families who share their homes because of economic constraints, common language and customs, the inability of older generations to adapt successfully to life in a new culture, or the desire to impart cultural heritage to younger generations. In any of these situations, family members from each generation experience unique stressors, burdens, and rewards that result from these household structures.

### PREVALENCE

The exact number of individuals living in multigenerational households is difficult to estimate. Many of these living arrangements are short-lived. Once the event that prompted different generations to live together passes—for example, an adult child gains employment or an older parent with dementia is placed in long-term care—the multigenerational household dissolves. Additionally, many of these living arrangements are informal. For example, in some African American families, the boundaries of who exactly resides in the home are more fluid, with some family members moving out and others moving in over a relatively short period of time.

Taking these problems into account, it is estimated that anywhere from 17 to 20 percent of individuals are residing in multigenerational households at any one time. The vast majority of these homes consist of only two adult generations; estimates for multigenerational households with three generations are approximately 4 percent at any one time. Further, between 32 and 40 percent of Americans are estimated to live in multigenerational households at some point in their lives. These figures suggest that parents, adult children, and grandchildren living together is more common than once suspected.

With the changing demographic profile of American society (for example, increases in longevity, increases in rates of substance abuse, rising numbers of individuals diagnosed with some form

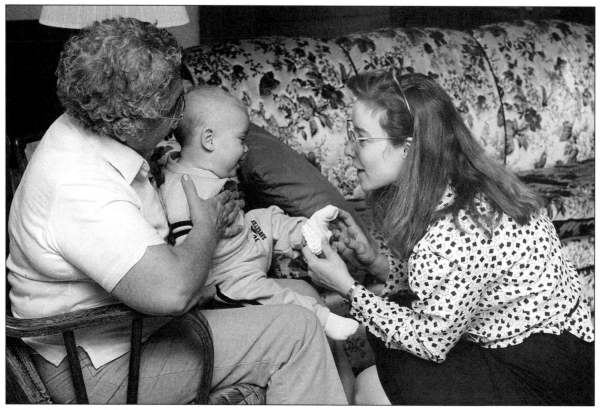

*Although the extended family as a typical model is not as common as in the past, many circumstances create temporary multigenerational households, such as divorce, death, or financial need.* (James L. Shaffer)

of dementia), the number of multigenerational households is expected to increase in the future. For example, 70 percent of all adult children have at least three other generations of family members currently living. Additionally, changes in family structure over the last one hundred years such as fewer siblings and more time spent in intergenerational roles have resulted in increased opportunities for members of different generations to communicate and forge relationships necessary for multigenerational households to occur.

### OLDER GENERATIONS

Mental or physical disability of an older parent is a primary reason for the formation of multigenerational households. It is important to note that adult child preferences precede disability level of the parent, indicating whether aging parents are placed in long-term care facilities or asked to join the adult child's household. Of the thirty-four million individuals over the age of sixty-five in

1995, between 10 and 20 percent resided with adult children. The vast majority of these older adults are unable to perform at least some of the instrumental activities of daily living such as shopping or dressing themselves.

These disabilities, along with memory difficulties associated with Alzheimer's disease, multiinfarct dementia, or other cognitive impairment place considerable strain on all family members involved. This burden falls disproportionately on middle-aged women, who perform the majority of caregiving for their aging parents. Higher levels of stress, lowered self-esteem, fatigue, increased marital difficulties, more family confrontations, and higher levels of depression have been frequently cited as consequences of caring for a disabled parent in the home.

Negative consequences for the older generation have also been reported as a result of living with adult children. Loss of independence, decreased feelings of competence, increased levels of depression, and feelings of being a burden or "in the way" have been reported by older individuals without moderate to severe cognitive impairment.

Despite the prevalence of negative consequences associated with multigenerational homes including a disabled parent, a growing body of literature supports positive consequences as well. Increased affection between the generations, the adult child having a confidant in the home, the older parent having companionship, and the opportunity for grandchildren to interact and learn from grandparents have been noted as positive aspects of the multigenerational living arrangement.

## YOUNGER GENERATIONS

Adult children return to live with parents for a number of reasons. Breakup of marriage, unemployment, financial constraints, and use of illicit substances have been cited as primary reasons. More often than not, adult children bring with them their own children, adding additional strain to the multigenerational household. It is estimated that approximately 15 percent of adults who are grandparents have their own children as well as at least some of their grandchildren also living with them.

Divorce in the middle generation is a precipitating event for the formation of these households, along with economic considerations, though the two do not necessarily occur together. For example, many adult children who experience divorce have adequate incomes but require extensive help with child care from their parents. A disproportionate number of African American multigenerational families live in poverty that is associated with single parenting.

Regardless of the cause of the formation of these multigenerational families, strains are apparent. Disputes surrounding authority in the home, child-rearing practices, contribution of income, and household chore responsibility are common. Negative consequences associated with living together in these families include increased intergenerational tension, increased anger and hostility over parenting responsibility, and lowered feelings of competence among the adult children (though these outcomes are moderated to a great extent by age of the parent, age of the grandparent, and age of the child).

Nevertheless, children and adolescents appear to benefit from having a grandparent in the home. For example, compared to children in single-parent homes, those in multigenerational households are more socially adapted, have better health, and perform better in school. Teenagers in these families have also been reported to be less deviant (have less trouble with law enforcement) than those raised in homes where only one parent is present.

## GRANDPARENTS AS CAREGIVERS

An extended definition of multigenerational households would also include those in which grandparents have primary responsibility for raising their grandchildren. In these homes, the parent may be present to differing degrees, from being totally absent to present much of the time. Substance abuse; child neglect, abandonment, or abuse; and incarceration (often associated with substance abuse) are the main reasons grandparents raise grandchildren. Currently, 5 percent of grandparents head these unique multigenerational homes. Members of ethnic minorities are more likely to be caregiving grandparents, with 20 to 29 percent of African Americans and 10 percent of Latinos performing this role.

Increased anxiety and depression, lowered feelings of self-esteem and well-being, less time with friends, increased marital conflict, and more health complaints have been cited as consequences of parenting grandchildren. Additionally, these individuals often struggle with trying to help their own children as well (for example, in recovery from substance abuse). Regardless, many report enormous satisfaction with being able to help their grandchildren by providing a stable and nurturing home environment.

## MINORITY POPULATIONS

Although exact estimates are lacking, immigrant and American Indian families may be more likely to form multigenerational family units.

Latino families often include numerous generations because many are recent immigrants to the United States. These families are more likely to live in poverty, have lower levels of education, experience higher levels of discrimination, and perceive their health to be poorer than their majority population counterparts. However, strong family ties, the desire to impart familial and cultural traditions, and traditions associated with providing support to extended family members appear to be the primary reasons individuals from different generations reside together.

Much less is known about Asian American multigenerational households. Restrictions on immigration throughout much of the twentieth century have resulted in a relatively small number of older adults living together among these groups. Despite persistent stereotypes of familial piety and communal living, recent research suggests that among the prevalent Asian ethnic groups (Japanese, Chinese, Filipino), family structure patterns more closely resemble those of the dominant culture.

Among American Indian families, multigenerational households are common, especially among those living on reservations. For the majority of tribes, the grandmother role has traditionally encompassed the raising of grandchildren. With increased exposure to Western culture through more frequent contact and the mass media, a greater emphasis is now being placed on forming multigenerational homes. This allows American Indian elders the opportunity to pass along important tribal heritage, customs, and language to younger generations.

—*Richard Wiscott and Karen Kopera-Frye*

**See also** African Americans; American Indians; Asian Americans; Caregiving; Children of Aging Parents; Cultural views of aging; Divorce; Family relationships; Filial responsibility; Grandparenthood; Great-grandparenthood; Latinos; Long-term care for the elderly; Parenthood; Poverty; Sandwich generation; Single parenthood; Skipped-generation parenting; Stepfamilies.

### FOR FURTHER INFORMATION:

Feinauer, Leslie L., et al. "Family Issues in Multigenerational Households." *American Journal of Family Therapy* 15, no. 1 (January, 1987).

Knipscheer, Cess P. M. "Temporal Embeddedness and Aging Within the Multigenerational Family." In *Emergent Theories of Aging*, edited by James E. Birren and Vern L. Bengtson. New York: Springer, 1988.

Power, Paul W. "Understanding Intergenerational Issues in Aging Families." In *Strengthening Aging Families: Diversity in Practice and Policy*, edited by Gregory C. Smith and Sheldon S. Tobin. Thousand Oaks, Calif.: Sage Publications, 1995.

## MULTIPLE SCLEROSIS

**RELEVANT ISSUES:** Health and medicine

**SIGNIFICANCE:** Multiple sclerosis (MS) is a debilitating disease affecting the central nervous system; the population of older MS sufferers is growing

In the late 1990's, it was estimated that 400,000 Americans had this disorder of the brain and spinal cord, which causes disruption in the smooth flow of electrical messages from brain and nerves to the body. The progress of the disease is slow and may take decades to achieve complete nerve degeneration and paralysis. New, effective medical treatments are available to slow the advance of the disease. Although often considered a disease of youth, MS has the potential to become an increasing problem in aging populations. More cases of late-onset MS are coming to light in individuals over fifty years of age, including such celebrities as comedian Richard Pryor, former Mouseketeer Annette Funicello, and talk-show host Montel Williams.

### WHAT IS MULTIPLE SCLEROSIS?

Multiple sclerosis is a chronic and disabling disease of the nervous system. Symptoms can be mild, such as limb numbness, or severe, such as paralysis and loss of vision. How the disease progresses and its severity in specific individuals is difficult to predict because it progresses differently in each of its victims.

The first written report of MS was published in 1400 when the famed Dutch skater Lydwina of Schieden was diagnosed. It was recognized initially as a wasting disease of unknown origin. The disease was described clinically by Jean-Martin Charcot in 1877. Charcot initially characterized the clinical signs and symptoms of MS. He recognized that the disease affected the nervous system and tried many remedies, without success. In 1890, the cause of MS was thought to be suppression of sweat; the treatment was electrical stimulation and bed rest. At the time, life expectancy for a sufferer was five years after diagnosis. By 1910, MS was thought to be caused by toxins in the blood, and purgatives were alleged the best treatment. In the 1930's, poor circulation was believed to cause MS, and blood-thinning agents became the treatment of choice. In the 1950's through 1970's, MS was thought to be caused by severe allergies; treatments included antihistamines. Not until the 1980's was the basis of MS understood and effective treatment developed.

Multiple sclerosis is caused by degeneration of the nervous system. A fatty substance called myelin surrounds and protects many nerve fibers of the brain and spinal cord, the central nervous system. Myelin is important because it speeds up signals that move along the nerve fibers. In MS, the body

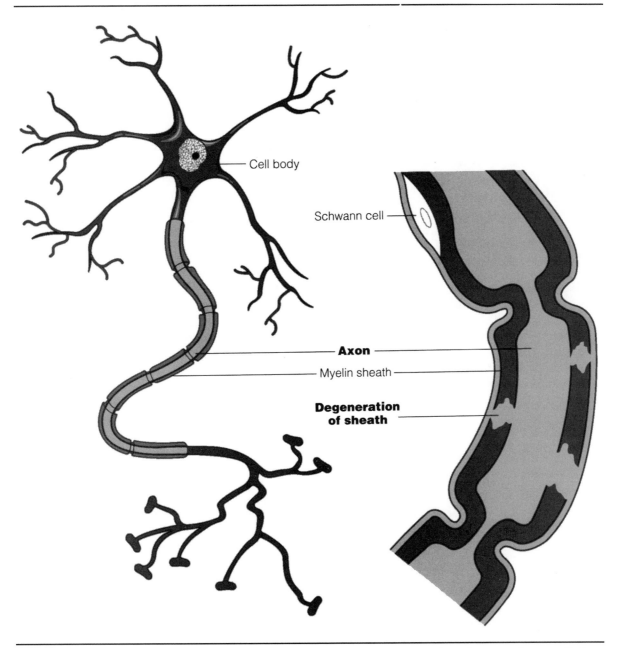

Cell body

Schwann cell

**Axon**

Myelin sheath

**Degeneration of sheath**

*Multiple sclerosis is caused by the degeneration of the myelin sheath (right) that insulates the axons of nerve cells (neurons); a neuron is shown on the left.* (Hans & Cassidy, Inc.)

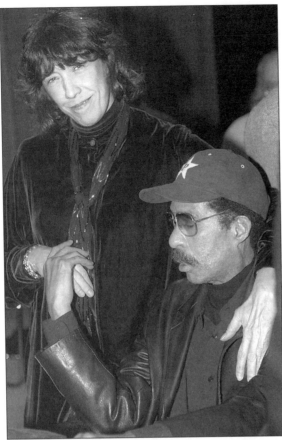

*The diagnosis of multiple sclerosis in such celebrities as comedian Richard Pryor, with actress Lily Tomlin at a 1995 tribute, raised awareness about the occurrence of this disease among the middle aged.* (AP Photo/ Kevork Djansezian)

attacks its own tissues, termed an autoimmune reaction, and a breakdown in the myelin layer occurs along the nerves. When any part of the myelin sheathing is destroyed, nerve impulses to and from the brain are slowed, distorted, or interrupted. The disease is called "multiple" because it affects many areas of the brain. Sclereids are hardened, scarred patches that form over the damaged areas of myelin.

The initial symptoms of MS may include tingling, numbness, slurred speech, blurred or double vision, loss of coordination, and muscle weakness. Later manifestations include unusual fatigue, muscle tightness, bowel and bladder control difficulties, sexual dysfunction, and paralysis. The most common cognitive functions influenced are short-term memory, abstract reasoning, verbal fluency, and speed of information processing. All the mental and physical symptoms listed may come or go in any combination. The symptoms may also vary from mild to severe in intensity throughout the course of the disease.

### THE DISEASE COURSE

The symptoms of MS not only vary from person to person but also may periodically vary within the same person. This makes the prognosis of the disease difficult to foresee. Although the general course of the disease may be anticipated, the symptoms and their severity seem to be quite unpredictable in most individuals. In the "classic" course of MS, as time progresses, chronic problems gradually accumulate over many years, slowly worsening the sufferer's quality of life. The total level of disability will vary from patient to patient.

The typical pattern of MS is marked by active periods of the disease during which the nerves are being ravaged by the immune system. These periods are called attacks, relapses, or exacerbations. The active periods of the disease are followed by calm periods called remissions. The cycle of attack and remission will differ from sufferer to sufferer. Some people have few attacks, and their MS disabilities slowly accumulate over time; in these sufferers, it takes decades to become truly debilitated. Most people with MS have what is known as the relapsing-remitting form of the disease. They suffer many attacks over time, and these attacks occur unpredictably; the attacks are then followed by complete remission which may last months or years. Again, the injuries may take many years to accumulate to complete disability.

The most aggressive form of the disease is primary progressive MS. In this type of MS, the disease follows a rapid course that steadily worsens from its first onset. Although there are still attacks and partial remission, the attacks are quite severe and occur more regularly in time. Full paralysis may develop in primary progressive MS in three to five years. Secondary progressive MS occurs in patients who initially have the relapsing-remitting type and later develop the more aggressive form.

### ONSET AND EPIDEMIOLOGY

Both genetic and environmental factors have been implicated in inducing the onset of MS. Viral infection has been suggested as a cause, but no single virus has ever been shown to be associated with MS. Risk may be conferred by exposure to a specific environment during adolescence, but that environment and the genetic risk factors have not yet been characterized.

Researchers Sharon Lynch and John Rose suggested that certain racial and geographic populations are less susceptible than others to the disease. MS is uncommon in Japanese people as well as among American Indians. The disease is more common among Northern European Caucasians as well as among North Americans of higher latitudes. There is an additional sexual dimorphism in the epidemiology of MS; the disease is found more frequently in women, by a ratio of 2:1.

The disease usually begins its first manifestations in late adolescence (around age eighteen) to early middle age (around age thirty-five). It is not clear how the interaction between the genetics of the sufferer and the environment may trigger onset. The progressive type of MS is more common over the age of forty, so those with late-onset MS often have the quickest deterioration of motor function. The reason that an older age predisposes someone to primary chronic progressive MS is still not clear.

Studies by Swiss researcher Avinoam Safran have shown that occasionally MS manifests after the age of fifty. This condition has been named late-onset multiple sclerosis. Late-onset MS is not rare. Nearly 10 percent of MS patients demonstrate their first symptom after the age of fifty. This type of MS is often not recognized by physicians, who do not expect it in the aged.

### MEDICAL TREATMENTS

There is no cure for MS, but there are many effective treatments. In most cases, steroidal drugs are used to treat relapses or attacks of the disease. Corticotropin was the first steroidal immunosuppressant to be used widely in MS treatment. The primary effect of the drug is to shorten the duration of an attack, although it does not appear to reduce the severity of the attack. Although it is still used with patients who respond well to it, corticotropin has been supplanted by the use of other drugs. Methylprednisolone is an immunosuppressant and steroid that has replaced corticotropin. It has been shown to control the inflammation that

accompanies demyelination. These steroids seem to work by sealing leaking blood vessels in the brain and coating the white blood cells of the immune system so that they cannot attack the myelin easily.

Several federally approved drugs can slow the rate of attacks: Avonex, Betaseron, and Copaxone. Although these drugs do not stop MS entirely, they actually limit the level of myelin destruction, as observed in magnetic resonance imaging (MRI) scans of the brain. Avonex slows down the rate of increased disability, and all three slow down the natural course of MS. University of Western Ontario researcher George Ebers performed experimental treatments on MS patients with interferons. Interferons are proteins produced by the immune system that enter cells and induce them to set up defenses against attack. The myelin sheath is actually produced by a special nerve cell called a schwann cell; presumably the schwann cells are stimulated to protect themselves by exposure to interferons. Patients treated with human interferons demonstrated a 34 percent reduction in frequency of attack; that reduction was sustained over five years of treatment. More impressive was the 80 percent reduction of MS activity detected in their brains. Steroid treatment was rarely required in these patients.

As additional therapy, patients with MS should participate in a regular exercise program. Exercise is vital to the maintenance of functional ability in MS sufferers. It strengthens muscles, benefits gait, and generally improves coordination. The best type of exercise is aquatic in nature. Sufferers are often heat-intolerant, and participation in a regular aerobic program would be unpleasant. Also, aquatic exercise is a low-impact activity that puts less stress on chronically sore muscles. Exercise programs also encourage socialization of patients and engender peer support.

*—James J. Campanella*

*See also* Disabilities; Illnesses among the elderly; Reaction time; Wheelchair use.

### FOR FURTHER INFORMATION:

Carroll, David, and Jon Dorman. *Living Well with MS: A Guide for Patient, Caregiver, and Family.* New York: HarperPerennial Library, 1993. A book for any person affected by MS. Information ranges from how to buy a wheelchair to staying out of one.

Halbreich, Uriel. *Multiple Sclerosis: A Neuro-psychiatric Disorder.* Boston: American Psychiatric Press, 1993. Describes the psychological conditions that often accompany multiple sclerosis.

Iams, Betty. *From MS to Wellness.* Chicago: Iams House, 1998. An autobiography of an MS sufferer who outlines treatments that have helped her overcome the disease.

Kalb, Rosalind, ed. *Multiple Sclerosis: The Questions You Have, the Answers You Need.* New York: Demos Vermande, 1996. A guide for everyone concerned about multiple sclerosis.

Sibley, William. *Therapeutic Claims in Multiple Sclerosis: A Guide to Treatments.* 4th ed. New York: Demos Vermande, 1996. A guide to treatments available for MS and their effectiveness.

Taggart, Helen. "A Multiple Sclerosis Update." *Orthopaedic Nursing* 17, no. 2 (March/April, 1998). Provides a history of MS and its treatments from a nursing perspective.

*Angela Lansbury and Claude Akins in an episode of* Murder, She Wrote. *(Archive Photos)*

## MURDER, SHE WROTE

**CAST:** Angela Lansbury
**DATE:** Aired from 1984 to 1996
**RELEVANT ISSUES:** Culture, media
**SIGNIFICANCE:** Television programs sometimes present characters in stereotypical roles; however, the character of Jessica Fletcher in *Murder, She Wrote* reflected positive aspects of aging

In 1984, the Columbia Broadcasting System (CBS) introduced what was to become the longest-running mystery drama in the history of television. *Murder, She Wrote,* starring Angela Lansbury as Jessica Fletcher, enjoyed prime-time popularity for twelve years. The series was set in the small coastal town of Cabot Cove, Maine, where the widowed Jessica made her home. A retired English teacher turned mystery writer, she had an uncanny knack for happening upon murders and becoming involved in the investigations. Fortunately, she also had a knack for solving the murders, often out-shining the detectives assigned to the case.

The character of Jessica Fletcher was not subject to stereotypes about aging. She traveled regularly, often in connection with her books. She remained active in her retirement, often bicycling around Cabot Cove or taking brisk walks to become acquainted with new surroundings. She was a widow who sometimes reminisced wistfully about her late husband, Frank, but who also entertained occasional flirtations. She had had a successful career as an English teacher but launched a new career as a successful author. She clung to her faithful manual typewriter for years but eventually adapted to writing on a computer. Faithful to long-time friends such as Seth Haslett, the irascible town physician, Jessica also made new friends in her travels. She was sensible without being a fuddy-duddy, adventurous but not foolish, and nurturing but not controlling. She had a sense of humor, and her infectious laugh was often highlighted in the ending shot of the show. Most of all, her keen intellect was reflected in her abilities to use logic, make deductions, remember important details, and, of course, solve murders. —*Elizabeth Ann Bokelman*

**See also** *Matlock;* Television; Wisdom; Women and aging.

## NATIONAL ASIAN PACIFIC CENTER ON AGING

**DATE:** Founded in 1979
**RELEVANT ISSUES:** Health and medicine, race and ethnicity, work
**SIGNIFICANCE:** This organization meets the special needs of the rapidly increasing number of older Asian Americans and Pacific Americans, particularly in the areas of health care and employment

The National Asian Pacific Center on Aging (NAPCA), with its headquarters in Seattle, Washington, is dedicated to serving aging members of the Asian and Pacific Islander communities in the United States. According to the United States Census Bureau, this segment of the aging population is growing at a faster rate than any other segment. The number of older Americans in this group is expected to increase nearly 1,000 percent from 1990 to 2050.

A unique problem addressed by NAPCA is the wide variety of languages spoken by this population. About one-half of the members of this group do not speak English well enough to communicate. NAPCA meets this need through the Capacity Building Project. This initiative brings together older Asian Americans and Pacific Islander Americans, service providers, and policy members in meetings held in the elders' native languages. NAPCA also provides information in all needed languages on health care, health insurance, managed care, and long-term care.

NAPCA is involved in two important national projects dealing with employment of older members of the Asian and Pacific communities. The Senior Community Service Employment Program (SCSEP), administered by the United States Department of Labor, provides low-income elders with part-time employment in community service programs. NAPCA's participation in this program involves more than one thousand elders in eight states. The Senior Environmental Employment Program (SEE), administered by the United States Environmental Protection Agency (EPA), provides part-time and full-time employment in EPA offices. NAPCA is involved in SEE in nine states and in the District of Columbia.    —*Rose Secrest*

*See also* Advocacy; Asian Americans; Employment.

## NATIONAL CAUCUS AND CENTER ON BLACK AGED

**DATE:** Founded in 1970
**RELEVANT ISSUES:** Economics, race and ethnicity, work
**SIGNIFICANCE:** The National Caucus and Center on Black Aged is the only national organization whose major focus is improving life for African American and low-income elderly

In 1970, a group of concerned citizens led by Hobart C. Jackson, a nursing home professional, organized the National Caucus and Center on Black Aged (NCBA) to ensure that the 1971 White House Conference on Aging would address the particular needs of the African American elderly. The caucus existed as an advocacy group until 1973, when it received a grant from the Administration on Aging to conduct research, train personnel, and serve as a technical resource. In 1978, the NCBA received a major grant from the U.S. Labor Department to operate the Senior Community Service Employment Program in five states. In 1983, the caucus expanded to include senior housing.

By 1999, the NCBA had become one of the largest minority-focused organizations in the United States, with thirty-two chapters, employment offices in nine states and the District of Columbia, and six owned and managed housing projects. The NCBA was recognized as a national leader in housing, employment, and advocacy on behalf of African American aged. Its Web site (http://www.ncba-blackaged.org/) provides links to a mission and goal statement, a capability statement, membership information, announcements of conferences and meetings, chapter locations with contacts, and historical information about the organization. It celebrated its twenty-fifth anniversary in 1995.

The NCBA publishes a newsletter entitled *Golden Page, Profile of Black Elderly*, a support service reference guide, a public policy statement, and several volumes entitled *Job Placement Systems for Older Workers*. NCBA programs include the Senior Employment Program, the Senior Environmental Employment Program, and the Wellness Promotion and Disease Prevention Program.    —*Mary E. Allen*

*See also* Advocacy; African Americans; Employment; Housing; White House Conference on Aging.

## NATIONAL COUNCIL OF SENIOR CITIZENS

**DATE:** Founded in 1961

**RELEVANT ISSUES:** Law, media, values

**SIGNIFICANCE:** The National Council of Senior Citizens is a nonprofit organization that works to advance the interests of aging people in the United States

The National Council of Senior Citizens (NCSC) was launched in 1961 as an organization designed to fight for the passage of legislation that would provide accessible, affordable health care for the elderly. In its early years, the NCSC coordinated its battle plans from an office in a tiny hotel room in Washington, D.C. After working tirelessly to promote passage of the Medicare Act, NCSC leaders and activists accompanied President Lyndon B. Johnson on Air Force One in 1965 to Independence, Missouri, where the president signed the bill into law.

The NCSC has become one of the largest nonprofit organizations in the United States, with more than five million members in over five thousand affiliated clubs and councils nationwide. The NCSC keeps track of the concerns of older Americans and then takes action for improvements. In the 1990's, the organization continued the battle to protect Medicare, Medicaid, Social Security, and other programs vital to older Americans. Although the U.S. Congress repeatedly proposed budget cuts that would drastically reduce the quality of health care that aging people receive and that would throw millions of elderly Americans into poverty, the NCSC successfully challenged these proposals by holding numerous press conferences, rallies, and congressional briefings.

The NCSC sponsors affordable housing, community service jobs, and other programs for the elderly. It lobbies for improved nursing homes and for the funding of Social Security and health care programs. Local senior citizen clubs help the aged with a variety of problems, provide social and recreational activities, and sponsor community service projects. In addition, the NCSC has been active in issues of general public concern, including the elimination of child labor, legislation mandating a minimum wage, antipollution laws, and the development and maintenance of the interstate highway system. 　　　　—*Alvin K. Benson*

*See also* Advocacy; Medicare; Politics; Senior citizen centers.

## NATIONAL COUNCIL ON THE AGING

**DATE:** Founded in 1950

**RELEVANT ISSUES:** Culture, law, media, values

**SIGNIFICANCE:** The National Council on the Aging seeks to improve public and private policies affecting older people

The changing age structure of the United States has thrust the elderly into the center of American politics, both as a political force and as a topic of debate. Since its founding in 1950, the National Council on the Aging (NCOA) has played a vital role in the development of key legislation to improve the life of older people. The primary short-term goal of the NCOA is to promote the dignity, well-being, self-determination, and contributions of aging people, while its long-term goal is to develop a caring, just world where the aging make vital and valued contributions to families, communities, the world, and future generations.

The NCOA is an association of organizations and individuals committed to enhancing the field of aging through leadership, education, advocacy, and service. To accomplish its goals, the NCOA works closely with professionals and volunteers, service providers, consumer and labor groups, businesses, government agencies, religious groups, and voluntary organizations. Members of the NCOA have many opportunities to participate in the development and expression of public policy views through participation in constituent units and through activities of the NCOA Annual Conference, held in even years in Washington, D.C.

The advocacy of the NCOA takes the form of testimony before the U.S. Congress and consultation with government agencies and private organizations. The NCOA has also engaged in fact finding to dispel destructive attitudes toward aging and has sought to counter ideas and campaigns that attempt to pit generations against each other. Two major concerns among the elderly are the maintenance of Social Security benefits and the establishment of a long-term health care program. The NCOA has long advocated national health care reform based on principles of universal access and comprehensive coverage that includes long-term care for all generations.

The NCOA provides strong lobbying support for the aging and has been instrumental in the development of the Older Americans Act, the Age Discrimination in Employment Act, Medicare, and Medicaid. It also has been active in protecting Social Security benefits for older people and plays a key role in promoting reform of the Social Security system to ensure that the program will be in operation for future generations of the elderly. The NCOA has helped transform the image of the elderly from one of an underprivileged and forgotten segment of society to one of a powerful and effective voting bloc.

The NCOA is a founding member and cochair in the Leadership of Aging Organizations, which meets in Washington, D.C. It is also represented among the nongovernmental organizations of the United Nations and is in touch with developments in aging throughout the world. The NCOA publishes a biennial statement of essential public policy principles, together with specific recommendations in the broad areas of health, economic security, community services, and housing. The organization also releases policy statements that provide access to its positions on Medicare, Medicaid, Social Security, the Older Americans Act, and other policy issues that relate to the elderly.

—*Alvin K. Benson*

***See also*** Advocacy; Age Discrimination in Employment Act of 1967; Health care; Medicaid; Medicare; Older Americans Act of 1965; Politics; Social Security; Voting patterns.

## NATIONAL HISPANIC COUNCIL ON AGING

**DATE:** Founded in 1980

**RELEVANT ISSUES:** Culture, demographics, family, race and ethnicity

**SIGNIFICANCE:** This advocacy group addresses concerns associated with aging among Latinos, the fastest-growing segment of the national population over age sixty-five

Founded in 1980, the National Hispanic Council on Aging (NHCoA) is a nonprofit organization whose mission it is to promote the health and well-being of Latino elderly people. A membership organization based in Washington, D.C., and governed by a board of directors, the NHCoA produces culturally and linguistically appropriate educational materials. The organization publishes a quarterly newsletter called *Noticias* (available in English or Spanish) and has published several books, including *Hispanic Elderly* (1988), edited by Marta Sotomayor and Herman Curiel, and *Empowering Hispanic Families* (1991), edited by Sotomayor.

The NHCoA is also involved in research, policy analysis, demonstration projects, and training. Members, in association with other organizations, address problems commonly encountered by the Latino elderly and their families, including poverty, limited access to health care, lack of affordable housing, and inadequate social services support. Among its accomplishments is Casa Iris, a forty-unit housing project in Washington, D.C., built in cooperation with the Department of Housing and Community Development. The council also sponsors a program promoting the early detection of cervical and breast cancer. As with other similar groups (such as the National Indian Council on Aging), the NHCoA acts as a network for organizations and community groups interested in their elderly. The council compiles and disseminates research data, sponsors workshops and a semiannual national conference, and maintains a speaker's bureau, thus providing national leadership in support of the Latino elderly.

—*Lee Anne Martínez*

***See also*** Advocacy; Housing; Latinos.

## NATIONAL INSTITUTE ON AGING

**DATE:** Established in 1974

**RELEVANT ISSUES:** Demographics, health and medicine, psychology, sociology

**SIGNIFICANCE:** The National Institute on Aging, a department of the National Institutes of Health, serves as a catalyst for innovative research, lifestyle-enhancing technologies, and health care services related to aging

Funded by public tax dollars, the National Institutes of Health (NIH) is one of eight agencies of the Public Health Service, which is part of the U.S. Department of Health and Human Services. The NIH consists of twenty-four separate institutes, centers, and divisions sponsoring biomedical research in the United States. The goal of NIH research is to acquire new knowledge to help prevent, detect, diagnose, and treat disability and disease.

*Senator and Mercury astronaut John Glenn speaks at a press conference in 1998 about exercise and fitness for people over fifty as part of a coalition that included the National Institute on Aging and NASA; later that year, at seventy-seven, he became the oldest person to travel into space when he flew onboard the shuttle* Discovery. (AP Photo/Joel Rennich)

The National Institute on Aging (NIA) was established as one of the NIH institutes in 1974. It is the main federal agency focusing on aging. The NIA guides and sponsors collaborative activities with other NIH institutes and other research and clinical agencies. This research is conducted on the NIH campus in Bethesda, Maryland, and also at research and training facilities in hospitals, medical centers, and universities.

The NIA's work focuses on diverse and specific areas of science, each in a specialized program emphasizing a different kind of investigation related to aging. The Biology of Aging Program focuses on basic biologic mechanisms involved in aging, the onset of age-related disease, and research and training in biochemistry, endocrinology, genetics, immunology, molecular and cell biology, nutrition, and pathobiology. The Behavioral and Social Research Program supports social and behavioral science research on the processes of aging, the

place of elders in society, demography and the age composition of the population, and the impact of the aging population on society as a whole. The Neuroscience and Neuropsychology of Aging Program supports research on the physiology of the aging nervous system and the behavioral characteristics of the aging brain. It also has a special focus on Alzheimer's disease, concentrating on its epidemiology, causes, diagnosis, treatment, and short- and long-term management. Finally, the Geriatrics Program supports research on the causes, prevention, and treatment of the health problems of elders, covering such topics as physical frailty and osteoporosis, pharmacology and elders, and rehabilitation. The program also provides such services as the physical and mental assessment of elders and specialty training for providers working with geriatric populations.

The NIA also has a public information office committed to fostering public education on aging through press releases, public service announcements, and the dispensation of science-based educational materials on lifestyle practices that affect health and the aging process. The materials produced cover a wide range of topics, including Alzheimer's disease, the menopause, aging and exercise, cardiovascular disease, and effective communication between professionals and older patients. In addition, the office publishes a directory of aging-related resources. The materials are written for use by the general public, patients and family members, health professionals, the media, and volunteer and community organizations. Booklets, brochures, and fact sheets are available via the Internet and in print for little to no cost.

—*Nancy A. Piotrowski*

*See also* Advocacy; Aging: Biological, psychological, and sociocultural perspectives; Aging process; Health care.

## NATIVE AMERICANS. *See* AMERICAN INDIANS.

## NEARSIGHTEDNESS

RELEVANT ISSUES: Biology, health and medicine

SIGNIFICANCE: Nearsightedness, a visual defect that impairs the perception of distant objects, is a prevalent problem for elderly people

Nearsightedness (myopia) occurs when light from distant objects reaches a focal point in front of the retina, the photoreceptive tissue of the eye. Consequently, vision of distant objects is blurred on the retina. The primary cause of myopia is an eyeball that is too long from front to back. Higher testosterone levels in the womb and a genetic predisposition have been advanced as possible causes of this condition. Research has also found that prolonged eyestrain, especially that which often accompanies long periods of reading, can distort the shape of the eye. This is one reason why well-educated people manifest higher rates of nearsightedness than less-educated individuals.

All children are born nearsighted; by the age of six months, however, vision begins to improve. Myopia is an uncommon problem in younger school-age children but begins to increase in prevalence as children move into their teenage years. From the twenties until the late sixties, the rate of visual deterioration tends to slow down. By the time peo-

ple reach their seventies, however, the rate of visual decline accelerates again. People past the age of seventy are fourteen times as likely to experience myopia resulting in legal blindness than those in their twenties.

For several centuries, nearsightedness has been corrected by the use of a concave lens, which moves the focal point of light in myopic eyes closer to the retina. The first evidence for the use of concave lenses is found in a 1517 painting of Pope Leo X by Italian artist Raphael. As the twentieth century drew to a close, innovative surgical approaches were developed. Most of these procedures, such as radial keratotomy or laser surgery, move the focal point of light closer to the retina by changing the shape of the cornea.

—*Paul J. Chara, Jr.*

*See also* Aging process; Cataracts; Glaucoma; Reading glasses; Vision changes and disorders.

## NEGLECT

RELEVANT ISSUES: Family, health and medicine, sociology, violence

SIGNIFICANCE: Elder mistreatment is a significant problem that can result in both physical and psychological neglect

Mistreatment is an underreported, undetected, and serious problem that affects more than 1 million elders each year. Neglect falls within the realm of domestic violence, seen or unseen acts of harm that lead to physical, emotional, or other injury to another person. Acts of omission usually lead to elder neglect. Two kinds of neglect may result: physical and psychological. Indicators of physical neglect include poor hygiene and lack of skin integrity, such as urine burns (skin redness and sores), insect bites, and abrasions; contracture of muscles; dehydration and malnutrition; intestinal blockage with fecal material; and inadequate living environment, such as the presence of physical hazards and insects, as well as insufficient heating and food supplies.

Characteristics of psychological neglect include habit disorders, such as sucking, biting, and rocking; conduct disorders, such as antisocial and destructive behaviors; neurotic traits, including sleep and speech disorders; and psychoneurotic reactions, such as hysteria, obsession, compulsion, and phobias. However, these attributes could also result from injury, trauma, illness, or chronic disease; they may not be in any way related to neglect.

The typical victim of neglect is a Caucasian woman over the age of seventy-five years, is physically or mentally impaired, and lives with a relative. The person who neglects the elder is most often a family member involved in a caregiving situation. Frequently, the elder is a source of stress and is dependent on the caregiver. Neglect cases highlight the role of this dependency.

Several specific stressors may lead caregivers to neglect the elders for whom they are caring. First, family dynamics may have included poor past relationships between caregivers and elders, or may have included a history of marital conflict and family violence. Second, physical and mental impairments among the elderly may cause increased demands on caregivers, which often results in physical, emotional, and financial stress for caregivers. Third, adult children or spouses who are mentally ill or substance abusers may be cognitively impaired themselves and neglect the elder. Fourth, problem behaviors among the elderly, such as combativeness, verbal belligerence, wandering, and bowel or bladder incontinence, may precipitate neglect. Fifth, caregivers may feel overwhelmed, unappreciated, isolated, and frustrated and may respond by neglecting elders who are viewed as the cause of isolation and frustration. Finally, a caregiver's external stress because of loss of job or poor health may interfere with caring and may trigger neglect.

Once risk factors for neglect are identified, several steps may be taken to remedy the situation: A community agency may be referred to for monitoring, strategies may be taught to decrease the caregiver's stress, or elders can be placed in another living situation. In cases of documented evidence of neglect, Adult Protective Services may initiate short- and long-term interventions for both victims and caregivers based on causation.

Detection of neglect remains a problem, as it is difficult to complain or report a person who is providing most of one's daily needs. Many victims of neglect fear reprisal or cessation of caring by caregivers or placement in a nursing home. Additionally, elders who suffer from mental impairment with memory loss, who lack communication skills, or who want to hide their predicament from family members or outsiders may be unable or unwilling to report neglect. Many elders who try to report neglect are faced with the stereotype of elderly people as confused or paranoid and therefore lacking in credibility. Another barrier to reporting neglect is the lack of consideration of neglect as a specific diagnosis by health care professionals. Much neglect is subtle in presentation and difficult to identify.          —*Linda L. Pierce*

**See also** Abandonment; Adult Protective Services; Caregiving; Elder abuse; Family relationships; Malnutrition; Mental impairment; Psychiatry, geriatric; Violent crime against the elderly.

*Not all older people have family members or friends who can be counted on for needed assistance; some suffer physically and emotionally from willfull or unintentional neglect.* (Archive Photos)

## NEUGARTEN, BERNICE

**BORN:** February 11, 1916; Norfolk, Nebraska

**RELEVANT ISSUES:** Family, health and medicine, sociology

**SIGNIFICANCE:** Bernice Neugarten conducted groundbreaking research on all aspects of aging, focusing on aging as a normal, rather than a pathological, process

Bernice Levin Neugarten, who focused on the study of aging people and changes in personality over the life span of adults, began her career with the intention of expanding the field of gerontology. She later came to wonder if there should be a field of gerontology at all. Her daughter, Dail Neugarten, said of her mother, "Given her innate curiosity, Neugarten constantly reinvented the field of adult development and aging, and in so doing, consistently revitalized her students, her colleagues, and herself."

A prolific writer in the field of adult development and aging, Neugarten brought previously unrecognized topics to light during her many years of research. Her research on the menopause, grandparenthood, and parent caring relied on careful and accurate quantitative and qualitative methods. She coined many phrases that are now used in common parlance, including "social clock," "young-old" and "old-old," "age-integrated society," and "age-irrelevance." Important areas of research to which she has contributed include age as a dimension of social organization, the life course, personality and adaptation, and social policy issues.

In 1968, Neugarten edited *Middle Age and Aging*, a collection of essays that discuss the manner in which society in general divides itself into different age-related roles. Neugarten paid particular attention to "social and psychological processes as individuals move from middle age to old age." She called attention to the question, "What social and psychological adaptations are required as individuals move through the second half of their lives?" Issues regarding health are often omitted in studies of the aging process. Neugarten viewed this as regrettable because, she believed, the issues of physical health must be considered in understanding the social and psychological behaviors in aging.

In 1981, Northwestern University founded the Human Development and Social Policy (HDSP) graduate program under the leadership of Neugarten. HDSP meets the growing need for researchers, decision makers, and professionally trained scholars who can evaluate critical issues that affect daily human life and public policy. Graduates of HDSP have a wide range of career choices that deal with critical issues of midlife and aging populations.

Neugarten's work reflected her belief that an individual's attitude toward health and changing roles through midlife and into old-age are important. Some of these attitudes, according to Neugarten, are changing family roles; work, retirement, and leisure; other dimensions of the immediate social environment such as friendships, neighboring patterns, and living arrangements; differences in cultural setting; and perspectives of time and death. "The aging-society," Neugarten claimed, "brings with it many challenges and opportunities for both aging persons and for the society at large." After her retirement, Neugarten was named professor emerita in the Department of Behavioral Sciences at the University of Chicago.

*—Virginiae Blackmon*

**See also** Aging: Biological, psychological, and sociocultural perspectives; Cultural views of aging; Erikson, Erik H.; Kübler-Ross, Elisabeth.

## NO STONE UNTURNED: THE LIFE AND TIMES OF MAGGIE KUHN

**AUTHOR:** Maggie Kuhn, with Christina Long and Laura Quinn

**DATE:** Published in 1991

**RELEVANT ISSUES:** Law, media, values

**SIGNIFICANCE:** This autobiography by Kuhn, the founder of the Gray Panthers, traces her many accomplishments before and after she became an advocate for older people

In her autobiography *No Stone Unturned*, Maggie Kuhn writes that she discovered "all injustices, however small or seemingly unrelated, are linked." Throughout her long and extraordinary life, she addressed the intertwined injustices of sexism, ageism, ableism, social elitism, and racism.

Born into an intergenerational home where "men were treated with great deference, but the house was ruled by women," she was the eldest daughter of an older, supportive mother and an adoring, demanding father. Why did she never marry, despite her enjoyment of men and sex? "Sheer luck," she writes.

Kuhn describes how she excelled in academic, social, religious, and career roles, all of which were constricted by society's definition of appropriate female roles. She completed college and studied at Columbia University Teacher's College and Union Theological Seminary. She first pursued a career in the Young Women's Christian Association (YWCA), one of the era's foremost feminist and so-

*Maggie Kuhn, the founder of the Gray Panthers and the author of the autobiography* No Stone Unturned. *(AP Photo/George Widman)*

cialist organizations, advocating full political and economic equality for women. Subsequently, she served as an advocate for hundreds of thousands of women who faced crushing problems in defense production plants during World War II. Kuhn explains how during the 1950's and 1960's, she took progressive stands on civil rights, homosexuality, and Medicare. At a Medicare hearing, President Gerald Ford addressed her as "young lady." She responded, "I am an old woman, Mr. President."

Forced into retirement at age sixty-five, Kuhn organized the Gray Panthers with the vision of a national grassroots organization including young and old activists. She describes her work with consumer advocate Ralph Nader, her challenges to the Gerontological Society of America and the American Medical Association, and her efforts to organize the Older Women's League (OWL), the National Citizens' Coalition for Nursing Home Reform, and the National Shared Housing Resource Center.

Advocating intergenerational social reform, she writes in *No Stone Unturned*, "We must act as the elders of the tribe, looking out for the best interests of the future and preserving the precious compact between the generations."  —*Anne L. Botsford*

**See also** Advocacy; Age discrimination; Ageism; Forced retirement; Gerontological Society of America; Gray Panthers; Job loss; Kuhn, Maggie; Medicare; Older Women's League (OWL); Politics; Women and aging.

## NURSING AND CONVALESCENT HOMES

**RELEVANT ISSUES:** Family, health and medicine
**SIGNIFICANCE:** Although only a small percentage of elderly people reside in nursing homes, many of them will require short-term care in such a facility at least once in their lifetime

In 1999, only about 5 percent of the elderly people in the United States resided in the nation's 20,000 nursing homes. Although 80 to 85 percent of people over sixty-five are in relatively stable health, as many as 30 to 40 percent of them will spend some time in a nursing home for short-term care at least once in their lifetime. About 50 percent of those admitted to nursing homes stay fewer than six months, 20 percent stay one year or longer, and 10 percent stay three or more years.

The terms "nursing home" and "convalescent home" are widely misused and misunderstood. They have been used to describe everything from shelter care to acute care hospitals. However, nursing homes are primarily designed to meet the needs of people convalescing from illness or to provide long-term nursing supervision for people with chronic medical problems. The goal of a nursing home is to provide care and treatment to restore or maintain the patient's highest level of physical, mental, and social well-being. This goal is ensured by strict federal legislation called the Omnibus Reconciliation Act (OBRA), which was implemented in October, 1990. The OBRA set minimum requirements for registered nurse staffing, training for nursing assistants, limited use of restraints (both physical and chemical), physical layout of the building, services, and patient rights.

### SKILLED NURSING FACILITIES

A skilled nursing facility (SNF) is required to provide twenty-four-hour nursing supervision by registered or licensed practical nurses. Commonly referred to as "nursing homes" or "convalescent hospitals," these facilities normally care for the incapacitated person in need of long- or short-term care and assistance with many aspects of daily living, such as walking, bathing, dressing, and eating. At a minimum, SNFs provide medical, nursing, dietary, pharmacy, and activity services.

Most SNFs have a certified distinct part (CDP) or transitional care/subacute unit that provides Medicare part A rehabilitative services by occupational therapists, speech-language pathologists, and physical therapists. Examples might include rehabilitation for a fractured hip, tube feedings, and ostomy care. The cost is nearly one-half of what would be charged in an acute care hospital, but the intensive, multidisciplinary approach to rehabilitation is excellent. Nursing homes are designed to help people recover strength and return to the activities of daily living with the goal of going back home; they are not, as is popularly believed, "warehouses" for infirm and dying elderly people.

Three areas have had a significant impact on the evolution of care in nursing homes: economics, attitudes, and education. Trends in nursing home care include short-stay rehabilitation, outpatient rehabilitation, managed care, and subacute care (which includes ventilator patients, wound management, postsurgical care, coronary care, enhanced rehabilitation, and the medically complex patient). Such trends have allowed the image of nursing homes to change rapidly to that of highly specialized health care centers.

The difference this transformation has made in care and outcomes has been significant. The exchange of skills and information not only has expanded the practice of the clinicians involved but also has benefited residents. The inclusion of occupational therapists who work on resident positioning offers new approaches and facilitates the reduction of the use of physical restraints. Recreational therapists and occupational therapists may collaborate to provide special classes using adaptive equipment for residents with residual disabili-

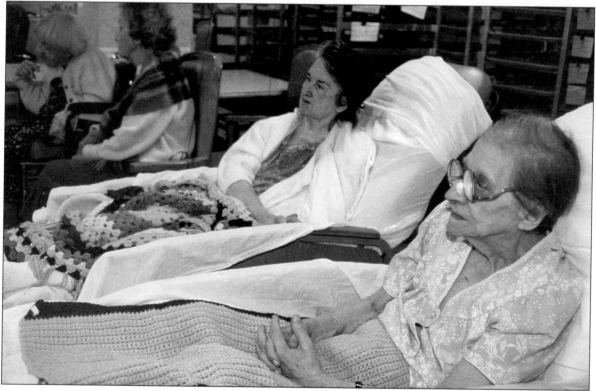

*Residents of a nursing home in Morristown, New Jersey, take part in daytime activities. Women predominate at such care facilities.* (Jeff Greenberg/Archive Photos)

## Nursing Home Beds

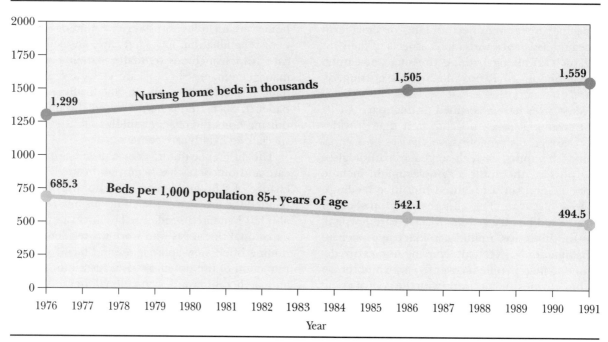

*Source:* Centers for Disease Control and Prevention, National Center for Health Statistics, National Health Provider Inventory (National Master Facility Inventory).

ties from stroke. Feeding and swallowing problems in the nursing home are now addressed by a team consisting of specialists in speech-language pathology, diet, nursing, and occupational therapy if necessary. Most of all, residents are involved in care decisions and choices about their daily activities, which enhances resident self-esteem and independence.

### SPECIAL DISABILITY UNITS AND INTERMEDIATE CARE FACILITIES

Skilled nursing facilities for special disabilities provide a protective or secure environment for people with mental disabilities, such as Alzheimer's disease. Residents in head injury units tend to be young and middle-aged adults. Many states reimburse the nursing home at a higher rate for these residents, who are sicker or require more complex care. Facilities are challenged not only to provide protection for these demented residents and others in the facility but also to devise prostheses and programs to enable these individuals to maintain their independent self-care abilities for

as long as possible with a minimum of psychotropic drugs. Mind-altering medications are considered chemical restraints that can immobilize an individual.

The advantage of this type of unit is that care can be specifically tailored to meet the special needs of these residents. For instance, activities for demented residents must be structured differently from those for residents who are not demented. The staff ratio may need to be higher than in the traditional nursing home unit because, depending upon the stage of the disease, more intense supervision may be needed. The unit must be safe, comfortable, and not overstimulating. These units usually have their own admission and discharge criteria.

An intermediate care facility (ICF) is required to provide eight hours of nursing supervision per day. Because of their physical appearance, these facilities are often confused with the SNFs. Intermediate care, however, is less extensive than skilled nursing care and generally serves clients who are ambulatory and need less supervision and care. Licensed nurses are not always immediately available in an ICF. At a minimum, ICFs provide medical, intermittent nursing, dietary, pharmacy, and activity services. Some states, such as Texas and Nebraska, have a large number of ICFs, while others, such as California, have very few. Approximately one-third of all nursing homes are certified to provide intermediate care, with most services performed by unlicensed staff members.

### LICENSING AND CERTIFICATION

Most nursing homes are certified to participate in both the federal Medicare and Medicaid programs, which pay certain funds for a "spell of illness." Some facilities, such as Mount St. Vincent's in Seattle, Washington, and the Mary Conrad Center in Anchorage, Alaska, have also emphasized the social aspects of care. Instead of meals being served on trays in the individual's room or in the dining room, the food is presented buffet style, with the residents choosing what appeals to them. "Pods" or "neighborhoods" are formed with clusters of residents to encourage friendships and bonding.

All state governments require that nursing homes be licensed. The licensing requirements establish acceptable practices for care and services. State inspectors visit nursing homes at least once each year to determine their compliance with state standards and their qualifications to receive Medicare and Medicaid reimbursement. This survey report of the facility's deficiencies is available for public scrutiny in the lobby of the facility, on the Internet, and upon written request from the state department of health.

Some licensed nursing homes may also be certified to designate what level of care they provide and how they may be reimbursed for that level of care. Depending upon the state, residents may be classified as light care, moderate care, heavy care, or heavy special care. Light care residents require less assistance with the activities of daily living (dressing, bathing, and feeding) than residents in other classifications.

### OWNERSHIP AND MANAGEMENT OF NURSING HOMES

Some nursing homes are operated as nonprofit corporations. They are sponsored by religious, charitable, fraternal, and other groups or are run by government agencies at the federal, state, or local levels. However, about 80 percent of nursing homes are proprietary, meaning they are businesses that aim to make a profit. They may be privately owned by small companies or individuals, or corporately owned by large chains, such as Beverly Enterprises.

Final responsibility for the operation of a nursing home lies with its governing body, which acts as the legal entity licensed by the state to operate the facility. The governing body sets policies, adopts rules, and enforces them for the health care and safety of the residents. The person in charge of the financial and day-to-day management is called the administrator. The nursing home administrator reports to the owner, board of directors, or corporate officer. Within the nursing home are many departments that either provide direct care, such as nursing, or provide such support services as dietary and laundry. The largest department is the nursing department, which provides twenty-four-hour resident care.

A person in a nursing home must be under the care of a physician. If the person's personal physi-

*Some convalescent homes are located in rural areas, where patients can enjoy the beauty and peacefulness of nature.* (Digital Stock)

## The Functional Status of Nursing Home Residents, 1985

| Functional status | All ages | Under 65 years | 65-74 years | 75-84 years | 85+ years |
|---|---|---|---|---|---|
| | | | Number of residents | | |
| All residents | 1,491,400 | 173,100 | 212,100 | 509,000 | 597,300 |
| | | | Percent distribution | | |
| **Dressing** | | | | | |
| Independent | 24.6 | 41.1 | 29.8 | 24.1 | 18.3 |
| Requires assistance[1] | 75.4 | 58.9 | 70.2 | 75.9 | 81.7 |
| **Using toilet** | | | | | |
| Independent | 39.1 | 57.1 | 43.4 | 39.7 | 32.0 |
| Requires assistance | 48.9 | 31.5 | 45.8 | 47.8 | 55.9 |
| Does not use | 12.0 | 11.4 | 10.8 | 12.6 | 12.1 |
| **Mobility** | | | | | |
| Walks independently | 29.3 | 51.0 | 39.6 | 30.4 | 18.4 |
| Walks with assistance | 24.8 | 13.5 | 20.4 | 24.7 | 29.6 |
| Chairfast | 39.5 | 29.3 | 33.7 | 38.7 | 45.1 |
| Bedfast | 6.5 | 6.2 | 6.3 | 6.1 | 6.9 |
| **Continence** | | | | | |
| No difficulty controlling bowel or bladder | 48.1 | 67.7 | 57.1 | 45.0 | 41.9 |
| Difficulty controlling— | | | | | |
|   Bowel | 1.9 | *1.5 | *2.0 | 1.7 | 2.2 |
|   Bladder | 10.3 | 6.4 | 6.8 | 11.0 | 12.0 |
|   Bowel and bladder | 31.7 | 16.8 | 27.5 | 33.6 | 35.8 |
| Ostomy in either bowel or bladder | 8.1 | 7.5 | 6.6 | 8.7 | 8.1 |
| **Eating** | | | | | |
| Independent | 60.7 | 68.5 | 66.6 | 60.9 | 56.1 |
| Requires assistance[2] | 39.3 | 31.5 | 33.4 | 39.1 | 43.9 |
| **Vision** | | | | | |
| Not impaired | 75.9 | 88.5 | 83.3 | 77.8 | 68.1 |
| Partially impaired | 14.6 | 5.9 | 10.0 | 14.2 | 19.1 |
| Severely impaired | 5.6 | *1.9 | 4.3 | 4.1 | 8.4 |
| Completely lost | 2.5 | *2.5 | *1.3 | 2.1 | 3.2 |
| Unknown | 1.4 | *1.2 | *1.0 | 1.8 | 1.2 |
| **Hearing** | | | | | |
| Not impaired | 78.5 | 96.1 | 90.4 | 82.6 | 65.7 |
| Partially impaired | 16.7 | *3.1 | 7.4 | 14.8 | 25.5 |
| Severely impaired | 3.4 | *0.1 | *1.1 | 1.5 | 6.8 |
| Completely lost | 0.6 | *0.1 | *0.4 | *0.6 | *0.8 |
| Unknown | 0.8 | *0.5 | *0.7 | *0.5 | 1.1 |

[1]Includes those who do not dress.
[2]Includes those who are tube or intravenously fed.
*Relative standard error greater than 30 percent.

*Note:* Data are based on a sample of nursing homes. Some figures have been rounded.

*Sources:* Hing, Esther. *Characteristics of Nursing Home Residents, Health Status, and Care Received: National Nursing Home Survey, United States, May-December, 1977.* Vital and Health Statistics 13, no. 51. DHHS Publication no. (PHS) 81-1712. Washington, D.C.: Government Printing Office, 1981; Hing, Esther, Edward Sekscenski, and Genevieve Strahan. *The National Nursing Home Survey: 1985 Summary for the United States.* Vital and Health Statistics 13, no. 97. DHHS Publication no. (PHS) 89-1758. Washington, D.C.: Government Printing Office, 1989.

cian will not continue to provide care, a new physician must be chosen who will evaluate the person's needs and prescribe a program of medical care. A nursing home is not free to initiate any form of medical treatment, medication, restraint, special diet, or therapy without the consent of a physician.

Prior to being admitted to a nursing home, most people undergo a complete physical examination to determine whether skilled nursing care or intermediate care is required, the person's diagnosis, the duration of the illness or need for nursing home care, what treatments are indicated, and the person's rehabilitation potential. Since physicians are slow to make nursing home rounds, more and more facilities have geriatric nurse practitioners on staff who relieve the physicians and provide on-site visits on a daily basis.

### FINANCING AND ADMISSION

In 1999, the basic charge for a double-bed room in a typical nursing home was in the range of $20,000 to $60,000 per year. Homes in rural areas tend to be slightly less expensive than those in the cities. The costs of medications and physician's visits are not included in the basic charge. Also, special treatments, such as physical, occupational, and speech therapy, often add to the cost. There are also possible additional charges for drugs, personal laundry, haircuts, and extra services.

Three out of four residents are dependent upon government assistance through Medicare (including supplementary Medicare insurance called Medigap) or Medicaid. Other financial aid might be available from private health insurance sources. Medicare part A will pay the entire bill for the first twenty days, then partially pay for the rest of the first one hundred days of skilled nursing home care in the CDP; however, Medicare pays nothing for care in an ICF. Medigap policies typically pay only a portion of the daily costs, and then only for a limited number of days. Long-term or catastrophic care insurance is designed to provide benefits for this type of care. Financial assets accumulated by the resident and spouse could be exhausted through prolonged care in a skilled nursing facility. Therefore, it is extremely important to plan ahead by determining all the benefits available under Medicare and Medicaid. A staff social worker can usually guide the resident and family through the maze of red tape and paperwork needed to qualify for available programs. Patients are routinely advised to contact the local state Medicaid agency for eligibility and program information as early in the placement process as possible.

Advance planning is one of the best ways to ease the stress that accompanies choosing a nursing home. Many good nursing homes have waiting lists, and the chances of getting placed in the home of choice will be greatly enhanced if placement is made on a waiting list prior to the actual time of need. Selecting a home is an important decision—one that deserves foresight and careful, clear-headed consideration rather than a crisis atmosphere. Professionals in the long-term care field may provide referrals to particular nursing homes. In addition, state inspection reports on nursing facilities will detail any code violations and provide information on how the facility treats its residents.

The home's contract or financial agreement is a legal contract, so it is advisable to have a lawyer review the agreement before signing it. Free legal assistance is usually available to senior citizens. The admission papers should include the following items: an agreement stating the terms and conditions, the daily room rate, and what services are covered by it; a list of optional services and the charges for them; a copy of each patient's bill of rights; a statement about eligibility for Medicaid; and a statement that the nursing home is or is not Medicare and Medicaid certified.

*—Maxine M. McCue*

**See also** Alzheimer's disease; Dementia; *Gin Game, The*; Health care; Housing; Independent living; Leisure activities; Long-term care for the elderly; Medicare; Medications; Mental impairment.

### FOR FURTHER INFORMATION:

Allender, Judith A., and Cherie L. Rector. *Readings in Gerontological Nursing*. Philadelphia: Lippincott-Raven, 1998. This book is written for the professional assisting the elderly in decision making.

*Guide to Choosing a Nursing Home*. Rev. ed. Baltimore: U.S. Department of Health and Human Services, Health Care Financing Administration, 1996. A step-by-step guide to choosing the right nursing home.

Ignatavicius, Donna D. *Introduction to Long Term Care Nursing: Principles and Practice*. Philadelphia: F. A. Davis, 1998. Written for student nurses, this book provides practical and accessible information in every chapter.

McConnell, John. "Reflections on the Evolution of Care in Nursing Homes." *Journal of Gerontological Nursing* 20, no. 6 (June, 1994). McConnell describes the changes in nursing homes made during the late 1980's and early 1990's.

"Nursing Homes: A Special Investigative Report." *Consumer Reports* 60, no. 8 (August, 1995). This series of articles on long-term care examines public policy on the financing of nursing homes and offers suggestions for families facing the cost of long-term care.

# NUTRITION

**RELEVANT ISSUES:** Health and medicine

**SIGNIFICANCE:** The requirements for certain nutrients change as people age; in addition, nutrition plays a prominent role in the prevention and treatment of chronic diseases that commonly occur in later years

Certain functions of the body change as a natural result of the aging process. Many organs are not as efficient as they once were. As these normal physiological changes occur, the requirements for certain nutrients also change. Some changes in the older body are pathological and represent chronic diseases of old age, such as hypertension, diabetes, cardiovascular disease, pulmonary disease, and cancer. Programs designed to prevent or delay the onset of these chronic conditions always include a nutritional component. Even after a disease is established, nutrition maintains a significant role in its treatment.

## CHANGING NUTRIENT REQUIREMENTS

Requirements for calories usually decline with age. This decline in caloric need is tied to the frequent decline in lean body mass and increase in adipose tissue that occurs with aging. This may be because of a decline in energy metabolism. Although some researchers feel that this is associated with an aging body alone, others believe that physical activity also plays a large role in determining what the basal energy metabolism will be. In fact, some experts beleive that most of these negative effects can be overcome by a vigorous exercise program.

Changes in protein requirements with age are more controversial because recommendations for both decreased and increased dietary protein intakes have been advocated by different experts. Many believe that dietary protein requirements decrease with age and that this decline is secondary to the decline in lean body mass. Less muscle tissue would require less dietary protein to sustain it. The lower dietary protein recommendation is also congruent with kidney function, which declines somewhat with age as well. The opposing argument claims that higher dietary protein intakes diminish the loss in lean body mass that occurs with aging and that these higher dietary protein intakes are not detrimental to renal function.

Of the vitamins for which there seems to be increased requirements during normal aging, vitamin $B_{12}$, vitamin D, and vitamin $B_6$ are most prominent. During aging, the amount of hydrochloric acid secreted by the stomach gradually decreases. For many people, this results in achlorhydria (lack of hydrochloric acid in gastric juice) or hypochlorhydria (low levels of hydrochloric acid in gastric juice). The reduction in hydrochloric acid secretion results in less intrinsic factor being secreted. Intrinsic factor is required for efficient absorption of vitamin $B_{12}$. Therefore, the decrease in intrinsic factor leads to a decrease in the absorption of vitamin $B_{12}$. This can partially be overcome by ingesting larger amounts of vitamin $B_{12}$, which will saturate the intrinsic factor carrier system and allow for some free diffusion of vitamin $B_{12}$. Some of the manifestations of vitamin $B_{12}$ deficiency are mental changes and dementia. Indeed, many elderly with dementia have subtle vitamin $B_{12}$ deficiencies.

Although the major dietary source of vitamin D is fortified milk, most vitamin D is synthesized by the skin after exposure to sunshine. The synthesis of vitamin D occurs primarily in the epidermis layer of the skin, where a precursor of vitamin D is metabolized to vitamin D. There is less of this precursor in the epidermis of older people; therefore, less vitamin D is synthesized. Both dietary vitamin D and vitamin D synthesized in the skin must undergo an activation reaction in the kidney. It is also believed that this activation process might be reduced in older people because of the decline in renal function that occurs in aging. Although specific recommendations for older people have not

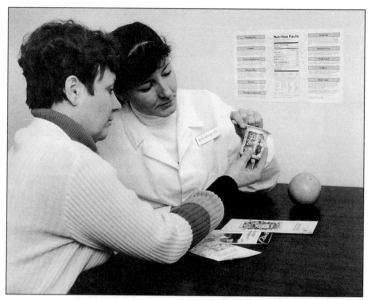

*Older women, especially those who have gone through the menopause, need to pay particular attention to their diets to ensure that they get enough calcium and do not gain excessive weight.* (James L. Shaffer)

been set concerning vitamin D, additional dietary sources or sunlight exposure are being considered by experts. This is especially important for housebound elders who would benefit by sun exposure on their face and hands for fifteen minutes several times per week.

Many elderly have indicators of poor vitamin $B_6$ status, although the cause for this marginal status is not clear. Vitamin $B_6$ requirements are linked to protein intake, so some of the variability may be because of a range of protein intake across many ages and body compositions.

Vitamin A is the only vitamin for which lower requirements have been discussed for the elderly. Preformed vitamin A is found in organ meats, eggs, some fish, and dairy products. Carotenoids found in vegetables and some fruits can be converted to vitamin A. Vitamin A is a fat-soluble vitamin, and excess is stored in the liver. However, vitamin A toxicity can occur when either the liver's capacity to store vitamin A is exceeded or the dose is so large that normal carrying and storage processes are overwhelmed. With a normal, varied diet, sufficient vitamin A will be stored in the liver. The quantity of vitamin A stored will increase as the person ages. Because of the probability of having enough vitamin A stored to cover vitamin A re-

quirements and the possibility that the liver's storage capacity could be exceeded because of long years of vitamin A deposition, experts are considering lowering the recommended intakes of vitamin A for the elderly. However, since carotenoids pose no health risk or threat of toxicity, no recommendation concerning carotenoids has been forthcoming.

Of the minerals, calcium is discussed most often in terms of recommending increased requirements during normal aging. The consensus statement from the National Institutes of Health (NIH) concerning optimal intake of calcium recommends almost twice the current recommended dietary allowance for those over sixty-five years. The reason for the increased calcium intake is based upon a lower intestinal absorption of calcium in the elderly and a decreased conversion of vitamin D to its active form by the older kidney. Vitamin D is necessary for calcium utilization. Higher intakes of calcium are thought to diminish the calcium losses from bone that result in osteoporosis.

Although intestinal absorption of other minerals, such as zinc and iron, may decrease during aging, studies do not suggest a need for an overall increase in dietary intake of these two minerals in general. Furthermore, despite considerable mythology, neither fatigue nor lack of energy seems related to iron status in the elderly. Changes in smell and taste that are common during aging do not seem related to zinc status. However, elderly people with very poor diets, or those who are malnourished, may develop a zinc or iron deficiency that would require dietary modifications.

### Osteoporosis and Cardiovascular Disease

Most chronic diseases begin to reveal symptoms in middle age. Such symptoms become more severe and impair quality of life in the later years if appropriate therapy is not begun or if such therapy proves ineffective. Chronic diseases for which there is a clear role for nutrition modification in prevention and treatment include osteoporosis, cardiovascular disease, cancer, and diabetes.

Calcium and vitamin D are essential for normal bone matrix to remain viable. Although not the only risk factors in the development of osteoporosis, poor calcium and vitamin D statuses contribute significantly to this risk. Bone health in later years depends upon the peak bone mass determined early in midlife and the rate of bone loss during advancing years. Dietary modification to increase calcium and vitamin D consumption should occur in the young to effect peak bone mass in midlife. However, even increasing calcium and vitamin D consumption in later years can have a favorable impact on the rate of bone loss.

Cardiovascular disease risk includes many factors, such as blood lipid levels, heredity, body weight, exercise level, and smoking history. Diet has been shown to affect blood lipid levels as well as body weight. The blood lipid levels of most concern are the low-density lipoproteins (LDLs), the high-density lipoproteins (HDLs), and the total cholesterol levels. Some discussion has occurred surrounding the cost-effectiveness and ramifications of screening blood lipids in the elderly. Some studies have shown that the risk value of elevated blood lipids is less in the elderly than it is in younger adults. Nevertheless, the consensus seems to be that blood lipid determination in older adults is warranted because the highest incidence of heart disease occurs in people older than age sixty-five.

For those who have high lipid levels, the National Cholesterol Education Program recommends that dietary modification be tried before medication therapy. Such dietary modification includes restriction of dietary fat to no more than 30 percent of total calories, saturated fatty acid intake to 8 to 10 percent, polyunsaturated fatty acid intake to less than 10 percent, monounsaturated fatty acid intake to less than 15 percent, and dietary cholesterol intake to less than 300 milligrams per day. In addition, total caloric intake should be monitored to achieve and maintain desired weight. Studies have shown that therapy that low-

*Some people suffer from poor nutrition in their later years as the senses of taste and smell decline, food preparation becomes more difficult, income decreases, and social opportunities for meals are limited. Restaurant specials and communal dining can encourage proper eating habits.* (PhotoDisc)

ers LDL and total cholesterol reduces coronary risk and the total mortality rate. These results include older people. Although some have advocated not restricting the elderly in diet or prescribing medications with possible side-effects, most medical practitioners agree that the high-risk older patient should not be denied the benefits of therapy that can prevent or delay the complications of heart disease.

## CANCER

Diet is known to be a risk factor for several types of cancer common in the older population. Diet is never the sole risk factor, but dietary modification is believed to reduce cancer risk in certain conditions.

There are three phases in the progression of a normal cell into a cancer cell: initiation, promotion, and progression. For cancer to be initiated, the deoxyribonucleic acid (DNA) must be damaged. This damage can occur because of viruses or chemicals. Even after being damaged, cancer will not occur unless the cells are promoted to increase cell division. After promotion, cell division must progress and interfere with normal physiological function. It is at the initiation and promotion stages that most nutrients are thought to have a role in cancer. Some nutrients might help prevent the DNA from becoming damaged, while some might decrease the chance that the damaged cells are promoted. Conversely, some nutrients might increase DNA damage or tumor promotion.

Certain nutrients are believed to increase the risk of cancer. Those include calories, fat, and alcohol. The association between cancer risk and a nutrient appears to be strongest for fat. High fat intake is strongly associated with cancer of the prostate, breast, and colon. There is also an association between cancer and high calorie intake. This might be because diets high in fat are also high in calories. However, it might be that the high caloric intake is really more related to cancer risk than is dietary fat. Nevertheless, high caloric intake is associated with an increased risk of breast and prostate cancer. Alcohol appears appears to act as a promoter associated with cancer of the esophagus, mouth, and larynx. This is especially true when alcohol is combined with smoking. Alcohol intake has been implicated in the development of breast cancer, although the results are inconclusive.

Certain nutrients seem to reduce the risk for cancer. These include fiber, vitamin C, and carotenoids. The association between fiber and the reduced risk for cancer has been studied for a long time. Fiber may decrease intestinal transit time and thereby decrease the amount of time any potential carcinogen might be in contact with the absorptive surfaces of the gut. Fiber might also trap carcinogens and carry them along to pass through the body unabsorbed. Fiber may also dilute the influence of dietary fat on cancer initiation or promotion. Increasing fiber-rich foods can decrease the proportion of calories coming from fat. However, the reduced risk of cancer associated with high-fiber diets may not be caused by the fiber alone. High-fiber foods such as fruits and vegetables are also high in vitamin C and carotenoids.

Vitamin C, or ascorbic acid, has been associated with a decreased incidence of stomach, larynx, and esophageal cancer. It also appears to decrease the toxicity of nitrosamines, which can be formed when meats are cooked at very high, quick-cooking temperatures and which have been associated with cancer development. Vitamin C, which can act as an antioxidant in certain conditions, can scavenge free radicals, which may have a role in the initiation or promotion stage of cancer development. Carotenoids can also act as antioxidants. Higher intakes of foods that are high in carotenoids, such as fruits and vegetables, are associated with reduced risk of breast, lung, prostate, and cervical cancers.

## DIABETES

Another chronic disease that affects millions of older adults is diabetes. In diabetes, the body produces inadequate amounts of insulin, or the insulin produced is not being used effectively. Insulin functions in the body by transporting the sugar from the blood into the cells of the body. The cells then use the sugar (glucose) for energy or store it as fat. If insulin is lacking, the cells are starved for energy, while the sugar in the blood reaches abnormally high levels. Although there are many risk factors for developing diabetes, aging itself is a risk factor. Adult-onset, or type II, diabetes often occurs so gradually that many adults will have had the disease six or more years before it is diagnosed.

Another risk factor for diabetes that is also associated with aging is obesity. More than 75 percent of adults diagnosed with diabetes are obese at the time the diagnosis is made. Indeed, the risk of developing diabetes doubles with every 20 percent of excess weight above desirable weight for gender, age, and height. Therefore, the nutritional prevention of diabetes involves the maintenance of a desirable body weight. Very often this is also the nutritional treatment, although a more rigid dietary structure may also be required.

*—Karen Chapman-Novakofski*

**See also** Antioxidants; Bone changes and disorders; Breast cancer; Cancer; Cholesterol; Dementia; Diabetes; Heart disease; Malnutrition; Obesity; Osteoporosis; Prostate cancer; Vitamins and minerals; Weight loss and gain.

### FOR FURTHER INFORMATION:

Morley, John E., Zvi Glick, and Laurence Rubenstein. *Geriatric Nutrition: A Comprehensive Review.* 2d ed. New York: Raven Press, 1995. Contributors offer reviews on nutritional deficiencies and diseases affected by nutrition in the elderly.

Munro, Hamish, and Gunter Schlierf, eds. *Nutrition of the Elderly.* New York: Raven Press, 1992. Examines the relationship between diet and disease in the elderly, especially osteoporosis and Alzheimer's disease.

Roe, Daphne. *Geriatric Nutriton.* 3d ed. Englewood Cliffs, N.J.: Prentice Hall, 1992. An overview of the aging process, nutritional assessment and dietary modifications, and drugs and nutrition in the elderly.

Schlenker, Eleanor D. *Nutrition in Aging.* 3d ed. Boston: WCB/McGraw-Hill, 1998. Includes discussions on the theories of aging, nutritional needs of the elderly, and food habits of ethnic groups.

Vellas, Bruno J., Paul Sachet, and R. J. Baumgartner, eds. *Nutrition Intervention in the Elderly.* Paris: Serdi/Springer, 1995. Contributors present nutrition studies of elderly people around the world and provide information about nutrient intake, nutrition status, and nutrition-related risk factors for disease.

Ziegler, Ekhard, and L. J. Filer, Jr., eds. *Present Knowledge in Nutrition.* 7th ed. Washington, D.C.: ILSI Press, 1996. A comprehensive overview of vitamins, minerals, and nutrition with reference to the elderly in several sections.

**OASDI.** *See* **Social Security.**

## Obesity

**Relevant issues:** Health and medicine

**Significance:** Obesity is an abnormally high percentage of body fat; it is important to understand the many factors that contribute to obesity in the aging population

The prevalence of obesity has been increasing in most industrialized nations. The prevalence is higher in certain population groups such as African American women and Latinas. The factors that contribute to obesity are numerous, but the key factor is energy imbalance, which means that calories eaten are greater than calories used. By definition, obesity is an abnormally high percentage of body fat; however, assessing the precise value of this measurement is subject to debate.

### Measurements of Body Fat

Body composition can be measured by several techniques, each with varying degrees of accuracy and cost. One of the best methods is underwater weighing. Using the principle of Archimedes, density is determined from weight of the body both under and out of water. Although this method is relatively easy to perform, people must agree to be submersed and many find the experience unpleasant.

A technique that uses the electrical conductivity of body tissues to estimate fat is based on the premise that lean tissue and fat tissue have differences in the ability to conduct electromagnetic waves. Measuring total body electrical conductivity is expensive. A less expensive technique is bioelectrical impedance, in which electrodes are placed on the arm and leg. Based on level of impedance, one can estimate body fat. This method is accurate provided that the subject is adequately hydrated.

Methods such as computed tomography (CT) scanning and nuclear magnetic resonance imaging (MRI) scanning give an accurate picture of regional fat such as intra-abdominal and extra-abdominal fat. Ultrasonic waves can also give a measure of regional fat. These techniques are impractical for determining total body fat and are expensive. Other accurate total-body composition techniques involve neutron activation, fat-soluble gas, heavy water techniques, and potassium isotopes. All these methods are expensive and impractical for broad scale use.

Simple techniques include height and weight measurement and skinfold thicknesses and circumferences. Skinfolds are a measure of fat under the skin, which perhaps should be more accurately called "fatfolds." The underlying premise is that a certain percentage of the body's fat depot is under the skin. The subject's skinfold measurements can be inserted into standardized prediction equations to estimate body fat. Common sites include the triceps and biceps (arm muscle areas), thighs, and the subscapular (under the shoulder blade) and suprailiac (above the hip bone on the abdomen) regions. Skinfolds are difficult to measure correctly, and practice and skill are required to obtain valid measurements. For the best estimates, multiple skinfold site measures are taken.

If health professionals are interested in assessing obesity on a large scale, the measurement techniques need to be inexpensive and easy to use and to involve little stress on the subject. A more practical technique is measuring height and weight. Measures can be compared to tables of acceptable weights for heights or converted into the body mass index (BMI), also called the Quetelet index. BMI gives a measure of weight relative to height. It is calculated as weight in kilograms divided by height in meters squared or as weight in pounds divided by height in inches squared, multiplied by 703.

In addition to knowing an individual's BMI, it is important to measure where that body fat is distributed. Abdominal fat, or central adiposity, is a more potent risk factor for obesity-related diseases than BMI alone. Central adiposity can be measured using a variety of techniques, from sophisticated and expensive techniques such as CT scans to a simple circumference ascertained with a tape measure. Waist circumference provides an estimate of central adiposity that is inexpensive and easy to do. Some experts measure both waist and hip circumference and calculate a waist-hip ratio (WHR). A desirable WHR is under .90 for a man and under .80 for a woman. Waist circumference alone is a useful measure of central adiposity that can be used by health professionals to assess an individual's risk for obesity-related diseases. Thus, two simple parameters, BMI and waist circumference, can be used to define obesity with reasonable accuracy, especially among the older population.

Healthy weight ranges reflect statistically derived values that appear to provide maximal protection against the development of chronic disease. A BMI of 19.0 to 25.0 seems to reflect a healthy weight. Overweight is defined as a BMI between 25.0 and 29.9, and obesity is defined as a BMI of 30.0 or greater. Extreme obesity is defined as a BMI of 40 or greater. For waist circumference, the cutoffs identifying increased disease risk for adults are greater than 40 inches (102 centimeters) for men and greater than 35 inches (88 centimeters) for women. High waist circumference coupled with a high BMI escalates the risk potential for disease.

Body fat composition increases with age. As men age, their fat content almost doubles, while women experience a 50 percent increase but their weight rises only about 10 to 15 percent, reflecting a reduction in lean body mass. When older people become obese, this change of proportion of fat to lean is further exaggerated. Contributing to the problem of obesity in the older population is that energy requirements also decrease with age. For example, basal metabolism, the energy required to rest, declines about 2 percent per decade in adults.

## CAUSES OF OBESITY

Although physiological changes in body composition might explain the tendency to gain weight with age, there are aspects of lifestyle that can accelerate or retard body composition changes. Numerous labor-saving devices have fostered a reduction in energy output. The physical activity patterns of older people tend to decline as well, further facilitating caloric output deficits.

Many changes in the food supply foster obesity. Numerous snack and convenience foods make it easy to procure and consume excess calories. Eating in restaurants and fast-food establishments is associated with consumption of larger portions of high-calorie, high-fat foods. For elderly on fixed incomes, inexpensive food choices are often nec-

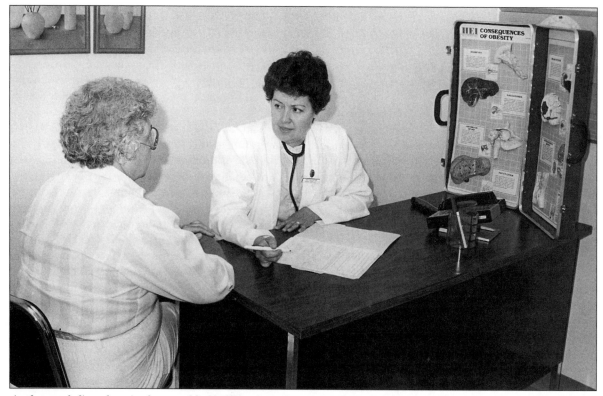

*As the metabolism slows in the second half of life, obesity becomes an increasing threat. Education about eating and exercise is the key to maintaining a healthy weight at any age.* (James L. Shaffer)

essary and are higher in fat and calories. Combining the reduction in energy expended and the increased variety of high-calorie food choices for energy consumed, it is understandable why obesity rates have risen.

## HEALTH RISKS OF OBESITY

Obesity is a risk factor for several diseases such as cardiovascular disease, hypertension, diabetes mellitus type II, arthritis, gallbladder disease, gout, and certain cancers. Aging itself is also a risk factor for these diseases. The lowest cardiovascular disease mortality is among those who remain lean throughout life. Obesity increases the risk of high blood cholesterol levels and is estimated to cause 40 to 50 percent of hypertension (high blood pressure). Obese people are five to six times more likely to develop hypertension than lean people. Weight reduction of as little as 10 to 15 pounds in many individuals, however, can reduce the dosage or eliminate the need for drugs to control blood pressure in many individuals.

The rate of type II diabetes rises as BMI increases, with the highest prevalence seen in those with a BMI greater than 28. This type of diabetes, characterized by the inability of body cells to use insulin, can be corrected with weight reduction. Many elderly with diabetes suffer from related complications, such as kidney disease, blindness, heart disease, and the destruction of sensory function.

Obesity is associated with some cancers. There is a consistent positive relationship between body weight and endometrial cancer, with risk starting at a BMI of 28 to 30 or greater. Postmenopausal women with a BMI of 27 or greater have an increased risk for breast cancer.

Research has estimated that a reduction in BMI of about two units can reduce later onset of knee osteoarthritis and decrease the rate of symptomatic occurrences. Obesity also increases the risk for gallbladder disease, especially among women. Obesity is a risk factor for the development of gout and sleep apnea (episodes of breath cessation during sleep), which is common among those with upper-body obesity.

## TREATING OBESITY

People need to reject the notion that increasing weight is a normal phenomenon of aging and begin to make lifestyle changes to prevent weight gain. Dieting alone is not an effective long-term solution because the recidivism rate is high. Restrictive dieting can also result in inadequate intake of nutrients.

Drug therapy is not recommended unless the person has a BMI of 30 or greater or a BMI of 27 or greater with concomitant risk factors or diseases. Weight loss surgery is reserved for those with severe obesity or a BMI greater than 35 who also suffer from related disease conditions, but only when all other medical therapies have failed.

Lifelong healthy weight maintenance requires a lifestyle that includes regular daily physical activity and consumption of a healthful diet that is calorically matched with energy output. Nothing else has been shown to work as effectively. Weight loss of as little as 10 percent is sufficient to reduce disease risks associated with being overweight. A loss of 5 to 10 pounds helps to lower blood pressure and can improve both blood cholesterol and blood sugar levels. For many elderly, this modest goal is attainable and could provide health benefits. Weight reduction among elderly must be monitored carefully, however, to prevent mistaking disease-related weight loss as the result of voluntary weight loss. With proper guidance, healthful eating patterns coupled with regular physical activity could afford the elderly with marked health benefits that are sustainable and substantial.

—*Wendy L. Stuhldreher*

*See also* Aging process; Arthritis; Cancer; Diabetes; Exercise and fitness; Gout; Heart disease; Hypertension; Malnutrition; Nutrition; Stones; Weight loss and gain.

## FOR FURTHER INFORMATION:

Bray, George A., Claude Bouchard, and W. P. T. James, eds. *Handbook of Obesity.* New York: Marcel Dekker, 1998.

Cassell, Dana K., and Felix E. F. Larocca. *The Encyclopedia of Obesity and Eating Disorders.* New York: Facts on File, 1994.

*The Clinical Guidelines on the Identification, Evaluation, and Treatment of Overweight and Obesity in Adults: Evidence Report.* Bethesda, Md.: National Institutes of Health, National Heart, Lung, and Blood Institute, 1998. Also available at www.nhlbi.nih.gov/guidelines/obesity/ob_home.htm or published as a supplement to the *Journal of Obesity Research,* September, 1998.

Jensen, Gordon L., and Joanne Rogers. "Obesity in Older Persons." *Journal of the American Dietetic Association* 98, no. 11 (November, 1998): 1308.

"Recommendations from the American Health Foundation's Expert Panel on Healthy Weight." *American Journal of Clinical Nutrition* 63, supplement (1996). Also available from the American Health Foundation, 320 East 43d Street, New York, NY 10001.

**OCCUPATIONS.** *See* **EMPLOYMENT.**

# OLD AGE

**RELEVANT ISSUES:** Biology, demographics, family, health and medicine, psychology, sociology

**SIGNIFICANCE:** Since most people born in the United States today will live to be old, the older population is increasing, providing not only challenges but also opportunities and the prospect of a positive aging experience

*Individuals can approach old age and its multiple effects with many different attitudes, ranging from despair to resignation to pride.* (James L. Shaffer)

Although youth may be desirable and "old age" alarming, many myths and stereotypes about older people are proving wrong. While old age presents challenges, much of the news is good. As a group, people are living longer because of medical advances and healthier lifestyles. Older people often retain their independence, and many remain healthy throughout life. For those who need them, many services are available, both formal and informal, to help maintain a high quality of life even into the later years.

## MIDDLE AGE

One can scarcely discuss old age without first describing the stage of life that precedes it. No one can say when middle age begins or ends, but many researchers place it as between the ages of forty and sixty-five. Its ending may be as difficult to determine as its beginning, and middle age and old age can overlap.

In their book *Aging, the Individual, and Society* (7th ed., 1999), Susan Hillier and Georgia M. Barrow call middle age a transition time. It is a good time for most. People often reach their peak earning power during these years and usually have established careers. They may see their children grown and gone and may experience new freedoms. Married couples may grow closer. In 1950, Erik Erikson called this a stage of "generativity" with, hopefully, a sense of productivity and creativity. Yet, middle age may also bring uncertainties. People tend to think they will always be young, and middle age comes gradually and unannounced.

Middle age is getting more attention as baby boomers are getting older. Some thought that baby boomers, the cohort born between 1946 and 1964, would change middle age as they had changed other aspects of American society. Many baby boomers may try to avoid "middle age" altogether since the stereotypes about the period, in many ways, do not fit them. They may simply give new meaning to "getting older."

## WHAT IS "OLD"?

What does it mean to age? When is a person old? Aging is both simple and complex. Getting older may sound simple, but why people age is still a mystery. Yet, research is beginning to find some answers.

Most gerontologists designate the start of old

age as sixty-five, the retirement age set by the Social Security Act of 1936. Yet sixty-five may also be considered young. Many researchers divide those over sixty-five into the "young-old," the "middle-old," and the "old-old." Hillier and Barrow believe that seventy-five, eighty, or even eighty-five might describe the beginning of old age.

### LIFE SPAN AND LIFE EXPECTANCY

Why are there so many older people? People are not living that much longer today; individuals have lived past one hundred years of age for quite some time. In other words, life span, the maximum age that one could live, has not increased greatly. Life expectancy, however, has increased as more people live into the later years. Most people born today will live to be old.

In 1990, life expectancy at birth was 75.4 for the U.S. population. Life span refers to the maximum age anyone has been known to live (now more than 120 years), and life expectancy is the average number of years that one might expect to live. Even though life expectancy may be seventy-five, many people live longer, and one's life expectancy increases as one gets older and evades the common causes of a shorter life.

### LIFE SATISFACTION

To be old does not necessarily mean to be sick, poor, unhappy, and unable to care for oneself. These are stereotypes and not true for everyone. An encouraging fact is that according to Duane A. Matcha in *The Sociology of Aging* (1997), only about 5 percent of people over sixty-five are in nursing homes in the United States at any given time. Most older people are able to take care of themselves and, with assistance, others also remain in their homes. Life satisfaction, for many, is high.

Many older people are enjoying their later years. Medical advances and an emphasis on healthy lifestyles can make old age easier and more enjoyable, and according to James A. Thorson in *Aging in a Changing Society* (1995), most older people report their health to be excellent or good. When they retire, many maintain their former lifestyles, often as actively as before or even more so. They may travel, golf, pursue hobbies, or climb mountains. Some keep working because they cannot afford to retire, and some work because they enjoy it.

Older people are a varied and productive lot. In *The Social Processes of Aging and Old Age* (2d ed., 1996), Arnold S. Brown lists three types of leisure roles emerging among the retired: volunteers, students, and those pursuing arts and crafts. Many continue busy lifestyles through personal activities or community service.

As reported by Jill Quadagno in *Aging and the Life Course* (1999), studies indicate that religion provides comfort, support, and meaning in life to many older people. According to Cary S. Kart in *The Realities of Aging* (5th ed., 1997), the positive values of religious faith and activities for older Americans include help when facing death, meaning and purpose in life, acceptance of unavoidable losses, and the discovery and use of the potential of old age. Harold G. Cox reports in *Later Life* (4th ed., 1996) that studies show a greater life satisfaction and better adjustment among those who attend church, possibly from a sense of community and well-being.

### HEALTH AND INDEPENDENCE

According to William C. Cockerham in *This Aging Society* (2d ed., 1997), older people as a group are healthier than in the past. Most older people feel their health is relatively good, and healthier lifestyles have given many a greater sense of control. The realities of aging may also include health problems. These conditions, which are often chronic, may not hold elders back significantly, however, and medical research is making progress toward understanding and conquering the more serious illnesses.

To most older people, home is best. An abundance of services, both formal and informal, help many elderly people stay at home longer than they might otherwise. Family members provide the most assistance, but neighbors, friends, and churches also help. Not everyone has family or others to whom they can turn, however, and community services may be helpful. Home-delivered meals, visiting nurses, and housekeeping assistance are only some of the services offered, often paid for on a sliding scale so that more people can afford them.

Some older people need the formal care that nursing homes can provide. Assisted-living facilities, a more recent concept, also offer a variety of services, sometimes at less cost. Assisted living may be suitable for those elders who no longer live in their own homes but can care for many of their own needs.

Researcher Robert C. Atchley, believing that people both change and stay the same with age, proposed the continuity theory. Cockerham explains the continuity theory in *This Aging Society*. It suggests that personality in old age tends to be much the same as in earlier years, with some change possible but global personality traits stable. Retaining certain traits through life can be helpful, and earlier coping strategies often prove useful.

### IMPLICATIONS FOR THE FUTURE

Thorson sees a trend of older people having more money and better education than previous generations. He believes that their political clout will be considerable, social programs will help them stay independent longer, and as professionals and the general public are increasingly aware of this growing group, their needs will be addressed. Healthy lifestyles will contribute to greater enjoyment of these years, with health problems squeezed into fewer years at the end. If Thorson is correct, many will embrace Robert Browning's invitation from his poem "Rabbi Ben Ezra": "Grow old along with me! The best is yet to be."

—*Mary L. Bender*

*See also* Aging: Biological, psychological, and sociocultural perspectives; Aging process; Alzheimer's disease; Arthritis; Bone changes and disorders; Brain changes and disorders; Canes and walkers; Caregiving; Cataracts; Centenarians; Cultural views of aging; Death and dying; Dementia; Demographics; Dentures; Diabetes; Disabilities; Discounts; Driving; Elder abuse; Emphysema; *Enjoy Old Age: A Program of Self-Management*; Erikson, Erik H.; Family relationships; Forgetfulness; Fractures and broken bones; Fraud against the elderly; Geriatrics and gerontology; Glaucoma; Grandparenthood; Great-grandparenthood; *Growing Old in America*; Health care; Hearing aids; Hearing loss; Heart attacks; Heart changes and disorders; Hip replacement; Home services; Homelessness; Housing; Illnesses among the elderly; Income sources; Independent living; Injuries among the elderly; Jewish services for the elderly; Leisure activities; Life expectancy; Life insurance; Long-term care for the elderly; Longevity research; Macular degeneration; Meals-on-wheels programs; Medical insurance; Medicare; Medications; Memory changes and loss; Men and aging; Mental impairment; Middle age; Mobility problems; Nursing and convalescent homes; Osteoporosis; Overmedication; Personality changes; Pets; Poverty; Prostate cancer; Prostate enlargement; Psychiatry, geriatric; Religion; Relocation; Respiratory changes and disorders; Retirement; Retirement communities; Safety issues; Sarcopenia; Senior citizen centers; Sensory changes; Skin changes and disorders; Sleep changes and disturbances; Social Security; Stereotypes; Strokes and TIAs; Successful aging; Transportation issues; Urinary disorders; Vacations and travel; Violent crime against the elderly; Vision changes and disorders; Widows and widowers; Wisdom; Women and aging.

### FOR FURTHER INFORMATION:

Atchley, Robert C. *Social Forces and Aging: An Introduction to Social Gerontology*. 9th ed. Belmont, Calif.: Wadsworth, 1999.

Brown, Arnold S. *The Social Processes of Aging and Old Age*. 2d ed. Upper Saddle River, N.J.: Prentice Hall, 1996.

Cockerham, William C. *This Aging Society*. 2d ed. Upper Saddle River, N.J.: Prentice Hall, 1997.

Cox, Harold G. *Later Life: The Realities of Aging*. 4th ed. Upper Saddle River, N.J.: Prentice Hall, 1996.

Erikson, Erik H., Joan M. Erikson, and Helen Q. Kivnick. *Vital Involvement in Old Age*. New York: W. W. Norton, 1986.

Hillier, Susan, and Georgia M. Barrow. *Aging, the Individual, and Society*. 7th ed. Belmont, Calif.: Wadsworth, 1999.

Kart, Cary S. *The Realities of Aging: An Introduction to Gerontology*. 5th ed. Boston: Allyn & Bacon, 1997.

Matcha, Duane A. *The Sociology of Aging: A Social Problems Perspective*. Boston: Allyn & Bacon, 1997.

Quadagno, Jill. *Aging and the Life Course: An Introduction to Social Gerontology*. Boston: McGraw-Hill, 1999.

Thorson, James A. *Aging in a Changing Society*. Belmont, Calif.: Wadsworth, 1995.

## OLD-AGE, SURVIVORS, AND DISABILITY INSURANCE. *See* SOCIAL SECURITY.

## OLD MAN AND THE SEA, THE

**AUTHOR:** Ernest Hemingway
**DATE:** Published in 1952
**RELEVANT ISSUES:** Culture, psychology, values, work
**SIGNIFICANCE:** This novel about the struggles of an elderly fisherman highlights issues that accompany aging in physically demanding work

Ernest Hemingway's novel *The Old Man and the Sea* concerns an elderly and solitary Cuban fisherman, Santiago, who has not caught a fish for eighty-four days. On the eighty-fifth day, Santiago hooks an enormous marlin while in his small boat, but Santiago has gone out to sea too far. He is unable to prevent sharks from devouring his catch as he tows it back to his village after three days of struggle.

Certain experts on this novel note that Santiago has been labeled as useless by his culture because he is elderly and without luck. Despite this label, Santiago continues his fishing. By drawing on his abundant experience and skill, Santiago catches a larger fish than any of the younger, but less experienced, fishermen who have alienated him. Seen in these terms, Santiago's catch is a triumph of the aging individual—possessing the unique abilities acquired only from many years of experience—over a youth-oriented culture trapped by its shortsighted attitudes toward elders. Other commentators, however, have chosen to highlight the fact that Santiago, in an act of desperation, knowingly goes out too far. In doing so, he is making a last attempt to prove to himself, and his critics, that he is still a capable man and member of the community.

Many critics point out that Santiago embodies the values that Hemingway thought one should possess as an elder: determination, humility, hopefulness, wisdom, skill, pride, and courage. Santiago is content with realizing these values in the course of his daily work. This picture of a poor but content elder has been contrasted with Hemingway's depiction of the younger fishermen who, while more successful, are preoccupied by material gain. Seen in this way, Hemingway's Santiago has arrived at a successful approach to life in his later years.
                                           —*Robert Landolfi*

*See also* Cultural views of aging; Latinos; Literature; Men and aging; Old age; Wisdom.

## OLDER AMERICANS ACT OF 1965

**DATE:** Passed on July 14, 1965
**RELEVANT ISSUES:** Economics, health and medicine, law
**SIGNIFICANCE:** In 1965, Congress passed legislation to provide funds for services for needy persons aged sixty and over; the law was designed to supplement Social Security benefits

Prior to 1965, research indicated that many senior citizens in the United States lacked adequate retirement income, health care, affordable housing, gainful employment, and meaningful civil, cultural, and recreational opportunities. In addition, as persons grew older, they were spending increasing percentages of their fixed incomes on medical care. Accordingly, as a part of President Lyndon B. Johnson's Great Society programs, Congress passed the Older Americans Act on July 14, 1965. Several amendments have been made to the act, including the Age Discrimination Act of 1975.

The act created the Administration on Aging (AoA), headed by a commissioner of aging within the Department of Health, Education, and Welfare. The Advisory Committee on Older Americans, consisting of the commissioner and fifteen people with relevant experience, was also established to provide expertise in designing new programs. In 1978, AoA was transferred to the new Department of Health and Human Services. Acting on recommendations of the 1992 White House Conference on Aging, Congress in 1993 amended the act by upgrading the commissioner to assistant secretary for aging; in addition, the Advisory Committee on Older Americans became the Federal Council on Aging.

The AoA provides grants to states. To obtain funds, each state must designate a state unit on aging (SUA), which must design a program to utilize the funds. SUAs then identify area agencies throughout each state, which form advisory councils to develop the area plan, hold hearings, represent older people, and review and comment on community programs. SUAs by law must have a full-time ombudsman to handle complaints.

The AoA awards two types of grants: for research and development projects (which make needs assessments, develop new approaches—including clinics to provide legal assistance to poorer senior citizens and multipurpose activity centers—develop new methods to coordinate programs and services, and evaluate the various programs) and for training projects for personnel to run the programs.

Each state receives at least 1 percent of the total funding, and American Samoa, Guam, and the Virgin Islands each receive 0.5 percent. The remaining 49.5 percent is allocated on the basis of the relative size of the state's population. No more than 10 percent of each state's allotment can support SUA administrative expenses. The AoA also provides consultants, technical assistance, training personnel, research, and informational materials to the states. Priority program recipients are those who are homebound because of disability or illness. Meals-on-wheels services provide hot meals directly to their homes, and they are eligible for in-home support services, including home health aides. Low-income minorities are especially targeted.

Programs operating under the act have been criticized largely because, although the quality of services is much better in some states than others, the AoA has neither developed nor enforced minimum standards. In 1991, Congress held up renewal of the act while it developed a means test to ensure that only needy older persons would take advantage.
                                          —*Michael Haas*

**See also** Advocacy; Age Discrimination Act of 1975; Home services; Meals-on-wheels programs.

## OLDER WOMEN'S LEAGUE (OWL)

**DATE:** Founded in 1980
**RELEVANT ISSUES:** Culture, health and medicine, sociology, violence
**SIGNIFICANCE:** The Older Women's League is a grassroots organization that addresses the special needs of midlife and older women in the United States

The Older Women's League (OWL), begun by Tish Sommers and Laurie Shields, is an organization that grew out of the 1980 White House Mini-Conference on Older Women in Des Moines, Iowa. The OWL is a nonprofit organization supported by membership, corporations, foundations, and individual donations. More than fifteen thousand members, most of them forty and older, support seventy local chapters with an annual bud-

get of $700,000. A telephone message about federal legislation affecting women, recorded weekly, is available to OWL members.

Local chapters have sponsored legislation for mammogram regulations, health and nutrition for the elderly, peer counseling for abused older women, peer-led divorce support groups for older women, and a pension information hotline. In the late 1990's, the national organization focused on a national universal health care system, equitable and adequate Social Security, more adequate Social Security Insurance (SSI), expanded employer-sponsored pension coverage, and increased access to housing and housing alternatives. Growing violence toward the elderly prompted the OWL to form a special committee on elder abuse victim support, a peer-support program especially for older victims of domestic abuse. Trained peer leaders facilitate all special-interest meetings.

The OWL provides educational programs and materials pertinent to older women, manages a speakers' bureau, and compiles statistics for public use. Its leadership directs attention to educating younger women about their critical stake in the issues of the OWL and encourages them in advocating for positive change. Educational materials include *Women and Job Discrimination: A Primer, Women and Pensions, The Future Face of Housing: Old, Alone and Female in the Twenty-first Century,* and *Divorce and Older Women.* Topics of the OWL's Mother's Day Report, distributed to members of Congress as well as the general public, include "Faces of Care: An Analysis of Women's Retirement Income" and "Ending Violence Against Midlife and Older Women."
                                    —*Virginiae Blackmon*

**See also** Advocacy; Elder abuse; Health care; Pensions; Social Security; Violent crime against the elderly; Women and aging.

## OLDER WORKERS BENEFIT PROTECTION ACT

**DATE:** Signed on October 16, 1990
**RELEVANT ISSUES:** Economics, law
**SIGNIFICANCE:** This act ensures that older workers cannot be tricked by employers into losing retirement benefits

The Age Discrimination in Employment Act (ADEA) of 1967 was designed to deter employers from discriminating against workers over the age of forty. Unscrupulous employers, however, decided to offer early retirement incentives to older workers—often threatening to lay off older workers just before they became eligible for a pension—provided that the workers waived their ADEA rights.

When one of these schemes was challenged, the U.S. Supreme Court ruled, in *Ohio v. Betts* (1989), that such waivers were perfectly legal. Congress then passed the Older Workers Benefit Protection Act (OWBPA) in 1990 to establish procedural safeguards so that such waivers could not be signed in haste and so employers could not target older workers in staff-cutting programs.

The OWBPA established the following requirements: The waiver must be written in a manner that can be understood by the average employee; the waiver cannot relinquish non-ADEA rights; the waiver cannot refer to rights subsequently established by an amended ADEA; the employee must be advised in writing to consult an attorney before signing a waiver; the employee can take at least three weeks before signing the waiver; and the waiver can be revoked within one week after signing.

The OWBPA provides that the burden of proof about the legality of a waiver falls on the employer. When an employer challenged the OWBPA, the Supreme Court, in *Oubre v. Entergy* (1998), affirmed that an employee has the right to sue under ADEA if an employer's waiver agreement fails to comply with these six procedural requirements. Moreover, an employee suing for a violation of the OWBPA need not return the severance pay provided in the waiver.

—*Michael Haas*

*See also* Age discrimination; Age Discrimination in Employment Act of 1967; Early retirement; Employment; Retirement.

## On Golden Pond

**Author:** Ernest Thompson
**Date:** Play produced in 1978, published in 1979; film released in 1981
**Relevant issues:** Death, family, health and medicine, marriage and dating, work
**Significance:** This play about an elderly couple highlights important issues of aging, including retirement and coping with failing health

Ernest Thompson's play *On Golden Pond* depicts an elderly couple, Norman and Ethel, on a summer vacation in Maine. They are visited by their daughter, her boyfriend, and his adolescent son. The boy stays the summer while the daughter vacations elsewhere with her boyfriend.

Much of the play concerns difficulties which may occur after retirement. Norman is an always-witty retired professor. In the opening act, however, one sees him searching through "help wanted" advertisements for unskilled jobs. Critics note that Norman is a victim of a youth-oriented culture that often fails to provide a dignified and active role for elders, reducing their self-esteem. Norman no longer believes he has much to offer and is willing to accept any job. In this sense, his relationship with the teenager later in the play represents a triumph. During their summer together, Norman becomes the boy's mentor and is rejuvenated by this relationship.

Health issues that may accompany aging are also central to this play. As Norman nears eighty, he experiences mild senility and heart palpitations. Commentators have noted that the younger and healthier Ethel compensates for her husband's failing health by taking on a parental role in their marriage. Ethel often attempts to structure Norman's time, for example, to help him with his tendencies toward forgetfulness.

Health issues are also a part of the play's treatment of the subject of death. Ethel and Norman have different attitudes toward death. Norman is preoccupied with the subject and Ethel, always the optimist, avoids it. In the final act, Norman has a mild heart attack. Through this experience, Ethel finally faces death. At the end of the play, Norman recovers and the couple appreciates life more than ever as a result of this experience.

A popular film adaptation of *On Golden Pond* was released in 1981. It starred Henry Fonda as Norman, Katharine Hepburn as Ethel, and Jane Fonda as their daughter. The film won Academy Awards for Best Actor for Henry Fonda, Best Actress for Hepburn, and Best Adapted Screenplay for Thompson.

—*Robert Landolfi*

*See also* Ageism; Death and dying; Death anxiety; Employment; Family relationships; Forgetfulness; Heart attacks; Literature; Marriage; Mental impairment; Multigenerational households; Successful aging; Vacations and travel.

# OSTEOPOROSIS

**RELEVANT ISSUES:** Biology, Health and medicine

**SIGNIFICANCE:** As the number of elderly people in the United States grows, an increasing number of women and a smaller but growing number of men will experience an osteoporotic fracture at some point in their lives

Osteoporosis is a major public health problem that affects at least 25 million Americans; about 1.5 million osteoporotic fractures occur each year. The condition is often silent until a fracture occurs. Up to one of every five older patients who sustains a hip fracture dies within six months of the fracture. One-half of the survivors need some help with their daily-living activities, and as many as 25 percent of these patients need care in a nursing home. The 1995 estimated cost for treating osteoporotic fractures was nearly $14 billion.

Bone is a metabolically active, dynamic tissue that is remodeled throughout life. Depending on a number of factors, the process is either in or out of balance. In children, formation exceeds loss, so bone mass increases. In adults, the two are about equal, so bone mass only changes if there is additional or less stress. In old age, bone loss exceeds bone formation, and bone mass is decreased. When bone mass is reduced, the bone becomes mechanically weak and vulnerable to fractures. The gradual loss of bone mineral density, or bone thinning, is a normal part of the aging process; osteoporosis occurs when this process exceeds what are considered normal rates, making bones exceedingly fragile and susceptible to breaks and fractures. There is no known cure for osteoporosis; prevention is the only strategy for combating bone mineral loss and the development of osteoporosis.

The osteoporosis of aging is designated as type I. It has two forms: postmenopausal and senile. Postmenopausal osteoporosis occurs in women between the ages of fifty-one and sixty-five and often results in fractures of the vertebrae and wrist; senile osteoporosis, which occurs in both men and women past the age of seventy, increases the danger fractures of the hip and vertebrae. A side effect of a hip fracture that requires surgery or immobilization is muscle wasting. With less muscle, the person is less stable and more likely to fall and re-injure the hip. Fractures of the hip are a significant medical problem: 12 to 20 percent of such patients die within six months of the fracture, and about one-half lose the ability to live independently.

### RISK FACTORS FOR OSTEOPOROSIS

A number of risk factors for osteoporosis have been identified, some of which cannot be changed. For example, the older a person is, the more likely he or she is to develop osteoporosis. Women tend to be more vulnerable than men because, in addition to the accelerated rate of bone loss that occurs at the menopause, women have

## Osteoporosis

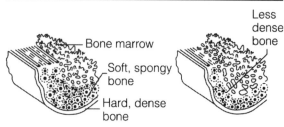

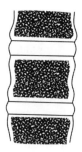

**Normal vertebral body**

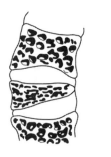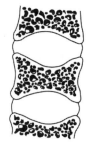

**Osteoporotic vertebral bodies**

*Osteoporosis leads to bone that is less dense, more brittle, more easily broken, and degenerative.* (Hans & Cassidy, Inc.)

smaller skeletons than men and, therefore, reach the threshold for bone fragility well before men.

People with large body frames are less likely to develop osteoporosis than those with small body frames, probably because their bone reserve allows them to lose bone for a longer period before reaching the threshold for fracture. Genetic research has also determined that variations in the gene for the vitamin D receptor may contribute to 7 to 10 percent of the difference in bone mass density because of its influence on calcium intake. For those with a family history of osteoporosis, this factor could lead to early identification and intervention.

A number of risk factors that can be reversed have also been identified. Even though osteoporosis is a disease of the elderly, identification of risk factors in the young will ensure that preventive measures can be followed. Normal calcium intake throughout life may do the most toward prevention of osteoporosis, even among high-risk populations. About 99 percent of the body's calcium is found in the bones and teeth, and daily intake is meant to keep these stores full. A low dietary calcium intake is associated with a reduced bone mass and an increased fracture rate. Conversely, an elevated calcium intake, particularly in children and adolescents, is associated with an increased mass.

In 1997, the National Academy of Science increased the dietary reference intake (DRI), formerly known as the recommended dietary allowance (RDA), from 800 milligrams to 1,300 milligrams per day for those between the ages of nine and eighteen. The ideal daily level for all adults was determined to be 1,000 milligrams. The academy also recommended that men increase intake to 1,500 milligrams after age sixty-five and that postmenopausal women who are not on hormone replacement therapy (HRT) take 1,200 milligrams. Women on HRT were advised to continue at 1,000 milligrams. It is preferable to get most of the calcium from the diet; it has been recommended that calcium supplied through supplements should be restricted to doses of no more than 500 milligrams at one time, preferably during meals. Calcium is not absorbed well, so the presence of stomach acid, as well as vitamin D and protein, enhances the absorption. Some research in the 1990's suggested that vitamin D deficiencies in the elderly may be a main cause of low calcium levels.

Physical inactivity is associated with a reduced bone mass. People who are sedentary are more susceptible to osteoporosis than those who are active. During the formative years, exercise helps develop higher bone density. Recommendations include a variety of weightbearing and vigorous exercises that are done regularly, for thirty to sixty minutes per day, three to five days per week. Variety is essential because no one exercise stresses all bones equally. In the elderly, exercise may have a secondary benefit. Fractures are often precipitated by falls that are caused by a loss of balance or coordination. Maintaining an active lifestyle helps with balance and coordination, as well as confidence, all of which may help in fall prevention. Studies on the elderly have demonstrated that general exercise, such as walking, does not maintain gains in bone density for very long. Many medical experts have therefore recommended adding a regular strength-training regimen, performed two or three times per week for twenty minutes, that targets the most common fracture sites. Research in the 1990's also suggested the benefits of jump training in the elderly to strengthen the hip and spine.

Other modifiable risk factors include smoking and excess alcohol consumption. Both of these are risk factors for a number of diseases, so they are discouraged in everyone. Some medications, such as glucocorticoids and anticonvulsants, can also interact with bone formation or increase bone loss; therefore, anyone on long-term prophylactic use of either is advised to consult a physician about bone health.

## TREATMENT AND THERAPY

In order to prevent osteoporosis, doctors often request baseline information on the bone densities of women before the menopause and of men between the ages of fifty and sixty. The most accurate technique available to measure bone density is dual energy X-ray absorptiometry (DEXA). Although it is an X ray, exposure to radiation is minimal. The same densitometry machine can do both whole-body and single-site readings. A technique using ultrasound received U.S. Food and Drug Administration (FDA) approval in 1998. The lower cost and lack of radiation may prompt more people to receive early screenings and to submit to repeated tests at critical times throughout their lives.

*One of the more serious effects of osteoporosis can be kyphosis or "dowager's hump," an extreme curve in the upper back.* (Ben Klaffke)

Osteoporosis therapy includes several options. The most commonly prescribed drug is HRT, which is effective in arresting the bone loss that occurs after the menopause. If use is initiated within five years of the menopause and is accompanied with calcium and exercise, bone mass may even increase. Although such therapy reduces the risk of developing cardiovascular diseases, it also increases the risk of breast cancer in some women; therefore, prescription is decided on a case-by-case basis.

Calcitonin, a hormone produced by the thyroid gland, specifically prevents bone breakdown. As a result, its use leads to a relative increase in the rate of bone formation. After the initial increase, however, the bone mass tends to stabilize, and continued administration may be associated with an actual decline in bone mass. Therefore, calcitonin is usually administered in cycles of six to twelve

months. One of the main advantages of calcitonin is that, unlike HRT, it is effective in both sexes and in patients of all ages, including the very old. Calcitonin also appears to have an analgesic effect, which may be quite useful following a vertebral collapse. In the past, calcitonin was an expensive drug that was administered through daily injection. In 1997, however, the FDA approved a synthetic form administered as a nasal spray. In general, calcitonin does not appear to be as effective in thickening bones as other drugs being studied.

Another drug, alendronate, received FDA approval in 1998 for use in women. It was the first nonhormonal osteoporosis drug. Several studies showed dramatic increases in bone mass, along with fewer fractures. The cost is about the same as calcitonin but considerably more than HRT. This, coupled with the lack of long-term use studies to determine side effects, makes alendronate a drug of choice for the elderly with severe bone loss rather than a preventive measure in newly postmenopausal women, unless their risks for osteoporosis are very high.

Other drugs that have shown promise in controlled studies include slow-release sodium fluoride, calcitrol, and raloxifene. Considerable research has been conducted on the use of different preparations, such as growth hormone, testosterone, and anabolic steroids, in the treatment of osteoporosis, particularly in men. Some experts have suggested that men with low testosterone may benefit from a biweekly injection or a daily application of a testosterone patch.

### PSYCHOSOCIAL FACTORS

Osteoporosis follows the psychological profile of other chronic diseases, causing anxiety, depression, and feelings of hopelessness. Diagnosis often causes a fear of loss of independence, fear of another fall, or fear of financial devastation from long-term health care, all of which lead to further limitation of activities and reduced physical conditioning.

Vertebral fractures, loss of height, protruding abdomen, or compressed lungs can ultimately lead to pneumonia in individuals who contract a viral or bacterial lung infection. Those same patients may experience challenges in tasks of daily living, such as reaching or walking; these limitations may add to feelings of frustration and ineffectiveness. Such people often withdraw from social activities, which are a big part of health and wellness in the elderly.

Pain is probably the primary physical problem associated with osteoporosis. It challenges coping skills and makes it difficult to deal with other aspects of the disease. Pain may be either acute and severe (following a fracture) or chronic (from spinal deformity and associated changes in the body, which often increase over time). Pain management is usually a significant part of the treatment program for people with osteoporotic fractures of the spine. *—Wendy E. S. Repovich*

***See also*** Back disorders; Bone changes and disorders; Estrogen replacement therapy; Exercise and fitness; Fractures and broken bones; Kyphosis; Malnutrition; Medications; Menopause; Nutrition; Safety issues; Vitamins and minerals; Women and aging.

#### FOR FURTHER INFORMATION:

American College of Sports Medicine. "American College of Sports Medicine Position Stand on Osteoporosis and Exercise." *Medicine and Science in Sports and Exercise* 27, no. 4 (April, 1995). A critical review of the benefits of exercise and the hazards of lack of exercise for osteoporosis, including the recommended kinds and amounts of exercise necessary.

Bilger, Burkhard. "Bone Medicine." *Health* 10, no. 3 (May/June, 1996). This article summarizes drugs approved by the FDA for the treatment of osteoporosis in women.

Heaney, Robert P. "Osteoporosis." In *Nutrition in Women's Health*, edited by Debra A. Krummel and Penny M. Kris-Etherton. Gaithersburg, Md.: Aspen, 1996. This chapter highlights the role of nutrition in the prevention and treatment of osteoporosis in the postmenopausal woman.

National Academy of Science, Institute of Medicine. *Dietary Reference Intake for Calcium, Phosphorus, Magnesium, Vitamin D, and Fluoride.* Washington, D.C.: National Academy Press, 1997. Revised dietary guidelines for the substances listed in the title.

Petersen, Marilyn D., and Diana L. White, eds. *Health Care of the Elderly: An Information Sourcebook.* Newbury Park, Calif.: Sage Publications, 1989. D. W. Belcher's article "Prevention of Osteoporosis in the Elderly" discusses accepted treatment modulations to reduce the acceleration of osteoporosis in patients at risk.

Snow-Harter, Christine, and Robert Marcus. "Exercise, Bone Mineral Density, and Osteoporosis." In *Exercise and Sport Sciences Reviews.* Vol. 19. Baltimore: Williams & Wilkins, 1991. This is a review of the role exercise plays in the development and retention of bone density and osteoporosis.

Van Horn, Linda, and Annie O. Wong. "Preventive Nutrition in Adolescent Girls." In *Nutrition in Women's Health*, edited by Debra A. Krummel and Penny M. Kris-Etherton. Gaithersburg, Md.: Aspen, 1996. Discusses the role that nutrition in the adolescent may play in the prevention of osteoporosis later in life.

## OURSELVES, GROWING OLDER: A BOOK FOR WOMEN OVER FORTY

**EDITORS:** Paula Doress-Worters and Diana Laskin Siegal

**DATE:** Published in 1987, revised in 1994

**RELEVANT ISSUES:** Family, health and medicine, psychology

**SIGNIFICANCE:** *Ourselves, Growing Older* is a guidebook for women over forty in dealing with changes in body, relationships, and health as they and their loved ones age

*Ourselves, Growing Older: A Book for Women over Forty*, edited by Paula Doress-Worters and Diana Laskin Siegal, was first published in 1987; it appeared in a revised edition in 1994 as *The New Ourselves, Growing Older: Women Aging with Knowledge and Power.* Doress-Worters and Siegal prepared this volume in cooperation with the Boston Women's Health Book Collective, the authors of *Our Bodies, Ourselves* (1971; revised as *The New Our Bodies, Ourselves* in 1992) and other health-related works. In fact, the idea for this book arose from the challenges associated with writing a single chapter on health concerns for the older woman for *Our Bodies, Ourselves.* It is based on the same principle as *Our Bodies, Ourselves*: that women must know themselves and their bodies to be free from mistaken notions about women and their health and well-being. Written from a feminist perspective, *Ourselves, Growing Older* is a collaborative effort by women in their mid-forties to their eighties aimed at exposing the effects of ageism and sexism on all people, not just on women.

The authors also hope to enable women to stay well as they move into their later years. They examine the ways that culture influences aging in women and argue against the medicalization of the menopause, as earlier women's health activists argued against the medicalization of childbirth. They believe that both of these events should be approached as normal parts of a woman's life, rather than as pathologic conditions. Instead of looking at women's health solely from a biomedical model, the authors also consider the effects of the environment, poverty, and injustice on aging. Their underlying philosophy is that the lives of older women can be rich and fulfilling. They consider this idea to be especially important because the greatest proportion of the older population is female.

*Ourselves, Growing Older* is divided into three sections. "Aging Well" includes six chapters devoted to dealing with the expected changes of aging and health habits associated with healthier aging. These chapters address diet, exercise, substance use, body image, stress, and other topics. "Living with Ourselves and Others as We Age" includes six chapters on topics ranging from sexuality in the second half of life, birth control and childbearing in midlife, the menopause, relationships, housing arrangements and work, retirement, and economics. The final section, "Understanding, Preventing, and Managing Medical Problems," begins by discussing the needed reforms to the health care system. Individual chapters cover common health problems of aging: arthritis, osteoporosis, dental problems, incontinence, hysterectomy, heart disease, cancer, diabetes, gallbladder problems, sensory changes, and memory loss. This section concludes with a chapter on death and dying. The final chapter discusses ways to change, both on a societal and on an individual level. Each chapter provides extensive references, and the authors offer more than sixty pages of resources, including other books and articles, agencies, audiovisual materials, and pamphlets.

—*Rebecca Lovell Scott*

*See also* Ageism; Arthritis; Cancer; Cultural views of aging; Death and dying; Dental problems; Diabetes; Estrogen replacement therapy; Exercise and fitness; Health care; Heart disease; Housing; Incontinence; Memory changes and loss; Menopause; Osteoporosis; Poverty; Psychiatry, geriatric; Retirement; Sensory changes; Sexuality; Stress and coping skills; Successful aging; Women and aging.

## OVER THE HILL

**RELEVANT ISSUES:** Culture, psychology, values
**SIGNIFICANCE:** This phrase presents a metaphorical image of aging that affords multiple angles for interpretation

"Over the hill," a popular expression to describe aging, is a metaphoric construct. As simple as it is, the inherent richness of this phrase affords people multiple angles from which to interpret what aging means. A few of them are discussed here.

Aging is often seen as a life journey. On the completion of climbing up a hill to the peak, going "over the hill" indicates the beginning of the rest of the journey.

Aging is coming down the path "over the hill," demonstrating a declining trend in contrast to upward growth. The peak marks the turning point of the developmental course, separating two qualitatively different stages in life: growth and aging.

Aging is a developmental process involving new tasks in a new context. The tasks may be difficult and the path may be rough, as expressed in the Chinese saying, "It is easy to climb up a hill; it is hard to go down a hill." Yet, aging can be exciting: The grass might be greener "over the hill." New growth and achievements are possible in a person's later life.

Aging varies in its internal meaning and motivational structure for individuals. Each person must locate his or her position on the hill of life. Even after going "over the hill," the individual decides the speed and style of descending.

Aging is an indicator of maturity and accomplishment, worthy of celebration. Having gone "over the hill" implies a successful past and opens up new prospects for the future, as depicted in an American Indian story in which once over the hill, a person sees another hill ahead yet to conquer. The number of people on each successive hill decreases.

—*Ling-Yi Zhou*

*See also* Aging: Biological, psychological, and sociocultural perspectives; Ageism; American Indians; Cultural views of aging; Humor; Maturity; Middle age; Old age; Stereotypes; Wisdom.

## OVERMEDICATION

RELEVANT ISSUES: Health and medicine

SIGNIFICANCE: Overmedication of the elderly causes great harm to individuals and results in unnecessary health care expenditures

The overmedication of older Americans is a serious problem with many dimensions—cultural, economic, political, and medical. Although health problems are the most obvious, overmedication of the old should be seen in a broad context. Among the contributing factors are aggressive promotion by drug companies, especially of drugs meant for long-term use; lack of training in aging on the part of most doctors; Americans' preference for quick solutions to medical problems; lack of understanding of bodily changes in the old that make prescription drug use by them riskier than for younger people; a widespread belief that the old need drugs because they are old; the absence of drug education programs to teach the old and their families safe and appropriate prescription drug use; undertesting of drugs on elderly populations; and the high cost of nondrug alternatives for treating chronic diseases of aging.

In the late 1990's, Americans spent eighty billion dollars a year on prescription drugs. People over sixty-five constituted 13 percent of the population but consumed 34 percent of the prescription drugs (as high as 45 percent, according to some estimates). Approximately 70 percent of men over sixty-five used drugs, compared to 75 percent of women in this age group. The number of old persons taking more than six drugs a day was not known, but geriatricians (specialists in the diseases of old age) believed the number to be large.

### ADVERSE DRUG REACTIONS

Each year, 100,000 Americans die of adverse drug reactions. The old are the most vulnerable, especially those who take several drugs daily. They are twice as likely to suffer ill effects from medications as persons in their thirties and forties, and their adverse reactions are more likely to be severe. An estimated nine million older Americans suffer adverse drug reactions each year. Approximately 17 percent of hospital admissions of people over seventy are caused by this problem. Not all adverse reactions are caused by overmedication, but gerontologists (those who study aging) surmise that among the elderly, overmedication is the most common cause. About 40 percent of respondents to a survey by the American Association of Retired Persons (AARP) reported side effects from the medications they were taking. Some of the side effects were presumably mild and acceptable, given the benefits of the drugs.

Because the metabolism of older people slows down and organs tend to function less efficiently, drugs can have a very strong impact on aging bodies. With age, less blood flows into the liver, which becomes smaller and less efficient in metabolizing some drugs. Drug clearance from the body declines with age. For example, reduced kidney function results in drug accumulation. Because the stomach empties more slowly with age, drugs remain there longer. Age-related changes in hormones mean that drugs have a stronger impact on the old than on younger people. For example, the elderly are more likely to develop drug-induced hypoglycemia.

With age, the brain becomes more sensitive to the sedative effects of drugs, so that oversedation is often found among the elderly. For example, excess sedation or confusion from too much Valium (diazepam) or Dalmane (flurazepam) may not occur until several weeks after well-tolerated doses were begun. Consequently, some geriatricians recommend that Valium not be given to old patients.

According to physician Margaret W. Winker, fat-soluble drugs, including those that affect the brain, are retained longer in the body with age, so that drugs prescribed for problems in the elderly such as anxiety or insomnia must be given in smaller doses and less frequently than they would be given to younger patients. Some narcotic medicines may cause serious side effects in older patients. Winker believes that medications commonly used in the past for insomnia, such as barbiturates, should now be avoided in old persons because they interact with many other drugs, slow respiration, and cause confusion. She also notes that prednisone should not be prescribed for osteoarthritis, the most common form of arthritis, because of its harmful effect on the endocrine system. In addition, the monoamine oxidase (MAO) inhibitors used to treat depression, a common complaint of the elderly, may interact with food to cause high blood pressure. Over-the-counter medicines such as cold remedies and nasal decongestants also interact with MAO inhibitors.

Other common reactions to overmedication include impaired movements, memory loss, anxiety, constipation, palpitations, depression, restlessness, insomnia, blocked thyroid function, mood swings or other emotional imbalances, blurred vision, urine retention, potassium depletion, and lessening capacity to smell and taste. In addition, overuse of drugs can cause nutritional depletion, resulting in such problems as hearing loss, anemia, breathlessness, and weakness. Among nutrients lost are vitamins A and C and beta carotene, all thought likely to help the immune system ward off cancer.

Alcohol and tobacco interact with prescription drugs, increasing risk factors for the old who take multiple drugs. Some arthritis medicines, for example, interact with coffee and alcohol to damage the lining of the stomach. When sleeping pills mix with alcohol, breathing can be impaired to a dangerous degree.

Nonbiological factors related to overmedication are drug swapping by the old, poor doctor-patient communication, and noncompliance on the part of patients. Sometimes an elderly patient will obtain prescriptions from various doctors or pharmacies, so that no one doctor or pharmacist sees the complete picture of the individual's drug consumption. Patients may not tell doctors what over-the-counter medicines they take. They may not understand, for example, that long-term use of laxatives for constipation can damage their intestines. Others may neglect to mention herbal medications that they take, anticipating the doctor's disapproval. Doctors may not have time for a thorough review of drug use history, current symptoms, and potentially harmful side effects. Limited knowl-

*Pharmacists can play an important role in preventing overmedication by watching for dangerous drug interactions and questioning suspicious prescriptions.* (Digital Stock)

edge of English, hearing loss, extreme deference to doctors, and a sense of powerlessness on the part of the patient may also be factors in incomplete drug assessment.

Although overmedication of the old affects those who live independently or with families as well as those who are institutionalized, overmedicating is especially serious among nursing home residents. Since this population is largely female, the problem of overmedicating nursing home residents is considered a women's issue. Over one-half of all nursing home residents are prescribed psychotropic drugs (those having an effect on the mind). Geriatricians are concerned that in many cases, no precise diagnosis indicates a need for these powerful drugs. They also believe that nursing home residents are often overdosed with medications marked "as needed." Another problem is that some drugs have very similar names, resulting in mix-ups. Many falls in nursing homes result from overmedication.

Sedating is a chemical restraint necessary for unruly or out-of-control patients but often unnecessary for the majority of nursing home residents. Cultural devaluing of the frail and dependent elderly and the convenience of often-underpaid staff may play a larger role in medicating decisions than the particular health needs of individual residents. Overdrugging of nursing home residents is a theme in May Sarton's novel *As We Are Now* (1973).

Many hip fractures occur each year among people over sixty-five who use tranquilizers. Both gait and balance are affected by these drugs. Hip fractures are an especially serious problem for women. For either sex, taking more than four prescription drugs is a risk factor for falls.

While the precise extent of overmedication remains uncertain, pharmacologists who specialize in aging—Peter Lamy, for example—believe that as much as 25 percent of the prescriptions given to the elderly are unnecessary. Other researchers estimate that approximately one-fourth of the elderly are given drugs inappropriate for their complaints. Prescription drugs are most effective for acute, short-term illnesses, but the health problems of the old tend to be chronic.

The estimates cited are probably conservative. Accepting them as accurate, an obvious inference is that overmedicating the old is an extremely costly problem in the United States today. At a time when other health care costs are rising, the cost of overmedicating is likely to increase as the number of older Americans increases. This is especially true since by the end of the twentieth century, the fastest-growing segment of the elderly population was people over eighty-five. It is they who are most likely to be institutionalized and to be given multiple drugs.

## RELATED SOCIAL AND CULTURAL ISSUES

Often when drugs cause the old to become confused or disoriented, these behaviors are attributed to dementia. When reactions to drugs are mistaken for normal signs of aging, elderly persons are unlikely to have their drug use evaluated carefully and adjusted for their individual needs. Perhaps much of what is called "aging" in the United States is actually a cumulative reaction to multiple prescription drugs taken over a long period. Those who live and work with the elderly and the elderly themselves may well believe that the problems they experience result from a slowing down natural to their age and not from overmedication.

The more frequently the old see mainstream doctors, the more often they get prescriptions for drugs and the more likely they are to get sick from side effects if they take several drugs. Thus, high consumption of medical services on the part of the old perpetuates itself. Typically, gerontologists say, if an old person leaves a doctor's office without a prescription, he or she feels neglected or believes that a health problem has not been taken seriously. The prescription represents a doctor's caring.

Given the rising numbers of Americans over sixty-five, the social policy implications of overmedicating the old need analysis. Should one consider it acceptable to sedate the old because they are old? How much social control, especially of the frail and dependent old, is appropriate? Do gender and racial differences affect drug prescribing and monitoring? Stanford gerontologist Gwen Yeo suggested, for example, that older Asian Americans may need only one-half of the drug dose prescribed for whites. Will baby boomers resist physical decline more vigorously than their parents and thus demand more careful drug prescribing? The high cost of medications is an increasingly serious problem for low- and middle-income people. Will politically active seniors demand that their expensive drugs be paid for by Medicare or by other government programs? Will resentment of the old increase as their consumption of costly prescription drugs drives up the cost of health care?

Heavy medication of the old is a fairly recent phenomenon, one more characteristic of aging in the United States than in other societies. In Germany and England, where homeopathy is widely practiced, nondrug treatment of the old is more prevalent. In Japan, Western drugs are available, but it is unusual for an elderly person to be on as many as four drugs, and doctors prescribe traditional Asian remedies as well as prescription drugs. In the United States, where drug companies are among the most profitable businesses, the use of many drugs by the old is repeatedly presented as a normal part of aging for all people, not only for those who are sick. Thus, overmedication of the old is both a health and medical problem and a sign of the American tendency to equate aging with illness. Potential dangers of multiple drug use need further study and public discussion. One solution to overmedication is to increase the number of geriatricians trained to meet the needs of an increasingly elderly population, especially those over eighty. Any senior who takes prescription drugs should heed the advice geriatricians give about medicating the old: "Begin low and go slow." Periodic revaluation of drug use can help prevent overmedication.                       —*Margaret Cruikshank*

**See also** Aging process; Alcoholism; Balance disorders; Depression; Forgetfulness; Gastrointestinal changes and disorders; Health care; Medical insurance; Medicare; Medications; Memory changes and loss; Mental impairment; Nursing and convalescent homes; Nutrition; Psychiatry, geriatric; Sensory changes; Sleep changes and disturbances; Thyroid disorders; Urinary problems; Vision changes and disorders; Vitamins and minerals.

**FOR FURTHER INFORMATION:**
Gomberg, Edith S. "Alcohol and Drugs." In *Encyclopedia of Gerontology: Age, Aging, and the Aged*, edited by James E. Birren. New York: Academic Press, 1996.

*Hearing on Adverse Drug Reactions in the Elderly.* Special Committee on Aging. U.S. Senate, 104th Congress, 2d session. Washington, D.C.: U.S. Government Printing Office, 1996.

Knight, Eric, and Jerry Avorn. "Older Adults' Misuse of Alcohol, Medicines, and Other Drugs." *The Gerontologist* 39, no. 1 (February, 1999): 109-111.

Lamy, P. P. "Physiological Changes Due to Age: Pharmacodynamic Changes of Drug Action and Implications for Therapy." *Drugs and Aging* 1 (September/October, 1991): 385-404.

Roberts, Jay. "Drug Interactions" and "Drug Reactions." In *The Encyclopedia of Aging*, edited by George L. Maddox. New York: Springer, 1995.

Winker, Margaret. "Managing Medicine." In *The Practical Guide to Aging*, edited by Christine Cassel. New York: New York University Press, 1999.

Woolhandler, Steffi, et al. "Inappropriate Drug Prescribing for the Community-Dwelling Elderly." *Journal of the American Medical Association* 272, no. 4 (July 27, 1994).

## PARENTHOOD

**RELEVANT ISSUES:** Family, psychology

**SIGNIFICANCE:** The role of parent continues into late life; for most elders, the positive aspects of this relationship far outweigh the negatives

Parenthood may not be a universal experience, but more than 80 percent of the adult population has at least one child. With the average life span increasing each decade, this means that most people alive today will spend most of the years of their lives as parents. This is a dramatic contrast to the situation in the early twentieth century, when the average life span was barely long enough to launch children into adulthood.

Today's generation of elders differs also in family composition. Families of the past had few generations but had many members in each generation, giving an older person during his or her lifetime many sons or daughters, a good number of siblings, plus a few grandchildren. Elders are now more apt to have fewer sons or daughters and fewer siblings, but chances are great that they will live to have grandchildren and great-grandchildren. In fact, most people in the United States over sixty-five are members of four-generation families.

Several pervasive, false myths pertain to the parental role in late life. One is that the role of parent ends at some point in the child's life, such as when the son or daughter reaches legal majority or moves out of the family home. This is no longer true of families in Western culture; according to anthropological surveys, it seems not to have been true in the past or in any other cultures. In almost all studies of family structure, contact between parents and their adult children continues after the children have married, even if they have moved to another location and become part of their new spouse's kinship group. In the United States, almost all parents over sixty-five

have regular communication of some kind with their adult children. Clearly, the myth of parenthood ending at any point in life is not based on valid evidence.

Another false myth of parenthood in later life is that the family unit now consists of young parents and their children, having shrunk from times past to exclude extended kin, such as grandparents. Census data on family units of the past show that extended families living under one roof were seldom a reality; furthermore, today's families have not excluded their elders, but instead include more generations than ever before. One in five adults between the ages of sixty-five and eighty-nine lives with his or her children and often grandchildren, and the proportion rises to one in two after the age of eighty-nine. Clearly the myth of truncated families is also a false one.

A third myth about parenthood in later life, equally false, is that there is a role reversal at some point in time during which the parents become like children and the adult children take over the parental role. Although this may be true in cases of extreme physical disability or dementia, almost all elders retain their roles as parents. Adult children

*As couples wait longer to have children and remarriage prompts the creation of second families, many people are finding themselves to be new parents in middle age.* (James L. Shaffer)

frequently assist in various tasks of daily living and even bring parents into their homes to live, but in very few instances do parents relinquish their status or do their children stop viewing them in their roles as mother and father.

### OLDER PARENTS AND ADULT CHILDREN

In addition to frequency of contact between older parents and their adult children, researchers have studied the types of contact these family members have and also factors that might influence which type of contact older adults have with their adult children. Most communicate via letters, telephone, and electronic mail (e-mail), but 40 percent of parents over the age of sixty-five have face-to-face contact with at least one of their children two or more times a week, and 20 percent see at least one of their children daily.

Among the factors that can affect frequency of contact between older parents and their adult children are gender, with daughters contacting parents more often than sons; race or ethnicity, with African Americans and Latinos contacting parents more often than Caucasians; stage of life, with young and middle-aged adults who have children at home contacting their parents less frequently than those who have either no children or whose children are already grown; age and health of parents, with adult children having more frequent contact as parents grow older or as their health declines; and socioeconomic group, with working-class families having more contact between parent and adult child than middle-class families.

Although it has been established that the relationship between parent and child is lifelong, the content of the parenting role changes. As children grow up and establish their own families, their childhood needs of parents as providers, protectors, and secure emotional bases change. Part of attaining maturity involves looking to oneself for the fulfillment of needs, perhaps through the process of developing mental representations of one's parents and using them as templates. Other needs formerly fulfilled by parents, such as secure emotional bases, are thought to be fulfilled by spouses. However, more than three-quarters of adults report that their relationships with their parents are emotionally close.

Although older parents do not typically provide financial support to their adult children, they do assist in time of need. This assistance includes lending money to an adult child for specific purposes, such as buying a house or starting a new business, or providing a home once again for an adult child who has serious needs because of illness or financial reversals. Another time older parents are particularly helpful to their adult children is in time of divorce, especially for daughters. Parents not only provide homes and financial assistance for their daughters, but they also may take over some aspects of the parental role if there are grandchildren. Grandfathers, especially, tend to provide the financial support and male influence that was previously the responsibility of their fathers. In some families, especially African American families, mothers play a substantial role in the lives of their adult daughters and often take over the responsibility of raising their grandchildren, even when the daughter is also living in the home. It is estimated that four million American children live in households headed by a grandparent; for one million of those children, the grandparent is the sole caregiver.

Older adults contribute more than tangible assistance to their adult children. Almost one-half of adults report receiving advice and counseling from their parents, particularly concerning health, work, family relationships, and finances. Middle-aged children, in turn, also offer advice to their parents, usually about where to live, how to handle their finances, and how to spend their time. Although more advice comes down from parent to child, older parents are more apt to act on the advice of their children than vice versa. Often the type of advice exchanged is specific to a particular family; that is, some families exchange advice between generations primarily about financial matters, while other families advise each other mainly on strengthening relationships within the family.

### BENEFITS OF PARENTHOOD IN LATER YEARS

Becoming a parent is a central goal and ultimate source of meaning for most people. The relationships parents have with their children are thought to shape them as individuals as much as the relationships they had in childhood with their own parents. One of the important psychological tasks of middle adulthood is theorized to be "generativity"—the need to create, to accomplish, to nurture. Although this can be done in many arenas, its most direct expression is found in having children and fostering their development into maturity. According to this theory, individuals who have accomplished this task are able to achieve higher levels of meaning in their lives than those who have not.

Besides individual fulfillment, parenthood also seems to contribute to marital happiness in later years. Older adult couples who are parents often have happier marriages than those who are not parents, although this is not true in the earlier years. Longitudinal research shows that during the years that parents have children living in the home, their assessments of marital happiness is lower than couples who have no children. Once the "nest is emptied," however, marital happiness increases. The difference is not a large one, but it is significant and consistently found in a number of studies. One explanation of these data is that couples who are parents spend more time and effort on effective parenting than on attaining marital happiness. Once the children are launched, they can focus again on each other, pleased that they have accomplished this important task together.

Less esoteric benefits of parenthood for older adults include the contribution adult children make to their welfare and well-being, including financial support and instrumental support. In nontechnical cultures, there is a direct economic benefit to having children, especially sons. Parents provide for children until they are grown, then the children provide for the parents as a fair exchange. This is not the general expectation of parents in the United States. Most parents consider themselves the providers for their children well into adulthood, and it is difficult when situations arise that make them unable to provide, or worse, force them to depend on their children. Although many adult children give to their parents financially and instrumentally, it is difficult when the parents feel they have become a burden. Optimal situations are found when elderly parents feel they are participating in a fair exchange with their children, such as baking a pie for the son who mows their grass each week or clipping grocery coupons for the daughter who drives them to doctors' appointments. Other elderly parents take pride in discussing their life insurance, family jewelry, or other inheritance they will leave for their helpful children.

Perhaps more important that instrumental help, adult children provide social and emotional support for their parents. After physical dependence, loneliness is the greatest fear of older adults. As age increases, the number of friends and acquaintances a person has decreases—some die, some become invalids in nursing homes, and others move away. Older adults who have children rely more and more on them for social and emotional support, especially if they are divorced or widowed. Research has shown that older adults who have close emotional ties to family members have better physical and psychological health than those who are isolated.

## NEGATIVE ASPECTS OF PARENTHOOD IN LATER YEARS

If older parents bask in the happiness and success of their adult children, the reverse is also true—having adult children who are troubled and unsuccessful can bring heartache and shame in the later years of life. Major problems reported by adults over sixty-five include concerns over their adult children's marital problems, financial problems, and physical and psychological health problems. Although these issues are unfortunate at any time, they are especially problematic in later years, when parents have fewer financial or emotional resources to offer.

Other negative aspects of parenthood in later life are intrusive children who often try to make decisions for their elderly parents on matters such as finances, health care, and living arrangements, regardless of the parents' own reasoning abilities. While some adult children no doubt have selfish motives of controlling the family resources, most are acting out of a sense of misplaced responsibility toward their parents or lack of knowledge about the normal aging process. Especially distressing for widowed parents are attempts by children to thwart social encounters with potential for romance. Whether out of loyalty to their deceased parent, motives to protect their future inheritance, or refusal to see one's older parent as having romantic interests, adult children can produce roadblocks when parents show an interest in seeking companionship or romance with a member of the opposite sex.

One surprising aspect of parenthood in old age is that having inattentive children does not pose a

*Parenthood does not end when children leave home—it is a lifetime relationship that grows and changes with age.* (Popperfoto/Archive Photos)

significant negative effect. Although adult children can be a major source of social support, older adults who have no children or who have inattentive or disinterested children report similar happiness if they have close relationships with their spouse or with close friends.

The truths of parenthood and aging are that multigenerational families are now common, that almost all older parents have frequent contact with all of their children and most have face-to-face contact with at least one child on a regular basis, and that parent-child role reversals in later years are not typical in physically and mentally healthy families. Parenthood can bring personal fulfillment, social support, and instrumental assistance as one ages. Drawbacks exist, but if one's adult children are reasonably happy and successful, if they allow parents to make their own major decisions as long as they remain capable, and if the parents have some close relationships with other family members or friends, the benefits far outweigh the negatives. —*Barbara R. Bjorklund*

**See also** Childlessness; Children of Aging Parents; Communication; Empty nest syndrome; Family relationships; Full nest; Grandparenthood; Marriage; Maturity; Multigenerational households; Skipped-generation parenting.

## FOR FURTHER INFORMATION:

Bee, Helen L., and Barbara R. Bjorklund. *The Journey of Adulthood.* 3d ed. Upper Saddle River, N.J.: Prentice Hall, 1999. This textbook is designed for undergraduate college students majoring in a number of subjects dealing with adulthood and aging. The book is written in a warm and friendly tone but includes research findings from a wide variety of fields that study the aging process. Particularly interesting are two chapters on social roles and relationships in adulthood.

Belsky, J. "Children and Marriage." In *The Psychology of Marriage*, edited by J. Fincham and T. Bradbury. New York: Guilford Press, 1990. Although Belsky researches the lives of young parents as they enter parenthood, the contrast to later stages of parenthood is valuable.

Bengtson, V. L., and W. A. Achenbaum. *The Changing Contract Across Generations.* New York: Aldine de Gruyter, 1993. This book offers a sociological perspective of parent-child relationships at different ages and in various cultures.

Erikson, Erik H. *Identity and the Life Cycle.* New York: Norton, 1980. Erikson, a leading neo-Freudian, discusses his theory of psychosocial development across the life cycle and the importance of parenthood (or similar generative endeavors) to the well-being of middle-aged and older adults.

Gutmann, D. L. "Parenthood: Key to the Comparative Psychology of the Life Cycle?" In *Life-Span Developmental Psychology: Normative Life Crises*, edited by N. Datan and L. Ginsberg. New York: Academic Press, 1975. This chapter discusses the vital importance of parenthood to humans and argues that it might very well be the organizing force in human lives across the entire life span.

Pillemer, K., and J. J. Suitor. "Relationships with Children and Distress in the Elderly." In *Parent-Child Relations Throughout Life*, edited by K. Pillemer and K. McCartney. Hillsdale, N.J.: Lawrence Erlbaum, 1991. This chapter discusses the effects on elderly parents of adult children's problems, such as physical disabilities, mental retardation, and psychological problems.

# PARKINSON'S DISEASE

**RELEVANT ISSUES:** Health and medicine

**SIGNIFICANCE:** Parkinson's disease arises from a progressive neural degeneration that leads to the death of specific cells deep within the brain; the disease has devastated the lives of millions of people

As the average life span has steadily increased, Parkinson's disease has become a growing problem; in 1999, there were approximately 500,000 patients with this disease in the United States alone. In fact, the number of people affected is higher than all patients of multiple sclerosis (MS), muscular dystrophy, and amyotrophic lateral sclerosis (Lou Gehrig's disease) combined. Most patients are above forty years old, although the disease has been found to affect younger people. A rare form of Parkinson's disease appears to also affect teenagers. Statistically, men have a higher incidence of the disease, and Caucasians are more affected than any other race.

## SYMPTOMS AND DIAGNOSIS

A human is born with all the brain cells (also known as neurons) he or she will ever have. This means that if, during lifetime, some of those neurons die, they will never be replaced. Extensive research has shown that people with Parkinson's disease have lost most of the neurons that produce dopamine, an important neurotransmitter that delivers messages within the brain. As the available dopamine is decreased, an imbalance of dopamine and acetylcholine occurs in the brain, leading to a lack of movement coordination.

Parkinson's disease is not diagnosed easily because various patients do not show the same symptoms and because there are no proven, specific tests for its identification. Moreover, Parkinson-like symptoms can often arise from head trauma or the use of tranquilizing drugs, such as phenothiazines and butyrophenones. Even carbon monoxide poisoning or Reglan, a common antidote against stomach upset, may provide these symptoms. The general diagnosis involves a neurological examination, which evaluates the symptoms and their severity. If the symptoms are judged as serious, a trial test of anti-Parkinson's drugs (such as primary levodopa) may be administered to establish the existence of the disease. If the patient fails to gain ground, other brain evaluations using such technology as computed tomography (CT) or magnetic resonance imaging (MRI) are used to rule out other diseases rather than certify the presence of Parkinson's disease.

Type A patients display an extensive degree of tremor, often on either the left or right side only, together with a muscle rigidity. Type B patients may not exhibit tremors at all but may show a great disturbance in balance and gait, as well as an inability to move easily. A more severe class involves the "Parkinson's plus" patients, whose cases are accompanied by six different types of neurological disorder, such as Shy-Drager syndrome, substantia nigra degeneration (SND), progressive supranuclear palsy (PSP), olivopontocerebellar atrophy (OPCA), or multisystem atrophy.

Despite the scientific breakthroughs in understanding various brain mechanisms, the cause of the disease is still unknown. In some cases, viral infections appear to have triggered the symptoms, such as in the worldwide encephalitis epidemic that took place between 1918 and 1922, in which the mortality rate reached 40 percent. Parkinson's disease has also been found among people whose pyramidal nervous system was damaged by the use of illegal drugs related to the narcotic painkiller meperidine (Demerol).

Comparisons of healthy and Parkinson's patients' brains have shown considerable differences in the substantia nigra and the striatum parts. Many of the substantia nigra's pigmented cells are damaged in the patients; instead of the normal black spots, they contain pink staining spheres called Lewy bodies. It is estimated that loss of approximately 80 percent of the substantia nigra's pigmented cells and 80 percent of the striatum's dopamine content results in the appearance of Parkinson's disease symptoms.

### HISTORY

Parkinson's disease took its name from nineteenth century British physician James Parkinson, who described the classic symptoms of resting tremor, propulsion, and stooped posture for the first time in a monograph entitled "An Essay on the Shaking Palsy" in 1817. In 1939, neurosurgeon Russell Meyers removed a brain tumor from a patient who also had Parkinson's disease. Further experimental surgery on the same patient involved a lesion in a neurosignal fiber bundle, called the ansa lenticularis, which reduced the patient's Parkinson's symptoms to a considerable degree. The same complex surgical procedure was later applied to about one hundred more people, thirty-nine of which showed improvement, while seventeen died.

In the early 1950's, Swedish neurosurgeon Lets Leksel applied a procedure called posterolateral pallidotomy to patients, with mixed results. In this approach, a small-diameter metal probe was inserted into the skull along the front hairline, deep into the globus pallidus part of the brain. However, missing the target by the smallest margin led to blindness or permanent impairment of other

*The problems with posture and tremors that can accompany Parkinson's disease make even simple tasks such as eating difficult.* (Ben Klaffke)

functions. Thirty years later, several other Swedish neurosurgeons attempted to implant surgically in the brain parts of the patient's adrenal gland that produces dopamine. Success, however, remained elusive. In 1985, Lauri Laitenen proposed a modified procedure of Leksel's original pallidotomy, called PVP pallidotomy. The process involved attaching a calibrated metal halo to the patient's head. The use of CT or MRI pictures with the calibration of the halo allowed the identification of the exact target spot during the surgery.

Transplanting small parts of live tissue from aborted fetuses into the brains of Parkinson's disease patients appeared to gain ground in the war against the disease in the late 1980's. This process, also called fetal tissue transplant, first involved fetal adrenal gland tissue and later fetal brain tissue and served as an attempt to enhance the production of more dopamine in the patient's brain. Pioneering neurosurgeons who used this procedure included Laitenen in Sweden, Z. S. Tang in China, and Robert Iacono in the United States. A fetal bank was established in Hua Shan Hospital in Shanghai, China, where the fetal brain tissue was held under cryogenic conditions. The actual transplants took place in China, since a long-standing ban on fetal tissue research made this kind of surgery practically impossible in the United States.

### TREATMENT

Apart from surgery, type A and B patients can be helped by medication prescription or neurosurgery. The primary medications are classified as anticholinergics, antihistamines, dopaminergics, and dopamine agonists. Unfortunately, all drugs used have side effects that may create a serious impact on the quality of life. Drug therapy attempts to maintain the patient on conservative levels of medication while maintaining mobility. Side effects include dry mouth, constipation, blurred vision, visual hallucinations, lethargy, confusion, and nausea.

Levodopa is the drug of choice for treatment of Parkinson's disease and is marketed as a mixture with carbidopa. Carbidopa is used as a blocker of the breakdown of levodopa in the peripheral organs in order to allow more levodopa to cross the blood-brain barrier. Through a series of complex enzymatic reactions, levodopa is converted to dopamine. As the disease progresses, however, the patients need much larger quantities of levodopa. During the administration of the medicine, patients appear to have a surge of energy, which quickly wears off as time elapses.

Interestingly, symptoms on the left side of the patient are relieved with an operation on the right part of the brain, and vice versa. Moreover, a brain whose problems arise from the death of some of the neurons can show signs of improvement by deadening some more of those cells in the critically overstimulated pathways. Thus, the activity that would result if all of the brain's circuits carried action commands appears to be controlled.

During the overall surgical procedure, the patient is awake and only lightly anesthetized, responding to the surgeon's commands to move various parts of the body, such as hands, fingers, eyes, toes, and tongue. With the help of the MRI pictures, the surgeon can pinpoint the cells that are to be neutralized. A probe is slowly entered into the brain, and its tip sends an electric signal back to the control panel, indicating the overall geogra-

phy of the brain map. Once it reaches the target spot, an electrical shock is applied at the probe tip that kills the overreacting cells. The patient has absolutely no feeling, and the electrical "cauterization" has no effect on the nearby capillaries and the blood flowing in them. The probe is then removed, and the penetrated skin is stitched up. After the surgery, the patient displays much less muscle tightening, as well as dramatic decreases in tremors. In most cases, the patient stays one night in the hospital for observation, then walks with no help out of the hospital the next day.

*—Soraya Ghayourmanesh*

**See also** Brain changes and disorders; Illnesses among the elderly; Mobility problems.

**FOR FURTHER INFORMATION:**

Bunting, L. K., and B. Fitzsimmons. "Depression in Parkinson's Disease." *Journal of Neuroscience Nursing* 23, no. 3 (June, 1991).

Cram, David L. *Understanding Parkinson's Disease: A Self-Help Guide.* Omaha, Nebr.: Addicus Books, 1999.

Duvoisin, Roger C., and Jacob Sage. *Parkinson's Disease: A Guide for Patient and Family.* 4th ed. Philadelphia: Lippincott-Raven, 1996.

Gerfen, C. R., et al. "D1 and D2 Dopamine Receptor-Regulated Gene Expression of Striatonigral and Striatopallidal Neurons." *Science* 250, no. 4,986 (December 7, 1990).

Giovannini, P., et al. "Early Onset Parkinson's Disease." *Movement Disorders* 6, no. 1 (1991).

Jahanshahi, Marjan, and C. David Marsden. *Parkinson's Disease: A Self-Help Guide for Patients and Their Careers.* London: Souvenir Press, 1998.

# PENSIONS

**RELEVANT ISSUES:** Economics, work

**SIGNIFICANCE:** Pension plans enable regular income or annuity payments to a retired former employee who is eligible for pension benefits through advanced age, total earnings, or years of service. Benefits may also be paid following total disability or job termination, with payments made to surviving beneficiaries following the death of the covered worker

Americans are becoming increasingly concerned about pension benefits following retirement because they are living longer: In the late 1990's, men could expect to live approximately fifteen more years after reaching sixty-five years of age, whereas women could expect to live approximately nineteen more years. Many financial and retirement planning professionals recommend that retirees plan for an income of 70 to 80 percent of their final annual work income in order to maintain a comfortable lifestyle for themselves and their spouses for the duration of the life span.

Congress has enacted several laws allowing workers to plan for their retirement that provide strong financial incentives for both employers and employees to set aside additional retirement funds by making them deductible from their current federal income taxes. Monies put into pension plans are allowed to accumulate on a tax-free basis until withdrawn during retirement, thus creating one of the best tax shelters available for persons with middle-class incomes.

## A HISTORY OF PENSION PLANS

The Roman Empire was the first government on record to establish pension plans for the provision of housing and board benefits for their disabled and aged soldiers. This practice was followed much later by the governments of France and Britain, as persons holding government offices began passing legislation to make retirement provisions for themselves by the early nineteenth century.

Although various forms of primitive pension plans have been awarded to American war veterans since the founding of the United States, the earliest highly organized American pensions were developed by railroad, banking, and public utility firms beginning in the late 1870's. Metropolitan Life Insurance Company issued the first group annuity contract in 1921, with the Equitable Life Assurance Society following suit and entering the pension business in 1924. By 1940, however, less than 20 percent of employees in business and government were covered by private pension plans.

Immediately following World War II, tremendous growth was seen in pension coverage of private citizens. By 1982, approximately 50 percent of all private business workers and 75 percent of all government workers were enrolled in some form of retirement program other than Social Security. As greater taxes began to be imposed on large corporations, particularly those that were highly profitable, financial incentives were established by the federal government to encourage the business sector to create pension plans for its employees.

## TYPES OF RETIREMENT BENEFITS

Pension plans offered by private employers are generally identified as being insured or trustee, group or individual, private or public, contributory or noncontributory, fixed or variable benefit, and single employer or multiemployer. Insured plans involve a life insurer as the funding agency, whereas a trust fund plan involves a commercial bank or individual trustee as the funding agency. Both funding methods are employed in a split-funded or combination plan. Insured plans enable the insurance company to invest the contributions and pay the retirement benefits using an allocated funding contract or an unallocated funding method.

Allocated funding contracts involve cash-value life insurance or deferred annuities that are immediately purchased for each employee. Individual policies, generally utilized by smaller businesses, are funded through individual insurance such as whole-life or retirement income contracts that deliver payment upon retirement. Group deferred annuities plans involve single premium annuities that are purchased yearly and then credited to individualized accounts.

Unallocated funding methods make up a vast majority of all insured plans and enable funds to accumulate and be used later to purchase annuities for employees upon retirement. Group deposit administration plans involve the accumulation and investment of employers' deposits to be used later to purchase annuities upon retirement. Immediate participation guarantee plans involve the immediate and full participation of the employer in the plan's investment, with the covered worker paid directly from the fund following retirement. Guaranteed investment contracts generally involve larger pension funds by which the insurer guarantees somewhat higher rates of interest for a period of several years.

Under a defined contribution arrangement such as a 401K plan, profit sharing, or money purchase plan, the employer, employee, or both contribute funds directly into the pension. This money is usually invested into one of several different mutual funds, with many plans leaving the specific allocations up to the individual worker. The money contributed is exempt from current income tax, with the earnings continuing to accumulate tax-free until retirement, when regular withdrawals begin to be made. Most pensions will pay benefits either in equal monthly payments or in a lump sum, depending upon the wishes of the retiree. Some plans may require that workers take a lump-sum distribution if they leave their jobs before retirement and the total value of their benefits is $3,500 or less. If the value of the benefits is greater than $3,500, workers may be given the choice of an immediate lump-sum payment or monthly payments that begin at retirement as specified in the plan. Choosing to take a lump-sum payment gives workers the choice of investing the money or spending it as they desire. Unless the funds are placed in an individual retirement account (IRA), however, the full amount received is taxable in the year that it was received. The only exception is "forward income averaging," which is available to persons receiving pension funds after 59.5 years of age. If the retiree is under age 59.5, the pension plan administrator is required to withhold 20 percent of pension funds and immediately forward that money to the Internal Revenue Service (IRS).

## GOVERNMENT REGULATION OF PENSION PLANS

Because the Social Security system in the United States was never designed to provide, and is not capable of providing, a majority of the income necessary following retirement, Congress has enacted laws encouraging both employers and employees to set aside additional funds for retirement. Some pension plans are designed to integrate the payments that retired workers receive with the amount of Social Security benefits provided.

The 1930's saw U.S. citizens become increasingly more concerned about the need to provide for their personal retirement, in addition to that of their spouses and other family members that survive them. This social and increasingly political movement culminated in the late 1940's, when the automobile, coal, and steel unions pushed to make pension plans one of the central issues in their labor negotiations. Pushes by various labor unions for pension benefits were assisted by a National Labor Relations Board (NLRB) ruling in 1948 that employers had a legal obligation to bargain with employees over the specific terms of the pension

plans offered. Military pensions are covered by the Servicemen's and Veteran's Survivor Benefits Act of 1957, whereby retired service men and women receive 50 percent of their base pay at time of retirement following twenty years of service, with regular increases as determined by the consumer price index.

The Federal Welfare and Pension Plan Disclosure Act of 1958—in combination with the Internal Revenue Code of 1921, which qualified taxation issues—provided the initial regulation of pension plans. A pension plan that qualified provided considerable tax advantages to the employer, such as the deduction of employer contributions as a business expense. These contributions are not considered taxable income until after payments begin following retirement. Investment earnings on assets are not taxable, and installment death benefits and lump-sum severance distributions also receive very favorable tax treatment.

The extremely complex Employee Retirement Income Security Act (ERISA) of 1974 allowed comprehensive regulation of pension plans from their inception to termination and greatly strengthened retirement benefits, mainly by reinforcing previous regulations. A major goal of ERISA was to protect the benefit rights of workers regarding pension qualification, participation, funding, vesting, actuarial soundness, plan termination, management of assets, annual reports, and fiduciary responsibility.

This act also established the Pension Benefit Guaranty Corporation, which administers plan termination insurance, thus assuring some level of benefits for pensions that are terminated as a result of inadequate funding. However, this federal insurance would not necessarily replace all benefits in the event that the employer and the related pension plan were not able to remain financially stable. Coverage by the Pension Benefit Guaranty Corporation does not extend to defined contribution plans or to other important benefits such as health or life insurance.

The Retirement Equity Act of 1984 and the Tax Reform Act of 1986 set the minimum standards for pension plans in private industry. Although these and other federal laws made several regulations for pension plans, employers are not legally required to provide any pension benefits whatsoever to workers. Although federal law protects some retired workers in the event that a company attempts to terminate their previously established pension contract, there is presently no similar protection when an employer terminates, for example, the health care benefits of retirees. An increasing number of workers who retire before age sixty-five and thus are not yet eligible for Medicare find themselves temporarily without health insurance as more companies are legally reducing health care benefits for early retirees.

### VESTING AND RETIREMENT AGE

The term "vesting" describes the covered worker's right to the monies contributed from the employer to the pension plan in the event that employment is terminated prior to retirement. Cliff vesting involves full vesting not later than following five years of service if the pension is administered by a single employer. Multiemployer pensions involve a collectively bargained plan to which more than one employer makes contributions and within which full vesting must occur no later than following ten years of service. Graded vesting requires that employees be at least 20 percent vested after three years of service and receive an additional 20 percent in each of the next four service years, so that they are fully vested after seven years. Workers have no vesting rights until they complete the appropriate years of service. Contributions made directly by workers to a pension plan, in addition to interest, are always fully vested.

Pension plans generally allow the retirement age categories of normal, early, or late. Normal retirement at age sixty-five corresponds with eligibility for Social Security benefits. Early retirement with an appropriately reduced pension is generally allowable if the employee is at least fifty-five years of age and has paid into the pension plan for at least ten years. Mandatory retirement before age seventy was prohibited in 1978 by an amendment to the Age Discrimination in Employment Act. Extremely late retirement (beyond seventy years of age) with increased benefits is then provided, but many pensions now simply pay normal retirement benefits even following late retirement to encourage retirement at age sixty-five.

### REGULAR CHECKS ON PENSION PLANS

The Employee Retirement Income Security Act (ERISA) of 1974 requires employers to provide written information regarding pension plans available to their covered employees. Summary plan descriptions, to be received within ninety days by all covered workers after becoming participants, provide information on operation of the pension plan, eligibility of a covered worker or surviving spouse to receive benefits, calculation of the anticipated benefits to be received, and the filing of claims. Federal law also dictates that any changes in the summary plan are to be provided within 210 days of the end of the plan year in which the change took place and that annual reports of the plan be available. Covered workers also have the right to receive an Individual Benefit Statement, which relates vesting status and the accumulated benefits in the plan.

ERISA also established complicated rules that prevent workers from losing pension benefits for a break in service, which depend on the timing of the break in employment and how long the break lasts. Employees can obtain information regarding the financial stability of their pension plan by requesting a copy of the plan's annual federal tax return from the U.S. Department of Labor Disclosure Office.

### PENSION RIGHTS FOR SURVIVING SPOUSES

Federal law requires that pension plans provide benefits for surviving spouses. Once an employee becomes fully or partially vested in a pension, survivor benefits are guaranteed upon death of the covered worker. This does not mean, however, that benefits are paid immediately in the event of death of a covered worker before retirement. For example, if the pension allowed early retirement benefits at age fifty-five and the covered worker died at age fifty, the surviving spouse would not receive benefits until the date that the worker would have turned age fifty-five. Additionally, the amount of payment is often only 50 percent of what would have been received if the covered worker had lived until retirement age and then retired.

When a covered worker dies after retirement, joint and survivor benefits require that the surviving spouse receive 50 percent of the previously received benefits, with payments continuing until the death of the survivor. Spouses are able to waive survivor benefits to get a larger monthly pension during the covered worker's retirement, but this is only recommended if the spouse is suffering from a terminal illness. —*Daniel G. Graetzer*

*See also* Age discrimination; Age Discrimination in Employment Act of 1967; Early retirement; Employment; Estates and inheritance; Forced retirement; 401K plans; Income sources; Individual retirement accounts (IRAs); Job loss; Older Worker Benefit Protection Act; Politics; Retirement; Retirement planning; Social Security; Widows and widowers.

### FOR FURTHER INFORMATION:

Gaudio, Peter E., and Virginia S. Nicols. *Your Retirement Benefits*. New York: Wiley, 1992. This excellent text highlights old-age pensions, pension trusts, and retirement planning.

Harris, Dan R. *The Aging Sourcebook: Basic Information on Issues Affecting Older Americans*. Detroit: Omnigraphics, 1998. An often-referenced resource manual that includes information on pensions as related to demographic trends, legal rights, and retirement lifestyle options.

Karpel, Craig S. *The Retirement Myth*. New York: HarperCollins, 1995. Describes what future retirees should know now regarding job security, pension plans, Social Security, the stock market, and housing prices.

Matthews, Joseph L., and Dorothy Matthews Berman. *Social Security, Medicare, and Pensions: Get the Most out of Your Retirement and Medical Benefits*. Thorndike, Maine: G. K. Hall, 1996. Highlights laws and legislation regarding pension trusts and Social Security.

Mooney, F. Bentley. *Creating and Preserving Wealth: Expert, Practical Advice You Can Use to Protect Your Estate*. Chicago: Probus, 1991. A well-written text that adequately meets its title. Gives practical advice about common decisions that retiring workers have to make regarding pensions.

Runde, Robert H., and J. Barry Zischang. *The Commonsense Guide to Estate Planning*. Burr Ridge, Ill.: Business One Irwin, 1994. A well-written text on personal finance and tax shelters, with several references to pensions.

U.S. Department of Labor. *What You Should Know About Pension Law*. Washington, D.C.: U.S. Pension and Welfare Benefits Administration, 1999. Provides information regarding the federal laws that regulate pensions. Available free from the Pension Benefit Guaranty Corporation.

## PERSONALITY CHANGES

**RELEVANT ISSUES:** Biology, psychology, sociology

**SIGNIFICANCE:** One of the fundamental questions regarding human functioning is whether personality changes or remains stable throughout the life course

Being able to predict what people will be like when they are older is a challenge to both professionals and laypersons. The impact of age upon people entails an investigation into styles of reacting, thinking, and feeling—better known as personality. Trying to unlock and identify the mechanisms underlying personality—as well as determining whether the essential characteristics of people change across the life course—is perplexing. Part of the problem stems from the lack of a comprehensive, universally accepted definition of personality.

This diversity in meaning stems from fundamental differences in how human functioning is viewed and is best conceptualized by clarifying the dimensions upon which personality is described and explained. Those seeking to explain the origin of personality generally concentrate on the roles of inheritance (biology) and experiential (environmental) factors in the development and sustainability of the essential qualities and characteristics of individuals. Another debate exists between the optimistic view that a person's character may change over time and the notion that by the age of thirty the character is stable. Although there are a number of other dimensions used to clarify differences in perspectives regarding personality functioning, the notions of inheritance-experience and change-stability are the primary points of comparison.

### STABILITY PERSPECTIVES

Perspectives that emphasize the role of biology in personality development have roots that go back to early Greek philosophy. However, contemporary views can be divided into two camps. The first incorporates theories referred to as psychoanalytic. Austrian psychoanalyst Sigmund Freud's view of human nature personifies this camp. Freud's notions regarding personality development revolve around satisfaction of biological urges and the belief that personality is frozen at adolescence. The second camp incorporates a view of human nature relying upon the biological concept of traits to describe and explain personality. The view that traits are psychological entities subscribes to the assumption that personality is made up of enduring and relatively stable characteristics, and differences among individuals merely reside in how much of each characteristic they possess. These characteristics may incorporate behavioral, mental, emotional, or temperamental traits. However, there appear to be just five dimensions or domains (neuroticism, extraversion, openness to experience, conscientiousness, and agreeableness), along with their associated traits, upon which everyone may be evaluated. Scientific studies originating from this particular camp find that adult personality changes very little and support the notion that by the age of thirty, the character is set. Although some psychological research supports biologically based contributions to the underlying stable nature of personality, there is a great deal of controversy and mixed results regarding whether characteristics or attributes of a more global nature can change well into advanced age.

Perspectives that subscribe to assumptions that people's character may change with age are more numerous and diverse. These views acknowledge the contributions that biology has made in the underlying nature of personality; however, they also emphasize and identify factors external to the person that may be responsible for change later in the life course.

### Self-Notions

There are a number of different positions regarding the role of external factors in personality change. One position has its origins in psychoanalysis. Unlike Freud's view, this view of personality is quite distinct in that growth, development, and change are thought to occur well into advanced age. The defining factor here is the concept of self (who one is). It is thought to evolve over the life course and allow individuals to unite both positive and negative aspects within themselves into an integrated, balanced, and whole notion of who they are. Some individuals never achieve an integrated personality, while others find that age grants them the ability to turn inward (introversion) and explore their inner selves. Whereas in youth, turning toward the outer world (extroversion) is paramount—establishing careers, finding

mates—the primary duty of the older person is to turn toward the inner, subjective world—acknowledging eventual mortality and abandoning youthful self-images. Although this position initially focuses on internal biological factors in personality functioning, it also enlists the aid of the external world in its definition and strongly supports the notion of change across the life course as fundamental.

Self, as a defining characteristic of personality, is also used by a number of other positions. Once again, these notions focus upon internal aspects of the individual; however, they are not strictly biological. The notion of self is a psychological construct and is composed of a number of related but separable facets. Similar to the trait concept, it helps explain, describe, and define personality; however, because it is a psychological concept, as opposed to a biological one, aspects of the self are thought to interact with the environment. Many scholars in this area, as well as such related disciplines as sociology, see the developing self as an outgrowth of interactions with others; self and its formation is a social phenomenon. The ways that people view and mentally represent themselves in the past, present, and future are pivotal to understanding whether personality changes or remains stable with age. Research in this area tends to support the potential for personality change, as well as the sustainability of it.

### Stage Concepts

The idea that there is a predictable sequence of age-related changes is another predominant view. Such normative crises models claim that changes in personality emerge as a result of adults progressing through a series of stages (life tasks), which are often marked by age-related role expectations and emotional crises. The notion of the midlife crisis, in which the early to mid-forties is thought to be a stressful period of time in which individuals reevaluate and reappraise their lives and change their personalities and lifestyles, is somewhat of a misnomer; however, the idea epitomizes these crises-model approaches.

Although these views emphasize commonality in personality change, they also leave room for variability in the human experience by focusing on changing personal meanings and values over the life course. This suggests that not everyone reacts in a similar way and that lives may not follow exactly the same course. The defining characteristic of personality advocated by these positions lies within the individual in the guise of age, but it is also impacted by age-related role expectations and life tasks constructed by society that are external to the individual.

### LIFE AND HISTORICAL EVENTS

Life experiences and historical events may also play a role in personality changes in later adulthood. Personality psychologists who emphasize life events (marriage, parenthood, retirement) as markers of change define and describe personality according to the various roles that people assume during the life course (spouse, parent, grandparent, worker), as well as to the historical influences (the Great Depression, World War II) embedded within those roles. According to this timing-of-events model, the "social clock" consists of cultural norms and expectations regarding when certain life events should occur. Life events that are anticipated and on time are less stressful than unanticipated, unusual events or events that occur at the "wrong" time. Being forced into an early retirement because of a physical disability would produce stress for many individuals and constitutes a life-altering event that not only is unanticipated but also occurs at the wrong time.

Historical events, such as the Great Depression of the 1930's and World War II, are also pivotal to understanding personality change. Scholars have found that boys whose family incomes were reduced by more than one-third during the Depression were profoundly impacted by the economic hardship. Men and women who had direct contact with war activities during World War II were, as older adults, more assertive and showed greater social competence and self-reliance than their cohorts who had no such experiences.

Overall, these personality models focus primarily upon social cultural constructs, external to the individual, to understand change and stability. Their exploration into both historical and social contexts does not easily support change over stability with respect to the effect of age on personality. However, this line of inquiry does support the importance of including both historical and social contexts in the study of personality development.

—*Rosellen M. Rosich*

*See also* Alzheimer's disease; Brain changes and disorders; Creativity; Dementia; Depression; Erikson, Erik H.; *Fountain of Age, The*; Maturity; Medications; Psychiatry, geriatric; Successful aging; Wisdom.

#### FOR FURTHER INFORMATION:

Friedan, Betty. *The Fountain of Age*. New York: Simon & Schuster, 1993.

Levinson, Daniel. *The Seasons of a Man's Life*. New York: Alfred A. Knopf, 1978.

_____. *The Seasons of a Woman's Life*. New York: Alfred A. Knopf, 1996.

Liebert, Robert M., and Lynn L. Liebert. *Liebert and Spiegler's Personality: Strategies and Issues*. 8th ed. Pacific Grove, Calif.: Brooks/Cole, 1998.

McCrae, Robert R., and Paul T. Costa. *Personality in Adulthood*. New York: Guilford Press, 1990.

Papalia, Diane E., Cameron J. Camp, and Ruth Duskin Feldman. *Adult Development and Aging*. New York: McGraw-Hill, 1996.

Perlmutter, M., and Elizabeth Hall. *Adult Development and Aging*. 2d ed. New York: John Wiley & Sons, 1992.

## PETS

**RELEVANT ISSUES:** Economics, family, health and medicine, recreation

**SIGNIFICANCE:** Elderly people who own or interact with pets often experience psychosocial and health benefits that impact quality of life

Pet ownership or interaction with companion animals has been found to contribute to psychological, social, and physical health and well-being, all important aspects of quality of life for the elderly. Pet ownership or contact appears to be associated with lower levels of anxiety and depression. The presence of animals appears to increase smiling, touch, and talk. Researchers report that animal interaction also tends to increase happiness and morale, alertness, feelings of affection, and security.

Elderly men and women, particularly those who live alone, may experience loneliness. Pet ownership can reduce loneliness by providing companionship and opportunities for socialization, interaction, play, and affection. Such effects may be direct, as a result of contact with affectionate and playful animals. Pet ownership may also reduce loneliness in indirect ways. For example, it has been found that elderly dog owners go for walks more frequently than nonowners. During such walks, opportunities for socialization with other people often arise. Indeed, there is a growing recognition that pet presence has the potential for giving people an excuse and a topic for conversation and that pets may function as "social lubricants" for their owners.

### HEALTH AND ECONOMIC BENEFITS

Pet ownership or contact appears to be associated with better health. Research shows that pet ownership or interaction reduces the risk of cardiovascular disease, heart attack, and stroke. Compared with nonowners, pet owners appear to have lower cardiovascular risk factors, lower systolic blood pressure, lower serum cholesterol, and lower triglyceride levels. Similarly, of people hospitalized for cardiovascular disease, pet owners have a greater chance of still being alive one year later than do those who do not own pets. Having (and

*A man with Alzheimer's disease pets his dog. The love and companionship provided by a pet are especially valuable in old age and can help alleviate the psychological effect of some age-related conditions.* (Ben Klaffke)

looking at) an aquarium of goldfish has been found to reduce stress and lower blood pressure in people already suffering from high blood pressure. Having a parakeet has been found to increase the health of noninstitutionalized British pensioners. Further, some aspects of pet ownership encourage healthy behaviors. For example, elderly dog owners appear to get more exercise than people who do not own dogs, probably because they take their dogs for walks.

Pet ownership may also have economic benefits. It appears that senior citizens who own pets visit the doctor less often and live longer than those who do not own pets. For example, a 1990 study of Medicare beneficiaries belonging to a large California health maintenance organization found that dog ownership was associated with fewer physician contacts. Similarly, a 1996 review of effects of pet ownership on health costs in Australia concluded that pet ownership could save Australia $800 million to $1.5 billion in its national health budget. Recognizing the economic implications of such findings, several insurance companies (such as Midland Life Insurance) have begun to offer reduced rates to pet owners.

### NEGATIVES OF PET OWNERSHIP FOR THE ELDERLY

Pets may also have negative effects on quality of life of the elderly. Animal care may be an economic burden that is beyond the means of some elderly people. The financial cost of feed, particularly for larger pets, and costs of veterinary care, particularly for older or ailing pets, may be unmanageable. Animal care may also require energy and strength beyond the abilities of some elderly people, particularly as the person's health declines. Larger, more energetic pets (some dogs, for example) could unintentionally hurt fragile or infirm elderly people by knocking them down. Further, not all pets are capable of interaction with humans. Goldfish provide less interaction than do dogs and cats. Some interactions may be harmful. Dogs may bite; cats may scratch. Finally, the death of a beloved pet may lead to considerable grief and distress.

Concerns about animal care and well-being may keep some elderly people from traveling, visiting relatives, and maintaining relationships with family or loved ones. Similarly, such concerns may delay or prevent some elderly people from getting the health care they need, as when they postpone an operation that requires hospitalization because they have no arrangements for pet care.

Concerns about pet care and well-being keep many elderly people from moving into apartments, nursing homes, or other assisted-living facilities, which tend to prohibit pets. Giving up a beloved pet in order to move into an apartment or nursing home may be as emotionally painful as a divorce or death for some elderly people. Indeed, many of the pets that are taken to vets or animal shelters in such situations are euthanized. As this problem is recognized, more nursing homes and assisted care facilities are adopting "pro-pet" policies. For example, residential care facilities operated by the Anchor Trust in England allow elderly residents to keep their pets.

### PET-ASSISTED THERAPY IN NURSING HOMES

Animal presence or contact has been found to increase social interaction, friendliness, cooperation, and self-care behaviors among elderly residents of nursing homes. Even having a wild bird feeder (and being given responsibility for it) has been found to increase happiness and activity in a nursing home setting. Observations of the positive effects of direct contact and interaction with animals have resulted in a dramatic growth, in recent years, of pet visitation programs in the United States. In the typical pet visitation program, volunteers bring their companion animals to interact with nursing home residents on a regular schedule. Research suggests that male residents of nursing homes, who tend to be less social and more reclusive than female residents, tend to benefit more and faster than female residents, who may be more adept at getting their needs met by interaction with humans. Research also suggests that the positive effects of contact with animals are not permanent. That is, for the positive effects to be maintained, the visits must be continued on a regular basis. Recognizing this, a growing number of facilities are providing resident companion animals for their patients as part of treatment programming. As nursing home and other health care facilities gain experience with pet-assisted therapy, issues have arisen regarding selection, training, and certification of both animals and their owners.

*—John W. Engel*

*Studies show that residents in nursing homes benefit physically and emotionally from contact with animals.* (Digital Stock)

***See also*** Death and dying; Depression; Grief; Health care; Loneliness; Nursing and convalescent homes; Psychiatry, geriatric; Social ties.

### FOR FURTHER INFORMATION:

Barba, Beth E. "A Critical Review of Research on the Human/Companion Animal Relationship." *Anthrozoos: A Multidisciplinary Journal of the Interactions of People and Animals* 8, no. 1 (1995).

Beck, Alan, and Aaron Katcher. *Between Pets and People: The Importance of Animal Companionship.* West Lafayette, Ind.: Purdue University Press, 1996.

Burch, Mary R. *Volunteering with Your Pet.* New York: Macmillan, 1996.

Crowley-Robinson, Patricia, and Judith K. Blackshaw. "Pet Ownership and Health Status of Elderly in the Community." *Anthrozoos: A Multidisciplinary Journal of the Interactions of People and Animals* 11, no. 3 (1998).

Cusack, Odean. *Pets and Mental Health.* New York: Haworth Press, 1988.

Cusack, Odean, and Elaine Smith. *Pets and the Elderly: The Therapeutic Bond.* New York: Haworth Press, 1984.

Palika, Liz. *Love on a Leash.* Loveland, Colo.: Alpine, 1996.

Perelle, Ira B., and Diane A. Granville. "Assessment of the Effectiveness of a Pet Facilitated Therapy Program in a Nursing Home Setting." *Society and Animals* 1, no. 1 (1993).

Sussman, Marvin B., ed. *Pets and the Family.* New York: Haworth Press, 1985.

Wilson, Cindy C., and Dennis C. Turner, eds. *Companion Animals in Human Health.* Thousand Oaks, Calif.: Sage Publications, 1998.

# PNEUMONIA

**RELEVANT ISSUES:** Death, health and medicine
**SIGNIFICANCE:** Pneumonia, an inflamed state of the lower lung, is a leading cause of sickness and death in those over the age of sixty-five, especially in individuals confined to nursing homes

Pneumonia has been a common and often lethal disease for centuries. "Captain of the men of death" was a description given to pneumonia by Sir William Osler over one hundred years ago. At the beginning of the nineteenth century, before the advent of antibiotics, pneumonia was responsible for the deaths of about 1 per 1,000 persons each year in the United States. The majority of these cases were caused by streptococcal infections.

In the era of antibiotics, the face of pneumonia has changed. Streptococcal pneumonia is no longer the major threat. In persons under sixty-five years of age and otherwise in good health, atypical organisms are found as increasing causes of pneumonia. Pneumonia is generally curable with current antibiotics; this type is sometimes called walking pneumonia. In about 80 percent of cases, it is treated at home with very good outcomes.

As the body ages, however, its defenses against microorganisms decrease. Older people are more susceptible to different microbiological organisms that are causing pneumonia in increasing numbers. In addition, with age, the body has an increasing chance of suffering from concomitant illnesses, such as diabetes, lung disease, heart disease, and malignant tumors. This situation increases the susceptibility to pneumonia.

Sociological factors also play a role. Aging increases the chance of not being able to remain at home for daily needs. Some individuals must enter nursing home facilities. Immobility and exposure to many bacterial and viral illnesses in a closed environment further predispose the body to the development of pneumonia.

## SYMPTOMS AND DIAGNOSIS

Pneumonia is an inflamed state of the lower lung, including the lung sacs (alveoli) and the smaller bronchial passages. In the majority of cases, the inflammation is caused by virulent bacteria and viruses that have entered these lower airways in sufficient numbers to overwhelm the lung defenses.

Most of the time, the response of the lung defense system is adequate to meet the infective challenge. The lungs call forth locally and from distant sites special cells that help to fight and contain the inflammation. Some of these cells also promote healing. If the defenses are sluggish, as might be seen in the very elderly, or if the person has chronic lung disease with poor phlegm ejection, pneumonia is more likely to develop. In addition, persons with diabetes and chronic kidney disease show a slower entry of the protective white cells into the inflamed area to fight off the infection.

Physicians or other health care workers use many different signs and symptoms to diagnose pneumonia. There is usually a fever of 100 degrees Fahrenheit or higher in younger individuals. In the elderly, however, the fever may be lacking. A rise in temperature is noted about 80 percent of the time in the diagnosis of pneumonia. In addition, one expects to see coughing that produces phlegm, as well as shortness of breath. The breathing rate, which is normally between ten and sixteen breaths per minute, is usually above twenty breaths. Upon examination, the health care provider may hear abnormal sounds in the lung, which suggests pneumonia. All these symptoms may be reduced, however, in the elderly above the age of seventy and in those individuals who have lost their ability for independent activity. The only telltale signs of pneumonia may be a breathing rate of thirty to thirty-five breaths per minute and a change in mental status, with confusion apparent.

Strictly speaking, an X ray showing abnormal shadows in the lungs is needed to confirm a suspected diagnosis of pneumonia. This finding may be falsely lacking, however, if the patient is very dehydrated or if the body cannot produce enough protective white cells to create a significant shadow on the X ray. In practice, many times an X ray is not taken, since more than 85 percent of the suspected cases of pneumonia acquired in the community will heal with the antibiotics available. In patients who display a high fever that does not respond in forty-eight to seventy-two hours and who remain sick with a breathing rate above thirty, low oxygen in the blood, and continued confusion, X rays are needed. In the most severe cases, a computed tomography (CT) scan of the chest is performed. The most severe cases of pneumonia are frequently seen in patients who have poor infection-fighting ability. Laboratory tests may be required to make a diagnosis of pneumonia and to plan the correct therapy. Testing includes measuring the number of white blood cells in the blood, searching for the offending infective agent in the blood, and performing other nonspecific indicators of severe infection. In severe and complicated pneumonias, a specialized needle may be inserted into the pleural space around the lungs to help diagnose and treat the pneumonia.

Once the diagnosis of pneumonia has been made, the next decision is whether to hospitalize the patient. In general, this assessment cannot be made with absolute certainty, but guidelines for the practitioner are available. When pooled together, these factors suggest and predict which patients would do better in a hospital environment. Factors predicting poorer outcome are age greater than sixty-five, preexisting disease or diseases, cough, mental confusion, fever above 101 degrees Fahrenheit, a breathing rate above thirty-five breaths per minute, and the presence of significant noise in the chest on physical examination.

### TREATMENT

Decisions about therapy for pneumonia, especially therapeutic action taken outside the hospital, often need to be made without knowing the infecting organism or organisms.

In the elderly, the choice of antibiotic should always include coverage of streptococcal pneumonia. Adequate antibiotic coverage would include amoxicillin or clavulanate, a second- or third-generation cephalosporin, trimethoprim or sulfa-

**Pneumonia**

Trachea

Bronchus

Bronchiole

Infected          Normal

*Pneumonia is a group of inflamatory diseases that affect the bronchi, bronchioles, and alveoli of the lungs.* (Hans & Cassidy, Inc.)

methoxazole, and a quinolone. In those confined to nursing homes, the antibiotic spectrum needs to be enlarged. Other potent organisms, known as gram-negative organisms, need to be considered and treated. In nursing homes, two antibiotics need to be used, at least initially. They may be given at the nursing home to spare admitting the patient to a hospital. The antibiotics are administered by injection, either intramuscularly or directly into a vein. Once the patient's temperature has normalized, usually after forty-eight to seventy-two hours, antibiotic delivery may be switched to the oral route. In younger individuals who are not confined to an institution, organisms such as mycoplasmal pneumonia and chlamydia pneumonia are encountered more frequently. These organisms respond nicely to macrolide or quinolone antibiotics in an outpatient setting.

Viral infections are also commonly involved in the causation of pneumonia. Antibiotics have no effect on the treatment of viral infections, and their administration is not justified to prevent possible secondary bacterial infections. Antiviral agents are becoming widely available, however, especially in the treatment of influenza and associated pneumonia. Rapid diagnostic testing for influenza is now available, allowing treatment for this viral illness to be more effective. Extensive use of amantadine and rimantadine, if given within the first forty-eight hours of the start of symptoms, reduces the severity and the length of influenza. Another antiviral agent, Zanamivir, not only decreases the severity of symptoms and reduces the course of illness caused by the influenza virus, but also stops viral replication and may reduce the risk of complications.

## PREVENTION

Pneumococcal and influenza vaccinations are valuable preventive measures. In institutionalized individuals, there is an increased risk of complicated pneumonia caused by streptococcal pneumonia, and these cases in turn lead to outbreaks of pneumonia at the institution. The vaccine available in the late 1990's contained antigens (substances that stimulate the immune system) against more than 90 percent of the causative streptococcal organisms.

The Advisory Committee on Immunization recommends that all individuals over sixty-five years of age receive the pneumococcal vaccine. The effectiveness of the vaccine does wane with time, and it is recommended that those who received it before sixty-five have the vaccine administered again after reaching that age. In addition, people under sixty-five years old who have chronic illnesses (such as diabetes, chronic lung disease, liver disease, kidney disease, and heart disease), those without a spleen, and those who are immunologically incompetent because of serious blood diseases should receive the pneumococcal vaccine.

The agents against viral infection are not as effective as those against bacterial illnesses. It is therefore of paramount importance that these illnesses be prevented. In those over sixty-five years of age and especially those confined to a nursing home, vaccination helps to reduce the severity of the illness in individuals and helps prevent outbreaks of viral disease in institutions. Convincing evidence shows that influenza-related pneumonias are reduced by 40 to 50 percent in those who are vaccinated. In nursing homes, influenza deaths are reduced by 70 to 80 percent in those residents that have received the influenza vaccine. In addition, health care workers, especially those who work in nursing homes, should be immunized to reduce the chance of transmission to patients under their care.

Pneumococcal and influenza vaccines do work. Their administration is a high priority among health care providers. Remaining mobile, retaining independence in daily living, and strict handwashing when exposed to a patient with a viral illness are all measures that help to prevent pneumonia.                       —*Thomas A. Ramunda*

*See also* Death and dying; Hospitalization; Illnesses among the elderly; Immunizations and boosters; Influenza; Nursing and convalescent homes; Respiratory changes and disorders.

### FOR FURTHER INFORMATION:

Bartlett, John G. "Approach to the Patient with Pneumonia." In *Infectious Diseases*, edited by Bartlett, Sherwood I. Gorbach, and Neil R. Blacklow. Philadelphia: W. B. Saunders, 1998.

_____, et al. "Community-Acquired Pneumonia." *The New England Journal of Medicine* 333, no. 24 (December, 1995).

Muder, Robert R. "Pneumonia in Residents of Long Term Care Facilities: Epidemiology, Etiology, Management, and Prevention." *The American Journal of Medicine* 105, no. 4 (October, 1998).

Mundy, Linda, et al. "Implications for Macrolide Treatment in Community-Acquired Pneumonia." *Chest* 113, no. 5 (May, 1998).

Seigal, Robert E. "Switch Therapy in Community-Acquired Pneumonia." *Pulmonary Infections Forum* 2, no. 2 (1998).

Sopena, Nieves, et al. "Comparative Study of the Clinical Presentation of Legionella and Other Community-Acquired Pneumonias." *Chest* 113, no. 5 (May, 1998).

Woodhead, Mark. "Management of Pneumonia in the Outpatient Setting." *Seminars in Respiratory Infections* 13, no. 1 (March, 1998).

# POLITICS

**RELEVANT ISSUES:** Demographics, economics, law, values

**SIGNIFICANCE:** As life expectancy has steadily increased, the concerns of the elderly have become a highly critical and controversial issue in American politics

Numerous issues directly affect the quality of life of the elderly. Skyrocketing health care costs and living expenses, concerns over whether various social programs—such as Social Security—can keep pace with inflation, and attempts by politicians to weaken the government's health care system have all inspired the emergence of a highly organized political constituency that demands legislative action for elderly concerns.

## SOCIAL SECURITY ACT OF 1935

Prior to the introduction of the Social Security Act, few Americans possessed any form of an old-age pension. While several industrialized nations provided a comprehensive system of pensions and health care plans, the United States provided its workforce with virtually nothing. Federal and state civil service employees, armed services veterans, and approximately 10 percent of all private sector workers enjoyed some form of a retirement plan, but the majority of Americans depended on either private savings or family support to offset the loss of wages following their withdrawal from the labor market. This situation, however, was drastically reversed during the 1930's, when Francis Everett Townsend launched a nationwide movement to help alleviate the suffering of the elderly during the Great Depression.

After a number of failed real estate schemes, Townsend achieved some degree of economic stability practicing medicine in Long Beach, California. During the 1930's, he became increasingly agitated as he watched elderly citizens starve and rummage through garbage heaps for food. He maintained that after a lifetime of employment, individuals should be entitled to a secure retirement income. His slogan, Youth for Work/Age for Leisure, implied that workers should be rewarded after years of service. Townsend argued that if the elderly received a monthly stipend and agreed to spend it, the economy would rapidly recover. He claimed that his plan could be financed by apply-

ing a 2 percent tax on all business and commercial transactions. This would guarantee each individual approximately $150 to $200 per month and would ensure a consistent source of consumer funds for the market. His ideas achieved instant success in Long Beach, and, by 1934, the Townsend Plan obtained widespread support from countless older Americans. By 1935, Townsend had organized more than three thousand clubs, each with anywhere from one hundred to one thousand dues-paying members. Local meetings resembled religious revivals, and Townsend secured a loyal following among middle-class farmers, skilled workers, small businesspeople, and insurance agents who were troubled about their own upcoming retirements.

As his movement spread, it generated a considerable amount of alarm within the political system. President Franklin D. Roosevelt, who had been devising his own pension plan, recognized that elderly Americans possessed considerable political clout. Based on the successful pension plan of General Electric, the president's advisers outlined a "social security" system that called for contributions from both employers and workers. After hearing congressional testimony from Townsend and other leading economists, the Social Security Act was signed into law by President Roosevelt on August 5, 1935. It created a system of old-age pensions, unemployment compensation, aid to dependent children, and federal support for various health care programs. It was jointly financed by payroll deductions and employer contributions; qualified individuals would receive pension benefits after their sixty-fifth birthday.

This act was the result of several years of political fighting, negotiation, and compromise. Early critics had charged that it represented a communist solution for a capitalist economy. They claimed that it would lead to a public dole and destroy the individual work ethic. Roosevelt countered these critiques by insisting that the plan was more of a social insurance program than a form of welfare. The government would serve as a banker, or fee collector, and when workers reached retirement age, their contributions would finance their benefits. Since it was a self-funding system, it would actually reward, rather than hinder, the American commitment to hard work and sacrifice. After retirement, Social Security would replace lost wages and provide the elderly with disposable consumer income.

Many workers, however, were initially omitted from this law. Townsend criticized the act since it did not apply to rural laborers, state employees, and domestic servants; despite the fact that they were obligated to begin payments immediately, individuals would not receive any actual benefits until the 1940's. Radicals, on the other hand, attacked the president on the basis that the governments of other industrial nations assumed full financial responsibility for old-age pensions. Roosevelt, however, believed that if workers were required to make contributions through payroll deductions, they would develop a vested interest in the act, which would ultimately insulate it from partisan politics. He was right. Since the program also affected a wide range of political constituencies and was not affected by job changes, Social Security evolved into one of the most popular pillars of America's welfare state. Constituted as a partici-

patory system, most Americans quickly perceived it as a just reward after years of service.

Townsend continued his efforts to seek out further assistance for the elderly. In October, 1935, seven thousand Townsendites met in Chicago for the movement's first annual convention. After the meeting, Townsend attacked both political parties and insisted that both President Roosevelt and Republican Party candidate Alfred Landon should endorse the Townsend Plan. When this failed to materialize, Townsend attempted to form a third political party but eventually decided to sponsor the Union Party and William Lemke. This action, however, failed miserably when Roosevelt attained a landslide victory. Townsend continued to hold meetings throughout the 1930's, but Roosevelt's actions had preempted his issue and coopted his support.

This period marked a historical turning point in the politics of aging. Townsend represented the first significant effort to organize the elderly into a

*Presidential candidate and vice president Al Gore holds a town meeting about health care for older Americans in New Hampshire in 1999. The influence of the "senior vote" compels candidates to address the issues that affect the elderly. (AP Photo/Jim Cole)*

cohesive political force, and, despite his personal failures, his actions helped produce a number of safeguards that would protect the elderly's interests for subsequent generations. Roosevelt's actions, moreover, created a system of contributory pensions that would allow millions of Americans to retire with some form of guaranteed income. Finally, with the passage of the Social Security Act, the elderly emerged as a powerful voting bloc within the American pluralist system; as a result, old-age concerns evolved into a permanent issue on the political agenda. Both the Harry S Truman and Dwight D. Eisenhower administrations extended Social Security to cover an additional 20 million Americans; politicians who suggested any cuts in this program encountered severe and hostile opposition from their constituencies.

## MEDICARE AND MEDICAID

Social Security did not address the elderly's concerns over rising health care costs. When President Truman first proposed a national health care plan, critics argued that government-sponsored health care represented "socialized medicine." Yet both President John F. Kennedy and Lyndon B. Johnson maintained that old-age pensions should not be depleted by medical expenses. While Kennedy's legislative package failed in 1962, Johnson secured passage of the Medicare and Medicaid programs in 1965. These acts, which guaranteed hospital insurance for all Americans over age sixty-five, were naturally very popular among the elderly.

Although Johnson initially intended for the bill to only cover hospital visits, Congress insisted upon a voluntary insurance program to help defray the costs of doctor visits and surgical fees. The government split the premium with the individual; as a result, more than 90 percent of all eligible Americans purchased government-subsidized health care. These programs marked a watershed for the elderly as they transferred responsibility for health care from the individual to the federal government. Within ten years, the number of Medicare recipients jumped from 4 million to 24 million, while government contributions soared from $3.4 billion to $18 billion during the same period. Consequently, millions of elderly individuals who had previously been unable to afford hospital visits now received guaranteed medical care

to supplement their Social Security benefits check. By 1976, approximately 20 percent of the nation's medical services were financed by these programs.

Medicare and Medicaid, however, did not provide a panacea for all of the elderly's ills. The American Medical Association's opposition to the bills was diffused only after it was decided that the legislation would not affect fees or private practices. Yet this decision generated a spiraling increase in health care costs. Doctors, profiting from government payments, raised fees, while patients, protected by guaranteed insurance, insisted on a variety of tests and procedures. Since the program did not impose any cost controls, hospital prices increased by an annual rate of approximately 14 percent throughout the 1970's. Doctor fees jumped an average of 7 percent per year.

Hospital administrators also placated doctors' concerns with welfare by ordering the latest technology, raising wages, and expanding patient capacity. The costs of expansion were ultimately passed on to the federal government. Misappropriation of funds exceeded $250 million per year in New York alone, and the largest benefactor of this program became the medical profession. The welfare state was extended to include guaranteed health care, along with Social Security pensions; however, this process also transferred taxpayers' money directly into the hands of high-priced doctors. As a result, while individuals were obligated to pay a smaller percentage of their medical expenses, out-of-pocket payments escalated. Retired people still had to purchase drugs, eyeglasses, and dental care; by the 1980's, it was apparent that Medicare and Medicaid had fallen quite short of their initial promise.

Yet despite these visible failures, these programs became the cornerstone of the welfare state as the politics of aging directly shaped and influenced the legislative agenda in the United States. The elderly often flexed their muscles when cuts were threatened. Old-age opposition could determine the outcome of an election and help shape a political party's platform and itinerary. For example, after orchestrating a Republican victory during the congressional elections in 1994, Congressman Newt Gingrich attempted to restructure the Medicare system, reduce benefits for millions of elderly, and push the political spectrum further to the right, away from entitlement programs. Se-

*A group of seniors applauds the passage of a Republican Medicare bill in the House of Representatives in 1995. The future of the Medicare and Social Security programs promises to remain politically controversial for years to come.* (AP Photo/Doug Mills)

niors responded with indignation and outrage and ultimately contributed to the demise of Gingrich's power.

### SENIOR POWER MOVEMENT

In the second half of the twentieth century, senior citizens acquired a considerable degree of political clout by forming energetic lobbying organizations. Committed to a high rate of voter turnout, they ultimately developed into one of the most energetic and persistent special-interest groups in American politics. Following the first White House Conference on Aging in 1961, a number of organizations began to agitate for a more unified approach toward senior citizen issues. Two groups, the American Association of Retired Persons (AARP) and the National Council on the Aging (NCOA), joined hands with the newly formed Gray Panthers and the National Council of Senior Citizens in order to raise awareness and increase activism among the elderly.

The movement, however, faced serious internal divisions. The AARP's membership came from middle- and upper-class seniors who were more concerned with consumer issues and retirement opportunities. The organization opposed mandatory retirement rules and insisted that individuals should not be penalized for working past the age of sixty-five. The AARP insists that senior workers be judged on merit and that any form of age discrimination must be eliminated from the economy. The Gray Panthers are more concerned with the poor and prefer to form coalitions with other working-class organizations in order to ensure a fair standard of living for all. The Gray Panthers concluded that the elderly should not be a segregated special-interest group but must work toward eliminating, rather than furthering, hostility among the various generations.

Although a great deal of diversity exists within the senior movement, all groups share an overriding commitment to the preservation of Social Security and Medicare. One of the most formidable beliefs among seniors maintains that every individual should be entitled to a dignified retirement, and, if personal savings prove to be inadequate, the government has a direct responsibility to subsidize the elderly's income. Health care costs, moreover, should never be permitted to obliterate a senior citizen's bank account. The elderly should be given every chance to enjoy a dignified, peaceful, and secure retirement. The AARP, the Gray Panthers, and others have been extremely successful in forcing politicians to abandon any plans that would eradicate old-age pensions or guaranteed health care benefits.

### POLITICS OF AGING

By the 1980's, Social Security and Medicare developed into two of the most firmly entrenched institutions and popular components of America's welfare system; they appealed to all segments of society. Social Security and Medicare guaranteed individuals a pension and health plan after retirement. As costs spiraled upward, various conservatives and economists called for program cuts, a balanced budget, and tax reform, but entitlement programs rarely came under attack. Senior citizens were active at the polls, and most candidates understood that they needed to court the elderly bloc if they hoped to succeed. Middle-aged voters, moreover, became more vocal and vociferous champions of these programs as they steadily approached retirement age. Consequently, Social Security and Medicare became virtually untouchable.

During Ronald Reagan's administration, these two programs represented 48 percent of the federal budget. The president often voiced criticisms of the system before his presidency, claiming that it was poorly structured, bad business, and an invasion of freedom. He initially entertained ideas regarding cuts and reforms; Reagan's budget director, David Stockman, suggested huge reductions and proposed to eliminate benefits for those retirees under age sixty-five. Reagan, however, enjoyed great popularity among America's older conservatives and allowed these entitlements to grow as Medicare costs increased by 12 percent during the 1980's. Tax cuts, defense spending, the savings and loan bailout, and social welfare programs eventually produced record deficits. Yet even conserva-

tive New York congressman Jack Kemp understood that an assault upon elderly programs would generate a considerable voter fallout. In fact, during the 1992 Democratic presidential primaries, future president Bill Clinton accused his opponent and fiscal conservative, Paul Tsongas, of planning a rollback of Social Security benefits. This undermined Tsongas's standing among senior citizens, and Clinton's commitment to elderly entitlement represented one of the factors that propelled him to the White House. Whether voters identified with the Religious Right or lower working class, elderly voters shared a consensus on the maintenance of all retirement benefits.

Congressman Newt Gingrich of Georgia unleashed a systematic assault upon the welfare state in 1994. Motivated by his desire to become Speaker of the House and by the opportunity to restructure the welfare state, Gingrich asked the American voters to embrace the Republican Party's "Contract with America" during the 1994 elections. In a two-hundred-page published document, he outlined his agenda and invited the public to grant him a mandate to initiate sweeping changes in the welfare system. Oddly enough, the contract offered more benefits for senior citizens. President Clinton had passed legislation in 1993 that required the elderly to pay higher taxes on their benefits and placed a lower ceiling on earnings. Part of the president's Omnibus Budget Reconciliation Bill stipulated that any individual earning more than $34,000 or any couple earning more than $44,000 per year would have to pay taxes on up to 85 percent of their benefits. Other senior citizens between ages sixty-five and sixty-nine lost one dollar in benefits for every three dollars they earned over $11,160.

Gingrich proposed to slash senior tax rates by the year 2000, dismantle limitations on income, and improve health care. His Senior Citizens' Equity Act would encourage seniors to remain in the workforce and would permit them to keep a larger percentage of their salaries. His legislation would also grant tax incentives for private long-term care insurance. Overall, Gingrich attempted to alleviate the burdens of middle- and upper-class senior citizens, who often had to choose between potential wages and the loss of Social Security benefits. Despite his overall offensive against the welfare state in his Contract with America, Gingrich was extremely careful to avoid all references to Social Security and Medicare as he proposed an exhaustive onslaught on entitlement. He may have been seeking to balance the budget by disposing of welfare programs, but during the campaign, Gingrich declared that Social Security and Medicare must be preserved intact. His efforts persuaded many senior citizens to elect a Republican Congress in 1994.

Upon assuming control as Speaker of the House, Gingrich succumbed to many problems. He specifically overestimated his popularity, and when his recommendations affected the lives of key constituencies, the public moved away from Gingrich's Contract with America. Assuming that the nation desired vast tax cuts and conservative reform, the Republicans submitted legislative plans for a curtailment in Medicare benefits. This reversal was based on the fact that Gingrich declared Medicare to be facing an imminent crisis. He claimed that reform was essential to save the system from eventual bankruptcy. However, few senior citizens accepted this picture and viewed Gingrich's actions as a betrayal. Faced with rising health care costs and an uncertain future, the elderly rebelled against Gingrich's leadership.

President Clinton exploited the Republican Party's tactical errors and utilized the politics of aging during his successful 1996 reelection campaign. Proposed cuts in social insurance programs literally destroyed Gingrich's relationship with the elderly, and Clinton became the beneficiary of this electoral backlash. Public opinion polls may have indicated that a majority of Americans desired a balanced budget and some degree of tax reform, but few embraced cuts in old-age benefits. Clinton recognized this, and, cloaking himself in the rhetoric of Roosevelt and other liberal reformers, he once again reaffirmed the Democratic Party's commitment to welfare entitlements and easily defeated Republican senator Bob Dole in the presidential election. Gingrich had underestimated the power of the politics of aging; as a result, his party's popularity plummeted.

## GRAYING OF AMERICA

Since the majority of Americans are under the age of sixty-five, the social insurance system has had little difficulty providing for the needs of the elderly. Yet as the United States experiences a rapid demographic transformation caused by an aging population and a declining birthrate, the financial solvency of this system could topple. Between the 1970's and the 1990's, the birthrate in the United States dropped from 18.4 births per 1,000 people to less than 16. At the same time, life expectancy dramatically increased: The number of individuals over age sixty-five rose from 8 percent of the population in 1970 to over 12 percent in 1990. In 1900, only 4 percent of the nation reached the age of sixty-five; by the 1990's, men lived an average of seventy-seven years, while women's average soared to age eighty-two. Experts predict that by the year 2030, 20 percent of the nation will be of retirement age. With more and more workers leaving the workforce, living longer, and depending upon the government for pensions and health care, the payroll deductions and contributions that are essential for maintenance of the programs are rapidly dwindling. The graying of America has also been accompanied by an escalation of health care costs. As a result, some experts doubt whether these entitlements will survive the first half of the twenty-first century.

The aging predicament will continue to plague politics as the baby boomers reach retirement age. Between 1946 and 1964, 74 million children were born in the United States, a birthrate increase of 12 percent. Upon reaching adulthood, many baby boomers had fewer children and often subscribed to family-planning schemes that deferred parenthood until they reached their thirties. This led to a sharp decline in the potential labor pool for the twenty-first century, and many are concerned that Social Security taxes will no longer be capable of meeting the elderly's expenses. During the 1940's and 1950's, there were approximately ten to fifteen workers for every beneficiary; by the 1990's, this rate dropped to three workers for every pensioner. Many experts predict that, by 2030, it will fall to a 2 to 1 ratio. Moreover, in the 1990's, over one-half of the baby boomers were not earning enough to supplement Social Security with private pension plans. Rising housing costs further contributed to this downward spiral, and there is a considerable degree of concern over whether the baby boomers can pay their own way after retirement.

This phenomenon has generated a significant degree of conflict in American society. Some younger voters, believing that Social Security will no longer be available for their retirement, want an immediate end to the program. Upset that they are forced to provide for the elderly when their chances for government pensions appear slim, they insist that they should be allowed to use their deductions to augment private pension and stock plans. The federal government has responded to the graying population by enacting several reforms to the system. The 1983 amendments to the Social Security Act eliminated excesses, brought more jobs into the program, and eliminated some unnecessary benefit categories. As a result, Social Security began enjoying a surplus in 1984. However, as the government draws upon this surplus for other bailouts and as the baby boomers prepare to retire, younger workers fear that they are being forced to pay for a system that will be defunct by the time they retire.

The AARP has attempted to counter this development through partisan politics. They have organized senior citizens into a viable and powerful voting bloc, and their lobbying efforts in Washington, D.C., receive a pivotal amount of respect. The AARP distributes voting guides to its members, sponsors candidate debates, and conducts extensive letter-writing and phone campaigns. It is committed to educating voters through workshops and town meetings. It directs voter registration drives, presents material to the media, and publishes a national newsletter. The AARP was instrumental in securing the passage of the Balanced Budget Act of 1997, which guaranteed the solvency of Medicare until 2008. While it maintains that Social Security possesses sufficient funds to survive until 2032, the AARP has demonstrated a willingness to work toward reform and greater privatization. It has also proposed tax reform measures to ensure that senior tax rates are fair, equitable, and progressive. These developments clearly indicate that seniors are willing to accept some adjustments to the system.             —*Robert D. Ubriaco, Jr.*

*See also* Advocacy; Age Discrimination Act of 1975; Age Discrimination in Employment Act of 1967; American Association of Retired Persons (AARP); Americans with Disabilities Act; Baby boomers; Consumer issues; Executive Order 11141; Forced retirement; Gray Panthers; Graying of America; Health care; Kuhn, Maggie; Life expectancy; Medicare; National Council of Senior Citizens; National Council on the Aging; Older Americans Act of 1965; Older Workers Benefit Protection Act; Social Security; Townsend movement; Voting patterns; White House Conference on Aging.

**FOR FURTHER INFORMATION:**

Dionne, E. J., Jr. *They Only Look Dead: Why Progressives Will Dominate the Next Political Era.* New York: Touchstone Books, 1996. Dionne discusses how Social Security and Medicare reform became contentious issues in American politics in the 1990's.

Gillespie, Ed, and Bob Schellas, eds. *Contract with America: The Bold Plan by Rep. Newt Gingrich, Rep. Dick Armey, and the House Republicans to Change the Nation.* New York: Random House, 1994. This is the original copy detailing the Republican Party's platform calling for changes in the welfare system. It offers insight into how the Republicans utilized the politics of aging during the 1994 election.

Graebner, William. *A History of Retirement.* New Haven, Conn.: Yale University Press, 1980. This book provides key insight into retirement issues and furnishes valuable information on the career of Francis Townsend.

Landis, Andy. *Social Security: The Inside Story.* Bellevue, Wash.: Mount Vernon Press, 1993. A critical source for understanding the various pension rates and Medicare benefits that each individual is entitled to after retirement.

Longman, Phillip. *Born to Pay: The New Politics of Aging in America.* Boston: Houghton Mifflin, 1987. Longman addresses various ideas associated with generational conflict and elderly entitlement programs. He also provides fundamental quantitative data outlining the demographic changes that could lead to a crisis for Social Security and Medicare recipients in the twenty-first century.

Matusow, Allen J. *The Unraveling of America: A History of Liberalism in the 1960's.* New York: Harper & Row, 1986. This book is a valuable source for understanding the origins of both Medicare and Medicaid; it also places elderly entitlement programs within the context of 1960's liberal reform.

Quadagno, Jill. *The Transformation of Old Age Security: Class and Politics in the American Welfare State.*

Chicago: University of Chicago Press, 1988. This book serves as a useful guide for understanding the historical significance of the politics of aging.

# POVERTY

**RELEVANT ISSUES:** Economics, race and ethnicity, sociology

**SIGNIFICANCE:** Despite widely held stereotypes depicting older Americans as being secure economically, a significant proportion of the elderly population is impoverished, some elderly subgroups experience extremely high poverty rates, and official guidelines underestimate real levels of elderly economic malaise

Issues relating to the socioeconomic status of the elderly population are more prominent in public discourse than they have been since the early twentieth century debates that culminated in the passage of the Social Security Act in 1935. During this earlier historical period, there was little question that a huge proportion of the elderly population was destitute and constituted a major social problem in need of public attention.

Contemporary discussions of poverty among the aged, however, are held against a backdrop of decades of marked economic improvement for the elderly. If such debates are to be meaningful, they must be based on detailed social scientific analyses of the economic conditions of the elderly. For example, those considering the myriad proposals for "reforming," or dramatically altering, the structure of publicly funded elderly support programs cannot depend on ideologically driven or "common knowledge" sources, or even objective official guidelines, to provide valid information on, or accurately assess, the needs of the fastest-growing age-based segment of America's population.

## ELDERLY STEREOTYPES

In the United States, there have always been popular socially constructed, generalized images of the elderly. Current elderly stereotypes differ dramatically from those of earlier historical eras. From the 1950's through the 1970's, older Americans were commonly viewed as being barely or not able to afford basic necessities, having been relegated to living on small fixed incomes, in poor

health and social isolation. It was commonly believed that industrialization and urbanization had weakened nuclear family ties, resulting in the widespread abandonment and neglect of older family members. The perception that the elderly were largely a dependent population led to what some authors call "compassionate ageism," that is, the general acceptance of negative images of the aged, resulting in a willingness to increase public support for their needs. However, the cultural image of the elderly as poor through no fault of their own, and therefore deserving of assistance, was to be displaced by the dawn of the 1980's.

The economic progress made by the elderly in absolute terms and relative to other age groups created the current, commonly held image of older Americans as being affluent and greedily seeking even more publicly funded assistance, even though elderly support programs collectively make up a large proportion of the overall federal budget. Macro-level analyses generate findings (for example, the lower rates of impoverishment for the elderly compared to the general population and children, and the relatively large proportion of U.S. collective wealth controlled by those over sixty-five) that lend support to this stereotype. Further support is found in anecdotal evidence involving stories of wealthy older persons receiving Social Security, Medicare, and other benefits that were made possible through withholdings from the paychecks of even the least-affluent Americans in the labor force who are struggling to support their families. This new cultural image depicts the elderly as people who are advantaged and affluent because they retired at relatively young ages with high levels of retirement income due to the fact that they worked during periods of economic expansion that provided them with generous private and public pensions, and who possess political power that has brought them a comprehensive collection of publicly funded programs to provide health care and other services. As a result, many blame the elderly for the economic problems of nonelderly Americans and those of the society as a whole.

While it is true that a large proportion of the elderly were poor and needy in the 1950's and 1960's, and that the standard of living for older Americans as a whole has improved substantially, the inherent inaccuracies of all stereotypes apply to these polarized collective images. The move from a sociopolitical atmosphere of "compassionate ageism" to "scapegoat ageism" denotes not only a failure to acknowledge the real socioeconomic diversity within the elderly population during both historical periods, but also a reluctance to recognize the potential consequences of the more recent mind-set. An examination of the social gerontological literature reveals the complexity of ascertaining levels of dependency and need among contemporary older Americans, and points out the inadequacy of the most commonly used standards for determining impoverishment, which underestimate the true extent of the elderly population's economic problems.

## POVERTY RATES AND MEASUREMENT ISSUES

One of the greatest success stories of the War on Poverty begun by President Lyndon B. Johnson is the reduction of elderly impoverishment. According to the most commonly used criteria, the poverty rate for Americans over sixty-five in the mid-1990's was one-third of its 1959 level of 35.2 percent, making it much lower than that for children. Social Security and other publicly funded elderly support programs are largely responsible for this accomplishment. However, this achievement has generated controversy in the form of resentment expressed by Americans in the labor force over their perception that they are being excessively taxed to provide the more than five hundred billion dollars annually to fund these programs, that benefits will be severely cut back or eliminated by the time they retire, and that the aged do not really need the assistance. Related ageist slurs have become increasingly commonplace as elderly Americans are collectively referred to by some as "greedy geezers," "woopies" (well-off older persons), or "the generation that hit the lottery."

Objective and critical analyses by social scientists have raised questions regarding the validity of the conventionally used "poverty line" and whether alternative measures of economic jeopardy might more accurately tap into true levels of need among the elderly. Being "poor" in America is defined for all official purposes by applying an income threshold that is determined by a formula established in the 1950's. Persons or households whose incomes fall below it are "poor." Trends in impoverishment for specific groups, for example,

the steady reduction in poverty among the elderly and the steady increase among children in recent decades, are almost always expressed in terms of the percentage who fall below the official government poverty threshold. The calculation of the poverty line is based on the cost of the minimal amount of food necessary for survival. Using current food prices, the threshold is established at any point in time by multiplying the cost of this minimally nutritious food plan by three, because a poll conducted in 1955 indicated that food made up about one-third of the average household budget. By this criterion, in 1995, a four-person family with two children would have to receive an income below $15,455 to be poor.

Critics of this measure claim that it has underestimated levels of extreme financial hardship since its adoption. To begin with, the official poverty threshold was never intended to describe a reasonable long-term level of living, but rather the barest requirements for subsistence during periods of emergency. In addition, it has been suggested that, at the very least, the formula should be adjusted to reflect the fact that the costs of basic necessities—housing, clothing, and transportation—are typically much higher than three times the family's food budget. Furthermore, it has been asserted that using the average household budget at any point in time as the basis for this calculation is inappropriate because the least-affluent families in America devote over 85 percent of their budgets to food and shelter alone.

Beyond these general issues relating to the poverty line, the official standards for defining elderly poverty are even more controversial because the income threshold is lower than for those under sixty-five. The underlying assumption is that older people have lower nutritional requirements than their more active younger counterparts, and, since the calculation is based on food costs, the elderly must have less income to be officially poor. In 1995, for example, a household with two people and an elderly head was poor if its income was below $9,219, compared to a threshold of $10,259 if the head of the household was under sixty-five. For individuals, the poverty line was $7,309 for those over sixty-five and $7,929 for the nonelderly. It has been asserted that the assumption of lower nutritional requirements for the elderly is subject to question and that the differential age-based thresholds ignore the dramatic increases in expenditures for many older people for such items as health care and prescriptions, home maintenance, and transportation. One of the architects of the original poverty line formula has stated publicly that if more reasonable food costs were used to calculate the elderly poverty line, the percentage of older impoverished Americans would increase to over 30 percent.

For some time, researchers have responded to the possibility that the poverty line underestimates true levels of economic vulnerability by reporting rates based on both people below the poverty line and the "near poor," that is, those whose incomes are 125, 150, or even 200 percent of the poverty threshold. Although the official definition of impoverishment remains unchanged, some government assistance programs now recognize its inadequacy. For example, people with incomes below 130 percent of the poverty line are eligible for food stamps. However, many assistance programs that serve the needs of the nonaffluent aged do not recognize "near impoverishment." In fact, the minimum income guaranteed to the elderly under Supplementary Security Insurance is well below the poverty line. Several authors contend that an accurate measure of financial marginality among the elderly should include the near impoverished, defined as those between 100 and 200 percent of the official income threshold. If this standard is applied, a vastly different picture of levels of need emerges. In 1995, when the elderly poverty rate was 10.5 percent, 40 percent of older Americans had incomes below 200 percent of the poverty line. Those between the line and 200 percent of it, the near poor, may be worse off in real terms than their officially impoverished counterparts, for they are not eligible for need-based assistance programs.

The perspective that conventionally calculated poverty rates underestimate levels of economic malaise among the elderly is not universally shared. There are those who posit that the current poverty line formula creates inflated estimates of elderly impoverishment and that factors currently excluded should be counted as income. "Income," as defined by the poverty threshold formula, includes money received from wages and salaries, private pensions, interest and dividends, Social Security, and public assistance programs. Some con-

tend that a more valid estimate of elderly poverty would result from counting the value of services provided through government programs, tax benefits received by the elderly, and potential income based on the value of home equity in addition to money income. The result would be a significant reduction in the elderly poverty rate. In 1994, when 11.7 percent of older Americans had incomes below the poverty line, this expanded definition of income would have produced an elderly poverty rate of only 5.7 percent.

Critics of proposals to redefine "income" to include factors other than money received believe that such policy changes would place large numbers of older Americans in economically untenable positions. They agree that direct money transfers through government programs should be counted, pointing out that if Social Security and other government assistance money was not counted as income, the elderly poverty rate would have been 52 percent in 1994, which demonstrates the need for and the success of elderly income maintenance programs. Yet, these critics claim that the value of services that the nonaffluent elderly could not afford were it not for government programs, such as a temporary stay in a nursing home, does not improve the recipient's ability to cover basic expenses. By the same token, imputed income from home equity does little to assist with increasing home maintenance costs. Charges are common that political motivations underlie suggested policy changes that would reduce levels of elderly eligibility for need-based assistance, in a political atmosphere that features budget reduction and deficit elimination and calls for a more equitable age-based redistribution of publicly funded assistance. The resolution of these debates over whether the current guidelines that officially define poverty should be maintained or amended to include more or fewer of the financially marginal elderly will have a marked effect on the economic well-being of older Americans.

## CAUSES OF POVERTY AND DISADVANTAGED SUBGROUPS

Disagreements over the validity of the poverty line notwithstanding, when the conventional poverty threshold is applied, the dominant fact regarding elderly impoverishment in America is its steady and dramatic reduction for several decades.

The two most compelling questions that remain are "Why do a significant minority of aged Americans still live in impoverishment?" and "Why does categorical economic diversity within the elderly population produce subgroups with poverty rates much higher than the overall average?" There is a single answer to both questions. Public elderly support programs do not serve the needs of all older Americans equally well. Those who enjoy a decent standard of living fit a profile that includes entering the paid labor force as young adults and contributing to Social Security throughout a long working lifetime, which results in relatively generous Social Security benefits that supplement private pensions, savings, and home equity. By contrast, the elderly poor tend to be people whose labor force participation histories are fragmented or involve the lowest-paying occupations with few or no benefits, and those who suffer from severe physiological or cognitive decline. As a result, the public assistance safety net works well for the healthy middle-class elderly and leaves women, racial and ethnic minorities, and the oldest old overrepresented in the ranks of the elderly impoverished.

Social scientists have sought to analyze the perpetuation of these pockets of severe economic jeopardy within the elderly population. In 1995, for example, when the overall elderly poverty rate was 10.5 percent, the rate for Latinos and African Americans was about 25 percent, was twice as high for women than men in every racial and ethnic category, was almost 50 percent for Latinas and African American women living alone, and increased for each older age group within the elderly population. "Cumulative advantage" and "cumulative disadvantage" are theoretical concepts developed by economic and social gerontologists to describe processes that perpetuate categorical elderly impoverishment. The former term refers to the fact that those who are advantaged early in life build on those advantages throughout the life cycle, and the latter concept posits that those who historically have had limited access to the structure of opportunities (for example, women and minorities) are affected by those disadvantages throughout their lives, often resulting in impoverishment in old age. Even the higher poverty rate for the oldest old compared to their younger elderly counterparts can be attributed, in part, to these life course processes. While factors such as failing health, a re-

duced ability to generate supplementary income, and the higher proportion of elderly women living alone do increase the poverty rate for the oldest Americans, the flow of relatively advantaged cohorts with higher average levels of education and income into the younger elderly age groups also contributes to the perpetuation of age-based economic diversity among the elderly.

Misconceptions and confusion regarding the economic well-being of older Americans are not uncommon because, too often, publicly disseminated information on the topic includes only some of the facts. It is true that, overall, the current cohorts that make up America's elderly population are the most economically secure in its history. It is also true that large numbers of older Americans continue to suffer in impoverishment, and there are only two other industrialized nations in the world with higher current elderly poverty rates than the United States. —*Jack Carter*

**See also** Abandonment; African Americans; Ageism; Homelessness; Income sources; Latinos; Neglect; Politics; Social Security; Stereotypes; Women and aging.

**FOR FURTHER INFORMATION:**

Barusch, Amanda S. *Older Women in Poverty: Private Lives and Public Policies.* New York: Springer, 1994. A thorough examination of the feminization of poverty as it affects older women.

Binstock, Robert, and Linda George, eds. *Handbook of Aging and the Social Sciences.* 4th ed. San Diego: Academic Press, 1996. Contains separate articles that address the economic status of the elderly, race and elderly inequality, differential aging experiences by gender, cumulative disadvantage, and the economics of aging.

Marmor, Theodore R., Timothy M. Smeeding, and Vernon L. Greene, eds. *Economic Security and Intergenerational Justice: A Look at North America.* Washington, D.C.: Urban Institute, 1994. Includes numerous readings that objectively assess the support needs and economic problems of the elderly.

Minkler, Meredith, and Carroll L. Estes, eds. *Critical Perspectives on Aging: The Political and Moral Economy of Growing Old.* Amityville, N.Y.: Baywood, 1991. Contributions critically examine "scapegoat ageism" and levels of elderly dependency, and the effects of capitalism on both.

Pampel, Fred C. *Aging, Social Inequality, and Public Policy.* Thousand Oaks, Calif.: Pine Forge Press, 1998. Focuses on the socioeconomic diversity among the elderly, levels of need and dependency, excessively economically disadvantaged subgroups, and appropriate policy responses.

## PREMATURE AGING

**RELEVANT ISSUES:** Biology, health and medicine

**SIGNIFICANCE:** People worry about aging prematurely, but with few exceptions, the rate of aging is mainly determined by genes and is beyond individual control

The best examples of premature aging in humans are the rare genetic diseases Werner's syndrome and Hutchinson-Gilford progeria syndrome, the latter also simply called progeria. People with Werner's syndrome age rapidly in their teens and twenties, often suffering from cataracts, heart disease, and diabetes and dying in their thirties. Progeria is even more dramatic. Children with progeria start to show signs of senescence a few months after birth. They age very rapidly, becoming white-haired and bald, developing coronary artery disease, and resembling little wizened octogenarians well before they are ten years old. They typically die of age-related diseases in their early teens. Both Werner's syndrome and progeria remain essentially untreatable. The accelerated rate of aging that characterizes these diseases, once begun, stops only with death.

Fortunately, both diseases occur extremely rarely, as little as once per million or more births. The lesson that these rare diseases teach is that genes control the normal rate of aging. In these families, mutant forms of normal genes lead to aging that is dramatically accelerated. Furthermore, these genes and the proteins that they determine implicate cellular metabolic processes such as deoxyribonucleic acid (DNA) damage and repair in the normal aging that occurs in everyone else.

Considerable evidence from other species such as mice, fruit flies, and higher animals often shows the principal role of genes in determining the rate of aging. In the small roundworm *Caenorhabditis elegans*, several genes, notably *ced-3*, control the rate of aging. Phenomena such as programmed cell death in many organisms show that aging is essentially an intrinsic cellular process, under the control of factors in the cell's nucleus, again implicating genes and DNA.

Some well-known risk factors for age-related diseases in humans can be within the control of individuals to affect. Obesity predisposes individuals to heart disease and diabetes. Strong sunlight causes skin cancer and damage to skin cells like that caused by aging. Lack of exercise can cause loss of muscle tone. In these particular regards, a person can prevent premature aging within his or her own genetic makeup.

Most people wish that they could delay aging, or at least avoid the reality or appearance of premature aging. Current fads include diet manipulation with calorie restriction, vitamin supplements, and antioxidants such as flavonoids. Little or no evidence, however, supports the effectiveness of these regimens in humans. Instead, genes appear to take the predominant role in controlling the rate of aging. One cannot determine one's genes, just as one cannot choose one's parents. Nevertheless, a person can try to live a well-balanced and healthy life, get reasonable diet and exercise, avoid too much sun on the skin, and not fret about the rest.

—*R. L. Bernstein*

*See also* Aging process; Antiaging treatments; Antioxidants; Caloric restriction; Cosmetic surgery; Face lifts; Genetics; Gray hair; Hair loss and baldness; Life expectancy; Longevity research; Nutrition; Skin changes and disorders; Wrinkles.

## PRESCRIPTION DRUGS. *See* MEDICATIONS.

## PROSTATE CANCER

**RELEVANT ISSUES:** Biology, death, family, health and medicine

**SIGNIFICANCE:** The 1990's showed a sharp rise in the occurrence of prostate cancer; research continues to show a close correlation with aging

The prostate gland is a walnut-sized gland just below the male bladder that encircles the urethra (the tube that carries urine through the penis). Any enlargement or abnormal growth of this gland may cause such symptoms as difficulty or discomfort in urination, excessive frequency of urination (especially at night), or inability to urinate. However, these symptoms by no means indicate cancer in all cases. Cancer is an uncontrolled, excessive reproduction of cells in the gland, which

*Former senator Bob Dole helps unveil a postage stamp promoting awareness of prostate cancer during the National Men's Health and Fitness Conference in 1999. Dole was diagnosed with prostate cancer in 1990. (AP Photo/Chris Gardner)*

may spread to other parts of the body through the blood stream or the lymph system.

### INCIDENCE AND RISK FACTORS

With the exception of skin cancer, prostate cancer is the most frequently occurring cancer in men; in the United States, it accounts for one out of every three cancers in men. Between 1987 and 1997, the estimated number of identified cases of prostate cancer grew from about 90,000 to 209,000 annually. The direct correlation with aging is shown by the fact that only 7 percent of these cases were discovered in men below the age of sixty. The average age at which prostate cancer was diagnosed was seventy-two.

There are some obvious ethnic factors in the incidence of prostate cancer. Black men have the highest incidence in the world, approximately one-third higher than Caucasian men, and their death rate is double that of Caucasians. Asian immigrants to the United States, on the other hand, have a much lower incidence. Researchers continue to look for explanations for these differences. Another risk factor involves having relatives with the disease. When a father or brother has the disease, the risk doubles; some studies have shown that when a man has three relatives with prostate cancer, he is more than ten times as likely to get the disease.

Environmental factors also seem to raise the risk of prostate cancer. Some studies have shown links between farmers and workers exposed to cadmium through welding, electroplating, and making batteries and an increase in incidence of prostate cancer. Workers in the rubber industry may also be a higher risk group.

### DIAGNOSIS AND PREVENTION

Preliminary tools for diagnosing prostate cancer are the digital rectal examination (DRE), the prostate-specific antigen (PSA) test, and the prostate acid phosphatase (PAP) test. The DRE consists of a doctor inserting a gloved and lubricated finger into the rectum and physically feeling for abnormal growths. The PSA test checks the blood for the level of a specific protein produced by the prostate gland, while the PAP test checks the level of prostatic acid phosphatase. Elevated PSA or PAP levels do not necessarily indicate cancer but do suggest the need for further testing. None of the tests are foolproof. While the PSA test is the most accurate of the tests, it still misses about one-third of cancers that have not spread outside the prostate gland.

In addition to these tests, some doctors may perform a urine test to check for blood or infection. An intravenous pyelogram—a series of X rays of the organs of the urinary tract—may also be used. In another procedure, called a cystoscopy, the doctor looks through a thin, lighted tube into the urethra and bladder.

If any of these tests suggests the possibility of a malignancy, the doctor may combine a transrectal ultrasonography (a procedure in which sound waves are sent out by a probe inserted into the rectum, allowing a computer to create a picture called a sonogram) with a biopsy. If an abnormal area is found by the DRE, tissue will be removed from the abnormal area by insertion of a hollow needle through a tube inserted into the rectum. If an elevated PSA is the indicator, random sections from the entire prostate gland may be taken. The only certain way to detect cancer is to observe the tissue under a microscope.

Perhaps the most important part of the diagnosis is determining the stage of the cancer when a biopsy reveals it to be present. One system is to rank the malignancy from 2 through 10, with the higher numbers being the more advanced stage. The more common system uses a grading of 1 through 4. Stage 1 means the cancer has not spread beyond the prostate gland, is causing no symptoms, and cannot be detected by the DRE. Stage 2 tumors may be felt by the DRE or detected by blood tests but have not spread beyond the prostate. Stage 3 means the cancer has spread to nearby tissues outside the prostate. Stage 4 means cancer cells have spread to lymph nodes or other parts of the body.

While research is ongoing in attempts to find ways of preventing prostate cancer, results have not been notable. High-fat diets have long been recognized as a risk factor; daily consumption of green and yellow vegetables, and especially tomato-based foods, has been shown by some studies to reduce the risk of several types of cancer, including prostate. The validity of such studies has not been universally acknowledged, however, and a strong question has been raised as to whether switching to a low-fat diet after years of ingesting high levels of fat can be effective. Regular amounts of raisins and other dried fruits in the diet have also been suggested as a preventive measure. Exercise is yet another factor. Several studies have suggested that exercise reduces testosterone levels and hence the odds of getting prostate cancer.

### TREATMENT

Primary methods of treatment include surgery, hormones, radiation, chemotherapy, and cryosurgery. The stage of the malignancy is a primary determinant of treatment methods to be used. Two types of surgery that are used are radical prostatectomy (surgical removal of the entire prostate gland) and radical orchiectomy (surgical removal of the testicles so that the prostate gland is deprived of testosterone needed for malignant cells to reduplicate and grow). The latter has shown dramatic results in the short term; in the long term, however, the cancers returned, usually with fatal results. Surgery is often accompanied by undesirable side effects, such as impotence and inability to control urination.

Radiation therapy is often combined with surgery or may be used independently. A machine may be used to direct radiation to the area of the malignancy (external radiation), or radioactive material may be placed directly in or near the infected areas (internal radiation). External radiation is administered on an outpatient basis, whereas internal radiation usually involves a brief stay in the hospital. For stage 3 tumors, radiation is the more common treatment. Like surgery, radiation therapy may have undesirable side effects, such as impotence, diarrhea, or frequent and painful urination.

The preferred treatment for stage 4 cancer is hormone treatment. One form consists of introducing luteinizing hormone-releasing hormone (LHRH) into the body, which prevents the testicles from producing testosterone. Another form is to introduce estrogen, a female hormone that stops the testicles from producing testosterone. These treatments are often accompanied by a drug called an antiandrogen, which blocks small amounts of male hormones produced by the adrenal glands.

Researchers have also tested chemotherapy. Although a variety of drugs have been administered, no consensus has developed as to their effectiveness. Also, such drugs usually cause undesirable side effects. The effectiveness of cryosurgery—the application of extreme cold directly to the tumor to freeze it and destroy the cancer cells—also remains questionable.

Sometimes the best treatment for prostate cancer is simply "watchful waiting." Prostate cancer cells are notoriously slow growing and are sometimes best left alone. About seven out of ten men diagnosed with prostate cancer will die of other causes. Medical experts advise aging males to have a DRE and PSA test annually after age fifty. In the case of high-risk people, these tests should probably begin around age forty. Early detection is a key factor in effective treatment.    —*Joe E. Lunceford*

*See also* African Americans; Cancer; Impotence; Men and aging; Prostate enlargement; Reproductive changes, disabilities, and dysfunctions; Urinary disorders.

## For Further Information:

Aigotti, Ronald E. *The People's Cancer Guide Book.* South Bend, Ind.: Belletrist, 1996.

Giovannucci, Edward, et al. "Intake of Carotenoids and Retinol in Relation to Risk of Prostate Cancer." *Journal of the National Cancer Institute* 87, no. 23 (December 6, 1995).

Klein, Eric A. "Hormone Therapy for Prostate Cancer: A Topical Perspective." *Urology* 47, Supplement 1A (January, 1996).

McKinnell, Robert G., et al. *The Biological Basis of Cancer.* Cambridge, England: Cambridge University Press, 1998.

Phillips, Pat. "Reports at European Urology Congress Reflect Issues of Interest to Aging Men." *Journal of the American Medical Association,* May 6, 1998.

Watson, Ronald R., and Siraj I. Mufti. *Nutrition and Cancer Prevention.* New York: CRC Press, 1996.

Winawer, Sidney J., and Moshe Shike. *Cancer Free.* New York: Simon & Schuster, 1995.

## PROSTATE ENLARGEMENT

**RELEVANT ISSUES:** Biology, health and medicine

**SIGNIFICANCE:** Problems associated with enlargement of the prostate gland affect more than one-half of all men in their sixties and up to 90 percent of men in their seventies and eighties

The prostate gland is a walnut-sized organ of the male reproductive system located just below the bladder. It consists of two halves (lobes) surrounded by an outer layer, or capsule. The prostate gland surrounds the urethra (the tube that carries urine from the bladder out through the penis) just as it leaves the bladder. The primary function of the prostate gland is to produce a milky fluid, which, along with other fluids, makes up semen. Semen carries and nourishes sperm cells and is expelled during ejaculation. There are three main problems that can affect the prostate gland and cause problems for men: benign prostatic hyperplasia, prostatitis, and prostate cancer.

The prostate gland goes through two main periods of growth. During puberty and young adulthood, the prostate grows rapidly, doubling in size. Around age forty to forty-five, the prostate begins to grow again, a condition called benign prostatic hyperplasia (BPH), and continues growing slowly until death. As the name implies, BPH is not cancer and does not turn into cancer. However, it is possible to have BPH and prostate cancer at the same time. The prostate enlarges from within and is kept from expanding by its surrounding capsule. This causes the gland to press against the urethra passing through it, much like a kink in a garden hose. This pressure on the urethra is responsible for the most common symptoms of BPH: difficulty starting or maintaining a stream of urine, the urge to urinate suddenly, the need to urinate more frequently (especially at night), and leaking or dribbling urine. BPH develops slowly over many years, and the symptoms usually develop slowly as well. This is why symptoms of prostate enlargement caused by BPH are more common among older men. When severe, BPH can cause serious health problems, such as bladder or kidney damage.

Prostatitis is inflammation of the prostate gland usually caused by a bacterial infection of the urinary tract. Prostatitis occurs in middle-aged men and is associated with BPH in older men. Symp-

## The Prostate Gland

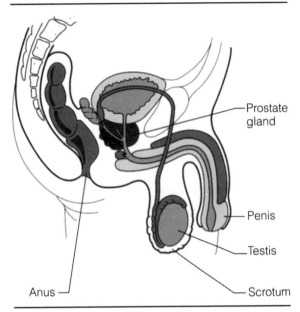

Prostate gland

Penis

Testis

Anus

Scrotum

(Hans & Cassidy, Inc.)

toms of prostatitis may be similar to those of BPH and may also include fever and burning or pain with urination. Prostatitis is generally treated with a course of antibiotics lasting several weeks or several months.

Several treatment options for BPH are available. Surgery generally involves removal of all or part of the gland. Other medical treatments involve the use of drugs to shrink the prostate gland or reduce symptoms, though these drugs are not effective in all cases.

Prostate enlargement is extremely common among older men. The symptoms of an enlarged prostate are not a necessary part of getting older, and men need not suffer from such symptoms. Medical experts advise all men over fifty to have an annual examination, including a digital rectal exam to screen for prostate problems.

*—William J. Ryan*

**See also** Men and aging; Prostate cancer; Reproductive changes, disabilities, and dysfunctions; Urinary disorders.

## Psychiatry, geriatric

**Relevant issues:** Family, health and medicine, psychology

**Significance:** As people age, mental and emotional problems may result from psychological and social stresses, genetic predispositions, or physical medical conditions; therefore, psychiatric care is a necessary component of geriatric health care

Psychiatric symptoms can occur at any point in life. Often, they are a sign of increased stress in the life of the individual; such stress may be mental, physical, financial, or social. Medical attention, such as visits to a primary care physician or a geriatric psychiatrist, can be beneficial at these times to help the affected person address the stress and decrease or eradicate the problematic symptoms. At other times, however, psychiatric symptoms can result from both stress and underlying vulnerabilities that a person may have, and may develop into a psychiatric illness that requires specialized medical attention. While it is possible that such symptoms might go away on their own, it is more likely that, without attention from a professional, the affected individual will suffer more intensely or for a longer period of time than necessary.

Since it is difficult to distinguish between these two types of psychiatric symptoms, consultation with a physician is almost always a good idea. Psychiatric symptoms can also be indicative of or confused with major physical problems, particularly in elders; a failure to evaluate and address the symptoms could put the affected individual at risk for major physical health problems or could exacerbate a condition that might already be life-threatening.

### Special Needs of Elders

Advances in medical science are allowing more and more individuals to live longer and more productive lives. Such advances, however, require a keen awareness of medical case management. The interaction of such medical procedures and drugs with the aging body systems may create physical, mental, and social challenges that can affect elders in significant ways. Simply put, older bodies do not react to drugs, injuries, and medical procedures in the same way that younger bodies do. Slower metabolism of substances, slower healing, and decreased immune system functioning can all play a role in the maintenance of health and mental well-being. In addition, the physical, psychological, social, and financial supports that buffer people from the stresses and strains of daily living may weaken over time, causing elders to suffer increased vulnerability to psychiatric disorders.

The specialty field of geriatric psychiatry was developed to focus on the prevention of major mental disorders and on the maintenance of mental health in the elderly. Because of the nature of social changes that coincide with aging—including decreases in independence and greater reliance on family or medical care assistants—geriatric psychiatry frequently involves family psychiatry and collaboration with other medical professionals.

## PSYCHIATRIC DISORDERS IN THE ELDERLY

The later years of a person's life can be a great time for enjoying the fruits of lifelong productivity. It is not uncommon, however, for elders to experience such psychiatric problems as depression, anxiety, substance abuse, and dementia. Even for the most well-adjusted elders, the challenges of later life can affect mental status. Such problems as illness, physical challenges, retirement, geographic relocation, financial and social stresses, and the loss of friends and significant others to death can lead to mild depression and anxiety. For many, these discomforts may simply pass, but for others, they will not. These stresses and strains, if left unattended, may result in more serious conditions, such as major depression. Major depression often causes individuals to exhibit decreased levels of activity, decreased levels of pleasure in activities normally enjoyed, and decreased levels of social interaction. Other symptoms may include notable changes in weight (either loss or gain), lack of interest in sex, difficulty sleeping, and suicidal thoughts or extreme feelings of guilt and worthlessness.

Changes in physical abilities, such as hearing, mobility, and strength, can also affect mental health; some individuals may become anxious about not being able to take care of themselves or manage daily activities as they once used to do. Certain activities that were once commonly engaged in (such as cooking, bathing, driving, or leaving the home) might be avoided out of fear or concern. Often, a critical incident, such as an accident, mishap, or misunderstanding, can lead to avoidance. Although cessation of the activity is sometimes appropriate (such as when driving abil-

ity becomes impaired), the primary problem may simply be fear of reoccurrence of the mishap. In such cases, avoidance often compounds the problem and may lead to the development of phobias and panic, which may impair normal behavior. Elders also can have problems with alcohol and drugs. For some, this may be a continuation of a lifelong problem, but for others, it can be a new development. Drugs prescribed to take care of pain, insomnia, or even anxiety or depression may create drug dependence and lead to additional physical, mental, and emotional problems. Prescription drugs may also create problems when they are combined with small amounts of alcohol or other prescription or over-the-counter drugs. Symptoms of substance misuse may include falls, accidents, slurred speech, increased sleeping, anxiety, insomnia, irritability, or social withdrawal.

Dementia is characterized by permanent, diffuse, profound, and significant decreases in mental and emotional functioning and abilities. These changes, which can occur gradually (over many years) or abruptly, are usually the result of damage to the brain from a variety of causes. Substance abuse and strokes may lead to localized dementia, while Alzheimer's disease has a global effect on functioning. The onset of Alzheimer's disease is often very gradual as it progresses through several recognizable, distinct stages. People suffering from dementia usually require the assistance of caregivers and long-term case management.

Some medical conditions common to elders can first show themselves as psychiatric symptoms that may seem small or inconsequential. To complicate matters, the reverse is true as well. Among the medical conditions that may cause psychiatric symptoms are cancer, diabetes, Alzheimer's disease and other dementias, strokes, hearing loss, and irregular heartbeat or heart palpitations. Symptoms of depression, for instance, can be the first sign of cancer or dementia. Difficulty hearing and understanding oral information can lead to isolation and the misperception of stimuli, fostering opportune conditions for anxiety and paranoia. Memory loss can be one of the first symptoms of dementia. Problems with anger or inappropriate emotional reactions to situations can be an early indicator of strokes and dementia. Confusion can be an indicator of problems with diabetes, hypoglycemia, or dementia.

## TREATMENT AND MANAGEMENT

An individual who visits a geriatric psychiatrist for the first time will typically be asked to supply a history, both recent and long-term, of the problems and symptoms. This gives the geriatric psychiatrist a functional picture of the symptoms to help determine causes and the best ways to treat the problem. This type of questioning is extremely important and, for some individuals, can even help to alleviate some symptoms. Sometimes simply describing a problem in detail and receiving some educational information from a professional is all that is needed to help alleviate the concerns an elder might have. If a problem is determined to be related to stress, the psychiatrist may recommend stress management procedures. Such procedures might involve setting up a daily routine, learning how to identify symptoms of stress, and learning to recognize stressful activities so they can be replaced by healthier, alternative activities.

When the cause or level of symptom severity is more pronounced and more of an ongoing impediment to well-being, regular meetings between a geriatric psychiatrist and the affected elder and his or her family might be suggested. Such meetings, typically called therapy or talk therapy, involve a process in which problems are discussed in greater detail. In the case of depression, for example, individuals might talk about the losses they have experienced and how they feel about them; psychiatrists may then suggest ways of thinking or behaving in response to such feelings that are more adaptive. For cases related to anxiety, discussions may center on specific ways of managing anxious feelings, understanding how certain thinking patterns might be making things worse, and learning new ways of behaving in response to anxiety. If talk therapy alone is not helpful, psychotropic drugs or drugs that affect thinking and feeling might be used to treat some disorders, such as anxiety and depression. In cases of severe depression where psychotropic drugs cannot be tolerated, electroconvulsive therapy may be used.

When psychiatric symptoms result from an underlying medical problem, treatment of the medical problem becomes primary. Typically, geriatric psychiatrists may provide supportive therapy to family members or affected elders as they go through treatment. In cases where the symptoms might represent a permanent disability, such as with dementia or stroke, supportive therapy may continue for all involved. The affected elder and his or her family or caregivers may be given some educational information regarding what can be expected in the future and how best to design a rehabilitation and adjustment program. This may involve ongoing contact with medical providers or home health assistance.

The geriatric psychiatrist may also recommend behavioral modifications for performing tasks of basic living to allow the affected elder to function as safely and as independently as possible. In these cases, the thoroughness of the initial and ongoing assessments of the elder's functioning and abilities is critical in order to keep the rehabilitation and adjustment program productive. If a program that was working suddenly becomes less effective or if additional problems develop, further assessment is needed. —*Nancy A. Piotrowski*

**See also** Aging: Biological, psychological, and sociocultural perspectives; Alcoholism; Alzheimer's disease; Cancer; Dementia; Depression; Driving; Grief; Hearing loss; Loneliness; Medications; Memory changes and loss; Mental impairment; Personality changes; Stress and coping skills; Strokes.

## FOR FURTHER INFORMATION:

Ford, Norman. *The Sleep Rx: Seventy-five Proven Ways to Get a Good Night's Sleep.* Englewood Cliffs, N.J.: Prentice Hall, 1994. This book provides suggestions for identifying common causes of sleep problems and ways to combat insomnia.

Gruetzner, Howard. *Alzheimer's: A Caregiver's Guide and Sourcebook.* New York: John Wiley & Sons, 1992. Useful, step-by-step information is presented for family members trying to identify different phases of Alzheimer's dementia; provides a well-rounded picture of treatment options and research findings.

Ilardo, Joseph A. *As Parents Age: A Psychological and Practical Guide.* Acton, Mass.: VanderWyk and Burnham, 1998. Ilardo highlights key psychological issues confronted by adult children and aging parents.

Mace, Nancy L., and Peter V. Rabins. *The Thirty-Six-Hour Day: A Family Guide to Caring for Persons with Alzheimer's Disease, Related Dementing Illness, and Memory Loss Later in Life.* New York: Warner Books, 1991. This frequently recommended book is full of suggestions for how and when to make difficult decisions for those caring for elders affected by the serious cognitive and emotional problems resulting from dementia.

Morris, Virginia. *A Complete Guide: How to Care for Aging Parents.* New York: Workman, 1996. This book describes common physical and other problems that may affect the elderly, while also presenting important information on legal issues and on dealing with emotional issues such as grief; includes contact information for useful organizations.

Restak, Richard M. *Older and Wiser: How to Maintain Peak Mental Ability for as Long as You Live.* New York: Berkley Books, 1999. Restak provides suggestions and easy-to-do exercises to maximize good memory performance in elders who wish to keep their mental abilities as sharp as possible.

Staudacher, Carol. *Men and Grief: A Guide for Men Surviving the Death of a Loved One: A Resource for Caregivers and Mental Health Professionals.* Oakland, Calif.: New Harbinger Press, 1992. This book covers common issues related to grief and loss, highlighting how men respond to grief and how they can be helped to cope with losses.

Weiner, Florence, Mathew H. M. Lee, and Harriet Bell. *Recovery at Home After a Stroke: A Practical Guide for You and Your Family.* New York: Berkley Publishing Group, 1996. This book provides information about psychiatric and other medical symptoms that are likely to be evident following a stroke, as well as practical suggestions useful in assisting family members and the affected stroke victim in their adjustment to and recovery from the stroke event.

## REACTION TIME

**RELEVANT ISSUES:** Biology, health and medicine, psychology

**SIGNIFICANCE:** As people age, their reaction times to stimuli tend to slow, causing safety concerns about such activities as driving; studies of reaction time have helped researchers learn about the effects of aging on cognitive performance

Reaction time refers to the amount of time that passes between the occurrence of a stimulus and the execution of a response to that stimulus. Factors that influence reaction time include the need to accurately perceive the stimulus, to decide what action needs to be taken, and to coordinate the actions of the relevant muscular systems involved in the execution of the response. There is little doubt that humans experience a gradual slowing in reaction time as part of the aging process. However, the significance of this finding for performance in everyday life and its relevance to issues such as driving safety is far less clear.

Reaction time remains relatively stable until the age of forty, at which point a gradual pattern of slowing begins. Comparisons between healthy younger and older adults typically show that the responses of older adults take approximately 30 percent longer to execute than those of younger adults. Estimates regarding the rate of slowing indicate that reaction times decrease by approximately 2 percent for every five years of age.

The size of age differences in reaction time varies widely from study to study. Larger age differences are found in studies in which there is greater difficulty in detecting the stimulus, less opportunity to prepare a response in advance, and a change in the rules that indicate the correct response to a given stimulus. In addition, the difficulty of the task has a large influence on the size of age differences in reaction time. More complex or difficult tasks are associated with larger age differences in reaction time. This result is usually thought to reflect a slower speed of information processing in the brains of older adults.

While older adults almost always display slower responses than younger adults, declines in the speed of cognitive operations may not provide a complete explanation of age differences in cognitive performance. For example, there is evidence that older adults make fewer errors on reaction time tasks than younger adults. This indicates that at least a portion of reaction time slowing in older adults may be explained by a style of performance that places more emphasis on accuracy than on speed. This stylistic difference may manifest itself in everyday life through more cautious driving habits.

Two other lines of research indicate that age differences in reaction time are not as absolute as once thought. First, age differences in reaction time are reduced with extensive practice in a particular task. Second, data suggest that physically fit older adults may not experience slowed reaction times to the same degree as less physically fit older adults.

*—Thomas W. Pierce*

***See also*** Aging: Biological, psychological, and sociocultural perspectives; Aging process; Brain changes and disorders; Driving; Safety issues.

## READING GLASSES

**RELEVANT ISSUES:** Biology, health and medicine

**SIGNIFICANCE:** With age, the lens of the eye hardens and becomes less able to focus on nearby objects; during middle age, all individuals will require reading glasses for near vision

The eye gathers visual information and sends that information to the brain, where it is put into a meaningful picture. In order to transmit the information, the lens focuses light on the back of the eye, or retina, where special cells, the rods and cones, process the light information. In order to focus the light precisely onto the retina, the lens must be flexible and able to elongate or shorten. When the lens cannot flex in order to position the light onto the retina, objects in the environment become out of focus or blurred.

The lens gradually loses its elasticity with age. In a very young child, the lens is highly elastic and flexible and has great focusing power. As an individual ages, however, the hardened lens loses its focusing power, and a person begins to notice that close-up objects become blurred. A forty-year-old will notice difficulty reading small print, will have to hold newspapers and books at arm's length, and may have trouble with close tasks such as threading a needle. Once the lens becomes unable to focus on small objects held even an arm's length away, a common complaint is, "My arms are too short."

The inability to focus on near objects as a result of lens hardening with age is called presbyopia and

*The requirement of glasses for reading and other close work is a natural part of the aging process of the eyes.* (PhotoDisc)

is a completely normal part of aging. Presbyopia is not a disease. Although this condition cannot be prevented, it is correctable with reading glasses. The prescription strength of the glasses will increase gradually as a person advances in age and the lens of the eye becomes more inflexible. The distance at which the patient works most often should be considered by the eye care professional when determining prescription strength for reading glasses.    —*P. Michele Arduengo*

**See also** Aging process; Cataracts; Glaucoma; Nearsightedness; Vision changes and disorders.

## RELIGION

**RELEVANT ISSUES:** Death, psychology, religion

**SIGNIFICANCE:** Belief in a higher power and being part of a caring community may help maintain a sense of well-being in the face of the almost inevitable losses faced as a result of aging

Religion, by its very nature, can be a controversial subject. It is most commonly thought of as involvement in an organization of people who share a common theology. Most of the literature on aging and religion seems to assume that being religious includes a belief in an ultimate being, God, and a belief in a relationship with God.

Faith is usually thought of as part of religion, and it is usually so. However, it has been suggested that all people have faith in something: in their intellect, in their ability to control their destiny by hard work and determination, in their family and friends and social connections, or just in themselves. Others, those considered religious, have faith in God. Religious faith, specifically, may be thought of as believing in God, experiencing a relationship with God, and acting on this belief in a way that is thought to be pleasing to God.

Spirituality is sometimes thought of as synonymous with religion, but one can be religious without being spiritual or spiritual without being religious. Some who equate God with the universe and thus see themselves as part of God may be quite spiritual but not religious. The other view, and the one that has been most investigated in successful aging, is that God is separate and distinct from the universe; if the universe ceased to exist, God would remain. People holding this belief would probably be considered religious. Some of those who consider themselves very religious and are very devout at church attendance and at obeying the strictures of their church may not be spiritual. According to the National Interfaith Coalition on Aging, "Spiritual well-being is the affirmation of life in a relationship with a God, self, community, and environment that nurtures and celebrates wholeness." This definition of spiritual well-being seems to include the idea of a connection with God, a caring for self, and an involvement in a corporate body that may minister to the group and to the individual.

Successful aging may have many meanings for many people. Some would consider successful aging to mean retirement with financial security, having grown children who are on their own and successful, and being in good health. However, success at any point in life often includes overcoming adversity, and successful aging is no exception. If successful aging only included those things mentioned, many people would find successful aging beyond their ability. Harold Koenig, a noted authority on aging, claims that successful aging involves how older people feel, think, and act in whatever circumstances they find themselves. Successful aging, he suggests, is defined by crisis. When crisis comes, religious faith may be the difference between successful aging and facing one's final years with despair.

## RELIGION AND AGING

Given such a definition of successful aging, the possibility of a special connection between religion and aging is easily understood. When people are young, especially in Western societies, the individual and individual accomplishment are stressed. As one ages, however, it becomes clear that the time left to accomplish goals is shortening and may even be gone. As younger people enter the workplace, elders have a choice: Accept the changing times and find another life-fulfilling goal, or fight to maintain their perceived positions. It has been suggested that in midlife, focus begins to shift from the outer world and turn toward the inner world. This may be a result of necessity. In fact, it is suggested that retirement may be the occasion that leads many older people to religion. Many people derive their sense of identity from their career, and leaving that career behind can create the need to answer one of life's basic theological questions: "Who am I?"

When people reach midlife and see the aging process at work in their lives, faith in self and in a sense of control over their destiny may begin to falter. The best efforts cannot always control health or finances. The death of close friends, family members, or a spouse can leave a person feeling at a loss and bring the realization that control over life is, at best, transitory and perhaps only an illusion. Thus, people may find themselves looking for something to fill a void in their lives. A resurgence of interest in religion has been noted among the huge cohort of postwar baby boomers that began to reach the fifty-year-old mark around 1996. This could be explained by the fact that many of these people experienced the loss of parents and even the loss of spouses to death by the time they reached their fiftieth birthday.

As people experience the almost inevitable losses that occur with aging, they may feel needs that have not previously been evident. They may feel a loss of connection with the world because of loss of companions. Older people are often heard to say that the world they live in has changed drastically since they were young. This may include relatively innocuous changes, such as technological advances, but it often includes such things as loss of homes because of financial reverses and loss of loved ones to death. Religious faith may offer answers in these circumstances. It can give a sense of connection with God and with an extended family of believers, which may help soften the blows of losing loved ones. Further, seeing God as an omniscient, omnipresent, omnipotent, and unchanging entity can offer great comfort in the face of changing circumstances.

Other evidence exists for a special connection between religion and aging. Many Eastern religions teach that elders have a clearer vision of divine reality and possess greater wisdom as a

*The rituals of religious faith can provide great comfort for those older people dealing with the loss of loved ones as well as their own mortality. (James L. Shaffer)*

result of their age. Hinduism teaches that, in contrast to one's earlier years and regardless of what one's vocation was during those earlier years, the final years should be a time of spiritual vocation, of forsaking the world and its vocations and devoting one's self to the soul's salvation. If love of God and others is learned over a lifetime, as suggested by early Christians, spiritual growth should be a natural result of aging.

## HEALTH AND RELIGION

According to Andrew Weaver and Koenig, research has shown consistently that nurturing, nonpunitive religion is good for mental and physical health. One-fourth to one-third of older adults find religion to be the most important factor in enabling them to cope with chronic illness and other stressors experienced as a result of aging. In one study, 60 percent of elderly people reported that they had become more devout with age, while only 5 percent stated that religion had become less important to them.

The connection between mental and physical states is generally accepted by the medical profession. However, there is great reluctance to mention religion as a factor in mental health. Religion's connection to good mental health seems directly related to successful psychological practices, according to Koenig. Psychology and religion overlap in many areas. For instance, psychology speaks of the importance of unconditional, positive regard in the development of self-worth and in the therapeutic relationship between counselor and patient. Religious faith offers the unconditional love of God. Many of the things psychological therapy offers are also offered by religion. Therapy offers a trained listener; most religions offer a God who is always interested and is always listening. Therapy offers to help people gain a sense of self-worth; many religions offer a sense of worth in that each person is loved by God just because he or she exists, not because of having earned that love. Psychology recognizes that suppressed guilt can be problematical; religion offers forgiveness for past mistakes and errors. Anger and hatred toward others is known to be a major factor in maladjustment; religion offers the means to forgive others. Further, involvement in a religious community can offer the social support so important to those experiencing grief over loss, physical problems as-

sociated with aging, or even the difficulties inherent in caring for a loved one who is ill.

It is generally accepted that many illnesses are stress-related. Cardiovascular disease, high blood pressure, ulcers, and autoimmune disease are all made worse by stress. In addition, long-term stressful situations may lead to changes in the immune system that can result in illness and infection. Further, long-term stress has been associated with increases in tumors and even loss of brain cells. Stress, by definition, is what one feels when one perceives something as stressful. Thus, it might be said that stress exists in the mind of the perceiver. Most religious faith offers the assurance that there is a God in control of life's circumstances. Thus, when bad things happen, God is present in that circumstance and will help in some way. This belief can make things that would normally be perceived as stressors lose their power to produce anxiety. Holding this kind of belief may be very important and comforting to aging people who are experiencing the losses and the changes life may bring.

Other reasons that religious faith may be a significant factor in health maintenance have been suggested. First, a community of caring may be important for maintaining physical and mental health. Second, a belief in a final destination may offer great comfort. If life is seen as a dead end, it may lose its purpose. However, if life is seen as a faith journey with a final destination that offers joy, peace, and a new beginning, it may be easier to face death without anxiety. Third, most religions stress growth throughout life. If one stops being mentally active or focuses on physical problems or on the past, life can quickly lose meaning. In fact, evidence suggests that continued mental activity may be important in helping to prevent dementia. Religious faith usually encourages continued spiritual growth, and this usually entails continued involvement with other people. Fourth, attitude is important. The Christian religion stresses peace, joy, love, and patience as fruits of a growing relationship with God. Few would dispute that these attitudes promote physical health.

## PSYCHOLOGICAL THEORIES OF DEVELOPMENT

Psychological development continues throughout life. One theorist who addressed the psychosocial development of adulthood and aging was Erik Erikson. He focused on interpersonal relationships and described eight stages of development throughout the life span, each of which was characterized by a central life task that needed to be completed for successful psychosocial development to take place. The stage of adulthood, from age forty to age sixty-five, is characterized by what Erikson termed "generativity versus stagnation." During this stage, adults must feel that they are accomplishing something important to them in their life; otherwise, they may feel that life has been without purpose. The final stage, called maturity and termed "integrity versus despair," corresponds to the last years of life. According to Erikson, integrity reflects an emotional integration, a belief that the life one has lived was acceptable and necessary, and includes a sense of life's order and meaning.

Erikson believed that failure to successfully negotiate any of these stages would compromise later stages. His theory, while making intuitive sense in many ways, proposes that the only way to achieve generativity or integrity is to complete each previous stage successfully. Misfortunes early in life, noncaring parents, accidents, and illness can all interfere with successful completion of earlier tasks.

Religious faith, however, may offer an alternative. For those who have faith, past errors can be forgiven, and a new life can be attained. One can achieve intimacy (one of the earlier life tasks, according to Erikson) with God, if no one else. The most basic of skills, learning to trust, is also a basic component of most religious faith, as trusting God is the first step in faith in God. Religion provides a belief that there is an order and a purpose to life, that life has meaning in spite of circumstances. It offers a sense of continuity between this life and the next.

According to Koenig, the physical illness, disability, and decreasing social, financial, and cognitive resources that often accompany aging can heighten the struggle between integrity and despair. Ill health, he claims, can adversely affect integrity by interfering with a person's ability to experience hope, meaning, and purpose in life, and can make it difficult to feel loved. These feelings can lead to despair and depression; studies show that nearly 40 percent of hospitalized patients age seventy or over evidence some form of depressive illness. Religious faith may offer the only sense of meaning and hope that people in these situations

can experience. A strong faith in God, an assurance of God's presence in the pain, and a belief in life after death can generate a sense of integrity or peace that might otherwise be impossible.

### THEORIES OF FAITH DEVELOPMENT

James Fowler has developed a theory of faith development that attempts to describe how faith develops across the life span, independent of the content of that faith. Fowler has integrated the developmental theories of Erikson and Jean Piaget, as well as Lawrence Kohlberg's theory of moral development, into his theory of how faith develops across the life span. Fowler defines faith as involving "people's shaping or testing their lives' defining directions and relationships with others in accordance with coordinates of value and power recognized as ultimate." These coordinates of power, according to Fowler, may refer to God, self, money, job position, family, sex, power, or anything that is of ultimate concern to the individual. This definition of faith and the stages he describes are meant to be applicable to all religious and nonreligious faiths in all cultures. Fowler carefully differentiates structure from content in his theory.

As is the case with Kohlberg's theory of moral development, Fowler suggests that the faith stages he describes increase in maturity as one ages and that each one is in some way "superior" to the one that came before. Stage 0, that of undifferentiated faith, occurs from birth until age two. It is a strictly preliminary stage. Stage 1, that of intuitive-projective faith, occurs from age two to seven. During this stage, the child begins to form pictures of God, heaven, and hell. Similar to Piaget's early stages and Kohlberg's preconventional stage of moral development, the child is egocentric, incapable of seeing things from another's point of view, and thus unable to differentiate God's point of view from his or her own.

Fowler calls stage 2 the mythic-literal faith stage, and it runs from age seven to twelve. Cognitively, the child is in Piaget's concrete operational stage, meaning that he or she can begin to use logic and understand what is real and what is make-believe but still interprets things in a very literal or concrete fashion. For the person at this stage of moral development, the world operates, according to Kohlberg, on the rule of reciprocity. At this point, the child's image of God corresponds to that of his

*Clergy members can offer guidance and conversation in care facilities for elders of all spiritual and religious persuasions.* (James L. Shaffer)

or her culture and family. God is seen as operating in a strictly reciprocal manner, giving bad things to bad people and good things to good people. It might be suggested that some people never progress beyond this stage.

Synthetic-conventional faith begins during adolescence. The opinions of peers begin to be of major importance to the individual. The young person becomes capable of seeing things from other viewpoints. However, because authority is located outside the self, the characteristic of this faith stage is the tendency to accept faith without critical examination (synthetic) and adhere to group norms (conventional). There is no view of faith independent of the community or family. Fowler suggests that much of church life in the United States works best when members remain at this stage, and he claims that perhaps only 50 percent of people in adulthood advance beyond it.

Stage 4, which coincides with the postconventional moral development stage of Kohlberg, is called the individuative-reflective faith stage; it begins in the early to mid-twenties or later. During this time, people are completing Erikson's tasks concerning intimacy versus isolation and are moving toward the generativity versus stagnation conflict. Fowler suggests that it may take a crisis, such as a divorce, health problems, or other loss, to move a person beyond stage 3 into stage 4. At this point, the person moves away from relying on external authority and a need for approval of the group. Faith is questioned, and the individual decides what will form the "faith coordinates" by which he or she will live. This stage of moral development includes the definition of moral values and principles apart from the authority figures that, in the past, have been the defining force. Thus, the individual turns inward, away from the external world, for answers to questions of belief.

The final stage, that of conjunctive faith, occurs at midlife and beyond. It is said to coincide with the crisis of generativity over stagnation postulated by Erikson and includes a recognition that an overdependence on logic and rational understanding may not make sense in the light of the limits of human reason. Some of the decisions made in stage 4 may be rejected. During this stage, a person must integrate past experience and childhood faith into a new vision of truth. This individual growth is accompanied by a new commitment to justice for everyone, regardless of perceived differences.

Koenig suggests that, while Fowler's stages of faith are intuitively reasonable, scientifically based, and socially conscious, there may be some difficulties with his theory, particularly when one tries to apply it to the aging population. While the effort to focus on a structure of faith that is totally separate from content is commendable, it may make the theory difficult to apply to individuals. Further, implying that higher faith stages are more valuable and contain more truth than lower stages may be problematical for two reasons. First, by implying that simple, childlike faith is somehow less mature, contains less truth, and is less valuable than the later stages, Fowler has added content to his theory. Many religious faiths, including Christianity, specifically require the believer to have "faith as a little child." Fowler's theory may be seen as devaluing this simple faith. Second, because Fowler links his theory to cognitive development, people who are not capable of progressing to these intellectual levels may be denied mature faith. Again, in spite of attempting to remove content from his theory, his insistence on looking inside of one's self for truth may be seen as contrary to some religious faiths, including some aspects of Christianity. Further, particularly when considering the elderly, whose reasoning ability may be impaired by illness or advancing age, individuals who maintain simple, devout obedience to their faith are considered to be stuck at a lower stage.

Koenig suggests that the opportunity to advance in faith should be available to all, including an elderly person with a stroke or a slowly advancing organic disease, such as Alzheimer's disease. In his book *Aging and God* (1994), Koenig offers a complete critique of Fowler's theory and presents a theory of his own, which includes content. Koenig hypothesizes that the most important aspect of Judeo-Christian religion that impacts on mental health is, in fact, the specific content of the tradition itself. The content of the belief is what determines attitude and behavior, which, in turn, influence the emotional state. His theory includes a description of mature faith as involving a complete and wholehearted trust in God, regardless of circumstances: believing that God is in control, knows best, and is always present.

Not all people turn to religious faith as they age. Some people never seem to need any religious faith, and some place their faith elsewhere. There is no guarantee that age brings spiritual maturity or even a desire to seek comfort in spirituality. If mature faith is defined as that which carries a person through difficult times and does not fluctuate in sorrow or happiness, some faith never matures. In addition, temptations do not automatically lose their appeal at age sixty-five. It is suggested that, for some people, the last years of life may bring a more acute awareness of spiritual impoverishment than of spiritual fulfillment. However, a Gallup poll revealed that 69 percent of people fifty to sixty years of age felt that religion was important in their lives, while 70 percent of those sixty-five and up felt the same way. Only 8 percent felt that religion was not important to them during their older years.

—*Gayle Brosnan-Watters*

***See also*** Aging: Biological, psychological, and sociocultural perspectives; Cultural views of aging; Death and dying; Death of a child; Death of parents; Depression; *Driving Miss Daisy*; Erikson, Erik H.; Funerals; Grief; Jewish services for the elderly; "Jilting of Granny Weatherall, The"; Marriage; Maturity; *Memento Mori*; Remarriage; Stress and coping skills; Successful aging; Widows and widowers.

## FOR FURTHER INFORMATION:

Fischer, Kathleen. *Winter Grace*. Nashville: Upper Room Books, 1998. Fischer discusses how to deal with many issues faced by the aging from a spiritual standpoint.

Fowler, James W. *Stages of Faith*. San Francisco: Harper & Row, 1981. Fowler presents his theory concerning the five stages of faith.

Johnson, Barbara. *Living Somewhere Between Estrogen and Death*. Nashville: Word, 1999. Although often humorous, this collection of thoughts for women deals with serious, age-related matters. Written from a strongly evangelical Christian perspective.

Koenig, Harold G. *Aging and God: Spiritual Pathways to Mental Health in Midlife and Later Years.* Binghamton, N.Y.: Haworth Pastoral Press, 1994. This complete treatment of the subject of aging and God covers psychiatry, mental health, theoretical issues, research on aging and religion, clinical applications, nursing homes, Alzheimer's disease, family, and bereavement.

Seymour, Robert E. *Aging Without Apology: Living the Senior Years with Integrity and Faith.* Valley Forge, Pa.: Judson Press, 1995. Seymour provides thoughts on aging, along with suggestions on how to do so successfully, including how to deal with impending death.

Weaver, Andrew J., Harold G. Koenig, and Phyllis C. Roe, eds. *Reflections on Aging and Spiritual Growth.* Nashville: Abingdon Press, 1998. A collection of authors' thoughts on aging and how one may grow spiritually during this process.

## RELOCATION

**RELEVANT ISSUES:** Demographics, economics, family, recreation

**SIGNIFICANCE:** Choice and personal freedom remain important as people age. One of those matters of choice is where to live and whether to relocate to a warmer climate or to housing for the elderly

By the end of the twentieth century, the United States was aging faster than ever. In 1996, the thirty-four million Americans aged sixty-five and older comprised 13 percent, or about one-eighth, of the population. Projections put the number of persons sixty-five and older at almost seventy million by 2030. While the Caucasian population of the aged was expected to nearly double, even larger increases were projected for African Americans, Latinos, American Indians, Inuits (Eskimos), Aleuts, Asian Americans, and Pacific Islanders.

Relocation upon retirement to Florida or Arizona is a stereotype for the elderly in the United States. Is it accurate? Where do senior citizens actually live? Do they flee ice and snow? Of the top ten states for the sixty-five and older population in 1996, only California, Florida, Texas, and North Carolina would be considered southern. Ten states had sixty-five and older populations greater than 14 percent of their total population: Florida, Pennsylvania, Rhode Island, West Virginia, Iowa, North Dakota, Arkansas, South Dakota, Connecticut, and Massachusetts. Only two of these states with high elderly populations are considered warm in climate: Florida and Arkansas.

Thus, it seems that retirees do not relocate to warmer climates in droves. Although the elderly often move to another residence in the same state

## Population 65+ by State, 1996

| | | | | | |
|---|---|---|---|---|---|
| 3,516,000 | California | 641,000 | Washington | 229,000 | Nebraska |
| 2,657,000 | Florida | 586,000 | Arizona | 189,000 | New Mexico |
| 2,434,000 | New York | 578,000 | Maryland | 183,000 | Nevada |
| 1,951,000 | Texas | 577,000 | Minnesota | 175,000 | Utah |
| 1,912,000 | Pennsylvania | 557,000 | Alabama | 173,000 | Maine |
| 1,497,000 | Ohio | 497,000 | Louisiana | 156,000 | Rhode Island |
| 1,486,000 | Illinois | 489,000 | Kentucky | 153,000 | Hawaii |
| 1,193,000 | Michigan | 470,000 | Connecticut | 140,000 | New Hampshire |
| 1,100,000 | New Jersey | 447,000 | South Carolina | 135,000 | Idaho |
| 917,000 | North Carolina | 445,000 | Oklahoma | 116,000 | Montana |
| 859,000 | Massachusetts | 433,000 | Iowa | 105,000 | South Dakota |
| 747,000 | Virginia | 430,000 | Oregon | 93,000 | Delaware |
| 742,000 | Missouri | 385,000 | Colorado | 93,000 | North Dakota |
| 735,000 | Indiana | 362,000 | Arkansas | 75,000 | District of Columbia |
| 730,000 | Georgia | 352,000 | Kansas | 71,000 | Vermont |
| 686,000 | Wisconsin | 333,000 | Mississippi | 54,000 | Wyoming |
| 667,000 | Tennessee | 278,000 | West Virginia | 31,000 | Alaska |

*Source:* AARP Research, *Profile of Older Americans.*

*Most seniors do not relocate to warmer climates, housing for the elderly, or smaller accommodations, instead preferring the comforts of home.* (James L. Shaffer)

(78 percent in 1993), few relocate to another state (6 percent) in comparison to persons under sixty-five (18 percent). Some retirees who do move to Florida become discouraged and migrate a second time north to the Carolinas or Virginia; they are called halfbacks. Other retirees relocate abroad. Others choose to move closer to adult children, grandchildren, or siblings or even to share housing with them. Most elderly, however, remain in their own communities. About 30 percent live in cities, and 46 percent choose the suburbs.

## LIVING ARRANGEMENTS

In the late 1990's, most aging people lived in their own homes (78 percent) or were renters (22 percent). Most of the homes of older people (53 percent) were constructed before 1960. Remaining in one's own home may have an economic advantage because it may be paid for, so that expenses are mainly repairs and taxes. Some elderly people congregate informally in neighborhoods; these pods of older persons have been dubbed NORCs, for "naturally occurring retirement communities." In the late 1990's, about 7 percent of elders lived with relatives and 2 percent more lived with nonrelatives. Only about 5 percent of the elderly resided in nursing homes.

The chance of living in a nursing home increases with age to 47 percent for those individuals that approach the century mark. About 90 percent of nursing home residents are, as would be expected, the elderly. Other levels of housing facilities include apartments or condominiums for those needing no assistance but using a common dining room, assisted-living arrangements within individual apartment or condominium units, nursing care for the bedridden, and special facilities for Alzheimer's patients. Assisted living means help with meals, shopping, money management, telephone use, housework, and medications. These institutions can be expensive—for example, $6,000 a month for nursing care in 1999. Some facilities may require the resident to buy a condominium, which may trap the individual in that location or generate problems for the estate regarding resale. Others permit a resident to rent a room or apartment.

The wide variety of other care options includes senior centers, hospitals, adult day care, home health care, and hospice. Hospitals have a high representation of the elderly, who account for 48 percent of the days of hospital care. In the late 1990's, about $5,000 a year was spent for an older person's health care, on average, which was three or more times that spent for a younger person. Elders contemplating relocation must also consider the availability of medical facilities such as hospitals, especially if they have special needs.

### OTHER IMPORTANT CONSIDERATIONS

Economics may dictate options for relocation. The poverty rate for those sixty-five and older is surprisingly a little less than for younger people, but it still includes 3.4 million elderly, with higher poverty rates among women, African Americans, and Latinos. Investment strategies are a big concern for retirees who are better off financially. Those who wish to relocate and who can afford to do so might choose a place where they always wanted to live. They may move to Mexico for the climate and economy. Estate tax laws and other taxes vary from state to state.

Planning any change is important for the elderly. Planning includes not only the possibility of relocation and financial investment but also the drawing up of a will, the assignment of durable power of attorney, and perhaps the creation of a living will regarding medical care.

Transportation is a concern in choosing living arrangements. First is personal transportation, as stairs become more difficult to ascend. Walking distances and the presence and location of elevators become important. Second, elders may lose the ability to drive a car, so that the availability of alternative transportation (buses, taxis) must be considered. Safety may be a concern, as the elderly may be victims of crime or scams. The elder may no longer be able to or wish to cook. In addition to restaurants, senior citizen centers that serve meals and services that deliver food to homes should be available.

The opportunity for a social life may be a consideration in relocating. Approximately 47 percent of women and 14 percent of men have lost their spouses by their senior years. Employment opportunities may also be a consideration in relocating, as many seniors want to work and volunteering is almost expected of active elders. Education is an attractive option for the aging; some colleges and universities are identifying and beginning to appeal to their housing needs and learning wishes.                                        —*Sue Binkley*

**See also** Adult education; Caregiving; Demographics; Driving; Early retirement; Home ownership; Home services; Homelessness; Housing; Income sources; Independent living; Leisure activities; Meals-on-wheels programs; Mobility problems; Multigenerational households; Nursing and convalescent homes; Poverty; Retirement; Retirement communities; Retirement planning; Safety issues; Senior citizen centers; Social ties; Temperature regulation and sensitivity; Transportation issues; Vacations and travel; Volunteering.

### FOR FURTHER INFORMATION:

American Association of Retired Persons. "Frequently Asked Questions Relating to U.S. Citizens Moving Abroad." www.aarp.org/intl/moving.html.

_____. *A Profile of Older Americans.* Washington, D.C.: AARP, 1997. Also available from AARP Fulfillment, 601 E. Street N.W., Washington, D.C. 20049.

Beddingfield, Katherine T. "Retire to Tuscany? We Found Better Places: Former War Zones Never Looked So Good." *U.S. News and World Report* 124, no. 25 (June 29, 1998): 82.

*Business Week*, no. 3587 (July 20, 1998). Special issue on retirement.

"Living Arrangements of the Elderly." *Information Please Almanac.* Boston: Houghton Mifflin, 1995.

Mitchell, Emily, and Rebecca Winters. "They Came, They Stayed." *Time* 153, no. 9 (March 8, 1999): S84.

Pifer, Alan, and Lydia Bronte, eds. *Our Aging Society: Paradox and Promise.* New York: W. W. Norton, 1986.

## REMARRIAGE

**RELEVANT ISSUES:** Culture, family, sociology

**SIGNIFICANCE:** After a marriage ends through death or divorce, demographics make it difficult for older Americans to find another partner

As the divorce rate rises in the United States, the spouses set adrift for one reason or another must seek out personally and socially acceptable ways of adjusting to their newfound "free" state. The search is exacerbated when the marriage is dissolved by the death of one or the other partner. Typically, women outlive men. Thus, widows find themselves, if they desire remarriage, in direct competition with many other single women—widowed, divorced, or never married—for a relatively smaller population of eligible and suitable men. In the United States, there are six million widows and one million widowers past sixty-five. Social gerontologists, health care professionals, sociologists, and (to some extent) clergy are involved in helping older unmarried persons find a solution to their unwed status in a manner that is beneficial to both society and to the individuals.

The reasons that people marry vary greatly and have changed over time. Traditionally, a man may be seeking someone to "keep the hearth fire burning"—to help gather food, cook food, bear children, offer companionship, and provide sexual access. A woman may be interested primarily in a protector, a provider of food and shelter, a father for children, a sexual partner, and a companion. Marriage changes the social roles of the man and woman: Before marriage, they are two individuals; after marriage, they are a couple, a sort of corporate entity.

All these relationships change with time. Although the married pair still exist as a couple, their roles as homemakers and providers may be switched. Except for childbearing, either person may assume the activities of the other. The end of a marriage, by divorce or other legal means or with finality in the death of one partner, changes the legal and often religious contractual arrangement. Some individuals are content to allow the end of marriage to be just that, with no thought of remarrying. Others, however, seek out another partner.

### WHY PEOPLE REMARRY

The reasons that people remarry are in many ways similar to the reasons that they married the first time, but with some exceptions and changes in priorities. For many, the prime reason is companionship. The fires of passion may merely be glowing or be only a fond memory, but the knowledge that another person who cares is close by, especially in the still of the night, is comforting. Childbearing is no longer important in the remarriage of older persons, but social and economic security are very important. One or both partners in the union may provide assets that, when joined, provide a level of living not available to either one living singly. (Conversely, some persons who are living on Social Security income find that their economic status is enhanced by not marrying but simply living together, or cohabitating.)

The loss of a marriage partner, especially through death, may impose heretofore unexperienced burdens on the surviving spouse. For example, a husband may find it more diffi-

*Remarriage in later life may combine two very different family structures, depending on the number of previous children and grandchildren and the presence of elderly parents.* (James L. Shaffer)

cult to cope with the death of his wife, not only dealing with the emotional loss but also facing the household tasks of cleaning and cooking. Moreover, although many women are capable, simple household or automobile repairs may prove to be formidable tasks.

In remarriage, older couples find that they often have more time together, further enhancing the companionship aspect. The wives no longer have to share their time with young children, and the husbands, no longer busy carving out a career, do not have to work late or be away from home on business trips.

Not everyone who loses a spouse through death or divorce will remarry. A common reason for not remarrying is the opposition of grown children. The offspring may suggest that their parent is too old for love. The potential marriage partner may be seen as an interloper, usurping the place of the deceased parent. Expected inheritances also play a role in efforts to sabotage a late marriage. Antagonism by the children toward the surviving parent's new romantic interest may quickly put an end to the relationship. In addition, many men and women, after the death of a spouse, simply do not want to remarry. Some have grown accustomed to single life and prefer not having to answer to someone. Others fear the death of a subsequent spouse, with the added burden of the entire grief process again.

## MARRIAGE AS A HUMAN INSTITUTION

The formality of marriage is relatively new for the human species. It grew out of a sense of cooperation—basic to human nature—and one of the many kinds of associations formed by humans to help solve the different sorts of problems with which people must cope. Basic problems include the need for food, protection from the elements, and protection from other individuals and from predators. These problems could be solved through group behavior (bands or tribes), but they also could be solved by a pairing of males and females, with the added benefit of easy access for sexual activities and the resulting procreation.

Hearth and home—the household—established the basic unit of human society. Typically, the household consists of some form of family, a grouping of relatives that rises, at its simplest, from the parent-child bond plus the interdependence of men and women. With the inevitable relationship between sexual activity and the production of offspring who must be nurtured, family and marriage arose as a human state.

Over the millennia of human existence, family structures have varied. They have included polyandry (one wife with several husbands), polygyny (one husband with several wives), monogamy (one wife and one husband), and, more recently, serial monogamy (one man or woman married to a series of spouses in succession). Although monogamy is most common on a global basis, serial monogamy prevails in North American society, where more than 50 percent of first marriages end in divorce.

The form or survival rate of marriage notwithstanding, the basic building block of human society, the household, gives identity and support to its members and provides a place for the organization of economic production, consumption of goods and services, inheritance, child rearing, and shelter.

As human culture evolved, the act of marriage took on a life of its own. It became a ceremony or sometimes a series of ceremonies, legal (that is, civil) and also religious, including combinations of the two. Often payment of monies or goods takes place, from the bride's family to the groom (a dowry) or from the groom's side to the bride's family (a bride price). The legal portion of a ceremony is to establish the legitimacy of children of the union and recognition of their place in the family or other kinship group.

Marriage also changes the social status of the couple. Prior to the ceremony, the man and woman exist in society as individuals. After marriage, they are considered to be a familial, inseparable unit, or corporate entity. The history of marriage is a complex that encompasses the legal and economic dependence of women upon men. It includes the not-so-ancient concept of the inability of women to legally own or deal with property—real, fiscal, or personal.

In marriage, children are looked upon as the key to ideal, happy family life. Children demonstrate to society the fruit of the union and the place of that family in the future life. Indeed, many sociologists consider the upbringing of children as the sole and primary function of the family. It is in the family that the children receive their primary socialization—the basic activities of language, correct behavior including eating and proper manners, and toilet training and personal cleanliness. Later, as the children grow, their world is expanded with secondary socialization such as education and the skills needed to live and interact with other individuals.

Ultimately, when the children leave home, they assume adult roles, marry, and establish families of their own. The aging parents of these grown children undergo a metamorphosis, and the parent-child relationship may be reversed. The children may provide financial support for now-retired parents, or the surviving parent if one has died. The children may provide shelter as well. Above all, the children may serve as guides and advisers to the parents, regardless of whether the parents are capable of caring for themselves adequately and making their own decisions.

What if the aging parent, now single as the result of divorce or the spouse's death, decides to remarry? Sociological research has shown that the family dynamics are basically different from those of the first marriage, even if that first marriage was a successful one. In fact, remarriages have a 60 percent divorce rate. The ingredients that made for a successful first marriage do not necessarily guarantee a successful second marriage.

### PROBLEMS IN REMARRIAGE

About one-third of all Americans will remarry at least once in their lives. The ratio is reduced as the individuals age. Most of the problems in remarriage stem largely from the "baggage" that each partner brings into the new relationship. The marital stresses occur largely in several areas: families, including children (grown or young), relatives, and possibly a divorced spouse; finances; and houses, furniture, and other belongings.

Young children, up to and including older teenagers, often resent the interloper who is now intruding in the cozy relationship they had with the parent, usually the mother. This is especially the case in a "May-December" remarriage in which one spouse, usually the woman, is much younger than the man. Occasionally, she may be young enough to be his daughter's age. Grown children with families of their own see the new spouse as a competitor for their parent's affections or as a free-booter come to take away the inheritance that rightfully belongs (in the minds of the children) to them. Relatives who had formed a close relationship with the couple, on the death of one member of the pair, may feel that they exist in a state of limbo. Are they in-laws, former in-laws, or simply friends? What is their status?

Any finances that the couple brings into the remarriage raise other issues. Do they consider the monies "his and hers" or "theirs"? To clarify the fiscal arrangements and establish ground rules, many couples prepare a prenuptial agreement. Executed with the help of a lawyer, this agreement spells out how the monies are

**First Marriages and Remarriages of U.S. Couples in 1998**

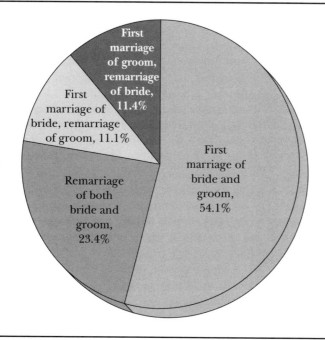

*Source:* U.S. Bureau of the Census, *Statistical Abstract of the United States: 1997.* Washington, D.C.: GPO, 1997.

to be handled. This is especially valuable in situations where one spouse has greater financial assets than the other. Occasionally, couples who, as unmarried individuals, relied on Social Security benefits for their income choose to live together as husband and wife without benefit of marriage rather than accept the reduced benefits they would receive as a married couple.

Where to live after the ceremony is a question frequently facing an older couple contemplating remarriage. One or both may have a home with all that goes with it—furniture, neighborhood, nearby friends. There is no simple answer to resolve this situation, and many a potential remarriage has foundered even before it began because of the property, real and personal, owned by the individuals.

One matter that may be important to older, remarried couples is how to spend their day. Perhaps one or both had a full-time job and is now retired. Conflicts can arise with owl/lark personality habits. One partner prefers to stay up catching the late news, then a late talk show, then a late movie, followed by a morning sleep-in. The other prefers to hurry off to bed, not even watching the late news, but instead rising with the sun to work on a favorite hobby or to engage in some early morning exercise. In too many couples, these differences in spending the day can result in a real problem unless there is some serious compromise. Unfortunately, the habits of a lifetime are hard to bend, let alone break, and frequently the late-in-life remarriage becomes seriously damaged.

### AGING AMERICA AND THE FUTURE OF REMARRIAGE

Demographic studies clearly demonstrate the differences in the survival rate of women versus men. Data show that almost half of all women more than sixty-five years old are widows and that in the sixty-five- to sixty-nine-year-old age group, there are only eighty-one men for each one hundred women. The ratio becomes even more lopsided as the population ages, so that for persons over eighty-five, there are only thirty-nine men for each one hundred women. Some of the single men over the age of sixty-five will undoubtedly choose not to remarry. The women must choose what to do with the rest of their lives.

Prior to World War I, many older widows and widowers moved in with their married children to fit in as best they could. Unfortunately, modern homes and households do not readily expand to include extended families. Unless the suddenly single older person finds that "special someone" or is able to fit in smoothly as a single, he or she effectively retires from society. —*Albert C. Jensen*

***See also*** Cohabitation; Death and dying; Demographics; Divorce; Family relationships; Marriage; Parenthood; Sexuality; Single parenthood; Widows and widowers.

**FOR FURTHER INFORMATION:**

Belovitch, Jeanne. *Making Remarriage Work.* Lexington, Mass.: D. C. Heath, 1987. The author provides advice and suggestions for improving the chances of success in remarriage, including among older persons.

Kate, Nancy T. "Housework the Second Time." *American Demographics* 18 (June, 1996). In second marriages, where the wife expects a more equal division of household labor, she often finds that helping around the house, for some men, is still optional.

Levine, Art. "The Second Time Around: Realities of Remarriage." *U.S. News and World Report* 108, no. 4 (January 29, 1990). Argues that newly remarried couples experience up to ten times the stress, including financial problems, than do those in first-time marriages.

Simpson, Eileen. *Late Love: A Celebration of Marriage After Fifty.* Boston: Houghton Mifflen, 1994. Interviews by the author, a psychotherapist, of fifty men and women concerning what makes for success in late marriage suggest that "all you need is love."

Talbott, Maria M. "Older Widows' Attitudes Towards Men and Remarriage." *Journal of Aging Studies* 12, no. 4 (Winter, 1998). A majority of the women interviewed were opposed to remarriage, citing persisting grief, the quality of the prior marriage, finances, age, and health.

Taylor, Alex, III. "How I Flunked Retirement." *Fortune* 133 (June 24, 1996). In an interview, former Chrysler executive Lee Iacocca discusses what went wrong in the two short-lived marriages that followed the death of his wife of twenty-seven years.

Westoff, Leslie Aldridge. *The Second Time Around: Remarriage in America.* New York: Viking Press, 1977. Remarriage affects not only the couple involved but also relatives and society as a whole. The advantage, however, is that one is able to see what one is getting into.

## REPRODUCTIVE CHANGES, DISABILITIES, AND DYSFUNCTIONS

**RELEVANT ISSUES:** Biology, health and medicine, marriage and dating

**SIGNIFICANCE:** Reproductive changes and disabilities, and the sexual dysfunctions that may arise from them, can greatly affect an elder's quality of life

Reproductive changes, or changes in a female's or a male's ability to conceive children, begin sometime between the ages of forty and fifty. For most people, these changes are gradual and result in little alteration in ability to maintain sexual relationships. For individuals who value their reproductive ability including sexual performance and enjoyment, these changes can cause concern. An understanding of the normal changes in female and male reproductive systems can help individuals deal with the normal changes and adapt their sexual behaviors to accommodate these changes.

The incidence of illness and disability increases as a person ages. Sometimes illness, disability, or the changes in the reproductive system can result in sexual dysfunctions or impairment in sexual arousal or orgasm. Sexual dysfunction is not a normal accompaniment to old age and can be treated in a variety of ways. For most people, reproductive aging, illness, or disability might challenge them to be patient, understanding, and creative in their sexual relationships, but it is not cause for ending a sexual relationship that was once enjoyable.

### FEMALE REPRODUCTIVE CHANGES

Female reproductive changes are greatly influenced by the menopause. Upon arrival of the menopause, a woman's ovaries will no longer produce estrogen and progesterone and ripen and release an egg each month; thus, she will no longer have the capability of becoming pregnant. In addition to the cessation of fertility, the severe decrease of estrogen and progesterone will cause several modifications in a woman's sexual anatomy and sexual arousal. A postmenopausal woman may experience changes in the appearance of her genitals. The folds of skin that cover the genital region

shrink and become thinner, exposing more of the clitoris. Increased clitoral exposure may reduce sensitivity or cause an unpleasant tingling or prickling sensation when touched. The opening to the vagina may become narrower, especially if a woman is not participating in vaginal intercourse. In addition, the natural swelling and lubrication of the vagina occurs more slowly during arousal because the vaginal walls have become thinner and drier. These changes may affect a woman's sexual arousal and response.

Because of decreased vaginal lubrication, more time might need to be spent on foreplay or a water-based lubricant may need to be used. Compared to younger women, an older woman's orgasm will probably be shorter, and it will take less time for her body to move from the height of orgasmic stimulation to a resting state. However, the capacity to achieve orgasm, even multiple orgasms, does not change with age. For many women, engaging in intercourse at least twice a week will cause these sexual arousal and response changes to be reduced or absent.

While the physical changes related to the menopause may cause an alteration in the way some women view sexual relations, in general, if a woman enjoys sexual relations when she is young, she will probably still enjoy those relations after the menopause. Sexual desire is largely determined by emotional and social factors, but hormones such as estrogen and testosterone do play a role. The menopause causes a cessation of estrogen production in the ovaries, but testosterone is produced in the adrenal glands. Thus, for the most part, testosterone levels are unaffected by the menopause. Sexual desire is affected mainly by testosterone rather than estrogen, so after the menopause most women still produce enough testosterone to maintain their interest in sex.

### MALE REPRODUCTIVE CHANGES

Beginning at about the age of forty, men will experience a gradual change in their sexual functioning. These changes parallel those seen in postmenopausal women. Male changes are marked by a gradual, partial decline in the amount of available testosterone in the blood. Less testosterone is produced by the testes, and a growing portion of it is inactivated by bonding with protein.

The gradual decline in a man's testosterone level will affect his sexual response in several ways. As a man ages, it will take longer to achieve an erection. A young man can achieve an erection just by watching someone whom he finds attractive, whereas an older man will probably require more direct stimulation of the penis in addition to visual stimulation or fantasies. Once an erection is achieved, it will not be as firm. Yet a man with good blood circulation to the penis can attain erections adequate for intercourse until death. As a man ages, he will have more ejaculatory control, enabling longer intercourse and greater partner satisfaction. Although older men find orgasms intensely pleasurable, the actual force of ejaculation and amount of ejaculate become diminished as a man ages. Sperm production declines somewhat during midlife and levels off at about the age of sixty. Despite the reduction in sperm count, most men still produce adequate sperm to father children. After ejaculation, the erection subsides more rapidly, and a longer time is needed between ejaculations. Older men require several hours or a day or two between ejaculations.

Despite these changes, most older men remain interested in sex and enjoy an active sex life. Sexual desire originates in the brain and is influenced by emotional and social factors, but a minimum of testosterone is needed for the desire to actually materialize. While men do experience a gradual decrease in testosterone levels, the great majority of men produce well above the minimum amount needed to maintain interest in sex into advanced age.

## THE EFFECT OF ILLNESS OR DISABILITY

The incidence of illness and disability increases with age. The presence of an illness or disability may require a modification in sexual activity, but rarely does it warrant stopping sexual activity altogether. Experiencing a heart attack leads many people to stop sexual activity for fear of causing another. Generally, if a person was sexually active before the heart attack, she or he can probably be sexually active again. If one can climb two flights of stairs without symptoms such as chest pain, palpitations, or shortness of breath, then sexual activity can usually be safely resumed. People who have had a heart attack are usually able to have sex two to four weeks afterward, while bypass patients may

reach this point in one to three weeks after they leave the hospital. Those who suffer from angina or chest pain may be able to take a nitroglycerin pill for the pain before sexual activity. For many people, an active sex life may decrease the risk of a future heart attack.

Atherosclerosis, or hardening of the arteries, can damage small blood vessels and restrict blood flow to the genitals. In men, this can interfere with erection. About half of all impotence in men past age fifty is caused by atherosclerosis. In women, this can interfere with the swelling of the vaginal tissues. Diabetes can also affect male and female sexual functioning. Diabetes can increase the plaque or fatty deposits in blood vessels. These deposits restrict the flow of blood to the penis, causing about half of men with diabetes to become impotent. The risk of impotence increases with age. Women with diabetes may experience vaginal dryness, painful intercourse, and a decreased frequency of orgasm. Females also may have more frequent vaginal and urinary tract infections.

Although arthritis does not directly affect sexual organs, the pain and stiffness caused by osteoarthritis or rheumatoid arthritis can make sexual relations difficult to enjoy. Certain surgeries and drugs can relieve these problems, but in some cases, the medication actually decreases sexual desire. Exercise, rest, warm baths or showers, changes in positions, and avoiding sexual activity in the evening and early morning hours, when pain tends to be the greatest, can be helpful. Communication is important. Generally, as long as partners communicate openly regarding their desires and capabilities, a satisfying sexual relationship can be maintained.

Prostate surgery for a noncancerous condition such as an enlarged prostate rarely causes impotence. After surgery there will be a decrease in the amount of seminal fluid, but sexual ability and enjoyment should remain unaffected. Prostate surgery for cancer causes impotence 50 to 60 percent of the time; however, this type of impotence can be treated with penile implants.

Hysterectomy is the removal of the uterus and cervix and in some cases the Fallopian tubes, ovaries, and lymph nodes. This surgery does not interfere with a woman's physical ability to have intercourse or experience orgasm. If the ovaries have been removed, then the woman instantly experiences the menopause. Hormone therapy can help to replace the estrogen and progesterone that the woman's body is no longer producing and reduce the physical and sexual changes that a woman experiences.

### SEXUAL DYSFUNCTIONS

Sometimes people's bodies do not respond the way they would like them to. A sexual dysfunction is a physiological impairment in sexual response that prevents sexual arousal or orgasm. While not a normal part of aging, sexual dysfunctions are more common among the elderly because of their higher prevalence of chronic illness and the side effects of some prescription medications. Impairment may be due to physiological or psychological factors of which most can be treated.

Changes that a woman's body goes through during the menopause as well as medications and alcohol use can affect a woman's sexual functioning. Reduced vaginal lubrication caused by the menopause; use of blood pressure medication, over-the-counter antihistamines and decongestants, alcohol, or illegal drugs such as cocaine, heroin, and marijuana; and reduced vaginal elasticity, a vaginal infection, or poor hygiene can cause persistent or recurrent pain during sexual intercourse (dyspareunia). Dyspareunia is one of the most common sexual dysfunctions. Among older women, dyspareunia may also occur during orgasm because of spastic uterine contractions.

A second type of pain disorder is called vaginismus. Vaginismus is characterized by involuntary contractions of the muscles surrounding the outer one-third of the vagina, thus preventing penile penetration or rendering penetration painful. Vaginismus may be associated with dyspareunia among older women. A psychological fear of penetration causes vaginismus, and that fear might have been brought about by experiencing dyspareunia in the past. Vaginismus may be the result of the woman involuntarily trying to protect herself from painful stimulation associated with intercourse.

Orgasmic dysfunctions are when a woman persistently or recurrently has difficulty reaching orgasm. In women, use of high blood pressure medications, barbiturates, antidepressants, or alcohol commonly causes loss of pleasure in sexual activity and difficulty in attaining orgasm. Some women have been anorgasmic (never have reached or-

gasm), and others have reached orgasm but not consistently enough to satisfy themselves or their partner (situational orgasmic dysfunction). Situational orgasmic dysfunction can be caused by feelings of guilt or performance anxiety.

Male sexual dysfunctions tend to be related to attaining and maintaining an erection and to ejaculation. Erectile dysfunction, or persistent difficulty achieving or maintaining an erection sufficient to allow the man to engage in or complete sexual intercourse, is the most common male sexual dysfunction. These erectile dysfunctions can be partial (an erection is achieved but cannot be maintained), or they can be complete (an erection is never achieved). It is believed to affect one in every three men over the age of sixty. Four factors are needed for a man to reach and maintain an erection: complete male sexual organs, normal hormone levels, an adequate nerve and blood supply to the penis, and good emotional health. If one or more of these factors are missing, a partial or complete erectile dysfunction may exist. Certain medications and drugs can interfere with nerve or blood vessel function or affect sex hormone levels. Medications used to treat high blood pressure, depression, and psychosis commonly cause decreased sexual interest and erectile difficulties. Alcohol and illegal drugs such as cocaine, heroin, and marijuana have also been found to cause erectile difficulties among men.

Ejaculation difficulties are a second sexual dysfunction that can affect older men. These difficulties result in impaired ejaculation (unable to ejaculate) or premature ejaculation (ejaculate sooner than desired). Premature ejaculation is generally considered to be more psychological in origin, while impaired ejaculation can be a side effect of certain medications including antihypertensives, antidepressants, and antipsychotics.

### DIAGNOSIS AND TREATMENT

Ultimately adults should be able to discuss sexual changes and difficulties with their physician, but studies have found elders to be reluctant to volunteer information regarding sexual behavior to a physician. Older adults may believe their problems are due to the normal aging process, minimize the importance of their sexual needs and desires, or be embarrassed to discuss sex. Whatever the reasons are, studies have found that when physicians do ask patients if a sexual problem exists, many will volunteer significant concerns.

Before a sexual dysfunction can be diagnosed and treated, a physical examination and medical history are necessary. Blood will be drawn and laboratory tests will be run to measure blood levels of testosterone and other hormones so hormonal problems can be ruled out. A medical history will include family disease history, alcohol and prescription drug intake, and a sexual history. A sexual history will include a history of present relationship with partner; level of communication with partner about sexual matters; social situation, including other life stressors; how illness affects sexuality; number and gender of sexual partners; desired level of sexual activity; satisfaction with frequency and variety of sexual activity; presence of pain during sexual activity; quality of orgasm; and, for men, the frequency, duration, and firmness of erections and the quality of erection and ejaculation.

The cause of a dysfunction is either psychological or physical or a combination of the two. Psychological causes of dysfunction include emotional stress, partner dissatisfaction, negative body image, and guilt. Physical causes can include heavy alcohol use, certain medical conditions, prescription medications, and over-the-counter medications. Limiting alcohol consumption, treating medical conditions, and altering prescription and over-the-counter medications will oftentimes remedy the problem. If this is not the case, there are specific treatments available for each type of sexual problem. It is important to note that while many women do experience sexual dysfunctions, there has been very little research on the diagnosis, treatment, and causes of dysfunctions in women.

The origin of the dysfunction will determine how it is treated. If the problem is caused by drug therapy, an alternate drug or lower dose of the drug can be prescribed. When dysfunctions are psychological in origin, both the person experiencing the dysfunction and his or her partner (if there is one) are referred to a sex therapist. Also available are hormone therapy and penile implants. —*Catherine Schuster*

***See also*** Alcoholism; Communication; Estrogen replacement therapy; Hypertension; Impotence; Infertility; Marriage; Medications; Men and aging; Menopause; Prostate cancer; Prostate enlargement; Psychiatry, geriatric; Sexuality; Stress and coping skills; Urinary disorders; Women and aging.

**FOR FURTHER INFORMATION:**

Butler, Robert N., and Myrna I. Lewis. *Love and Sex After Sixty.* Rev. ed. New York: Ballantine Books, 1993. Discussion of how aging affects sexual desire and sexual activity.

Doress-Worters, Paula B., and Diana Laskin Siegal. *The New Ourselves, Growing Older: Women Aging with Knowledge and Power.* New York: Simon & Schuster, 1994. Useful and easy-to-understand information for both women and men.

Mayo Foundation for Medical Education and Research. "Sexuality and Aging: What It Means to Be Sixty or Seventy or Eighty in the '90's." *Mayo Clinic Health Letter* (February, 1993). Useful discussion of solutions to sexual changes that take place after age sixty.

Roberts, Amanda, and Barbara Padgett-Yawn, eds. *Reader's Digest Guide to Love and Sex.* Pleasantville, N.Y.: Reader's Digest Association, 1998. Colorful and easy-to-understand descriptions of female and male reproductive changes.

Whitaker, Julian, and Carol Colman. "Revitalize Your Sex Life: Restore Your Sexual Vitality, Enhance Your Sexual Function and Performance, Extend Your Sex Life into Your Sixties, Seventies, Eighties, and Beyond." In *Shed Ten Years in Ten Weeks.* New York: Fireside, 1997. Mainstream and alternative therapies for enhancing sexual functioning.

## RESPIRATORY CHANGES AND DISORDERS

**RELEVANT ISSUES:** Biology, health and medicine

**SIGNIFICANCE:** Respiratory changes during aging are of fundamental importance because they can affect quality of life and exercise tolerance; they are also associated with overall mortality

The ultimate purpose of the respiratory system is the transport of oxygen into cells and carbon dioxide out of cells. This is accomplished by moving air in and out of the lungs (ventilation), distributing the air within the lungs to areas that are perfused in blood (ventilation/perfusion), exchanging gas mixtures between the alveoli and blood (gas transfer), and transporting these gases in the blood to tissues. The respiratory system thus includes com-

*A nurse administers a respiratory test to an older patient. The lungs of elderly people are particularly vulnerable to disease and infection.* (Digital Stock)

ponents of the musculoskeletal system, the circulatory system, and the nervous system. All components may age or decline in function efficiency. These changes, as well as lifelong behaviors, make the elderly prone to chronic diseases of the respiratory system.

### Ventilation

Moving air into and out of the lungs occurs through changes in the size of the thoracic cavity. Upon inspiration, the thoracic cavity enlarges; during expiration, the thoracic cavity becomes smaller. The diaphragm is the most important muscle during ventilation. Auxiliary muscles include the intercostal muscles, located between the ribs, and the abdominal muscles. As the diaphragm contracts, the thoracic cavity enlarges, the lungs expand, the intrapleural pressure decreases, and air flows into the lungs. When the diaphragm and intercostal muscles relax, the tissues recoil, and air is expired. The amount of air entering or

leaving the lungs during a single normal breath is the tidal volume. The total amount of air that is exhaled following a maximal inhalation is called the vital capacity. The amount of air remaining at the end of a maximal exhalation is the residual volume. Added together, the vital capacity and the residual volume equal the total lung capacity.

Most increases in lung volume occur during a person's late teenage years or early twenties. The residual volume increases with age. Air remains trapped in the peripheral airways because of a loss of elastic fiber attachments. These elastic fiber attachments usually keep small conducting airways open and patent. During aging, these fibers appear to be disrupted and lose some of their function. Because the total lung capacity remains constant with age and the residual volume increases, the vital capacity decreases with age. That is, the amount of air that can be maximally exhaled decreases with age. Pulmonary function tests that indicate expiration capacity, such as the forced expiratory volume in one second ($FEV_1$), also decrease with age.

During expiration, the small airways at the base of the lung may close. This prevents the air at the base of the lung from being expired. The lung volume at which this closure occurs is called the closing capacity. The closing volume equals the closing capacity minus the residual volume. Closing volume has been shown to increase as people age. Therefore, older people exhale less air than younger people, and the air comes more from the upper parts of the lung than from the lower parts. When combined with other conditions, such as smoking or lung infection, ventilation can be significantly impaired, causing blood oxygen to become low.

Approximately 4 liters of air per minute enter the alveoli of the lung. Approximately 5 liters of blood per minute pass through the lungs. How completely the air and blood mix is termed the ventilation/perfusion ratio. Some researchers have shown ventilation/perfusion ratios to be less in the elderly than those found in younger adults. This means that the gases are not mixing as well with the blood, so that less oxygen or carbon dioxide can be exchanged. The lowered ratio, if it occurs, is often not significant to the average healthy older person. In fact, some scientists have reported a decrease in arterial oxygen content with age, but others have failed to demonstrate this association. Normally, the lungs will increase respiration or the heart will increase output to overcome the lower ventilation/perfusion ratio. However, when heart disease or chronic pulmonary disease is also present, the decreased ventilation/perfusion ratio may become worse. In such cases, lower blood oxygen and higher carbon dioxide can begin to be problematic.

## GAS TRANSFER AND BREATH CONTROL

The diffusion of gas from the end branches of the lung (the alveoli) into the blood depends on the total surface area of the alveoli, the thickness of the membrane across which the gas diffuses, and the capacity of the blood to absorb gas. Age-related decreases in gas transfer are usually the result of a loss of aveolar surface area, less perfusion of the lung by blood, or decreases in blood flow. All of these impact the ventilation/perfusion ratio.

The striated muscles of the respiratory system are under voluntary and autonomic control. Autonomic input to the muscles comes from both peripheral chemoreceptors and stretch receptors, which regulate the frequency and depth of breathing. The chemoreceptors are sensitive to the amount of carbon dioxide and, to a lesser extent, oxygen in the blood. The stretch receptors are sensitive to the contraction and relaxation of respiratory muscles. Although a fall in the oxygen content of the arteries can stimulate the chemoreceptors to increase breathing, arterial oxygen content is not normally an important part of the drive to breathe. Chemoreceptors are usually much more responsive to carbon dioxide concentrations. Researchers have shown that responsiveness to both oxygen and carbon dioxide decreases with aging.

Age-related respiratory changes do not appear to have a substantial impact on the normal, healthy older person. However, these changes do make the aging lung more susceptible to respiratory diseases, and the consequences of cardiac diseases and infectious diseases may be more severe. Certainly, pneumonia and upper respiratory infections become more serious for the older person who may have decreased ventilation and perfusion, as well as increased closing volume. In addition, chronic respiratory diseases are very common in the elderly.

## CHRONIC RESPIRATORY DISEASES

Chronic obstructive pulmonary disease (COPD), the fourth leading cause of death in the United States, usually manifests itself after the fifth decade of life. The term COPD is often used to include both bronchitis and emphysema because these two conditions often coexist. However, some scientists and physicians prefer to differentiate between the two based on the person's symptoms, history, and test results.

Bronchitis is closely associated with smoking and is typified by a productive cough for at least three months during the year for at least two consecutive years. The cough develops because of increased production of mucus and obstruction of the lower airways. The person with bronchitis cannot expire efficiently and so may retain carbon dioxide in the blood. Blood oxygenation may also decrease because of poor gas exchange in the alveoli. The person with bronchitis is often of normal weight or heavier. Although common to both conditions, the person with emphysema may appear to have more shortness of breath than someone with bronchitis. Gas exchange in the lungs worsens because of alveolar wall destruction, which decreases alveolar surface area. Measures of expiration decline, and arterial carbon dioxide is often elevated, although less so than is often seen in bronchitis. The person with emphysema is usually thin and becomes short of breath with little exertion.

The chronic respiratory diseases common in later years impair quality of life by curtailing activities. As respiratory disease progresses, activities may be limited to only those of personal hygiene. Additional exertion that would be needed to complete household tasks or leisure activities causes such people to become alarmingly short of breath. Combining medication with lifestyle changes and exercise can be successful, however, in many people. Surgical techniques that modify lung capacity also show great promise. For the older person without a chronic respiratory disease, the changes experienced with aging should not affect his or her quality of life. The changes in the respiratory system that occur as the result of aging alone are not significant enough to impact activities. People who have maintained an active lifestyle and developed their respiratory and cardiovascular systems will exhibit less decline than those who have been inactive for a lifetime. —*Karen Chapman-Novakofski*

**See also** Aging: Biological, psychological, and sociocultural perspectives; Aging process; Emphysema; Exercise and fitness; Illnesses among the elderly; Pneumonia; Smoking; Sports participation.

**FOR FURTHER INFORMATION:**

Abrams, William, Mark H. Beers, and Robert Berkow. *The Merck Manual of Geriatrics.* 2d ed. Whitehouse Station, N.J.: Merck Research Laboratories, 1995.

Derenne, Jean-Philippe, William Whitelaw, and Thomas Similowski, eds. *Acute Respiratory Failure in Chronic Obstructive Pulmonary Disease.* New York: Marcel Dekker, 1996.

Emslie-Smith, Donald, et al. *Textbook of Physiology.* 11th ed. New York: Churchill Livingstone, 1988.

Guyton, Arthur, and John Hall. *Textbook of Medical Physiology.* 9th ed. Philadelphia: W. B. Saunders, 1996.

Tockman, Melvyn. "The Respiratory System." In *Principles of Geriatric Medicine and Gerontology,* edited by William Hazzard, Reubin Andres, Edwin Bierman, and John Blass. 2d ed. New York: McGraw-Hill, 1990.

**REST HOMES.** *See* **NURSING AND CONVALESCENT HOMES.**

## RETIRED AND SENIOR VOLUNTEER PROGRAM (RSVP)

**DATE:** Founded in 1971

**RELEVANT ISSUES:** Demographics, recreation, work

**SIGNIFICANCE:** The Retired and Senior Volunteer Program is a national network of Americans, age fifty-five and over, who volunteer in their communities in an effort to improve the overall quality of life in the United States

The Retired and Senior Volunteer Program (RSVP) was founded by the Community Service Society of New York in 1971 as a pilot project designed to provide retirees with the opportunity to volunteer in ways that utilize their work and life experience. RSVP is one of three National Senior Service Corps programs administered by the Corporation for National Service, established in 1993 to promote community-based service programs. All three Senior Corp programs—the Foster Grandparent Program, the Retired and Senior Volunteer Program, and Senior Companion Program—provide volunteer opportunities for older citizens. More than 450,000 Americans volunteer their skills as part of RSVP annually.

RSVP members are not required to possess any minimum educational background or work experience, only the desire to volunteer on a regular basis. In 1999, RSVP volunteers actively served the needs of communities in more than 1,500 counties across the United States. At the local level, RSVP is typically affiliated with service providers, educational facilities, cultural organizations, and government agencies. Opportunities to volunteer vary widely, depending on the needs of the community. Skills or experience with adult day care, child care, classroom teaching, counseling, public speaking, and tutoring are utilized in most communities. Interested individuals are screened by RSVP staff and matched with the requirements of agencies prior to placement in the community at a volunteer site.

—*Donald C. Simmons, Jr.*

**See also** Mentoring; Retirement; Volunteering.

# RETIREMENT

**RELEVANT ISSUES:** Demographics, economics, law, race and ethnicity, work

**SIGNIFICANCE:** Formal retirement from work is a process that began in the late nineteenth century in Western societies because the industrial system needed to remove older workers in a socially acceptable manner

Beginning in the nineteenth century, formal retirement with pension payments provided a socially acceptable means for industries to reduce the size of their workforce. The welfare state in Western industrial countries worked with industries to achieve the goal of providing retired workers with a steady source of income. The retirement policies of the welfare state have helped determine the age at which individuals can retire from work. For example, the ability of individuals to receive lower Social Security payments at sixty-two years of age in the United States has been instrumental in lowering the age of retirement for many individuals in the population.

Women and racial minorities have different retirement patterns than Caucasian males because of their different work experiences. The increased size of the baby-boom population may lead to generational conflict in the United States if there are insufficient economic resources to support the current group of workers.

## RETIREMENT PRIOR TO THE INDUSTRIAL REVOLUTION

There was no formal universal retirement system in the world prior to the Industrial Revolution. Some occupations, such as the military, did provide care for their incapacitated members in good standing and provided shelter and food for them and their immediate family members. There were also benevolent work societies that cared for their indigent members. However, no universal system existed to provide a steady income for those no longer capable of working. Individuals continued working until their death, or they ceased working and were supported by either their accumu-

lated wealth or their family members. In colonial America, the landed elites, such as George Washington and Thomas Jefferson, used their personal wealth and the services of their slaves to support themselves in retirement.

The economic system did consider the diminished capacity of individuals to work by developing age-graded tasks. The system of slavery illustrated this process, with the younger slaves being engaged in field work and the older slaves doing lighter agricultural tasks or working in the plantation home. Slaves who could not work at all were either supported by the plantation owners or set free and left to the care of the state. In extreme cases, the incapacitated slave would be abandoned and left to die, as illustrated by Frederick Douglass's grandmother, who was left by her owners in a little hut to die after having provided a lifetime of service to them.

The family was required to bear the costs of maintaining those elderly who were no longer capable of working. This obligation was a heavy burden on most families, since, in some instances, they had to provide long-term care to their elderly relatives. Proportionally few individuals survived to old age prior to the Industrial Revolution, which limited this burden for most families. In eighteenth and nineteenth century America, many individuals were mobile, as illustrated by the case of Abraham Lincoln, who was born in Kentucky, lived as a child in Indiana, and eventually settled in the frontier town of Springfield, Illinois. These mobile individuals had limited contact with their relatives and were unable to offer them much aid. Propertied and elite elderly individuals, such as Benjamin Franklin in Philadelphia, were venerated by the larger community and received social support from this community, leading a comfortable existence in their older years. Ordinary elderly people with limited wealth were dependent on family members for support; without this support, they often endured extreme poverty.

## THE INDUSTRIAL REVOLUTION

In the nineteenth century, the evolution of the factory system changed the nature of work. Large numbers of individuals labored in this setting, producing mass goods efficiently and at a low cost. The factory system needed to replace older workers with younger ones, since the physical difficulty of the work made the elderly inefficient workers. There were age-graded tasks in these industries, but not enough for all elderly laborers. Since the older workers had no steady source of income if they ceased working, they resisted being removed from the workforce. In the early stages of industrialization, the owners of factories proceeded arbitrarily to dismiss their older workers and replace them with younger ones, sentencing these dismissed workers to a life of poverty. Such a policy created resentment among the workers, as well as discontent in the larger community. Violent labor disputes in the late nineteenth century, such as the Pullman Strike and the steel strike in Homestead, Pennsylvania, demonstrated that management needed a better means of managing their workforce. Part of this management involved the retirement of older workers without creating mass discontent.

One mechanism that industry found to accomplish this goal was to offer retired workers a pension as a reward for their lifetime of service to the organization. The railroad industry in the latter part of the nineteenth century began to offer a pension to its retired workers, easing the economic pain of their being removed from the workplace. However, most industries found that they could not afford to offer such a pension, and such economic incentives were used sparingly until the New Deal era in the 1930's. Companies were engaged in competition with other industries, and they found it unprofitable to offer their workers a pension and not have their competition provide a similar pension for their workers. In the southern United States, the workers were poorly organized and were split along racial lines, so the business community had less to fear from these workers. If a national retirement system was to be developed, a uniform national means of providing a retirement income for the older workers was required.

### THE WELFARE STATE

The welfare state was developed in Western industrialized societies to provide an income, as well as health benefits, for the older population. This welfare state, which provided state pensions for all

*Gardening is a favorite activity for many retired individuals.* (James L. Shaffer)

workers in society, was instituted in Germany in the 1870's by Prime Minister Otto von Bismarck. Bismarck, a staunch conservative, was engaged in a political struggle with the democratic socialist parties and needed some way to counter their appeal to the workers. He devised a uniform state pension system as a means of reducing the political radicalism of the workers, while at the same time tying them to the state. In the twentieth century, many of the other nations in Europe, including Sweden and Denmark, began to adopt such a pension system. Great Britain and France lagged behind other European nations in this development, but after World War II, they and other industrialized Western nations adopted similar retirement systems.

Left-wing and socialist worker parties were instrumental in the development of these retirement systems in Western democratic societies. These parties saw this type of pension system as being beneficial to their constituents. In political campaigns, the adoption of such a system became a major platform of these parties. In many instances, this type of campaign led to political victory and the national adoption of pension support for the elderly, as occurred in Great Britain in 1945 with the victory of the Labour Party.

The United States instituted retirement welfare later than other industrially developed nations. An early attempt at a welfare retirement system in the nation involved the federal government's payments, after 1890, to the 1.8 million individuals who served in the Union Army during the Civil War. This national welfare system was limited in scope, since it naturally excluded Confederate veterans, as well as the elderly immigrants who arrived in the United States after the war. Prior to the 1930's, some states developed pension systems, but their scope was limited, and the dollar amount of their pensions was small.

The Great Depression, which began in 1929 and lasted until World War II, provided the impetus for the creation of a national, although restricted, pension system. The Depression dramatically increased the level of poverty among the elderly and called forth social movements designed to reduce this poverty. In California, the Townsend movement, which advocated a fixed pension for all elderly citizens of the state, formed many clubs throughout the state. In 1934, the movement was instrumental in nominating writer and activist Upton Sinclair as the democratic candidate for governor. Franklin Delano Roosevelt was elected president in 1932 and started the New Deal program designed to help end the Depression. The New Deal came to see the development of a national pension system as an important goal, since such a system would offer aid to the poverty-stricken elderly population while at the same time stopping them from supporting more radical relief measures. In 1935, the Social Security Act was proposed by the Roosevelt administration and was passed by Congress. It was modest in scope, offering limited monthly pensions for workers in certain industries. In the South, African American sharecroppers were excluded from the system. After 1935, however, the scope of the program was expanded by successive Congresses, and the system became more inclusive. In 1965, the Lyndon B. Johnson administration passed the Medicare Act, providing medical care and services for those sixty-five years of age and older.

The total number of pension systems available to the American population significantly expanded after 1935. Most individual states offer extensive pension systems for state workers, with the state of California having the largest one in the nation. Many industries, including the automobile industry (which offers high pensions and medical benefits to workers who have thirty years of service), have expanded their pension offerings. By the 1970's and 1980's, individual pension systems, financed by tax subsidies, were instituted. Individual retirement accounts (IRAs) allowed individuals to invest up to $2,000 in most investment plans and claim it as a tax deduction, while supplemental savings accounts (SRAs) allowed workers to invest a larger amount in specified investment accounts and deduct the amount from their gross earnings. These government-subsidized accounts allowed individuals to make investments and defer their taxes on these investments until after they retired, when they would be in a lower tax bracket. These government-subsidized investment plans favored middle- and upper-income individuals, since lower-income individuals did not possess the extra income needed for investment. While large numbers of Americans have limited pension protection, being dependent on Social Security and Supplemental Social Security for their retirement

*For active seniors with adequate income, retirement often means the chance to travel at home and abroad.* (Jeff Greenberg/Archive Photos)

income, many Americans have been allowed to expand their pension coverage.

### THE AGE OF RETIREMENT

When the Social Security Act of 1935 was passed, it specified sixty-five years as the age when individuals or their spouse might receive a retirement pension. This age became accepted as that at which an individual should retire, and a vast majority of Americans prior to the 1960's retired at this age. However, after the Social Security Administration in the 1960's allowed individuals to retire with reduced benefits at the age of sixty-two, there was a decline in the age of retirement, with many Americans retiring before sixty-five. The growth of state pensions, which allow retirement either after thirty years of service or at age sixty, has further increased the number of individuals who retire prior to sixty-five. Many industries, such as the automobile and steel industries, grant retirement and medical benefits to workers after thirty years of service, and this policy has also increased the number of individuals who retire prior to the age of sixty-five.

Many individuals who retire relatively young, such as police officers or military personnel (who can retire after twenty years of service), start a second career. While some individuals follow a path of full work and then totally retire, others hold "bridge jobs" that provide lower levels of employment before they fully retire from work. This gradual reduction of work allows individuals to ease themselves into the retirement role, which requires some adjustment in their lifestyle. By the age of seventy, most individuals have removed themselves from the workforce or have involuntarily been removed because of illness or disability. Higher status professionals and managers are more likely to continue working beyond sixty-five, since their work activity is less strenuous and since they are in greater demand because of their skills. Many of these individuals can continue to work part-time by consulting with firms and organizations with which they had contact during their career.

In a study that examines the evolution of retirement between 1880 and 1990, Dora L. Costa provides a coherent explanation for the falling age of retirement in the United States. The increased retirement income available to the elderly is a necessary condition for explaining this process, but it does not totally explain it. Another factor is the improved health of the elderly population, which makes it possible for them to be active in their later years. There has been a steady rise in the life expectancy of all Americans, with the current overall life expectancy being seventy-five years of age, although it is higher for women and lower for African Americans. The education level of Americans has also increased appreciably. In 1945, at the end of World War II, the median formal education of all Americans was approximately eight years of schooling, while at present it is more than thirteen years of schooling.

The growth of an elderly population that is healthier and better educated, and possesses more discretionary income, has triggered the growth of a leisure and recreational industry that can serve this market at a competitive low cost. The expansion of cable television and rental films has provided the entire population with inexpensive entertainment in their homes. The development of the Internet, which can be accessed by all individuals with inexpensive computers, has given the elderly access to many sources of information and entertainment. The travel and tourist industry has expanded the services available to the elderly and has given them travel opportunities not available to earlier generations. Prior to World War II, travel to Europe and outside the country was only available for the wealthy or the elite elderly. In the nineteenth and twentieth centuries, wealthy Americans, such as John D. Rockefeller and Andrew Carnegie, or elite Americans, such as Ulysses S. Grant and Theodore Roosevelt, traveled and toured abroad, but such travel was not feasible for the average American. However, the development of low-cost air travel and the packaging of relatively inexpensive foreign tour packages reduced the cost of international travel and allowed lower income individuals the opportunity to travel abroad. Market changes related to leisure and recreation have made retirement more attractive for elderly Americans, who have readily availed themselves of these opportunities when they possess the economic resources.

The increased number of elderly citizens as a result of the aging of the baby-boom population, as well as the falling age of retirement for senior citizens, has prompted policymakers to attempt to reduce the number of retirees by raising the age at which individuals can receive their Social Security benefits. Those individuals born in 1943 and later must be sixty-seven years of age before they can receive full benefits, although there has been no change in the policy of giving reduced benefits for those who retire at sixty-two. This policy change may have some impact on the age of retirement, but since more elderly citizens have other sources of income beyond Social Security, its impact will be minimal. Because there will probably be fewer younger workers to support older workers in the future, it may be necessary to increase the age of retirement.

A larger concern with the increased number of retirees in Western industrialized nations is the impact of this change on economic growth. If the elderly dependent population becomes too large, this increase may reduce the capital available in the society for economic growth. In the 1950's and 1960's, a similar concern arose with the high number of young dependent people (fourteen years of age and younger) in underdeveloped nations.

Some demographers supported birth control policies in these nations as a means of reducing their young dependent population, which would make more capital available in these countries and stimulate economic growth.

## GENERATIONAL CONFLICT AND RETIREMENT

The increased number of elderly individuals who live a long life because of improved health, while at the same time receiving improved government benefits, has raised the fear of greater intergenerational conflict in American society. It is true that the baby-boom generation born between 1945 and 1964 has placed a strain on the Social Security and Medicare systems. It is estimated that these government transfer programs will pay out more than they take in during the early decades of the twenty-first century. The only means of correcting this situation is to either increase taxes or reduce benefits, neither choice being politically popular. The increased cost of caring for the elderly population led to the establishment of Americans for Generational Equity (AGE), a pressure group that criticizes the redistribution of social transfer payments in favor of the elderly. There are legitimate financial concerns about the increased economic cost of the elderly population for the remainder of society, but a part of this concern involves an ideological battle by conservative groups to end, or at least curtail, all government programs.

Demographer Samuel Preston has statistically demonstrated that, since the 1960's, proportionally more government transfer payments and funding are going to support the elderly, and proportionally less are going to the younger population. The Clinton administration's welfare reform package of 1996 is an illustration of this process, with the federal and state governments' transfer payments being cut for children and unwed mothers, as well as illegal immigrants. No such similar reform has been instituted for Social Security and Medicare, and no legislation has been proposed to reduce tax credits for IRA and SRA accounts. The elderly are a well-organized political group, and they can be mobilized to protect their vested interests.

Those who attack high government transfer payments for the elderly usually have no political desire to expand the scope of the welfare state and provide more government aid to children and those in poverty. Rather, they wish to cut or eliminate all government programs that aid the former groups, while also reducing government aid to the elderly. The support by business groups to privatize Social Security or to have a proportion of Social Security taxes go toward private investment is a step in the elimination of the program. Stock investments might aid some middle- and upper-income elderly, but they will be risky for lower-income individuals, as well as for those individuals who have a limited knowledge of personal investment.

Critics of the Social Security system often fail to see the insurance nature of the program and its ability, with full citizen participation, to provide aid to elderly and other individuals who need government support. Partially or totally privatizing the system would reduce funds for the Social Security trust fund required to pay its insurance claims, such as disability claims and Supplemental Social Security claims for the poverty-stricken elderly. The Social Security system is both a retirement system and an insurance system, with no payments for those who fail to survive long enough to collect payments. If an individual and his or her spouse die before retirement, the money they have paid into the system reverts back to the federal government. However, throughout their lives, they have been insured by the system.

In discussing the elderly and their cost for the younger working population, one should differentiate among three categories of elderly. The young-old, between sixty and seventy-five years of age, are relatively healthy and active. The middle-old, seventy-six to eighty-five years of age, experience more health problems and require a higher level of social support. The old-old, those over eighty-five years of age, are a fast-growing segment of the elderly population who experience high levels of health-related problems and require more social services, including long-term care in nursing homes or in their residence. This group places a significant burden on social and medical facilities.

Those individuals who stress the intergenerational conflict approach fail to consider the benefits that the elderly population transfers to the younger population. As a result of the growth of the American economy, the elderly population has accumulated vast amounts of wealth in property, stocks, bonds, and other forms of investments. In the first several decades of the twenty-first century, trillions of dollars of this wealth will be transferred to the younger generation through family inheritance. In evaluating the burden that the elderly population imposes on the younger generation, one should also consider these asset transfers between the generations.

## AFRICAN AMERICANS AND WOMEN

Elderly African American workers are often marginalized and have often experienced racial discrimination throughout their work careers. They are more likely to have worked in low-status jobs characterized by sporadic work patterns and low income. This job pattern means that they are less likely than Caucasians to have a pension beyond Social Security or Supplemental Social Security. Some of them work beyond sixty-five years of age because of economic necessity, but, as a group, they are likely to retire earlier than Caucasians, at fifty-five to sixty-four years of age. Their relatively poor health and more sporadic employment are the major reasons for this early retirement. African Americans who have similar work careers as Caucasians have similar types of retirement patterns. The lower life expectancy of African Americans implies that they receive less total retirement income from the system than Caucasians. However, they pay less than Caucasians into the Social Security system, and they are more likely to receive Supplemental Social Security benefits, balancing out inequities in payments from the system.

Women have become more active in the labor force since World War II. They often balance work and family needs. Women are more numerous in lower-paying occupations, such as teaching and social work, and suffer economic discrimination even when they perform the same tasks as men. As a result of these two factors, they have lower wages and a shorter job tenure than men. They also receive lower levels of Social Security benefits than men and are less likely to receive private pensions. The Social Security system discriminates against women when computing their benefits in that it fails to count their child rearing and family work when determining their benefits. Social Security benefits are determined on the basis of years worked and maximum salary during this work career, which is assumed to be thirty years. If a woman works fewer than thirty years, often because of family obligations, she receives fewer benefits. Women who are married and share in their husbands' benefits usually receive adequate retirement benefits, but divorced, widowed, and single women are likely to suffer economic deprivation.

—*Ira M. Wasserman*

**See also** African Americans; Early retirement; Employment; Forced retirement; 401K plans; Income sources; Individual retirement accounts (IRAs); Internet; Leisure activities; Life expectancy; Medicare; Men and aging; Old age; Pensions; Politics; Poverty; Retired Senior Volunteer Program (RSVP); Retirement communities; Retirement planning; Social Security; Townsend movement; Vacations and travel; Volunteering; Women and aging.

## FOR FURTHER INFORMATION:

Atchley, Robert C. *Social Forces and Aging: An Introduction to Social Gerontology.* 9th ed. Belmont, Calif.: Wadsworth, 1999. This standard social aging text discusses retirement, as well as economic and political issues related to aging.

Cockerham, William C. *This Aging Society.* 2d ed. Upper Saddle River, N.J.: Prentice Hall, 1997. Cockerham discusses the aging process and its social impact on the larger society.

Costa, Dora L. *The Evolution of Retirement: An American Economic History, 1880-1990.* Chicago: University of Chicago Press, 1998. A brilliant study of the economic history of retirement in the United States and the role of the market place in shaping retirement decisions.

Hooyman, Nancy R., and H. Asuman Kiyak. *Social Gerontology: A Multidisciplinary Perspective.* 5th ed. Boston: Allyn & Bacon, 1999. A discussion of retirement and other issues related to social gerontology.

Quadagno, Jill. *Aging and the Life Course: An Introduction to Social Gerontology.* Boston: McGraw-Hill, 1999. This study of the social aging process provides a historic and policy perspective for studying retirement and other aspects of aging.

Quadagno, Jill, and Debra Street, eds. *Aging for the Twenty-first Century.* New York: St. Martin's Press, 1996. This set of readings considers the impact of retirement on various class and status groups.

## RETIREMENT COMMUNITIES

**RELEVANT ISSUES:** Demographics, economics, family, recreation

**SIGNIFICANCE:** Retirement communities are a relatively new alternative for older citizens, who now can live in an age-segregated environment while receiving a varying range of services

Some people have described retirement communities as halfway stations between preretirement residences and nursing homes, but formal definitions of these communities are as varied as the services they provide. Retirement communities differ greatly in terms of their physical characteristics, organization, amenities and recreation opportunities, fee structure, and other aspects.

### VARIETY

The breakdown of retirement communities into categories often includes retirement towns and villages, retirement subdivisions, retirement residences, and continuing care retirement communities (CCRCs). The type of ownership also can be used as a basis for classification. Some are owned by residents and others rented by residents. In one hybrid form, residents buy their dwellings, but ownership reverts back to the corporate owner upon their death.

Many of these settlements have developed an autonomous community life, but others depend to varying degrees on the services of the outside community. A retirement community may take the form of a service-oriented mobile home park, a series of detached residences, or a high-rise public housing project, or even extend to an entire leisure community or a full-service continuing care retirement community.

Services provided may include housing, housekeeping services, recreation, therapy, sit-down meals (including those for special diets), social services, transportation, storage, parking, and, most important, medical care if necessary. In the more modest communities, the services may be limited to housing and one or two meals a day served cafeteria-style. Fees would be correspondingly lower. In CCRCs, there is often an entrance fee, part of which may be refundable upon the resident's relocation or demise (payable to the estate), in addition to the customary, usually high, monthly fee. Some of the newer CCRCs are based on the concept of owner equity, somewhat like a cooperative or condominium. In short, the variety is impressive.

The numbers are impressive as well. It was estimated that by 2000, there would be about fifteen hundred CCRCs in the United States with about half a million residents. That population would come out of more than three million elderly—about 10 percent of those older than sixty-five—who live in congregate residential facilities. Half of that population would live in nursing homes. Unlike nursing home patients, members of retirement communities are expected to be in fairly good health and sufficiently active to participate in community events.

Communities offer a variety of programming for residents. A typical week's activities at one community that emphasizes an active social life for residents include such organized events as church services, exercise classes, bingo, cinema, barbecues, ice cream socials, piano instruction, sing-alongs, crafts classes, baking instruction, lunch out, social night, and shopping and banking expeditions. Clubs might be organized around activities, such as a walking club to combine socialization with exercise.

### Origins

Although California had a statute as early as 1939, most of the other states that regulate retirement communities at all enacted their legislation between 1975 and 1986. Existing statutes vary widely in purpose, coverage, certification or registration requirements, disclosure provisions, contract content, and enforcement agencies (if any).

Retirement communities started as real estate developments planned somewhat offhandedly by public and private sponsors for an elderly clientele. Sponsors have included government agencies, fraternal lodges, labor unions, religious groups, voluntary associations, and real estate developers. In some way or another, the above were responding to the expressed desire of some older people to live with others of similar age and stage of life, often in warmer climates such as those of Florida and California. The mobility of older citizens in the automobile age, their willingness to relocate, and their desire to live in a special age-segregated environment also help to explain the acceptance and spectacular growth of these communities.

Subsequently, retirement communities were established in northern states—for example, New Jersey and Pennsylvania—as well as in Canada, where they are usually smaller than in the United States but otherwise do not differ in any systematic way. Retirement communities arose in these locations because some older adults preferred to remain in familiar surroundings.

### Pros and Cons

Criticisms of retirement communities, where they occur, are principally focused on the fact that the relatively homogeneous age groups—and often racial, social, religious, and income groups—create an artificial environment. Anthropologist Margaret Mead characterized retirement communities as "golden ghettos" untypical of the natural world. Other critics have stressed the stultifying atmosphere that a group of bored or listless senior citizens leading a hedonistic life in pursuit of happiness can generate. Most observers, however, view a retirement community as a unique opportunity to remain physically and socially active and to be relieved of many household responsibilities.

Other reasons for the success and growth of these communities are the increasing pool of elderly in both the United States and Canada, their longer life expectancy, and their better financial standing, which makes retirement facilities more affordable. The latter is a result of increased government Social Security and Medicare payments, as well as the increasing prevalence and benefits of pension plans and personal retirement savings options. The elderly of the late twentieth century will be among the last Americans to be able to rely to any significant degree on pensions for their retirement, but the elderly of the future have been warned, and many are saving to pay for a comfortable retirement.

### Relationships

The tradition of elderly parents moving in with their children or even grandchildren upon retirement or when they become unable to care for themselves is no longer as strong. There may be other "push" factors encouraging the growth of retirement communities, such as the deterioration of the elderly's earlier residential neighborhoods, the loss of their friends through relocation or death, or even an excessive number of children in their vicinity. Finally, developers have found the establishment of such communities—especially at the upper end of the scale—very lucrative.

Various polls and anecdotal reports suggest that retirement community residents tend to be satisfied with them, especially because of the socializing possibilities such congregate living affords. Malcontents tend to compare the services of staff unfavorably with the personalized touch of family members. In addition, sometimes the type of retirement community selected may not be tailored to meet the needs and desires of particular residents.

Staff often fulfill a surrogate family role, as do other residents and peers, through socializing and support. Family assistance, support, or merely presence often is unavailable because of estranged relations, lack of sustained contact with family over many years, distance, or simply personal preference. With loners excepted, those who are thus unattached must rely on on-site support systems. Even when the younger family members live nearby, the prevalence of working couples makes it difficult for the younger set to care for older relatives.

### A CASE STUDY

Pine Woods is an adult home community in central Florida covering some three hundred acres of land. The site was purchased by an insurance company in 1972 because of its mild climate, rolling hills, woodlands, waterways, and isolation from congested areas. The community was deliberately planned to be relatively small to maximize a friendly village atmosphere. In 1992, Pine Woods had nearly two thousand residents.

A sixteen-hundred-seat auditorium in the clubhouse is the hub of social and recreational life. The facility has covered shuffleboard courts, a swimming pool, saunas, whirlpools, and a marina with access to a lake for boating and fishing. Other activities take place in smaller meeting rooms. The retirement community has a closed-circuit television system, cable television, paved and lighted streets, an around-the-clock security system and security gate, and a call-button system linking residents to security for emergencies.

A residents' cooperative association board of directors is responsible for overall policy and financial arrangements. A general manager has day-to-day responsibility for the community and for the paid staff, including a recreation director. In the course of its life cycle, new and younger residents move in as some older settlers move out or die,

thus helping to energize the facility and take over voluntary leadership roles. Other types of retirement communities with older clienteles would tend to focus more on health services rather than recreation, or at least on those activities that require less physical exertion. *—Peter B. Heller*

*See also* Friendship; Home ownership; Housing; Independent living; Laguna Woods, California; Leisure activities; Nursing and convalescent homes; Relocation; Retirement; Retirement planning; Senior citizen centers; Social ties.

**FOR FURTHER INFORMATION:**
Beesley, Kenneth B. *Social Well Being in Planned Retirement Communities: A Review and Pilot Study.* Peterborough, Ontario, Canada: Trent University, 1989.

Down, Ivy M., and Lorraine Schnurr. *Between Home and Nursing Home: The Board and Care Alternative.* Buffalo: Prometheus, 1991.

Moss, Rudolf H., and Sonne Lemke. *Group Residences for Older Adults.* New York: Oxford University Press, 1994.

Osgood, Nancy J. *Senior Settlers: Social Integration in Retirement Communities.* New York: Praeger, 1982.

Sherwood, Sylvia, et al. *Continuing Care Retirement Communities.* Baltimore: Johns Hopkins University Press, 1997.

Smithers, Janice A. *Determined Survivors: Community Life Among the Urban Elderly.* New Brunswick, N.J.: Rutgers University Press, 1985.

Teski, Marea. *Living Together: An Ethnography of a Retirement Hotel.* Washington, D.C.: University Press of America, 1981.

## RETIREMENT PLANNING

**RELEVANT ISSUES:** Economics, psychology, work
**SIGNIFICANCE:** Retirement planning is essential to people throughout life if they are to enjoy their retirement years

Retirement is a time requiring many significant changes in the life of the individual. At retirement, the individual suddenly has more time on his or her hands, fewer commitments, more time for other people, and a change in level of income. One who plans ahead for retirement generally will have an easier time accomplishing these transitions successfully. Preretirement planning is considered one of the major developmental tasks of middle age according to Robert J. Havighurst's theory of development. In reality, in order to be prepared adequately for retirement, one needs to begin planning by young adulthood.

## FINANCIAL PLANNING

An individual facing retirement must first make a decision about when to retire. This decision has been heavily influenced by changing life ex-

---

## Planning for Retirement

---

These excerpts are from a survey by the Pew Research Center for the People and the Press on "Public Attentiveness to Social Security and Medicare." Results are based on telephone interviews conducted under the direction of Princeton Survey Research Associates. The survey was among a nationwide sample of 1,002 adults, 18 years of age or older, during the period October 29-November 9, 1997. For results based on the total sample, the sampling error is plus or minus 3 percentage points.

Q: (IF NOT RETIRED) Do you personally have any money saved to live on when you get older? (IF RETIRED) Do you have any personal savings or investments now?

| Percentage of total | | Not retired | Retired |
|---|---|---|---|
| 57 | Yes | 55 | 67 |
| 41 | No | 44 | 26 |
| 2 | Don't know/Refused | 1 | 7 |
| 100% | | 100% | 100% |
| | Number of respondents | (830) | (172) |

Q: (IF ALREADY RETIRED) How has your standard of living changed since you retired? Would you say it has gone up, gone down, or stayed about the same? (IF NOT RETIRED) How do you think your standard of living will change when you retire? Do you think it will go up, go down, or stay about the same?

| | Retired | Not retired |
|---|---|---|
| Gone/Go up | 14 | 14 |
| Gone/Go down | 30 | 36 |
| Stayed/Stay about the same | 55 | 47 |
| Don't know/Refused | 1 | 3 |
| | 100% | 100% |
| Number of respondents | (172) | (830) |

Q: (IF NOT RETIRED/DISABLED) When you retire do you expect you'll have enough money to . . . (IF RETIRED/DISABLED) Do you currently have enough money to . . .

| Percentage of total | | Not retired/disabled | Retired/disabled |
|---|---|---|---|
| 22 | Live very comfortably | 22 | 22 |
| 34 | Meet your expenses with a little left over for extras | 36 | 25 |
| 31 | Just meet your basic living expenses | 30 | 35 |
| 11 | Not enough to meet expenses | 10 | 14 |
| 2 | Don't know/Refused | 2 | 4 |
| 100% | | 100% | 100% |
| | Number of respondents | (811) | (191) |

pectancies. With life expectancies reaching nearly seventy-seven years and increasing, people realize that they will probably be alive for many years after retirement and need money to live on for quite some time. The age at which one will be able to collect Social Security is also a factor influencing retirement. People born prior to 1938 can collect full benefits at sixty-five, while those born after 1960 must wait until sixty-seven. The existence of private pension plans (if any) will also influence the timing of retirement and the socioeconomic status afterward.

It has been estimated that in order to be financially secure at retirement, an individual must have at least two-thirds of his or her preretirement income (with three-quarters of prior income giving one a more comfortable margin). In order to decide precisely what people will need, they should estimate the number of years that they will probably be retired, the style of living that they would like during those retirement years, and the rate of inflation likely between now and retirement. The earlier one starts saving, the more time money has to grow. A twenty-two-year-old who sets aside $50 per month will have approximately $319,000 at the age of sixty-two (with a 10 percent annual return). By waiting ten years until he or she is thirty-two, that individual will have to invest approximately $140 per month to reach that same goal.

Clearly, one needs to begin saving early in life. In planning for retirement, one needs to take into account Social Security and employer pension plans, as well as individual savings for retirement. Annual deposits into traditional or Roth individual retirement accounts (IRAs) or 401K plans are highly beneficial to the individual. Many families today are creating "kindergarten capitalists," investing for their children to better secure their futures.

## MEDICAL AND LEGAL PLANNING

No matter how well one plans financially for retirement, there are certain expenditures that one cannot foresee. Most typically, these are medical expenses. While most retired elderly have Medicare health coverage, this does not include coverage for eyeglasses, hearing aids, dental work, or prescriptions. These expenses pose a large financial burden for the retired person, but may still be manageable. When one is hit with a long-term or catastrophic situation, medical expenses mount dramatically, often wiping out retirement savings and any legacy for one's survivors. In order to avoid this situation, in preretirement planning one might acquire long-term care insurance to cover catastrophic medical expenses. Approximately 70 percent of couples over the age of sixty-five can expect one spouse to require long-term care.

Reports in the *New England Journal of Medicine* indicate that, in the late 1990's, 50 percent of those who entered nursing homes would spend an average of two years there, at over $36,000 per year. While long-term care insurance can help cover these costs, other safeguards might be employed to protect one's estate. One of the ways commonly chosen is the establishment of a living trust.

Aside from financial concerns associated with medical conditions, people should have very real concerns about how they will be treated medically in the future if they are unable to make decisions for themselves. The existence of advanced directives should allow people to make their desires known, as well as appoint an agent to make these decisions if so desired. By creating a living will or durable power of attorney for health care, all adults can ensure that their medical treatment will be consistent with their wishes. This is one very important part of planning (like financial planning) that is best dealt with initially by early adulthood.

## PLANNING A NEW LIFE

Planning for retirement includes planning ways to make life pleasant and productive. As such, this includes planning where one wants to live both in terms of locale and type of housing. In recent years, large numbers of retirement living options have come to exist. Prior to deciding on the type of housing desired, one needs to decide to which area he or she would like to retire. This decision should be based on a familiarity with the area (including actual time spent there), as well as research into such areas as the cost of living, opportunities available including part-time jobs, volunteering, and leisure activities, and the existence of programs designed specifically for the elderly. By engaging in appropriate research, in the years prior to retirement, the individual or couple can make decisions confidently about which options best suit their desired lifestyle. Much of this research can be conducted on the Internet; information is available on a large number of housing options.

People can plan to remain in their own homes, move to smaller houses that are easier to care for and provide them with additional financial resources, or move to condominiums, retirement communities, senior high rises, or assisted-living situations. A newer alternative to be considered has been developed in New Jersey and is known as ALLY (Alternative Living in Later Years). This consists of a nonprofit situation that purchases large houses and subdivides them to be shared by a number of senior citizens. This allows seniors who have lived in their own houses to continue doing so without the burden of living alone, overwhelming financial responsibility, and sole responsibility for upkeep. Additionally, it provides the single senior with a new network of support, which in many instances comes to serve as a surrogate family.

Consideration of these many different housing alternatives while planning for retirement should leave one ready to initiate changes upon retirement. When an individual or couple has decided on a type of housing and an area for retirement, they would do well to actually "try it out" rather than moving permanently. This trial move can be accomplished at the very beginning of retirement (since most people do not have the flexibility to do this while still working). People would begin by subletting their house (rather than selling it), renting an apartment or house (rather than buying one) in their new desired location, and getting involved in the types of activities that they hope to engage in throughout retirement. By spending the first year of their retirement in this manner, they are engaging in a trial run (and still continuing to plan for a long and happy future). Too many retired individuals burn all their bridges behind them as soon as they retire, only to find out that living in an area and vacationing there are two different things entirely. After a year of living in the new "desired" situation, the individual or couple is ready to make this commitment permanent or go back to their previous way of life (which they can easily do since they have not made any permanent changes). In so doing, they are able to determine that they do have enough money to live on, a liking of the area in which they have settled, satisfaction with their housing situation, enjoyment of the leisure, volunteer, and work opportunities available, and adequate social support systems available to them.

Middle-aged adults should consider the social lifestyle changes that they will face in retirement. Typically, one will spend a lot more time with one's spouse or significant other than while working. This relationship is likely to be more pleasant if the middle-aged couple deliberately plans to spend time alone together (to "date"), concentrating on one another (talking, holding hands, reminiscing) and continually planning their future together.

The other consideration that requires planning is adaptation to a relatively unstructured day. The individual is no longer faced with a routine. One must think about and plan for activities to fill the gap left by loss of career at retirement. By planning in young adulthood or middle age, individuals can uncover and develop hobbies or hidden talents into which they can channel time and energy in retirement.

## CONCLUSION

Retirement is a period involving many major adaptations to a changing lifestyle. These adaptations and transitions occur most smoothly when they have been planned for ahead of time. Planning should include all the following areas: financial, legal, medical, social, housing, and activities. A person who plans accordingly can then look forward to the "golden years" of retirement.

—*Robin Kamienny Montvilo*

**See also** Durable power of attorney; Early retirement; Employment; Estates and inheritance; Forced retirement; 401K plans; Home ownership; Housing; Income sources; Individual retirement accounts (IRAs); Leisure activities; Life insurance; Living wills; Long-term care for the elderly; Medical insurance; Relocation; Retirement; Retirement communities; Social Security; Social ties; Trusts; Wills and bequests.

## FOR FURTHER INFORMATION:

Belsky, J. *The Adult Experience.* St. Paul: West, 1997.

Binstock, R. H., and L. K. George. *Handbook of Aging and the Social Sciences.* 4th ed. San Diego: Academic Press, 1996.

Hoyer, W. J., J. M. Rybash, and P. A. Roodin. *Adult Development and Aging.* 4th ed. Boston: McGraw-Hill, 1999.

Johnson, E., and K. McFadden. *Senior Net's Official*

Guide to the Web: The Complete Guide to the Web for People over Sixty-five. Emeryville, Calif.: Lycos Press, 1997.

Papalia, D. E., J. C. Camp, and R. D. Feldman. Adult Development and Aging. New York: McGraw-Hill, 1996.

## RHINOPHYMA

**RELEVANT ISSUES:** Biology, health and medicine

**SIGNIFICANCE:** Rhinophyma, a complication of rosacea, is a buildup of excess tissue on the nose and cheeks, leading to a bulbous red nose and puffy cheeks

Rosacea is a chronic inflammation and redness of the face that usually affects people between the ages of thirty and fifty. It is more common in women but is more severe in men. Guy de Chauliac, a French surgeon, first described rosacea medically in the fourteenth century, attributing the condition to the excessive consumption of alcoholic drinks. It is now known that, although alcohol may exacerbate the condition, rosacea can develop in individuals who have never consumed alcohol. While the actual cause is unknown, rosacea is more common in fair-skinned people who flush easily. The most common triggers for this flushing are hot drinks, alcohol, spicy foods, stress, sunlight, and extreme heat or cold. There is no cure for rosacea, but it can be treated with oral and topical antibiotics and avoidance of triggers.

Untreated, rosacea may progress from facial redness to slight swelling, pimples, pustules, and prominent facial pores on the nose, mid-forehead, and chin. In some patients, particularly in men, the oil glands enlarge, causing a bulbous, enlarged red nose and puffy cheeks. Thick bumps can develop on the lower half of the nose and nearby cheeks. This stage is known as rhinophyma, a condition made famous by actor W. C. Fields with his red, bulbous nose. Rhinophyma can be extremely disfiguring, and its mistaken association with alcoholism can cause embarrassment and affect self-esteem. Like rosacea, rhinophyma cannot be cured, but the symptoms can be lessened or even eliminated. Rhinophyma is usually treated with surgery. The excess tissue that has developed can be removed with a scalpel or a laser, or through electro-surgery.

—Lisa M. Sardinia

**See also** Skin changes and disorders.

## ROBIN AND MARIAN

**DIRECTOR:** Richard Lester

**CAST:** Sean Connery, Audrey Hepburn, Robert Shaw, Ian Holm, Nicol Williamson, Richard Harris

**DATE:** Released in 1976

**RELEVANT ISSUES:** Culture, media, psychology, values

**SIGNIFICANCE:** This film explores the response of the aging hero and heroine whose powers fade, making it impossible for them to repeat the famous feats of their youth

Upon the death of King Richard (Richard Harris), Robin Hood (Sean Connery) returns, having served in the Crusades and other wars for twenty years. He goes to Sherwood Forest, where he lived as an outlaw during the struggle against King John (Ian Holm) and the sheriff of Nottingham (Robert Shaw, in a marvelous, humane performance). Many of his band have died or given up the outlaw life. Marian (Audrey Hepburn), with whom he is still in love, has become the abbess of a nunnery.

Sean Connery and Audrey Hepburn in the film Robin and Marian. (Archive Photos)

Marian does not wish to leave the religious life, but Robin's love combines with the new king's machinations against the Church to bring them together again. They live in Sherwood as lovers and as leaders of the fight against royal power. Robin is now in his forties, however; he is battle-scarred and stiff. The adventures which follow show that he no longer has the endurance and strength of his youth. Despite his age, he defeats the sheriff of Nottingham in single combat, though he is wounded. Marian and Robin's friend Little John (Nicol Williamson) help him to the nunnery. Robin has not observed that the royal troops, violating Nottingham's order to withdraw should Nottingham be defeated, have destroyed the uprising.

Marian prepares "medicine" that she and Robin both take. She has poisoned them both to protect them from the ravages of age and the destruction of the bright legend that was Robin Hood. When Robin realizes what she has done he says, "I'd never have a day like this again, would I? It's better this way." He asks Little John to bury them both where his last arrow falls in the forest.

*Robin and Marian* is a subtle and moving examination of the response to the failing of one's powers with age.                    —*Robert Jacobs*

*See also* Films; Middle age; Suicide.

## "ROMAN FEVER"

**AUTHOR:** Edith Wharton
**DATE:** Published in 1933
**RELEVANT ISSUES:** Family, marriage and dating
**SIGNIFICANCE:** This short story explores bitterness over sexual rivalry that lasts decades, continuing even after the loved one's death

Edith Wharton's "Roman Fever" tells the story of two lifelong acquaintances who loved the same man, now deceased. He became the husband of one and, as revealed in a surprise ending, the father of the child of the other. Mrs. Delphin (Alida) Slade and Mrs. Horace (Grace) Ansley, "two American ladies of ripe but well-cared-for middle age," meet in Rome while each is traveling with her daughter. The daughters, like their mothers a generation ago, are seeking romance and marriage.

As the two older women while away the afternoon sitting on a terrace overlooking the Palatine and the Forum, the reader learns that Alida Slade harbors a resentment against Grace Ansley, who had been her girlhood acquaintance and then her New York neighbor for many years. Mrs. Slade is proud of her status as the widow of a brilliant lawyer, but holds a grudge against the other woman for having been a competitor for her husband's hand in those far-off years. Her sense of unease is aggravated by the fact that Mrs. Ansley's daughter is more brilliant than her own.

Mrs. Slade gradually reveals that before her engagement to Delphin, she had used the ruse of writing a letter to Grace inviting her, in the name of her lover, to meet him at the Coliseum, hoping that Grace would catch a chill (the "Roman fever" of the title) and be out of commission for some weeks so that Alida could cement her relationship with Delphin. Grace reveals that she kept the rendezvous—and that Delphin had met her, she having answered the letter. Alida's sense of superiority is dashed, and her wish to hurt the other woman is turned back on herself when Grace reveals that the rendezvous produced a child, the brilliant young woman with whom Alida's own daughter compares unfavorably.                    —*Charlotte Templin*

*See also* Literature; Marriage; Middle age; Widows and widowers; Women and aging.

## SAFETY ISSUES

**RELEVANT ISSUES:** Health and medicine

**SIGNIFICANCE:** Many of the physical changes related to aging put elderly people at higher risk of injury from accidents

The age-related changes that elderly people experience often alter what constitutes a risk to their safety. The family home environment can be dangerous for an elderly person, not because the aspects of the house have changed, but because of the change in the physical abilities of the elderly person. Elderly people with intact cognitive abilities may choose to take the risk of staying in their familiar home environments with full knowledge of the increased risk. The dilemma for others, especially health providers, is defining what constitutes an acceptable level of risk for the elderly.

Unintentional injuries (accidents) are the sixth leading cause of death in people over sixty-five years of age. The death rate is 51 per 100,000 people for those sixty-five to seventy-four years of age, rises to 104 per 100,000 for those aged seventy-five to eighty-four, and reaches a high of 256 per 100,000 for those who are eighty-five years of age or older. In the over-eighty-five age group, accidental injury is the fifth leading cause of death. Injuries cost the United States between 75 and 100 billion each year. Accidents are usually viewed as random events over which individuals have little or no control. Many other types of injuries are preventable, and safety enhancement may decrease the number of serious outcomes.

### FALLS

Falls account for a considerable number of deaths and injuries among elderly people. They are the second leading cause of death related to unintentional injury, after motor vehicle deaths. Falls are not an uncommon event for elderly people; approximately 30 percent of noninstitutionalized elders report a fall each year. One-half of the people who report falls experience multiple falls. Although falls are a common occurrence, they are not always dangerous: Only 11 percent result in a serious injury, and an estimated 1 percent result in hip fractures. The number of hip fractures yearly in the United States (200,000) is substantial and serious. They lead to death in 12 percent to 20 percent of cases and account for 2

percent of the mortality rate in the United States. More than 40 percent of deaths from falls occur in the home. Stairs account for a large proportion of falls, many occurring because the elderly individual misses the last step. Falling injuries account for 40 percent of nursing home admissions; however, more than 20 percent of all fatal falls occur in the nursing home setting.

Falls among the elderly may be caused by a variety of factors: physical frailty, pathological states, psychological stress, drug interactions, and multiple environmental hazards. The risks of falling increase with increasing age, the number of chronic diseases present, the number and type of medications being taken, cognitive impairment, and physical disability. The risk of falling is often associated more with the intake of some types of drugs (antidepressants, sedatives, or vasodilators) than with medical conditions. Most doctors provide elderly patients with information concerning the effects of drugs that they may be taking, including the risk of a drop in blood pressure related to these medications. Instruction concerning how to decrease the effects of orthostatic hypotension, such as dangling feet before getting out of bed and rising slowly from a sitting or reclining position, is important in the prevention of falls.

Falls may cause bruises, abrasions, pain, swelling, or fractures. Changes in cognitive function related to pressure from edema or blood clots within the brain may also be evidenced. Psychological damage resulting from falls is more subtle. An older person who sustains little or no injury in a fall may delay or avoid discussing it in order to avoid embarrassment or risk of being viewed as less competent. Falls may also prompt changes in behavior, such as decreased thoroughness in housekeeping tasks or discussion of fears of living alone. Changes in grooming, dress, and personal appearance may also be observed. Increased fear of venturing out into the neighborhood may lead to a decreased ability to meet the daily requirements of shopping and food preparation.

### THE PREVENTION OF FALLS

Falls are better prevented than treated. Because quality of life is as important as length of life, limiting activity in the hope that falls will not occur is the least acceptable method of prevention. A more realistic approach is to modify the environment.

Although cost may be a limiting factor, many alterations can be implemented that are both acceptable to the older person and minimal in expense. Many environmental modifications are relatively easy to perform.

Many falls occur in the bathroom. Nonslip bath mats and adhesive-backed, nonskid strips in the bathtub or shower are important safety measures. Grab bars may be placed at critical locations near the bathtub and toilet to lend support. Railings may be installed on stairways for support. A piece of fabric, a knob, or some other marker can be attached to the rail to indicate the level of the top and bottom steps.

The need for light increases with age. The environment can be lighted at a safe level by increasing either the number of lights or the intensity of the light bulbs. Adequate illumination that does not cause shadows, which may cause problems with perception, is extremely important in high-hazard areas, such as stairways and stair landings. Night lights or lighted switches enable those who get up at night to orient themselves more easily within the environment and minimize the risk for falling. The removal of obstructions and obstacles can also help increase the safety of the home. Among the objects that may cause elderly people to trip are extension cords and long phone cords, low furniture, carpet edges, and throw rugs. These can easily be removed from high-traffic areas or taped down to minimize the risk of causing injury.

## TRAFFIC INJURIES

In modern societies, an important rite of passage for adolescents is to receive a driver's license. Driving an automobile is viewed as the first step toward adult life because it fosters independence. On the other hand, driving a car also calls for a sense of responsibility to others who share the roads. Many roads are crowded, and traffic moves at a rapid and sometimes confusing rate. Drivers must be physically and mentally alert to handle the hazards of the roads. Elderly people with impaired physical capabilities must make a choice between continuing to drive, and therefore maintaining their independence, or taking measures to increase safety for themselves and others on the road.

Traffic injuries in the elderly population are divided into two categories: pedestrian injuries and vehicle-related injuries. Elderly people are more at risk for injury at street intersections than anywhere else, both as pedestrians and as drivers or passengers in an automobile. As pedestrians, many elderly people are at risk because of an inability to cross the street in the time allotted between changes in the traffic lights. Factors that may influence pedestrian injuries are curb height, driver error, and physical and cognitive impairment of the elderly pedestrian.

A major problem for older drivers is the multivehicle accident, and the risk for injury in these crashes increases dramatically with age. The majority of such accidents take place in daylight, on good roads, and with no alcohol involvement. Elderly people experience a higher mortality rate with less severe injuries in vehicle crashes; the risk of death is three times greater for a seventy-year-old person than for a twenty-year-old person. The major factor that influences the high susceptibility of involvement in traffic injuries may be the decreased skill of the elderly person in operating an automobile. This change in skill level may be caused by age-related changes, such as decreased visual acuity or a slower neurological response time.

Citations for traffic violations, such as failure to yield right-of-way and failure to obey traffic signs, increase after the age of sixty. Although older adults have lower accident rates and fewer traffic violation citations than those under twenty-five years of age, elderly people have an increased risk of fatality in traffic accidents. One group of elders at increased risk for vehicle-related injury are those who are experiencing the early signs and symptoms of dementia. The American Association for Retired Persons (AARP) operates special classes in driver education to help older adults cope with age-related changes that affect their driving abilities.

## SAFETY CONSIDERATIONS

Safety is a major concern when assessing living conditions. Many older adults live in unsafe housing. Relatively minor nuisances—such as excessive clutter, loose flooring or floor coverings, poor lighting, and unstable stairs—can pose safety risks for the older adult. Financial constraints may prompt older adults to settle for living in less desirable areas. Other safety concerns are related to the older adult's physical or mental functioning. People who have trouble walking or climbing stairs are prime examples of those at risk as the result of impaired physical functioning. People who are forgetful or who wander off and get lost pose a significant risk to themselves and others as the result of impaired mental function.

It may be necessary to observe the elderly actually moving about in their environment to locate any potential problems. If the elderly person uses an assistive device, such as a cane, walker, or wheelchair, the environment may require further modifications. Ramps may need to be installed, or living arrangements may need to be changed to accommodate these ramps.

Most elderly people prefer to stay in their own homes in familiar communities for as long as possible. As people get older, they often fear that they may have to leave home for health reasons. Such fears are realistic because acute and chronic health problems associated with aging often dictate at least temporary changes in environment, leading the elderly to reside in places they do not prefer. Their desire to stay at home challenges the health care system to study their special needs and devise solutions that will accommodate them in the most acceptable way.

Elderly individuals who live alone are well advised to learn how to summon emergency help and to make home adaptations to compensate for decreased mobility and dexterity. Cognitive impairments often present a more serious threat to safety than physical impairment. People who know they are having problems are likely to call for help and remain safely in the home until help arrives. However, individuals with impaired judgment may present a hazard to themselves, as well as to their neighbors, through such behavior as forgetting to turn off the stove. In isolated instances, a choice may be made to preserve such a person's autonomy at the risk of serious injury; however, few would agree that the impaired older person has a right to put others at risk of serious injury.

Medication usage is another important factor to consider when evaluating whether or not an older person can safely remain at home alone. Sometimes the deciding factor in whether a cognitively impaired individual can remain at home alone is the nature of the medication regimen. Some individuals must have regular medication to maintain health. There are various systems to help forgetful people take their medicines. Preparing and labeling medications for each day is one strategy for simplifying medication administration. Medication calendars, which show each type of pill with its time of administration and which have a space for marking when the pill is taken, are useful to individuals with early memory impairment. Functionally impaired individuals who want to stay at home but require assistance or supervision with activities of daily living are often helped by paraprofessional personnel.

—*Jane Cross Norman*

**See also** Alzheimer's disease; Balance disorders; Canes and walkers; Death and dying; Dementia; Disabilities; Driving; Forgetfulness; Hip replacement; Housing; Independent living; Injuries among the elderly; Mental impairment; Mobility problems; Overmedication; Wheelchair use.

## FOR FURTHER INFORMATION:

Abramson, Alexis. *Home Safety for Seniors*. Atlanta: Mature Mart Press, 1997.

Gill, T. M., C. S. Williams, J. T. Robison, and M. E. Tinetti. "A Population-Based Study of Environmental Hazards in the Homes of Older Persons." *American Journal of Public Health* 89, no. 4 (1999): 553-556.

Howland, J., et al. "Covariates of Fear of Falling and Associated Activity Curtailment." *Gerontologist* 38, no. 5 (1998): 549-555.

Kannus, P., et al. "Fall-Induced Injuries and Deaths Among Older Adults." *JAMA* 281, no. 20 (May 5, 1999): 1895-1899.

Lachman, M. E., et al. "Fear of Falling and Activity Restriction: The Survey of Activities and Fear of Falling in the Elderly (SAFE)." *Journals of Gerontology Series B—Psychological Sciences and Social Sciences* 53B, no. 1 (1998): 43-50.

Lachs, Mark S. "Caring for Mom and Dad: Can Your Parent Live Alone?" *Prevention* 50, no. 10 (October, 1998): 155-157.

Lisak, Janet M., and Marlene Morgan. *The Safe Home Checkout: A Professional Guide to Safe Independent Living*. 2d ed. Chicago: Geriatric Environments for Living and Learning, 1997.

Means, K. M., D. E. Rodell, and P. S. O'Sullivan. "Obstacle Course Performance and Risk of Falling in Community-Dwelling Elderly Persons." *Archives of Physical Medicine and Rehabilitation* 79, no. 12 (1998): 1570-1576.

Myers, A. H., M. Van Natta, E. G. Robinson, and S. P. Baker. "Can Injurious Falls Be Prevented?" *Journal of Long Term Care Administration* 22, no. 2 (1994): 26-29, 32.

Ryan, J. W., and A. M. Spellbring. "Implementing Strategies to Decrease Risk of Falls in Older Women." *Journal of Gerontological Nursing* 22, no. 12 (1996): 25-31.

# SANDWICH GENERATION

**RELEVANT ISSUES:** Demographics, family

**SIGNIFICANCE:** As longevity has increased in late twentieth century North America, adults have been increasingly obliged to care for two generations, their parents and children, contributing to the growth of the sandwich generation

In late twentieth century North America, people are living longer and having fewer children. This has changed the age composition of the North American population. The "graying" of the population is a major factor contributing to the growing number of sandwich generation families. The expanding proportion of older persons is bringing with it dramatic changes in family structure. People are giving more thought to the nature and extent of services necessary to support older persons and to their views on the respective roles of family and society in providing for these needs.

## CARING FOR TWO GENERATIONS

As persons live longer, the aged have a greater need for assistance from their families. The term "sandwich generation" refers to adults who provide financial or task assistance to their parents while also caring for their own dependent children. Adults may assist their parents by providing them with emotional support, financial assistance, transportation, shopping and cleaning, meal preparation, and personal hygiene. At the same time, they may assist their children financially and emotionally and even care for grandchildren. Thus, members of the sandwich generation serve as a support system for both their aging parents and their dependent children. They are, in essence, "sandwiched" between the needs of two generations, balancing the needs of their children, the needs of their parents, and their own needs, obligations, and ambitions in the home and workplace.

With longer life spans and later childbearing, more middle-aged persons find themselves sandwiched between providing child and elder care. Estimates of the percentage of sandwiched persons vary widely. Corporate studies suggest that as many as 40 percent of the population belong to this category, while other studies suggest that the figure is only 6 percent. In 1986, the huge corporation IBM reported that 6.3 percent of its employees were responsible for both their children and parents. By 1991, this figure had risen to 11 percent. Regardless of the actual percentage, experts agree that in the twenty-first century there will be greater numbers of sandwiched persons.

## FINANCIAL RESPONSIBILITIES OF SANDWICHED FAMILIES

The financial choices facing sandwiched families are difficult. Even if parents are healthy, sandwiched persons still have to juggle between parents' eventual needs and their responsibilities to their children. Compromises are inevitable. The parents of sandwiched persons require much more financial support than the children of sandwiched persons. Sandwiched families that do not have the financial resources to help parents may bring their parents into their communities or households or offer them nonmonetary assistance.

Because there is no national health care program in the United States as there is in Canada, the U.S. government is quick to stress the financial responsibility of families for the health care and other needs of aged family members. In thirty states, Supplemental Security Income (SSI), which assists low-income older persons, requires of children who are financially capable that they help support their parents. However, this law is rarely enforced. As a result of the proposed health care reforms that were under debate in the U.S. Congress in the 1990's, families may be asked or even required to shoulder ever-increasing responsibility for elderly family members. Limiting persons' access to nursing home care and reducing support services may become policy. Proposed reforms may include increased community-based supportive services and mandated assistance from families. Regardless of the outcome, the growing message has been that families must bear responsibility for aged parents and children. In the United States, this may result in nursing homes for the very rich or the totally destitute, leaving most elderly people in the care of their families.

### HELPING CHILDREN

One trend contributing to the financial burden on the sandwich generation is the prolonged financial dependence of children. In 1990, 23 percent of the U.S. population between the ages of twenty-five and thirty-four lived with their parents—an increase of 45 percent since 1970. A combination of attitudes, economics, and demographics underlies this phenomenon. Adult children have begun to marry and establish their careers later in life. In a 1990 *Newsweek* special issue on "Families in the Twenty-first Century," one article stated that American youth, in a sharp reversal of historical trends, were taking longer to mature. Although more young people were enrolled in college than previously, fewer graduated and many took longer to get their degrees.

Some researchers have blamed the economy for the prolonged dependency of young adults on their parents. In the 1990's, the younger half of the baby-boom generation—that is, adults in their mid-twenties to mid-thirties—seemed to have taken the brunt of economic downturns. Many young adults have joined the labor force at a time of stagnant wage growth and have been trapped in a rental market that has seen apartment rents increase at double the inflation rate since 1970. Higher rents have meant that the adults in this age group have been less able than older age cohorts to save for down payments on homes. Unable or unwilling to establish their own households, many young adults have lived longer with their parents. The phenomenon of adult children leaving home and returning several times for brief periods because of economic difficulties or changes in marital status has been called the boomerang effect. As a result, typical young adults of the 1990's lived with their parents for a total of twenty-four to twenty-six years.

*Middle-aged women may find themselves part of the "sandwich generation"—caring for both children and parents.* (Jim Whitmer)

## HELPING PARENTS

It is believed that one out of six parents or spouses aged sixty-five or older will require some form of assistance—either from their children or other sources. Daughters and daughters-in-law provide care more often than sons. In the United States, the average sandwiched caregiver in the late 1990's was a woman in her forties with a family income of less than $40,000. Parents most frequently required assistance with shopping, transportation, and household chores, such as meal preparation, housecleaning, and laundry. More daughters (69 percent) than sons (59 percent) assisted their parents with personal functions such as eating, toileting, and dressing. Often daughters have helped their parents to use the telephone, make visits, and perform household tasks.

Overall, caregiving daughters have spent an average of 4.0 hours per day and sons 3.5 hours per day on caregiving tasks. Yet, sons have been more likely than daughters to help parents financially in writing checks, paying bills, and assisting in the preparation of income tax returns. Sons have also helped more often than daughters with home maintenance. As aging persons have fewer adult children and perhaps no daughters, sons may be required to provide help with a wider variety of tasks than has previously been the case.

One-third of all women above the age of eighteen will care for both children and parents during their lifetimes. Many will spend more years helping a parent than in raising their own children. Half of caregivers provide care for two to five years, but only 6 percent provide it for more than five years. Women's roles as caregivers remain entrenched in the expectations of society and individual families. Caregiving tasks are often viewed as the responsibility of females. Women are the most likely to have little intergenerational support during their middle years. This phenomenon is called the "generational squeeze," because women in the middle generation give significantly more support than they receive.

## THE EFFECTS ON WORK

The 1982 Informal Caregivers Survey revealed that 44 percent of caregiving daughters and 55 percent of caregiving sons were in the workforce. Within these two groups, about 25 percent of working daughters and sons reported conflicts between work and caregiving responsibilities. For many, the conflict forced them to cut back on work hours, change their work schedules, or take time off from work without pay. The strains on women have shown up at the workplace: Of caregivers to the elderly, most of whom are women, some 14 percent have switched from full-time to part-time jobs, another 28 percent have considered quitting their jobs, and 12 percent have left the workforce because of caregiving responsibilities.

## LOOKING TO THE FUTURE

Longer life spans will continue to put more middle-aged and older family members in the position of providing care to elderly relatives. The chances are increasing that a retired person will also have a living parent who needs care. As a result, care for the disabled elderly may increasingly fall on those who are old themselves.

What the future holds in store for sandwiched persons is an open question. Intergenerational support and cooperation will be more critical. Older persons may help younger relatives with child care when they are able, and as they age, the persons whom they help may provide reciprocal care for them. Parents will probably rely more on friends and volunteers because fewer family members will be able to provide assistance. Communities may need to provide more services to support the independence of older persons when families cannot provide support. With families, friends, and communities working together to balance their needs, older persons will be able to live with dignity, and their younger relatives will be able to meet the demands of their own busy lives.

—*Virginia W. Junk*

**See also** Absenteeism; Baby boomers; Caregiving; Children of Aging Parents; Death of parents; Demographics; Employment; Family relationships; Filial responsibility; Full nest; Grandparenthood; Great-grandparenthood; Middle age; Midlife crisis; Multigenerational households; Parenthood; Single parenthood; Women and aging.

## FOR FURTHER INFORMATION:

Durity, A. "The Sandwich Generation Feels the Squeeze." *Management Review* 80 (1991).

Junk, Virginia, Laurie A. Stenberg, and Carol A. Anderson. "Retirement Planning for the Sandwich Generation." *Journal of Home Economics* 85 (Summer, 1993).

Schurenberg, Eric. "The Crunch of Caring for Both Parents and Kids." *Money* 18 (March, 1989).

Van Caspel, V. *Money Dynamics for the 1990's.* New York: Simon & Schuster, 1988.

Woodward, Kenneth L. "Young Beyond Their Years." *Newsweek Special Issue: Families in the Twenty-first Century* 114 (Winter/Spring, 1990).

# SARCOPENIA

**RELEVANT ISSUES:** Biology, health and medicine
**SIGNIFICANCE:** Reduction in muscle mass with aging is associated with weakness, decreased physiological functioning, and decreased physical activity, which can result in functional impairment, disability, loss of independence, and increased risk of fall-related fractures

Sarcopenia, when translated from its Greek roots, means "flesh" (*sarx*) "loss" (*penia*). Thus, the syndrome for the loss of muscle mass (also known as lean body mass or fat-free mass) that often accompanies aging is called sarcopenia. This is differentiated from the general terms "wasting," which refers to the unintentional loss of weight attributable to a loss of both fat and muscle mass from insufficient caloric intake, and "cachexia," which refers to the loss of muscle mass without weight loss as a result of an overactive metabolism. Therefore, the term "sarcopenia" is often used to describe muscle wasting in old age.

## PREVALENCE

The extent of sarcopenia in the aged population suggests that less than 25 percent of persons under seventy years of age are afflicted with this syndrome, whereas more than 50 percent of those aged eighty or more are likely to be affected. Beginning in the seventh decade of life, approximately 25 percent of people report difficulty in walking and carrying heavy packages. Those older than seventy years of age report decreased ability to carry out common daily activities such as going down stairs or performing housework, and some even have difficulty using the toilet without assistance. These self-reported difficulties in functional ability occur regardless of gender, ethnicity, income, or other health behaviors.

The combination of inadequate dietary intake combined with decreased strength from declining muscle mass results in a progressive decline in physical activity and accelerates muscle atrophy, or shrinkage, as a result of disuse. This condition adversely affects functional mobility, as evidenced by slower walking speeds, shorter walking strides, and a decrease in the amount of work a muscle can tolerate.

## ETIOLOGY

Since skeletal muscle stores great quantities of protein for the body, tracking protein synthesis can verify subsequent muscle mass loss. A reduction in muscle mass occurs when muscle protein content is reduced. The protein content is determined by assessing the balance between protein synthesis and protein breakdown. With aging, protein synthesis slows, thereby resulting in decreased muscle synthesis. This can be aggravated by poor nutritional status, low caloric intake, and low protein intake.

Nutritional surveys have reported that individuals over age sixty-five consume an average of 1,400 Calories (kilocalories) a day, or less than 25 Calories per kilogram of body weight (1 kilogram = 2.2 pounds; 1 pound = 3,500 Calories). This average daily caloric intake of 1,400 Calories is approximately 500 Calories less than that which is recommended for optimal health for individuals over fifty years of age. Thus, based upon the average energy allowance recommendations, older adults should be consuming 5 Calories more for every kilogram of their body weight if they are to meet or exceed the current U.S. recommended daily allowances (RDAs) for caloric intake and optimal health. Lower caloric intakes imply lower nutritional status: less fat, carbohydrate, and/or protein consumption, potentially leading to nutritional deficiencies in important vitamins and minerals.

The current nutritional guidelines also suggest that adults in the United States only need 0.8 gram of protein per kilogram of body weight daily; however, some researchers contend that this value is based primarily on the needs of young adults, not older adults. Based on data which showed that many adults over the age of sixty consume less than 0.8 gram per body weight daily, researchers from the Noll Research Laboratory at Pennsylvania State

University suggested that older adults should consume between 1.0 and 1.25 grams of high-quality protein per kilogram of body weight daily. This would potentially help to prevent the compensatory loss in muscle mass resulting from long-term deficits in dietary protein intake.

The negative age-related changes in body composition are reflected in decreased muscle, bone density, and water content of the body, with a corresponding increase in body fat. Muscle tissue plays an important role in the regulation of metabolic rate (the burning of calories). It is generally agreed that muscle mass is maintained up to about age forty; however, the gender issue as to who loses muscle mass faster is not resolved. Some reports state that men begin to lose muscle mass between forty and sixty years of age, with women not experiencing similar declines until after age sixty; other reports declare the opposite or find no difference between the genders. Regardless of gender, however, by eighty years of age, the cumulative muscle mass loss is estimated to average 30 percent, with a corresponding decline in muscle strength. Ultrasound estimates of muscle mass loss suggest that older subjects lose between 0.5 and 0.7 percent of muscle annually. Muscle tissue is more metabolically active than fat tissue, meaning that muscle burns more calories than fat. Beginning in the third decade of life, metabolic rate, or the rate at which calories are burned by the body, decreases 2 to 3 percent per decade. Taken together, the loss in muscle tissue and the decrease in metabolic rate results in a gradual percent body fat increase from the second through the eighth decades of life, resulting in a net percent body fat gain of 20 percent for men and 10 percent for women. Hence, as muscle tissue atrophies, the unused "leftover" space is replaced by fat tissue, which is not used to perform muscular work.

Cross-sectional studies comparing athletes to sedentary controls, as well as studies with non-athletes, suggest that large muscle mass is predictive of higher bone mass. Thus, age-related sarcopenia and osteopenia (loss of bone) may be related. Research suggests that age-related changes in the dynamics of muscular contractions might contribute to bone remodeling imbalances, resulting in bone loss. The loss of motor units, activation, and synchronization of these units not only impairs bone integrity but also contributes to the loss of strength that accompanies muscle mass loss. Muscle strength is the ability to generate a maximal force by a muscle group. This strength is determined not only by total muscle mass but also by the individual muscle fibers. When muscle mass atrophies with aging, there is a decrease in fiber size, fiber number, and selective shrinking of type II, or fast-twitch, muscle fibers. Fast-twitch fibers are responsible for anaerobic, power-type strength activities. In addition, the loss of muscle mass may contribute to the reduction in aerobic capacity as the total amount of mitochondria, the powerhouses of cells, is reduced when muscle mass is lost.

### PREVENTION AND TREATMENT

Research is inconclusive as to whether age-related skeletal muscle wasting is preventable. It appears to be an inevitable part of aging. It may be, however, that the rate of skeletal muscle loss can be slowed down with progressive resistance (strength) training. This type of exercise has been shown to increase muscle size and strength even in the oldest of old. If strength training is to be used as a potential preventive measure, research suggests that high-intensity training (50 to 70 percent of one's maximal strength) with low repetitions should be implemented no later than fifty years of age; after age sixty, strength training is considered to be therapeutic, compensating for the age-related muscle mass wasting.

This is not to say, however, that after age sixty strength training should not been done. This situation is quite the contrary. While sarcopenia may not be preventable after age fifty, it has been proven that the frail elderly as well as community-dwelling healthy elderly can increase muscle mass by as much as 17 percent and maximal strength by as much as 110 percent with an aggressive strength training program. Contrary to the "moderate" exercise guidelines used for improving aerobic fitness, low-level resistance training only yields modest increases in strength and muscle mass. In addition to the use of exercise for maintaining and improving muscle mass and strength, the judicious use of hormone replacement therapy (estrogen, testosterone, growth hormone) may also assist in maintaining muscle protein synthesis, thereby preventing and/or reducing muscle wasting.

—*Bonita L. Marks*

*See also* Aging process; Balance problems; Estrogen replacement therapy; Exercise and fitness; Fat deposition; Malnutrition; Mobility problems; Nutrition; Old age; Weight loss and gain.

## FOR FURTHER INFORMATION:

Baumgartner, R. N., K. M. Koehler, D. Gallagher, L. Romero, S. B. Heymsfield, R. R. Ross, P. J. Garry, and R. D. Lindeman. "Epidemiology of Sarcopenia Among the Elderly in New Mexico." *American Journal of Epidemiology* 147, no. 8 (April 15, 1998): 755-763.

Dutta, Chhanda. "Significance of Sarcopenia in the Elderly." *Journal of Nutrition* 127, no. 5 supplement (May, 1997): 992S-993S.

Evans, William J. "Reversing Sarcopenia: How Weight Training Can Build Strength and Vitality." *Geriatrics* 51, no. 5 (May, 1996): 46-47, 51-53.

_____. "What Is Sarcopenia?" *The Journals of Gerontology, Series A* 50A (November, 1995): 5-8.

Nair, K. Streekumaran. "Muscle Protein Turnover: Methodological Issues and the Effect of Aging." *The Journals of Gerontology, Series A* 50A (November, 1995): 107-112.

*Recommended Daily Allowances.* 10th ed. Washington, D.C.: National Academy of Science, National Academy Press, 1989.

Roubenoff, R. "The Pathophysiology of Wasting in the Elderly." *Journal of Nutrition.* 129, 1S supplement (January, 1999): 256S-259S.

Rowe, John W., and Robert L. Kahn. *Successful Aging.* New York: Pantheon Books, 1998.

Sexell, Jon. "Human Aging, Muscle Mass, and Fiber Type Composition." *The Journals of Gerontology, Series A* 50A (November, 1995): 11-16.

Shepard, Roy J. *Aging, Physical Activity, and Health.* Champaign, Ill.: Human Kinetics, 1997.

Tseng, Brian S., Daniel R. Marsh, Marc T. Hamilton, and Frank W. Booth. "Strength and Aerobic Training Attenuate Muscle Wasting and Improve Resistance to the Development of Disability with Aging." *The Journals of Gerontology, Series A* 50A (November, 1995): 11-16.

## SARTON, MAY

**BORN:** May 3, 1912; Wondelgem, Belgium
**DIED:** July 16, 1995; York, Maine
**RELEVANT ISSUES:** Family, sociology, work
**SIGNIFICANCE:** Sarton gained critical notice and public recognition late in life as a feminist

*Author May Sarton.* (Gabriel Amadeus Cooney)

writer and poet; she is best known for her personal journals dealing with change, creativity, and aging

Eleanor Marie "May" Sarton was born into a cultured and artistic family. Her father, George Sarton, taught at Harvard University. May Sarton nurtured her European roots. Her mother bequeathed to her an intellectual curiosity, a love of art, and a love of nature, all of which became core aspects of Sarton's personality. The beauty of nature and the power of words are themes repeatedly reflected in her writings. Her later poetry and journals clearly mirror the insights gained over time, as she seeks solace in memories and gains wisdom through a renewed understanding of the value of change. Sarton's work is at once her legacy and her reflection upon that legacy as it unfolds.

Sarton's personal history provided both turmoil and inspiration. Her life is recorded in her poetry and prose. Read chronologically, Sarton's works reveal the fire of a young artist-writer tempered over time. The middle-aged Sarton struggles with love, acknowledges her lesbianism, and overtly struggles with inner conflicts concerning her relationships to others and to her writing. As she gains the public attention she craves, she recoils from the demands of fame and seeks solitude. Her work resounds with tension between her contemplative side and her need for attention. Sarton's novels, poetry, and journals reflect the changes brought by time and age and capture with poignant clarity her burdens and joys, the daily struggles of the artistic soul growing older in the modern world. In *Journal of a Solitude* (1973), she notes, "I have written novels to find out what I *thought* about something and poems to find out what I *felt* about something."

Sarton's novels generally reflect issues faced by independent-minded women or artistic souls in search of a muse. The protagonists of *Joanna and Ulysses* (1963) and *The Poet and the Donkey* (1969) each struggle with the artistic elements of their being in order to bring the muse to fruition. Each of these books reappeared in the 1980's as Sarton's audience broadened.

Sarton's body of poetry shows the tenacity of her muse as well. *A Grain of Mustard Seed* (1981) is reflective of her lyricism, but with an edge, as Sarton, the mature poet, puts to pen the political and religious turmoil of the volatile 1960's. In *Coming into Eighty* (1994), Sarton clearly accepts the limitations of age and embraces the poetry that is the fruit of her experience. She states in the preface to the poems, "These poems are minimal because my life is reduced to essences." She notes, "I am a foreigner in the land of old age and have tried to learn its language." Sarton never lost her muse. Through her final years, she continued to write about the limitations and the freedoms that come with age. Her final work, *At Eighty-two: A Journal* (1996), was published posthumously. Sarton's work is a testament to the resilience of the creative human spirit.                    —*Kathleen Schongar*

*See also* Literature; Women and aging.

## SCAMS AND CON ARTISTS

**RELEVANT ISSUES:** Economics, law

**SIGNIFICANCE:** Although victimization rates underestimate true offense levels, researchers and law enforcement officials now assert that the elderly are overrepresented among those who have been swindled by confidence artists, whose illicit schemes often target older people

Deceptive and dishonest business practices have always been a fact of life in capitalistic societies.

Many consumers have learned to question the claims of every seller with whom they do business. Others remain more trusting and thus more vulnerable. As disturbing as conventional consumer fraud is, with its overpriced or shoddy goods and services, even more insidious are the scams of professional confidence artists and swindlers who make false promises or "sell" nonexistent goods and services, leaving victims bilked and humiliated. These scams often target the elderly.

### COMMON CON GAMES

Swindles perpetrated by con artists begin with establishing a strong sense of trust with the strangers that they victimize. Professional grifters pride themselves on being gifted actors who project the apparent charisma and sincerity necessary to gain the confidence of potential marks, which is the key to the success of the "game." Once a sense of trust has been established, con artists can persuade their prey to engage in actions that are designed to separate them from their money. There is some disagreement about the extent to which the elderly are specifically targeted by hucksters, but several authors now contend that some perceived general characteristics of older people make them popular marks. For example, the perceptions that the elderly grew up in simpler times when fraud in all of its forms was less common, have relatively lower average levels of education and technological expertise, are often home during the day, and lead more isolated lives than younger people might make them more likely to talk to, and believe, a personable, clean-cut stranger.

Scams that do not necessarily focus on the elderly have had their share of older victims. Among these classic cons are the block hustle, in which the victim is sold worthless goods that are supposedly valuable and possibly stolen; the bank examiner swindle, which involves a mark withdrawing savings and giving them to an "official" to aid in a banking investigation; the pigeon drop, in which money "found" by the con artist will be divided with the victim if they put up some good faith money; and the lottery swindle, in which the mark buys "winning" counterfeit lottery tickets from people who cannot cash them in for some reason, such as being wanted by the law.

Many time-honored scams focus on the needs and characteristics of the elderly, and thus claim large numbers of elderly victims. Estate cons take many forms, for example, those in which con artists claiming to set up trusts for the relatives of the elderly steal the money. Others involve establishing friendships with older, often frail, elderly people to obtain powers of attorney, giving them free access to their assets. Phony social referral services charge large fees to lonely widows and widowers to find them prospective dates or mates. Life and health insurance scams sell practically or totally worthless policies to the elderly. Land swindlers offer dirt-cheap prices for real estate in what are to be fully developed retirement communities, but the development never occurs or the "developers" do not own the land. Large proportions of the elderly are homeowners, and are inordinately victimized by home equity schemes in which "financial experts" end up with the money from a loan to be repaid by the homeowner or with the title to the home itself. There are also numerous variations of home improvement scams that include unnecessary or very shoddy repairs being performed, or "contractors" absconding with large deposits or payment in full for work that is never done. Numerous medical cons offer miracle cures for ailments that plague older people (such as arthritis and cancer), or the restoration of youth, or at least its appearance. The wealthy and nonaffluent elderly alike fall for cons based on their desire to supplement retirement income, for example, investments involving nonexistent businesses or fake stock certificates and work-at-home schemes that promise significant income once start-up materials are paid for. These few examples represent only a small fraction of elderly oriented swindles perpetrated by a growing number of creative con artists. One author asserts that at least 30 percent of all victims of confidence games are elderly.

## Telemarketing Scams

While there are still old fashioned con artists who ply their trade by establishing relationships with their victims face-to-face, the vast majority of swindles are now carried out over the telephone. Telemarketing flim-flam artists have perfected the art of establishing trust and perpetrating practically every conceivable type of con game. Researchers and law enforcement officials agree that, in the era of telemarketing swindles, the elderly are by far the preferred and most often exploited

victims. Con artists themselves have testified that older people possess characteristics that make them perfect telemarketing marks. Many older Americans are financially well-off, and many more have assets from Social Security and private pensions or money from life insurance on a deceased spouse—some sort of nest egg to sustain them through their elderly years. They also grew up in earlier eras, when people were much more trusting and courteous, and therefore are more reluctant to hang up on persistent telephone solicitors and less likely to be suspicious of their claims than younger adults. Moreover, the elderly are often at home during the day and are often anxious and have the time to talk to an apparently empathetic caller. The result, according to Federal Bureau of Investigation (FBI) estimates, is that the elderly are bilked out of forty billion dollars a year.

Telemarketing cons have become a major industry in America. Some states have hundreds of boiler room operations—rented office space with numerous employees making thousands of phone calls a day, pitching every scam imaginable. These crooks work from "sucker lists" that they buy and sell among themselves or obtain from legitimate sources such as the obituaries or lists of people who entered contests. Leads can sell for from ten to hundreds of dollars apiece, the highest prices going for names of people who have fallen for cons in the past. The American Association of Retired Persons (AARP) asserts that a majority of elderly people are on some sucker list and that practically every woman over seventy-five is on one.

Telemarketing con operations have become very specialized and legally sophisticated. There is a hierarchy among their employees, starting with those who make the initial calls to potential marks. Those who make subsequent calls to marks that did not bite yet are called closers. No-sales men and women work on the skeptical and recalcitrant, while reload men and women make pitches to those who have been victimized in the past. Amazingly, the most highly paid category of boiler room employee is the recovery room specialist, who cons people who have been bilked multiple times and have sworn never to be conned again. Typically, they kick the repeatedly fleeced while they are down by claiming to be district attorneys or other court officials who will return all the money stolen from victims if they will pay sizable "court costs" or "recovery fees" associated with recovering swindled funds. These *coup de grâce* specialists can make more than $300,000 per year.

Many telemarketing operations tend to specialize as well. Some are termed badge rooms because they claim to be raising funds for the families of slain police officers and fire fighters or police and fire fighters associations. Others feature recovery room operations exclusively. Other lucrative specialties include contest prizes or inheritances that can be had for a "recovery fee," and nonexistent charities. Fraudulent investment rooms have bilked the elderly out of millions. Often this con involves a promise of high percentage returns on regular investments. Victims turn over large sums of money regularly for an extended period of time, not realizing that their "dividends" are paid from money bilked from new marks, no real investments exist, and their money is lost.

These types of offenses are very difficult to prosecute for a number of reasons. Many victims are embarrassed and believe that the police cannot help, so they do not report the incidents. Others are reluctant to report these crimes because they fell for the con due to a desire to expand their retirement nest egg to avoid burdening their families and do not want to acknowledge their losses to their children. The same mind-set causes the victims of reload and recovery room specialists to incur further losses in the hope of replacing the initial ones. Telemarketing hucksters are adept at closing down operations and setting up new ones as the law closes in, and they know that calling victims in other states helps them evade prosecution because there are two different jurisdictions involved. Because incidence rates are underestimated and successful prosecution rates low, elderly activist groups and law enforcement agencies have set up programs and task forces to inform older people of the real dangers posed by con artists, suggest guidelines for avoiding financial exploitation, and amass evidence against grifters through sting operations. Some authors speculate that cons of the elderly will be less effective as the more skeptical baby boomers become the elderly population, but others point out that, so far, con artists have used their creativity to make successful adjustments in their games based on the characteristics of elderly cohorts and the state of the art of technology.

—*Jack Carter*

*See also* Advertising; Advocacy; Consumer issues; Fraud against the elderly; Income sources; Violent crime against the elderly.

**FOR FURTHER INFORMATION:**
Alston, Letitia T. *Crime and Older Americans.* Springfield, Ill.: Charles C Thomas, 1986.

Bekey, Michelle. "Dial S-W-I-N-D-L-E." *Modern Maturity* 34 (April/May, 1991).

Camille, Pamela. *Getting Older, Getting Fleeced: The National Shame of Financial Elder Abuse and How to Avoid It.* Santa Barbara, Calif.: Fithian Press, 1996.

Fattah, Ezzat A., and Vincent F. Sacco. *Crime and Victimization of the Elderly.* New York: Springer-Verlag, 1989.

Gladdis, Stephen D., ed. *The F.B.I. Law Enforcement Bulletin* 2, no. 2 (February, 1994).

## SENILITY. *See* ALZHEIMER'S DISEASE; DEMENTIA.

## SENIOR CITIZEN CENTERS
**RELEVANT ISSUES:** Demographics, psychology, sociology, recreation

**SIGNIFICANCE:** As increasing life expectancy has created a larger elderly population and changing family structures have minimized extended families, many elderly people have their social and service needs met through alternate sources

In 1965, the groundwork was laid for the provision of a variety of social services for the elderly in the United States with the passage of the Older Americans Act (OAA). This legislation provided funding for many programs, including senior citizen centers, which tended to take the form of social clubs for the aged. These centers were needed, to some extent, because of an increase in the population of older persons.

### THE AGING OF NORTH AMERICA
In 1995, persons sixty-five years of age or older constituted 13 percent of the U.S. population and 12 percent of the Canadian population. By 2030, when most of the baby-boom generation will have retired, it is expected that 21 percent of the United States population will be aged sixty-five or older, along with 20 percent of the Canadian population.

In ageist societies, retirees often are excluded from much social participation with those other than age peers. Social isolation, although detrimental to persons of all ages, has been shown to be especially problematic to those in late life. Thus, a place for older people to gather had become important. There were approximately 450 of these seniors' clubs in the United States in 1965.

In slightly more than a decade, however, it became clear that more than just a club-type setting was required. In 1978, amendments to the reauthorization of the OAA called for the creation and support of multipurpose senior centers. This change was the result of recognition that many older persons had a variety of needs that were not being met adequately under other circumstances.

For various reasons, older persons are less likely to live with extended family members than in the past, and even if they do, they may not have someone with them in the home as much as they want or need. Many older persons therefore might have to rely on outsiders to meet some of these needs. Multipurpose senior centers developed as community focal points where elderly people could come together for services and activities to help support their independence.

### TYPES OF AVAILABLE SERVICES

The services available at these centers typically include transportation, legal assistance, health screening, congregate dining, and "meals on wheels" delivered to those unable to get to the senior center. Activities may include regular dances, arts and crafts training, exercise programs, and board or card games.

As many as 15 percent of the elderly population, or more than five million people, may have participated in some programs at a U.S. senior center in the 1990's. In 1997, more than two hundred centers and clubs were registered with the Canadian Senior Citizens Information and Service Center.

By the late 1980's, a prominent researcher on senior centers estimated that there were as many as thirteen thousand senior centers in the United States. By the late 1980's, however, the Administration on Aging had ruled that allocations under the OAA no longer could be used to support the ad-

*A group of seniors express their creativity at an adult day care facility.* (Ben Klaffke)

ministration of these senior centers. Consequently, most of them have had to resort to seeking operating capital through the support of foundations and holding various kinds of fund-raisers.

## Adult Day Care

Many multipurpose centers offer what is sometimes referred to as respite care or adult day care (ADC). This service is designed to provide the primary caregivers—usually family members—time off so that they do not suffer unduly from the burden of caregiving, which can become a twenty-four-hour-a-day job. Provided on a more long-term basis, it may also enable the primary caregiver—often an adult daughter or daughter-in-law of the elderly person—to return to the work for pay she may have left so that she could provide this care.

ADC centers are often attached to long-term care (LTC) facilities, even though ADC is designed to delay the older person's entry into LTC. In Canada, eligibility for ADC is established along the same lines as for LTC, and it is almost invariably provided by nonprofit organizations. In the United States, ADC is available in some senior residential facilities, some hospitals (nonprofit or otherwise), and some churches.

Wherever ADC services are provided, they enable elders to continue living at home while getting the supervision, assistance, and interaction they need during the day. ADC services may include physical rehabilitation, nursing, and transportation. This latter service may include home pickup and return. Overall, 90 percent of ADC users in the United States live within an hour of the center providing service to them. About 70 percent of ADC participants are women. Most live with family: 29 percent with children, 20 percent with a spouse, and 13 percent with other relatives or friends. One-fifth live alone.

## The Need for Advanced Services

In the late 1980's, 23 percent of U.S. elders living in the community had health-related difficulties with at least one of the activities of daily living (ADL), including dressing, bathing, and eating. Twenty-eight percent of them had difficulty with at least one of the instrumental activities of daily living (IADL), such as laundering, cooking, or housekeeping. Less than half of those with ADL difficulty were receiving some sort of help, but

most of those with IADL difficulty were receiving assistance. Most ADC center users indicate at least mild levels of the age- and disease-related confusion commonly called senility.

The U.S. National Center for Health Statistics indicates that rates of impairment of one sort or another vary by region. This variance leads to a differential incidence of need for ADC services. These different levels of physical need are one factor in the level of demand relative to capacity. Forty-three percent of ADC centers in the South had waiting lists, whereas only 15 percent of such centers in the Midwest had waiting lists. Other factors in demand include marital dissolution rates, which are considerably higher in the South than in the Midwest. Spouses are a significant source of care, and lack of a spouse may increase the need for outside caregiving.

ADC centers date back to 1947 in the United States, with one begun at the Menninger Clinic in Kansas. Their growth had been curtailed until recently by the introduction of Medicare and Medicaid legislation, which provided only for payment of medical services rendered by physicians, hospitals, and LTC facilities. With increased efforts at containing costs and finding options that provide for more independence and dignity for elders, health service providers have looked more closely at ADC as an option.

Some organizations have begun to explore novel ways of combining child and adult day care services, which may allow young children and their grandparents or great-grandparents to spend more time together, being cared for in proximate or even interrelated facilities. This could be a great boon to the parents of these children, members of the so-called sandwich generation that have the responsibility of caring for both their children and their parents. —*Scott Magnuson-Martinson*

**See also** Exercise and fitness; Friendship; Home services; Housing; Independent living; Leisure activities; Long-term care for the elderly; Meals-on-wheels programs; Nursing and convalescent homes; Older Americans Act of 1965; Retirement; Retirement communities; Social ties; Transportation issues.

## For Further Information:

Heide, Julie, and Linda C. Webb. *Day Care Programs and Services for Elders in Rural America.* Kansas

City, Mo.: National Center for Rural Elderly, 1991.

Kirwin, Patricia M. *Adult Day Care: The Relationship of Formal and Informal Systems of Day Care.* New York: Garland Press, 1991.

Krout, John A. *The Organization, Operation, and Programming of Senior Centers: A Seven Year Follow Up.* Fredonia: Department of Sociology and Anthropology, State University of New York, College of Fredonia, 1990.

_____. *Senior Centers in America.* Westport, Conn.: Greenwood Press, 1989.

Myerhoff, Barbara. *Number Our Days.* New York: E. P. Dutton, 1978.

Siler, Cinda. "Finding Day Care for Your Aging Parent." *Money* (December, 1987).

Weissert, William G., et al. *Adult Day Care: Findings from a National Survey.* Baltimore: The Johns Hopkins University Press, 1990.

## SENSORY CHANGES

**RELEVANT ISSUES:** Health and medicine

**SIGNIFICANCE:** As people age, their ability to perceive the information received from their senses is often impaired or distorted

The richness of the human experience is perceived through the senses, especially through vision and hearing. Aging dulls the senses, and the frail elderly must find ways to compensate for this change. A decline in sensory functioning is a silent, unnoticed process that may go undetected by both elderly people and their families.

### SIGHT

Vision is the result of the sense of sight being stimulated by patterns of light that are external to the person. Human sight is limited by a field of vision that excludes approximately 40 percent of the surrounding environment. Normal aging brings changes to the eye and to the sense of sight. These changes affect the functional level of sight referred to as "vision." Aging brings an increase in the susceptibility to pathological conditions that affect vision. It has been estimated that 1.3 million elderly people experience some loss of vision. There is a need for early intervention and rehabilitation, as many of the visually impaired elderly have conditions that are amenable to treatment. Among the tasks of the caregiver are the prevention, screening, restoration, and rehabilitation of the elderly who are subject to visual impairment.

The normal eye undergoes significant age-related changes. The eye's external changes show evidence of advancing age. These changes result from multiple, normal changes, such as loss of orbital fat, loss of elastic tissue, and decrease in muscle tone. The skin around the eye darkens, and wrinkles appear. These age-related changes may give rise to two conditions: senile entropion (in which the lid margin turns inward) and senile ectropion (in which the eyelid margin turns outward). Although not threatening to vision, these conditions may cause the older person to experience discomfort and may become severe enough to cause psychosocial problems because of cosmetic effects. In senile entropion, the turning inward of the eyelid may cause the lashes to rest against the conjunctiva, often resulting in ocular irritation. This can be corrected by a surgical procedure. In contrast, senile ectropion exposes the conjunctiva and may lead to inflammation of the affected eye.

The eye itself undergoes major changes during the aging process. The cornea tends to flatten, which reduces its refractory power. Also, the sensitivity of the cornea decreases, which limits its protective function. The sclera, although it remains white throughout the life span, tends to take on a yellow coloration because of fatty deposits. The pupil becomes smaller, and the response to different levels of illumination lessens because of a loss of range in pupil dilation and constriction. The retina of an older individual receives only one-third the amount of light that the retina of a younger person receives. This change necessitates a higher level of illumination for reading. Older people also have difficulty in color perception, especially the blue-green distinctions. The lens of the aging eye loses its elasticity and increases in density. Because of the change in the lens, glare becomes a more severe adaptive problem for elderly people, which increases their need for sunglasses. Floaters—opacities occurring in the vitreous humor—may appear in the elderly person's field of vision.

The most common, although not universal, clinical change in the cornea is arcus senilis, in which a grayish-yellow ring forms around the iris. This usually begins on the upper portion of the eye. It then continues to develop until the entire iris is encircled. Arcus senilis is common in people over the age of sixty-five and does not cause any visual problems. An accompanying age-related change that causes many minor eye problems is diminished tear secretion. This natural protective device of the human body slows in its ability to defend the eye against the pollution of the environment. This predisposes the eye to more infections of the conjunctiva.

The most frequent condition that results from the age-related changes in the human eye is called presbyopia. This change is caused primarily by a loss of flexibility of the lens and results in the loss of range of accommodation for near vision. Corrective lenses are extremely helpful in assisting the elderly person to maintain visual function.

### HEARING

The prevalence of hearing loss in the elderly population in the United States is significant; of people sixty-five to seventy-four years of age, 25 percent experience hearing loss, while 50 percent of those over the age of seventy-five experience hearing loss. Some studies report that 90 percent of those over eighty suffer from hearing impairment. The number of hearing-impaired adults is estimated at about 10 million people.

Hearing loss can occur at any age as the result of a variety of causes, such as otitis media, intense noise exposure, head trauma, and the use of some drugs. Age itself seems to be a cause for hearing loss. The ability to hear is one of the fundamental skills that enable people to communicate with others and therefore to live within a community. Without the ability to hear and to differentiate the meaning of sounds, hearing-impaired elders are at risk for a loss of communicative skills, which may result in social isolation. Hearing is fundamental to human interaction. Without the ability to hear, the older person is deprived of the total experience of life. There may be a loss of intimacy, friendship, and significant roles, such as musician or teacher. Hearing also allows the individual the opportunity to discern the sounds of the external environment and to judge whether the sounds convey any danger, such as the ringing of a smoke alarm.

The early, insidious signs and symptoms of hearing loss often go unrecognized and untreated. Behaviors such as withdrawal from social activities, suspiciousness, and loneliness are among the behaviors that many people consider to be normal, age-related changes but that may be symptoms of hearing loss that are often amenable to treatment. These significant behavioral clues to the insidious nature of hearing loss may go unnoticed by elderly patients and their families because of the gradual nature of the changes.

Elders who are hard of hearing lose the ability to understand information from media sources, such as radio and television. Establishing new friendships is increasingly difficult when communication is hindered by hearing loss, and many elderly people worry that they will embarrass themselves by responding inappropriately. It is not surprising that studies show that people with hearing problems are more dissatisfied with life and are more depressed than are people with no hearing problems.

The process of hearing involves the transmission of sounds from the external environment, through the mechanism of the ear and the auditory neural pathways, to the brain. The normal auditory process begins when sound enters the external ear. The sound then vibrates and is transmitted as neural impulses through the inner ear. The function of the middle ear is to amplify and transmit sound to the inner ear. The sensory cells play a significant role in the transmission of the neural impulses to the brain. The age-related loss of these important cells is thought to be a primary source of hearing loss in the elderly population.

The term "deaf" refers to a condition in which a person is born without the ability to hear or suffered hearing loss before the advent of speech. The term "hearing-impaired" refers to a condition in which the person has enough residual hearing to process some but not all speech information through hearing or through the assistance of a hearing aid. "Presbycusis" is the term used to describe hearing loss associated with normal aging. This hearing loss may include impairment of the ability to hear high-frequency tones, to localize sound, or to understand speech.

There are three classifications of hearing loss: conductive, sensorineural, or mixed. Conductive hearing loss occurs when normal sound waves are not transmitted through the external auditory canal. Sensorineural hearing loss occurs when there is dysfunction of the inner ear. A mixed hearing loss is a combination of both conductive and sensorineural losses.

The symptoms of hearing loss include gradual loss of auditory sensitivity, with perception of high-frequency sounds diminishing first. This loss leads to a distortion of words, and sounds become jumbled. The resultant effect is poor speech discrimination. This is characterized by the often-heard remark of the hearing-impaired person, "I can hear you but I can't understand what you are saying."

Hearing loss is not uniform; some sounds are heard, while others are not. For example, hearing loss is worse for high frequencies and is greater for consonants than for vowels. This loss makes word discrimination extremely difficult, leading to inappropriate responses, ensuing embarrassment, and perhaps social withdrawal for the hard-of-hearing elderly person. Anyone with a hearing disorder is advised to have a medical evaluation of the ear, nose, and throat to rule out a treatable condition. One common, recurring factor that increases hearing loss for elderly patients is impacted wax. After this and all other treatable conditions have been ruled out as causing or contributing to the hearing loss, an evaluation by an audiologist is essential for assessment of the appropriate steps for rehabilitation. Assisted-listening devices (hearing aids), instruction in speech reading (lipreading), and motivational counseling are important components of a rehabilitation program.

### Smell, Taste, and Touch

Imagining the smell of a wood fire in a campground evokes other sensory memories, such as images of companions and the taste of food. The smell of coffee in the morning prompts a conscious anticipation of the taste of the hot coffee. This sense of awareness and anticipation of taste is denied to elderly people who have experienced a diminished sense of smell. Aging generally reduces but does not extinguish the sense of smell.

Psychological, cultural, and social factors influence a person's perception of taste. Research suggests that elderly people have a higher threshold for sensing sour, bitter, and salt tastes, while the taste for sweetness does not seem to undergo any age-related change. A higher threshold means that it takes more sensory stimulation to trigger the sensory experience of taste. Thus, in the case of salt intake, elderly people would use more salt to

experience the same level of salt taste than they did when they were younger.

The importance of touching and being touched begins in humans during infancy. Without some form of touch, a newborn infant cannot survive; so it is with all states of life. Touching allows physical connections among people. The sense and the perception of touch is influenced not only by physical properties but also by emotional and cultural factors. With touch, as with all other forms of communication, the receiver's interpretation of the message is an important link in the communication. How the elderly person responds to the care provider's communication of caring through the physical act of touching will be influenced by each person's past experience with touch as a meaningful form of communication. —*Jane Cross Norman*

*See also* Aging: Biological, psychological, and sociocultural perspectives; Aging process; Cataracts; Communication; Glaucoma; Hearing aids; Hearing loss; Malnutrition; Nearsightedness; Nutrition; Reaction time; Reading glasses; Vision changes and disorders.

**For Further Information:**

Barresi, B. J., and H. J. Kaplan. "Managing Vision Care for the Medicare Population: Strategies for Success." *Health Care Innovations* 8, no. 6 (1998): 17-20.

Blankenship, G. W., and A. Iwach. "Toward Optimal Health: The Experts Respond to the Aging Eye." Interview by Jodi Godfrey Meisler. *Journal of Women's Health* 7, no. 9 (1998): 1089-1092.

Braus, P. "Vision in an Aging America." *American Demographics* 17, no. 6 (1995): 34-39.

Carnevali, Doris L., and Maxine Patrick. *Nursing Management for the Elderly.* 3d ed. Philadelphia: J. B. Lippincott, 1993.

Cohen, Stephen. *Sensory Changes in the Elderly.* New York: American Journal of Nursing, 1981.

Colavita, Francis B. *Sensory Changes in the Elderly.* Springfield, Ill.: Charles C Thomas, 1978.

Cruikshanks, K. J., et al. "Prevalence of Hearing Loss in Older Adults in Beaver Dam, Wisconsin: The Epidemiology of Hearing Loss Study." *American Journal of Epidemiology* 148, no. 9 (November 1, 1998): 879-886.

Ferrandez, Anne-Marie, and Normand Teasdale. *Changes in Sensory Motor Behavior in Aging.* New York: Elsevier, 1996.

Lueckenotte, Annette G. *Gerontologic Nursing.* St. Louis: C. V. Mosby, 1996.

Moeller, Tamerra P. *The Sixth Sense: A Learning Guide About Sensory Changes and Aging.* Washington, D.C.: National Council on the Aging, 1985.

Schmall, Vicki L. *Sensory Changes in Later Life.* Rev. ed. Washington, D.C.: U.S. Department of Agriculture, 1991.

## SEXUAL DYSFUNCTION. *See* IMPOTENCE; REPRODUCTIVE CHANGES, DISABILITIES, AND DYSFUNCTIONS.

## SEXUALITY

**RELEVANT ISSUES:** Health and medicine, psychology, sociology, values

**SIGNIFICANCE:** Sexual intimacy among the elderly has been a taboo subject until recent years, as researchers in psychology and sociology have recognized sexual activity as a normal function in aging

Young and old alike are often astounded at the notion that people are able to remain sexually active into their seventies, eighties, and beyond. It is frequently assumed by younger Americans that older persons do not have sexual desires or that the elderly are physically unable to perform sexually. The media portrays sexuality as something possessed solely by the young and older persons as being sexually undesirable or incapable. The idea of elderly persons having sexual relations is considered by many people as shameful and perverse.

Yet, it has become increasingly clear that the desire to remain sexually active is a major concern in many elderly people's lives. Fear about the loss of sexual prowess in older men is a common concern. Many older women also express interest in sex but fear that it is undignified or somehow disgraceful. Some elderly freely accept their interest in sex, but their children or grandchildren may disapprove, causing the elder to experience guilt and shame for remaining sexually active or having an interest in sexual activities.

Many jokes about elderly men interested in sex portray them as impotent or as "dirty old men." A bumper sticker on some vehicles protests this notion: "I'm not a dirty old man. I'm a sexy senior citizen." Elderly women can fare even worse in the public eye. They are often the social neuters of American culture. The mysterious metamorphosis of turning from the desirable younger woman to a mature and intriguing thirty-something woman soon diminishes in the steady decline into the fifties and sixties, when a woman becomes publicly sexually undesirable.

Nursing and retirement homes may also add to the portrayal of older people as sexless beings. Some institutions continue to segregate the elderly and offer little or no provisions for privacy. Conjugal visits between husband and wife are rarely provided in some nursing homes in the United States, and even husbands and wives who live in the same institution may be segregated. This problem is no less difficult when the elderly choose to live with their adult children in shared housing arrangements, as adult children often fail to consider their elder parents' sexual needs.

### THE CHANGING PHYSIOLOGY OF THE ELDERLY AND SEXUALITY

The fear of dying from overexertion is a factor affecting sexuality in the elderly. There are many symbolic associations between sexual activity and death. Even the French term for orgasm, *petit mort,* means literally "little death." Fear of the occurrence of heart attacks or strokes during sexual intercourse frequently can lead to older couples abstaining from such activities, regardless of a doctor's advice to the contrary.

Female longevity creates another barrier to sexual activity in later years. On average, women outlive their male counterparts by seven years, leaving many women without partners in later life. Collectively, women have not had the societal prerogatives of men to socialize and mate with younger members of the opposite sex. Further, there are not enough eligible older men available for older women. As Richard Schulz and Robert B. Ewen argue in *Adult Development and Aging: Myths and Emerging Realities* (2d ed., 1993), extramarital affairs are difficult for many elderly to reconcile religiously, ethically, or morally, and masturbation, although increasingly more acceptable, is still considered shameful or harmful by many older Americans.

Research on the sexual activities of the elderly generally supports the view that sexual capacity has been underestimated, except where chronic or debilitating illness or the lack of a sexual part-

*The need for sexual contact and affection does not diminish with advancing age.* (Jim Whitmer)

ner is a factor. However, people do experience age-related sexual changes as they grow older.

Older men generally take longer to obtain erections, but they can remain erect and make love longer before attaining an orgasm. Older men also experience a reduction in the volume of seminal fluid and a decrease in pressure to ejaculate, according to Robert N. Butler, Myrna I. Lewis, and Trey Sunderland in *Aging and Mental Health: Positive Psychosocial and Biomedical Approaches* (5th ed., 1998).

One of the biggest fears of older men is impotency. Dacey and Travers found that physical changes, loss of a partner, nonsupportive peers, and internal fears may be enough to inhibit or terminate sexual activity in older men. Older men are usually able to continue some form of sexual activity well into their eighties and beyond. Schulz and Ewen point out that loss of interest or impotence can be due to a number of factors, including boredom, fatigue, overeating, excessive drinking, medications, and medical or psychiatric disabilities.

Older men rarely suffer from symptoms related to hormonal decline analogous to the hot flashes in menopausal women. More typically, there is a gradual decline in testicular functioning, with a change in fertility and potency, beginning with middle age. Nonetheless, men can remain sexually active and even fertile well into an advanced age, argues Carel B. Germain in *Human Behavior in the Social Environment: An Ecological View* (1991).

Women experience little change as they age. A woman in reasonably good health can expect to remain sexually active well into late life. The menopause, the gradual cessation of menstruation, usually begins in the late forties to early fifties. Many myths surround the menopause, including fear of insanity, the end of sexual desires and attractiveness, depression, adverse physical symptoms, and defeminization, claim Butler, Lewis, and Sunderland.

Some women may experience menopausal discomforts such as hot flashes, heart palpitations, and vaginal shrinking and dryness because of hormonal changes. Hormone replacement therapy (HRT) such as estrogen can relieve these symptoms in many cases. HRT is also believed to protect older women from heart disease and osteoporosis, a bone-thinning disease that can lead to complications and bone fractures. As noted by Germain, replacement of estrogen and progesterone in a combination regime is thought to protect against the risks of uterine cancer as well, but may actually increase the risk of an older woman developing heart disease.

Although many women do not suffer adverse symptoms related to the menopause, many find the middle years a difficult and stressful time. Elderly women are at an increased risk of suffering from depression, loneliness, reduced life satisfaction, or lowered self-esteem. In her 1981 article "Abstract of a Lecture on Menopause," gynecologist Malkah T. Notman observed that physicians tend to connect everything that occurs in a woman's middle years to problems associated with the menopause. As a result, Germain argues, older women are likely to be treated with more prescription and over-the-counter medications than older men are.

The physiological situation of older women during and after the menopause commonly affects gradual steroid insufficiency, which causes a thinning of the vaginal walls. Cracking, bleeding, and pain can result during sexual intercourse. A woman may experience vaginal burning and itching, the urethra and bladder can become irritated as the vaginal walls atrophy, and burning or increased frequency in urination may occur for several days after sexual intercourse. The loss of steroids also reduces the length and diameter of the vagina and may shrink the major labia. Secretions that lubricate the vagina may decrease with age; this does not seem to occur as commonly in older women who are sexually active on a regular basis from youth onward. As with men, a consistent pattern of sexual activity is beneficial to women in maintaining sexual capacities. Muscle toning, also known as Kegel exercises, can affect the grip of the vagina on the penis during intercourse and lead to greater sexual gratification, according to Robert C. Atchley in *Social Forces and Aging: An Introduction to Social Gerontology* (9th ed, 1999).

Noted by several geriatric specialists are certain personality changes that occur in men and women that begin in the middle years. Men tend to become more nurturing and expressive and to shift from a more active, assertive role to a more passive role. Women, on the other hand, tend to become more active, assertive, and independent. David L. Gutmann, who developed this hypothesis, explained the shift as a "return to the repressed." That is to say, early gender role socialization erases one side of each gender's total humanness. Matilda W. Riley suggested in a 1985 essay that this capacity to combine traditionally masculine and feminine traits, replacing earlier gender roles, may be the best means of coping with aging. She believes that such role changes in later life may actually contribute to the social adaptation of older persons.

## ELDERLY WIDOWS AND THE VERY-OLD

A number of factors account for gender differences in the attitudes toward and interest in sexual relationships. Women outlive men by approximately seven years, and most married women will become widows because the average woman marries a man about four or five years older than herself. In contrast, men are not as likely to become widowers unless they reach age eighty-five or over, according to John S. Dacey and John F. Travers in *Human Development Across the Lifespan* (4th ed., 1999). Due to this significant imbalance of elderly men and women, it is more difficult for older women to find sexual partners in later widowhood.

Whether a woman is sexually active as she ages frequently depends on her marital status. In contrast, older single men are just as likely to be sexually active as their married counterparts. Dacey and Travers argue that men generally have more opportunities to meet women as they age.

An interesting study was conducted in 1988 on the sexual activities of the very-old, people aged 80 to 102 years, using 182 subjects. It was found that 63 percent of the men and 30 percent of the women that were studied admitted to having sexual intercourse at least occasionally and that 76 percent of the men and 39 percent of the women said they still enjoy sexual activities. Despite the results of this study, most very-old men are concerned about their ability to consummate intercourse, according to Germain.

## PSYCHOLOGICAL NEEDS OF THE ELDERLY

Like most people, the elderly thrive on human contact and touch. Deprivation of sexual contact can result in an elderly person reaching out to medical and mental health professionals who work in geriatric specializations. The inexperienced helping professional may feel uncomfortable, especially if the elderly person has implied sexual connotations or expressed sexual desire. Those who work in professions that help the elderly need to accept the central importance of sexuality throughout the life cycle and the need for the elderly person's sexual expression.

Understanding of an elder person's past methods of sexual expression is helpful in judging the significance of verbal and nonverbal cues that might indicate sexual interest. Mild flirtation may only require the geriatric professional's or helper's gentle acknowledgment of the elderly person as a sexual human being. The senior who is withdrawn since the loss of a partner may need to see a trained geriatric professional for more in-depth exploration and discussion of sexual needs.

Seniors who do not discuss sexual issues openly may still wish to explore them but may feel restrained because of the topic. This can be especially difficult for a heterosexual elder who has a helper of the opposite sex. Some elderly persons may fear ridicule or embarrassment for having sexual feelings, and a trained helping professional needs to work carefully with the elder on this subject.

The geriatric specialist should be prepared to provide the elderly person with consistent and nonpunitive responses combined with realistic efforts to provide the elder with an outlet for sexual expression. Geriatric helping professionals should also serve as advocates in helping to remove the stigma, shame, and secrecy of sexuality of older adults.

## CONCLUSION

Sexual activity in later adulthood is viewed by old and young alike in American society as abnormal or nonexistent. Many elderly Americans conform to this stereotype and abandon efforts to engage in normal, healthy sexual relationships and miss the interpersonal rewards and satisfaction that sex can offer. Sexual activity in later life is strongly associated with life satisfaction, whereas lack of sexual expression is often associated with depression. The experience of sexuality is and can be a natural occurrence throughout a person's life cycle, argue Butler, Lewis, and Sunderland.

Self-esteem, self-image, and sexuality are interrelated in each human being's life. The task of the geriatric professional in working with older persons is to acknowledge sexual expression and provide for open dialogue about sex. The geriatric specialist should be aware of feelings, fears, and possible misunderstandings about sexuality in old age and be able to recognize and support the special qualities of sex and intimacy in later years. If sexual activity and potency decline while intimacy and interests remain high for an elderly couple, the helping professional should consider whether improvement in sexual functioning is possible. If it is not, then divergent activities and different levels of achieving or maintaining higher levels of intimacy and sexual satisfaction should be discussed.

—*Cathleen Jo Faruque*

**See also** Ageism; *Change: Women, Aging, and the Menopause, The*; Cohabitation; Communication; Impotence; Loneliness; Marriage; Men and aging; Menopause; Psychiatry, geriatric; Remarriage; Reproductive changes, disabilities, and dysfunctions; Social ties; Stereotypes; Widows and widowers; Women and aging.

**FOR FURTHER INFORMATION:**

Atchley, Robert C. *Social Forces and Aging: An Introduction to Social Gerontology.* 9th ed. Belmont, Calif.: Wadsworth, 1999. This text examines various social issues in the United States that affect people as they age.

Butler, Robert N., Myrna I. Lewis, and Trey Sunderland. *Aging and Mental Health: Positive Psychosocial and Biomedical Approaches.* 5th ed. Boston: Allyn & Bacon, 1998. This text provides an in-depth examination of the psychological, sociological, and medical issues of the elderly.

Dacey, John S., and John F. Travers. *Human Development Across the Lifespan.* 4th ed. Boston: McGraw-Hill, 1999. This text discusses developmental issues of human beings from early childhood to late adulthood.

Germain, Carel B. *Human Behavior in the Social Environment: An Ecological View.* New York: Columbia University Press, 1991, pp. 397-398. This text takes an ecological perspective in examining human beings in their social environment.

Gutmann, David L. "The Cross-Cultural Perspective: Notes Toward a Comparative Psychology of Aging." In *Handbook of the Psychology of Aging*, edited by James E. Birren and K. Warner Schaie. New York: Van Nostrand and Reinhold, 1977. This paper examines cultural issues that affect the older American directly.

Notman, Malkah T. "Abstract of a Lecture on Menopause." *Hot Flash* 1, no. 3 (Fall, 1981). This abstract examines the unique issues of women and the menopause.

Riley, Matilda W. "Women, Men, and the Lengthening Life Course." In *Gender and the Life Course*, edited by Alice S. Rossi. New York: Aldine Press, 1985. This paper looks at men and women as they grow older.

Schulz, Richard, and Robert B. Ewen. *Adult Development and Aging: Myths and Emerging Realities*. 2d ed. Upper Saddle River, N.J.: Prentice Hall, 1993, pp. 246-252. This textbook examines human development and the aging process.

Silverstone, Barbara, and Ann Burack-Weiss. *Social Work Practice with the Frail Elderly and Their Families*. Chicago: Charles C Thomas, 1983, pp. 175-183. This textbook addresses social work practice issues for professionals who work with the elderly and their families.

## SHEEHY, GAIL

**BORN:** November 25, 1937; Mamaroneck, New York

**RELEVANT ISSUES:** Family, health and medicine, psychology, sociology

**SIGNIFICANCE:** Sheehy is the author of widely read self-help books dealing with midlife crises and passing through life stages, particularly middle age through the menopause and beyond

In Gail Sheehy's career as a journalist, she won many awards and published numerous books. Sheehy's most popular published works are *Passages: Predictable Crises of Adult Life* (1976), *The Silent Passage: Menopause* (1992), and *New Passages: Mapping Your Life Across Time* (1995). A survey conducted in 1991 for the Library of Congress on the most influential books in people's lives listed *Passages* as ninth.

In *The Silent Passage*, Sheehy discusses what she calls one of the few remaining taboos in modern society. She states that she was surprised to find out how little had been written about the menopause but came to realize that in earlier times, women rarely lived to the menopausal years. Sheehy was

criticized for not taking into account the existing body of work on the subject. According to *Washington Post* reviewer Diana Morgan, "Sheehy focuses excessively on her own experiences in the book. The reader is told an astounding amount about the angst of Gail Sheehy." Barbara Ehrenreich, noted feminist author and *New York Times Review* contributor, applauded Sheehy for meeting the challenge of putting "the Change" on public view. Ehrenreich took exception to descriptions of the menopause as "an almost invariably volatile, frightening experience" and stated that Sheehy's book "actually supports a far less alarmist view."

*New Passages* began as an effort to revise *Passages*, but Sheehy soon realized that an entirely new book was needed. Cheryl Lavin, *Chicago Tribune* contributor, wrote that, "Sheehy wandered into a revolution of life cycles. People were taking longer to grow up and longer to die." Lavin reported, "Sheehy said men move from competing to connecting, while women graduate from pleasing others to realizing their own goals." Sheehy told Lavin that she intended *New Passages* to be a wake-up call to help people see themselves as they are, celebrate that they have a second adulthood, and get on with planning and enjoying it.

Nancy Matsumoto of *People Magazine* challenged the author to speak to the charges that Sheehy had shied away from dealing with the problems associated with growing older. Sheehy replied that, "Getting yourself into the second adulthood is not easy. It is about allowing yourself to experience this little psychic death and not trying to deny that you're moving into another stage. But society has always focused on the deficits, not on the gains." Sheehy argued that the gains far outweigh the losses.

Sheehy had many experiences abroad as a journalist throughout her career. She was in Thailand writing a story on Cambodian refugees for the *New York Times Magazine* when she first met her adopted daughter, Mohm. Mohm was eleven and had been orphaned at age six by the Khmer Rouge. She became the subject of Sheehy's seventh book, *Spirit of Survival* (1986). Sheehy believed that Mohm's story offers lessons of self-help for everyday misfortunes. "Above all Mohm reminds us we have the power to prevail," Sheehy wrote. Both Mohm and Sheehy's biological daughter, Maura, became writers.

—*Virginiae Blackmon*

*See also* Aging: Biological, psychological, and sociocultural perspectives; Men and aging; Menopause; Middle age; Midlife crisis; Women and aging.

## SHOOTIST, THE

**DIRECTOR:** Don Siegel
**CAST:** John Wayne, Lauren Bacall, Ron Howard
**DATE:** Released in 1976
**RELEVANT ISSUES:** Culture, death, media, values
**SIGNIFICANCE:** This film depicts the last days of an aging Western gunfighter who has discovered that he is terminally ill with cancer

In *The Shootist*, John Wayne plays the part of aging gunfighter John Bernard Books. The film covers the last weeks of this man's life as he tries to reconcile his past glory with the reality that his life is rapidly approaching its end.

*The Shootist* opens with actual scenes from Wayne's early film career, and the audience is able to observe how Books (and Wayne) has aged over the course of four decades. Visiting the town doctor, Books learns that he is terminally ill; he wishes only to avoid suffering as death nears. Among the questions with which Books must deal, however, is whether his life has been worthwhile. He has no family, and while his life had no shortage of adventure, he wonders about the legacy that he is leaving behind.

Books arranges to spend his last days in the home of a widow, Bond Rogers (Lauren Bacall), and her teenage son Gillom (Ron Howard). The widow and son display ambivalent feelings toward their tenant; Gillom is enthralled by the presence of a famous gunfighter, while Bond has mixed emotions for the same reason. Still, she cannot avoid pitying the man. Eventually, all feelings are reconciled. Books dies a hero's death, and Gillom realizes the futility of a gunfighter's life.

Wayne's character, although placed specifically in a Western setting of the late nineteenth century, exhibits many feelings that are common among the terminally ill, such as the desire to not suffer,

*John Wayne in a scene from the film* The Shootist. (Archive Photos)

worries about dying alone, and doubts about whether one's life has been worthwhile. Ironically, Wayne himself was diagnosed with stomach cancer shortly after completion of this motion picture. He died from the disease in 1979.    —*Richard Adler*

*See also* Cancer; Death and dying; Death anxiety; Films; Terminal illness.

## SIBLING RELATIONSHIPS

**RELEVANT ISSUES:** Death, demographics, family, psychology

**SIGNIFICANCE:** Brothers and sisters occupy an important position in the lives of many older adults, and sibling relationships will increase in significance as the baby boomers reach older ages

Siblings are assumed to be offspring of the same parents, thereby sharing, on average, 50 percent of the same genes. Most adult sibling research is limited to biological and adopted siblings. Little is known at this time about adult stepsiblings or half siblings who share one biological parent and quasi siblings with different biological parents living together. Less is known about fictive siblings who achieve sibling status by formal ritual. The steadily increasing rate of divorce and remarriage will undoubtedly affect sibling relationships. With the increase in blended families through remarriage, there will be more half siblings and stepsiblings. For divorced older people who do not remarry, sibling interaction may become more important than when they were married. The degree of commitment to these new and varied relationships is unknown at this time.

The sibling relationship is unique. Siblings share the same biological heritage, cultural heritage, and family history. They have a relationship that can last a lifetime, and they are members of the same generation.

### ROLE OF SIBLINGS IN LATER LIFE

Sibling relationships assume, or reassume, critical importance in the lives of older adults. After young adult siblings leave home to establish their own life, the relationship between them often goes underground until they are older. For many older adults, siblings are the only surviving support system. The nature of sibling relationships also changes over the life course. Sibling ties may be strong among children, then become weaker as jobs, marriage, and parenting make demands on time and energy. During the middle years, siblings may live far apart and have little in common in terms of values and interests. Later life events like the departure of children from the home, retirement, and widowhood often bring siblings closer together. Older adults often mention the importance of their brothers and sisters, and as people age, the sibling bond becomes even more important. Siblings often provide support to each other and are a source of psychological well-being in old age.

Sometimes siblings become closer when they have to plan for an aging parent. Caring for their parents can renew and enhance sibling relationships. The siblings have to refocus their attention on their family of origin. Role and power reversals occur. When there is more than one adult child in the family, caring for parents has an impact on all siblings. Siblings who may have little contact find themselves in more frequent contact as they coordinate care arrangements. Caring for ailing parents does not always enhance relationships among older adult siblings. The stress of the caregiving and the parents' illness may break through the veneer of politeness covering the anger that underlies many sibling relationships.

Siblings may also care for each other as they grow older, although more likely, they only provide emotional support. Siblings can function as an insurance policy for older adults. The demographics of the American family are changing caregiving patterns. The growth in the number of single elders and the geographic mobility of adult children increase the need for siblings to be part of each other's social support systems. Research results are mixed in the area of siblings as caregivers for each other. In one study of persons aged fifty-five and older, the majority of respondents felt that their siblings would help them in a crisis, although only 25 percent had actually received such help. Illness often reconstitutes the sibling social support network. One widow explained how her sisters pitched in when her husband became sick. Having peer or same generational status was found to give siblings more empathy for and identification with their ailing brothers and sisters. Some research concluded that for some older adult siblings, giving or receiving help was distressful.

## SIBLINGS IN CONFLICT

Past tensions and family feuds can keep siblings in conflict. If parents have kept their children in emotional bondage by withholding approval and love, children compete for affection and become alienated from each other. In such families, adult siblings may be unable to reconcile until one or both parents die. Instead, they may continue to re-play earlier sibling rivalries in their old age. Gender differences in sibling conflict are interesting. Women express more conflict about sisters than men express about brothers. High levels of conflict between sisters have been attributed to the greater intensity of feeling in the relationship. Sister-to-sister expressions of conflict may also be a result of cultural devaluation of female characteristics, which women themselves have internalized. Women, however, devalued brothers as well as sisters, suggesting a gender difference in expression of strong feelings.

Overall, older persons express lower negative ratings of siblings than younger persons. This is perhaps due to the successful completion of the developmental task of resolving sibling conflict in old age. The older adult years can provide siblings who have been estranged from each other with a rich opportunity to move toward reconciliation. Even older adult siblings who have had especially close relationships often find that the later years can be a time of increased closeness and sharing. It is at this time that many older adult siblings rediscover each other as travel companions, as a source of emotional support, and as fellow travelers back into the land of family memories and nostalgia.

## INFLUENCE OF FAMILY SIZE AND GENDER

The nature of sibling relationships is partly determined by the size and gender composition of the sibling group. A brother whose siblings include a sister is more likely to be close to his siblings than one who has only brothers.

The bond between sisters is closest, and sisters are more likely to take care of each other. For example, a seventy-five-year-old widow left her children in the East when her husband died and returned to her Ohio hometown to be near her two sisters. The three sold their own homes, bought a home together, and pooled their possessions and other resources. When one of the sisters became ill, they hired an aide to provide some daily care.

And because all the sisters pitched in, no single individual had to bear a large burden.

Men's ties to their siblings are likely to be of longer duration than any other relationship in their lives, especially in families in which children are closely spaced. Because of divorce, men may become outsiders in their family of procreation, and as a result, siblings may play an increasingly important role in men's lives as they grow older.

## DEATH OF SIBLINGS

The first death among older adult siblings has a profound effect on each sibling. It is a break in the mental and emotional armor that protects them from their own sense of mortality. Most research emphasis has been placed on the impact of the death of parents of older adults. The first and subsequent deaths of siblings remove or reduce any chance for siblings who are emotionally distanced from each other to resolve their differences. Each death also removes one more member of the childhood memory bank. Another person with whom early family experiences were shared is gone forever.

Sibling sharing of memories can serve as a buffer for some older adults as they struggle with the more difficult aspects of aging. As older adult siblings begin to die, the sibling structure changes profoundly. Younger members in a large family can become the oldest, or the youngest can become the only child at the death of the last older sibling.

## TRENDS

Current demographic trends will affect these relationships in future decades. As more couples remain childless or have only one or two children, siblings will become even more important supports. Greater longevity and better health among the current middle-aged cohort imply greater availability of living siblings in the future. This is a particularly salient issue for baby boomers who are rapidly approaching sixty-five years of age. This group tends to have more siblings than children as potential support providers. However, reduced fertility rates in the current period will mean that later cohorts will have fewer siblings on whom to rely.

*—Peggy Shifflett*

*See also* Caregiving; Childlessness; Communication; Family relationships; Friendship; Social ties; Stepfamilies.

**FOR FURTHER INFORMATION:**

Bedford, Victoria. "Sibling Relationships in Middle and Old Age." In *Handbook of Aging and the Family*, edited by Rosemary Bliesner and Victoria Bedford. Westport, Conn.: Greenwood Press, 1995.

Connidis, Ingrid Arnet. "Sibling Support in Old Age." *Journal of Gerontology* 49 (1994).

Gold, Deborah. "Continuities and Discontinuities in Sibling Relationships Across the Lifespan." In *Adulthood and Aging*, edited by Vern Bengston. New York: Springer, 1996.

Matthews, Sarah. "Men's Ties to Siblings in Old Age: Contributing Factors to Availability and Quality." In *Older Men's Lives*, edited by E. Thompson. Newbury Park, Calif.: Sage Publications, 1994.

Moyer, Martha Sebastian. "Sibling Relationships Among Older Adults." In *Families and Aging*, edited by L. Burton. San Francisco: Baywood Press, 1993.

Scott, Jean Pearson. "Sibling Interaction in Later Life." In *Family Relationships in Later Life*, edited by T. Brubaker. Beverly Hills, Calif.: Sage Publications, 1990.

Weisner, T. S. "Comparing Sibling Relationships Across Cultures." In *Sibling Interaction Across Cultures: Theoretical and Methodological Issues*, edited by P. G. Zukow. New York: Springer-Verlag, 1989.

# SINGLE PARENTHOOD

**RELEVANT ISSUES:** Economics, family, psychology, sociology

**SIGNIFICANCE:** According to the United States Census Bureau, the number of single-parent families more than doubled from the mid-1970's to the end of the twentieth century and 59 percent of the nation's children will live in a single-parent home at least once before attaining adulthood

Parenting is no longer primarily taking place in the traditional two-parent family. Previous to the current accelerated growth in number of single-parent families, one-parent families were 10 percent of the total. This percentage was a consistent and stable proportion of families until the 1980's. In 1999, more than sixteen million children lived in single-parent households. According to census data, 63 percent of African American children lived in single-parent homes, while 19 percent of white children resided in one-parent situations.

Single parenthood arises at any age through the death of a spouse, divorce, or childbearing without benefit of a partner. Children growing up in a one-parent family face multiple challenges. In approximately one-half of the cases of single parenthood, poverty or strained economic resources exist.

The greatest problem associated with single parenthood has long been identified as a lack of financial resources. Nearly half of single mothers live below the poverty line, compared to 10 percent of married couples with children. Although some women are poor prior to motherhood, the majority become poor at the time of marital disruption or the arrival of children.

Poverty in these families can result from many factors. Single mothers tend to have a lower earning capacity, and they can work few hours. In 1998, the Field Institute of San Francisco discovered in a survey that 49 percent of households headed by a single parent earned less than $20,000 a year. This contrasts with 21 percent in two-parent households. For single-parent homes, 60 percent reported difficulties in trying to live on their current income.

## DIVORCE

Based upon statistics provided by the Population Reference Bureau in 1996, the divorce rate in the United States was nearly twice that found in other industrialized countries. Each year, more than one million American families go through the experience of divorce. The Children of Divorce Intervention Program found that children rate the stress of parental divorce second only to the death of a parent. Divorce can place added burdens on the single parent as he or she copes with financial restraints, parenting role overload, maintenance of a social life, and problems with former spouses.

In a 1993 survey of divorced parents published in *Family Relation*, 78 percent of single mothers reported that money was their biggest problem following divorce, compared with 18 percent of single fathers. The single fathers tended to identify their former spouses as the major source of stress in fulfilling their role as a single parent. One year after divorce, the income of single-mother families is only 67 percent of the predivorce level. Single mothers have lower incomes for at least three basic reasons: lower earning capacity of the mother, lack of child support from the father, and low benefits provided by assistance programs. It is usually estimated that single mothers earn only one-third of the income of married fathers.

Divorce can disrupt the developmental stages of parenthood. According to Ellen Galinsky, parenthood unfolds in a predictable series of stages. A parent's self-image is shaped by interactions with his or her child. In the first stage, the parental-image phase, parents seek to treat their children as they wish their parents would have treated them. Images of perfection dominate this stage. The second stage is the nurturing phase; it lasts until the infant's second year. Bonding and attachment are major tasks that need to be addressed. The third stage is the authority stage, in which the child and parent test autonomy. Parents must come to grips with fantasy notions of perfection in themselves and the child. The integrative stage follows and lasts throughout middle childhood. Parents must permit initiative on the part of the child and accept their son or daughter's uniqueness. The teenage phase requires a redefinition of authority as parents need to assist their child in gaining independence. Next comes the departure stage, when the child leaves home. Parents must deal with how to interact with their child as an adult.

The orderly progression of the parenthood stages of development can be impeded by a break in the family structure. Financial strains created by a divorce can change the patterns of interactions between parent and child. Family routines such as eating meals together, enjoying recreational time together, monitoring a child's social activities, providing advice on daily decisions, and helping with schoolwork can suffer. The single parent must cope with financial concerns and feelings of social isolation. Social isolation may result from the need to move to a new residence, change lifestyle, or take a new job. Multiple demands on a single parent may leave little time for participation in a social network or progression through the stages of parenthood. Many single parents become task-oriented as a way to manage time and focus less on the emotional concerns of their children.

Nearly 50 percent of the children in mother-only households do not see their fathers in the course of a year. If divorced men remarry, they typically assume child-rearing responsibilities in their new household. They typically become more involved financially and emotionally with the new children or stepchildren than with the biological children from a previous marriage. This loss of contact continues throughout the life span.

## WIDOWHOOD AND SINGLE PARENTING

Although widowhood is a common status among elderly women, losing a spouse is not common among women or men with young children. The death of a husband or wife is a severe crisis, as it abruptly removes the major source of human companionship from a person's life. The remaining spouse is faced with an assortment of financial, emotional, and social pressures. These stresses can have an impact on the interactions between parent and child. As both grieve the loss of the loved one, the widow or widower serving as a single parent must assume added responsibilities that were not expected. Plans, hopes, and dreams for the future are disrupted. The single parent must adjust to new role realignments and new self-images.

## SINGLE FATHERHOOD

The United States Census Bureau estimates that the number of unmarried fathers living with children more than doubled from 1980 to 1999. Single fathers constituted 14 percent of single-parent households. Approximately 1.5 million single fathers were primary caretakers for their children.

Rather than the financial restraints and social isolation reported by the single mothers, single fathers experience problems with parenting in two areas: uncertainty of role and discipline. Single fathers report that feelings of isolation are a major concern. Many single fathers lack the role models necessary to fulfill successfully all the demands associated with being a parent. Conflicts arise when the father attempts to be a disciplinarian and friend at the same time to the child.

Because American society has been mother-centered in its philosophy of child care, single fathers have a difficult time fulfilling the expected nurturing role. More recently, American society has seen the emergence of "new fathers." These men do not want to be absorbed by vocational and social pursuits. The "new father" voluntarily devotes significant time to child care responsibilities.

## OUTCOMES

Traditionally, single-parent families have been considered to have a negative impact on children. There is evidence that academic performance is negatively affected by divorce and living in a single-parent household. These negative results are seen in grades rather than in scores on intelligence tests. Juvenile crime and early sexual activity have also been associated with children reared in single-parent homes. Long-term consequences of growing up in a one-parent family can include being disadvantaged in terms of educational opportunities and becoming a single parent at an early age. These outcomes can be explained by economic disadvantages, poor parent-child interactions, or lack of social supports. On the other hand, many children from single-parent households display more androgynous behaviors, exhibit more responsibility, and feel greater efficacy than those reared in traditional two-parent households.

Mothers in single-parent families report more worries, use more mental health services, and express less satisfaction with their lives than married mothers or women without children. Single-parent mothers usually are less consistent in their discipline, hold less restrictive attitudes toward sexual expression, and are less consistent in household routines than are married women.

A growing number of women are becoming single mothers by choice. These women enter parenthood without any expectation or illusion that anyone else will do anything for the child. The women who select parenthood typically have their children at a later age than the norm. Demographics of single mothers by choice suggest that they have substantial education levels and are financially able to provide the time, money, and emotional commitment to their children. A number of organizations, including Single Mothers by Choice, have emerged to provide support for these women.

*—Frank J. Prerost*

**See also** Biological clock; Divorce; Family relationships; Marriage; Men and aging; Parenthood; Remarriage; Skipped-generation parenting; Stepfamilies; Widows and widowers; Women and aging.

## FOR FURTHER INFORMATION:

Brott, Armin. *The Single Father: A Dad's Guide to Parenting Without a Partner.* New York: Abbeville Press, 1999.

Dulaney, Sara. *The Complete Idiot's Guide to Single Parenting.* New York: Alpha Books, 1998.

Engber, Andrea, and Leah Klungness. *The Complete Single Mother: Reassuring Answers to Your Most Challenging Concerns.* Holbrook, Mass.: Adams Media, 1995.

Hunter, Lynda. *A Comprehensive Guide to Parenting on Your Own.* Grand Rapids, Mich.: Zondervan, 1997.

Ludtke, Melissa. *On Our Own: Unmarried Motherhood in America.* New York: Random House, 1997.

Mattes, Jane. *Single Mothers by Choice: A Guidebook for Single Women Who Are Considering or Have Chosen Motherhood.* Rev. ed. New York: Times Books, 1997.

Tippins, Prudence, and Sherill Tippins. *Two of Us Make a World: The Single Mother's Guide to Pregnancy, Childbirth, and the First Year.* New York: Henry Holt, 1996.

## SINGLEHOOD

**RELEVANT ISSUES:** Family, psychology

**SIGNIFICANCE:** People who have never married often experience a level of satisfaction in many aspects of late adulthood equal to that of married people; both groups tend to experience greater satisfaction than do their divorced and widowed agemates

Although the vast majority of adults in all societies marry at some point in their lives, a small number of individuals reach old age having never married. Once known as "avowed bachelors" or "aging spinsters," this group of elders is now referred to as never-married or ever-single people, or lifelong singles. The rate of lifelong singles within a population differs significantly among technological societies, from a low of 5 percent in the United States to 10 percent in most European countries and as high as 22 percent in Scotland. Reasons suggested for these differences are varying economic conditions, marriage customs, and attitudes toward adults who remain unmarried. History plays a role also, with more lifelong single women found in countries that have experienced recent wars or large-scale emigration.

Popular myths depict this group of older, never-married adults as being unhappy, regretful, and even bitter. Society expects adults to fulfill certain roles as they go through the life span, and people who do not marry are typically viewed as shirking social responsibility or missing out on some of life's pleasures. However, the research findings on the lives of older adults who have never married show a much different picture than this stereotype.

Reasons for remaining single throughout life range from caring for elderly parents to being homosexual. Many lifelong singles report being too involved with careers in early adulthood and then realizing in middle adulthood that they prefer the independence of being single. Few plan to remain single, but small decisions made at different points in life seem to conspire to produce the lifelong single.

Popular wisdom and gerontological research concur that married people fare better than unmarried people throughout life, especially in late adulthood when they enjoy the benefits of better health, wealth, and happiness than their unmarried counterparts. However, the question arises over what aspects of married life contribute to this outcome. Is it the presence of a spouse in later years? Is it because married people have not experienced the negative consequences of being widowed or divorced? A closer examination of lifelong single people in their later years has provided compelling support for the latter.

## LIFELONG SINGLES AND HEALTH

Several studies have divided older single people into four categories: divorced, widowed, separated, and never married. When comparisons are made among these groups, those who have never married report having the best health and fewest disabilities than those in the other three groups. Older adults who have never married also have the lowest incidence of suicide and report higher levels of mental health than the divorced and separated elders.

Even though never-married individuals enjoy better mental and physical health than those who are divorced, widowed, and separated, they are more apt to spend the later years of their lives living in nursing homes. Among people seventy-five years of age or older in the United States, 20 percent of those who never married live in institutions, compared to 14 percent of those who were formerly married and 4 percent of those who are still married. However, these data do not necessarily reflect a sudden decline in health for the life-long single elders, but rather a lack of traditional caregiving options. When an older person can no longer live independently, the first option is to remain at home and be cared for by a healthier spouse. If no spouse is available, the second option is to remain at home and be cared for by a son or daughter. A person who has never married usually does not have these options and, as a result, enters assisted living facilities or nursing homes at a younger age and in better health than older adults who have spouses or children.

## LIFELONG SINGLES AND WEALTH

Most of the information on lifelong singles in late adulthood comes from studies of women. The major reason for this is simply that older women outnumber older men in almost every category, and lifelong singles are no exception.

Women who have never married achieve more in their careers than women who marry. They have more education and advance further and more quickly in their jobs. One reason for this is that lifelong single women typically work steadily throughout their career years and do not take time off for childbearing and child rearing. In addition, women who have never married seldom have children to support and educate or the unexpected financial responsibilities of single parenthood after divorce or widowhood. Furthermore, women who have never married are more apt than other women to plan for retirement. With high and steady incomes during early and middle adulthood, no dependents, and the opportunity to focus most of their time and energy on their careers, women who have never married tend to go into retirement with solid assets and good pensions.

Although never-married women have higher incomes in retirement than divorced or separated women, they have lower incomes than widowed women who are collecting pensions from their late husband's earnings because of the income differential between equally qualified men and women that was common and substantial in decades past. Formerly married women with histories of low wages, and those who did not work at all, can collect retirement benefits based on their late husbands' higher wages. In spite of having lower incomes than widows, lifelong single women report equal satisfaction with their retirement incomes, while divorced and separated women report signif-

## Single U.S. Men and Women Living Alone in 1996

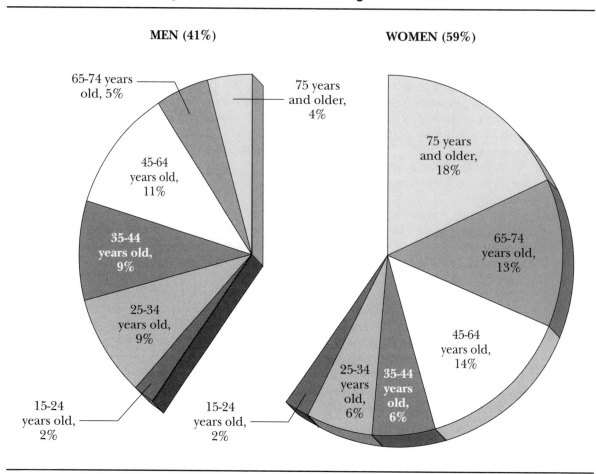

MEN (41%)

WOMEN (59%)

65-74 years old, 5%

75 years and older, 4%

45-64 years old, 11%

35-44 years old, 9%

25-34 years old, 9%

15-24 years old, 2%

15-24 years old, 2%

75 years and older, 18%

65-74 years old, 13%

45-64 years old, 14%

25-34 years old, 6%

35-44 years old, 6%

*Note:* In 1996 approximately 24,900,000 Americans aged 15 years and up were single and living alone. Percentages are rounded to the nearest whole number.

*Source:* U.S. Bureau of the Census, *Statistical Abstract of the United States: 1997.* Washington, D.C.: GPO, 1997.

icantly less satisfaction with this aspect of their retirement years.

### LIFELONG SINGLES AND HAPPINESS

The happiness and life satisfaction of married couples has been studied across the life span. General findings have been that early adulthood is a happy time for couples, middle adulthood is a little more difficult, and the later years bring renewed happiness and life satisfaction. One of the major causes of the middle adulthood dip in happiness is children. Couples with no children report more stable levels of happiness and life satisfaction across the life span.

When taken as a group, men and women who have never married are happier than married people in early adulthood and less happy in late adulthood. However, when the happiness levels of men and women are considered separately, older never-married women are significantly happier than their male counterparts. In fact, comparing never-married women with married women in later years shows little difference in happiness levels, while never-married men are significantly less happy than their married counterparts.

Another important factor in the happiness of older adults is the presence or absence of social support, which is defined as having people in one's life in whom one may confide and from whom one receives caring, positive attention. The typical source of social support for adults is a spouse, and those who have lost spouses through divorce or widowhood report lower levels of life satisfaction and adjustment.

Studies of people who do not marry, especially women, show that they maintain close ties with their parents during early and middle adulthood, often being the primary caregivers of elderly parents. They also have close relationships with their siblings throughout adulthood and foster close relationships with nieces and nephews. Furthermore, the lifelong single person often has close and long-term friendships with people they consider family, a relationship sociologists refer to as "fictive kin." Lifelong single women report less loneliness than divorced or widowed women in late adulthood, and they give indications of satisfaction with their social support equal to that of married women. Apparently, the relationships lifelong singles cultivate throughout adulthood provide social support in the later years similar to that enjoyed by married couples. In contrast, it seems that married people do not seek out these additional sources of social support during early and middle adulthood, and if they are widowed or divorced, they experience more social isolation than the lifelong single person.

In general, it seems that marriage is the best life situation for older adults who chose to marry, and singlehood is the best life situation for older adults who chose not to marry. Problems arise when those who chose to marry find themselves living alone for reasons beyond their control, such as the death of their spouse or divorce.

—*Barbara R. Bjorklund*

*See also* Divorce; Family relationships; Marriage; Men and aging; Nursing and convalescent homes; Retirement; Single parenthood; Social ties; Widows and widowers; Women and aging.

## FOR FURTHER INFORMATION:

Aiken, L. *Aging*. Thousand Oaks, Calif.: Sage Publications, 1995.

Barresi, C., and K. Hunt. "The Unmarried Elderly: Age, Sex, and Ethnicity." In *Family Relationships in Later Life*, edited by T. Brubaker. Newbury Park, Calif.: Sage Publications, 1990.

Bee, Helen L., and Barbara R. Bjorklund. *The Journey of Adulthood*. 3d ed. Upper Saddle River, N.J.: Prentice Hall, 1999.

Keith, P. *The Unmarried in Later Life*. New York: Praeger, 1989.

Newtson, R. L., and P. M. Keith. "Single Women in Later Life." In *Handbook on Women and Aging*, edited by J. M. Coyle. Westport, Conn.: Greenwood Press, 1997.

## SKIN CANCER

**RELEVANT ISSUES:** Health and medicine

**SIGNIFICANCE:** The skin is the most common site of cancer in older light-skinned residents of North America

The largest organ in the body, the skin is the body's interface with the physical and chemical constituents of the external world, many of which are harmful and can cause cancer in the long term. Human skin is composed of two layers: The outer, protective epidermis covers a deeper layer called the dermis. The basal layer of the epidermis adjacent to the dermis contains a number of specialized cells, melanoblasts and melanocytes, that produce the pigment melanin, which gives the skin its color. The dermis contains blood and lymphatic vessels, sensory nerve endings, and specialized structures such as sweat glands, sebaceous glands, and hair follicles. Epidermal cancers are overwhelmingly more common than cancers of the dermal components (nonepithelial skin cancers). The common types of epidermal cancers are discussed here.

### TYPES AND CAUSES OF SKIN CANCER

Of the many different varieties of skin cancer, the three most common are basal cell carcinomas, squamous cell carcinomas, and melanomas or malignant melanomas. The first two behave in a distinctly less aggressive fashion than the last and are generally discussed under the rubric nonmelanoma skin cancers.

Skin cancers are not inherited, although conditions favoring skin cancer formation are. Because external or internal irritants take considerable time to result in cancer, skin cancers are often seen in aging populations. The most common cause of skin cancer production is the sun's ultraviolet (UV) rays. Vertical rays of the sun are particularly dangerous, as the atmospheric ozone layer can screen out considerable portions of the UV rays. Equatorial latitudes and the sun exposure between 10 A.M. and 3 P.M. are particularly potent in causing skin cancer. UV rays are also reflected by sheets of water or snow and from sandy beaches. The effect of the sun's rays is mainly on the melanoblasts in the basal layer of the skin. Natural pigmentation of the skin is the best protection against the UV rays. Hence, skin cancers are significantly more prevalent in light-skinned individuals.

Other, rare causes of skin cancer include chronic nonhealing scars from injuries or burns and prolonged exposure to arsenicals, as in a contaminated water supply. Some forms of medical treatment can also be carcinogenic: Special types of X rays, hydroxyurea derivatives used in the treatment of myeloproliferative disorders, and immunosuppression for organ transplantation can all increase the incidence of nonmelanoma skin cancers.

### INCIDENCE

Basal cell carcinomas and squamous cell carcinomas are the most common type of skin cancers in the United States and also the most easily treated. Customarily, their numbers are not recorded, whereas those of melanomas and nonepithelial cancers are. The projected incidence and lethality in the United States of melanomas and nonepithelial skin cancers for 1999 are shown in table 1.

---

### 1999 Skin Cancer Incidence and Death in the United States (projected)

**Melanomas**

|            | Total  | Males  | Females |
|------------|--------|--------|---------|
| Incidence  | 44,200 | 25,800 | 18,400  |
| Deaths     | 7,300  | 4,600  | 2,700   |

**Nonepithelial (Nonmelanoma) Skin Cancers**

|            | Total | Males | Females |
|------------|-------|-------|---------|
| Incidence  | 9,800 | 7,600 | 2,200   |
| Deaths     | 1,900 | 1,200 | 700     |

---

*Source:* Landis, S. H., T. Murray, S. Bolden, and P. S. Wingo. "Cancer Statistics, 1999." *CA: A Cancer Journal for Clinicians* 49 (1999): 12-13.

For melanomas, the highest incidence is in light-skinned populations in sunny climates. Thus, according to D. M. Parkin, P. Pisani, and colleagues in their 1999 article "Global Cancer Statistics," Australia and New Zealand have high rates, with an age-standardized incidence rate of 27.9 in men and 25.0 in women. (The corresponding figures for North America are 10.9 in men and 7.7 in women.) Nonmelanoma skin cancers should also have a high incidence in these countries, as the predisposing factors are the same.

### NONMELANOMA SKIN CANCERS

The skin shows a number of changes with increasing age. Of these, superficial flaky lesions called solar or actinic keratoses on the sun-exposed skin of the head and neck and extremities, especially the backs of the hands, are considered to be premalignant, or precursors of later basal cell carcinomas and squamous cell carcinomas. These cancers arise in skin as a result of chronic sun exposure. Other rare precursor conditions include abnormal lack of pigmentation, such as that found in xeroderma pigmentosa, albinism, and Bowen's disease.

In North America, basal cell carcinomas are about four times more common than squamous cell carcinomas. Basal cell carcinomas are especially common on the head and neck and may have a number of different appearances. Generally, they are pearly, discrete plaques in the skin with a long history of slow growth. They may be pigmented (and therefore can be mistaken for melanoma) or ulcerated with serpiginous edges (sometimes called a rodent ulcer). Long-neglected basal cell carcinomas can produce monstrous local deformities. They rarely spread to distant organs (metastasize) and are quite amenable to the standard treatment modalities.

Squamous cell carcinomas are the less common but more threatening nonmelanoma skin cancers. Arising on nonexposed as well as sun-exposed skin, they are usually red, ulcerated, and raised above the skin, although clinical differentiation between them and basal cell carcinomas is usually impossible. If they are neglected, a number of them will proceed to the local and then distant lymph nodes and even to distant viscera, such as the lungs. Cancers arising on burn scars (Marjolin's ulcer) are often squamous cell carcinomas. This type of skin cancer is eminently curable with early surgical excision.

## MALIGNANT MELANOMAS

Melanomatous skin cancers arise from the melanoblasts in the epidermis. These cancers are more common in light-skinned people, especially those with light-colored or blond hair, blue or green eyes, and of Celtic descent. Malignant melanomas are the most rapidly increasing type of cancer in the United States. Acute intensive sunburn, particularly in children or teenagers, is thought to cause these cancers in later life.

Melanomas are seen at ages earlier than nonmelanoma skin cancers. Four clinical types are recognized, based on appearance, both clinical and histological, and the natural history of the disease: superficial spreading melanoma, nodular-type melanoma, acral lentiginous-type melanoma, and lentigo maligna.

Superficial spreading melanoma (50 to 70 percent) is the most common type. These malignant cells spread horizontally along the dermal-epidermal plane, with little tendency to penetrate the dermis. Thus, they are distant from the lymphatic and venous channels thought to be necessary for distant spread. The peak incidence is in the fourth and fifth decades of life, and common sites are on the legs and backs of white women and the upper backs of white men.

Nodular-type melanoma (15 to 30 percent) is less common but considerably more dangerous than superficial spreading melanoma. The cells proliferate in a vertical plane. Therefore, they form nodules on the skin and also invade the dermis. Their propensity to spread (and hence their potential lethality) has been shown to relate to the depth to which they penetrate both by histological layer and by measured thickness.

These two types constitute the great majority of melanomas. Clinically, melanomas have a variegated appearance with varying shades of brown and black in the lesion, which is generally more than 6 millimeters in diameter. The colored patch may be in the plane of skin or raised even into the nodules. Its margins or borders are uneven. The lesions often arise spontaneously and progress relatively rapidly; they may occasionally rise on preexisting moles that suddenly change their appearance and start to grow. Some ulcerate, and others itch. In advanced cases, evidence of distant spread may be manifested by enlargement of draining lymph nodes or symptoms related to distant viscera.

Acral lentiginous-type melanomas (2 to 5 percent) are seen in the palms, soles, and under the nails of the hands and feet. This type is often seen in African Americans and generally appears in the seventh decade of life. Nail apparatus melanoma starts off as a flat, variegated, black patch that destroys the nail and soon becomes nodular. These lesions are particularly invasive.

Lentigo maligna (Hutchison's freckle) or lentigo maligna melanomas (1 to 2 percent) appear as broad, brown, and irregular patches on the sun-exposed skin of older persons. After a prolonged indolent course of many years, they start to proliferate rapidly and take on the characteristic appearance and lethality of nodular melanoma.

## SOME SPECIAL CONSIDERATIONS

Immunosuppression in transplant patients causes cancers at various sites, including melanoma. The rate and site seem to be genetically influenced. According to C. S. Ong, A. M. Keogh, and colleagues, among light-skinned heart transplant patients in Australia, 31 percent developed nonmelanoma skin cancers after ten years and 43 percent developed them after twenty years; squamous cell carcinomas were three times more common than basal cell carcinomas. As reported by H. Kishikawa, Y. Ichikawa, and colleagues, among renal transplant patients in Japan, the new cancer rate was much lower, 3.9 percent at ten years and 13.9 percent at twenty years, and mainly in the digestive tract and not on the skin.

Genetic influences undoubtedly play a part in melanoma development and spread, though the exact relationship is currently unclear. Melanomas are often associated with defective p53 tumor suppressor genes (also seen in other cancers). The HLA-DR4 phenotype is associated with an increased risk of both melanomas and basal cell carcinomas.

## DIAGNOSIS AND TREATMENT

Exact identification of the type of lesion is essential for appropriate treatment, follow-up, and prognosis of skin cancer patients. Therefore, it is essential to do a biopsy of any lesion that cannot be excised with an adequate margin. Microscopic examination is generally adequate, although more sophisticated methods such as staining for tumor-specific markers have to be used.

Surgical excision is the current preferred treatment for both nonmelanoma skin cancers and melanomas. A special combination of excision and chemosurgery (Moh's technique) may be used under special circumstances. Excisions of nonmelanoma skin cancers must be complete, with adequate and clear margins. Early surgery cures almost all basal cell carcinomas and over 95 percent of squamous cell carcinomas. Radiation therapy is effective in treating nonmelanoma skin cancers when surgery is refused or is impossible.

For melanomas, the width and depth of the excision are dependent on the thickness of the lesion. According to W. H. McCarthy and H. M. Shaw, for a thin melanoma, a 0.5 centimeter margin is probably adequate; deeper penetration requires a 1 to 3 centimeter margin of excision. The results of surgical treatment of melanomas have significantly improved in recent years. A near 100 percent cure can be expected with early superficial spreading melanomas. Nodular-type melanomas that are still limited to local tissues can be cured in 60 to 80 percent of patients. The modern technique of mapping sentinel lymph nodes to determine if there has been spread to the lymphatic system (in the absence of clinical findings) allows early clearance of affected nodes. With metastasis to the local lymph nodes, however, the cure rate drops to around 30 percent. With generalized spread to the visceral, a cure is unattainable by current methods.

No specific chemotherapeutic drugs are currently useful against nonmelanoma skin cancers. Interferon has shown some promise in the short-term relief of malignant melanomas.

## PREVENTION

Of the inciting causes of skin cancer, the one that is easiest to control is solar UV rays. Nonmelanoma skin cancers are caused by long-term or chronic exposure to these rays. They can be avoided by leaving as little of skin exposed as possible when outside. Skin that cannot be covered should be protected with repeated applications of a sunscreen with a sun-protecting factor (SPF) of at least 15. The practice of sunbathing not only ages skin but also increases the possibility of skin cancers, especially if exposure is to the vertical solar rays between 10 A.M. and 3 P.M. (Such sun protection does not decrease the important formation of vitamin D analogues by the skin.) Whether suntanning using machines promotes the development of skin cancer has not been clearly determined, but this effect would seem possible.

The key to the prevention of skin caner in middle and old age is caution in youth. Acute significant sunburn in children is particularly conducive to malignant melanomas in later life. It is therefore important to protect children from this type of exposure, especially on playing fields and beaches and on hiking trips. While parents should be aware of this, children also need to be taught the dangers of exposure to UV rays.

Finally, recognition of the health hazards of ozone depletion is needed by the business and manufacturing communities, lawmakers, and the public. Skin cancers, both nonmelanoma skin cancers and melanomas, in older adults are among the many unwelcome legacies of this human assault on the environment.

—*Ranès C. Chakravorty*
*See also* Cancer; Skin changes and disorders.

**FOR FURTHER INFORMATION:**
Arnold, Harry L., Richard B. Odom, and William James. *Andrews' Diseases of the Skin.* 8th ed. Philadelphia: W. B. Saunders, 1990.
Kishikawa, H., Y. Ichikawa, et al. "Malignant Neoplasm in Kidney Transplantation." *International Journal of Urology* 5, no. 6 (November, 1998): 521-525.
Landis, S. H., T. Murray, S. Bolden, and P. S. Wingo. "Cancer Statistics, 1999." *CA: A Cancer Journal for Clinicians* 49 (1999): 8-31.
Lookingbill, Donald P., and James G. Marks. *Principles of Dermatology.* Philadelphia: W. B. Saunders, 1986.
McCarthy, W. H., and H. M. Shaw. "The Surgical Treatment of Primary Melanoma." *Hematology/Oncology Clinics of North America* 12, no. 4 (August, 1998): 797-805.
Ong, C. S., A. M. Keogh, et al. "Skin Cancer in Australian Heart Transplant Recipients." *Journal of the American Academy of Dermatology* 40, no. 1 (January, 1999): 27-34.

Parkin, D. M., P. Pisani, et al. "Global Cancer Statistics, 1999." *CA: A Cancer Journal for Clinicians* 49 (1999): 33-64.

Rook, Arthur, et al., eds. *Textbook of Dermatology.* 4th ed. 3 vols. Oxford, England: Blackwell Scientific Publications, 1986.

Siegel, Mary-Ellen. *Safe in the Sun.* New York: Walker, 1990.

## SKIN CHANGES AND DISORDERS

**RELEVANT ISSUES:** Health and medicine

**SIGNIFICANCE:** Changes in skin and hair are the most visible signs of aging; skin changes predispose the elderly to develop age-related skin disorders

Structurally, the skin is composed of three layers: the outer epidermis, the middle dermis, and the underlying hypodermis or subcutaneous layer. Specialized cells in the skin include keratinocytes, which produce keratin, a fibrous, horny material that acts as a protective, mechanical shield. Melanocytes produce melanin, the substance that gives the skin its color tones and acts as a screen to protect the body from ultraviolet rays. Langerhans cells in the skin are part of the immune system and protect the body against harmful substances. The appendages of the skin include the eccrine and apocrine sweat glands, sebaceous glands, nails, and hair.

Functionally, skin acts as a barrier that provides protection against loss of body fluid, trauma, and microbes and other harmful agents. Skin also assists in the regulation of body temperature, secretes sweat and sebum, participates in the synthesis of vitamin D, and contains sensory receptors to touch, pain, and temperature.

### THE EFFECTS OF AGING

All skin structures and functions are adversely affected by the aging process. Skin changes occur because of intrinsic factors related to inevitable tissue aging, as well as extrinsic factors, primarily exposure to ultraviolet light. Skin damage caused by ultraviolet light is referred to as photodamage, while skin change caused by ultraviolet rays is referred to as photoaging or dermatoheliosis. The extent of change to the epidermis and dermis is related to the cumulative effects of the aging process and sun exposure. Chronically sun-exposed skin looks leathery, thickened, and deeply creased. A comparison can be made between the sun-exposed skin of the face and the covered skin over the buttock. Overall, melanocytes decrease in number with age, leaving the skin more sensitive to ultraviolet rays. Darker skin has more protective melanocytes and therefore shows less damage from the sun's ultraviolet rays. The development of many noncancerous (benign) and cancerous (malignant) skin lesions is related to the effects of ultraviolet rays.

Cigarette smoking contributes to an aged appearance of the skin. Characteristic skin changes associated with smoking include "purse-string" wrinkles around the lip border and increased wrinkles over the face. Skin changes correlate to length and quantity of smoking (pack years).

Changes occur in the structure of all layers of the skin with age. As cell reproduction in the epidermis declines, the skin layer becomes less dense, and the skin will appear thinner. In the very old, the skin looks like parchment; the fragile, thinner skin is easily torn. Superficial blood vessels are more prominent, and easy bruising occurs because the small blood vessels lose the support originally provided by the connective tissue and subcutaneous pad. The blood vessels are more easily traumatized, resulting in irregular-shaped, purplish, superficial hemorrhages of various sizes called actinic or senile purpura, which can last for several weeks. These purpuric areas can occur spontaneously from the leakage of superficial capillaries. Senile purpura are frequently seen on the hands and forearms. The area of attachment between the epidermis and dermis decreases with age, enabling the skin to tear more easily with shearing force.

Other age-related changes include a decrease in the function of the sebaceous and sweat glands located within the skin. The sebum produced by the sebaceous glands lubricates the hair follicle and, to a lesser degree, lubricates the skin. A decline in function results in a diminished production of oil and drier skin. Sebum has antimicrobial properties, so the decrease makes the skin surface more vulnerable to infection. The decline in sweat production contributes to dryness of the skin. Drier skin with less perspiration results in a condition called xerosis. The exact cause of xerosis is unknown, but it is typically, and commonly, seen in the elderly. The skin is rough, dry, and flaky. The dryness causes skin to itch (pruritus). Low humidity, harsh soaps, hot baths, rough clothing, and exposure to sun can compound the itchiness. Scratching can cause breaks in the skin that can become infected. With less sweat production, the cooling mechanism of perspiration and evaporation is lost or diminished. This increases the risk of hyperthermia or heat stroke in the elderly.

Structural changes in the collagen and elastic fibers of the dermis of the skin cause a loss of suppleness and elasticity. The skin becomes progressively more inelastic and lax, resulting in wrinkling and sagging. Facial wrinkling begins as early as the second decade of life as a result of repeated muscle movement associated with facial expressions. These wrinkles can be seen around the eyes and mouth and over the forehead as aging occurs. Additional fine, diffuse wrinkles appear over the skin with the loss of moisture and elasticity of the dermal layer and the decrease in the subcutaneous or fatty layer of the skin. A decrease in the elasticity and turgor also results in loose or drooping skin seen most obviously under the chin, along the jaw, beneath the eyes, and in the earlobes.

The lax, loose skin can result in overlapping folds, creating intertriginous areas where two skin surfaces are in constant contact. One such area is the corner of the mouth, where the loose skin from the cheek and upper lip overlaps the lower, outer lip. Overlapping is exaggerated in those individuals who are edentulous (without teeth). Other intertriginous areas are under the breasts and in the groin area. Moisture collects where skin surfaces overlap; this creates an environment conducive to skin breakdown and the development of skin infections.

Age changes cause the barrier functions of the skin to be less effective, and the elderly are more prone to develop contact dermatitis caused by sensitivity to such substances as leather goods, certain metals, and formaldehyde in clothing fab-

*Years of sun exposure and natural changes in elasticity and underlying fat deposits can alter the appearance of the skin significantly.* (Jim Whitmer)

ric. A decrease in Langerhans cells leads to a decline in immune response by the skin and an increased risk for skin infection. The elderly are also more prone to photosensitivity reactions when exposed to the sun. Photosensitivity is a side effect of a number of medications frequently taken by older adults.

Nerve endings for pain and temperature perception that are located in the skin decline with age. The decrease in function can lead to frostbite and burns. Once injury to the skin occurs, tissue repair and healing will be a slower process in the elderly, partly because of the decreased vascularity of the dermis and decreased cell reproduction. This is true of all wound healing; the process takes longer in the elderly, and wound separation is more likely to occur.

With a decrease in the subcutaneous layer, which serves as a "padding" or "cushion," bony prominences and joints appear more conspicuous, sharper, and more angular; at the same time, hollows around the bony skeleton deepen. These changes are apparent over the upper chest, shoulders, and neck. Because of the loss of padding, the elderly are more likely to sustain injuries from a fall, and bedridden elderly are more prone to developing pressure ulcers (bed sores) over bony prominences. Since the subcutaneous fat pad also serves as insulation, other consequences of loss of the subcutaneous layer are feeling cold more easily and vulnerability to hypothermia.

With age, skin color appears less uniform and more blotchy. Functioning melanocytes do not spread evenly, so areas of hyperpigmentation and hypopigmentation occur. These changes are generally related to photodamage and are more apparent in fair-complected individuals. Increased freckling and lentigo are common. Senile or solar lentigines, also called age spots or liver spots, are round, flat, brown areas of various sizes with well-defined borders. They occur in chronically sun-exposed areas, usually over the face and back of the hands and wrists. Lentigo appear during the middle decades of life, and the number and size increase with age. Whitish, depigmented patches, termed pseudoscars, appear as well.

Senile or cherry angiomas are tiny, red, slightly raised lesions that turn brown with age. Cherry angiomas are vascular in origin. They appear over the trunk and arms in midlife and increase with age. Telangiectasias, which are small, superficial, dilated blood vessels, are frequently seen over the nose, cheeks, and thighs.

A decrease in melanocytes results in the graying of the hair. The age of onset for graying is typically in the thirties, although darkly pigmented individuals begin graying approximately one decade later. A decline in sebaceous oil production causes the hair to feel more coarse and to look less shiny. The rate of hair growth declines. Although more pronounced in men, scalp hair in both men and women becomes sparser with increased age. There is an increase in coarse facial hair in women and an increase in nasal, ear, and eyebrow hair in men. With aging, nails thicken, take on a yellowish color, and develop heavy vertical ridges. The nail plate becomes more brittle and can split or peel. Changes in the toenails are more apparent than in fingernails. Thickening of the toenails can make them difficult to trim. An inability to keep the feet and nails clean can lead to fungal infections of the toenails.

### SKIN DISORDERS

Senile or seborrheic keratosis is a common, pigmented skin growth that usually first appears in middle age. They develop from the keratin-containing cells of the skin; increased melanocytes give them their dark color. Keratoses are yellow-brown to black, raised, wart-like lesions that become darker and larger over time. They vary in size and have a sharp border, and most appear to be set on top of the skin surface. Sun exposure does not seem to be a factor in their development, since they appear on covered body surfaces, such as the back. It is not clear what factors do contribute to their development, but there appears to be a familial tendency. Seborrheic keratoses originally appear as small, flat, tan areas. They most commonly develop on the trunk, face, scalp, and neck, and increase in number with age. They can appear singularly or in profusion over the body. Dermatosis papulosa nigra is a form of seborrheic keratosis seen in darkly pigmented individuals. These lesions are small and raised, and may be pedunculated. Multiple lesions develop over the face and neck. Seborrheic keratoses are benign growths, creating a cosmetic rather than a medical problem. The growths can be removed with cryotherapy, electrodesiccation, or laser therapy.

Actinic or solar keratoses, unlike seborrheic keratoses, are precancerous. They appear as tannish-red or pigmented, roughened or scaly patches on sun-exposed areas, such as the hands, forearms, face, bald scalp, and ears. Solar keratoses are treated with cryotherapy, fluoroplex cream, or laser therapy. Cutaneous horns, which develop from one type of actinic keratoses, are skin-colored, hard projections of keratinized skin. They vary in size from a few millimeters to several millimeters and usually grow on the hands or forehead. Although usually benign, in some cases the base can be cancerous, so removal and biopsy is usually recommended.

Skin tags or acrochordons are also more common with increasing age. They are soft, skin-colored or pigmented, pedunculated growths that develop frequently on the neck, axilla, inner thigh, and other areas of friction. Skin tags are small, usually 1 to 3 millimeters. They can appear singly or in large numbers. Skin tags present no health problem and are easily removed. Keratoacanthoma is a skin-colored elevation of the skin with a central area of keratin. These lesions develop rapidly, usually on sun-exposed areas in individuals over fifty years of age, and resolve spontaneously over a few months. Because they closely resemble squamous cell carcinomas, a biopsy is indicated.

Sebaceous gland hyperplasia frequently occurs on the forehead and nose. The lesion appears as a yellow, slightly raised area with a central depression, ranging in size from 1 to 3 millimeters. It is important to differentiate these benign lesions from basal cell carcinoma. Sebaceous hyperplasia is most often the result of chronic sun damage. Sun damage can also lead to solar elastosis, a condition characterized by a thickening of the fibers in the dermal layer. Other features of sun-damaged skin are nodularity, comedones or blackhead, ruddiness, and telangiectasias. Treatment generally includes topical tretinoin (Retin A).

Although herpes zoster (shingles) can occur at any age, the vast majority of cases occur in those over forty years of age, perhaps because of the decline in immune system functioning with age. In a significant number of elderly persons, postherpetic neuralgia or pain persists after the herpes lesions have healed. The pain can continue for months or indefinitely.

Although two malignant skin cancers, basal cell and squamous cell carcinomas, commonly occur in the elderly, they rarely metastasize beyond the site of origin. Both types occur more often in males and in fair-skinned individuals.

Skin manifestations can occur with systemic medical disorders. One common example in the elderly is the skin changes that occur in the lower extremities resulting from circulatory problems. When venous blood drainage from the lower extremities is slowed, increased blood pressure in the venous system results (venous insufficiency). The increased pressure causes leakage from the blood vessels, which creates edema or fluid accumulation in the tissue. If the condition persists, the skin becomes tight, red, and scaly. The condition is referred to a stasis dermatitis or gravitational eczema. Hyperpigmentation develops over the anterior, lower leg from iron in the red blood cells being deposited in the tissue, a condition referred to as hemosiderosis. A chronic situation of decreased circulation and edema can result in skin breakdown or ulcer formation. Leg ulcers can also be the result of decreased arterial blood flow.

Regardless of the amount of previous sun damage, all individuals benefit from using sunscreen and protective clothing when they are exposed to the sun's rays. Totally avoiding sun exposure during midday is recommended. Moisturizers provide temporary relief from skin dryness. Mild soaps and bath oil clean the skin without further drying. Closely trimmed fingernails are less likely to cause abrasions if itching results in scratching. Adding humidity to the environment during the winter increases comfort. It is important to report any new, unusual, or changing skin lesions to a primary health care provider. —*Roberta Tierney*

**See also** Age spots; Aging process; Cancer; Cosmetic surgery; Face lifts; Gray hair; Hair growth; Hair loss and baldness; Skin cancer; Smoking; Temperature regulation and sensitivity; Wrinkles.

**FOR FURTHER INFORMATION:**
Freedberg, Irwin M., Arthur Z. Eisen, Klaus Wolff, K. Frank Austen, Lowell A. Goldsmith, Stephen I. Katz, and Thomas B. Fitzpatrick, eds. *Fitzpatrick's Dermatology in General Medicine.* 5th ed. New York: McGraw-Hill, 1999. An in-depth, comprehensive text describing etiology, morphology, symptoms, and treatment of skin disorders.

Ham, Richard J., and Philip D. Sloane. *Primary Care Geriatrics: A Case-Based Approach.* 2d ed. St. Louis: Mosby Year Book, 1992. Case studies featuring geriatric patients in an ambulatory health care setting.

Porth, Carol Mattson. *Pathophysiology.* 5th ed. Philadelphia: J. B. Lippincott, 1998. Presents anatomy and physiology of body systems followed by pathophysiologic changes; includes one chapter on skin.

Sams, W. Mitchell, Jr., and Peter J. Lynch, eds. *Principles and Practice of Dermatology.* 2d ed. New York: Churchill Livingstone, 1996. Comprehensive discussion of skin disorders.

Singleton, Joanne K., Samuel A. Sandowski, Carol Green-Hernandez, Theresa V. Horvath, Robert V. DiGregorio, and Stephen P. Holzemer. *Primary Care.* Philadelphia: J. B. Lippincott, 1999. Care of adult patients seen in a medical office, with one section focusing on the care of skin problems.

## SKIPPED-GENERATION PARENTING

**RELEVANT ISSUES:** Demographics, family

**SIGNIFICANCE:** Grandparents who are raising their grandchildren have specific stresses that result from child rearing; support services can assist them with providing care

In the 1990's, the number of grandparents raising their grandchildren tripled. In 1999, about 1.5 million children lived in these "skipped-generation" or "parent-absent" families. While grandparents have always been a source of support in child rearing, the contemporary practice of providing primary care for their grandchildren can present older people with stressful family issues and need for support.

Several factors account for the increase in this family form. The most common, and devastating, reason is the increase in crack cocaine use among women in childbearing years. Their addiction demands the entire attention of these women, who often neglect their children or leave them in the care of their own parent. Other reasons that children are not living with their parent include the rise of women who are imprisoned, increased rates of human immunodeficiency virus (HIV) infection and acquired immunodeficiency syndrome (AIDS) in the heterosexual community, and community violence, such as domestic violence and homicide, which takes the life of the parent.

In situations where a child permanently or temporarily loses a parent, the grandparent typically becomes the next available care provider in the family. While some grandparents may care for only one child, others raise several children who may range in age from infancy to late adolescence. Some grandchildren live with their grandparents for a time-limited period, such as a prison sentence, while others will be raised by their grandparents until adulthood.

Grandparenthood is a role that is not exclusively held by people in later life. Examples of grandparents who are in their late thirties is not uncommon. Yet, many grandparents who are raising their grandchildren are past the usual age of child rearing, such as their fifties, sixties, or seventies. These older grandparents may have a difficult time readjusting to their caregiving role. In addition, these older adults are beginning to experience some age-related changes that can compromise their ability to provide care.

### FAMILY ISSUES

Grandparents who are in midlife or later life may be experiencing the physical, social, and economic changes associated with the aging process. These age-related changes can compound the usual stresses that are associated with raising children. Grandparents often describe the physical exertion that is required in caring for younger children. The consequence ranges from "feeling run down" to exacerbating an existing health problem such as hypertension or diabetes. In addition, the time expended in child rearing leaves fewer hours for the grandparents to spend in other activities. Grandparents may eliminate positive health practices, such as exercising and sleeping, which also takes a negative toll on physical health.

There are also social costs related to caregiving. The child-rearing role can decrease the quality of the grandparents' marriage and other social relationships. One stressful aspect can be a lack of opportunities to spend time as a couple or with friends. The outcome can be a sense of isolation or loneliness for the grandparents.

The nature of the relationship with the parent of the child can also create tension within the family. A crack-addicted mother, for example, may re-

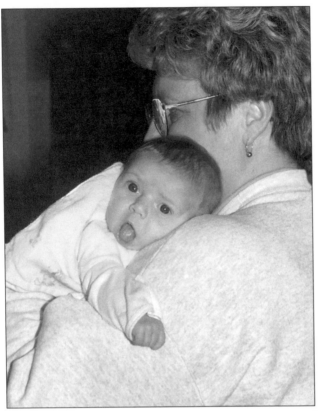

*Problems with younger mothers such as teen pregnancy and drug abuse can result in the phenomenon of skipped-generation parenting in which grandparents raise their grandchildren.* (Marilyn Nolt)

parenting competence also rises. Contemporary youths face different social situations and pressures—including violence in school, gangs, sexual relationships, and drugs—than those existing when many grandparents raised their own children. Grandparents may not possess the knowledge or experience to know how to guide their grandchildren through these difficult issues.

The economics of child rearing can also present a stressor for these grandparents. While skipped-generation families are found in all income and racial groups, a disproportionate number are in low-income, African American families. These grandparents often have more limited financial resources to support a child. In addition, many of these child care arrangements are informal; therefore, the family does not receive the social welfare benefits, such as cash subsidies or allowances, that may be available in formal custodial or guardianship situations.

While several stressors have been highlighted, grandparents also report positive experiences in raising their grandchildren. For some, this opportunity is one that allows them a second chance to rectify mistakes that they may have made with their own children. A strong motivator is that the grandparent is able to keep the child out of the foster care system and provide a home with family members. In spite of the physical, social, and emotional consequences, the grandparents would feel worse if their grandchildren were raised by nonfamily care providers.

appear for a time and temporarily reunite with her children. This "sometimes parenting" can be frustrating and confusing for the children and create an additional strain around the caregiving relationship with the grandparent.

The relationship with the child's parent can also have an emotional price for the grandparents, who may feel a sense of guilt over the problems experienced by their own son or daughter. At the same time, they may struggle to continue hoping that their son or daughter can overcome his or her problems by being granted parole or overcoming an addiction. The outcome can be a confusing set of loyalties for the grandparents—being divided between having hope for their own son or daughter and feeling a sense of responsibility for their grandchildren.

Since many of these grandparents have passed their own child-rearing years, the question of

### SUPPORT PROGRAMS

Because of the demands of raising a grandchild, several communities have instituted support programs for grandparents. Many such programs are aimed at decreasing isolation of the caregivers by helping them make contact with others of the same family form. Support groups may be sponsored by schools, churches, or other child welfare organizations for this purpose. These groups provide grandparents with a social outlet and an opportunity to discuss their experiences with others who share similar situations.

Respite care is another support program that can assist grandparents. Respite is a brief period of relief from the responsibilities of child rearing. This type of support can provide grandparents with an opportunity to spend time with their spouses or on themselves. This relief can come from someone taking care of the children within the household or from a group, such as an outing for the children to a community event.

Grandparents may also benefit from education on child development and social issues. Education groups can address a number of topics that help grandparents learn more about their grandchildren's social development. Particular topics may range from dealing with unmanageable behaviors of the grandchildren to contemporary social pressures such as sexual relationships, drugs, and violence. These sessions can provide information and opportunities for grandparents to build different parenting styles.

One area in which grandparents may need particular assistance is legal issues. There are often questions about terminating parental rights and gaining legal custody of the grandchildren. This process is one that is very emotional and complicated for grandparents. In addition, other legal issues need to be pursued carefully, such as estate planning and drafting a will. Often, legal issues come to attention in the case of a crisis, such as the health problem of a grandchild, when there is no formalized process to gain legal consent from the grandparents. To the greatest extent possible, grandparents should be aided in considering the legal action that needs to be taken prior to the occurrence of an emergency.

Children who are being raised in skipped-generation families may exhibit challenging child-rearing issues. Many of the children who are in the care of their grandparents have been through traumatic experiences with their parents. These backgrounds include physical or sexual abuse, neglect, or abandonment. In addition, the health status of the mother, especially if she had an addiction or was HIV-positive, can contribute to the health and mental health problems of the children. Because of such early life experiences, these children may present challenging behaviors to the grandparents, such as detachment, over-dependency, or oppositional behaviors. Grandparents who have these experiences with their grandchild may need to have intensive support from a child mental health or guidance agency.

## SUMMARY

The number of grandparents who are primary care providers of their grandchildren is on the rise. Many grandparents in these roles are past the period of caregiving for their own children and are experiencing some age-related changes that can add stress to child rearing. As these family forms increase in frequency, various programs will be constructed to help and support these families. Demographics suggest that an even-greater array of these types of services may be needed in the United States as the older population continues to expand. —*Nancy P. Kropf*

*See also* African Americans; Caregiving; Family relationships; Grandparenthood; Multigenerational households; Parenthood.

## FOR FURTHER INFORMATION:

Burton, L. M. "Black Grandparents Rearing Children of Drug-Addicted Parents: Stressors, Outcomes, and Social Service Needs." *Gerontologist* 32, no. 6 (December, 1992).

Chalfie, D. *Going It Alone: A Closer Look at Grandparents Parenting Grandchildren.* Washington, D.C.: American Association of Retired Persons, 1994.

Creighton, L. L. "Silent Saviors." *U.S. News and World Report* 111, no. 25 (December 16, 1991).

Gross, J. "Collapse of Inner-City Families Creates America's New Orphans." *The New York Times,* March 29, 1992, section 1, p. 1.

Jendrek, J. P. "Grandparents Who Parent Their Grandchildren: Circumstances and Decisions." *Gerontologist* 34, no. 2 (April, 1994).

_____. "Grandparents Who Parent Their Grandchildren: Effects on Lifestyle." *Journal of Marriage and the Family* 55, no. 3 (August, 1994).

Minkler, M., D. Driver, K. M. Roe, and K. Bedeian. "Community Interventions to Support Grandparent Caregivers." *Gerontologist* 33, no. 6 (December, 1993).

Minkler, M., and K. M. Roe. *Grandmothers as Caregivers: Raising Children of the Crack Cocaine Epidemic.* Newbury Park, Calif.: Sage Publications, 1993.

## SLEEP CHANGES AND DISTURBANCES

**RELEVANT ISSUES:** Biology, health and medicine, psychology

**SIGNIFICANCE:** A sizable proportion of the elderly report sleep disturbances, which can lead to problems in daytime functioning and dissatisfaction with quality of life

The reasons why people sleep, like the reasons why people age, are not well known. Many researchers believe that sleep serves a restorative function. Indeed, it appears that sleep is necessary to keep the brain functioning normally; sleep deprivation can lead to distortions in perception and cognition. Rapid eye movement (REM) sleep is apparently necessary for brain development and learning. Whatever its function, sleep is irresistible and universal in all vertebrates.

### STAGES OF SLEEP

There are several well-known stages that occur during a typical night's sleep. These stages are distinguished primarily by the electrical activity of the brain, as measured by an electroencephalogram (EEG), that occurs during each stage. These EEG recordings are in the form of wave activity and are described according to the frequency and amplitude of the wave. While awake but relaxed, a person's EEG will show electrical activity characterized by medium-frequency (8 to 12 hertz) and low-amplitude waves. Such activity is called alpha activity. When awake and alert, an individual's EEG activity will consist of beta activity—irregular, low-amplitude waves of 13 to 30 hertz.

During sleep, a person's EEG record will show regular movement among various stages, each characterized by a particular pattern of electrical activity. After becoming drowsy and falling asleep, a person enters stage 1 sleep, characterized by the presence of brain waves of 3.5 to 7.5 hertz. Approximately ten minutes later, the sleeper will enter stage 2 sleep, which consists of wave activity whose overall frequency is less than in stage 1. There will also be brief bouts of 12- to 14-hertz wave activity called sleep spindles during this stage. Stage 3 sleep, which follows about ten minutes after the onset of stage 2, consists of brain wave activity that has a lower frequency, but higher amplitude. The same is true for stage 4. Both stage 3 and stage 4 are considered deep sleep, or slow-wave sleep, and are characterized by the presence of bursts of very high amplitude delta activity (brain waves less that 3.5 hertz).

Approximately ninety minutes after the onset of sleep, the EEG pattern undergoes a drastic change in appearance. The waveform is indicative of a person who is awake. Other measurements (such as respiration and heart rate) also suggest that the person is awake. In spite of these measures, the person is still asleep but has entered a stage called REM sleep, named for the rapid eye movements that accompany this stage. An additional feature of REM sleep is the occurrence of dreaming. During a typical night's sleep, a person will experience four to five regular cycles of REM and non-REM sleep.

### SLEEP CHANGES WITH AGE

Sleep problems are reported in approximately 40 percent of the elderly population and can result from a number of causes. For example, the changes seen in sleep might be the result of a normal aging process. They might also be secondary to a medical or psychiatric condition, or they might be the result of poor sleep hygiene. Sleep hygiene includes, among other factors, sleep schedule, bedroom acoustics and lighting, daytime napping, dietary habits, exercise (or lack of), exposure to daylight, and use of alcohol and caffeine. Each of these can affect the quality of an individual's sleep.

In general, older individuals experience a number of age-related changes in their sleep patterns. Included among these changes are spending more time in bed, spending less time asleep, decreased sleep efficiency (spending less time in stages 2, 3, and 4, but more time in stage 1), and taking more time to fall asleep. Research suggests that much of this change in sleep quality is not accounted for by medical or psychiatric problems. Some sleep disturbances are affected by diseases (such as dementia), which increase in prevalence with age; however, most research suggests that when health factors are controlled for, the prevalence of sleep complaints in the elderly are less than previously thought.

Sleep disorders that are age-related include sleep-related breathing disturbance (SRBD), or sleep apnea, and periodic leg movement during sleep (PLMS), or nocturnal myoclonus. However, it is not clear whether the presence of SRBD or PLMS has any debilitating effect on daytime functioning in the elderly, so the clinical significance of these disorders is questionable.

A disproportionate number of prescriptions for sedatives are given to the elderly who complain of poor sleep quality. These sedatives, while perhaps useful for the transient relief of sleep disorders, have limited usefulness for the chronic treatment of sleep disturbances. Tolerance develops, and the administration of these drugs, ironically, can worsen the quality of sleep in those individuals already experiencing sleep disturbances.

### CIRCADIAN RHYTHMS

Sleep is clearly a behavior that follows a rhythmic pattern. Not only does an individual cycle between sleep and wakefulness during a twenty-four-hour period, but also sleep itself follows a regular pattern of REM and non-REM sleep during the night. Research suggests that some of the disturbances in sleep seen with age are the result of changes in circadian rhythms. However, these changes in circadian rhythmicity and sleep quality with age might be reversible.

Circadian rhythms are regulated by the brain structures (the suprachiasmatic nucleus and the pineal gland) and neurochemicals (serotonin and melatonin) that make up the circadian system. This system regulates a number of physiological and behavioral functions, including body temperature and hormonal rhythms, in addition to the sleep-wakefulness rhythm. Age-related changes in the circadian system include a decrease in amplitude (the range of changes between the maximum and minimum values) and an advance in phase (a specific measuring point linked to a particular clock time). The most consistently reported change with age is diminished amplitude (reduced release of melatonin), which affects sleep quality by decreasing time spent sleeping during the night. This reduction in sleep quality can result in impaired alertness and performance the following day. Phase shifting results in a particular phase (for example, temperature regulation) occurring earlier according to clock time. For example, older adults regularly go to bed earlier than younger adults, and this change in behavior might be a function of an earlier phase of the body temperature rhythm. Declines in body temperature are a cue for sleeping, and if these declines occur earlier in the evening, a change in sleeping behavior could follow.

These changes in rhythmicity might result from a number of factors, including decreases in the sensitivity of the eye to light, changes in the bio-chemistry or structure of key sites in the circadian system, and reduction in exposure to light in the elderly. It has also been found that there are reductions in the release of melatonin, a hormone with soporific qualities. If reduced light and reductions in melatonin underlie the changes in the circadian system that occur with age, it is possible that these changes can be attenuated with therapy. Phototherapy and exogenous administration of melatonin are examples of therapies that might restore circadian rhythmicity and improve the overall quality of sleep in aging individuals.

Sleep changes with age can result from a number of causes. Some of these disturbances might be secondary to other medical or psychiatric problems; some are caused primarily by aging itself. In addition, judgement of sleep quality is, in many ways, a subjective appraisal. Disruption of sleep during the night might be very troubling for one individual but merely annoying for another. For these reasons, a careful examination of the overall health of the aging individual, as well as that individual's sleep hygiene, are necessary in any evaluation of sleep disturbance. The growth in the number of sleep laboratories and sleep disorder clinics in the United States has made such evaluations more feasible than in the past.

*—Kevin S. Seybold*

**See also** Aging: Biological, psychological, and sociocultural perspectives; Aging process; Brain changes and disorders; Circadian rhythms; Depression; Medications; Menopause; Overmedication; Temperature regulation and sensitivity.

### FOR FURTHER INFORMATION:

Carlson, Neil R. "Sleep and Biological Rhythms." In *Physiology of Behavior,* by Neil Carlson. 6th ed. Boston: Allyn & Bacon, 1998.

Cowley, Geoffrey, and Anne Underwood. "Exploring the Secrets of Age." *Newsweek* 132, no. 17 (October 26, 1998).

Medina, John J. *The Clock of Ages: Why We Age—How We Age—Winding Back the Clock.* New York: Cambridge University Press, 1996.

Myers, Bryan L., and Pietro Badia. "Changes in Circadian Rhythms and Sleep Quality with Aging: Mechanisms and Interventions." *Neuroscience and Biobehavioral Reviews* 19, no. 4 (1995).

Turek, Fred W. "Sleep/Rhythm: Aging and John Glenn's Return to Space at Age Seventy-seven."

*Journal of Biological Rhythms* 13, no. 6 (December, 1998).

Vitiello, Michael V. "Sleep Disorders and Aging: Understanding the Causes." *The Journals of Gerontology* 52A, no. 4 (July, 1997).

# SMOKING

**RELEVANT ISSUES:** Death, health and medicine

**SIGNIFICANCE:** Smoking poses important health risks that are significantly decreased by smoking cessation, even in older age

Smoking is the main avoidable cause of death in the United States and many other developed nations. More than 10 percent of North Americans over the age of sixty-five smoke cigarettes, putting themselves and those with whom they live at risk for significant health problems. These risks appear to increase both with age and with the number of years of smoking. After World War II, more women began smoking. Because the diseases related to smoking usually take years to develop, it was only in the last part of the twentieth century that rates of smoking-related disease among women began to approach those of men. On the other hand, research indicates that smoking cessation appears to be beneficial, even in a person who has smoked for many years.

### THE HEALTH EFFECTS OF SMOKING

Cigarette smoking has long been known to have adverse effects. Smokers get more wrinkles than nonsmokers, so they tend to look older than their chronological age. They also are more likely to develop gum disease and lose teeth, adding to the changes related to eating, such as alterations in sense of smell and taste, that are normal as people age. Loss of teeth leads to difficulty chewing, which in turn leads to difficulties with digestion. Most people who lose teeth eventually develop loss of the bone that should support their teeth, making it increasingly difficult to fit dentures.

Smokers are ten times more likely to get lung cancer than nonsmokers. Lung cancer is now the number one cause of cancer death in women, as well as in men. In addition to lung cancer, smokers have a higher incidence of cancers of the head and neck, esophagus, colon, rectum, kidney, bladder, and cervix. Smokers are twenty times more likely to have a heart attack than nonsmokers. In older people, the major risk factor for disease of the coronary arteries is hypertension, but smoking is still significant, especially when combined with other risk factors for heart disease, such as diabetes or high cholesterol. Smoking and diabetes are also the two most important risk factors for diseases of the veins and arteries of the lower leg. Those who continue to smoke once these diseases develop are much more likely to require limb amputation than those who quit. Smokers may develop chronic obstructive pulmonary disease (COPD), which includes emphysema and chronic bronchitis, and are eighteen times more likely than nonsmokers to die of diseases of the lungs other than cancer. Older smokers also show decreases in muscle strength, agility, coordination, gait, and balance. The changes in these areas make them seem five years older than their actual age.

Smoking has long been thought to be associated with peptic ulcer disease. In addition, smoking makes the symptoms of many diseases worse or increases the risk of complications in patients with

*Some seniors continue to enjoy cigars and cigarettes despite warnings about the health risks involved and studies showing that quitting can improve lung function and circulation greatly.* (James L. Shaffer)

allergies, diabetes, hypertension, and vascular disease. Male smokers are at greater risk of experiencing sexual impotence. Female smokers tend to experience an earlier menopause and are at increased risk for hip fracture than nonsmokers. Smokers are more likely to develop glaucoma than nonsmokers. Studies completed in 1996 indicated an increased risk with smoking for macular degeneration, the leading cause of blindness in older adults. The evidence is mixed on smoking and Alzheimer's disease, but a 1998 study contradicted earlier work and found that the risk is greater in smokers than nonsmokers. Finally, smokers are at greater risk of death or injury caused by cigarette-related fires.

### Smoking and Medications

Cigarette smoking tends to speed up the processes in the liver for breaking down, using, and eliminating medications, both nonprescription and prescription. This means that medications may not perform as expected in the body. Smokers may need to take medications more frequently or in greater doses than nonsmokers, so it is important for health care providers to know that a person smokes. The drugs known to be affected by smoking include sedatives, narcotic and synthetic narcotic painkillers, certain antidepressants, anticoagulant medications, asthma medications, and beta blockers. These changes are of particular concern in the older population for a number of reasons. First, older people (whether smokers or nonsmokers) tend to need more medications than younger people. With each additional drug, the risk of serious drug interaction and other adverse effects increases. Second, changes in body composition and function that alter the metabolism of drugs come with age, making medication use somewhat riskier in older persons, in terms of adverse effects and complications. The additional changes associated with smoking increase these risks significantly.

The dangers of passive smoking are well documented. The effects seem to be more harmful in children than in adults, but adults who are affected are at increased risk for cancer, heart disease, noncancerous lung diseases, and allergies.

### The Benefits of Smoking Cessation

Numerous studies have shown that smoking cessation has health benefits in as little as one year, such as reducing the risk of heart attack and coronary artery disease. Within two years of smoking cessation, the risks of stroke and diseases of the blood vessels in the lower leg are reduced as well. Even though chronic lung disease is not reversible, those who quit smoking slow the decline in lung function considerably. Risks for cancers also decrease significantly with smoking cessation and are similar to the cancer risk for nonsmokers in ten to thirteen years. These findings indicate that it is worthwhile even for older people to give up smoking.

Because smoking is an addiction, it may be difficult to quit, particularly after years of cigarette use. Most smokers have to stop several times before quitting permanently. Setting a quit date, attending support group meetings, taking it one day at a time, undergoing hypnosis, making a contract with a friend or a health care provider, substituting carrot sticks for cigarettes, increasing exercise (particularly swimming), and breathing deeply all seem to be helpful techniques. Nicotine replacement systems are available in the United States on a nonprescription basis, but it is important for older people, particularly those with health problems or who are taking multiple medications, to consult a health care professional prior to using them. It is also important that anyone using these aids stop smoking completely. It is possible to get a toxic dose, perhaps even a fatal one, by smoking and using nicotine replacement simultaneously.

*—Rebecca Lovell Scott*

**See also** Cancer; Dental disorders; Emphysema; Fractures and broken bones; Glaucoma; Heart attacks; Impotence; Macular degeneration; Medications; Osteoporosis; Respiratory changes and disorders; Skin changes and disorders; Strokes; Vision changes and disorders; Wrinkles.

### For Further Information:

"The Agency for Health Care Policy and Research Smoking Cessation Clinical Practice Guideline." *JAMA: The Journal of the American Medical Association* 275, no. 16 (April 24, 1996).

Christen, William, et al. "A Prospective Study of Cigarette Smoking and Risk of Age-Related Macular Degeneration in Men." *JAMA, The Journal of the American Medical Association* 276, no. 14 (October 9, 1996).

Hales, Diane. "Tobacco Use." In *An Invitation to*

Health, 9th ed. Pacific Grove, Calif.: Brooks/Cole, 1996.

Hermanson, B., et al. "Beneficial Six-Year Outcome of Smoking Cessation in Older Men and Women with Coronary Artery Disease." *New England Journal of Medicine* 319, no. 21 (November 24, 1988).

Ott, A. "Smoking and Risk of Dementia and Alzheimer's Disease in a Population-Based Cohort Study: The Rotterdam Study." *The Lancet* 351, no. 9119 (June 20, 1998).

Seddon, Johanna, et al. "A Prospective Study of Cigarette Smoking and Age-Related Macular Degeneration in Women." *JAMA: The Journal of the American Medical Association* 276, no. 14 (October 9, 1996).

"Smoking, Not Drinking Worsens Physical Functioning in Aging." *Brown University Long-Term Care Quality Advisor* 7, no. 8 (April 24, 1995).

Vogt, Molly, et al. "Smoking and Mortality Among Older Women: The Study of Osteoporotic Fractures." *Archives of Internal Medicine* 156, no. 6 (March 25, 1996).

## SOCIAL SECURITY

**RELEVANT ISSUES:** Demographics, economics, law, work

**SIGNIFICANCE:** Social Security provides protection against income losses that can accompany the disability, death, or old age of working persons

The Old-Age, Survivors, and Disability Insurance (OASDI) programs, commonly known as Social Security, provide monthly benefits to retired and disabled workers, their dependents, and survivors. In December, 1995, average monthly benefits of $720 were paid to 43.4 million persons, or 16 percent of the U.S. population. Retired workers, widows, widowers, parents, and disabled workers were 84 percent of OASDI beneficiaries and together received 71 percent of benefits; children of deceased, disabled, or retired workers made up 8 percent of beneficiaries and received 21 percent of benefits; and wives and husbands of disabled or retired workers made up 8 percent of beneficiaries and received 8 percent of benefits. Approximately 65 percent of all beneficiaries were between the ages of sixty-five and eighty-four; 14 percent were between the ages of fifty and sixty-four; and about 7 percent each were between the ages of eighteen and forty-nine, eighty-five and older, or under eighteen. About 60 percent of the 40.4 million adult beneficiaries were women.

Social Security provides at least half of total income for a majority of beneficiaries. In 1994 Social Security accounted for 50 percent or more of income for 66 percent of beneficiaries and 90 percent or more of income for 30 percent of beneficiaries. Social Security helps reduce poverty. In 1994 Social Security enabled 42 percent of all aged households—either married couples living together with husbands or wives aged sixty-five or older or persons sixty-five or older who did not live with spouses—to live above the poverty level. Social Security as a share of total income varies greatly by income level. In 1994 Social Security was 23 percent of total income for the highest income quintile of the aged, compared to 81 percent for the lowest quintile. In general, aged households with less income from assets, earnings, and private pensions increasingly rely on Social Security as a main source of economic well-being.

The OASDI programs have been the subject of public concern in large part due to anticipated costs associated with the growing and increasing life expectancy of the elderly population. In 1995, 12.5 percent of the total U.S. population was sixty-five years of age and over. By 2040, the number of U.S. elderly was expected to double, with one in five individuals sixty-five years of age and over. This increase is primarily attributed to the aging of some seventy-six million baby boomers, those born between 1946 and 1964. Life expectancy was estimated to increase from 72.5 years for men and 79.3 years for women in 1996 to 78.4 and 84.1 respectively in 2070. Federal expenditures for the OASDI programs increased from $11 billion in 1960 to $117.1 billion in 1980 to $301.1 billion in 1993. As a percentage of total federal expenditures for public programs, however, the costs of the OASDI Programs have actually declined from 44.2 percent in 1960 to 38.6 percent in 1980 to 37.4 percent in 1993.

Costs of Medicare, the related health care program for the elderly, increased from $7.1 billion in 1970 to $34.9 billion in 1980 to $148 billion in 1993. Unlike the OASDI program, Medicare as a percent of total federal expenditures for public programs increased from 9 percent in 1970 to 11.5 percent in 1980 to 18.4 percent in 1993. As the population

## Social Security and Poverty Rates, 1992

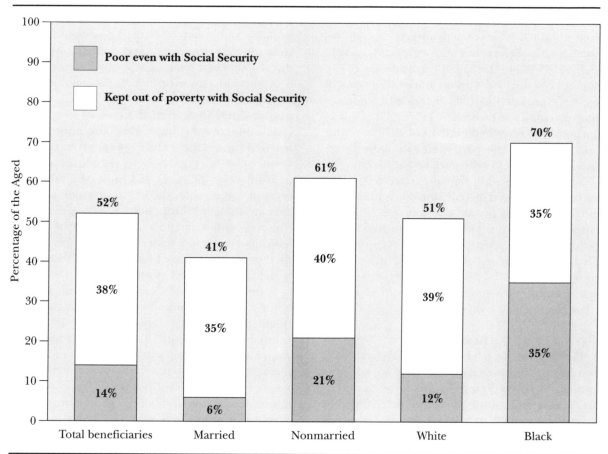

*Note:* Data are based on family income rather than aged unit income to conform with official measures of poverty.
*Source:* U.S. Department of Health and Human Services, Social Security Administration, Office of Research and Statistics. *Facts and Figures About Social Security.* Washington, D.C.: U.S. Government Printing Office, 1994.

of the United States ages, related expenses are expected to rise in real dollar terms as well as a share of total federal expenditures on public programs, driven more by the costs of Medicare than by the OASDI programs. Unless something is done to control modern spending levels, Social Security and Medicare are expected to run cash deficits, increasing from $232 billion and $114 billion respectively in 2020 to $1.3 trillion and $1.9 trillion respectively by 2040. Invariably, these projected increases in program costs are likely to create much pressure to curtail or crowd out means-tested, selective programs, such as Supplemental Security Income and food stamps, which benefit primarily low-income individuals and families.

## THE DEVELOPMENT OF SOCIAL SECURITY IN THE UNITED STATES

Old age benefits were provided for retired workers in the original Social Security Act of 1935, which covered only workers in commerce and industry, then about 40 percent of the workforce. The 1935 act provided monthly benefits to retired workers sixty-five years of age and over and a lump-sum death benefit to the estate of these workers. In 1939 benefits were extended to dependents of retired workers (wives sixty-five years of age and older and children under sixteen) and to survivors of deceased workers (widows sixty-five years of age and older, mothers caring for an eligible child, children under the age of sixteen, and dependent parents).

In 1956 benefits were further extended to disabled workers fifty to sixty-four years of age and to the disabled children over the age of eighteen of retired, disabled, or deceased workers, if they became disabled before they were eighteen (changed to disabled before the age of twenty-two in 1973). Benefits for disabled workers under fifty years of age were provided in 1960. The Medicare insurance program was created in 1965. As a result of the Social Security amendments of 1972, monthly cash OASDI benefits have been automatically adjusted since 1975 to keep pace with inflation.

Social Security was originally conceived as one leg of a three-legged income stool for retirees. Personal savings and private pensions were the two other legs, and both of these were expected to constitute the major portion of retirement income. That view was challenged by a 1975 Advisory Council, which saw Social Security as the nation's primary pension plan, providing more retirement income than private savings.

### BENEFITS

Benefits can be paid to workers and their dependents or survivors if workers have worked long enough in covered employment to be "insured" for these benefits. Insured status is determined by a formula applied to workers' average monthly earnings indexed to the increase in average annual wages. For workers with many years of low earnings, Social Security provides a special minimum benefit based on the number of years of covered employment.

Workers must be at least sixty-two years old to be eligible for retirement benefits. There is no minimum age requirement for disability benefits. A benefit is payable to a spouse of a retired or disabled worker when a currently married spouse is at least sixty-two years old; is caring for one or more of the worker's entitled children who are disabled or have not reached the age of sixteen; or when a divorced spouse is at least sixty-two, is

not married, and the marriage lasted at least ten years before the divorce became final. A divorced spouse may be entitled independently of the worker's retirement if both the worker and divorced spouse are sixty-two years of age and if the divorce has been final for at least two years.

A monthly survivor benefit is payable to a widow, widower, or divorced spouse of a worker who was fully insured at the time of death. The widow, widower, or divorced spouse must be unmarried (unless the remarriage occurred after the widow or widower first became eligible for benefits as a widow or widower) and must be either sixty years of age or older or fifty to fifty-nine years of age and disabled throughout a waiting period of five consecutive calendar months that began no later than seven years after the month the worker died or after the end of his or her entitlement to benefits as a widowed mother or father.

A monthly benefit is payable to an unmarried child; eligible dependent grandchild; or a retired, disabled, or deceased worker who was fully or currently insured at death. The child or grandchild must either be younger than eighteen, a full-time elementary or secondary student younger than nineteen, or a disabled person eighteen years of age or older whose disability began before twenty-two years of age. A grandchild is eligible for benefits on a grandparent's earning record if the

### Gradual Increase in the Age for Full Social Security Benefits

| Full benefit at age— | Applicable to workers who attain age 62 in year— |
|---|---|
| 65 | 1994-1999 |
| 65 and 2 months | 2000 |
| 65 and 4 months | 2001 |
| 65 and 6 months | 2002 |
| 65 and 8 months | 2003 |
| 65 and 10 months | 2004 |
| 66 | 2005-2016 |
| 66 and 2 months | 2017 |
| 66 and 4 months | 2018 |
| 66 and 6 months | 2019 |
| 66 and 8 months | 2020 |
| 66 and 10 months | 2021 |
| 67 | 2022 and later |

Source: U.S. Department of Health and Human Services, Social Security Administration, Office of Research and Statistics. *Facts and Figures About Social Security.* Washington, D.C.: U.S. Government Printing Office, 1994.

## Distribution of Social Security Benefits Among Adults, by Gender, in December, 1993

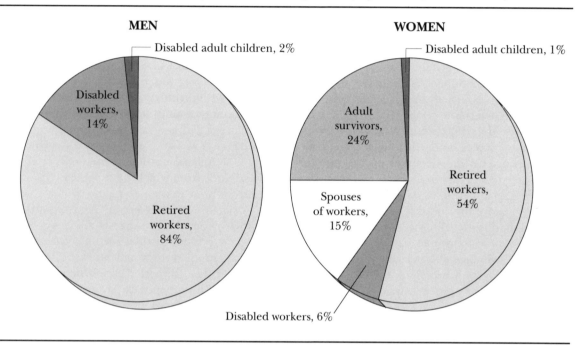

MEN

Disabled adult children, 2%

Disabled workers, 14%

Retired workers, 84%

WOMEN

Disabled adult children, 1%

Adult survivors, 24%

Spouses of workers, 15%

Retired workers, 54%

Disabled workers, 6%

*Source:* U.S. Department of Health and Human Services, Social Security Administration, Office of Research and Statistics. *Facts and Figures About Social Security.* Washington, D.C.: U.S. Government Printing Office, 1994.

grandchild was adopted by the grandparent and may be entitled under certain circumstances even if no adoption took place. If adopted by the surviving spouse of that grandparent, the child would be eligible if he or she lived with or received one-half support from the grandparent prior to the grandparent's death.

A monthly survivor benefit is payable to a mother, father, surviving divorced father, or surviving divorced mother if the deceased worker on whose account the benefit is payable was fully or currently insured at the time of death and the mother, father, surviving divorced father, or surviving divorced mother is not married and cares for one or more entitled children of the worker. These payments continue as long as the youngest child being cared for is younger than sixteen or disabled. A monthly survivor benefit is payable to a parent sixty-two years of age or older of a deceased fully insured worker. The worker must have been providing at least one-half of the parent's support.

Social Security benefits are often discussed in terms of how much of a person's preretirement earnings the benefits represent. Replacement rates (the percentage of a person's earnings in the year before retirement) vary by income level. For example, for individuals born in 1935 and expected to reach normal retirement age in 2000, replacement rates are 51.7 percent for low earners (those whose earnings are equal to 45 percent of the Social Security average-wage index), 42.4 percent for average earners (those whose earnings are equal to the Social Security average-wage index), and 25.6 percent for maximum earners (those whose earnings are equal to the maximum wage taxable for Social Security purposes).

Social Security benefits may be reduced, withheld, or increased for various reasons, thereby affecting the economic well-being of families. Individuals may be entitled to benefits both as workers, based on their own earnings, and also as dependents (spouse, widow, or widower) of other workers. In these cases, individuals do not collect both benefits. The amount of benefits that spouses, widows, or widowers receive is offset dollar for dollar by the amount of benefits to which they are entitled as workers. The benefit based on one's own work record is always received first, and the only part of the dependent benefit payable is that which it is greater than the worker benefit. In her essay in *Social Security in the Twenty-first Century* (1997), Karen Holden has shown that two-earner couples are at a distinct economic disadvantage when one spouse dies. In effect, the replacement-rate formula used to determine benefit levels of different couples with identical covered annual incomes is such that as couples share earnings more equally, protection against the death of one spouse declines. Such declines are more likely to plunge into poverty the far larger percentage of elderly widows who hover above the poverty line. Ironically, the increased sharing of earning roles between spouses, assumed to increase women's access to protective wage-based insurance, substantially lowers the economic protection provided to them as widows, compared with one-earner couples.

Social Security law also reduces benefits for non-disabled recipients who earn income from work above a certain amount. In 1997 recipients under sixty-five years of age could have earned up to $8,640 a year in wages or self-employment income without having their benefits reduced. Individuals between the ages of sixty-five and sixty-nine could have earned up to $13,500. For earnings above these amounts, recipients under age sixty-five lose $1 of benefits for each $2 of earnings, and those between sixty-five and sixty-nine lost $1 in benefits for every $3 of earnings. The earnings limit does not apply to recipients who are older than sixty-nine or to those who are disabled. The earnings limits rise each year indexed to the rise in average wages in the economy. At issue is the extent to which the incentive structure of Social Security encourages retirement (discourages work) for those under age seventy. Research has shown that labor force participation rates of older workers, particularly men, have decreased over the past several decades, but the influence of Social Security compared to other factors on this trend remains questionable.

## THE FINANCING MECHANISM OF SOCIAL SECURITY

There has been much debate about how financially sound Social Security is. The primary source of revenue of OASDI is the payroll tax paid by covered workers and matched by covered employ-ers (7.56 percent of wages in 1996). In 1996 approximately 96 percent of the paid workforce in the United States was covered under Social Security. Excluded were state and local employees, federal civilian employees, and students. Taxes are based on earnings up to the annual maximum taxable wage base, which was $62,700 in 1996. Self-employed individuals pay contributions on their annual net earnings up to the same maximum as employees, but at a rate that is equal to the combined employee-employer tax rate. Revenue from the OAS and DI portion of the tax is credited to trust funds from which monthly benefits and administrative expenses are paid.

A declining trend in the ratio of workers to OASDI beneficiaries suggests that fewer workers contribute more of their incomes to support increasing numbers of beneficiaries. In 1960, 5.1 taxpaying workers supported each beneficiary, whereas in 1995 the number of taxpaying workers supporting each beneficiary had declined to 3.3. As the number of taxpayers per recipient declined, Social Security as a percentage of workers' payroll increased from 1.2 percent in 1955 to 11.5 percent in 1995. By 2040 no more than two, and perhaps as few as 1.6, taxpaying workers are expected to support Social Security beneficiaries, while Social Security is expected to range between 17.5 percent to 22.2 percent of workers' payroll. At issue is the extent to which all retirees come to rely on Social Security as a larger share of total income, thereby becoming increasingly dependent on workers whose proportionately shrinking take-home pay must also meet workers' own financial obligations. The debate over Social Security reform promises to be lively, as workers seek to maximize their take-home pay and elders seek to protect their economic well-being. —*Richard K. Caputo*

*See also* Baby boomers; Disabilities; Dual-income couples; Health care; Income sources; Life expectancy; Medical insurance; Medicare; Pensions; Politics; Poverty; Retirement; Retirement planning; Townsend movement.

## FOR FURTHER INFORMATION:

Berkowitz, Edward D. *America's Welfare State from Roosevelt to Reagan.* Baltimore: The Johns Hopkins University Press, 1991. Historical overview of Social Security and other programs, tracing the ebb and flow of OASDI's popularity.

Committee on Ways and Means, U.S. House of Representatives. *1996 Green Book*. Washington, D.C.: U.S. Government Printing Office, 1996. Provides detailed background material and data on programs within the committee's jurisdiction, including Social Security, Medicare, and the Railroad Retirement System.

Kingston, Eric R., and James H. Schultz, eds. *Social Security in the Twenty-first Century*. New York: Oxford University Press, 1997. Collection of essays that examines how Social Security affects families and the economy, including such issues as its impact on work, its fairness to women, and its financial stability.

Peterson, Peter G. *Will America Grow Up Before It Grows Old?* New York: Random House, 1996. Alarming view of how changing demographics may adversely affect families and the economy unless major changes are made in how the U.S. finances and limits Social Security benefits, such as switching from an income-based to a consumption-based tax and raising to seventy the age at which persons become eligible for Social Security.

Schultz, James H. *The Economics of Aging*. 6th ed. Westport, Conn.: Auburn House, 1995. Thorough examination of changes in retirement patterns, problems of older workers, and the complexity of retirement preparation and a discussion of pension plans and health costs.

Social Security Administration. *Annual Statistical Supplement, 1996 to the Social Security Bulletin*. Washington, D.C.: U.S. Government Printing Office, 1996. Presents more than 250 tables of detailed data on the U.S. network of income programs, as well as brief historical summaries of and discussions about recent legislative changes that affect these programs.

## SOCIAL TIES

**RELEVANT ISSUES:** Culture, family, sociology, values

**SIGNIFICANCE:** As the link not only between social ties and social well-being but also health and emotional stability is further established, research is increasingly focusing on social ties and aging

Age plays a basic role in determining how societies are structured or organized. It influences the allocation of social resources and social roles which, in turn, influence the patterns of everyday living. The patterns and networks of social ties, for instance, differ for persons at various stages of their life. As the everyday activities of children differ from adults, so the pattern of daily life for the elderly tends to differ from that of either children or nonelderly adults.

The role of social ties and social networks is of particular importance in defining the aging process. Considerable research has indicated that the way people live—how and with whom they interact day after day—significantly affects everything from their health to their mental, emotional, and economic well-being. The types and quality of social ties an individual maintains with others are paramount. These ties involve contacts of all sorts with family, friends, and acquaintances. The social ties and the networks they represent provide a certain level of support, both emotionally and practically.

To have a significant and supportive network of social relationships means individuals are interconnected through a number of meaningful and ongoing social ties. The ties themselves, rather than the attributes of the individuals in the network, are most important. To be immersed in a web of group affiliations is the very basis of social, emotional, and practical support. Someone who is isolated and experiencing problems will not receive support to the same extent as individuals who are engaged in a wide range of significant social ties. For instance, family, friends, and acquaintances may help ensure compliance with a treatment regimen by reminding the elderly to take their medicine on time or by arranging for transportation to the doctor's office or a clinic.

Social networks are intimately interconnected with life events and life changes, both positively (weddings, births, and anniversaries) and negatively (deaths, divorces, and the loss of a job). Potentially disruptive life changes such as the death of a spouse and being forced to move or forced to retire—events which regularly confront the elderly—represent the disruption or termination of social ties. Social networks are apparently "coping recourses" that can serve as a buffer to the stressful impact of such life changes. When social ties are disrupted, the "adaptive energy" of the participants diminishes and their ability to cope with changing circumstances lessens, as does their ability to alter their social milieu. This is an especially difficult challenge for the elderly living in fast-paced, rapidly changing societies such as contemporary America where change is seldom easy to anticipate or handle.

Although the link between social ties and aging is well established, a number of unanswered questions remain. Why do stressful events call forth such differing outcomes in individuals with similarly structured social networks? Short-lived problems, chronic problems, minor problems, and acute problems can all be produced in similarly situated individuals by the same stressful event. Is the quality of relationships more important than the quantity of relationships? In studying situations in which the elderly receive support, some of their social ties provide support while others are not supportive. How does the configuration or structure of their social networks affect the level of support for the elderly? Is the effect of either social support or of increasing isolation cumulative? Although social ties influence health and illness, to what extent does prior illness influence the configuration of an individual's social networks? The inability to meaningfully participate in a network of social relationships may be primarily due to an individual's health status. As health continues to deteriorate, isolation usually increases, which in turn may contribute to further deterioration in health status.

A particularly interesting question concerns the relative importance of strong ties and weak ties for the elderly. Research suggests that strong ties (defined as close, intimate, and emotionally significant) and weak ties (those less intimate, less emotionally significant, and more often task-oriented) play somewhat different roles in the lives of the elderly. After the death of a spouse, for example, the emotional support needed by the widow or widower is usually most effectively provided through strong ties to close family and friends. As the widow or widower begins to adjust to their new life

*Friendship among women is valuable at all ages and especially when facing the challenges of midlife and beyond.* (James L. Shaffer)

and look to the future, their less intimate and less emotionally significant or weak ties may be more useful in providing them with valuable information, ideas, and contacts. The importance of weak ties is seen in their potential to foster social cohesion through expanding social networks as a conduit to influence, information, and social mobility and as the basis for community and political organizing.

Although the relationship between social ties and aging is complex and further examination is needed, the importance of social ties for the elderly is undeniable. People who have frequent and meaningful contacts with neighbors, friends, family, or organizational associates report "being happy" more frequently. People need social ties to fulfill numerous basic, practical needs. Although different people have different needs depending on their personal circumstances, the elderly in particular have needs that must be met through social contacts. These include obtaining help when ill, locating and acquiring medical assistance, shopping, house cleaning, borrowing money, and other types of caretaking.

### CROSS-CULTURAL DIFFERENCES IN AGING

In addition to the differing patterns of age-related activities and expectations within a society, the social activities and social roles performed by the elderly also differ from one society to another. In some societies, aging enhances prestige and social standing while in other societies aging depreciates prestige and social standing. In some societies, the elderly are assigned and perform functional roles that contribute to the well-being of the group. In these societies, the elderly maintain their employment, continue to work, and generally remain active in a variety of social roles. In other societies, the elderly systematically relinquish socially valued positions such as their job and other formal positions, including being officers and active members in a variety of organizations and associations. These differing patterns are modified by such factors as social class, gender, and physical and psychological capabilities.

In those societies where the status of the elderly is depreciated, the loss of formal roles means the elderly move into informal or what are referred to as tenuous social roles. In such settings, the elderly find themselves drawn into such activities as caring for children, storytelling, preparing food, and mending, washing, and ironing clothing. Such roles typically exclude the elderly from many areas of social life. This, in turn, diminishes their network of meaningful social ties, which can have a variety of negative outcomes for the elderly, including the loss of social value as well as social identity. The absence of meaningful roles and relationships means older people not only tend to experience the loss of social identity but isolation and withdrawal as well. This contributes to the elderly suffering from diminished social integration, which in turn furthers the decline in the breadth and strength of their social ties.

In extreme cases, particularly where the conditions of life are difficult, such as in harsh climates and where the very survival of society or the group is questionable, the sick and very old have been abandoned to die. Examples from the past can be found among nomadic groups such as the Lapps of northern Europe and the Hopi Indians of the southwest United States. In contrast, where aging contributes to social standing, the elderly are seen as having greater wisdom based on their having lived a long life and having accumulated a wealth of experiences. In these societies the elderly are often in the mainstream or very core of social life. This is seen in both the respect and deference they receive as well as the richness of their social ties which, in one way or another, link them in meaningful ways to a wide range of significant others.

Having briefly reviewed the diversity of expectations, roles, and relationships characterizing aging cross-culturally, it is necessary to identify the sociocultural trends that affect the elderly in the modern Western world, including the United States. This requires examining not only the trends, but their impact on the process of aging, and their significance for understanding social ties and aging.

### SOCIOCULTURAL TRENDS AND AGING

A wide range of significant political, economic, and cultural trends have unfolded in the modern Western world in recent years. Many if not most of these trends have contributed to redefining the process of aging, including the pattern of social ties among the elderly. With the evolution from a traditional agrarian to industrial and eventually to postindustrial or information-based society, the

*Family members are an important source of social interaction for the elderly, particularly those who have relocated to senior housing or nursing homes.* (James L. Shaffer)

size of the core or nuclear family, composed of husband and wife and children, if any, has declined dramatically.

Having large numbers of children was commonplace and economically viable when America was largely a nation of farmers, for many hands were needed to work the fields. The advent of industrialization and subsequently the postindustrial society, coupled with inflation, rendered having children less economically feasible. Smaller families mean fewer children to assist parents and grandparents as they age. The decline of the larger or extended family (where contact with nieces, nephews, cousins, and other distant relatives is less regular, frequent, and meaningful), the fast pace of modern life, increased geographic mobility with family members often living and working some distance from one another, and the appearance of two-working-parent families have contributed to the elderly increasingly turning to social service personnel rather than family members as care-

givers who assist with shopping, transportation, health, and housekeeping needs.

The "senior boom" America is experiencing, in which both the total number of elderly and the overall percentage of the elderly in America's population have increased, has affected society in many ways, not the least of which is the quantity and quality as well as the types of social ties the elderly experience. Although millions of elderly Americans are self-sufficient, live at home, and continue to actively participate in the life of society, millions of others face difficult physical, mental, emotional, and financial problems. Many struggle to remain in their homes. For those whose families cannot or choose not to be caregivers to their elderly relatives, a variety of programs, both public and private, exist to assist many elderly people to remain in their homes. These programs include meal delivery, in-home health services, in-home social visitations, and transportation assistance for the elderly.

One of the fastest growing segments of the population is the very-old, those over seventy-five years of age. As the baby boomers age, the number of old people, generally, and the very old, in particular, will continue to expand. The role of modern medicine and medical technology, coupled with improved sanitation, are major contributors to increased longevity. This has and will continue to place increasing demands on society to provide the necessary resources to care for the elderly. Not only will in-home social services expand, but the need for specialized facilities to care for those elderly who require additional care and can no longer live alone will continue to increase. In addition, the need for nursing homes and centers for the aged where various social service and health care personnel provide differing levels of care from residential to skilled nursing will grow. Clearly, the living arrangements of the aged exert a considerable influence on their social ties. Those who live in specialized facilities for the elderly, particularly when they are no longer mobile, usually experience diminished contact with the non-elderly.

## CONCLUSION

Although there is much that is not well understood about the relationship between the process of aging and social ties, much is known. The aged, like all human beings, are most appropriately thought of in holistic terms. That is, they are simultaneously physical beings, social beings, and emotional beings. The significance of social ties in everyday life is seen in the fact that the patterns, extensiveness, and strength of the social ties of the elderly are linked to their social well-being, which in turn is related to both their physical and emotional well-being. This is not only the case for the elderly, but is characteristic of each stage in the process of aging.

There is a definite pattern to the process of aging; however, the elderly are clearly not as homogeneous a category as many people believe. Stereotypes about the elderly, however misinformed they might be, persist in many societies including the United States. Common thinking and attitudes toward the elderly portray them as dependent, submissive, isolated, and often abused. While this is true for many, others are independent, definitely not submissive, actively integrated and involved in a wide range of social activities, and not

abused. Many others represent various combinations of these traits.

The aged are truly a diverse group. Even their ages vary dramatically. Being ninety is far different than being sixty or seventy. Social class, gender, and racial and ethnic differences among the elderly are as consequential as for other age categories. One constant factor surrounding social ties and aging is that both, in addition to their relationship, are dynamic. As societies change, so the process of aging changes, which then feeds back and influences the society of which it is a part.

*—Charles E. Marske*

*See also* Abandonment; Adult education; Aging: Biological, psychological, and sociocultural perspectives; Aging: Historical perspective; American Association of Retired Persons (AARP); Caregiving; Childlessness; Cohabitation; Communication; Cultural views of aging; Death of a child; Death of parents; Depression; Divorce; Empty nest syndrome; Family relationships; Friendship; Full nest; Gray Panthers; Home services; Housing; Internet; Leisure activities; Loneliness; Marriage; Meals-on-wheels programs; Men and aging; Mentoring; Multigenerational households; Neglect; Nursing and convalescent homes; Parenthood; Personality changes; Pets; Psychiatry, geriatric; Relocation; Remarriage; Retired Senior Volunteer Program (RSVP); Retirement communities; Senior citizen centers; Sexuality; Sibling relationships; Single parenthood; Singlehood; Skipped-generation parenting; Sports participation; Stepfamilies; Stress and coping skills; Successful aging; Vacations and travel; Volunteering; Women and aging.

## FOR FURTHER INFORMATION:

Atchley, Robert C. *Social Forces and Aging: An Introduction to Social Gerontology.* 9th ed. Belmont, Calif.: Wadsworth, 1999. A thorough overview of the social aspects of aging. Social ties and aging are touched upon through the examination of numerous topics.

Berleman, Lisa F., and Lester Breslow. *Health and Ways of Living.* New York: Oxford University Press, 1983. A useful presentation of the myriad of ways lifestyle and health are interrelated. The role of social ties is addressed.

Granovetter, Mark. "The Strength of Weak Ties." *American Journal of Sociology* 78 (1973). A classic article on the function and nature of social ties with emphasis on "weak ties."

Keith, Jennie. *The Aging Experience: Diversity and Commonality Across Cultures*. Thousand Oaks, Calif.: Sage Publications, 1994. This work provides valuable information on how the elderly are alike and how they differ.

Matcha, Duane A. *The Sociology of Aging*. Boston: Allyn & Bacon, 1996. A basic textbook that offers a comprehensive yet very readable review of the social and cultural dimensions of aging.

Morgan, Leslie, and Suzanne Kunkel. *Aging: The Social Context*. Thousand Oaks, Calif.: Pine Forge Press, 1998. A work that examines aging from a sociohistorical perspective.

## SPORTS PARTICIPATION

**RELEVANT ISSUES:** Culture, psychology, recreation, sociology

**SIGNIFICANCE:** Participation in recreational and competitive sports provides an avenue for socialization while enhancing self-efficacy and improving overall health

Recreational activities and sports participation are options available for older adults to meet the need to be more active for optimal health. Sports can be enjoyed individually or within a group setting, thereby providing social interactions through club memberships, tournaments, and masters level competition. The negativism often associated with aging will be deemphasized as more middle-aged and older adults become involved in physical activity and sports participation. It has been projected that the baby-boom generation is going to change dramatically the perception that aging is synonymous with being frail and unproductive.

### FACTORS AFFECTING RECREATIONAL PATTERNS

Several factors are associated with an older adult choosing to be active in recreational pursuits. A very important factor is attitude. Younger and middle-aged adults with positive attitudes toward aging and activity continue to be active, productive older adults as long as they remain healthy. Recreational preferences are based upon past experiences established earlier in life. If the experiences were enjoyable and the opportunity to continue participation are present, the older individual is likely to continue his or her activities. It has also been reported that the most active older adults have attained a higher educational level and belong to a higher socioeconomic group. Those individuals who have the support and encouragement of a "significant other" or caretaker will be the most successful in accomplishing their recreational goals.

On the other hand, older adults who were brought up with preconceived notions that people must slow down as they age will not be very active. In addition, those who were brought up with a strong "work ethic" tend to have a difficult time engaging in leisure activities unless there is a specific purpose behind the action (other than simple enjoyment). Furthermore, recreational participation is often lower in older adult minorities due to lack of exposure to many leisure activities in their youth.

Often times, the reason why many older adults do not participate in recreational activity and sports programs is due to poor environmental planning, poor maintenance, or safety issues regarding facilities. A recreational facility must be in a safe, easily accessible location. Faucets in showers need to be large enough to enable arthritic hands to turn the shower on and off. Asphalt walking paths should be covered with crushed bark to absorb moisture and reduce slippery surfaces. Swimming pool ladders should be a height that requires a minimum of shoulder strength, and nonskid mats and handrails should be placed in and around the pool and shower areas.

Being more active means a greater risk for incurring an activity-related injury. However, a 1996 report issued by the United States Department of Health and Human Services on injury rates in senior athletes concluded that age did not predict injury and age increments were not related to increments in self-reported injuries. In fact, they stated that the oldest age group was less likely to report an injury. Sports that have the lowest risk of injury include walking, swimming, dancing, Tai Chi, golf, tennis, volleyball, and softball. Activities such as yoga and Tai Chi are good options for older adults since they focus on body awareness and flexibility rather than strength and speed. Other activities that are popular for both middle-aged and older adults include hiking, cycling, fishing, and bowling.

## SPORTS PARTICIPATION CHOICES

When choosing a sport, several factors need to be considered. First is sport category preference. There are three general sports categories: individual sports that can be performed alone (walking, swimming); dual sports that require a partner (racquet sports); and team sports that require more than two players (basketball, softball). Second, the individual's fitness level must be taken into consideration. While many sports can accommodate a range of fitness levels, certain ones, such as squash, handball, and downhill skiing, require high levels of physical fitness. Third, if expense is an issue, activities that cost the most money are ones requiring special fees and equipment rentals (or purchases) such as golf and skiing.

Adults tend to be more self-conscious when learning a new sport skill. If an older adult becomes socially embarrassed because he or she was unable to execute a simple athletic movement, he or she will be less likely to attempt that sport again. Therefore, to reduce the anxiety of new-sport participation, the new sport chosen should have similar motor skills already learned from a previous activity. For instance if an individual used to play softball, those same motor skills can be applied to tennis doubles. The hand-eye coordination and arm strength will transfer and having a partner will lessen the intensity of the activity. It is also suggested that novice participants start off in a low-pressure situation—for instance, golfing during off-peak times.

## SPORTS PROGRAMS

The thrill of victory has been shown to be significantly related to aging, especially among the seventy- to eighty-nine-year-old age group, thereby contradicting the stereotypical impression that in-

*Around middle age, most people begin to notice limitations in their ability to participate in sports activities in relation to younger individuals.* (James L. Shaffer)

terest in competition declines with aging. A tremendous surge of interest in the masters athletic competition occurred beginning in the late 1970's. A "master athlete" is any individual who exceeds a minimum age requirement and competes in a given sporting event. Several specialized senior and masters athletic competitions are held at the regional, national, and international levels; they are sponsored by sporting good manufacturers, health care systems, and communities. However, there still remains to be developed a good system for dispersing athletic training advice for this population.

In an attempt to meet this need, a variety of recreational club memberships have been formed. Organizations such as the Sporting Good Manufacturer's Association (SGMA), at www.sportlink.com, and the American Association of Retired Persons (AARP), at www.aarp.org, have set up computer Web sites to access senior-oriented sports and leisure activities. The United States Tennis Association (USTA) sponsors tennis programs for older adults; its address is Senior Tennis programs/USTA Education and Research Center, 729 Alexander Rd., Princeton, NJ 08540. The National Senior Sports Association (NSSA) offers golf, tennis, bowling, skiing, plus other sports programs for older adults; its address is National Senior Sports Association Inc., 317 Cameron St., Alexandria, VA 22314.

Well-known athletic competitions include the World Masters Championships and the World Veterans Games, both track and field competitions, and the World Masters Swimming Championships. However, the most widely known masters competition in the United States is the United States Senior Sports Classic, formerly known as the Senior Olympics. Founded in 1969 by Warren Blaney, the first Senior Olympics had 175 participants and consisted of three events—the marathon, swimming, and track and field. By 1999, this event had grown to ten thousand master athletes competing in eighteen events, which include archery, badminton, basketball, cycling, softball, volleyball, a 10 kilometer road race, tennis and table tennis, swimming, and track and field as well as less strenuous events such as croquet, golf, horseshoes, and shuffleboard. The minimum age to compete is fifty-five years, and the competition is broken down into six age groups: fifty-five to fifty-nine, sixty to sixty-four, sixty-five to sixty-nine, seventy to seventy-four, seventy-five to seventy-nine, and eighty and older. Individuals are limited to entering a maximum of eight events. While awards are given for first, second, and third place (gold, silver, and bronze medals), plus ribbons for fourth to sixth place, a major emphasis is placed on participation in order to encourage all adults to exercise regularly for better health, happiness, and productivity. The most important reasons given by older adults for participation in the Senior Olympics were enjoyment of the activity, the sense of accomplishment, the thrill of competition, and winning. Information about Senior Olympic events can be obtained by contacting Warren Blaney, Senior Olympics, Senior Sports International Inc., Wilshire Blvd., Suite 360, Los Angeles, CA 90026 or the U.S. National Senior Sports Organization, 14323 S. Outer Forty Road, Suite N300, Chesterfield, MO 63017.          —Bonita L. Marks

**See also** Exercise and fitness; Independent living; Injuries among the elderly; Leisure activities; Reaction time; Safety issues; Social ties.

**FOR FURTHER INFORMATION:**

Ettinger, Walter H., Brenda S. Mitchell, and Steven N. Blair. *Fitness After Fifty.* St. Louis: Beverly Cracom, 1996.

Flatten, Kay. "Senior Athletes: A Profile in Courage and Spirit." *Journal of Physical Education, Recreation, and Dance* 62, no. 3 (May/June, 1991).

Hastings, John. "Trying on a New Sport." *Health* 8, no. 7 (Nov-Dec., 1994).

Leitner, Michael J., and Sara F. Leitner. *Leisure in Later Life.* 2d ed. New York: Haworth Press, 1996.

Schreck, Maryann. "Factors Influencing Participation in Senior Olympic Competition." In *Proceedings of the Sandra A. Modisett Symposium on Aging and Leisure in the 1990's*, edited by Barbara A. Hawkins and Ron Rothschadl. Indianapolis: AALR and AAHPERD, 1992.

Segal, Doralie D., Carlos J. Crespo, and Ellen Smit. "Active Seniors: Protect Them, Don't Neglect Them." *Public Health Reports* 113, no. 2 (March/April, 1998).

Seidler, Todd L., Edward T. Turner, and Larry Horine. "Promoting Active Lifestyles Through Facilities and Equipment: A Look at Children, Seniors, and People with Disabilities." *Journal of*

*Physical Education, Exercise, Recreation, and Dance* 64, no. 1 (January, 1993).

Spiriduso, Waneen W. *Physical Dimensions of Aging.* Champaign, Ill.: Human Kinetics, 1995.

Wellner, Alison S. "Getting Old and Staying Fit." *American Demographics* 20, no. 3 (March, 1998).

## STEPFAMILIES

**RELEVANT ISSUES:** Family, marriage and dating, values

**SIGNIFICANCE:** A stepfamily is composed of a group of people who come together after a loss, such as divorce or death. The creation of a stepfamily presents parents and grandparents of all ages with many challenges

The stepfamily is not a new phenomenon. Prior to the early twentieth century, medical care and safety measures were inadequate, leading to the death of some parents at an early age. Mothers died in childbirth or of postpartum infections, and many fathers were not able to raise their children alone. Economic challenges required these men to continue working to provide for their families. They were not taught the intricacies of household management, nor were they expected to be primary nurturers. Fathers, the breadwinners for their families, often died in farming or industrial accidents, leaving mothers with sometimes poor educational and vocational skills to struggle to feed their families and provide a home for them. Both types of situations prompted remarriage and the formation of stepfamilies. These families often came together out of economic need and not always out of love.

Stepfamilies still arise from loss in a family, whether it is the death of a parent, divorce, or nonmarital childbirth. Divorce often takes place at family milestones: when a first child is born, when children become teenagers, when adult children leave home, or when one or both partners retire. Although these milestones appear to occur during the developmental phases of children's lives, the responsibility for divorce rests with the adults, who have not maintained emotional closeness in their marriage.

As the divorce rate increased in the 1960's and 1970's, and the stigma of divorce and remarriage decreased, there was a rise in the number of stepfamilies. By the late 1980's, it was estimated that more than half of Americans had been or would be in a stepfamily situation during their lives. Statistics are difficult to obtain, however, because many parents living together are not married and those who are married do not always have custody of their children.

### CHANGES IN ROLES

When parents divorce or one of them dies, there is not only a loss in the roles played by family members and a change of their places in the family but also a loss of lifestyle and of family celebrations and rituals. A period of mourning for the past is necessary before family members can move on to a new phase of life. The timing of this period differs among individuals and among adults and children, as the knowledge of death or divorce becomes a reality. The loss of a parent can redefine the role of an older child to one of a "co-parent" to younger children or a pseudo head of household. The custodial parent may be forced to seek employment or additional employment to supplement the household income, placing the most responsible child in this co-parenting position.

Grandparents often take on a surrogate parent role with their grandchildren or are requested to share their home with the family for awhile. They can have a stabilizing influence on the family. On the other hand, the parenting styles of parent and grandparent may differ, providing further instability for the children. Grandparents also struggle with the changing family situation and may mourn the loss of a son-in-law or daughter-in-law. They may also mourn the loss of grandchildren if the custodial parent does not want contact between the generations.

With remarriage, life changes again for both children and adults as holiday and birthday celebrations have to be shared or reorganized to accommodate new living arrangements. The combining of two households often forces children to lose their special place as the only, oldest, or youngest child. Sharing a bedroom, toys, and their biological parent with another child or children requires adjustments and creates disagreements beyond the normal sibling rivalry for children from different households. The loyalty of children is divided between two or more households as the adults try to regroup their lives. Being asked to share information between households makes boundaries hard to maintain for both adults and children.

In the latter half of the twentieth century, role models for successful stepfamilies were numerous, as television glorified the status of blended families and set the stage for disillusionment and yet another loss for both children and adults. Expectations that the newly married adults will provide instant love and caring for each other's children and that the children will be instantly happy and blend with the stepparent's family are often unrealistic.

## LATER-LIFE STEPFAMILIES

Remarriages in later life also focus on issues of loss, divided loyalty, and the reorganization of space, but in a different way. When older couples are faced with divorce or widowhood, the age, health, prior marital experience, and economic status of older men or women become factors in their desire or ability to remarry. Geographic distance from family support may make remarriage for companionship attractive. The experience of friends who have remarried and the availability of suitable partners are considerations. The ratio of men to women after the age of sixty places men at an advantage, as there are more single women than single men in this age bracket. Physical needs, emotional fulfillment, and financial strategies are motivations for remarriage.

The reaction of adult children to a parent's remarriage can range from shock, disbelief, and disapproval to acceptance and support for the new couple. In addition to divided loyalties, ageism in regard to a parent's sexuality and issues regarding finances or inheritance are factors that may interfere with acceptance of the new couple. These issues can be circumvented by thoughtful preplanning by the older couple. A prenuptial agreement, although considered a predivorce before marriage agreement by some people, is a good insurance policy for harmony between two or more sets of children. Assuring children that their own parent's memorabilia and family heirlooms will not go to "the other family" can be vital to the success of stepparent-stepchild relationships.

The importance of communication with children regarding inheritance and possessions is secondary to the agreement between the marrying couple. As in remarriage with younger couples, resolution of issues from a prior marriage or relationship promotes well-being for the new marriage. Issues of death and dying of former spouses can promote a need for tolerance and understanding between the new couple. Respect for the past life of each partner can have great rewards and can strengthen the bond between an older married couple through acknowledgement that the past is part of who they are in the present. Time to adjust to a recent loss and time to adjust to each other are necessary elements to the success of the new marriage. Resolution of financial difficulties (such as credit card debt or loans) and a clear understanding of finances between the couple allow a clean slate for the new relationship. Agreement on how to handle the children, presenting a united front in regard to time and space, is as important in a later marriage as it is in one with young children. Talking openly about time spent with children and grandchildren and time reserved for oneself and a new spouse can prevent much resentment and anger.

The position of an elderly stepparent in a new family is not easy for the stepparent either. Celebrations, holidays, responsibilities, and gift giving vary greatly from family to family and can be sources of stress for the new couple. Geographic distance between family members and the new couple may be desirable in times of good health but may be difficult as the older couple age and become ill. Preplanning and a clear understanding with the younger generation can keep boundaries and relationships clear.

## CONCLUSIONS

Taking a step in a new direction is a difficult task at any age. Many remarriage issues are the same for parents with young children as for those people who have raised their children and are ready for a new relationship.

Issues of finances, divided loyalty, the establishment as a couple both to themselves and to society are challenges. Premarital education and therapy are good investments in any new relationship. Preplanning for this step is as important for older couples as it is for those with young children. Statistics report that married couples live longer and are healthier than those people who live alone. Companionship, better nutrition, and someone to care about and be cared for by are three of the reasons given for this statistic. Thus, remarriage for older individuals who have faced widowhood or divorce is often a step in the right direction.

—*Carolyn L. Scholz*

*See also* Death and dying; Divorce; Family relationships; Grandparenthood; Marriage; Parenthood; Remarriage; Single parenthood; Skipped-generation parenting; Widows and widowers.

### For Further Information:

Bray, J. H., and S. H. Berger. "Developmental Issues in Stepfamilies Research Project: Family Relationships and Parent-Child Interactions." *Journal of Family Psychology* 7 (1993).

McGoldrick, Monica. *The Changing Family Life Cycle.* Boston: Allyn & Bacon, 1989.

Roha, Ronaleen P. "How Late Bloomers Marry Assets." *Kiplinger's Personal Finance Magazine* 53, no. 4 (April, 1999).

Silver, Marc A. "Case Study: Aging Dad Finds Romance." *Nation's Business* 86, no. 8 (August, 1998).

Smith, Ken R., Cathleen D. Zick, and Greg J. Duncan. "Remarriage Patterns Among Recent Widows and Widowers." *Demography* 28 (August, 1991).

Strong, Bryan, Christine DeVault, and Barbara W. Sayad. *The Marriage and Family Experience.* 7th ed. Belmont, Calif.: Wadsworth, 1998.

Wilson, Barbara F., and Sally C. Clarke. "Remarriages: A Demographic Profile." *Journal of Family Issues* 13 (June, 1992).

## STEREOTYPES

**Relevant issues:** Culture, media, psychology, sociology

**Significance:** Stereotypes about the elderly are widely shared and are capable of affecting interpersonal relationships as well as self-image

Age is culturally defined. Most cultures, including that of the United States, define age chronologically, while others define age in terms of accomplishments. While all cultures differentiate between children and adults, some cultures (for example, the United States) utilize many more categories. Each age category has its own socially prescribed roles based on the respective beliefs and stereotypes associated with it. Age categories, together with their accompanying beliefs and stereotypes, are subject to change; as life expectancy increases, the designation of old age tends to change accordingly.

In the United States, the recognized age categories are infancy (birth to about age two), childhood (ages two to twelve), adolescence (ages twelve to eighteen), and adulthood, which is subdivided into young, middle, and old age. Since the advent of Social Security in the 1930's, sixty-five, which was the usual age for retirement, has been commonly identified with old age. Gerontologists have since subdivided this category into young-old (ages sixty-five through seventy-five), middle-old (ages seventy-five through eighty-four), and old-old (age eighty-five and over). Aging occurs biologically (organs, bodily functions, and systems), psychologically (personality, perceptions, and mental functions), and socially (roles, relationships, and stereotypes).

### Meaning, Functions, and Consequences

The word "stereotype" comes from a Greek word meaning "hard core." Stereotype has come to mean a set of largely static and oversimplified ideas about a group or social category. These ideas may be either positive or negative but usually include both types. Stereotypes may arise from personal contact with members of a group or social category, but more commonly they are learned through socialization. They are taught—directly or indirectly—in homes, schools, churches, other groups, and mass media. These stereotypes can be held and shared regarding groups and social categories of people with whom personal contact has never been made.

The primary function of stereotypes is to reduce uncertainty by simplifying reality and allowing people to live in a complex world without the necessity of dealing with individual differences. Thus, when individuals are identified with a particular group or social category (such as the elderly), they are assumed to possess certain characteristics and are treated accordingly. This situation may result in a self-fulfilling prophecy wherein the elderly are admonished to "act their age" as defined by society. Sometimes, elderly individuals accept the role expected of them because, they believe, it is natural and inevitable.

One consequence of negative stereotypes regarding the elderly is "ageism," a term coin by Robert N. Butler, the former director of the National Institute on Aging. Like racism and sexism, ageism is an ideology of superiority and inferiority that results in prejudice and discrimination aimed at the elderly. Stereotypes are problematic because they influence people's behavior toward the elderly. They not only affect interpersonal relations but also are capable of affecting social policies and even elderly individuals' sense of self. Beliefs that the elderly are physically and mentally impaired led to the passage of laws requiring mandatory retirement and a proliferation of nursing homes that were little more than warehouses where residents waited to die.

Even positive stereotypes can have negative consequences. For example, voters and legislators who believe that the elderly are independent and financially well off are unlikely to support public aid, which is viewed as unnecessary. Also, the belief that grandparents are exceptionally good with children and have free time to do what they want has resulted in using elderly retired parents for free babysitting. Finally, stereotypes that portray the elderly as religious, trusting, and helpful make them frequent targets for unscrupulous individuals who want to defraud them of their life savings.

## COMMONLY HELD STEREOTYPES

Stereotypes of the elderly fall mainly into three categories: physical, psychological, and social. Common physical stereotypes include gray hair, balding, wrinkled skin, false teeth, poor eyesight, hearing impairment, gnarled hands, and impotence. Psychological stereotypes include memory loss, forgetfulness, irritability, feelings of isolation, lower self-esteem, and lack of interest in sex. Social stereotypes include being old-fashioned, living on a low income, needing nursing care, being dependent on family members, being poor drivers, and proving to be unproductive or unreliable workers.

A youth-oriented culture such as that found in the United States tends to have more negative than positive stereotypes regarding the elderly. This is compounded by the fact that in the United States, a person's social identity, worth, and status are all tied to employment, and employment declines with age. In a study to determine how older workers were perceived, perspective business managers indicated a belief that older workers (age sixty) were lower than younger workers (age thirty) in efficiency, motivation, productivity, ability to work under pressure, and creativity. They be-

lieved, however, that older workers were higher in dependability, trustworthiness, and reliability and were less likely to miss work for personal reasons. In reality, data show both high productivity and low rates of absenteeism among older workers. Because of the strong cultural emphasis on work and productivity, retired Americans are sometimes reticent to admit that they are no longer employed and often identify themselves with their past occupation or profession.

Another study testing the accuracy of commonly held stereotypes found that the elderly are believed to have high levels of poor health, poverty, fear of crime, feelings of not being needed, loneliness, and isolation. In addition, they are believed to lack friends, have little or nothing to do, and have been forced to retire. While the study found that these characteristics did exist to some degree, they were not true of the majority of elderly persons. Thus, stereotypes often persist even when there is evidence to the contrary. Elderly individuals who exhibit the expected traits are seen as proof of the stereotype, while the individuals who do not exhibit that trait are considered exceptions, regardless of their number.

Some positive stereotypes are that old people are wise and experienced, do not like handouts, are good with children (especially grandchildren), are willing to help, and are concerned for family. Politicians also see the elderly as conservative and politically active, which makes them important constituents.

## ELDERLY IMAGES ON TELEVISION

Television, which is very influential in how people view the world, tends to portray old people negatively or not at all. For the most part, they have been underrepresented. They have rarely been used in commercials except to advertise products associated with poor health and debilities such as hearing aids, bonding material for dentures, and diapers for incontinence. During the 1990's, some change was initiated as advertisers began to utilize elderly actors to advertise a variety of products from food to automobiles in order to attract the growing elder consumer market.

When old people appear in programs, it is seldom in starring roles. Instead they are often portrayed as dependent, sickly, old-fashioned, senile, and asexual. During the 1980's, there was a notable exception to this trend. *The Golden Girls* was a popular prime-time situation comedy that featured four older women who were portrayed as lively, interesting, healthy, independent, and sexually active. Some of the negative stereotypes were also presented; they could be irritable, moody, and occasionally morbid. On the popular prime-time variety program *The Carol Burnett Show,* comedian Tim Conway drew laughs with his portrayal of an old, disheveled man who barely shuffled along, his mouth open and eyes half closed, as he mumbled in response to questions that he either did not hear or could not comprehend. This character was also prone to doze off in the middle of a sentence.

Some social scientists have pointed out that in addition to reinforcing negative stereotypes regarding old age, television has a negative impact on the elderly in another, more indirect way. Television as a medium is concerned with immediate responses, sound bites, and temporary images. Unlike traditional cultures that prize old age for its connection with the past and accumulation of knowledge, modern television-dominated cultures treat young and old alike in its dissemination of information and presentation of experiences. Through television, people of all ages can witness and experience events that would normally come with old age. The modernization theory of aging suggests that there is an inverse relationship between technological advances in a postindustrial society such as the United States and the status of the elderly. —*Philip E. Lampe*

**See also** Advertising; Age discrimination; Ageism; Aging: Biological, psychological, and sociocultural perspectives; Aging: Historical perspective; Aging process; Cultural views of aging; Employment; Films; *Golden Girls, The*; Humor; Literature; Loneliness; Over the hill; Politics; Retirement; Sexuality; Television; Wisdom.

## FOR FURTHER INFORMATION:

Atchley, Robert C. *Social Forces and Aging: An Introduction to Social Gerontology.* 9th ed. Belmont, Calif.: Wadsworth, 1999.

Barrow, Georgia M., and Susan Hillier. *Aging, the Individual, and Society.* 7th ed. Belmont, Calif: Wadsworth, 1999.

Cox, Harold G. *Later Life: The Realities of Aging.* 4th ed. Upper Saddle River, N.J.: Prentice Hall, 1996.

Hooyman, Nancy, and H. Asuman Kiyak. *Social Gerontology: A Multidisciplinary Perspective.* 3d ed. New York: Allyn & Bacon, 1993.

McPherson, Barry. *Aging as a Social Process.* 2d ed. Toronto: Butterworths, 1990.

Moody, Harry. *Aging: Concepts and Controversies.* Thousand Oaks, Calif.: Pine Forge Press, 1994.

## STONES

**RELEVANT ISSUES:** Health and medicine

**SIGNIFICANCE:** While there is no evidence of increased incidence of urinary stones with increasing age, stones of the biliary tract (cholelithiasis) do increase with age, affecting approximately 33 percent of the U.S. population over seventy years old

Stones, or calculi, are hard deposits of material in the body associated with urine and bile. Unlike the typical calcium-based composition of kidney and ureter stones, bladder stones are most frequently composed of uric acid (a byproduct of protein metabolism) or struvite (a result of chronic urinary infection). Gallstones contain very little calcium; they are primarily composed of cholesterol.

### KIDNEY AND URINARY TRACT STONES

Kidney stones or stones in the urinary tract affect 5 to 10 percent of the general population of the United States. The likelihood of a person to form a stone for the first time in their life decreases with advancing age. In people who have a prior history of urinary stone formation, however, the incidence, recurrence, and severity of urinary stone disease is similar between the geriatric and younger population. The composition of urinary stones in the older population is no different from those found in younger patients, however the underlying urinary abnormality leading to the stone formation is different. More frequently, urinary stones in the elderly are caused by high uric acid levels and low citrate levels in the urine. Similar difficulties in the disposal of protein metabolites can lead to gouty arthritis.

The symptoms that accompany urinary stone disease are dependent on the location of the stone, the size of the stone, how long the stone has been present, whether infection is associated with the stone, and the degree of obstruction to urinary flow caused by the stone. Urine, which is produced

## Kidney Stones

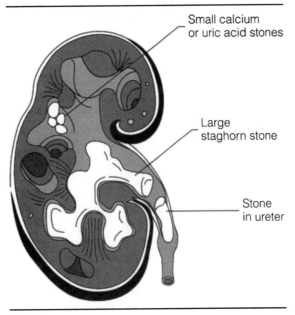

Small calcium
or uric acid stones

Large
staghorn stone

Stone
in ureter

(Hans & Cassidy, Inc.)

by the kidneys, located beneath the ribs of the back, is collected into a structure just outside the kidney known as the renal pelvis. From the renal pelvis, urine passes into a thin narrow tube called the ureter and travels a relatively long distance to the urinary bladder. It is easy to envision how a stone traveling along such a narrow, long tube can get stuck and dam the further flow of urine.

Stones caught in the renal pelvis, prior to entry into the ureter, generally cause an intermittent, sharp pain in the back or side. Stones that pass into the ureter can cause pain in the back as well as points distant to the urinary system (the groin, the lower abdomen, and the testicle and penis in men); this phenomenon is known as referred pain. Occasionally, stones in the lowest portion of the ureters will cause pain only with urination or produce the desire to urinate frequently but only in small amounts. Often, blood not visible to the naked eye can be found in the urine with a simple chemical dipstick or by looking at the urine under a microscope, both easily accomplished in most doctors' offices.

Several radiological tests can be performed to pinpoint the location of a stone lodged in the urinary tract. An intravenous pyelogram (IVP) is a series of X rays performed following the administration of a dye into the patient's vein. This dye is concentrated in the urine and can be visualized as it travels through the urinary tract. High-frequency sound waves, or ultrasound, can determine if obstruction is present in the kidneys but will frequently miss stones lodged in the ureters. A computed tomography (CT) scan is similar to an IVP but uses advanced computer technology to visualize better all contents of the body. While the CT scan is the most sensitive test for the detection of urinary stones, certain situations may necessitate the use of different tests. Frequently, people with poor renal function cannot receive the X-ray dye because of its potential harmful effects on the kidneys. A CT scan without contrast or ultrasound will frequently be performed in this situation.

Treatment of any stone depends on the location of the stone, its size, the time it has been in place, and any complicating issues such as infection. The methods for treatment are broad, and the specific means by which a stone is removed is often debated among the experts in this field. Some stones—especially if they are small, cause no pain, and are not significantly obstructing—are given a chance to pass on their own, a treatment termed watchful waiting. The most frequent noninvasive means to treat a small stone located in the urinary tract above the pelvic bone is extracorporeal shock wave lithotripsy (ESWL). This procedure involves the use of high-energy sound waves created by a machine outside the body and focused through the skin onto the stone. These sound waves break the stone into fine sand, which passes in the urine without symptoms. This is frequently the best method to deal with stones in elderly patients who have other medical problems that can make surgical means of removing a stone risky. Endoscopic removal of a stone involves the use of small telescopes passed into the urinary tract either through the urethra or through the back directly into the kidney. Different means of fragmenting the stone into smaller pieces for direct removal are then employed through the telescopes. This method is highly successful and often used for larger stones. Like ESWL, this low-invasive, endoscopic means of removing the stone places minimal stress on the elderly patient with other medical problems.

The development of these minimally invasive procedures for stone removal has led to a significant decrease in the need for open surgery. Nevertheless, there are special situations when an open surgical procedure may be the first reasonable option for the elderly patient with a urinary stone. These situations include abnormal urinary tract anatomy, concurrent urinary tract pathology other than the stone, or the failure of less invasive means to remove the stone.

### BLADDER STONES

Bladder stones are found much less frequently than stones in the kidney and ureter. Perhaps the most famous person to have suffered from bladder stones is Benjamin Franklin, who reportedly stood on his head to urinate. Throughout the world, bladder stones are almost exclusively a disease of the older, male population. They are most frequently found in association with enlargement of the prostate that obstructs the bladder's ability to empty and allows these stones to crystallize in the urine. Other causes of bladder stone formation should be excluded, such as a narrowed urethra, an abnormal pouching of the bladder, a chronic urinary infection, or a neurologic dysfunction leading to poor bladder emptying.

Symptoms of a bladder stone are pain in the lower abdomen that worsens with movement, intermittent blockage of the urinary stream, a weak urine stream, increased frequency of urination often associated with a strong and urgent need to void, recurrent urinary tract infections, or blood in the urine. Definitive diagnosis of a stone can be made with a simple X ray of the abdomen alone; however, the physician will often need to perform additional tests, including a direct look into the bladder.

Treatment is very successful and appropriate for the elderly. As with stones of the kidney and ureter, endoscopic removal of a bladder stone using small telescopes frequently can be performed. Most bladder stones, however, are removed with open surgery. Paramount to the successful treatment of a bladder stone is the treatment of the underlying cause for its formation, which frequently dictates the method of removal. Whether endoscopic or open surgery is chosen, both are generally well tolerated by elderly patients even if significant other medical problems exist.

### GALLSTONES

The biliary system stores bile formed in the liver and delivers it to the intestines following a meal, aiding in the digestion of fat and the absorption of certain vitamins. The gallbladder is a blind-ending pouch that comes off of the bile duct as it courses from the liver to the small intestine. After consumption of a fatty meal, its muscle-lined wall contracts to release bile into the intestine. Stones can form in the gallbladder and can cause pain or infection when lodged in the bile duct or common hepatic (liver) duct. If a stone causes blockage and infection, the patient can become very sick and require emergency medical care.

Diseases affecting the gallbladder and bile ducts occur commonly in the elderly. By the age of seventy, stones in the gallbladder and bile duct represent the most frequently occurring disorder affecting this organ system. In the late 1990's, it was estimated that 33 percent of the U.S. population over seventy would be diagnosed with gallstones at some point in their lives.

The symptoms associated with stones in the gallbladder or bile duct are numerous and depend on the location and size of the stone and whether there is an associated infection. Frequently, pa-

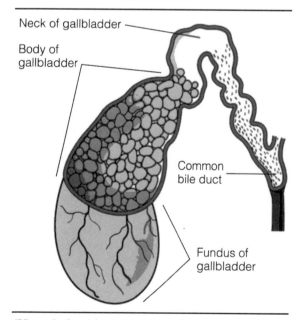

**Gallstones**

Neck of gallbladder

Body of gallbladder

Common bile duct

Fundus of gallbladder

(Hans & Cassidy, Inc.)

tients complain of pain in the right upper part of the abdomen. This pain often occurs after the consumption of a fatty meal, which causes the gallbladder to contract and release its bile. Fever, sweats, and chills may accompany the pain if there is infection present. Jaundice, a yellowish discoloring of the skin, may occur if the common bile duct or hepatic duct becomes obstructed with a gallstone. As with stones in the urinary tract, it is the blockage of flow of bile from the gallbladder that leads to the symptoms. Elderly patients who appear jaundiced may not always be suffering from gallstones, especially if there is no associated pain. Other diseases of the liver and biliary system, such as cirrhosis of the liver or hepatitis, will also cause jaundice and are frequently found in the elderly.

Unlike kidney stones, gallstones are frequently not visible on plain X-ray examination of the abdomen. Despite their hard nature, gallstones contain very little calcium. They are primarily composed of cholesterol which, unlike calcium, is not dense enough to be visible on an X ray. Ultrasound examination of the liver and gallbladder is almost always the first test ordered by a physician who is suspicious that a patient may have a gallstone. To determine if obstruction of the bile duct is present, a physician can also use nuclear medicine studies, which uses a radioactive material concentrated by the gallbladder, similar to the concentration of X-ray dye used in the diagnosis of kidney stones. On occasion, the diagnosis of a gallstone lodged in the bile duct requires the placement of a telescope into the patient's stomach and intestine and direct visualization of the common bile duct's entry into the intestine.

Treatment of symptomatic gallstones almost always involves surgery using lighted telescopes passed either directly into the abdomen (laproscopes) or through the stomach and intestine (endoscopes), or open surgery. Unlike the removal of kidney and bladder stones, which most often merely involves the removal of the actual stone and not the kidney, ureter, or bladder, treatment of gallstones usually also involves the removal of the gallbladder itself. The loss of this unpaired organ often does not lead to significant digestive problems, though in the elderly loose, foul-smelling bowel movements may result from the altered digestion of fats.

The choice of surgical approach again depends on whether an infection is associated with the stone, how severe the symptoms are, whether any liver dysfunction is associated with the stone, and the overall health of the patient. Gallstones not causing symptoms are generally not removed. Patients with diabetes mellitus and other complicating medical conditions are dealt with in a more cautious manner and frequently undergo surgery to remove the gallstone and gallbladder even if symptoms do not exist.

*—John F. Ward and Prodromos G. Borboroglu*
**See also** Gastrointestinal changes and disorders; Gout; Nutrition; Urinary disorders.

**FOR FURTHER INFORMATION:**
Gentle, D., M. Stoller, J. Bruce, and S. Leslie. "Geriatric Urolithiasis." *Journal of Urology* 158, no. 6 (December, 1997): 2221.
Glenn, F. "Surgical Management of Acute Cholecystitis in Patients Sixty-five Years of Age and Older." *Annals of Surgery* 193, no. 1 (January, 1981): 56.
Hosking, M., M. Warmer, C. Lodbell, et al. "Outcomes of Surgery in Patients Ninety Years of Age and Older." *Journal of the American Medical Association* 261, no. 13 (April 7, 1989): 1909.
Vieweg, J., et al. "Unenhanced Helical Computerized Tomography for the Evaluation of Patients with Acute Flank Pain." *Journal of Urology*, 160, no. 3 (September, 1998): 679.
Walsh, P., A. Retik, E. Vaughan, and A. Wein. *Campbell's Urology*. 7th ed. 3 vols. Philadelphia: W. B. Saunders, 1998.

## STRESS AND COPING SKILLS

**RELEVANT ISSUES:** Family, health and medicine, psychology

**SIGNIFICANCE:** Understanding stress and coping across the life span has both practical and empirical implications; however, relatively little is known about normal changes in these processes with age

Much of what is known about the physiological effects of stress on the body came from animal researchers in the early 1930's. Findings suggest that emotional experiences, such as pain and fear, act as a mobilizing force by producing physiological changes in the body (such as increased adrenal gland output) to help an organism ward off the threat and take action. The general adaptation syndrome is a model of the body's response to stress that involves three stages: alarm, resistance, and exhaustion. Stress across a short period is adaptive; however, with prolonged exposure to a threat and commensurate bodily alterations, it could be harmful. Important parallels apply to humans and the stress process: Stress affects health by overcoming capacities for adaptation; there are individual differences in each person's abilities to adjust to stress; and everyday life changes can have negative effects on the health of the mind and the body.

Early measurement of stress involved case studies of select events and their accompanying psychological consequences. Stressful life events, such as death of one's spouse, are frequently investigated. Some measures focus on the combined effects of aggregate or multiple stressful life events on well-being. Despite this different approach, the mechanisms responsible or processes underlying the negative effects on health are still largely unknown. Common aggregate measures of life stress involve asking individuals to indicate which events (from a list of possible stressful events) have occurred in some time interval and how upsetting it was. Stress is, by definition, an interaction of the stressor, or life event, and the meaning an individual attaches to that event. However, there is an ongoing debate about the best way to assess stress: via subjective self-report measures or objective measures. Self-reports may be influenced by negative affect states at the time of report, while the objective approach may be constrained by only querying about a select number of events. A larger problem involves the fact that stressful life events can be both a cause and a consequence of stress; however, the bulk of research with adults has focused on the consequences of experiencing stress in terms of costs to physical and mental health.

Early studies of life events found significant but weak relationships between stress and physical health, mental health, and immune functioning. However, this weak relationship may have been caused, in part, by nonsensitive measures of stress, well-being, or other indicators of health. Further, passage of time alone seemed to diminish the reported impact of stress on the individual. Researchers began to realize that certain personal and social resources of the individual could ameliorate the effects of stress. Higher income and occupational prestige, in addition to the availability of social support, have all been found to buffer or minimize the negative consequences of stress.

## STRESS AMONG OLDER ADULTS

Older adults report the occurrence of fewer life events and lower perceived stress than younger adults. Stressful events most commonly reported by older adults include death of a spouse, retirement, illness or hospitalization, and decreased income. Estimated one-year prevalence for such events was approximately 2 percent for death of spouse or retirement, 13 percent for decreased income, and 55 percent for illness. These frequently reported events all involve role losses of some type for older adults. Additionally, they are inextricably related to other life circumstances of an individual, such as their social relationships. For example, while death of spouse involves grief and psychological distress, this experience may also result in decreased number of friends and income. Research on stress has discovered links with congestive heart failure, decreased well-being, disrupted family life, anxiety, and depression.

Further research highlights yet another type of stress among adults: hassles. Hassles are everyday stressors that result in negative affect (such as a flat tire en route to an appointment). Middle-aged adults tend to report twice as many hassles when compared to the oldest-old, with hassles primarily focused on child issues.

## COPING WITH STRESS

Researchers realized that in order to understand the adaptive capability of individuals dealing with stress, they must understand the processes or individual responses to that stress. The coping process involves the behaviors and actions that an individual engages in to manage stress. Strong evidence supports the position that there are marked individual differences in how people manage stressful situations. Coping attempts also change over time and as a function of the particular stressful situation one is trying to manage.

According to one of the leading authorities in the stress and coping field, there are three common misunderstandings about the coping process: the tendency for researchers to treat the functions of coping as if they are single behaviors; the tendency to measure the coping process in isolation without an understanding of individual factors that affect coping; and a tendency to examine coping as separate from the emotion process.

Age-related coping has been conceptualized in several different ways by researchers. The developmental interpretation suggests that there are real changes in how people cope as they age. The underlying implication is that the coping change reflects developmental change and is not merely determined by environmental circumstances. Early researchers suggested that older adults regressed or became less sophisticated in their coping as they aged, typically utilizing more egocentric or impulsive approaches. Others researchers argue that individuals become more mature in their coping with age, frequently utilizing humor, distancing, and reflective thought.

A contextual interpretation of how people change in coping postulates that age differences occur because of changing life contexts and demands with age. This interpretation promotes examining the person-environment interactions in order to better understand coping. For example, knowing the age, available social resources, and type of stress are all critical to gain an appreciation of the coping strategy employed.

A third interpretation focuses on examination of historical experiences and birth cohort (group) to which an individual belongs in order to identify how that individual may cope. Other researchers have described marked gender differences, with men becoming more passive in strategy use and women becoming more aggressive.

The measurement of coping, like stress, has taken a variety of forms. Typically, checklists of various coping strategies are offered to the individual, and frequency of type of coping strategy used is quantified across some time interval. Others have asked individuals to recount a stressful event and describe how they handled it within an open-response framework; still others have used some combination of these approaches. Checklist analyses suggest three major types of coping strategies. Emotion-focused strategies are directed at managing the harm or threat by changing the meaning of the threat. They typically involve emotional expression to regulate the stress, such as finding ways to let feelings out. Problem-focused strategies involve actions designed to alter the conditions that arouse stressful emotions, such as finding out more information about the problem. Finally, cognitive-focused strategies are directed at thoughts of how to solve the problem or tackle the situation, such as thinking about how somebody one admires would handle the situation and using them as a model.

### COPING AMONG OLDER ADULTS

Research by Richard Lazarus and colleagues found extensive normative differences in the types of stresses experienced by younger and older adults. For the younger sample, the majority of stressors revolved around financial problems, work, taking care of the household, and dealing with personal problems and family; for older adults, health issues and lack of ability to carry out everyday tasks as easily as before predominated. Not surprisingly, the younger sample appraised their stressful circumstances as more changeable and reported more sense of control over the situations than older adults. This pattern was reflected in the predominant types of coping strategies reported by younger and older adults. Younger adults used more problem-focused strategies (seeking social support, planned problem solving), while older adults more frequently engaged in emotion-focused coping (distancing, acceptance, positive reappraisal).

Other researchers, however, found fewer age differences between different age groups and more stability to coping approaches. Part of this disagreement may be because of differences in research design. Despite differences in research methods, it appears that research supports the contextual interpretation of age differences in coping. That is, age differences in coping are a function of what situation people cope with and how they interpret the stressful circumstance rather than just the presence of stage-related developmental changes through which all individuals progress.

*—Karen Kopera-Frye and Richard Wiscott*
**See also** Death and dying; Death anxiety; Death of a child; Death of parents; Depression; Divorce; Forgetfulness; Grief; Heart attacks; Heart disease; Hospitalization; Loneliness; Psychiatry, geriatric; Relocation; Retirement; Social ties; Widows and widowers.

**FOR FURTHER INFORMATION:**

Aldwin, Carolyn M. *Stress, Coping, and Development.* New York: Guilford Press, 1994.

Goldberg, Leo, and Shlomo Breznitz, eds. *Handbook of Stress: Theoretical and Clinical Aspects.* New York: Free Press, 1993.

Lazarus, Richard S., and Susan Folkman. *Stress, Appraisal, and Coping.* New York: Springer, 1984.

# STROKES

**RELEVANT ISSUES:** Health and medicine

**SIGNIFICANCE:** Strokes are a leading cause of death and long-term physical problems among the aged; recognizing the early warning signs of impending stroke could save a person's life

According to the National Stroke Association (NSA), more than 500,000 people in the United States experience a stroke each year. Strokes are one of the leading causes of death in those over sixty-five and account for about 145,000 deaths each year. Two-thirds of those experiencing a stroke are elderly. Strokes can have devastating physical, financial, emotional, and social effects that impact the entire family. Strokes are also a major cause of elderly people going to live in a nursing home.

The medical term for stroke is cerebrovascular accident (CVA), suggesting that this event happens suddenly and is related to brain circulation. A stroke is defined most simply as an interruption in the blood supply to the brain. When the brain does not get enough oxygen for whatever reason, brain cells can die and leave permanent damage. A transient ischemic attack (TIA) can be a warning sign of stroke. TIAs occur when the brain lacks sufficient oxygen to cause a person to exhibit some signs of stroke, such as slurred speech, difficulties with vision, weakness or numbness in the face or extremities, loss of balance, or altered consciousness. However, the effects of a TIA last no more than twenty-four hours and go away without leaving any deficits. Sometimes laypeople refer to TIAs as ministrokes, but people experiencing TIAs should consider this a warning sign of a future stroke and seek medical treatment.

### CAUSES AND RISK FACTORS

There are several common causes of stroke. Strokes can be caused by clots, hemorrhage, nar-

rowing of vessels, and high blood pressure. The most common cause of stroke is a thrombus, a clot that originates in the brain because of narrowing of blood vessels. Narrowing of vessels can also lead to lack of oxygen to the brain. Such narrowing is often related to arteriosclerosis, or fatty deposits along the vessel walls, as seen in the carotid arteries of the neck. Older people may have an occlusion in these major arteries, which supply the brain with blood, and may need surgery to clean them out to avoid having a stroke. Clots can also come from other parts of the body. For example, a blood clot in the leg could break off and travel to the brain, causing an occlusion. This type of clot is

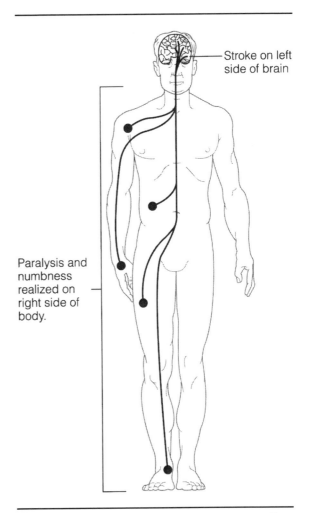

*A major stroke to one hemisphere of the brain generally results in impaired motor functions on the opposite side of the body.* (Hans & Cassidy, Inc.)

called an embolus. A hemorrhagic stroke results when a weakened blood vessel leaks or bursts. This could be from an aneurysm, a defective artery, high blood pressure, or a combination of these. In this case, blood leaking into brain tissue causes damage and results in the effects seen after a stroke.

There are several factors that put a person more at risk for stroke. Some of these can be controlled and others cannot. Risk factors that a person cannot do anything about include age, gender, race, and heredity. The risk for stroke increases with age. Men generally experience more strokes than women; after menopause, however, the numbers are more equal. African Americans, especially African American men with heart disease, have more strokes than Caucasians. Finally, a family history of strokes also increases the risk. Such information should be given to one's primary care provider.

The risk factors that can be controlled are many. These include high blood pressure (also called hypertension), high cholesterol, heart disease, diabetes, smoking, obesity, a sedentary lifestyle, and stress. The good news is that these risk factors can be changed to reduce the risk of stroke. Prevention of stroke thus centers on making changes related to these factors.

### WARNING SIGNS AND EFFECTS

It is essential that older people be aware of the warning signs of stroke. Knowing these symptoms can help a person decide when to seek help and can provide a better chance for recovery. TIAs happen before at least 10 percent of strokes, so they should be considered a warning sign. The NSA gives several warning signs of strokes. These include numbness or tingling in the face, arms, or legs; difficulty speaking; headache; blurred or other disturbed vision; dizziness; loss of consciousness; and sudden weakness or paralysis (often affecting just one side of the body). If any of these signs are manifested in an older person, they should seek medical treatment right away.

The effects of strokes are numerous and vary from person to person. No one can predict the exact effect of a stroke, as the deficits seen depend on the area of damage within the brain. Since a large portion of the brain controls speech and cognition, communication is often affected. People surviving a stroke may not be able to speak or may

have trouble understanding what is said to them. These types of problems with the use of language are referred to as aphasia. The muscles involved with speech and swallowing are closely related, so individuals may experience deficits in both of these areas. Certain swallowing problems may lead to aspiration and subsequent pneumonia. Thus, a speech therapy evaluation is often needed for any individuals exhibiting problems with eating, swallowing, or speech. Dietary modifications may be necessary for the person to swallow safely. Additionally, some stroke survivors require a feeding tube to maintain proper nutrition while participating in rehabilitation of the swallowing muscles and retraining of the swallowing mechanism.

Other problems can affect such senses as sight and touch perception. Visual problems may range from blurred vision to double vision to partial or total blindness. Stroke survivors may also experience cognitive difficulties, including memory loss, trouble recalling words, inability to remember how to perform familiar tasks, and difficulty sequencing things. They may also neglect the part of the body that is paralyzed or weak, or they may not recognize a paralyzed arm as part of their own body. A shorter attention span is also common after stroke.

Weakness (hemiparesis) and paralysis (hemiplegia) occur on the side of the body opposite the damage within the brain; if a person suffers damage from a stroke on the left side of the brain, one may observe right-sided weakness of the arm and leg. Strength generally returns to the legs first, but weakness or paralysis of the arm and hand may be slower to return or may even be permanent. These types of problems lead to difficulty in performing activities of daily living, such as dressing, eating, and bathing. Other tasks that may be harder after a stroke include using the telephone, cooking, shopping, doing laundry, resuming a job, and driving. The inability to perform some of these key life functions has a serious impact upon the stroke survivor and his or her family.

Other physical changes are noted after strokes. People may lose control over bowel and bladder function. The resulting incontinence can be embarrassing and humiliating to a person recovering from a stroke. With rehabilitation, nurses will work with patients to establish new patterns that can return control of these bodily functions to the person in a relatively short amount of time. Many people have a urinary catheter placed in the bladder immediately after a stroke. This is generally removed as soon as possible, and bladder retraining is begun, usually beginning with a program where the person is encouraged to go to the toilet every two hours or so. This time is gradually lengthened to a more usual number of hours as bladder control returns. People may require stool softeners or even suppositories to maintain bowel regularity after a stroke, but natural means are best. This includes increasing fluid intake, increasing activity, having adequate fiber in the diet, sitting up on the toilet to have a bowel movement (avoid bedpans), and taking advantage of normal reflexes. Recalling when the person formerly had a bowel movement during the day may help, but those having particular difficulties with constipation may find that sitting on the toilet within fifteen minutes after breakfast will help reestablish a regular pattern.

Changes in sexual function are also common. All people have the right to be respected as sexual beings. While many changes normally occur with aging, the effects of stroke add additional stressors to the aspect of sexuality. Those with one-sided weakness may need to learn different positions for intercourse. Openness to discussing the subject of sexuality with one's partner, as well as with health care professionals as needed, is often emphasized. Medications taken after a stroke or for prevention of recurring stroke can affect libido and function. Most rehabilitation units have pamphlets and brochures that provide specific suggestions for adapting to changes that affect one's sex life. It is important to note that sexual function is only one aspect of sexuality and that self-image and self-esteem can also be affected by stroke.

Many psychosocial and emotional changes may occur after a stroke. Sometimes changes in personality are noted. Emotional swings are common, particularly crying spells that may seem unrelated to the person's true feelings. This is called emotional lability, and family members should realize that these crying outbursts are not generally connected with the person's feelings but result from chemical imbalances in the brain that occur because of the stroke. A good way to tell if the stroke survivor is experiencing emotional lability is to distract him or her when it occurs by changing the topic of conversation, saying his or her name, or

making a loud noise. While others should not assume that the stroke survivor is crying because of emotional lability, it is an important event to note. Stroke survivors may go through a process of grieving the losses that the stroke has inflicted. They may feel angry, depressed, apathetic, or powerless. Depression in stroke survivors can be treated with counseling or medication. Fatigue is a common problem with stroke and may continue for months, even years, after treatment. Insomnia is also common. Stroke survivors and their families must learn new ways to cope and adapt to life after the stroke. Good social support and use of spiritual support systems, such as church involvement, may be of assistance. Knowing the resources of the community is also essential.

Some deficits are more common with right- and left-sided brain damage. Those with a left-sided stroke (right-sided weakness) tend to have swallowing problems and may require a feeding tube for some time after the stroke. They generally have a slow and cautious behavior style and may be fearful when learning new tasks. Those with a right-sided stroke (left-sided weakness) tend to be more impulsive and may not acknowledge that anything is wrong with them. They pose a safety risk to themselves by overestimating their abilities and have a high rate of falls. Disabilities in those with a right-sided stroke may be less obvious to others but nonetheless put the person at risk for injury.

### TREATMENT

The acute medical treatment of strokes begins with emergency care. Older adults should know the warning signs of a stroke and go to the nearest emergency medical facility if exhibiting such symptoms. Medical treatments, such as the use of tPa (a medication that may be given to dissolve blood clots), are available in many hospital emergency rooms. This drug can actually reverse the stroke effects in many people, leaving no residual impairment if given appropriately. However, tPa is only used in the case of a stroke caused by a clot and is only effective if given within the first three hours after the onset of symptoms. For this reason, it is crucial for a person suffering from a stroke to get to an emergency room where a computed tomography (CT) scan or magnetic resonance imaging (MRI) of the head can be performed so that a proper diagnosis can be made.

Rehabilitation is most crucial in the three-month period following the stroke. According to the Copenhagen Stroke Study, people with minimal weakness in the legs after stroke made optimum progress within three weeks and not much progress after nine weeks. For those with more severe weakness or paralysis, not much recovery was seen after eleven weeks. Overall, however, most stroke patients did recover the ability to walk within the first eleven weeks after the stroke. These research findings underscore the importance of early rehabilitation.

Stroke survivors have better recovery when treated by a team of rehabilitation professionals in a setting designed specifically for this type of recovery. Physical, occupational, and speech therapy (if needed) should begin in the hospital as soon as possible. Physical therapy focuses on lower extremity strengthening, helping the person learn exercises for the legs and regain walking skills. Occupational therapy centers attention on use of the arms and hands to perform key life activities, such as dressing, bathing, and eating. The occupational therapist also assists the person in resuming home management skills, such as doing laundry and cooking, as well as in reentering the community with a physical limitation. The speech therapist, also called a speech-language pathologist, assists patients in regaining speech, relearning skills that may be impaired because of memory problems or aphasia, and setting up an appropriate diet. Nurses in inpatient rehabilitation help patients with medication schedules, nutrition, skin care, bowel and bladder retraining, and family education. The social worker helps patients and families connect with resources in the community, figure out insurance problems, and make discharge plans. The patient's physician will help diagnose and treat medical problems and complications, and a psychologist or psychiatrist is generally available for counseling with the person and the family if needed. Together, this interdisciplinary rehabilitation team helps patients and families achieve their goals. Most patients get better outcomes if transferred to a rehabilitation unit or center soon after the stroke to receive more intensive therapy with the goal of home discharge.

—*Kristen L. Easton*

*See also* African Americans; Arteriosclerosis; Brain changes and disorders; Communication; Hypertension; Incontinence; Mobility problems; Personality changes; Vision changes and disorders.

**FOR FURTHER INFORMATION:**

Gresham, Glen E., Pamela W. Duncan, and Harold P. Adams, Jr., et al. *Post-Stroke Rehabilitation: Clinical Practice Guidelines*. Rockville: U.S. Department of Health and Human Services, 1995. Poststroke clinical guidelines compiled for health care professionals by a panel of nineteen experts in the field.

Nakayama, Hirofumi, Henrik Stig Jorgensen, Hans Otto Raaschou, and Tom Skyhoj Olsen. "Recovery of Upper Extremity Function in Stroke Patients: The Copenhagen Stroke Study." *Archives of Physical Medicine and Rehabilitation* 75 (April, 1994). A landmark study using a large sample that studied the length of time taken for return of arm and hand function in stroke survivors.

Paullin, Ellen. *Ted's Stroke: The Caregiver's Story*. Cabin John, Md.: Seven Locks Press, 1988. The wife of a stroke survivor discusses their journey after his stroke.

Sandin, Karl J., and Kristin D. Mason. *Stroke Rehabilitation*. Boston: Butterworth-Heinemann, 1996. A practical and informative guide to stroke care with a strong medical focus; written by physicians but in user-friendly terms.

## SUBSTANCE ABUSE. *See* ALCOHOLISM; MEDICATIONS; OVERMEDICATION.

## SUCCESSFUL AGING

**RELEVANT ISSUES:** Biology, culture, health and medicine, psychology

**SIGNIFICANCE:** Considering the attention that the world's aging population has received from the media, almost everyone who has reached middle age wants to know how to age successfully

Successful aging can have any number of different interpretations depending on the person asked. Most people would probably have the feeling that financial security and good health would be the critical factors in successful aging. Gerontologists, including specialists in psychology and sociology, have identified a number of factors besides financial security and good health that would most certainly contribute to aging successfully.

## BACKGROUND

The process of aging, which includes physical, psychological, social, and institutional dimensions, has been of interest to social scientists for many years. Perhaps the best-known theory of aging is that of Erik Erikson, who said that older adults face the psychosocial crisis of integrity versus despair. Many other theorists have also focused on the losses and declines that older people inevitably face as they move closer and closer to death. Overall, there has been an essentially pessimistic view of the nature of aging among social scientists for a long time. William Shakespeare's statement about the nature of very old people, "sans [without] teeth, sans eyes, sans taste, sans everything," may have been a poetic overstatement about the condition of very old people, but much of the research in developmental psychology until the 1970's seemed to reflect Shakespeare's negative view.

The traditional theories of aging among developmental psychologists emphasized the declines and losses that old people would suffer as they continued to age. They were to expect changes in their eyesight, hearing, taste sensitivity, and the ability to adapt to heat and cold. Additionally, older people could expect slower motor responses, lapses in memory, and other negative declines. The general assumption was that after a person reached maturity in late adolescence and early adulthood, the path was all downhill from there. In the 1970's many researchers were finding evidence that did not bear out the assumptions of traditional developmental theories. Since then more and more researchers have turned their attention to both the problems and promise of development and aging in the later years of life. This new perspective, known as life span developmental psychology, concentrates on changes in human behavior from conception to death. A major emphasis is on longitudinal studies and what they reveal about changes within individuals.

## BALTES'S THEORY OF SUCCESSFUL AGING

Premier among these researchers is Paul Baltes who saw that the results of most empirical studies of old people did not match up with traditional theories of aging. Baltes put forward a number of ideas in the form of a model of successful aging. He acknowledged that some physical and mental declines with old age are universal in humans, but he also identified major strengths that many old people have. These strengths help to compensate for the losses that go along with aging. Baltes based his model on the analysis of many longitudinal studies of people who have grown old in Europe and the United States.

Baltes's model rests on several assumptions about the nature of the process of aging; these assumptions differ considerably from those used for the traditional theories of aging. Among the most important of these assumptions are the following. First, normal aging differs from aging complicated by disease. The impression that many people have of the elderly is based on their observation of old people who suffer from chronic diseases. Normal aging unaffected by disease, on the other hand, is a gradual process without many drastic changes in appearance and functioning. Second, there is great variability among old people. There is a common notion that old people are very much alike in terms of their interests, motivations, feelings, habits, lifestyle, and aspirations. In fact, as research has shown, individual differences among old people as

*According to Paul Baltes, those who have aged "successfully" show a sense of resilience in the face of physical and social changes.* (James L. Shaffer)

a group are much greater than in a comparable group of young adults. Third, there are many untapped reserves and areas of strength in old people. The idea that old people cannot learn and cannot change is not at all supported by current research. Fourth, with aging, the balance between gains and losses becomes less positive. Although there are substantial strengths among old people, the biological clock is ticking. There is a gradual decline in many capabilities as older people become more vulnerable to the effects of undesirable changes in their physical functioning and in their environment. Fifth, contrary to common stereotypes, the self remains resilient in old age. People who have weathered the storms of life for many years have by definition adapted well. Old people are survivors, and they can continue to adjust to many stressors. Adjusting to the various demands of life does, however, become more taxing for them as the years wear on.

Based on these assumptions, Baltes's model of successful aging is much more optimistic than were the traditional theories of aging. According to Baltes, successful aging depends on three components: selection, optimization, and compensation. Selection relates to the fact that as a person ages, the individual can probably not do everything so well as he or she did in the past. General slowness, reduced muscle mass, poorer eyesight, and poorer hearing, for example, will make life's tasks more difficult. As a result, according to Baltes, older people will select those areas that they find most important as the objects of their greatest attention. This means, of course, that other areas will no longer be of such concern to them and that they will spend relatively little time in dealing with them. Baltes argues that selection is an adaptive response to the changes brought on by the process of aging; because of age-related loss, old people focus on fewer domains of activity. As a result, their physical and mental resources can actually be used more effectively.

Optimization, the second component of Baltes's model of successful aging, means that after older adults have selected the major areas of their concern they will spend much of their strength, time, and energy to maintain and to improve their functioning in those areas. This behavior pattern theoretically has the potential to result in meaningful tangible products, improved skills in some intel-lectual field, services to other people or the community at large, and feelings of accomplishment and self efficacy.

Compensation, the third component of the model, means that with the passage of time losses associated with aging may become extreme, considering the resources available to the old person. In this context, the individual can theoretically adapt to life tasks by developing new behaviors in place of those physical, intellectual, and psychological skills that served so well in the past but are no longer effective in present circumstances. Compensation involves acknowledging the need for some degree of assistance in order to achieve success in life tasks. That assistance can take many different forms, ranging from a hearing aid to adult day care.

It is important to recognize that selection, optimization, and compensation will differ in form, degree, and effect for different old people. Baltes has not given a recipe that can be applied indiscriminately to old people as a group, but rather a plan that can be applied by an older person and family and associates to assist the older person in aging successfully. It is also important to recognize that the three factors are interactive—each component influences all the others.

### EXAMPLES OF SUCCESSFUL AGING

A few examples may serve to illustrate the workings of the model. A major example used by Baltes concerns a marathon runner who has excelled in the sport for most of his life and wants to continue the activity into old age. If the runner wishes to stay at the same performance level, he will need to invest much more time and effort in running. Consequently, he will necessarily have to reduce or give up entirely other activities. At the same time he will need to increase his training and become more fully aware of products and techniques that could reduce the wear and tear of running on his body. In addition, he might need to have special attention from an expert in treating athletic-related injuries. It may well be in time that he would choose to cut down the distance he expects to run in the light of his recognition of the stress that marathon running places on his body. If this selection, optimization, and compensation process works out well in his particular set of circumstances, there is the possibility that he could continue his running well into old age and enjoy many physical and psychological advantages as a result.

Another example would be a woman in her eighties who has for her lifetime been a member of a local church. She has been faithful and has found her niche as the person who "does everything" around the church, such as singing in the choir, teaching Sunday School, keeping the nursery, serving on committees, and the like. She has recognized in recent years that she tires more quickly than in the past and she decides that she must reduce her level of activity. Instead of "doing everything," she focuses only on her role as teacher of the class for the eldest women of the church (selection). She now uses her full energy in preparing for her class and in keeping tabs on the health and family circumstances of the class members. She uses teaching materials written in large bold type and orders lesson-related material in contrasting colors for use in her class presentations (optimization). She finds over time that she has trouble getting around to visit her class members during the week because her driving skills have deteriorated to the point that she is worried about safety. She accepts the offer of a middle-aged neighbor to drive her to the local hospital to see her class members and to visit her other members at home (compensation).

One final example comes from B. F. Skinner, who was the foremost American behavioral psychologist for several decades. Skinner was an incredibly productive scholar and published hundreds of books and articles during his career as professor at Harvard University. He found with his passage into old age that he needed to take steps to continue doing the work that he loved to do. He found that in intellectual work lapses in memory were particularly bothersome. Skinner reported that he intentionally refocused his work to concentrate on that part that he thought to be most important and was to him the most satisfying (selection). He also took advantage of his knowledge of the importance of creating the right environment to do the kind of work that needed to be done. He, therefore, was careful to insure that the lighting and temperature and humidity levels were right and that he had all the materials he might need at hand, such as a word processor with spell check, a thesaurus, and other reference books. In addition, he determined that he would do his important

work at the time of day during which he was most alert (optimization). As time wore on, Skinner dealt with lapses in memory by carrying a notepad and tape recorder with him so that when he had an idea he very much wanted to remember, he could make an immediate note. In addition, he hung his umbrella on the doorknob so that he would remember when leaving to take it with him. When he was scheduled to attend a class reunion, he made it a point to look at his yearbook before departure so that he could improve the chances of remembering names (compensation). Many other examples of Baltes's idea of selection, optimization, and compensation could be added. The ease of citing many examples testifies to the practical importance of his model to a productive understanding of the process of aging.

### STRATEGIES FOR SUCCESSFUL AGING

Baltes offered five strategies that would help older people toward successful aging. It is important to note that these strategies are a pattern of beliefs and behaviors. If adopted and used both individually and at random, the effect may not be satisfactory, but if received as a perspective and a plan of action, the result may be desirable. These strategies can be personally valuable, but over time their greater significance may come in their guidance for makers of social policy as related to the aging population.

The first strategy involves the purposeful adoption of a healthy lifestyle in order to delay biological decline. The second is to be aware of the heterogeneity of the old adult population. What seems to work for one person may not be at all satisfactory for another of the same age. The third strategy is to strengthen reserve capacity in middle and in old age via education, motivation, healthy living, and the building of strong social ties, especially with age-mates. The fourth is to recognize that because of inevitable physical decline there will be the need for compensatory supports of one form or another. The fifth strategy, in terms of the physical, psychological, and social aspects of life, is to recognize that the gain-loss ratio will decline in time. One should be prepared to adjust by planning to modify aspirations and goals according to changing life circumstances.

These strategies can be collapsed into the single idea that people can actually create their own successful aging process. This is done by focusing on the positive and by working actively to change the environment, rather than by passively accepting physical and mental declines as "just the way life is."

### IMPLICATIONS OF THE MODEL FOR SUCCESSFUL AGING

Tithonus was an ancient mythical figure who found favor with the gods and was granted one wish. He wished to live forever. The wish was duly granted, but Tithonus was disappointed. He continued to live but he also continued to age, and with aging came inevitable decline. The goal of successful aging, as stated in the motto of the Gerontological Society of America, is "to add life to years, not just years to life." Successful aging concerns living a fuller and richer life. The specific qualities of successful aging identified by Baltes are length of life, biological, health, mental health, cognitive efficacy, social competence, and feelings of personal control and life satisfaction. In these terms, successful aging for individuals is certainly to be universally desired. Achievement of successful aging may someday help set the agenda for a social policy that respects the value and strength of the world's old people.

*—Roger G. Gaddis*

**See also** Creativity; Driving; *Enjoy Old Age: A Program of Self-Management*; Erikson, Erik H.; *Fountain of Age, The*; Independent living; Social ties; Sports participation; Stereotypes; *Virtues of Aging, The*; Wisdom.

### FOR FURTHER INFORMATION:

Baltes, Margaret M., and Paul B. Baltes, eds. *The Psychology of Control and Aging*. Hillsdale, N.J.: Lawrence Erlbaum Associates, 1986. A collection of essays concerning the importance of individuals having a sense of autonomy, control, and personal efficacy in adjusting to old age.

Baltes, Margaret M., and Hans-Werner Wahl. "The Behavior System of Dependency in the Elderly: Interaction with the Social Environment." In *Aging, Health, and Behavior*, edited by Marcia G. Ory, Ronald P. Abeles, and Paula D. Lipman. Newbury Park, Calif.: Sage Publications, 1992. A chapter about the inadvertent fostering of dependent behavior by well-meaning but poorly informed attendants in a nursing home setting.

Baltes, Paul B., and Margaret M. Baltes. "Psychological Perspectives on Successful Aging: The Model of Selective Optimization with Compensation." In *Successful Aging: Perspectives from the Behavioral Sciences*.: Cambridge, England: Cambridge University Press, 1990. The definitive discussion of the assumptions and the empirical research basis of Baltes's theory of aging and a discussion of strategies for successful aging.

Baltes, Paul B., Hayne W. Reese, and John R. Nesselroade. *Life-Span Developmental Psychology: Introduction to Research Methods*. Monterey, Calif.: Brooks/Cole, 1977. A major discussion of the research methods that characterize the life span perspective as opposed to those which were commonly used in the traditional theories of development.

Baltes, Paul B., and Sherry L. Willis. "Toward Psychological Theories of Aging." In *Handbook of the Psychology of Aging*, edited by James F. Birren and K. Warner Schaie. 4th ed. San Diego: Academic Press, 1977. A discussion of the results of a series of longitudinal studies and their relationship to traditional theories of aging.

Belsky, Janet. *The Psychology of Aging: Theory, Research, and Interventions*. 3d ed. Pacific Grove, Calif.: Brooks/Cole, 1999. A textbook with an extended treatment of the concept of successful aging.

Rybash, John M., Paul A. Roodin, and William J. Hoyer. *Adult Development and Aging*. 3d ed. Madison, Wis.: Brown & Benchmark, 1995. A textbook on aging emphasizing the methods and findings of current research.

Skinner, B. F. "Intellectual Self-Management in Old Age." *American Psychologist* 38, no. 3 (March, 1983). A personal essay by the leading behavioral psychologist concerning his coping with physical and mental losses in old age.

## SUICIDE

**RELEVANT ISSUES:** Death, health and medicine, violence

**SIGNIFICANCE:** Elderly individuals have higher rates of suicide than other age groups

From 1980 to 1992, suicides among persons aged sixty-five and older in the United States increased 36 percent, from about forty-five hundred to more than six thousand. In 1992, persons aged sixty-five and older accounted for 13 percent of the population, but almost 20 percent of suicides. As people age, their suicide risk increases. Persons eighty-five and older have the highest rates of suicide in the United States.

## GROUP DIFFERENCES

Suicide rates among the elderly vary by gender. As with other age groups, the suicide rate is higher among men than women. One possible reason is that women cope better than men. They adjust better to role shifts and have better social support systems. Another possibility is that men are much more likely to use violent methods of suicide, particularly firearms, than women are.

Suicide rates among the elderly also vary by ethnicity. Among the most prominent ethnic groups, the suicide rate is highest among American Indians. Rates are also high among Caucasian Americans, and relatively low among African Americans, Asian Americans, and Latinos. Each of these cultural groups are diverse. Within each there are subgroups with both higher and lower rates.

Other group differences in suicide exist as well. At all ages, suicide is higher among single, separated or divorced, or widowed persons as compared to married persons. The methods for committing suicide vary by age and gender. About two-thirds of elderly suicides are committed with guns, compared with only about 57 percent of suicides among those younger than sixty-five. Elderly Caucasian American men are the group most likely to use guns, particularly if they live in a rural area and have not completed high school.

## RISK FACTORS FOR SUICIDE IN LATE LIFE

Psychiatric disorders, such as depression, schizophrenia, anxiety disorders, and alcohol abuse or dependence, are the most important risk factors for suicide in the elderly. In one study, 80 percent of those who attempted suicide were admitted to an adult psychiatric inpatient hospital. They were found to have experienced major depression of late onset, especially psychotic depression. Among the elderly aged seventy-five and older who committed suicide, 71.4 percent had a mood disorder. This contrasts with 63.9 percent of those aged fifty-five to seventy-four who had a mood disorder.

Chronic physical illness is another risk factor for suicide among the elderly. In one study, 94 per-

cent of older suicides had physical problems at the time of death, and 57 percent had seen a health professional in the previous thirty days. The illnesses most frequently cited were diseases of the central nervous system (especially Alzheimer's disease), malignancies, cardiopulmonary conditions, and urogenital diseases. Those with mixed Alzheimer's and vascular dementia may be at a particularly high risk for suicidal thinking. The prospect of living many years with chronic pain or disability and subsequently becoming dependent upon the health care system or family members may be especially difficult for older persons who have traditionally achieved an independent lifestyle.

A previous history of suicide attempt is a risk factor for suicide. Among all age groups, those who attempt suicide once are more likely to try again than those who have never attempted suicide. Previous history may be especially risky for elderly individuals because they have fewer failed suicide attempts than younger people. Other risk factors include hopelessness, stressful life events, and biological susceptibility. Financial trouble is less important as a risk factor for the elderly than for younger populations.

Thus, the elderly people who are at most risk for suicide have probably had a major psychiatric disorder and attempted suicide in the past. They may also have a chronic physical problem, a sense of hopelessness about the future, other recent social stresses, and some biological susceptibility.

## ASSESSMENT AND INTERVENTION

Asking simple, direct questions is recommended for evaluating suicide risk. A direct question such as, "Have you ever thought of hurting or killing yourself?" can convey understanding and the willingness to take a person seriously. This does not provoke people to become suicidal. Most people will answer truthfully. Other useful inquiries include asking about vague suicidal thoughts, wishes to die, past attempts, and suicide plans.

If someone reveals suicidal thinking or plans, follow-up questions should be about specifics. Does the person have a concrete plan? Does he or she have the means to carry out the plan? For example, does the person have a gun and know how to use it? When a person is suicidal, he or she may need a referral to a mental health professional, medication, or hospitalization.

Mental health professionals who are treating a suicidal person begin with crisis intervention. The first priority is to preserve the person's life, so the professional may violate confidentiality if the person is of imminent harm to himself or herself. Initially, clinicians try to establish a good working relationship in order to see the person through the immediate crisis. Clinicians may find that at times, a no-suicide, no-harm agreement can be useful. The clinician will often elicit support from the suicidal person's social support system. The suicidal crisis is typically short term, lasting perhaps a few days. When it is resolved, the clinician can begin to address long-standing problems. For the underlying problems, psychotherapy and/or medication may be useful.

Community strategies can also be helpful with suicidal older individuals. According to a 1995 article by D. De Leo and colleagues, ongoing phone calls and reminders to take their prescribed medicine decreases the expected frequency of suicide among elderly individuals. Educating health care providers and the general public about risk factors for elderly suicide may reduce the conditions that can lead to suicide. Reducing the availability of firearms decreases suicide risk, especially among men.

## EUTHANASIA

In modern times, euthanasia has come to mean a physician actively causing a patient's death. This contrasts with physician-assisted suicide, in which the patient self-administers a lethal dose of a drug that was prescribed by a physician who knew that its purpose was to induce death. One piece of evidence that attitudes in the United States toward euthanasia have become more positive is the acceptance of living wills, in which individuals decree that no heroic procedures or exceptional life-sustaining measures be employed in the event of their incapacitation. Another indicator of changing attitudes is the popularity of *Final Exit*, a best-selling book by Derek Humphrey that describes how to commit suicide.

The prototype of the elderly suicide is a widower who is retired and lives alone. He is isolated from family and friends and is not active in church, community, or other social activities. He feels lonely, depressed, and helpless to do anything about his situation, and he may have other psychi-atric problems as well. Though not terminally ill or in debilitating pain, he has recently seen a physician. He feels hopeless about the future and finds no meaning in his existence. He has turned to alcohol or other drugs to drown his sorrows. He has relatives who have committed suicide. He has attempted suicide in the past and has thought about suicide recently. He has a gun in his home.

Though the myth is otherwise, the overwhelming majority of people who are terminally ill fight for life to the end. Only 2 to 4 percent of suicides occur in the context of terminal illness. A request for death comes from a person who is desperate, whether he or she is medically ill. In such cases, a comprehensive psychiatric assessment should include inquiring into the source of the person's desperation. It should also include trying to relieve this source. Elderly individuals who are informed of acute, potentially fatal medical conditions may express angry preoccupation with suicide and request assistance in carrying out these wishes. The majority are motivated primarily by dread of what will happen to them, rather than by current pain or suffering. They fear debilitating pain, dependency on others, loss of dignity, the side effects of medical treatment, burdening of their family and friends, and death itself. Those who are medically ill may not know what to expect. When they can express their fears, their request for euthanasia may quickly disappear.

Sociologists note that arguments about the right to suicide and assisted suicide for the elderly is a symbol of society's devaluation of old age. Ageism results in easy acceptance of the concepts of euthanasia, rational suicide, and assisted suicide. It creates a society in which suicide is not only expected but even demanded of all who might be a burden. —*Lillian M. Range*

*See also* American Indians; Death and dying; Depression; Euthanasia; Living wills; Men and aging; Terminal illness; Widows and widowers.

**FOR FURTHER INFORMATION:**

De Leo, D., G. Carollo, and M. L. Dello Buono. "Lower Suicide Rates Associated with a Tele-help/Tele-check Service for the Elderly at Home." *American Journal of Psychiatry* 152, no. 4 (April, 1995): 632-634. A description of an actual telephone service for the elderly.

Humphrey, D. *Final Exit.* Eugene, Oreg.: Hemlock

Society, 1991. This best-seller describes how to commit suicide.

Osgood, N. J. *Suicide in Later Life: Recognizing the Warning Signs.* New York: Macmillan, 1992. A well-done overview of facts, case studies, and ideas for intervention and prevention.

Stillion, J. M., and E. E. McDowell. *Suicide Across the Life Span: Premature Exits.* 2d ed. Washington, D.C.: Taylor & Francis, 1996. The chapter "Suicide Among the Elderly" gives facts and vivid case studies.

## SUNSET BOULEVARD

**DIRECTOR:** Billy Wilder

**CAST:** Gloria Swanson, William Holden, Erich Von Stroheim

**DATE:** Released in 1950

**RELEVANT ISSUES:** Media, psychology, values

**SIGNIFICANCE:** This satiric film explores the consequences of false values that make it impossible for a formerly glamorous film star to accept both her own aging and changing times

*Sunset Boulevard* is largely set in the Hollywood home of the faded silent screen star Norma Desmond (played by silent screen star Gloria Swanson). After the advent of talking pictures, the imperious Norma retreated to her sumptuous but decaying mansion, living in almost complete isolation. The illusion that she is still a popular star is sustained by her devoted butler, Max Von Mayerling (Erich Von Stroheim), who is Norma's first husband and her former director. Living in the glory days of her past, the aging Norma is unable to acknowledge that time has gone by—she still hopes to return to the big screen with a script in which she will portray the seductive biblical temptress Salome.

Hoping that he will rejuvenate her professionally and personally, Norma employs young, good-

*Gloria Swanson in the final scene from the film* Sunset Boulevard. *Erich Von Stroheim is at left.* (Archive Photos)

looking screenwriter Joe Gillis (William Holden) to work with her on the script. Pressed by his creditors and pitying Norma's desperation and neediness, Gillis also agrees to become her kept man. As Norma becomes increasingly overbearing and possessive, Gillis breaks off with her and, in a moment of bitterness, reveals the devastating fact that both she and her screenplay have been rejected by the film industry that had once celebrated her as a great star. Haggard and despairing, Norma shoots him with the gun that she had intended to use on herself. Placed under arrest, Norma walks down her staircase to a waiting squad car in a state of utter self-deception, convinced that she is performing the role of the bewitching Salome for her admiring fans.

*Sunset Boulevard* won Academy Awards for Best Screenplay, Best Art Direction, Best Set Decoration, and Best Score. It was adapted into a musical play by composer Andrew Lloyd Webber in 1993.

*—Margaret Boe Birns*

**See also** Age discrimination; Ageism; Beauty; Films; Women and aging.

# TELEVISION

**RELEVANT ISSUES:** Culture, demographics, media, sociology

**SIGNIFICANCE:** As a conduit of information and a socializing agent, television plays a crucial role in the formation and perpetuation of attitudes about aging

Television is viewed as both a mirror and a molder of societal values and attitudes. Its depiction of the elderly solidifies preconceptions of older people held by many younger viewers who have not experienced intergenerational family life. Its depiction also affects, to some extent, the self-image the elderly have of themselves.

Projections indicate that the number of people fifty years old and older will increase by more than 60 percent by the year 2020 in the United States. The eighteen to forty-nine age group, historically targeted and catered to by the television networks, will experience no significant growth during that same period. Moreover the projected adult median age for 2020 is forty-nine. To many, these demographics predict a shift from television's current neglect and misrepresentation of the older segment of the population. As the baby-boom generation enters the fifty-plus age group, the sheer weight of their numbers and the amount of their discretionary incomes will likely bring about a change in the image of the elderly depicted on television and an increase in their visibility.

### IMAGES OF THE ELDERLY ON TELEVISION

Collectively, the many and diverse content analyses of television programming provide an overall view of the image of the elderly in television programs: Older people are underrepresented, they are frequently stereotyped, and they are often pictured negatively. These studies call for improvement in terms of both the visibility and the image of older people on television.

While underrepresentation affects both genders, it is most striking for older women. A rough average of various studies indicates that old men appear on television two to three times more frequently than old women. One study claimed that a viewer could expect to see an elderly man on prime time television every twenty-two minutes. To see an elderly woman, a viewer must wait four or five hours. This disparity reflects the industry's tendency to cast attractive females at least ten years younger than attractive males. A female is less likely to be seen on screen once she exceeds thirty. On television, women are valued for the appearance of youthful beauty, while men are valued for their power, which is a function of maturity. Since society often equates what is seen on television with what is important, the lack of visibility on television of older people, especially older women, easily translates into a sense that the old are of no social consequence.

Because the elderly seldom play central roles in network programming, they are often subject to stereotyping. With little time to develop minor characters fully, writers often resort to stereotypes and idiosyncrasies that viewers can grasp and assess immediately. This stereotyping tends to depict the elderly as flat and one-dimensional with a narrow range of emotion. While stereotypes consist of simplified and inaccurate conceptions, constant usage makes them a standardized and readily held form of prejudice. Prejudice is said to wear three faces: discrimination, affecting the right to own; segregation, affecting the right to belong; and caricaturization, affecting the right to be and to be known. This stereotyping of the elderly curtails their ability to be seen as multifaceted individuals.

Projected stereotypes are often negative. Some of the commonly acknowledged negative characteristics attributed to the elderly on television include rigidity and inflexibility; a decline in intelligence, sometimes to the point of senility; lower productivity; health problems and dependence on others; and a lack of interest in romance or sex. Most of these negative images have become so common that researchers coined the term "reverse stereotype" to describe depictions of elderly people as physically and socially active, romantically involved, and independent.

### IMAGES OF THE ELDERLY IN COMMERCIALS

In general, more money, time, and effort are spent producing commercials than in producing a comparable program time segment. Production values are often greater. In commercials, the secondary content often carries the promise. Neutral products, therefore, are often associated with images of youth, sexuality, attractiveness, and vitality. It is not surprising, then, that content analysis of television commercials yields similar findings in terms of visibility of the elderly and gender inequity to those found with television programming.

Studies indicate that while the characters within commercials varied over several different character dimensions, age remained unchanged. The majority of commercials are delivered by young and attractive characters. In the case of a celebrity salesperson, physical attributes become less relevant. When older people do appear in commercials, they tend to be men. In commercials, men are permitted to look older as long as they retain an image of virility and sexual appeal. Older women are rarely seen in commercials.

One role reserved for older people in commercials is as authority figures and givers of advice. Even here, however, their depiction is problematic. Often the products they pitch are designed to eradicate the signs of aging. Thus, they reinforce the message that aging is bad and should be combated with the designated product. Studies also indicate that younger women sell beauty products, even products designed to mask aging. Middle-aged women often sell products that are designed specifically for older people: digestion aids, laxa-

tives, denture fixtures and cleansers, and arthritis remedies.

Advertisements generally carry two inherent messages: Youth is glorious, and people are what they buy. The elderly know that youth cannot be purchased. Since youth is glorified and age is discredited in commercial television, advertising sends the message that the elderly deserve little respect.

### VIEWING HABITS OF THE ELDERLY

Many researchers find that a person's age is not a prime indicator of a person's preferences; many other factors determine choices, especially in terms of television-watching patterns and program choices. One person may be experiencing the empty nest syndrome, while another person of the same age is still engaged in raising a family. These researchers prefer to calculate viewing patterns in terms of life stages rather than age. In any case, most studies identify television watching as one of the most important leisure pursuits of older people. For many people, increased viewing takes place after middle age and continues to increase until well past retirement, which most studies give

*For many older people, television is the primary form of entertainment and information.* (James L. Shaffer)

as seventy. Thereafter, there is a slight decline in viewing. Female viewers tend to watch slightly more television than do male viewers.

Studies indicate that elderly viewers use television in several ways. For many, television provides a strong sense of involvement. Many elderly people who no longer interact with peers in the workforce and who are past the task of child rearing use television as "a window on the world." Television provides information and allows people to share experiences in common with others. To some researchers, television makes possible for viewers with diminished interpersonal relationships a "parasocial" experience that substitutes for real-life experience. Others have found that television programming provides conversational topics that fuel real-life social interaction.

Because many of the commitments that formerly structured the elderly person's day no longer exists, television often serves as a means of demarcating time and structuring the day. Older people tend to establish daily routines that center around viewing favorite television programs. In a similar way, weekly programs may demarcate certain days of the week and provide a pleasurable experience to which one can look forward. For many, television not only structures time but also serves to fill it. While many older people engage in a variety of hobbies and other leisure activities, many find that they have an overabundance of time to fill. Television provides something to do. People between the ages of fifty and seventy watch television more than any other group.

### VIEWING CHOICES OF THE ELDERLY

Almost every study of the viewing choices of the elderly asserts that the group's overwhelming choices are news and public affairs programming. These programs may be sought out as a substitute for the loss of other sources of information, such as the workplace. Those with impaired vision may turn to television as a source of information to replace the newspaper or magazines. Cost, too, may be a factor for people on a fixed income since television is relatively inexpensive, while subscriptions cost money. Polls consistently indicate that the largest audience segment of all network newscasts are people aged fifty and older.

Soap operas also rate high among the viewing preferences of the elderly, both male and female,

though more women watch than men. Many reasons have been cited for this preference. Soap operas often provide a fictive family with which people can identify. More than in any type of programming, older people are respected and even revered as authority figures and advice givers in soap operas. There is also evidence that such programs are enjoyed because of their complex exploration of character, plot, and subplot. The programs themselves provided a common interest among viewers and therefore become sources of conversation.

Older viewers also tend to favor programs with strong family-centered themes. They also reportedly tend to like wholesome, happy, and less intense kinds of programming. Although news programs are highly rated, the entertainment and relaxation functions of television also hold high appeal to this age group. Fiction and nonfiction programs that feature older characters or celebrities remain popular. Programs that feature older actors appeal to the elderly. Syndicated programs (those that had previously run on television and have been purchased from independent distributing organizations to be reshown) were also well-received. However, feature-length films, even old films, are not highly regarded by the older audience. When surveyed, elderly people usually indicate that they would like to see more older people on television on a regular basis.

### THE ELDERLY AS A TELEVISION MARKET

Television, in addition to being a channel of information and entertainment and a shaper and mirror of attitudes and values, is also an industry. As such, it is susceptible to the laws of supply and demand. Advertising is its lifeblood. In effect, television does not exist simply to provide programs to an audience. Instead, it supplies an audience to sponsors who, in turn, provide money for programming. Television networks sell time to advertisers. Federal Communications Commission (FCC) regulations and National Association of Broadcasters (NAB) codes govern the amount of time that can be sold at any given time during the broadcast day. Advertisers, therefore, want reliable data about the nature of the audience who will view their commercials. A crucial factor is the number of viewers, the idea being that the more people who see the advertising, the more profit there will be. Increasingly, advertising agencies are using more sophisticated research methods to find out more about the makeup of audiences throughout the day: their ages, their financial status, and their product needs.

Advertisers seem to prefer a younger audience that has money to spend and a need for a wide variety of consumer goods; therefore, television programming and commercials remain skewed toward the younger segment of the population. This pattern contradicts the irreversible shift in demographics. Advertisers who continue to cling to the hypothesis that the eighteen to forty-nine segment of the population has the most discretionary funds to spend on their products are actually ignoring the largest growth market: the over-fifty portion.

There are several reasons why advertisers still court the young despite the increasing preponderance of older people in the population. Although the adult median age has been steadily rising in the United States, that fact has been obscured by the promulgation of a youth culture. Many researchers note the youth of the people in the advertising profession and point out their propensity to market to the young. They also argue that marketing to inexperienced consumers is easier than trying to sell to older consumers who have had much experience with buying and selling. It takes more time, effort, and money to persuade older consumers to switch brands or to try new products. In middle age, people's spending habits become more discretionary; while they have money to spend, they usually need to buy less because they already own products that the young must still purchase. Persuasion, therefore, becomes a more difficult task.

In addition to those factors, there has been a growing consciousness of issues of race, ethnicity, and gender. Television has shown itself sensitive to these issues by taking steps to reduce or eliminate negative stereotyping of women and minorities and by providing more visibility for these groups. As the general population becomes aware of ageism, television is likely to react favorably to an improved image of the elderly. Television is in a position to play a leading role in reflecting a changing consciousness about aging and can become an important catalyst for change.

—*Christine R. Catron*

**See also** Advertising; Antiaging treatments; Beauty; Communication; Consumer issues; Cul-

tural views of aging; Films; Leisure activities; Stereotypes; Women and aging.

**For Further Information:**

Danish, Roy. *Television Looks at Aging.* Washington, D.C.: Government Printing Office, 1985. This publication of the Television Information Office gives a comprehensive overview of television's coverage of the issue of aging, claims that the image of older people is changing positively, and highlights television programs dealing with issues of concern to the elderly.

Falk, Ursula A., and Gerhard Falk. "Ageism in Popular Culture." In *Ageism, the Ages, and Aging in America: On Being Old in an Alienated Society.* Springfield, Ill.: Charles C Thomas, 1997.

Grossman, Lawrence K. "Aging Viewers: The Best Is Yet to Be." *Columbia Journalism Review* 36, 5 (January, 1998). Grossman points out that while television news targets the younger audience, the over fifty group is growing in size and the news media will need to respond to their needs for more serious newscasts.

Kubey, Robert, and Mihaly Csikszentmihalyi. *Television and the Quality of Life: How Viewing Shapes Everyday Experience.* Hillsdale, N.J.: Laurence Erlbaum Associates, 1990. The authors examine the experience of viewing television in its natural context, emphasizing how television viewing fits into people's schedules and how they feel when watching it.

Palmore, Erdman B. *Ageism: Negative and Positive.* New York: Springer, 1990. Palmore examines many aspects of ageism, including the way television supports prejudicial attitudes.

## Tell Me a Riddle

**Author:** Tillie Olsen

**Date:** Published in 1961

**Relevant issues:** Death, family, psychology, values

**Significance:** Olsen's novella powerfully delineates the last life stage of a Russian Jewish immigrant who defies conventional expectations for older women as she struggles to find her individual voice

Readers of all ages respond to Tillie Olsen's poignant story of one woman's late-life anguish and struggle. The main character, Eva, is larger than

*Tillie Olsen, the author of the novella* Tell Me a Riddle. (Leonda Fiske)

her roles of wife and mother but constrained by them in ways that become intolerable in the last year and a half of her life. An orator in the 1905 Russian Revolution, she rebels against her husband's plan to move them to a senior residence. Angry, tired of sacrificing for others, and intent on solitude, Eva wants "never again to be forced to move to the rhythm of others." She refuses to be a sweet grandmother who tells riddles to amuse her grandchildren. Metastasized cancer heightens her withdrawal.

Olsen richly details Eva's painful dying as thoughts of past and present stream through her consciousness and she accepts devoted nursing from a granddaughter. She reaches out to her husband in a gesture of reconciliation. Although Eva dies with parts of herself unfulfilled, giving the story a somber tone, Olsen also expresses faith in human endurance and family ties and hope in rebellion against confining roles. The novella illumi-

nates the capacity for change in old age, even in unpromising circumstances, and suggests that the search for life's meaning is truly lifelong.

—*Margaret Cruikshank*

**See also** Cancer; Death and dying; Family relationships; Grandparenthood; Literature; Loneliness; Old age; Women and aging.

## TEMPERATURE REGULATION AND SENSITIVITY

**RELEVANT ISSUES:** Health and medicine

**SIGNIFICANCE:** The human body functions efficiently and comfortably within a very narrow temperature range; aging can decrease the body's ability to tolerate extremes of environmental temperatures

Normal internal (core) body temperature is around 37 degrees Celsius (98.6 degrees Fahrenheit). Core temperatures below 35 degrees Celsius (95 degrees Fahrenheit) are considered abnormally cold (hypothermia), while temperatures above 38.3 degrees Celsius (101 degrees Fahrenheit) are too hot (hyperthermia) for normal function. Thermoregulation, the monitoring and controlling of body temperatures, is primarily coordinated by the hypothalamus, located in the brain. The process of thermoregulation becomes active when air temperature rises above or drops below approximately 22 degrees Celsius (72 degrees Fahrenheit), depending on the relative humidity.

Tolerance of cool temperatures increases with body size, body fat, and muscle mass. The body also has two active strategies to maintain body temperature in cool environments: reducing heat loss or increasing internal body temperature. Body heat is normally lost through the skin's surface. Blood vessels in the skin can narrow with cold temperatures and decrease blood flow, thus reducing heat loss. Shivering, which involves contraction of muscles, can rapidly raise metabolism and body temperature. Inactive older people tend to lose muscle mass with aging, thus decreasing the ability to raise body metabolism and temperature. In addition, elderly people are usually not able to contract skin vessels as efficiently as the young, thus decreasing their ability to minimize heat losses.

Increased blood flow to the skin and sweating are the two primary body changes involved in reducing body temperature, thus preventing hyperthermia. Widening of skin blood vessels, increased blood flow from the heart, and redistribution of blood flow from the intestines, kidneys, and other organs can increase blood flow to the skin. Widening of skin blood vessels does not occur as efficiently in older people as it does in the young. In addition, the ability to increase blood flow from the heart and redistribute blood flow from vital organs to the skin can decrease with aging. Sweating also decreases with aging, possibly because of the increased sun damage to the skin over time. Hydration status also influences both sweating and the ability to redistribute blood flow to the skin. Older people tend to be less hydrated than the young, further decreasing their ability to thermoregulate in hot environments.

Illnesses and a sedentary lifestyle are considered the greatest threats to thermoregulation in the elderly. Therefore, a healthy and active lifestyle is probably the best way to preserve thermoregulatory functions with aging. Proper nutrition helps reduce dehydration and overheating, while sunscreens may help preserve the structural functions of the skin, which are vital for thermoregulation. Appropriate clothing can also help with thermoregulation. Research suggests that postmenopausal women taking estrogen maintain better hydration status and have improved functions of the skin, which helps with thermoregulation.                              —*Laurence M. Katz*

*See also* Aging process; Menopause; Skin changes and disorders.

## Terminal illness
**Relevant issues:** Death, health and medicine, law, psychology
**Significance:** Many controversial issues surround what determines when a disease process is terminal and the resulting choices and options for care

*Taber's Medical Dictionary* defines "terminal illness" as an illness that, because of its nature, can be expected to cause the person to die. Usually, it is a chronic disease for which there is no known cure.

The top four fatal illnesses in the United States are ischemic heart disease, chronic obstructive pulmonary disease, diabetes mellitus, and malig-nant neoplasms or cancers. When an individual is diagnosed as terminally ill, his or her social status changes radically. Even though an individual was previously an important contributing member of the community, since the person is now dying, he or she may therefore be seen as less "valued." The sick individual may be ignored by many former friends because of their personal discomfort with death. On the other hand, the sick person may no longer desire to interact with more than a handful of friends and family. As a result, the social sphere of the dying person becomes very small. Many former activities and broader interests disappear as the sick person becomes more focused on the task of dying.

### Stages of Dying
Elisabeth Kübler-Ross, the Swiss-born psychiatrist who did extensive work with the dying, described five distinct stages through which many terminally ill patients pass. In 1969, she wrote that each stage acts as a defense mechanism against the fear of death.

The first of Kübler-Ross's stages is known as denial. When first learning of a terminal illness, the patient registers shock and disbelief. The individual may argue with the physician that a wrong diagnosis has been made and that the laboratory reports are in error. The patient may demand a second opinion and perhaps a third and fourth. Usually, this stage is relatively short unless the family members also continue to deny the illness.

The second stage of dying is often anger. The diagnosed terminally ill patient may fret, "Why me? What did I do to deserve this?" The person may strike out verbally at others, whether family or health professionals. Sometimes, the person may blame himself or herself for some indulgent habit. The person's anger may also be unfocused. He or she may be irritable, complaining, and a challenge for others.

Kübler-Ross's third stage is termed bargaining. Most deals are secret and with God, even if one has never talked to God previously. Alternative medicines, herbs, faith healers, vitamin supplements, and experimental drugs are explored by the dying individual. Almost anything is acceptable to postpone death.

The fourth stage of dying is depression. When it becomes obvious that no bargains are available, depression sets in. The dying person withdraws into a silent cocoon to mourn losses of capabilities and relationships. Death is recognized as inevitable, and the feelings of loss are often overwhelming.

Kübler-Ross found the fifth and final stage of dying to be acceptance. Acceptance comes after the dying person has given up the fight. All emotions are spent. No longer talkative, crying, agitated, or seeking sympathy, the dying individual is often tired and weak and spends the day sleeping, resting, and reminiscing with only one or two close people.

Since Kübler-Ross, many other researchers have attempted to more accurately describe the dying process—particularly E. Mansell Pattison, who defined three stages of the living-dying interval in 1977. Pattison's stages are acute, chronic, and terminal. In the acute stage, individuals face the knowledge of their imminent death and may react with anxiety, denial, or anger. In the chronic phases, individuals begin to confront their fears of dying, such as loneliness and pain. They also deal with fears of what will happen after death. The final or terminal phase signals the end of hope and the beginning of withdrawal from the outside world upon realization of the inevitability of death. The goal of treatment for the dying, according to Pattison, is to help them cope with the first phase, help them live through the second, and move them toward the third.

## RIGHTS OF THE DYING

The process of dying takes a great deal of physical and psychic energy. Sedatives, painkillers, and some treatments can further reduce energy and cause disorientation and diminishing capabilities. As strength decreases, the dying are progressively less able to carry out activities of daily living. They become very vulnerable. Because those who are dying are generally in a weakened state, family members and health professionals are responsible to ensure their rights are not violated. The following are some of these rights.

Patients have the right to open communication about death. Because individuals commonly deny that they are dying in the early stages, it is generally most sensitive to inform them first that their condition is serious and to allow them to ask more questions as they are ready to hear it. Knowledge

of impending death allows dying persons to complete certain tasks before dying and to close their life in accordance with personal wishes. Additionally, full awareness of impending death allows an individual to make responsible decisions, such as where to die and what treatments to allow.

The terminally ill have the right to a painless death, to the greatest extent possible. The dying want to be free from pain. A common fear among the terminally ill, especially the elderly, is that their death will be painful. Patients considering suicide most often cite fear of prolonged suffering and painful death as a reason. Pain is more than just an unpleasant physical sensation. It may impair function, lead to fear and anxiety, interfere with social relationships, and cause spiritual distress.

Patients benefit from having been given "permission" to discuss their feelings about pain. They may have to unlearn reluctance stemming from previous encounters with unsympathetic or uninformed clinicians. Sometimes the terminally ill feel they must be brave or put on a front to help ease their family's distress. Pain can isolate patients, especially when they must hide it from others, and isolation in itself increases the risk of suicide.

Health professionals need to be reminded that the patient is the best judge of his own pain. Therefore, the terminally ill person needs to be involved in his or her own pain management. It becomes the individual's responsibility to tell caregivers when the medication has not relieved the pain. Some physicians, unfortunately, have received little training in pain management and may not prescribe the right drug, dosage, or route. When concerned about regulation of controlled substances or concern about the individual becoming tolerant to analgesics, it can be difficult to convince a physician to change a medication order. Clinicians may be reluctant to give high doses of opioids to patients with advanced disease because of a fear of side effects such as constipation, nausea and vomiting, sedation and mental clouding, and respiratory depression. The clinician's ethical duty—to benefit the patient by relieving pain—supports increasing doses, even at the risk of side effects. Because many patients with pain become opioid-tolerant during long-term opioid therapy, the clinician's fear of shortening life by increasing opioid doses is usually unfounded. It may help to refer to the *Patient Guide: Managing Cancer Pain* (1994) published by the Agency for Health Care Policy and Research (AHCPR). The terminally ill person, too, may worry about becoming addicted to painkillers. They may worry about costs of the medication, or show concern about becoming tolerant to pain medications. It is feared, even though the medication is currently working, it will not work when the pain becomes worse.

Noninvasive physical and psychosocial modalities can be used concurrently with drugs and other interventions to manage pain during all phases of treatment. Some physical modalities such as cutaneous stimulation, heat, cold, massage, pressure, vibration, exercise, repositioning, and acupuncture can involve family members, giving them interventions so they do not feel so helpless. The cognitive-behavioral interventions are an important part of pain management. Most of all, they help to give the patient a sense of control and to develop coping skills to deal with the pain. So, interventions like relaxation and imagery, cognitive distraction and reframing, short-term psychotherapy, support groups, and pastoral counseling introduced early in the course of illness are more likely to succeed because they can be learned and practiced by patients while they have sufficient strength and energy. With rare exception, the less invasive analgesic approaches should precede invasive palliative approaches as radiation therapy, nerve blocks, or neurosurgery to implant devices to deliver drugs to electrically stimulate neural structures.

Those who are dying have the right to the presence of concerned others. One of the terminally ill person's greatest fears is abandonment at the time of death. They fear that they will die alone. A high proportion of elders may spend their dying interval without a concerned person to help make medical decisions or advocate adequate medical treatment. The importance of a support person, especially during the final days, becomes apparent as the dying generally begin to lack interest in all visitors except one or two significant persons.

Terminally ill people have the right to as much control over environment as possible. Because the dying so often experience loss of control over their environment and declining health, it is imperative that family and health professionals allow the dying person as much control as possible, even in little things. Allowing patients some choice over meals, visiting hours, roommates, frequency of nursing interruptions, and medical treatments can greatly enhance their feelings of autonomy.

The dying, like other patients, have the right to have all medical treatments fully explained. This includes a description of the prognosis and methods of treatment, as well as the potential risks, benefits, and side effects. Individuals also have the right to refuse treatment for their illness and to seek out alternative medicine, even those not condoned by the medical profession. For example, chemotherapy has a variable success rate and is accompanied by many uncomfortable side effects. Because of this, the patient may refuse the therapy, opting for a more comfortable, although perhaps shorter, life. The terminally ill seek quality of life over quantity of hours. Patients have the right to refuse all heroic, artificial efforts to sustain life. These issues are best spelled out in a living will. Living wills are advance directives that express the desires of competent adults regarding terminal care, life-sustaining measures, and other issues pertaining to their dying and death.

## UNDERSTANDING THE PATIENT SELF-DETERMINATION ACT

On December 1, 1991, the Patient Self-Determination Act, a federal law enacted to ensure patient rights, went into effect. This law required Medicare- and Medicaid-certified hospitals, nursing homes, home health agencies, hospices, and health maintenance organizations to implement procedures to increase public awareness regarding the rights of patients to make treatment choices. The law was particularly concerned with advance directives, documents specifying the type of treatment individuals want or do not want under serious medical conditions in which they might be unable to communicate their wishes to the physician.

Advance directives generally take one of two forms: a living will or a durable power of attorney for health care. Living wills, which may vary from state to state, outline the medical care individuals want if they become unable to make their own decisions. A durable power of attorney for health care, on the other hand, designates another person to act as an "agent" or a "proxy" in making medical decisions if the individual becomes unable to do so. Substitute decision makers, however, are not necessarily perfect executors of patients' wishes. In one study, family members named as surrogates were asked for their view of patients' preferences on resuscitation. The surrogates correctly guessed what the patients (who were chronically ill, but still competent) wanted only 68 percent to 88 percent of the time. The study, however, pointed out a likely cause for surrogates' misunderstanding: lack of discussion. Patients by and large simply assumed their families and physicians would know what they wanted.

So, directives that include information on the patient's attitudes on life, health, and health care eliminate guessing. The medical directive should ask what the goals of treatment in various clinical situations should be (for example, to prolong life, to provide comfort). Such information helps the proxy and health care professionals because the question is not always "What do you want to do with the ventilator?" but "What does quality of life mean to you?" Clinicians and ethicists in recent years have increasingly come to view artificial nutrition (tube feedings) and hydration (intravenous fluids) as medical treatment rather than as food and water. As such, they may be withdrawn, much like a ventilator. A family may not share that view, however, even if withdrawal of artificial nutrition and hydration is consistent with the terminally ill person's wishes. Health care professionals must support the family by telling them that they are not "starving" the person but that these invasive procedures are only prolonging the dying process without curative powers.

The burden of responsibility needs to be removed from the shoulders of family members, who may feel a duty to make sure caregivers continue treatment. Clergy and other support people need to be available to help the family deal with any lingering doubts. More often than not, however, families react to the change of focus from cure to ensuring a comfortable death not with guilt but with relief, especially when the patient's wishes have been respected—that, in some measure, the dying person has been allowed to face death on his or her own terms.

## KNOWING EACH STATE'S LAWS

States vary in their acceptance of living wills; there may even be variation among agencies as to the conditions under which this document will be entered into the medical record. In most states, at least one physician (and sometimes two) must certify that the patient is terminally ill before an advance directive can be fulfilled. But in Idaho, a patient does not have to be terminally ill or permanently unconscious for the living will to be fulfilled. Rather, the individual must be a qualified patient: someone who is of sound mind and eighteen years of age or older.

A patient must have a certain medical condition (such as terminal illness) and a lack of mental capacity for a durable power of attorney for health care to go into effect in some states. In 1999, all states except Delaware, New Jersey, New Mexico, and Ohio provided a living will form that the patient could (but was not required to) use. However, Oregon and Rhode Island required that patients use the statutory durable power of attorney for health care form. In Arkansas, Arizona, Louisiana, and South Carolina, a living will was valid only if it was in compliance with the law of the state in which it was created. In Hawaii and Minnesota, a living will was valid only if it was in compliance with the law of the state in which it would be fulfilled.

*—Maxine M. McCue*

**See also** Acquired immunodeficiency syndrome (AIDS); Breast cancer; Cancer; Communication; Death and dying; Death anxiety; Death of a child; Death of parents; Depression; Durable power of attorney; Funerals; Grief; Health care; Kübler-Ross, Elizabeth; Living wills; Medications; Prostate cancer; Psychiatry, geriatric; Skin cancer; Suicide; Widows and widowers.

## FOR FURTHER INFORMATION:

*Compassion in Dying: Guidelines and Safeguards.* Portland, Oreg.: Compassion in Dying Federation, 1999. http://www.compassionindying.org/support/guidelines.htm.

Ferdinand, Rosemary. "'I'd Rather Die than Live This Way.'" *American Journal of Nursing* 95, no. 12 (December, 1995): 42-48. A terminally ill patient who expresses suicidal ideation can present both a clinical challenge and an ethical dilemma. These guidelines explore the reasons for a patient's desire to die.

Ferrini, Armeda F., and Rebecca L. Ferrini. *Health in the Later Years.* 3d ed. Boston: McGraw-Hill, 1999. Easy-to-read textbook for students preparing to work with older people; provides a broad overview of health and aging.

Ignatavicius, Donna D. *Introduction to Long Term Care Nursing: Principles and Practice.* Philadelphia: F. A. Davis, 1998. Written for student nurses, this text provides practical, accessible, need-to-know information in every chapter.

Meyer, Charles. "End-of-Life Care: Patients' Choices, Nurses' Challenges." *American Journal of Nursing* 93, no. 2 (February, 1993). Argues that a patient has a right to decide how far caregivers should go to keep him or her alive.

Murphy, Patricia A., and David M. Price. "ACT: Taking a Positive Approach to End-of-Life Care." *American Journal of Nursing* 95, no. 3 (March, 1995). Discusses how to use "aggressive comfort treatment" to ensure that the end comes peacefully for dying patients.

Parkman, Cynthia A., and Barbara E. Calfee. "Advance Directives: Honoring Your Patient's End-of-Life Wishes." *Nursing* 27, no. 4 (April, 1997). This guide is useful for nurses in helping patient's exercise their right to make end-of-life decisions.

*Patient Guide: Managing Cancer Pain.* AHCPR Publication no. 94-0595. Rockville, Md.: U.S. Department of Health and Human Services, 1994. A free booklet about cancer pain and how it can be controlled with the patient in charge.

Pinch, Winifred J., and Mary E. Parsons. "The Ethics of Treatment Decision Making: The Elderly Patient's Perspective." *Geriatric Nursing* 14, no. 6 (November/December, 1993). The vast resources—and costs—of available technology make it crucial that health care professionals understand what the patient wants.

Pokalo, Cheryl. "Understanding the Patient Self-Determination Act." *Journal of Gerontological Nursing* 18, no. 3 (March, 1992). Gives addresses and sources of more information on advance directives as the American Bar Association, American Health Decisions, and the U.S. Department of Health and Human Services.

## THYROID DISORDERS

**RELEVANT ISSUES:** Biology, health and medicine

**SIGNIFICANCE:** Normal functioning of the thyroid gland is essential for overall health; thyroid disorders can cause significant illness and are often difficult to diagnose in elderly individuals

The thyroid gland is one of several organs or glands that compose the endocrine system. Endocrine glands produce substances, called hormones, which are released into the bloodstream and distributed throughout the body, where they act upon specific target tissues or organs. Hormones control most of the chemical reactions of the body.

The thyroid gland is a butterfly-shaped organ located in the neck just in front of the trachea (windpipe) and just below the larynx (voice box). It produces two principal hormones, triiodothyronine ($T_3$) and thyroxine ($T_4$), which act on most tissues of the body by increasing metabolic rate. The thyroid gland is stimulated to produce $T_3$ and $T_4$ by a hormone called thyroid-stimulating hormone (TSH) produced by the pituitary gland, which is located in the brain and known as the master gland.

With aging, the thyroid gland atrophies or shrinks somewhat; however, it continues to function adequately and remains sensitive to the stimulating effect of TSH from the pituitary gland. In elderly people, the most important thyroid disorders are hypothyroidism and hyperthyroidism.

Hypothyroidism is a deficient production of $T_3$ and $T_4$ by the thyroid gland. It is the most common thyroid disorder, occurring in 2 to 5 percent of those aged sixty-five and older. It is much more common in women than men and in institutionalized than community-living elderly people. The main causes of hypothyroidism in adults are damage to the thyroid gland from radiation therapy, surgical removal of the gland (for cancer treatment), Hashimoto's disease (a disorder in which a person's immune system erroneously attacks the thyroid gland and destroys it), and other unknown (idiopathic) causes. Iodine deficiency is another cause for hypothyroidism, though this is rarely a problem in the United States.

The classic symptoms of hypothyroidism typically develop slowly over months or years and include a low metabolic rate, cold intolerance, tiredness, and lack of energy. Elderly people commonly develop nonspecific symptoms such as depression, mental confusion, constipation, loss of appetite, and weight loss, making diagnosis of hypothyroidism difficult. While its diagnosis may be tricky, treatment of hypothyroidism is readily accomplished by giving supplemental thyroid hormone in pill form.

Hyperthyroidism is an excess production of thyroid hormone. The most common causes of hyperthyroidism are Graves' disease (in which the immune system produces substances that act like TSH and stimulate the thyroid gland to overproduce $T_3$ and $T_4$) and thyroid tumors or nodules that secrete excess thyroid hormone. Typical symptoms of hyperthyroidism include increased metabolic rate, heat intolerance, increased appetite, weight loss, rapid heart rate, restlessness, and goiter (enlarged thyroid gland). In the elderly, hyperthyroidism often is confused with other disorders related to gastrointestinal, cardiac, muscular, or psychiatric function and is easily misdiagnosed. Treatments for hyperthyroidism include surgical removal of the thyroid gland and the use of radioactive iodine and other drugs.

Thyroid disorders are relatively common, frequently misdiagnosed in the elderly, and easily treated. Early detection and treatment can spare elderly individuals unnecessary suffering and disability.                                    —*William J. Ryan*

*See also* Illnesses among the elderly; Weight loss and gain.

## TOWNSEND MOVEMENT

**DATE:** Launched in September, 1933
**RELEVANT ISSUES:** Economics, sociology, work
**SIGNIFICANCE:** A movement to design an old-age pension plan, the Townsend movement attempted to end the Great Depression of the 1930's and bring about a general economic recovery

In response to his own desperate situation and the general collapse of the American economy during the Great Depression, Francis Everett Townsend (1867-1960) developed a plan that was intended to assist elderly Americans directly and to stimulate an economic recovery throughout the United States. In September, 1933, Townsend announced a pension plan that would eliminate the economic distress being experienced by senior citizens and provide the U.S. economy with an influx of capital. He proposed that all Americans age sixty and older who had been citizens for at least five years receive $200 monthly for the remainder of their lives on the condition that they spend it within thirty-five days of receiving it. To finance this twenty-billion-dollar pension scheme, a 2 percent sales tax on all transactions would be imposed. Townsend maintained that his plan would restore confidence in the American economy and family-based values.

Within ninety days of his announcement, Townsend's proposal was transformed into a major social movement. Local and regional Townsend clubs were established and *The Townsend National Weekly* began publishing in 1934. Although his plan was denounced by economists and officials in the administration of President Franklin D. Roosevelt, Townsend continued to attract support during 1935. Townsend entered into an anti-Roosevelt coalition with the Share Our Wealth Society, founded by Louisiana governor Huey P. Long, and the National Union for Social Justice of the reactionary, anti-Semitic priest Charles E. Coughlin. Their Union Party failed to achieve a credible level of support in the 1936 election. The movement collapsed with the gradual economic recovery of the late 1930's.                            —*William T. Walker*

*See also* Advocacy; Income sources; Pensions; Politics; Poverty; Social Security.

## TRANSPORTATION ISSUES

**RELEVANT ISSUES:** Culture, demographics
**SIGNIFICANCE:** The elderly have the same need for transportation as younger people; however, most American communities fail to provide adequate transportation services for the aged

Whether people can maintain independence in their communities as they age depends, in part, on their access to the goods, services, and social contacts necessary for a good quality of life. This access relies largely on whether they have transportation choices that serve their personal mobility needs and preferences. For the older adult who chooses to maintain an independent residence, reliable transportation is the link between home and a variety of social and medical services. Several factors can complicate the older adult's access to transportation.

Although many older adults retain their own automobiles, declining vision and other physical impairments may affect their ability to drive. To compensate, they may simply limit their driving to essential trips, which may be made only during the day and only in good weather. As the cost of maintaining a rarely used vehicle mounts, the older adult may opt to rely on others to provide transportation, which can severely limit the older person's lifestyle.

The trend of building accommodations for the elderly in outlying areas, inconveniently located away from stores, hospitals, and other vital services, further complicates transportation needs. Older adults who no longer have the use of their automobiles may find themselves relying on public transportation to access vital services. With public transportation options decreasing nationwide, it is clear that society is unable to meet this growing need. Where public transportation is available, the older adult's ability to take advantage of it is severely restricted by its high cost, limited access, or inconvenient scheduling.

The availability of a support network is sometimes a decisive factor when making a choice among a selection of transportation arrangements. Some communities have a wide variety of formal services available. Friends, family, and church or other organizations are all potential sources of transportation. Unpaid caregivers provide aid to more than 1 million noninstitutionalized older adults. Three-fourths of the community-living elderly who need assistance get help only from family or friends. Almost three-quarters of unpaid caregivers are middle-aged women, and approximately one-half of the caregivers reside with the care recipient.

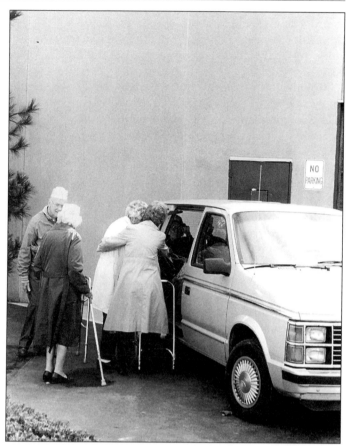

*Special transportation services for seniors can allow them to take part in community activities.* (Ben Klaffke)

## TRANSPORTATION SERVICES

Older people are often given discounts for bus, taxicab, subway, and train services. Commissions or offices on aging, health departments, departments of social services, and local chapters of the American Red Cross are often able to direct people to services accommodating wheelchairs and other special needs. Various health and medical facilities provide transportation for people using their services. For example, nursing homes may provide transportation for their residents to dentists, physicians, and rehabilitation services. Health services for the aged are provided by health departments, hospital clinics, and private practitioners. These providers may also assist the elderly in obtaining transportation and financial assistance for their health care. A variety of life-care communities, villages, mobile home parks, and apartment complexes, specifically designed for older people, include transportation services for residents to health services and recreational activities.

Surveys have examined sociocultural and quality-of-life variables as they affect use of health care and transportation services. Most respondents reported their health status as poor or very poor, and more than one-half had no medical care during the preceding six months despite the presence of multiple physical symptoms. Social isolation from family or neighborhood support systems exacerbated problems with transportation, and most of the elderly people relied on public transportation to gain access to health services. Public transportation services posed additional barriers to health care use, including fear of making trips alone within the complex urban transportation system.

Mobility for the elderly means having access to the goods, services, and social interactions that are necessary to independent living. A standard measure of mobility is the number of trips that people make away from their homes. Mobility may be affected by numerous factors, including emotional and physical health, economic well-being, and the ease or difficulty in getting around one's community. However, little research has been done on how older people themselves perceive their transportation options or the reduced mobility that accompanies old age.

### AARP Transportation Survey

A community transportation survey conducted in conjunction with the American Association of Retired Persons (AARP) questioned 710 respondents seventy-five years of age and older about such issues as how they travel, how often they travel, and features of the environment in which they travel. The survey also explored perceptions of comfort with two alternatives to driving—walking and public transportation. In addition, the survey investigated the mobility of nondrivers and potential solutions to helping nondrivers become more mobile.

Of those surveyed, 73 percent drove. Approximately 89 percent of males reported that they drove, compared to 64 percent of females. Older people with higher incomes were much more likely to drive. One-half of the people who responded, regardless of whether they drove, reported that they took five or fewer trips—without reference to the means by which these trips were made—per week. Men, people seventy-five to eighty-four years of age, and older people with incomes of $25,000 or more reported making a greater number of trips than women, people age eighty-five or older, and older people with more limited financial resources. The median number of trips by older drivers was three times that of older nondrivers. Regardless of age or sex, older drivers reported taking more trips than older nondrivers. For example, the median number of trips made by older male drivers was seven, compared to two for older male nondrivers.

Among all older drivers, 63 percent avoided driving at night, and 51 percent avoided driving during rush hour. Among older people who had ceased driving within the last three years, 61 percent had discontinued driving because of physical impairments. Other reasons offered for the discontinuation of driving included the inability to afford a car (7 percent), not having a need to drive (7 percent), being too old (6 percent), and getting rides from a spouse (6 percent).

As many as 30 percent of the drivers surveyed reported that they felt uncomfortable with specific physical design aspects of roads or traffic situations they encountered, while 33 percent reported that they avoided certain routes. Among the drivers who said they avoided certain routes, 34 percent cited heavy traffic and 30 percent cited interstate highways as reasons.

Among the nondrivers surveyed, one-half reported making two or fewer trips per week. Two-thirds of nondrivers said they relied on rides from family members or friends to get where they needed to go, while 86 percent reported that they did not use public transportation. Of the nondrivers who did not use public transportation, 33 percent said that they preferred to rely on rides from family and friends. Other reasons for not using public transportation included lack of availability, inconvenience, and individual physical problems.

One-half of nondrivers said they could not walk to a bus stop, and 53 percent said they could not walk to a grocery store. Among nondrivers who could not walk to a bus stop, 32 percent said that a resting place along the way would make it possible to do so, and 27 percent reported that a bus stop within five blocks of their home would make it possible to do so. Among nondrivers who could not walk to a grocery store, 37 percent reported that a store within five blocks of their home would make it possible to do so, and 35 percent said a resting place along the way would make it possible to do so.

### Correcting Transportation Problems

Key questions emerged from the report's findings that require further research about how best to meet the transportation needs of people age seventy-five and older. These questions include: To what degree is the reduced mobility of older people dependent on personal health status? To what degree is reduced mobility dependent on external barriers, such as crime or limited community transportation resources? How do older people perceive public transportation as an alternative to the automobile? Is the level of mobility of older drivers sufficient to assure access to the goods, services, and social contacts necessary to independent living? Are older drivers satisfied with their level of mobility? Do they simply prefer or need less mobility, or do they accept reduced mobility as part of getting old? Are nondrivers as immobile as these data suggest? How do they connect to their communities? Do they have sufficient access to the goods, services, and social contacts necessary to independent living? Do the families and friends of older people believe that they can meet the mobility needs of older people?

Because the majority of people rely on driving themselves well into their later years, public policies should support maximizing the capacity for safe driving through the life span. These policies include improvement of road design and signage, regulation of drivers on the basis of individual functional ability and driving record, and automobile design that addresses the needs of an aging population.

The fact that one-quarter of the seventy-five and older population are nondrivers means that federal, state, and local governments must identify and support transportation options designed to meet currently unmet transportation needs. These policies would be most useful if they were founded on the habits, preferences, and attitudes of older people to increase the likelihood that older people will use and be satisfied with their transportation choices. Zoning laws, transportation planning, regulation of public transportation, and allocation of federal funds for transportation services all have an impact on the short-term and long-term ability of people of all ages to connect with their communities and to maintain independence throughout their lives.

Other surveys have attempted to understand the needs of physically handicapped and elderly people and to recommend appropriate operational and physical changes within the system to meet these needs. The secondary intent of such studies is often to bring about public awareness of the mobility problems of the physically limited and the elderly.

Transportation and the quality of available health care are major problems for rural senior citizens because of the lack of rural public transportation. Although 30 percent of the population of the United States lives in such ares, only about 1 percent of the capitol federal investment and annual operating moneys spent on public transportation are allocated to help meet rural needs.

### TRANSPORTATION PLANNING

Communities develop planning guides designed to aid service agencies in their choices for setting up transportation services for the elderly. Alternatives to actual service include special buses for the elderly. This service may be provided directly by the coordinating agency and may include such vehicles as specially equipped vans, school buses, and station wagons. Another alternative is the reduced fare program whereby older adults may ride existing public transit at a reduced fare.

In some communities, buses provide scheduled trips to such destinations as grocery stores, medical appointments, and community centers. For many, buses are the vital link to a variety of activities, including doctor visits. Door-to-door and curb-to-curb service is often available. Most buses are wheelchair accessible. Some entrepreneurs have established businesses focused on the needs of the elderly that provide multidimensional services, including transportation, bill paying, and assisted-living options.

All evidence suggests that the elderly population will continue to depend on the private car to give them freedom, independence, and choice—as do younger travellers. It seems unlikely that other modes or options can provide anywhere near the level of mobility that the elderly want or need. Almost three-fourths of those over age sixty-five live in suburban or rural areas, where transit and paratransit options are inherently impractical or costly. These elderly individuals make choices about doctors, hospitals, friends, and social and recreational options based on their lifelong access to the car. When they can no longer drive or receive rides, their mobility will drop, and they may have to make drastic changes in their life network to be able to access just a few necessary services.

Those concerned with the use of medical services by the elderly population must focus not only on transportation but also on other variables that create the need for a car. Transportation needs are clearly linked to where and how medical and social services are made available. As the aging population grows, medical and human service agencies are likely to make an effort to make their programs accessible to the elderly population rather than simply locating their facilities where they please and assuming that elderly people or transportation planners will somehow deal with the resulting loss of mobility. —*Jane Cross Norman*

*See also* American Association of Retired Persons (AARP); Discounts; Driving; Independent living; Mobility problems; Nursing and convalescent homes; Safety issues; Vacations and travel; Wheelchair use.

**FOR FURTHER INFORMATION:**

Abdel-Aty, M. A., C. L. Chen, and J. R. Schott. "An Assessment of the Effect of Driver Age on Traffic Accident Involvement Using Log-Linear Models." *Accident Analysis and Prevention* 33, no. 4 (1999): 470.

Coughlin, Joseph F., and Annalyn Lacombe. "Ten Myths About Transportation for the Elderly." *Transportation Quarterly* 51, no. 1 (Winter, 1997): 91-100.

Eberhard, J. W. "Driving Is Transportation for Most Older Adults." *Geriatrics* 53, supplement 1 (1998): S53-S55.

Forrest, K. Y., et al. "Driving Patterns and Medical Conditions in Older Women." *Journal of the American Geriatrics Society* 45, no. 10 (1997): 1214-1218.

Johanssen, K., et al. "Can a Physician Recognize an Older Driver with Increased Crash Risk Potential?" *Journal of the American Geriatrics Society* 44, no. 10 (1996): 1198-1204.

Jolly, B. T. "Older Drivers: Growth Industry for the Future." *Annuals of Emergency Medicine* 33, no. 4 (1999): 470.

Keplinger, F. S. "The Elderly Driver: Who Should Continue to Drive?" *Physical Medicine and Rehabilitation: State of the Art Reviews* 12, no. 1 (1998): 147-154.

McGwin, G., Jr., and D. B. Brown. "Characteristics of Traffic Crashes Among Young, Middle-Aged, and Older Drivers." *Accident Analysis and Prevention* 31, no. 3 (1999): 181-198.

McGwin, G., Jr., R. V. Sims, L. Pulley, and J. M. Roseman. "Diabetes and Automobile Crashes in the Elderly: A Population-Based Case-Control Study." *Diabetes Care* 22, no. 2 (1999): 220-227.

Stamatiadis, Nikiforos, Thomas R. Leinbach, and John F. Watkins. "Travel Among Non-Urban Elderly." *Transportation Quarterly* 50, no. 3 (Summer, 1996): 113-121.

**TRAVEL.** *See* **VACATIONS AND TRAVEL.**

## TRIP TO BOUNTIFUL, THE

**DIRECTOR:** Peter Masterson
**CAST:** Geraldine Page, John Heard, Rebecca De Mornay
**DATE:** Released in 1985
**RELEVANT ISSUES:** Death, family
**SIGNIFICANCE:** In this film, an elderly woman's trip home serves as a type of life review and preparation for death

A life review can be important in late adulthood as a way of reaching ego integrity. In the film *The Trip to Bountiful*, which takes place in the 1940's, this life review is represented in the main character's desire to return to her home in the town of Bountiful, Texas. Carrie Watts (played by Geraldine Page) is an elderly woman who now lives with her son and daughter-in-law in Houston. Carrie feels driven to take a trip to Bountiful to see her old home and friends before she dies. The trip serves as an opportunity for the aging woman to remember her past and become better prepared for her future.

When she arrives in Bountiful, she realizes how it has changed during the twenty years she has been away. Everyone has either moved or died, and the town consists of just a few empty buildings. Nevertheless, Carrie feels at home as she arrives at the house in which she was raised. Being in Bountiful makes her feel safe, at peace, ready to return to her son's home in Houston—ready, eventually, for death.

Based on the 1953 play by Horton Foote, who also wrote the screenplay, *The Trip to Bountiful* is a moving drama about searching for peace by returning home. Page won an Academy Award for her portrayal of Carrie Watts. Throughout the film, the hymn "Softly and Tenderly" provides musical support for the theme. The hymn includes these words in the chorus: "Come home, come home. Ye who are weary, come home." Going home can be a powerful drive for those who are tired and in need of peace. Carrie found that peace during her trip to Bountiful.

—*Kevin S. Seybold*

*See also* Death and dying; Death anxiety; Films; Literature; Women and aging.

# Trusts

**Relevant issues:** Death, family, law

**Significance:** A trust—an entity enabling people to pass title to property to others during their lifetime or at death—can be used to implement many estate-planning techniques

Trusts are often referred to as gifts with strings attached: instructions and conditions given to the trustee as to whom, how, and when property contained in the trust can be distributed. Trusts can be cancelled or changed during the lifetime of the settlor or grantor (creator of the trust) so long as he or she remains competent.

## Characteristics of a Trust

A trust is a legal entity in which one person or corporation holds property for the benefit of another under written instructions and directives. A trustee (holder of the property for another's benefit) can be either an individual or a bank or other corporate institution. Banks generally have a trust department to administer assets held in trust in exchange for payment of a fee, usually based on a percentage of the value of the trust's assets (corpus). Using a bank or other corporate entity eliminates the need to name a successor trustee to act upon the death, resignation, or incompetence of the original trustee. In other circumstances, however, where a close friend or family member is named trustee, it is a good idea to name a successor. If there are minor children, a guardian and successor guardian should be named.

The settlor owns equitable title to the trust corpus: the right to use, possess, and enjoy the property; the trustee owns bare legal title (property in the name of the trust). Trustees are fiduciaries and have entered into a trust relationship with the settlor—the ultimate duty imposed by law. Trustees are absolutely mandated to follow instructions of the settlor, to exercise good judgement, responsibility, and objectivity. If this duty is breached, trustees can be sued for breach of fiduciary duty.

Trusts cannot last forever. The rule against perpetuities limits the length of a trust, generally specifying that a trust can last no longer than the lifetime of the beneficiary alive at the time the trust was created plus twenty-one years.

## Types of Trusts

The inter vivos trust (also called a living trust) can be structured so that settlors retain the right to change or terminate the trust during their lifetime. This type of trust is revocable; those that cannot be changed are irrevocable. In the revocable trust, settlors give what is owned to whomever they wish, whenever they wish, subsequent to death; terms and requirements about how the property passes can be spelled out. Settlors can control, coordinate, and distribute all property interests during their lifetime and at death. The inter vivos trust ensures privacy on death or incapacity because probate is not required. It is easy to create and maintain, and it can be changed or amended at the will of the settlor. For these reasons, the inter vivos trust is often referred to as a will substitute. Property not placed in trust during the settlor's lifetime can still be placed in trust after death through use of a "pour-over will" stating that any property not in trust will pass to the trust (pour over to it) after death.

A testamentary trust created in a valid will is not operative until death. The testamentary trust is never created to benefit the settlor and is subject to probate. Testamentary trusts are often set up as A-B trusts when a married couple is involved and when their combined estate may be taxable. The single trust is divided into two trusts (A and B) at the death of the first spouse. The deceased spouse's share flows into the B trust, containing flexible and discretionary provisions. The surviving spouse's share and the remaining share of the deceased spouse, if any, is placed into the A, or survivor's, trust (also called the marital trust). The surviving spouse normally has complete control over the A trust. This manner of dividing trust corpus may result in considerable tax savings, depending on the size of the estate.

Qualified terminable interest property (Q-TIP) trusts provide for children from different marriages. The marital deduction allows spouses to leave entire estates to each other without paying taxes. If there are children from other marriages, settlors might prefer that their biological children receive more from their estate than their current spouse's children from a previous marriage. The Q-TIP trust allows one to leave property in trust for one's spouse; after the spouse's death, it goes to whomever the settlor specifies.

Totten trusts are accounts at commercial banks or savings and loans that are registered "A in trust for B." It is presumed that the account belongs to the adult named as trustee unless the trust was irrevocable. On the death of the adult trustee, the account proceeds would belong to the minor beneficiaries but would be controlled by the local probate court on behalf of the minor until he or she reaches adulthood. This should be distinguished from a Uniform Gifts to Minors Act account, where an adult is named as custodian to manage the account until the minor reaches adulthood; in a savings account trust at a savings and loan, a minor can deposit or withdraw at will with no liability to the savings and loan.

Children's trusts are irrevocable trusts used to make gifts to children or grandchildren, providing for their future education and benefit. Appreciated assets are removed from the testator's estate and placed into the children's trust, where they will continue to grow. This is another tax-saving technique because the asset is taken from the estate of the testator and placed in a separate trust for the benefit of another, thus reducing the amount of testator's taxable estate. One caveat is that testators should not name themselves as trustee of the children's trust to ensure that the property will not be included in their taxable estate.

Prior to 1976, it was possible to avoid federal estate tax when property passed to future generations by means of a generation-skipping trust. In this situation, a settlor creates a trust funded at the settlor's death. His or her spouse receives all income and principal as needed. At the spouse's death, the children receive all income and principal as needed. At the children's death, the principal passes to the grandchildren. Another variation specifies that the settlor can mandate that on the death of his or her spouse, the property passes di-rectly to the grandchildren, bypassing the children and bypassing estate tax on these transfers. The Tax Reform Act of 1976 subjected generation-skipping assets to federal estate tax on the deaths of the beneficiaries of the generation-skipping trust. The Tax Reform Act of 1986 subjects an estate to double tax—the normal estate tax at the settlor's death and the generation-skipping tax at the death of the skipped individual. Exemptions from estate tax under current law nevertheless make this trust advantageous to the very wealthy.

Discretionary trusts contain provisions under which trustees can distribute the income and principal among various beneficiaries, or control disbursements to a single beneficiary, as they see fit. Spendthrift trusts can be set up for people whom the settlor believes would not be able to manage their own affairs because of their extravagance, immaturity, or mental incompetency. Support trusts direct the trustee to spend only as much income and principal as needed for the education and support of the beneficiary. Charitable remainder trusts are irrevocable. The settlor gives up control of appreciated assets placed in trust. In so doing, the settlor receives current tax deductions and a lifetime income without paying gift tax or capital gains tax. Assets can also be used for donation to private foundations rather than a public charity.

—*Marcia J. Weiss*

**See also** Estates and inheritance; Living trusts; Wills and bequests.

**FOR FURTHER INFORMATION:**
American Bar Association. *The ABA Guide to Wills and Estates.* New York: Times Books, 1995.
Bove, Alexander A., Jr. *The Complete Book of Wills and Estates.* New York: Henry Holt, 1989.
Burris, Donald J. *Protecting Your Assets: Wills, Trusts, and Other Estate Planning Options.* Philadelphia: Chelsea House, 1994.
Esperti, Robert A., and Renno L. Peterson. *The Handbook of Estate Planning.* 2d ed. New York: McGraw-Hill, 1988.
Lynn, Robert J. *An Introduction to Estate Planning.* St. Paul, Minn.: West, 1975.
Maple, Stephen M. *The Complete Idiot's Guide to Wills and Estates.* New York: Alpha Books, 1997.

# URINARY DISORDERS

**RELEVANT ISSUES:** Biology, health and medicine

**SIGNIFICANCE:** Decreases in the functional efficiency of the kidneys are associated with a number of diseases and pathological conditions; urinary disorders are among the leading causes of death in the elderly

As a by-product of its everyday activities, the human body produces wastes that must be eliminated. A number of organs excrete cellular wastes: the skin, lungs, large intestine, liver, and kidneys. Of these organs, the kidneys are, by far, the most important for maintaining the body in a healthy state. Kidney failure is fatal unless treatment is initiated promptly.

The two kidneys are the major organs of the urinary system; they are located on either side of the spine just below the rib cage. The urinary system is composed of two ureters, which pass from the kidneys to the urinary bladder, and the urethra, which moves the urine from the bladder to outside of the body. Kidneys are the major excretory organs, but other organs have excretory function as well. For example, along with excreting carbon dioxide, the lungs may also excrete ammonia. The liver and skin also excrete metabolic wastes.

## KIDNEY FUNCTION

The functional unit of the kidney is the nephron; each kidney contains about 1 million of them. The nephron is an exquisitely designed structure. It consists of a glomerulus, a ball of capillaries designed to act as a filter through which a fluid is separated from the blood and passes into Bowman's capsule, an expanded chamber in the kidney that surrounds the capillaries. Under normal conditions, the fluid is free of cells and larger molecules, and consists of mostly water and certain small molecules, including urea, a waste product of metabolism. The fluid that enters the kidneys is mostly water, and large amounts would be eliminated in the urine if nothing further was done in the kidneys. In a typical person, some 200 quarts of fluid pass into the kidneys each day, but only about 2 quarts end up being eliminated as urine. Most of the water that passes into the kidneys is reabsorbed back into the blood stream, as are most of the small molecules, including glucose. There are well over 100 miles of filtering

units and tubules in the kidneys to keep substances at normal levels in the body.

Although there is a decrease in the number of nephrons with the aging process, a decrease can also occur with certain diseases. However, kidneys have a considerable reserve capacity and can function at a level many times greater than under normal conditions. It is estimated that a person may live successfully with a 60 to 80 percent loss of their nephrons. In some cases, people can be born with only one kidney and never know it.

The kidneys produce urine but perform several other important functions to help maintain the chemical constancy of the blood by regulating both the volume and specific composition of body fluids. To accomplish this regulation function, about 1,700 quarts of blood, representing about 25 percent of the blood pumped by the heart into the aorta, passes through the kidneys of an average person every day.

Ureters drain urine, produced in the kidneys, into the urinary bladder, which is the temporary holding site for urine. The urinary bladder also functions in the process of elimination (also known as urination or micturition). The bladder is a hollow, baglike structure that, under normal conditions, holds between 300 and 500 milliliters of urine. Both voluntary and involuntary nerves control bladder functions. As the bladder begins to fill with urine, sensory receptors in the bladder wall are stimulated. Typically, a person has been toilet trained, and bladder control is usually voluntary; however, some elderly people may experience a loss of voluntary bladder control. Incontinence is the inability to retain urine until an appropriate time and place can be found for elimination. Urinary incontinence may be of considerable importance among the elderly and may be a problem in 10 percent of the population over sixty-five. It is especially common in older women but occurs in men as well.

Given the amount of blood that passes through the kidneys each day, it is evident that most of the fluid must be reabsorbed back into the bloodstream to conserve it from being eliminated in the urine. The process of water reabsorption is controlled by several hormones. One, the antidiuretic hormone (ADH), is produced in the pituitary gland. ADH acts on the distal tubules in the kidneys by increasing the rate of water reabsorption,

## Common Urinary Disorders

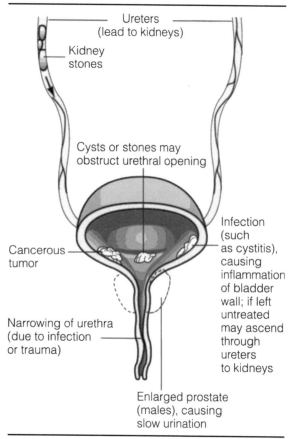

Ureters (lead to kidneys)

Kidney stones

Cysts or stones may obstruct urethral opening

Cancerous tumor

Infection (such as cystitis), causing inflammation of bladder wall; if left untreated may ascend through ureters to kidneys

Narrowing of urethra (due to infection or trauma)

Enlarged prostate (males), causing slow urination

(Hans & Cassidy, Inc.)

thereby reducing urinary output. Certain diseases can interfere with the production of ADH. A form of diabetes called diabetes insipidus leads to inadequate amounts of ADH. Affected people may produce gallons of dilute urine each day.

Kidney function is critical for life, and a complete loss of functioning brings death within just a few weeks. Serious kidney problems or renal failure may be caused by severe infections, an immune reaction to antibiotics, or a sudden and significant decrease in blood flow. Some impairment of kidney function may be related to the processes of normal aging.

### CHANGES WITH NORMAL AGING PROCESSES

Although several anatomical and physiological changes occur in the kidneys as a result of aging, they can continue to function well enough to maintain a homeostatic balance and keep the proper salt and water balances. Problems are likely to arise when conditions outside of the normal range, such as disease or excessive stress, place additional demands on the system.

The kidneys are dependent on an adequate blood supply for normal functioning. A decrease in blood to the kidneys may be caused by several conditions. In general, cardiac output tends to fall with age. The heart puts out less blood, and the proportion going to the kidneys also decreases. In young adults, 25 percent of the blood pumped by the heart reaches and is processed by the kidneys. A noticeable decrease is evident by forty to fifty years of age; by the age of seventy to eighty, blood flow to the kidneys may be one-half of what it was at age twenty. Ultimately, the decreased blood flow results in less efficient functioning of the kidneys.

Additional changes that further compound the problems caused by decreased blood flow take place in the kidneys themselves. Of the 2 million nephrons present in the kidneys of young adults, up to one-half will be lost by the age of seventy to seventy-five. Those nephrons that remain show degenerative changes that result in decreased functioning. The detection of large molecules—such as proteins, red blood cells, white blood cells, and glucose—in the urine during a urinalysis are indicative of some sort of disease or malfunction in the urinary tract.

In addition to changes in blood flow to the kidneys and a decrease in the functional efficiency of cells in the kidneys, problems can occur in the actual structures of the lower portion of the urinary tract. Loss of muscular tone with age may affect functioning of the ureters, bladder, and urethra. People may experience incomplete and difficult emptying of the bladder if there is a sufficient decrease in muscle tone. There also is a tendency for bladder capacity to decline in older people to less than one-half of that of young adults. Some older people may therefore experience more frequent and urgent urination.

### CHANGES WITH DISEASE CONDITIONS

Diseases of the urinary tract occur in young and middle-age adults; in specific cases, they may be even more common in these age groups than in the elderly. However, a number of urinary system disorders are age related and are likely to have more severe symptoms and outcomes; of special significance to the elderly are infections (including cystitis, pyelonephritis, and glomerulonephritis), kidney stones, cancers, incontinence, and renal failure.

The National Kidney Foundation has provided a list of symptoms that are warning signs of kidney disease: burning or difficulty during urination; more frequent urination, particularly at night; passage of bloody urine; puffiness around eyes and swelling of hands and feet, especially in children; pain in the small of the back just below the ribs; and high blood pressure. However, some diseases can be present without any overt symptoms, and other types of tests are required for diagnosis. As a part of an annual physical checkup, routine urine and blood analysis can detect many forms of kidney disease. Accurate diagnosis is essential, as the type of treatment and outlook for recovery depend upon the nature of the disease and its early detection.

Kidney stones, or renal calculi, are small when they first form, not much bigger than the size of a grain of sand. They form when crystals of salt become concentrated in the urine and, as long as they remain small, will usually wash out with the urine. However, if water reabsorption by the kidneys is high and the volume of urine is low, the stones will grow and may become stuck in the ureter as urine passes from the kidneys to the bladder. The pain produced by the stones irritating the ureter is extreme. If large enough, the stones can actually block the ureter and may cause a backing-up and flooding of the kidneys. Bleeding may occur from the irritation of the walls of the ureter, the condition being one of the reasons for the appearance of blood in the urine.

A number of factors are associated with the formation of stones. Atypical diets can shift the acid-base composition of the urine. If the pH shifts to either extreme, stones can form. Excessive loss of water or inadequate water consumption may concentrate the urine, creating an environment conducive to forming crystals. Kidney infections and a lack of exercise or situations of extreme inactivity also can contribute to the process. Overlying all of these factors is the observation that kidney stones tend to run in families, indicating that there is likely a genetic component. Prevention and treatment may involve procedures to ensure good dietary practices, adequate water intake, and an exercise program. Conventional surgery and ultrasonic techniques may be required to break up and dislodge the stones.

An urgency to urinate, burning and pain during urination, and a need to urinate frequently, which may require getting up several times during the night, are symptoms of urinary tract infection. Infections may occur in the kidneys, bladder, and lower urinary tract. They can be chronic and are often difficult to cure. Urinary tract infections are more common in women than in men and are most likely caused by the shorter urethra of females and its anatomical placement. Infection of the urinary bladder is known as cystitis and, in addition to causing an urgency of urination and pain on urinating, may produce pain in the lower abdominal region. Patients are asked to drink large amounts of water to increase their frequency of urination; antibiotics may be required to control the bacterial infection. Infections of the lower urinary tract may spread to the kidneys, possibly damaging them and, more critically, possibly leading to kidney failure. In addition, bacteria may spread to other parts of the body and cause other types of severe complications.

Bacterial infection of the kidneys is known as pyelonephritis or nephritis. The chronic form is more common in the elderly than is the acute form. Either form can lead to kidney failure and cause waste products to accumulate in the blood. If untreated, toxic substances will continue to accumulate, possibly resulting in death.

Although it is not a fatal disorder, urinary incontinence is a major physiological, psychological, health, and social problem among the elderly. Incontinence is almost twice as common in women as in men; the incidence may approach 50 percent or higher among the elderly. There are several types and causes of incontinence, making diagnosis and treatment difficult. Incontinence may be caused by certain drugs or medications. Exercise, sneezing, and even laughing may induce what is known as stress incontinence. Loss of mobility and psychiatric disorders can also lead to incontinence. Depending on the diagnosis of the cause, treatment might include exercise, drug therapy, counseling, and behavioral modification.

The prostate is a small gland found only in males; it is one of the sexual accessory glands that functions in reproduction. Its secretions contribute to the seminal fluid and probably assist in the activation of sperm. The prostate surrounds the urethra just as it leaves the urinary bladder; certain conditions that affect it can have serious consequences for the functioning of the urinary system. Any disorder of the prostate that leads to an increase in size may interfere with the passage of urine through the urethra. Extreme cases may even cause a complete obstruction of urine flow. Partial obstruction, if prolonged, can lead to bladder and kidney damage. Although the precise cause is not known, prostate enlargement (benign prostatic hypertrophy) is common among aging men and may require treatment if urine flow is impeded.

Cancerous growths, or carcinomas, may occur at various sites throughout the urinary system, including the kidneys, bladder, and prostate gland. Prostate cancer is the most common cancer in men and, although usually not fatal, is still the third leading cancer that causes death in men. Bladder cancer is also more common in males, and its incidence may be related to smoking or exposure to certain types of chemicals, especially aniline dyes. In the case of all types of cancer, early detection is critical so that treatment can be effected before it has spread (metastasized) to other sites.

—*Donald J. Nash*

*See also* Diabetes; Heart changes and disorders; Incontinence; Prostate cancer; Prostate enlargement; Stones.

**FOR FURTHER INFORMATION:**

Blaivas, Jerry G. *Conquering Bladder and Prostate Problems.* New York: Plenum Trade, 1998. Blaivas discusses the anatomy, physiology, and diseases of the bladder and prostate. A list of patient and advocacy organizations is included.

Chalker, Rebecca, and Kristene E. Whitmore. *Overcoming Bladder Disorders.* New York: HarperPerennial, 1991. This book is devoted solely to urinary bladder disorders. It includes an index of diagnostic tests, a drug glossary, a glossary of urological terms, and a list of more than one hundred references.

Dollinger, Malin, and Ernst H. Rosenbaum. *Everyone's Guide to Cancer Therapy.* Toronto: Summerville House, 1998. Causes and treatments of cancers of the urinary tract and prostate gland are included in this overall summary of cancer therapy.

Saxon, Sue V., and Mary Jean Etten. *Physical Change and Aging.* 3d ed. New York: Tiresias, 1994. This basic text on the biology of aging has separate chapters on the urinary system and the reproductive system.

Walsh, P. C., and J. F. Worthington. *The Prostate: A Guide for Men and the Women Who Love Them.* Baltimore: The Johns Hopkins University Press, 1995. This book covers the causes, tests, and treatments for benign prostate enlargement, cancer, and urinary problems.

## VACATIONS AND TRAVEL

**RELEVANT ISSUES:** Culture, economics, recreation, values

**SIGNIFICANCE:** The freedom to explore vacation and travel options is one of the benefits of aging; the options taken largely depend on habits acquired over a lifetime

The desire to see new parts of the world and extend cultural horizons is a large part of the impulse that sends people of all ages on exploratory voyages. This impulse can be of particular importance to those older citizens who have fulfilled their familial obligations, achieved some financial security, and acquired leisure time to devote to travel. This age group is a growing market for travel opportunities of all kinds.

### TRAVEL AND VACATION CHOICES

Travel by seniors can take many forms and satisfy a variety of needs. One choice that must be made is whether to travel alone, with a companion, or in a group. Seniors might also decide to combine travel with some kind of cultural or educational venture. A further choice is whether to travel abroad or to rediscover one's own county, state, country, or continent. Some seniors travel independently, perhaps in a vehicle leased or purchased for that purpose or on scheduled mass transportation, while others seek the services of a professional tour operator. In addition, a wide range of accommodation may be considered, from providing one's own shelter to renting a cabin, engaging in a home or apartment exchange, or staying in a luxurious hotel or resort.

The travel choices that seniors make will depend on a variety of factors, including lifestyle, physical condition, kind of experience sought, and personal preference. No matter where the older traveler decides to go, a wide variety of travel books can help in deciding how to get there, what to see and do upon arrival, where to stay, and what or where to eat. Increasing numbers of shops catering to the needs of the traveler exist, often owned by people glad to share their knowledge and experience. Most countries, and many tourists destina-

*Older people often have the time for more leisurely forms of sightseeing such as walking or bike riding, which also help them stay fit.* (Bavaria-Verlag/Archive Photos)

tions, have offices or agencies that provide free brochures upon request.

## Foreign Travel

Many factors might motivate senior travel to countries abroad, including curiosity about people and cultures different from one's own; the desire to see and photograph beautiful landscapes, visit famous art and archaeology museums, or explore fabled cities; and interest in attending sporting events, visiting summer festivals of music and the arts, or trying new cuisines in their natural setting. The older traveler might also develop an interest in discovering or connecting with family roots or wish to try out recently acquired language skills. The novelty of this kind of travel, particularly for those whose lives have been devoted to caring for family and pursuing a career, may be one of its most compelling features. Whether one is naturally gregarious or solitary, foreign travel affords many opportunities to expand awareness of the world.

People who engage in travel, particularly abroad, are often divided into one of two categories: travelers or tourists. While any person may partake of both worlds, there is a difference in how these two categories are perceived and, sometimes, treated. For the tourist, the hazards and uncertainties of the journey are kept to a bare minimum, while the comforts of home are, if not guaranteed, at least provided in some measure. Many tour operators provide older people with food, lodging, sightseeing, and recreation that is predictable and not too unlike the daily routine of home. The tour operator arranges transportation, makes hotel and other reservations, organizes sightseeing expeditions, chooses restaurants, and sets up a timetable, presumably on the basis of past satisfactory experience with similar age groups. An itinerary is delivered that meets the desires of the clientele for safety, comfort, cleanliness, and order.

This type of group travel arrangement is often promoted for older people because of their ability to pay the concomitant higher price and to allay their anxiety about traveling in countries where language, money, time, food habits, and living standards may be different from that to which they are accustomed. Quite often, these package tours are small group expeditions that may be targeted to a particular age, sex, occupation, or socioeco-

nomic category. For the older first-time tourist, this may be a wise option, since it removes some of the anxiety-causing elements of solo travel.

Among the chief joys of travel are the associated experiences of planning the trip, often in considerable detail, and in reminiscing about it after the trip or vacation is over. The highlights of the trip may be shared with friends and family through photographs or slides, video recordings, or stories about the inevitable mishaps that occur. While the predictability of guided tourism may be tempting, there is much to be said for the extra involvement of planning one's own itinerary.

Youth hostels, in spite of their name, are open in most countries to all ages. These are among the most cost-effective lodging choices for international travelers. If the older traveler has a spirit of adventure, likes to meet people of all ages and backgrounds, and does not expect too much in the way of creature comfort, youth hostels offer a good deal. When planning to engage in this more adventurous style of travel, however, it is important to invest in some of the basic necessities of any traveler: good walking shoes, plastic zippered bags, antidiarrheal medicine, photocopies of medical prescriptions, a Swiss Army knife, a pocket flashlight, and spare batteries. When planning to travel by rail, a bottle of mineral water is essential. For those seniors who prefer a higher level of comfort, however, there are many privately owned pensions and inns that offer comfort and hospitality but still provide amenities that the older traveler might prefer. It is wise to pack as little as possible, since carrying unnecessary baggage can make traveling much more exhausting than it has to be. A medical examination before setting out on a long trip is a wise idea, since not all medicines are readily available abroad; any prescriptions should be renewed and purchased beforehand.

Tourists planning to travel by rail in Europe have the advantage of being able to purchase numerous rail passes that make train travel there quite affordable. They must be purchased before arrival in Europe, however. This feature is enhanced by the ease of accessing rail timetables, and even purchasing rail passes, on the Internet.

## Security Measures

A frequent concern of older travelers is personal security. While almost everyone who travels

*Camping with a motor home in RV parks, sometimes traveling for months at a time, is a popular type of vacation among senior citizens.* (Ben Klaffke)

frequently has some stories to tell of untoward occurrences, from purse snatching to loss of personal possessions, commonsense precautions will alleviate most of these concerns. It is wise to conceal large amounts of convertible currency in a money belt worn next to the body and to carry travelers' checks separately from the receipt so that they can be replaced if lost or stolen. Passports should also be worn next to the body, since replacing a lost or stolen passport can be a time-consuming and exasperating experience. Copies of the front page of the passport, address book, and a list of all credit card account numbers should also be made and stored separately from the items themselves. A small purse slung over the shoulder that hugs the body is preferable to a large one that hangs loosely from the arm.

These security precautions repay the small effort they take to lessen the impact of an unfortunate incident. The traveler usually wants to view travel as an opportunity to make new friends, however, and an undue concern about security should not be allowed to limit the inevitable and welcome opportunities for interpersonal relations. A supply of visiting cards may come in handy when making new friends on the road.

## MONEY, COMMUNICATION, AND EDUCATIONAL TRAVEL

A real boon to the modern traveler is the automatic teller machine (ATM), available virtually everywhere, which makes carrying large amounts of cash unnecessary. It is wise to check with one's own bank before traveling abroad to make sure that the personal code and type of machine can be used in other countries. Credit cards can be useful when traveling since exchange rates are often more favorable via a credit card than at a currency exchange office, many of which charge high commissions. They also obviate the need for carrying large amounts of cash.

Another concern of older travelers is in knowing how to find out whether everything is going well back home. Although it is possible to call a neighbor or family member from abroad, one must keep in mind the time difference and the cost of international telephone calls. It might be easier and cheaper to arrange to connect with home via the Internet. A number of Internet sites provide free electronic mail (e-mail), which can be accessed for sending and receiving messages while traveling. Once the account and logon information has been set up, preferably before leaving, one can then correspond on the road with friends or family, which can be important for peace of mind. Special Internet cafes, often called cybercafes, exist all over the world. They are usually inexpensive and service-oriented, and they can provide assistance for new users. Many libraries, particularly in the United States and Canada, also provide this service, sometimes at no charge. In fact, the plethora of Web sites facilitating travel planning of all kinds make the Internet a basic resource for older persons who do not want unanticipated surprises while traveling.

Opportunities for extending educational horizons can be found through many programs that provide travel opportunities, both in one's own country and abroad. A program that caters to seniors in particular is called Elderhostel. This program is conducted through universities and colleges throughout North America. Courses ranging from nuclear physics to Sufi dancing and Russian literature are offered in attractive college settings. Dormitory space and food are provided, and opportunities to meet like-minded older people are abundant. Many foreign universities promote similar programs, particularly in the summer months when dormitory space is available and tourism is an objective. For those who feel that education is a lifelong enterprise, these options should be seriously considered.

### TRANSPORTATION

Senior travel in the United States and Canada, particularly by citizens of those countries, may differ considerably from travel overseas. A large market exists for recreational vehicles (RVs), many quite luxurious, that make it possible to travel in comfort and to bring items from home that are felt to be necessary, as well as to travel with pets. For many people, the ease of movement and flexibility of planning make this type of travel very attractive. Well-marked RV parks in scenic areas and a wide variety of public parks throughout North America are features that attract travelers from all over the world.

On the other hand, the poorly developed land transportation system for mass transit on the North American continent, particularly the United States, hampers the kind of unencumbered travel possible in other countries, especially those in Europe. In the United States, some form of private automotive transport is almost a necessity, whereas trains and buses serve tourists well in Europe and much of Asia and South America. For those wishing or needing to rely on public transportation in North America, however, there are special discount fares for senior citizens on Amtrak trains and on the Canadian rail system. Perhaps the best travel bargain for those over sixty-two in the United States, where air transport over vast distances is often needed, is a booklet of four senior air fare coupons, each for a single flight anywhere within the United States. They are sold by all the major airlines and are inexpensive.

### VACATION HOMES AND TIME SHARES

Some older persons who like to encounter new places but do not like to feel uprooted prefer to set up home exchanges, to buy a vacation house, or to purchase shares in a time share resort. Each of these options has its advantages and limitations. A caveat on time shares is to avoid those who lurk at tropical resorts and lure unsuspecting tourists to high-pressure sales rooms. One should investigate purchasing a vacation home or time share as carefully as any other major purchase, since such a choice may limit one's freedom to travel elsewhere. A number of home exchange organizations exist, easily found in most travel guides or at various Internet sites.

### CONCLUSION

The travel industry is the world's largest economic enterprise. Although much has been written about the colonial aspects of travel and its association with class, privilege, and economic disparity, observation indicates that the desire to travel, to see new places, and to meet new people is almost a universal human trait. Although the comforts of home may beckon, the lure of the unknown has an equally persuasive attraction. The freedom to travel that comes with retirement and increasing age is a powerful palliative to the much-touted discomforts of growing older.

—*Gloria Fulton*

**See also** Adult education; American Association of Retired Persons (AARP); Communication; Discounts; Early retirement; Friendship; *Harry and Tonto*; Housing; Immunizations and boosters; Internet; Leisure activities; Pets; Relocation; Retirement; Social ties; Transportation issues.

### FOR FURTHER INFORMATION:

Goeldner, Charles R. *Mature Traveler Bibliography: An Information Source Guide*. Lexington, Ky.: National Tour Foundation, 1997.

Heilman, Joan Rattner. *Unbelievably Good Deals and Great Adventures That You Absolutely Can't Get Unless You're over Fifty*. 10th ed. Lincolnwood, Ill.: Contemporary Books, 1998.

Martin, Anne F. *The Travel Behavior of the Elderly and the Attitudes of the Aged Towards the Transportation Environment: A Critique of the Literature*. Berkeley: Institute of Transportation Studies, University of California, 1992.

Massow, Rosalind. *Travel Easy: The Practical Guide for People over Fifty*. Glenview. Ill.: Scott, Foresman, 1985

Mills, Eugene S. *The Story of Elderhostel*. Hanover, N.H.: University Press of New England, 1993.

St. Claire, Allison. *Travel and Older Adults*. Santa Barbara, Calif.: ABC-Clio, 1991.

Sullivan, Donald L. *A Senior's Guide to Healthy Travel*. Hawthorne, N.J.: Career Press, 1994.

Williams, Anita. *The Fifty Plus Traveler's Guidebook: Where to Go, Where to Stay, What to Do*. Thorndike, Maine: Thorndike Press, 1992.

## VANCE V. BRADLEY

**DATE:** Decided on February 22, 1979

**RELEVANT ISSUES:** Law, values, work

**SIGNIFICANCE:** The U.S. Supreme Court decided that mandatory retirement at age sixty for U.S. Foreign Service officers does not violate equal protection under the Fifth Amendment, nor does mandatory retirement constitute age discrimination under the Constitution

*Vance v. Bradley* involved Holbrook Bradley and several other productive Foreign Service officers who were forced to retire at age sixty in accordance with Section 632 of the Foreign Service Act passed by Congress in 1932. Bradley sued the federal government, claiming that Congress and the State Department had violated the equal protection component of the Constitution's Fifth Amendment due process of law clause. By requiring the retirement, at age sixty, of able Foreign Service officers but not those in the Civil Service, Congress had made an unconstitutional, discriminatory distinction. A three-judge federal district court upheld Bradley's complaint, noting that little evidence was presented by the government to support its legal argument. Employees aged sixty and over were not shown to be less able, competent, productive, or dependable than younger Foreign Service officers.

On direct appeal by Secretary of State Cyrus Vance and others, the U.S. Supreme Court reversed the lower court decision. Eight members of the U.S. Supreme Court ruled that Congress did not deny equal protection of the law when it required mandatory retirement for Foreign Service officers. Congress sought to assure the professional competence and mental and physical reliability of the diplomatic corps that serves overseas under hardship conditions. Moreover, compulsory retirement at age sixty creates predictable opportunities for promotion and, thus, stimulates superior performance and enhances morale among junior Foreign Service personnel. Those above sixty are sufficiently old and less capable than younger persons of confronting the rigors of overseas duty.

It is constitutionally permissible to place a high value on the proper conduct of U.S. foreign policy, to subject Foreign Service officers to an earlier retirement age than occurs in the Civil Service, and to assure that promotion opportunities would be available among the limited number of Foreign Service officers. The goal of maintaining a competent Foreign Service is rationally related to the means of mandatory retirement at age sixty. In 1978, Congress repealed the mandatory retirement age for Civil Service personnel (5 percent of those who serve abroad) but left untouched mandatory retirement for those under the Foreign Service system, 60 percent of whom serve overseas at any given time.

Justice Thurgood Marshall dissented and argued that the Court should afford those terminated by age a heightened level of judicial scrutiny and protection. The prevalence of age discrimination in American society should require government to show a substantial relationship between a mandatory retirement system and actual governmental objectives. The federal government failed to provide evidence that it has encountered age-related problems with Foreign Service officers age sixty and over, and federal officials failed to show that forced retirement that affects one's livelihood and dignity boosts productivity.

—*Steve J. Mazurana*

**See also** Age discrimination; Age Discrimination Act of 1975; Age Discrimination in Employment Act of 1967; Employment; Forced retirement; *Johnson v. Mayor and City Council of Baltimore; Massachusetts Board of Retirement v. Murgia;* Retirement.

## VARICOSE VEINS

**RELEVANT ISSUES:** Health and medicine

**SIGNIFICANCE:** Although varicose veins can occur at any time, they are particularly predominant among the elderly; 50 percent of all individuals can expect to develop varicose veins by the age of fifty

The main task of normal leg veins is to return blood to the heart and lungs. This is difficult because the blood must be pushed upward, against the constant force of gravity. The force that propels the blood up the leg comes from the contraction of the calf muscles surrounding the deep veins that occurs during the act of walking. This forward momentum is quickly lost as gravity pulls the blood back down; however, one-way valves attached to the inside of the vein wall allow blood to pass up the leg freely, then close before the blood can be pulled back down. With each step taken, the column of blood moves up the leg until it eventually reaches the heart.

### DAMAGE TO THE VALVES

The system works well until one of the valves fails. Valves may fail because of congenital defect or because of damage from venous thrombosis (blood clots in the veins of the leg). As one ages, long periods of standing or straining eventually cause even normal veins to become stretched out and dilated, causing the valve leaflets to close improperly. When the vein valves do not close correctly, blood leaks backward, placing extra pres-

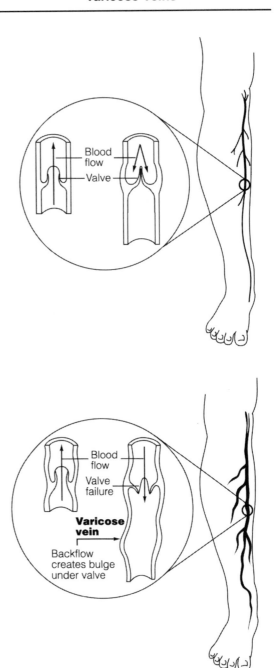

**Varicose Veins**

*In normal veins, the wings of the valves shut completely, preventing backflow of blood; with varicose veins, backflow creates a bulge that leads to the characteristic appearance of branched blue veins on the legs. (Hans & Cassidy, Inc.)*

sure on the valve beneath it. This increased pressure causes the vein to become dilated and twisted. Such veins are said to be "varicose." If this vein is near the skin, they will bulge out and become visible. These unsightly veins become more pronounced while standing and disappear or become less noticeable when lying down.

Once damaged, the valve cannot repair itself. The increased pressure continues to damage valve after valve until the small bump eventually becomes a large, bluish rope. Varicose veins are frequently accompanied by an aching sensation or a feeling of heaviness in the legs. These symptoms are aggravated by sitting or standing. People who must be on their feet all day usually experience severe discomfort. As the condition worsens, the legs and feet swell. These symptoms, which are often absent upon arising from bed in the morning, usually become more severe as the day progresses.

## POSSIBLE COMPLICATIONS

Although varicose veins are embarrassing and sometimes painful, they are not always a serious condition. Most people experience only minor inconvenience from them. However, if allowed to progress, varicose veins lead to more serious conditions. One of the most common—and most serious—of these complications is a blood clot within the varicose vein. As long as blood is moving quickly in a vessel, it is very difficult for it to clot. When a vein becomes varicose, the dilated portion of the vein allows blood to pool. If blood stagnates, it can become a solid mass of blood called a thrombus, or a blood clot. This blood clot may continue to grow up the vein. It can fill the entire vein from the foot to the groin and enter the deep veins of the leg.

A clot in a deep vein is a potentially life-threatening condition, as it may break loose, pass through the heart, and lodge in the arteries that take blood to the lungs. This condition is referred to as a pulmonary embolism. If this happens, and the blood clot is small, the patient experiences shortness of breath and chest pain. If the clot that breaks loose is big and lodges in a larger lung artery, it can result in sudden death. Blood clots limited to the superficial veins (near the skin) are far less likely to break loose and result in a major pulmonary embolism. The symptoms of clot in the superficial veins are pain and redness directly over

the vein involved. The varicose vein may also become hard. This is called a superficial cord. As the clot grows, the redness, pain, and cord move up the leg. This is a serious condition and requires immediate medical attention.

Other complications associated with varicose veins relate to the impact of having increased venous pressure in the legs over a long period of time. When the valves are working, the pressure in the tissue at the ankle is kept at a low level. When varicose veins are severe, the pressure in the tissue becomes so high that blood flow to the skin decreases. If this occurs over a long period of time, the skin becomes discolored and hardens. Ultimately, the skin breaks down, and venous ulcers occur. These open, weeping sores can become infected and become a chronic problem.

## TREATMENT AND PREVENTION

Minor varicose veins are managed quite effectively—if caught early—with well-fitting elastic compression stockings. These place pressure over the superficial veins, giving them support and preventing additional damage to them. This also forces blood into the deep veins. Assuming the deep veins have functioning valves in them, this provides relief and slows progression of the problem. Another popular approach is to surgically remove the damaged vein. This operation, called stripping, removes the veins with damaged valves, forcing blood to go through healthy veins. This can resolve the symptoms of varicose veins altogether. However, other veins may eventually become varicose.

Another intervention to get rid of varicose veins is injection therapy, or sclerotherapy, in which the patient is injected with a material that irritates the varicose vein, causing a clot to form in it. The clot is carefully controlled so that it stays only in the vein being treated. The clot attaches to the vein wall, causing the vein to shrink. This shrinking of the vein makes it seem to disappear. Sclerotherapy is not appropriate in more serious cases of varicose veins.

There is nothing that can be done to change congenital or inherited factors that cause varicose veins. There are, however, simple measures that can prevent the development of varicose veins before they occur or can slow their progression once they have developed. These preventive measures all have a common theme: avoiding long periods of sitting or standing and keeping the calf muscle active. Doctors advise people who must sit or stand for any length of time to flex and relax their calf muscles by pulling their feet up and pushing them back down. This keeps the blood moving and keeps it from pooling. Other measures include breaking up long periods of inactivity by walking a few minutes every hour, elevating the legs from time to time, and wearing loose clothing that does not restrict blood flow. Some doctors also recommend eating a high-fiber diet since some varicose vein problems result from straining during difficult bowel movements. —*Steven R. Talbot*

**See also** Aging process; Cosmetic surgery; Health care.

## FOR FURTHER INFORMATION:

Cranley, Jack J. *Vascular Surgery. Volume 11: Peripheral Vascular Diseases.* Hagerstown, Md.: Harper & Row, 1975.

Hobbs, J. T. *The Treatment of Venous Disorders: A Comprehensive Review of Current Practice in the Management of Varicose Veins and the Post-Thrombotic Syndrome.* Philadelphia: J. B. Lippincott, 1977.

Kumar, Vinay, Ramzi Cotran, and Stanley L. Robbins, eds. *Basic Pathology.* 6th ed. Philadelphia: W. B. Saunders, 1997.

Sabiston, David C., Jr., ed. *Textbook of Surgery.* 15th ed. Philadelphia: W. B. Saunders, 1997.

Wyngaarden, James, et al., eds. *Cecil Textbook of Medicine.* 19th ed. Philadelphia: W. B. Saunders, 1992.

## VIOLENT CRIME AGAINST THE ELDERLY

**RELEVANT ISSUES:** Demographics, family, sociology, violence

**SIGNIFICANCE:** The declining physical, and sometimes mental, abilities of the elderly make them particularly vulnerable to criminal victimization

Two primary sources supply official information on the extent of crime in the United States: the Uniform Crime Reports and the National Crime Victimization Survey. Both are published by the United States Department of Justice. The Uniform Crime Reports are compiled by the Federal Bureau of Investigation (FBI) and contain crime data on arrests and offenses that law enforcement agencies know have been committed. The National Crime Victimization Survey is based on self-reports of criminal victimization by a random sample of the population. Each year, a representative sample of the population is asked to identify the extent to which they have been criminally victimized during the preceding six months. Both sources examine crimes by age of offender and victim. Generally, the elderly population consists of those age sixty-five or older.

### CRIME AND THE ELDERLY

Those crimes that are considered to be serious violent crimes are homicide, forcible rape, aggravated assault, and robbery. Simple assaults do not entail the use of a weapon or result in serious injury to the victim. Aggravated assault involves attacks with a weapon that may or may not result in bodily harm. Robbery is defined as taking something from another by force or the threat of force, with or without a weapon, and with or without personal injury. Although low compared to other age groups, assaults (both simple and aggravated) and robbery rank highest among the violent crimes suffered by the elderly. Their frequency of robbery victimization indicates to the U.S. Department of Justice that the elderly are particularly prone to crimes whose motive is economic gain.

Although the elderly rank among the highest in terms of fear of crime, they rank the lowest in terms of criminal victimization. According to U.S. Department of Justice evidence, people age fifty and older represent about 30 percent of the population and only 12 percent of murder victims and 7 percent of serious violent crime victims. In contrast, those between the ages of twelve and twenty-four represent less than 25 percent of the population but nearly 50 percent of all those victimized by serious crime. Victimization rates for crime generally increase through the teenage years, then steadily decrease after age twenty.

Elderly violent crime victims are more likely than younger victims to suffer serious physical injury. Among those sixty-five and older, about 9 percent are the victims of serious injuries (broken bones, lost teeth, internal injuries, lost consciousness, rape or attempted rape injuries, or undetermined injuries requiring two or more days of hospitalization). Only about 5 percent of younger victims of violent crime suffer such serious injuries.

The elderly are much more likely to be victimized near their place of residence than younger people. For example, elderly victims are twice as likely as younger victims to be raped, robbed, or assaulted near their homes. The relative immobility of the elderly and the fact that many are retired and less inclined to socialize away from home or attend public events after sundown are thought to be primary contributing factors for this finding.

### VICTIMIZATION BY STRANGERS

Compared to younger people, the elderly are more likely to be violently victimized by a stranger. Furthermore, 38 percent of elderly people who are victimized by strangers are confronted by armed offenders, compared to 35 percent of those under the age of sixty-five; of these, 41 percent of elderly people and 36 percent of younger people are accosted by an offender with a gun.

Generally, victims of violent crime are confronted by a single offender. The likelihood of being victimized by multiple offenders varies by crime and age. In the case of robbery, one-half of elderly victims are the victims of multiple offenders, while more than one-half of younger victims are the victims of single offenders. In the case of aggravated assault, younger victims are more likely to be victims of multiple offenders.

The elderly are less inclined than younger people to protect themselves when violently victimized. Self-protective measures are sought by elderly victims in about 58 percent of their victimizations, as compared to 73 percent for younger victims. Elderly victims who do seek to protect themselves tend to use nonviolent means (arguing, attempting to reason with the offender, screaming, or fleeing). Elderly victims are more likely than younger victims to report a robbery but not an aggravated assault to the police.

Elderly men are much more inclined than elderly women to be violently victimized. However, elderly women are much more likely than elderly men to be the victims of personal larceny, particularly purse snatching. Further, elderly African American and Latino males are more likely than elderly Caucasian males to be victimized by violent crime. Higher violence rates are also experienced by those elderly with the lowest family incomes. Elders who are divorced or separated, live in apartments, and live in urban areas experience the highest criminal victimization rates for both violent and property crime.

### VICTIMIZATION BY INTIMATES

It is generally understood that the elderly are subject to much more abuse and criminal victimization than is reported to official agencies. It is also commonly thought that elder abuse and violence at the hands of intimates (spouses, former spouses, children, relatives, and friends) is more likely to go unreported than that perpetrated by strangers. Diminished physical and financial ability to challenge perpetrators, fear of retaliation, and dependence on caregivers are among the more prominent reasons for this. Whatever the reasons, violent criminal victimization of the elderly by intimates is highly prevalent and is a problem worthy of much greater official and public attention.

Based on reports from law enforcement agencies in nine states, the U.S. Department of Justice found that about 15 percent of all assaults on those over age forty were perpetrated by intimates. Intimate assaults include murder and both simple and aggravated assaults. Women, regardless of age, are much more likely than men to be murdered by an intimate. Among those sixty or older, about 20 percent of female murder victims were murdered by an intimate. For men the same age, the corresponding figure is 7 percent.

When rates of nonlethal violence inflicted by an intimate are considered, those sixty-five or older record a figure of 0.2 per 1,000 members of the population, the lowest of any age category. Nonlethal violence includes forcible rape, sexual assault, robbery, and both aggravated and simple assault.

In 1994, the United States began to experience a consistent decline in crime rates. Not surprisingly, given the fact that they have the lowest rates of criminal victimization, elderly victimization rates were little influenced by the general trend. Violent crime rate declines were highest in those disproportionately involved in its perpetration and victimization, most notably males between sixteen and thirty years of age. With the exception of the homicide rate, which steadily declined during the 1980's and 1990's, violent victimization rates among the elderly population were noteworthy for remaining rather steady. Victimization rates for rape and sexual assault among those sixty-five or older showed no significant change. However, there was a slight increase in elderly victimization rates for robbery and assaults, both simple and aggravated. —*Calvin J. Larson*

**See also** Elder abuse; Injuries among the elderly; Safety issues.

**FOR FURTHER INFORMATION:**
Bachman, Ronet. "The Double Edged Sword of Violent Victimization Against the Elderly: Patterns of Family and Stranger Perpetration." *Journal of Elder Abuse and Neglect* 5, no. 4 (1993).
Bachman, Ronet, et al. "Violence Against the Elderly." *Research on Aging* 20, no. 2 (March, 1998).
Decalmer, Peter, and Frank Glendenning, eds. *The Mistreatment of Elderly People*. 2d ed. Thousand Oaks, Calif.: Sage Publications, 1997.
Report of the American Psychological Association Presidential Task Force on Violence and the Family. *Violence and the Family*. Washington, D.C.: American Psychological Association, 1996.
U.S. Department of Justice. *Age Patterns of Victims of Serious Violent Crime*. Washington, D.C.: U.S. Government Printing Office, 1997.
_____. *Elderly Crime Victims: National Crime Victimization Survey*. Washington, D.C.: U.S. Government Printing Office, 1994.
_____. *Violence by Intimates*. Washington, D.C.: U.S. Government Printing Office, 1998.

## VIRTUES OF AGING, THE

**AUTHOR:** Jimmy Carter
**DATE:** Published in 1998
**RELEVANT ISSUES:** Family, health and medicine, religion, work
**SIGNIFICANCE:** Carter's book emphasizes the importance of quality of life rather than quantity of years or possessions for senior citizens

In *The Virtues of Aging* (1998), former president Jimmy Carter reveals his philosophy of aging; the book is an inspirational autobiographical account that he prepared as a guide for how the elderly can seek an improved lifestyle. He addresses the social, physical, and emotional aspects of aging and encourages readers to welcome opportunities that being elderly offers them.

Carter, writing in his seventies, describes the despair he felt when he lost the 1980 presidential election. He endured a personal crisis, feeling hopeless about the future. Gradually, he became involved in new projects and realized that aging did not require him to cease activity. Retirement enabled him to have time to grow spiritually and intellectually and to explore previously unconsidered options.

Carter describes how attitudes toward retired Americans changed during the twentieth century, comparing different generations, cultural perceptions of work, and the establishment of government policies for the elderly. Carter laments that ageism exists. He cites statistics showing that life spans are increasing, resulting in longer retirements and greater numbers of senior citizens. Carter urges the elderly to accept the challenges and changes presented by aging and advises people to seek knowledge and plan for the future, especially regarding financial decisions. He provides exercise and nutritional tips to offset physical limitations caused by aging. Carter believes senior citizens should volunteer, sharing their talents to improve their communities.

Love for self and others is Carter's main theme. He discusses aged mentors who have influenced him. He explains how his spirituality has enhanced his happiness as he has aged and how he hopes to enlighten others with his awareness of aging as a positive experience to be savored.

—*Elizabeth D. Schafer*

**See also** Religion; Successful aging; Volunteering.

## VISION CHANGES AND DISORDERS

**RELEVANT ISSUES:** Biology, health and medicine
**SIGNIFICANCE:** The eye is a highly specialized and intricate organ; many of the normal biological changes associated with aging affect the structure and function of the eye, resulting in changes in vision and increased occurrence of eye diseases

The job of the eye is to gather visual information and transmit these images to the brain, where they are synthesized into a meaningful picture of one's surroundings. These images provide information for balance, direction, and safety. Vision also plays a role in intellectual development and learning

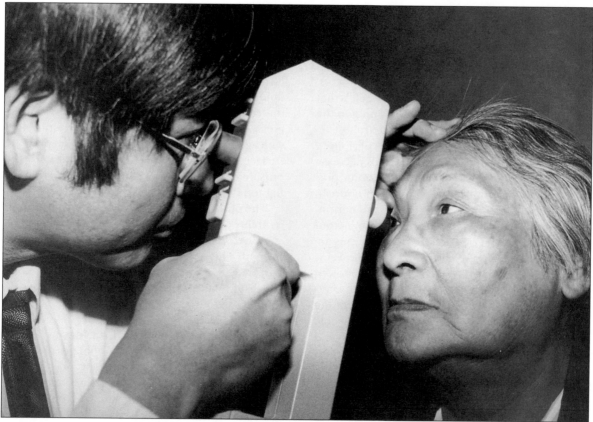

*Regular screenings for such vision disorders as cataracts and glaucoma are vital in later life.* (Frances M. Roberts)

through activities such as reading and writing. The eye develops through an involved process in which it must be properly positioned, supplied with nutrients through blood circulation, supported with bone and fat, moved by an intricate set of muscles, and directed by a complex set of nerves. The proper functioning of the eye is so important to human life that the eye is serviced by four major nerves that arise from the brain.

Light enters the eye through an adjustable opening called the iris. The iris is the part of the eye that determines a person's eye color. In the middle of the iris is a black hole, called the pupil, which is made larger or smaller depending on the availability of light. In bright sunlight, the iris contracts and makes the pupil opening very small, limiting the amount of light that enters the eye. In dim light or at night, the iris creates a very large pupil opening in order to gather as much light as possible. The part of the eye that is responsible for focusing the light is the lens, a transparent cover over the iris and pupil. The lens focuses the light on an area at the back of the eye called the retina, where special cells called photoreceptors process the light information and send it to the brain. In order to focus light properly, the lens must be flexible and able to elongate or shorten. The front of the eye is completely covered by the transparent cornea. A series of six muscles moves the eye from side to side, up and down, and inward and outward.

### NORMAL AGE-RELATED CHANGES IN THE EYE

The eye is supported and cushioned in the eye socket, or orbital, by a layer of fat called orbital fat. As a person ages, this fat breaks down and degenerates, and the eye may appear sunken or hollow. A second change that is easily observed is the loss of tone and elasticity of the skin and muscle that surrounds the eye. The skin around the eye loses the ability to stretch and snap back into shape, much like the elastic in an old pair of underwear.

The result is that the skin above the eye tends to fold over the upper eyelid. Sometimes this extra fold of skin can increase the pressure on the eye or reduce overhead vision.

The retina is also affected by the aging process. The cells of the retina, the photoreceptor cells that receive the light information and transmit it to the brain, are gradually lost over time and are not replaced. Also, the blood supply to the periphery (outer parts) of the retina decreases. This decrease in blood supply means that cells in the outer portion of the eye are not receiving as much nourishment from the blood. Sometimes a loss of peripheral vision, the ability to see things coming from the sides of the field of vision, results from this decrease in blood supply. All the arteries and veins that supply the eye with blood become narrower, or sclerosed, with age, just like all the other arteries and veins of the body. The macular area of the retina—the area of the retina that is responsible for the sharpest, central sight—collects the end products of the aging and dying photoreceptors.

Many changes also occur with the outer components of the eye. The most obvious change is the hardening of the lens, causing an inability to focus objects that are close to the eye. The inability to see near objects (presbyopia) affects all individuals and usually begins around age forty-five. People who had completely normal sight will require reading glasses to correct this, while people who are nearsighted often need bifocals.

The lens also becomes less transparent or more opaque. Sometimes this loss of transparency results from changes in lens proteins caused by exposure to ultraviolet (UV) light over time. The lens becomes brownish-orange or yellow in appearance. The yellowing causes changes in color vision; for instance, the perception of different shades of blue is more difficult because the yellowish color filters out blue light (like wearing a yellow pair of sunglasses) and allows more red and yellow light to enter the eye. This gradual loss of transparency of the lens can also lead to cataracts.

The eye is filled with a watery, gelatinous substance called the vitreous humor. The vitreous humor may collect particles of debris that can be seen by the individual as "floaters" that occasionally cross the field of vision. The vitreous humor may become more watery and less gelatinous over time. This causes the gel to shrink, and it can become

detached from the retina, resulting in visual impairment.

With age, the cornea of the eye can lose its natural transparency and become more opaque, much like the lens does. Additionally, deposits of fats and lipids may accumulate in a circular ring bordering the cornea, known as the arcus senilis. Often decreased tear flow, or dry eye, becomes a problem with age. Since tears are important for keeping the surface (cornea) of the eye well lubricated, the outside of the eye can become damaged from being too dry.

The pupil itself changes with age as well. It loses its ability to quickly accommodate, or change in response to, differences in the brightness or dimness or light. The pupil generally becomes smaller as a person ages, giving the individual an increased depth of focus in the central field of view but reducing the total size of the visual field.

### AGE-RELATED PERCEPTUAL CHANGES IN VISION

Because of the many physical changes of the eye with age, the individual will experiences perceptual changes in vision. For instance, dark adaptation becomes more difficult since the pupil is less able to respond to changes in light brightness. Glare becomes a significant problem. Glare reduces the ability of all individuals to see because it creates a scattering of light that reduces the sensitivity of the viewed objects. Although people of all ages are affected by glare, this scattering is even more pronounced in older individuals who have much yellowing of the lens and cornea. Headlights from oncoming cars, for example, can literally blind the aged driver.

Visual acuity—the ability to see small objects under normal lighting and contrast—also may suffer with age. Since the pupil opening is smaller (thus letting less light into the eye) and the lens and cornea are less transparent (thus scattering the light that does reach the eye), acuity decreases significantly with age. For every thirteen years of life, the amount of light needed for the eye to function properly increases twofold because of the changes in the pupil, lens, and cornea. More light is needed for such tasks as reading and writing; this condition is sometimes called night blindness. This reduction in acuity may decrease visual performance in unfamiliar environments as insignificant objects become distracting. Also, the person will experience changes in color vision as already described, having more difficulty perceiving blues that are filtered out by the increasingly opaque lenses.

### AGE-RELATED EYE DISEASES

One of the most common reasons for loss of sight in the elderly is age-related macular degeneration (ARMD), also known as senile macular degeneration. The macula is the part of the retina where most of the photoreceptor cells are located. The macula is responsible for the sharp, central line of vision; when a person looks directly at an object, the macula is the part of the retina that collects the light information and transmits it to the brain. People who stare too long at a solar eclipse destroy their sight because the intense light damages the macula.

There are two types of macular degeneration: dry and wet. Dry macular degeneration is caused by a decrease in the nutrient supply reaching the macular tissue. This is usually caused by a loss of blood vessels supplying this region of the eye. Vision loss from this type of macular degeneration is generally slow and less severe than the vision loss associated with wet macular degeneration. Often diet (eating foods rich in vitamins A, C, and E or taking ocular vitamin supplements) can slow or prevent dry macular degeneration.

Wet macular degeneration is more serious, and the vision loss occurs more rapidly than with dry macular degeneration. With wet macular degeneration, waste products fail to be transported away from the retina. This results in an increase in fluid within the macula, and this fluid can accumulate in small pools. The pools of fluid stimulate the growth of small, weak blood vessels, which can hemorrhage (rupture) and cause vision loss. This type of macular degeneration is usually treated by laser surgery to seal off small vessels, keeping them from growing into the pools of fluid.

Some of the risk factors that seem to be associated with macular degeneration not only include age but also include smoking in males; a family history of the macular degeneration; light-colored eyes; a history of heart disease; a history of recurrent, severe respiratory infections; and a decrease in hand grip strength. All of these factors do not directly contribute to macular degeneration, but they are associated with an increased risk of the disease.

A second age-related eye disease is glaucoma. Approximately 1 percent of all people over age forty have glaucoma. Glaucoma is an increase in pressure within the eye. This increase can be caused by overproduction of fluid by the eye or failure to drain eye fluid properly. The most common kind of glaucoma results from blockage of the fluid drainage system of the eye. The optic nerve that transmits the information collected by the photoreceptor cells to the brain is particularly sensitive to this increase in pressure. The increased pressure will damage the nerve and will ultimately cause blindness if the condition is not treated.

Early symptoms of glaucoma are very hard to detect, and the pressure from fluid buildup can stay high for many years, causing the optic nerve to atrophy. The central vision of the eye is the last to be lost from glaucoma. Undiagnosed glaucoma results in approximately five thousand new cases of blindness each year in the United States. In the population over age seventy, glaucoma is one of the top three causes of blindness. Factors that increase the risk of developing glaucoma include smoking, stress, consuming large quantities of alcohol, high blood pressure, and prolonged use of steroid medication. The nerve damage from glaucoma is irreversible, but the disease can be slowed and vision loss prevented or lessened through medications.

Cataract, or lens opacity, can develop any time from infancy to adulthood. The most common cataracts are age-related and often occur after age fifty. Although cataracts can result from a variety of causes, such as injury to the eye or toxins, most age-related cataracts result from the gradual decrease in transparency of the lens that happens with age. Cataracts are removed surgically when vision loss causes difficulty in performing daily activities, such as reading or watching television. Medications, particularly the prolonged use of steroids, may cause cataracts. Systemic illnesses, such as diabetes, can also cause cataracts. Symptoms of cataracts include blurred vision that is often noticed when reading or driving. Other symptoms include double vision, a decrease in the ability to judge distances, and increased sensitivity to glare.

A final common eye disease among older individuals is diabetic retinopathy. This condition affects diabetics and results from the weakening of the small blood vessels that nourish the retina; it is the leading cause of blindness in individuals aged twenty to seventy-four. These weakened vessels can be damaged, leading to hemorrhage. New, weaker vessels may try to grow into the area of the hemorrhage and result in the formation of scar tissue. This scar tissue may eventually lead to retinal detachment and vision loss. Unless the macula is affected by this scar tissue, the diabetic will be unaware of the disease process. Therefore, diabetic patients should have annual eye examinations to screen for this problem. Patients with diabetic retinopathy do benefit from early intervention, such as laser treatment to seal leaky blood vessels and prevent fluid buildup.

A healthy lifestyle that includes a well-balanced diet is essential to visual health throughout the life span. The diet should be low in fats and salts but high in dietary fiber. Supplementing the diet with vitamins A, C, and E provides some protection against eye degeneration, and the diet should include plenty of water. Maintaining normal body weight, not smoking, and limiting alcoholic intake will also benefit eye health. As with all medical problems, early diagnosis of eye diseases is key to successful treatment; individuals are advised to have regular eye exams to screen for glaucoma, age-related macular degeneration, and other eye diseases.
                                                —*P. Michele Arduengo*

*See also* Aging: Biological, psychological, and sociocultural perspectives; Aging process; Cataracts; Diabetes; Glaucoma; Macular degeneration; Nearsightedness; Reading glasses.

## FOR FURTHER INFORMATION:

Beresford, Steven, D. W. Muris, M. J. Allen, and F. R. Young. *Improve Your Vision Without Glasses or Contact Lenses.* New York: Simon & Schuster, 1996. A discussion of exercises, habits, and diets that contribute to visual health.

D'Alonzo, T. L. *Your Eyes!* Clifton Heights, Pa.: Avanti, 1991. A reference guide to the working of the eye and explanation of eye diseases, risk factors, and treatments.

Gooding, Edward G., and John S. Hacunda. *Computers and Visual Stress.* Charleston, R.I.: Sea Coast Information Services, 1990. A brief description of the impact of video display terminal work and eye strain, including suggestions for prevention of eye-strain problems.

Shier, David, Jackie Butler, and Ricki Lewis. *Hole's Human Anatomy and Physiology.* Dubuque, Iowa: Wm. C. Brown, 1996. Chapter 12 provides information about the development and structure of the eye, with many figures and drawings to illustrate.

Shulman, Julius. *Cataracts.* Rev. ed. New York: St. Martin's Press, 1993. A patient's guide to symptoms, diagnosis, surgery, and recovery of cataracts.

Zinn, Walter J., and Herbert Solomon. *Complete Guide to Eyecare, Eyeglasses, and Contact Lenses.* 4th ed. Hollywood, Fla.: Lifetime Books, 1996. Chapter 34 provides a concise description of age-related vision problems.

## VITAMINS AND MINERALS

**RELEVANT ISSUES:** Health and medicine
**SIGNIFICANCE:** As the body ages, it utilizes vitamins and minerals less efficiently, placing the elderly at risk for nutritional deficiencies

Vitamins are micronutrients that function as coenzymes, which are at the foundation of all bodily functions. Recommendations for vitamin and mineral requirements are issued by the Food and Nutrition Board of the National Research Council, National Academy of Sciences. The daily value (DV) has replaced the recommended dietary (or daily) allowance (RDA), which is still commonly used. Because the body becomes less efficient at using nutrients as it ages, the older population is at risk for several vitamin deficiencies; standard DVs may not fully meet their micronutrient needs.

### VITAMINS A AND B

Vitamin A is an immune system booster that protects against diseases of the respiratory system and gastrointestinal system and decreases the risk of cancer and heart disease. An antioxidant, it destroys free radicals that may make the body more susceptible to cancer, cardiovascular disease, arthritis, and signs of aging. Beta carotene is the plant precursor of vitamin A, which enables the body to make active vitamin A. The requirement for beta carotene may increase with age. It is possible that beta carotene can reduce the incidence of eye disease associated with aging. The DV for vitamin A is 30 milligrams, or 5,000 international units

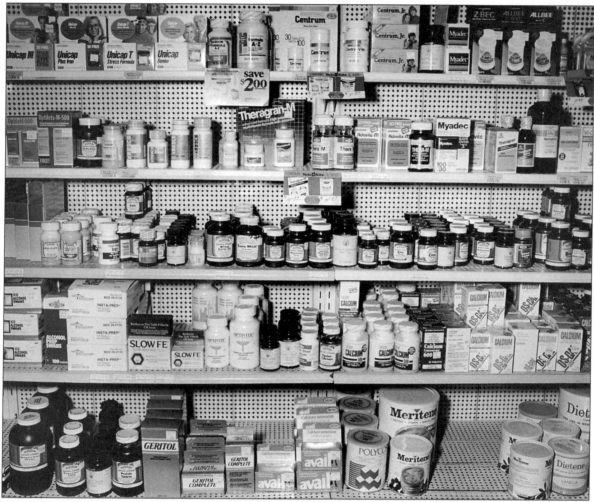

*The elderly are faced with a wide selection of over-the-counter vitamin and mineral supplements from which to choose. A doctor should be consulted to determine what is needed and to ensure proper doses.* (James L. Shaffer)

(IU), although some nutritionists recommend 10,000 to 50,000 IU. The active form of vitamin A can cause adverse effects at a daily dosage of 50,000 IU, but it usually takes a dosage of 100,000 IU for a period of months to notice negative effects. Any adverse effects are reversible.

The B vitamins are useful in healing nerves and muscles. They enhance the immune system, ease the physiological wear of aging, and may alleviate mild depression, anxiety, and poor memory. Supplementation usually includes the entire B complex. Since they work in concert, when individual B vitamins are recommended for a medical condition, additional amounts of the B complex should also be taken.

Vitamin $B_1$ is called thiamine. Thiamine deficiency is common among the elderly; symptoms may include fatigue, depression, confusion, nervousness, memory loss, and numbness of hands and feet. The DV is only 1.4 milligrams for males and 1.1 milligrams for females, but nutritionists tend to recommend 25 to 300 milligrams. Vitamin $B_2$, also known as riboflavin, may prevent or delay cataracts and is useful for neurological problems. Vitamin $B_3$, which comes in the form of niacin and niacinamide, is helpful in treating circulatory problems, and large doses can cause the skin to flush. Pantothenic acid, formerly called vitamin $B_5$, is important to nerve transmission and the immune system. It seems to protect against stress.

Vitamin $B_6$ is one of the most widely utilized vitamins, but many studies have found the elderly to be deficient. Inadequate intake means poorer immune function and higher risk of heart attack in older people. The DV is 2.2 milligrams. Doses of one hundred times the DV can cause nerve damage, but it is reversible. Supplementation of 200 milligrams per day for more than one month can sometimes cause dependency and so should not be stopped abruptly.

Vitamin $B_{12}$ (cobalamin) and folate deficiencies are common in the elderly. The DV is only 0.03 milligrams, but people over the age of sixty do not absorb vitamin $B_{12}$ from foods as well as younger people; for this reason, the National Academy of Sciences recommends that older people take vitamin $B_{12}$ supplements; 200 to 500 percent of the DV is recommended. Folic acid (also called folate) protects the heart and may help prevent colon cancer. The recommended DV is 4 to 12 milligrams.

### VITAMINS C, D, AND E

Vitamin C plays a major role in maintaining the immune system, handling stress, and preventing cancer, and also functions as an antioxidant. Elderly, nonsmoking men have lower levels of vitamin C in blood plasma than young men with the same intake. The DV is only 60 milligrams, which may be too low; the National Institutes of Health (NIH) regards 200 milligrams as ideal. Many nutritionists suggest 200 to 500 milligrams. It is believed that supplementation of 120 to 180 milligrams lowers the risk of cancer and cataracts in the elderly. People with kidney problems are advised to consult with a qualified professional about vitamin C supplementation. Bioflavonoids are antioxidants that are present with vitamin C in citrus pulp. They strengthen capillary walls, which protects against black-and-blue marks and varicose veins.

Vitamin D in its active form is considered to be a hormone. It helps absorb calcium and metabolize phosphorus and contributes to bone density. Calcium and magnesium should be taken with vitamin D to treat the thinning bones of menopausal women. Although the human body can make vitamin D from sunshine, many elderly people may not be exposed to enough sun to get a sufficient dose. There is no DV, but most professionals regard 400 IU as a reasonable amount. Up to 1,000 IU appears to be safe, although most nutritionists advise against taking more than 800 IU.

Vitamin E is a powerful antioxidant that may slow aging by promoting cell vitality; it also protects the body against various carcinogens and toxins, and improves blood flow to the extremities. Vitamin E is possibly helpful in treating circulatory problems to which older people are more susceptible, such as angina, arteriosclerosis, thrombophlebitis, and intermittent claudication. It may even alleviate lipofuscin, commonly known as liver spots or age spots. The DV is 10 to 20 IU, but many researchers suggest 400 IU, and some cardiologists recommend 200 to 600 IU.

### MINERALS

Some minerals are also essential to health, functioning like vitamins as coenzymes. In addition to building strong bones, calcium is important to white blood cells and helps ward off infections. Calcium also aids blood clotting, helps tired muscles, and also protects against high blood pressure. The DV is 800 milligrams, but 1,000 to 1,500 is recommended. Phosphorus contributes to the hardness of bones and plays a role in utilization of food. In most diets, phosphorus intake exceeds calcium intake, but nutritionists recommend as much calcium as phosphorus.

Zinc promotes a strong immune system and wound healing and helps prevent colds, but excess zinc interferes with absorption of copper; therefore, a zinc supplement should be taken with copper. One study found that zinc and selenium seemed to reduce infections in the elderly. Zinc is also helpful in treating the benign prostate enlargement common in older men. The decrease in taste that the elderly often experience may be alleviated by zinc supplementation. The DV for zinc is 15 milligrams, but some nutritionists suggest 22 to 50 milligrams. In one study, the zinc intake of elderly people was less than one-half the DV. Senile purpura (purple spots under the skin) may be caused by zinc deficiency. Copper is helpful in bone and heart health, blood sugar regulation, and iron absorption. The DV for copper is 2 milligrams. Copper deficiency is rare, but taking 1 milligram of copper for every 10 or 15 milligram of zinc will maintain the proper balance.

Chromium is the major mineral involved in insulin production, and low levels may result in hypoglycemia and increase risk of adult-onset diabetes. The DV has not been established; the National Research Council suggests 0.5 to 2 milligrams, and, in 1996, the Food and Drug Administration (FDA) recommended 1.2 milligrams. Some nutritionists recommend 2 to 6 milligrams. The average American diet provides only 1 milligram, and chromium deficiency is believed to be relatively common.

Selenium is an antioxidant synergistic with vitamin E; it may lower risk of prostatitis, lung, and colon cancer. Selenium deficiency may be associated with cardiovascular disease. A Finnish study of elderly people who were given selenium and vitamin E supplementation found improvement in mental states. The recommended DV is 1 milligram. Magnesium helps convert food into energy and is required for strong, healthy bones. It is linked to protection from diabetes, osteoporosis, atherosclerosis, and hypertension. The DV for magnesium is 400 milligrams. People with abnormal kidney function are advised to take magnesium supplements only under a physician's supervision.

Manganese is essential to many enzyme systems involved with metabolism and is required for proper functioning of the nerves. Manganese deficiency may affect the immune system and may play a role in glucose tolerance. There is no established DV, but the Food and Nutrition Board recommends 2.5 to 5 milligrams, and some nutritionists recommend 15 to 30 milligrams. Potassium is necessary for the fluid balance of cells, healthy skin, and stable blood pressure. Soft drinks contain large amounts of phosphorus, which depletes potassium. A potassium deficiency can cause a calcium deficiency. No DV has been established. Iron makes hemoglobin. Postmenopausal women need less iron. Only people with iron-deficiency anemia should take more than the DV, and some physicians suggest men avoid iron supplements.

—*William L. Reinshagen*

**See also** Age spots; Antiaging treatments; Antioxidants; Cancer; Free radical theory of aging; Malnutrition; Nutrition; Osteoporosis; Prostate enlargement; Skin changes and disorders.

### FOR FURTHER INFORMATION:

Gallagher, John. *Good Health with Vitamins and Minerals: A Complete Guide to a Lifetime of Safe and Effective Use.* New York: Summit Books, 1990.

Golgan, Michael. *Your Personal Vitamin Profile: A Medical Scientist Shows You How to Chart Your Individual Vitamin and Mineral Formula.* New York: William Morrow, 1982.

Lieberman, Shari, and Nancy Bruning. *Design Your Own Vitamin and Mineral Program.* Garden City, N.Y.: Doubleday, 1987.

Mindell, Earl. *Shaping Up with Vitamins: How the Right Foods and Nutrition Can Help with Your Body, Your Mind, and Your Sex Life.* New York: Warner Books, 1985.

Scala, James. *Making the Vitamin Connection: The Food Supplement Story.* New York: Harper & Row, 1985.

## VOLUNTEERING

**RELEVANT ISSUES:** Recreation, sociology, values, work

**SIGNIFICANCE:** Volunteering provides many health benefits and gives older people an opportunity to participate in activities that they may not have been able to pursue when they were employed or raising a family

Many Americans retire by the age of sixty, and almost all Americans have retired by the age of seventy. Yet the average American life expectancy is well beyond seventy; in fact, many people lead active, vital lives into their eighties and nineties. Thus, many retirees and people who spent their youth and middle years raising a family find that they have twenty or thirty years of free time. Some of these people choose to work at part-time jobs or in paid consulting positions. Others, however, turn to volunteer activities as a way to develop themselves, help their communities, and help their fellow citizens.

### TYPES OF VOLUNTEER ACTIVITIES

Elderly Americans volunteer in a multitude of ways and in a wide variety of settings. Any community service position or profession can have a volunteer aspect to it. For example, many people volunteer in the public school systems. They do not serve in the professional capacity of classroom teacher, but they aid the classroom teachers by performing many tasks—such as grading papers, making photocopies, and keeping records—that the classroom teacher does not have time to complete. Also, many classroom volunteers tutor in subject areas and in basic skills such as reading and mathematics. In kindergarten and first- and second-grade classrooms, elderly volunteers sometimes read to children, thus helping the children to develop a love of reading and learning.

Older Americans may also volunteer to be on community councils and boards, such as town councils, boards of education, planning commissions, and other civic committees. Volunteers answer phones, edit newsletters, write reports, prepare press releases, organize fund-raising campaigns, and organize and train other volunteers. Older Americans make up many of the boards of directors of civic organizations across the United States, and they serve as officers for many of these organizations.

Many of the retirees who volunteer are also veterans. Often veterans are interested in helping other veterans; thus, they volunteer to perform nonprofessional services in veterans' hospitals throughout the United States. Other volunteers serve in nonprofessional positions, such as greeters and patient aides, in community hospitals. Libraries benefit from the services of older Americans who volunteer to shelve books, collect fines, check books in and out, and assist library patrons in locating reference materials. Children are the concern of many volunteers who regularly lead Boy Scout and Girl Scout trips and chaperon church youth groups on trips and at meetings.

Another area where volunteers have been especially helpful is in advocacy positions in the courts. Special volunteers, appointed as advocates by the courts, advocate for the rights of children who have to appear in court proceedings but who have no adult to advocate for their rights. These court-appointed advocates receive special training from the court system. Other groups, such as the indigent, the homeless, and the mentally impaired, also sometimes receive volunteer help from people who advocate for them. The homeless and the indigent are also the recipient of volunteer ser-

*Retirees can use their lifetime of work experience to help young people. For example, teachers and others may volunteer to read to children.* (Marilyn Nolt)

*Many older people use volunteering as a way to stay in touch with younger generations and to give back to their communi-ties.* (James L. Shaffer)

vices in shelters, where much of the work, such as securing food and supplies, writing grants, meal preparation, and food service, is done by volunteers.

Many older Americans also volunteer in the private sector. Many people who have been successful in business serve as volunteer consultants, helping fledgling businesses and young entrepreneurs to become financially and personally successful. People retired from professions such as law, medicine, education, journalism, and engineering often choose to be volunteer mentors to young people who are entering, or who plan to enter, the profession from which the volunteer has retired. The retired professionals help the novices to understand how the profession works and how to avoid certain pitfalls that the professional life might present.

### VALUE OF VOLUNTEERING

Volunteering has value for the person who volunteers, for the community as a whole, and for the people who are recipients of the volunteer services. There are enormous social, intellec-tual, emotional, and physical benefits for the older person who volunteers. Almost all volunteer activities require the volunteer to come into contact with other people. This contact helps the volunteer retain social bonds with others and assures that elderly people, whose family members may not live with them or even in the same community, do not become recluses. Volunteering helps the volunteer retain and develop intellectual functioning. Many volunteer activities, such as tutoring, require the volunteer to think and to solve problems, which keeps the elderly person mentally active.

Many volunteer activities also require volunteers to assume professional roles that they have never before assumed. As the volunteer thinks about the new role, adjusts to it, and considers its various aspects, he or she must exercise a type of mental flexibility. The ability to be mentally flexible keeps the mind active. There is evidence that elderly people who use their minds to engage in problem solving and who are flexible in their approach to life's problems live longer, healthier lives and are able to perform daily tasks further into old age than are people who do not attempt to problem solve or to perform mental tasks.

Volunteering contributes to the volunteer's emotional well-being. This is true for a variety of reasons. First, as has been mentioned, the person who volunteers makes social contacts. The social contacts themselves help volunteers feel more at ease in their environment and feel emotional satisfaction. Also, the knowledge that they have helped others is emotionally satisfying to nearly all volunteers. Finally, many volunteers do things that they would have liked to do at a younger age but were prevented from doing because they had to earn a living or care for a family. Thus, many older people find it satisfying to be able to fulfill their youthful dreams. Volunteering can also contribute to a person's physical well-being. Leaving the house, moving around, and meeting appointments may cause retirees to become more physically alert and more conscious of their physical health.

Volunteer services have great financial and social value to the communities in which they are performed. Each year, in every community across the United States, volunteers contribute literally thousands of service hours that the community would have to pay for if there were no volunteers. Beyond the financial value, these volunteer hours have enormous social value. Volunteer services help all citizens come together to work for the common good and for the survival of the community. No price tag could be put on the importance of citizens working for the common good. Citizens working together is what makes a community truly a community, rather than just a collection of houses, businesses, and public institutions.

Individuals who use volunteer services receive both general and specific value from these services. In general, the individuals receiving the services understand that they are part of a larger community that cares about their welfare and their future; the knowledge of this caring is important for the individuals' well-being. Also, individuals receive a multitude of specific good from volunteers—tutoring, counseling, meal preparation, disaster aide, transportation, and so forth. Specific services are important and often life-sustaining for the people who receive them.

Serving as a volunteer enriches the life of the volunteer, the life of the community in which the volunteer services are performed, and the lives of those who are recipients of the volunteer services. Some volunteers even go beyond the bounds of their own communities to perform work. Some older Americans join the Peace Corps and go to developing countries, where they teach, train farmers, serve in hospitals, and help local people develop businesses. Some retired medical personnel go to Africa, Eastern Europe, or Central America to help people who are victims of civil unrest. Others volunteer to help the Red Cross and other disaster relief agencies to get food and medical supplies to parts of the world where disaster has occurred.                              —*Annita Marie Ward*

**See also** Advocacy; Caregiving; Employment; Home services; Leisure activities; Mentoring; Politics; Retired and Senior Volunteer Program (RSVP); Retirement; Social ties; *Virtues of Aging, The*; Wisdom.

**FOR FURTHER INFORMATION:**

Bull, C. Neil, and Nancy D. Levine, eds. *Older Volunteers: An Annotated Bibliography*. Westport, Conn.: Greenwood Press, 1993.

Carter, Jimmy, with Peter Gethers. *The Virtues of Aging*. New York: Ballantine Books, 1998.

Driskall, J. Lawrence. *Adventures in Senior Living: Learning to Make Retirement Meaningful and Enjoyable*. Binghamton, N.Y.: Haworth Press, 1997.

Hennon, Charles B. *Lifestyles of the Elderly*. New York: Human Sciences Press, 1989.

## VOTING PATTERNS

**RELEVANT ISSUES:** Demographics, sociology
**SIGNIFICANCE:** Older voters are a growing segment of the electorate; however, the senior vote is rarely monolithic

Senior entitlements have been referred to as the "third rail" of American politics: A legislator who threatens them dies politically. Like other interest groups, aging American voters are believed to put their own financial interests first. Few politicians have come to grief from following this rule. To the contrary, representative Claude Pepper of Florida held his seat from 1963 to 1989 largely on the basis of defending his older constituents' interests. Like most political nostrums, this simple rule conceals as much as it reveals. Few people of any age are one-issue voters. While the senior vote can be pivotal in a few situations, the voting patterns of older Americans vary widely.

## OBSERVED PATTERNS

Older Americans vote in relatively large numbers. Surveys show the over-sixty-five group either to have the highest turnout rate of any age cohort or to rank only slightly behind the fifty-five to sixty-four age group. In contrast, citizens aged eighteen to twenty-nine participate the least; a sixty-five-year-old is three times as likely to vote as a twenty-year-old. Earlier theories predicted that health problems or "disengagement" would cause less voting after age sixty-five. Actual studies show these theories to be wrong. Only among those over eighty is there any drop-off effect, presumably because of ill health. However, the drop in participation is very small, and increasing use of absentee ballots and mail-in voting may counteract it.

Party or partisan affiliation increases with age. Fewer people over sixty than younger citizens call themselves independents or support third parties. In 1980, only 4 percent of the over-sixty voters supported presidential candidate John Anderson, who ran as an independent. This contrasts with the 7 percent vote Anderson drew from the overall electorate and his 11 percent rate among eighteen- to twenty-nine-year-olds. Likewise, in the 1992 presidential election, Reform Party candidate Ross Perot received only 12 percent of the over-sixty votes but won 19 percent of the whole electorate. In 1998, former professional wrestler Jesse Ventura, running on the Reform Party ticket, defeated two conventional party politicians to become governor of Minnesota. Ventura carried all age groups except those over sixty.

Older voters' stronger party affiliations do not stop them from ticket splitting. Rather, research shows that age brings more attachment to traditional institutions, including political institutions. Lifetime experience may also have induced doubts about "wasting" their vote on an independent. Beyond these trends, the same traits that affect voting in general apply to older voters. These include socioeconomic status, educational level, party identification, political ideology, and gender. These factors, singly or together, determine older voters' choices on candidates and issues far more than does their age per se.

## UNSETTLED QUESTIONS

American politics offers few chances for voters to express their views on issues directly at the ballot box. Exceptions include certain local measures, such as school bonds, and statewide referenda. Such occasions offer a unique opportunity to see if elderly voters skew away from the mainstream on specific issues.

Some Florida residents complain that their schools are poorly funded because the state's many elderly voters refuse to support education. In six Florida counties during the late 1980's, a sizable senior electorate (people age fifty-five and over constituted 61 percent of voters) turned out to vote overwhelmingly against school bonds. Such events reinforce the image of older voters defending their own short-term financial interests. In other places, however, this phenomenon has not occurred. In fact, childless liberals, including older voters, in Orange County, California, have supported school funding at a higher rate than conservatives with school-age children. Most aging Floridians are migrants who lack community ties or the personal interest that the presence of grandchildren might provide; this may explain their negative vote.

The elderly are often believed to have a more conservative social outlook. Votes on referendum issues should provide the opportunity to test this belief. In the 1990's, ballot initiatives in various states touched on abortion, civil rights protection for homosexuals, and other important issues in the so-called culture wars. Measures to legalize medical marijuana and doctor-assisted suicide pit conservative social tenets against possible future self-interest. The "forced choice" made by senior voters on these last two questions would be especially interesting. Unfortunately for political analysis, such questions are part of general election ballots. Without very detailed exit poll data, it is not clear whether older voters diverged from others on these issues.

Another unsettled question is whether older voters' behavior reflects the aging process per se. The pattern of turnout increasing with age exists cross-culturally. If it is a general rule, it probably stems from life cycle changes rather than physiological ones: Young people are more mobile and more focused on establishing themselves in careers and personal relationships.

Other patterns may be caused by cohort or generational effects. Social change was rapid in the twentieth century, and each generation's socialization includes different values and experiences. Birth cohorts thus share a worldview that subtly distinguishes them from older or younger generations. One example of this effect is the voting rate of older women. Some years ago, it was noticeably lower than that of their male age peers. As seniors who grew up before women had the right to vote have died, however, this difference has narrowed dramatically.

Period effects, those of unique social changes or historical events, are a third factor. The generation that first voted during the prosperous 1920's was heavily Republican. Those coming of age in

the Great Depression were much more likely to be Democrats, reflecting President Franklin Roosevelt's massive efforts to mitigate economic misery. In both cases, party identities tended to stay with voters throughout their lives. It is harder to find pure cases of period effects on later generations in the United States. The Vietnam War was traumatic to both the draft-age generation and their parents, but it seems to have skewed both ways in impacting political views. However, definite period effects on the elderly can be seen in other nations. For example, in 1990's Russia, aging voters gave strong support to Communist Party candidates. This may have been partly from the conservatism of age (communism is the "conservative" ideology in Russia), but it also draws on anger at an economy

*As a group, senior citizens are the most likely to cast their ballots in an election.* (James L. Shaffer)

in which the pensions of elderly people have shrunk or vanished.

Aging itself, age cohort worldview, and unique period effects, along with socioeconomic factors, all impact the behavior of older voters. This makes their voting patterns complex but fascinating to observers of political trends. As the over-sixty-five population swells from 16 percent of voters in the 1980's to a possible 34 percent in 2038, new patterns are likely to emerge.

### FUTURE POSSIBILITIES

Will there be intergenerational war at the ballot box? Will the elderly vote to defend their entitlements, while younger people vote to cut or abolish them? This scenario is not impossible, but it is unlikely. Successful politicians tend to seek compromise, and most voting for candidates—by all age groups—is based on multiple issues.

The senior vote in the future will almost certainly reflect different social or political values. Such rolling change is a constant feature of American politics. A divorced and remarried man was once considered a damaged candidate because traditional older voters would not support him. The election, in 1980, of President Ronald Reagan (a charismatic senior citizen himself) dissolved that taboo. Less predictable is the question of what new values will become attractive for older voters in the future. Some accepted axioms about the senior vote may change as well. In the 1996 presidential election, the gender gap turned into a chasm among over-sixty voters, with older men voting for Republican candidate Bob Dole at a higher rate (48 percent) than those in any other age group. If the gap persists in other elections, gender may become a more salient factor than age.

Even the rule that aging voters will not vote against their economic interests may not always apply. Anti-Social Security measures will not win seniors' votes, but other issues are multidimensional. In early 1999, residents of Leisure World, a retirement community in California where the average age is seventy-seven, voted to incorporate. Despite the fact that the elderly residents knew that the resulting city of 18,000, called Laguna Woods, would need new taxes for street upkeep and police and fire departments, they voted for autonomy rather than for monetary savings.

*—Emily Alward*

**See also** Advocacy; Baby boomers; Laguna Woods, California; Politics; White House Conference on Aging.

### FOR FURTHER INFORMATION:

Binstock, Robert. "The Influence of Elderly Voters Is Exaggerated." In *The Elderly: Opposing Viewpoints*, edited by Karin Swisher. San Diego: Greenhaven Press, 1990.

_____. "The 1996 Election: Older Voters and Implications for Policies on Aging." *The Gerontologist* 37, no. 1 (February, 1997).

Flanigan, William, and Nancy Zingale. *Political Behavior of the American Electorate*. 6th ed. Boston: Allyn & Bacon, 1987.

Hornblower, Margot. "Elderly Voters Influence American's Elections." In *The Elderly: Opposing Viewpoints*, edited by Karin Swisher. San Diego: Greenhaven Press, 1990.

Peterson, Steven, and Albert Somit. *The Political Behavior of Older Americans*. New York: Garland, 1994.

Peyser, Marc. "Home of the Gray." *Newsweek* 133, no. 9 (March 1, 1999).

**WALKERS.** *See* **CANES AND WALKERS.**

## WEIGHT LOSS AND GAIN

**RELEVANT ISSUES:** Biology, economics, health and medicine

**SIGNIFICANCE:** Aging of the body causes many of its functions to slow down, altering body composition and resulting in changes in weight

Aging is not merely the passage of time; it is the manifestation of biological events that occur over a span of time. Chronological age is a poor measure of aging; how many birthdays a person has celebrated does not reveal much about him or her. The changes seen with aging are highly individualized. Some of the changes that occur with advanced age are the result of genetic factors, others are the result of environment, and some are the result of lifestyle choices.

Gain or loss of weight with advancing age is partly attributable to all these factors with disease added to the mix, a more rapid loss or gain depending on the manifestation of the particular disease. Through most of the twentieth century, the progression of weight in both men and women followed a consistent pattern. Following adolescence, when maturation causes gains in weight, weight tends to stabilize for five to ten years. When middle age begins, weight increases to a maximum in men at about age fifty and in women at about age sixty-five. Afterward, there is a steady decline until around age eighty, where weight remains stable until death. There might be a dramatic decline in weight if the cause of death creates body wasting, as with cancer, but that loss is attributable to the disease process, not the aging process. In the 1990's, the U.S. population as a whole increased in weight, from youths through the elderly, but the chronological ages for weight changes seemed to remain stable. As more Americans live to one hundred years and beyond, research may find a second decline in weight noted after age eighty.

### THE ROLE OF GENETICS

Genetic factors influencing weight occur through metabolic processes that affect body composition. Body composition is the relative amounts of lean mass, composed of more dense tissues such as bones and muscles, to fat mass, composed of less dense tissue or energy fat stores. The more dense the tissue present, the greater the weight of the person. Males, with a higher level of the hormone testosterone, have more dense bones, more muscle mass, larger organs, and less body fat. Their average weights are higher beginning at puberty and continuing throughout life. Females have higher levels of estrogen, the hormone to support pregnancy, so they have relatively more body fat in addition to the smaller lean mass and thus lower average weights. This gender variation is about 10 pounds throughout life.

Some genetic variations exist among racial groups that also create similar differences for the sexes. African Americans tend to have more dense bones and a slightly higher percent of body fat. Mexican Americans, Pacific Islanders, and American Indians tend to have a higher percent of body fat, while Asian Americans generally have a lower percent body fat.

The genetics of aging and its effect on weight revolves around the control of metabolism and

*Older men tend to gain weight in the abdominal area.* (Jim Whitmer)

how nutrients are absorbed and digested. Metabolism is the sum of all the chemical events that occur in a living organism. The relationship to aging and also weight is how the fuel that runs the body is stored and utilized. How quickly fuel is used is the metabolic rate. An analogy is gasoline consumption in a car, measured in miles per gallon. It is not unusual for consumption to decrease as a car gets older and is less efficient. Aging causes fuel to be used less efficiently, demonstrated by a drop in the metabolic rate. If calories taken in exceed what is needed by the body, then the excess is stored as body fat. If a person does not decrease caloric intake in conjunction with the decrease in metabolic rate, the result will be increased fat weight. Because of the concomitant decrease in lean tissue, the change in body composition might not affect body weight for a time, but it appears that at least in the United States, body fat is increasing at a faster rate than lean mass is decreasing, as demonstrated by the increase in obesity across the life span.

### THE ROLE OF ENVIRONMENT

Several environmental factors can affect body weight, but probably the most influential is financial. In the elderly, low income is often associated with poor nutrition, especially in urban regions where food costs tend to be higher even for staples. In at least one study of disease progression, the Baltimore Longitudinal Study on Aging, however, it was found that the greater the body weight, the longer time until death during chronic illnesses. This would suggest that a slight excess of body fat may be protective in the elderly and if economics prevent a healthy diet or even enough calories, then that outcome would not be possible.

Adequate protein intake is essential to maintaining lean mass. Often the most common protein food source, meat, is also the most expensive item on the grocery list. If the elderly have not been given adequate information to know that other, cheaper sources are just as good, such as combining incomplete proteins from vegetable sources, the tendency is simply not to buy meat. This situation might even manifest itself in a higher body weight if the calories replacing the protein come from carbohydrates or fats, as excesses of both are stored as body fat.

Unfortunately, lack of adequate protein affects not only lean mass but also overall health. Many of the essential parts of the immune system are made of proteins as well as the enzymes that help in cellular function. Lack of both reduced the ability to adapt to environmental stressors and is one of the main reasons the elderly often succumb to a viral disease such as pneumonia when a younger person would not.

Another environmental factor relates to the weather and temperature. There is a tendency for everyone, not only the elderly, to put on fat weight during the winter. Subcutaneous body fat is the insulator that helps regulate body temperature, so repeated exposure to cold causes an increase in body fat stores for more efficient regulation. In many people, it is probably not so much the temperature directly—the microclimate can be managed with clothing and shelter—but the tendency to be less active in inclement weather. If the calories eaten are not used for activity, they are stored as fat. There may also be a relationship to the economic issue: More financially stable retirees might move to a warmer climate or travel to one for the winter; if they remain, they can afford to join a health club to exercise. Any of these factors could mitigate the weather problem associated with weight.

### THE ROLE OF LIFESTYLE

There may be a strong association between lifestyle and economics, but some lifestyle choices can be made independent of finances. As with genetics and environment, lifestyle can affect weight in either direction. Education probably has the greatest effect on lifestyle. For a person to make the choices necessary to optimize health, he or she needs to have been given the information necessary to make educated decisions.

Because lifestyle diseases became the greatest causes of death early in the twentieth century, in the latter half of the century researchers studied everything that can affect health, with weight as a major factor. The leading cause of death, cardiovascular disease, includes obesity as a major modifiable risk factor. Even with this knowledge, however, the American population as a whole grew progressively fatter, especially in the 1990's. Research suggests that mortality and morbidity both decrease when weight, or more specifically fat, is kept within normal ranges.

The lifestyle choice to be active has been a major component of education, both in schools and the media, and it seems that those who have had the greatest exposure to the message are also the most compliant. Activity, both cardiovascular (such as running, walking, biking, dancing, and swimming) and strength training (such as weight lifting) have been shown to affect body composition and in turn health in all age groups. Studies of both men and women in their sixties, seventies, eighties, and even nineties have demonstrated similar effects across all age groups. Cardiovascular exercise causes a decrease in body fat and thus weight from energy use, and strength exercise causes an increase in lean mass, both muscle and bones, increasing weight.

### SUMMARY

It is clear that weight varies both throughout life as well as between individuals. When considering the effect of weight in older individuals, it seems safe to say that maintaining an ideal weight throughout life would be optimum, that there is no additional benefit from being underweight and there is a definite problem with being obese. Genetics cannot be changed, so manipulating lifestyle and/or the environment is necessary to obtain this goal.　　　　—*Wendy E. S. Repovich*

**See also** Cancer; Exercise and fitness; Fat deposition; Malnutrition; Nutrition; Obesity; Thyroid disorders.

### FOR FURTHER INFORMATION:

Castleman, Michael. "What Your Shape Doesn't Say About You." *The Walking Magazine* (March/April, 1997).

Evans, William, and Irwin H. Rosenberg. *Biomarkers: The Ten Keys to Prolonging Vitality.* New York: Simon & Schuster, 1991.

Hayflick, Leonard. *How and Why We Age.* New York: Ballantine Books, 1994.

Nuland, Sherwin B. *The Wisdom of the Body.* New York: Alfred A. Knopf, 1997.

U.S. Department of Health and Human Services. *Physical Activity and Health: A Report of the Surgeon General.* Atlanta: U.S. Department of Health and Human Services, Centers for Disease Control and Prevention, National Center for Chronic Disease Prevention and Health Promotion, 1996.

## WHEELCHAIR USE

**RELEVANT ISSUES:** Culture, health and medicine, recreation

**SIGNIFICANCE:** The huge number of people in the United States who are of senior citizen status makes it likely that hundreds of thousands of elderly Americans will be using wheelchairs during the first decades of the twenty-first century. This pervasive wheelchair use will contribute to changes in cultural attitudes, building construction, and social environments

In the year 2000, more Americans were over fifty than there were children enrolled in public school classes. In the United States, someone turned fifty-five years old about every eight seconds. These statistics leads one to believe that the American population as a whole is growing older very quickly. While many Americans spend their old age without the aid of mobility assistance, many others require the use of walkers and wheelchairs to move from place to place.

Wheelchair use is not confined to the elderly. People of every age group use wheelchairs. Many of the issues related to wheelchair use by the elderly are also applicable to wheelchair use by people of all ages. As the American population overall becomes older, however, these issues will become more significant and will likely affect the population at large.

While people who do not use wheelchairs for mobility may view the wheelchair as a symbol of disability and confinement, many of those who must use the device are likely to see it as a symbol of liberation. This attitude is especially prevalent among disabled elderly who, after leading active lives, would find themselves confined to a house, apartment, or long-term care facility if wheelchairs were not available.

The perception of wheelchairs as tools of liberation has caused all sorts of modifications to them. Motorized chairs are now available at relatively low prices. These chairs are truly liberating, since they make it possible for the occupant to operate the vehicle without an aide. Motorized wheelchairs have baskets that can be attached so the occupant can move belongings from one place to another or can shop for many items at a grocery or department store. Various accessories, such as cup holders and shopping bags, are available for attachment to both motorized and manually operated chairs, making the use of the chair both more comfortable and more convenient.

Many businesses provide motorized wheelchairs for the use of the disabled of all ages. As the number of elderly who need wheelchairs to shop and conduct other business increases, so will the number of businesses that provide these chairs. A business that had one chair available in 1999 may find that in 2010, it must have two or three chairs available. Increasingly, such businesses will have to think about establishing rules and regulations relative to the use of motorized wheelchairs. For both businesses and individuals, there may be insurance issues related to the use of such chairs.

As more elderly people use wheelchairs, there will be modifications in home and building construction as well as employment of more people to assist wheelchair users. These modifications will include such things as lower curbs on showers and lower kitchen counters and range tops. Places of business will have to increase the space allocated for loading and unloading chairs so that several wheelchairs can be unloaded to sit side by side. As more elderly people use wheelchairs, the widths of wheelchair ramps and paths may have to be increased to at least 5 feet so that chairs moving in opposite directions can pass each other. Airports, restaurants, hotels, and motels are likely to employ more people who are trained to assist disabled elderly customers in wheelchairs.

*—Annita Marie Ward*

**See also** Americans with Disabilities Act; Canes and walkers; Disabilities; Mobility problems.

## WHEN I AM AN OLD WOMAN I SHALL WEAR PURPLE

**EDITOR:** Sandra Martz

**DATE:** Published in 1987

**RELEVANT ISSUES:** Culture, family, psychology, values

**SIGNIFICANCE:** This collection of prose and poetry deals with women's adjustments to and perceptions of the aging process

*When I Am an Old Woman I Shall Wear Purple* is an anthology of well-written prose and poetry about women and their adjustments to and reflections on aging. The title of the book comes from the first line of a poem by the Englishwoman Jenny Joseph. Her selection, like many of those included, reveals the emotional confidence of a woman who looks forward to using the opportunities of aging to appreciate the fullness of both the past and the present times of her life.

The majority of the authors are American, representing the high quality of writing on aging being done throughout the country. Brief biographies of each author are included at the end of the book. Although more poetry than prose is offered, arresting black-and-white photographic portraits of older women are also featured. Selections are short to permit the widest variety of themes and writing styles. Representative themes include the influence of physical appearance on perceptions of aging ("The skin loosens; everything moves nearer the ground"), decision making in old age, mother-daughter relationships, caregiving ("I now mother my mother"), memories in time, women's roles, and cultivating aging. Many lines are likely to echo in the mind: "I watch my aging face . . . become yours"; "Memorizing the seasons, I touch things as if my fingers will learn them"; "Lipstick ran all over her face like a map of Chicago"; "I just sit and try to blend into the walls"; " . . . tending time more fragile than youth."

Women's attitudes toward the aging process have been associated traditionally with both their chronological age and the role in which they find themselves. The selections reflect the finely tuned individuality of the women described and their acute sensitivity to ordinary details from everyday experiences.

*—Enid J. Portnoy*

**See also** Aging: Biological, psychological, and sociocultural perspectives; Aging process; Beauty; Caregiving; Cultural views of aging; Family relationships; Literature; Women and aging.

## WHITE HOUSE CONFERENCE ON AGING

**DATE:** Every ten years; conferences held January, 1961; November/December, 1971; November/December, 1981; and May, 1995

**RELEVANT ISSUES:** Law, sociology

**SIGNIFICANCE:** The White House Conference on Aging is a national political and advocacy forum that addresses the issues of aging in the United States; decisions about policies and programs for older people are made from conference recommendations

The White House Conference on Aging (WHCoA) is a political mechanism that allows for public participation in the development of national policies for older persons in the United States. In 1958, the U.S. Congress enacted legislation requesting the first WHCoA. This legislation was in response to three successful national aging conferences that were sponsored by the Federal Security Agency in 1950, 1952, and 1956. It was Congress's intention that a WHCoA be held every ten years.

Representatives, or delegates, from each state attend the WHCoA. These delegates are appointed by either the governor of each state or Congress members. Delegates represent the concerns of their geographical area at the WHCoA.

The WHCoA provides the opportunity to highlight the needs and interests of older persons and makes recommendations about what actions, programs, and services would meet those identified needs. Each WHCoA features preliminary meetings with older persons, professionals, private citizens, and state and local political leaders. These preliminary meetings are used to advance issues for the conference. Each conference forms a set of concrete conference recommendations. Follow-up procedures are developed to monitor progress on the recommendations.

Congress authorized the first conference to occur in 1961 during the final days of President Dwight D. Eisenhower's administration. The main focus of this conference was the medical problems of the elderly and how to finance medical costs. The work accomplished at this conference contributed to the enactment of Medicare, Medicaid, and the Older Americans Act of 1965.

The second WHCoA, which was held in 1971 during Richard M. Nixon's administration, recommended the development of a wide range of services for the elderly. It supported the establishment of a network of federal, state, and local planning and advocacy agencies, including the National Institute on Aging and the House Select Committee on Aging. Delegates advocated for an expansion of programs under the Older Americans Act and the development of the Supplemental Security Income program.

The third WHCoA occurred in 1981 at the beginning of Ronald Reagan's administration. This conference recommended increases in government services for older Americans, including the maintenance of current Social Security benefits and the expansion of health insurance benefits for the elderly, which led to the Social Security Reform Amendments of 1983. It was influential in recommending amendments to the Older Americans Act and in supporting an emphasis on Alzheimer's disease research by the National Institute on Aging.

Bill Clinton's administration hosted the fourth WHCoA in 1995. The focus of this conference was on economic security, health, and social well-being. Major recommendations from this conference included preservation of the Older Americans Act, Social Security, Medicaid, and Medicare. Delegates advocated for housing options, as well as health and social service programs that provide elders with a continuum of care.

—*Colleen Galambos*

*See also* Advocacy; Housing; National Institute on Aging; Medicare; Older Americans Act of 1965; Politics; Social Security.

## WHY SURVIVE? BEING OLD IN AMERICA
**AUTHOR:** Robert N. Butler
**DATE:** Published in 1975
**RELEVANT ISSUES:** Culture, sociology, values
**SIGNIFICANCE:** Butler, who invented the term "ageism" to refer to the prejudicial stereotypes Americans assign to old people, wrote this book to show that the stereotypes are untrue and to reveal the extent of the neglect of the elderly

As medical advances have steadily increased the life span of Americans, the aging population has grown, and their problems have increased. Among these problems are a growing number of misconceptions about the elderly, including the idea that most are infirm and live in rest homes, hospitals, or with their children; that they are emotionally disengaged and bored with life; that senility is inevitable and pervasive; and that they are unproductive and resistant to change. The elderly are often considered a burden to society and are shunted into retirement communities and nursing homes, where they are ignored and neglected.

In 1975, Robert N. Butler published *Why Survive? Being Old in America* to show the public that old people are not all the same and that many of them are not helpless; some even want to work. As a psychiatrist, he has confronted all the cultural problems of aging in his own patients. He maintains the view that most of the old can continue to make decisions regarding their lives, including the decision to let someone else decide matters for them. In great part, the problems of the aging are reparable if more social support systems are created to help people take care of themselves. The aged can remain in their own homes, for example, if help could come on a regular basis to perform chores that an infirm person cannot perform for themselves and to remind them to do things they might otherwise forget. This recourse is economically sound compared with consigning them to a nursing home.

Another theme of Butler's book is an examination of the economic reasons for the poverty of so many of the old. Pension plans may disappear during a person's lifetime if a business fails or business policy changes. The Social Security system provides inadequate support: Payments have not increased at the same rate as inflation. Inflation reduces lifetime savings and investments below the expected standard of living for which the saver planned. In such circumstances, people often become destitute.

Butler's final point is that the issues he discusses belong to American culture as a whole and not just to the aged. Everyone lives side by side with those who are currently experiencing life as aged citizens, and everyone will eventually face these problems as they, too, age. As Butler predicted when he wrote the book in 1975, these problems have only worsened and become chronic with the passing of time.                                                 —*Ann Stewart Balakier*

*See also* Ageism; Poverty.

## WIDOWS AND WIDOWERS

**RELEVANT ISSUES:** Demographics, economics, family, marriage and dating

**SIGNIFICANCE:** Widowhood has been identified as the most stressful life event in adulthood; it is anticipated that the number of older adults experiencing widowhood every year will increase

Widowhood is a common, very stressful life event for older adults, particularly women; yet in comparison to loss of a spouse at a younger age, widowhood in older adulthood is considered a more "normal" life transition. Most older women are widows by age seventy and, since they do not tend

to remarry, may experience two decades or more of widowhood. According to Nancy Hooyman and H. Asuman Kiyak in *Social Gerontology* (3d ed., 1993), there are five widows to every widower in American society, and the majority are older adults. Men tend to remain widowers for a much shorter period of time since they are much more likely to remarry, often within the first eighteen months after the spouse's death. The impact of widowhood, particularly in the short term, is significant and multidimensional, regardless of gender.

### THE IMPACT OF WIDOWHOOD

Widowhood has physical, emotional, social, and economic impacts on the spouse, regardless of gender, and affects almost every aspect of daily life for the older adult. The impact of widowhood on day-to-day functioning is particularly significant when it occurs in later life since that is the time when other physical, functional, and cognitive impairments are most likely to be experienced. In *Widower: When Men Are Left Alone* (1996), Scott Campbell and Phyllis Silverman suggested that the process of bereavement, or getting over the death of another, is different for men than for women, but not less significant. The process of grieving the loss of a spouse is uniquely different for each individual and is influenced by a variety of factors, such as age at the time of the loss, length of the marriage, quality of the marriage, physical health status, socioeconomic status, and cultural mores and norms. However, some common adaptations are experienced and some fundamental tasks must be accomplished.

Researchers have recognized that the process of grief and mourning takes place over a period of one to three years rather than the six months that society has widely come to expect. In comparison to younger widows and widowers, older adults have been found to demonstrate a more prolonged grief reaction, extending beyond the "traditional" six-month grieving process. Additionally, older adults often experience other losses during the bereavement process, such as loss of a friend or even loss of personal health, which may further complicate the grieving process.

Resolution of grief includes acceptance of the loss and willingness to begin the transition to a different life without the deceased spouse. This may be particularly difficult for middle-aged or older

*Widows have outnumbered widowers because of the greater life expectancy of women. For many older women, the transition from wife to widow is a traumatic one.* (James L. Shaffer)

adults, who are more likely to be in long-term marriages, which tend to be associated with a higher level of interdependence. As couples age together and experience the narrowing of support networks that often occurs, they tend to more exclusively meet each other's needs without the help of others.

Physical reactions to grief—such as gastrointestinal disturbances, shortness of breath, difficulty sleeping, and loss of energy—are common immediately after a death and generally diminish over time. According to Robert C. Atchley in *Social Forces and Aging* (9th ed., 1999), the mortality rates of widowed people are slightly higher than those of married people, particularly among older adults. When the loss of a spouse occurs during older age, the physical responses to grief may be worsened or exacerbated by preexisting or latent disease processes, and grief may exacerbate or precipitate an underlying disease pathology. During the grief process, the bereaved commonly experience vacillating emotional responses, including disbelief, numbness, anxiety, relief, guilt, and profound sorrow. Depression frequently occurs and,

along with other symptoms, is found to lessen over time. Widowhood increases social isolation for both men and women, and loneliness is identified as a major problem by both widows and widowers, especially the aged.

The death of a spouse requires the development of a new social identity and social role: that of the widow or widower. According to Helen Lopata in *Current Widowhood: Myths and Realities* (1996), American society lacks a distinct role that lasts beyond the earliest stages of widowhood; widows and widowers, particularly when also elderly, can be viewed as a minority in society, often perceived as lacking in social value. Race and ethnicity compound the problem. Women in particular, especially if they were highly dependent upon their spouse, frequently encounter a drop in status, both socially and economically. Middle-aged and young-old women often drop out of their familiar circle of social activities with married friends and experience both social and emotional loneliness. In contrast, women who are older when widowed are more likely to be able to join the ranks of friends who are also widows and to benefit from that support network. Men who become widowers are often the most isolated because they are less likely than women to have established close friendships and because they tend to grieve more in isolation. Widowed older men often encounter more difficulties in day-to-day functioning because they have relied heavily on their wives, particularly in domestic areas, and may have difficulty completing such basic tasks as cooking and washing clothes.

Older widows are more likely to suffer negative economic consequences, particularly if they were economically dependent on their husbands' earnings or were unfamiliar with the household finances. Often, the widow does not qualify for Social Security, there are inadequate or no pension benefits, and any insurance benefits are quickly exhausted. This situation is worsened if the woman had been caring for an ill husband for a long period of time before death. As a result, according to Timothy Smeeding in *The Handbook of Aging and Social Sciences* (1990), it is estimated that 40 percent of older widows live at or near poverty level.

### ADJUSTMENT TO WIDOWHOOD

Despite the highly stressful nature of bereavement and the pain experienced during grieving, older adults usually cope quite well with the loss of

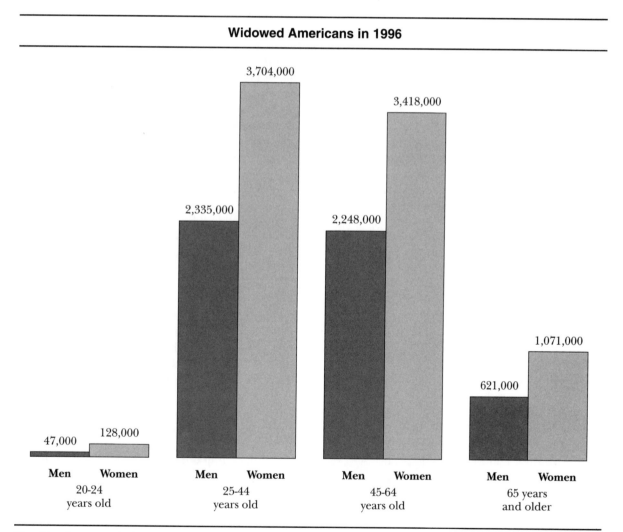

**Widowed Americans in 1996**

- Men 20-24 years old: 47,000
- Women 20-24 years old: 128,000
- Men 25-44 years old: 2,335,000
- Women 25-44 years old: 3,704,000
- Men 45-64 years old: 2,248,000
- Women 45-64 years old: 3,418,000
- Men 65 years and older: 621,000
- Women 65 years and older: 1,071,000

*Note:* Numbers rounded to nearest 1,000.
*Source:* U.S. Bureau of the Census, *Statistical Abstract of the United States: 1997.* Washington, D.C.: GPO, 1997.

a spouse. The experience of widowhood is often not entirely negative, and positive life transitions can even occur. For example, a woman who had been in a stable and successful marriage but who had been highly dependent upon her husband may, while grieving the loss of her spouse, achieve a sense of satisfaction and accomplishment from her new level of independence. Alternately, a spouse from a long-term but unhappy marriage may experience contentment for the first time, despite being alone and sometimes lonely. A husband or wife who has spent many years caring for a sick spouse may experience both a sense of relief and a sense of freedom, alternating with a sense of guilt, particularly early in the bereavement process, when those burdens are lifted. A widower may become active in a support group and gain new friendships and emotional experiences. Many younger widows continue in or return to work; this option is not available to women who are widowed at an older age, however. Women tend to be less interested in marrying again and are much less likely to remarry than are men; in contrast, more than one-half of widowed men will remarry.

Some factors that have been found to facilitate adjustment to widowhood include the quality of social support (including family and friends), the individual's ability to cope with stress, religion, health, and economic stability. Quality of relationships with family and friends is more important than quantity, and diversity of support networks is very important. Women are more likely than men to have had strong friendship relationships prior to widowhood, and these are often strengthened after the spouse's death. Friendships often provide more meaningful support than children in terms of reducing loneliness and providing recreational activities. Yet family relationships are extremely important, and children provide meaningful, tangible, and varied types of assistance. Men may have more difficulty maintaining family relationships than women and are less likely to have a confidant. Widows and widowers prefer to continue living away from their children as long as possible. According to Hooyman and Kiyak in *Social Gerontology*, socioeconomic class and ethnic status also influence whether the widow has an adequate social network.

Past experience and abilities in coping with life stressors are important in coping with loss of a spouse. In general, individuals who have had prior major losses and have coped with them successfully are better able to adapt positively to widowhood. Some examples of positive coping strategies used by widows and widowers include staying busy, maintaining a regular routine, using distraction, expressing emotion, and owning pets. Religion is often important in coping during bereavement. In *Dimensions of Grief* (1986), Stephen Shuchter claims that faith or belief in God is one of the most effective means of coping with death. Faith enhances coping in a variety of ways, including facilitating acceptance, offering support, promising continued relationship with the deceased, and combating loneliness.

The health status of the surviving spouse is an important contributor to adjustment to bereavement. Individuals with poor health are more likely to suffer worsening health status and additional health problems during the bereavement period. Health problems can often exacerbate or even trigger financial hardship in the bereaved person. Older widows are more likely to suffer from financial difficulties, and employment is generally not a reasonable option.

## WAYS TO FACILITATE ADJUSTMENT TO WIDOWHOOD

In *Widowed* (1996), Joyce Brothers recognizes that family and friends of the grieving person are often also grieving and would like to help the bereaved to get through the process. She suggests several ways that family members and friends can assist the widow or widower, including calling or writing, trying to put oneself in the bereaved's place, avoiding asking such questions as "How are you?", encouraging the bereaved to talk, letting the bereaved talk and express emotion, showing love, and refraining from giving advice.

Brothers also offers several suggestions to the bereaved during the grieving process, including staying in charge of one's life, avoiding hasty decisions, planning for the future, maintaining regular routines, getting out of the house, crying, and being wary of pills and alcohol. Many of these recommendations are particularly relevant to the widowed older adult since loved ones, particularly children, often feel the need to take charge and sometimes, in haste, encourage such decisions as selling a home or relocating. These actions are usually taken out of love and the perceived need to protect the older adult but instead have the potential to compromise both the future of the relationship and the widower's independence.

While most bereaved older adults cope successfully with the loss of their spouse, some experience a more intense, protracted, or "pathological" grief response and may benefit from professional assistance. Extensive feedback from widowed people themselves has generally demonstrated, however, that the bereaved benefit most from mutual help or support from other widowed people or peers. Numerous studies have shown that widows participating in these programs adapt more quickly and more positively. One of the first peer programs, the Widow-to-Widow Program, was developed by Phyllis Silverman. This program has been replicated numerous times throughout the United States, Canada, and Western Europe. The American Association of Retired Persons (AARP) offers more than two hundred local programs for older widows and widowers. Numerous other mutual help programs also exist and are commonplace in collaboration with hospice organizations and funeral services. *—Cynthia A. Padula*

**See also** Death and dying; Depression; Grief; Loneliness; Marriage; Men and aging; Poverty; Religion; Relocation; Remarriage; Stress and coping skills; Women and aging.

### FOR FURTHER INFORMATION:

Brothers, Joyce. *Widowed.* New York: Simon & Schuster, 1996. Brothers discusses her personal experience with widowhood and the grief process, and offers several chapters that provide helpful and specific advice about coping with loss of a loved one.

Campbell, Scott, and Phyllis Silverman. *Widower: When Men Are Left Alone.* New York: Baywood, 1996. Devoted entirely to the male experience of widowhood, this book begins with introductory information about widowhood, followed by several interesting and widely diverse case studies of widowers. Excellent and informative reading for both men and women.

Hooyman, Nancy, and H. Asuman Kiyak. "Death, Dying, Bereavement, and Widowhood." In *Social Gerontology: A Multidisciplinary Perspective.* 3d ed. Boston: Allyn & Bacon, 1993. This chapter provides a comprehensive review of the processes of death, dying, and bereavement; includes a section devoted exclusively to the demographics, issues, and impacts of widowhood.

Lopata, Helen. *Current Widowhood: Myths and Realities.* Thousand Oaks, Calif.: Sage Publications, 1996. This book presents a comprehensive review of widowhood in the United States and elsewhere, from a sociological perspective. Topics discussed include emotional experiences, kin roles, friendship roles, and community and society responses. Scholarly yet easily readable.

Shuchter, Stephen. *Dimensions of Grief: Adjusting to the Death of a Spouse.* San Francisco: Jossey-Bass, 1986. This book is organized according to the multiple dimensions of grief from the perspective of the bereaved, including such topics as the experience of bereavement, emotional and mental responses, coping, continuing ties to the deceased, how relationships change, and the evolution of identity. Excellent use of actual situations as examples.

Silverman, Phyllis. *Widow-to-Widow.* New York: Springer, 1986. Silverman provides an overview of the bereavement process, reports on the findings of the landmark Widow-to-Widow project, and illustrates how the program was of benefit to widows.

Smeeding, Timothy. "Economic Status of the Elderly." In *Handbook of Aging and the Social Sciences.* New York: Academic Press, 1990. Comprehensive discussion of the issues and facts about the economic status of older adults.

## WILD STRAWBERRIES

**DIRECTOR:** Ingmar Bergman

**CAST:** Victor Sjöström, Bibi Andersson, Ingrid Thulin

**DATE:** Released in 1957 as *Smultronstället*; released in the United States in 1959

**RELEVANT ISSUES:** Death, family, psychology, work

**SIGNIFICANCE:** Bergman's most honored film is a meditative analysis of an old scientist's quest to come to terms with the inhumanity and lovelessness of his past life

Like William Shakespeare's *King Lear,* Ingmar Bergman's *Wild Strawberries* is a study of an old man's need to discover painful truths about himself. Lear makes these discoveries through heart-wrenching sufferings leading to madness; Isak Borg (Victor Sjöström), the emeritus professor of medicine at the center of Bergman's film, finds out about his profound human failings through a succession of events and dreams during a trip to Lund, Sweden, where he is to receive an honorary degree. Borg, a bacteriologist and teacher, has sacrificed his humanity to his scientific work, leaving him an emotionally arid and spiritually adrift old man.

The film's story, which occurs during a single summer's day, focuses on the car trip that Borg makes to attend the ceremony with his daughter-in-law Marianne (Ingrid Thulin), who sees through his charming facade to his egocentric core. By the way Borg interacts with Marianne, his mother, and some hitchhikers, he is indeed revealed as cold-natured and authoritarian, and his dreams reveal him as fearful of death but also afraid of life. For example, he dreams of his former sweetheart Sara (Bibi Andersson) as she picks wild strawberries (Bergman's symbol for the fleeting happiness of youth), but she prefers his passionate brother to him, whom she regards as egotistical and aloof.

After these and other incidents in dream and reality, Borg emerges chastened by his confrontations with these repressed memories and hidden truths about himself. He receives his honorary degree, treats his son and daughter-in-law with a newly minted compassion, and retires to his bed, where he has another set of dreams. He again sees Sara, who takes him to an idyllic country setting where he waves to his young parents, whom he can now view with forgiveness and love. He has finally found a fulfilling meaning for his life, since he has been transformed into a human being with a growing awareness of the importance of emotional warmth and generosity.          —*Robert J. Paradowski*

*See also* Films; *King Lear*; Maturity; Old age.

## WILLS AND BEQUESTS

**RELEVANT ISSUES:** Death, family, law
**SIGNIFICANCE:** A will is a legally enforceable document defining in writing how a person wishes his or her property distributed after death; bequests are specific gifts provided for by will

A will takes effect on death and is revocable at the discretion of the maker, called a testator (testatrix,

if female) during his or her lifetime. The validity and execution of a will requires certain legal formalities and may vary from one state to another according to state law. People who die without a will are said to die intestate, and their property will be distributed according to state intestacy laws under the state statute of descent and distribution. This scheme may be contrary to decedents' wishes.

People must have testamentary capacity in order to execute a will. That is, they must be adults (of legal age), mentally competent (of sound mind), and aware of the nature and extent of property owned and the natural "objects of their bounty" (recipients of property). They must also realize the implications and consequences of what they are doing.

### TYPES OF WILLS

The "simple" will is the most widely utilized method of directing the administration and disposition of assets. It names an executor (executrix, if female) or personal representative to carry out the directions in the will. The executor may have special powers to sell property and settle claims. If one dies intestate, the probate court (also called orphan's court or surrogate's court) must appoint an administrator (administratrix, if female) to complete the same tasks as an executor.

Additionally, that person may have to post a security bond. In the United States, a will drawn up in one state will be good in another. If the testator dies owning property in more than one state, however, the will must be probated in more than one state. This second or ancillary administration requires proof of proper certification in the state of domicile. Generally, it is the laws of the state of domicile (where the testator has his or her primary residence) that govern probate of an estate.

While the formalities required in the execution of a will vary slightly from state to state, the most striking difference lies in the requirement of the witnesses. All wills must be signed by the testator, generally at the end of the document. Most states require that testators "publish" their wills (declaring it to be their will and the means by which they are directing disposition of their property) before witnesses who also sign the will. The purpose of witnesses is to establish that the will was voluntarily signed by the testator. Witnesses should be disinterested parties, not beneficiaries under the will.

Some states, such as Pennsylvania, do not require wills to be witnessed. The practice, however, is advisable.

Certain property does not pass under a will: jointly held property; life insurance payable to a named beneficiary; trust property; retirement plans, including individual retirement accounts (IRAs), Keough accounts, and pensions; Totten trusts or pay-on-death bank accounts payable to a named beneficiary; deeds in which decedent held only a life estate with property going to a named beneficiary after death; and gifts in contemplation of death.

Statutory wills are available in California, Maine, Michigan, and Wisconsin. Created by state law, these are forms available in stationery stores that can be completed and witnessed. They are limited and cannot be changed, but they can be modified by adding codicils and specific bequests.

A joint will is a contract between two people requiring the consent of each to modify. Provisions generally state that each spouse's property will pass to the other and then specify what will happen to the property when the second person dies. In cases of simultaneous death, the heirs of the survivor even by one second will inherit the property of the other. Because this may have unintended consequences, the parties can specify by will who is to be the survivor. Property will pass accordingly. Divorce or annulment will revoke the entire will or at least those provisions in favor of the former spouse.

A testator may also place conditions on bequests received under a will, such as that the person receiving the bequest perform certain conditions in order to inherit. It is also permissible for a testator to disinherit anyone except a spouse. Under state law, a spouse is entitled to a portion of the estate even if the other spouse dies and makes no provision for the surviving spouse or conveys less than a certain percentage of decedent's assets. In that case, the surviving spouse can "take against the will" or choose to accept an amount allowed by law (usually one-third or one-half of the estate) instead of the amount bequeathed in the will. The surviving spouse is not required to take against the will. If he or she chooses not to do so, the property bequeathed will pass according to the terms of the will. This is called the "elective" or "forced share" provision. Revisions of the Uniform Probate Code have adopted a sliding scale for widows or widowers who take against the will: the longer the marriage, the higher the elective share.

A holographic will is a document entirely in decedent's handwriting, signed and dated. If executed with testamentary intent, it can be considered a valid, enforceable will. A nuncupative will is an oral will used by sailors on the high seas. This will is upheld if circumstances show that at the time of the oral will the decedent believed death to be imminent. A "pour-over" will accompanies a living (inter vivos) trust, stating in effect that any property not in trust will pass into the trust (pour over to it) through probate administration and the distribution provisions in a will. Living wills are not wills at all, but rather a signed and witnessed advance directive stating that, in the event of a catastrophic illness, the person does not wish to be kept alive by artificial means or heroic measures. Living wills can also specify which therapies the person does or does not wish to undergo in a terminal situation. All states recognize living wills.

### PROBATE

The probate process consists of "proving" the decedent's last will (proper signature, validity, and the fact that it is the last will). This is also the court that deals with disputes concerning transfer of the property of decedents and claims against their estates. If the will is determined to be valid, the estate will be distributed according to the terms of the will. If it is invalid or if the decedent dies intestate, the estate will be distributed according to the state intestacy statute. If the original will is lost or destroyed, a certified copy is submitted to the court. The executor named in the will must petition (request) the court to probate the will. Notice of the petition is given to the decedent's heirs and other interested parties; some states require "publication" or placing a legal notice in a local newspaper listing death of the decedent, the name of the executor, and a date by which to object to the petition. From one to three months after appointment, the executor must file with the court an inventory of the estate's assets, including stocks, bonds, real estate, and jewelry owned by decedent at time of the death. Assets are not distributed until debts, fees, expenses, and federal and state taxes have been paid and accepted. "Small" estates are not required to file a federal tax return. Allowable amounts have been increased gradually through revisions in the tax code. State law governs amounts payable for state inheritance tax. When tax returns are accepted, the executor receives a "closing letter" stating that no further taxes are due in the estate.

After debts and expenses are paid and taxes are settled, the executor may prepare to distribute amounts remaining to beneficiaries according to the terms of the will. Beneficiaries must sign a release signifying acceptance of the distribution and releasing the executor from future claims. The executor must then file a final accounting with the court detailing all transactions made on behalf of the estate. When accepted by the court, the estate is closed, and the executor dismissed. The executor's fee is paid according to a sliding scale based on the size of the estate. The rate is fixed under state law.

### CODICILS, REVOCATION, AND RULE OF ADEMPTION

A codicil is an addition or amendment to a preexisting will and must incorporate the preexisting will by reference. Otherwise, it may by considered a new will. The codicil must conform to the same requirements and formalities of the will. Codicils can also correct a deficiency or error in the original document.

Will revocation is necessary when the testator's intent changes with respect to the distribution of assets at death. When a new will is executed, all previous wills are revoked and invalid. Even if a new will is not executed, the testator can revoke the old will by physically destroying it or doing some act with the intention of revoking the will. Marriage after the will is made revokes the will unless it was made in anticipation of marriage. A previously revoked will can also be revived if it was based on a material mistake. Divorce generally does not revoke a valid will. It does, however, revoke bequests to the former spouse or appointment of the former spouse as executor of the estate.

If a testator mentions a specific bequest of property in the will but disposes of the property during his or her lifetime, it will not be in the estate at death. The bequest, therefore, is said to be "adeemed," and the beneficiary gets nothing, regardless of the circumstances surrounding the disposal of the property. The subject of the bequest must exist and be owned by the testator at the time

of death. Where the form of the bequest is altered, ademption also occurs because the property cannot be restored to its former state (for example, where wool is woven into cloth or cloth is made into a garment). If the original property is adeemed but a similar property exists at the time of death, the law presumes that the testator restored the adeemed property, and the bequest will be honored. The rule of ademption applies only to specific bequests or legacies other than money. Where a group of items is involved (a collection of objects), the bequest could be adeemed totally or partially if some of the articles are not part of the testator's estate.

### ABATEMENT, LAPSE, AND INTESTACY

When the testator's estate does not contain sufficient assets to pay debts, expenses, and bequests in full, bequests are "abated," or reduced, according to certain rules unless the will specifies otherwise. The first to be reduced is the residuary bequest ("the rest, remainder, or residue of my estate"); some use personal property to pay costs before the sale of real estate, while others treat real estate and personal property alike for abatement purposes. Bequests will be abated proportionately.

Because a will "speaks at death," property cannot be transferred by will until the testator dies. An intended beneficiary under a will might predecease testator. If so, the intended gift to that person "lapses." In anticipation of this situation, the will can provide an alternate beneficiary. If lapse occurs and the state has an "antilapse" statute, a gift by substitution might occur, and a deceased beneficiary's children can accept the gift.

The scheme of distribution for a person who dies intestate (without a will) is generally the same in all states, although differences may occur under various state laws. If there are spouse and children, the estate passes one-half to the surviving spouse and one-half to the children. If a child is deceased but has offspring, the deceased child's share passes to his children. If there is a spouse but no children or grandchildren, one-half goes to spouse and one-half goes to blood relatives in the following order: parents, brothers and sisters, grandparents, aunts, uncles, cousins. If there are children or grandchildren but no spouse, the children will divide the entire estate equally. If one is deceased, his or her share passes to his or her children. Stepchildren are not considered next of kin, but children born after the decedent's death will inherit just as if they had been born during the decedent's lifetime. Adopted and natural children are treated the same for inheritance purposes. If no blood relatives survive the decedent, the estate will pass to the state of his or her principal residence at the time of death (escheat). Intestate succession may defeat the intent of the decedent and result in inheritance by certain unintended family members.

### WILL SUBSTITUTES

An inter vivos, or living, trust is often called a will substitute because settlors or grantors (the person creating the trust document) can be their own primary beneficiaries and can also pass property to beneficiaries at their death. Inter vivos trusts can be structured so that settlors retain the right to change or terminate the trust during their lifetime and control the use of their property. Inter vivo trusts do not require probate. At the settlor's death, the property is immediately available for the use and benefit of the settlor's beneficiaries. Property held jointly with right of survivorship also does not require probate. During their lifetimes, each joint tenant owns an equal share of the property. At the death of the first tenant, the survivor retains his or her own interest and gets the interest of the decedent automatically by operation of law.                   *—Marcia J. Weiss*

### FOR FURTHER INFORMATION:

American Bar Association. *The ABA Guide to Wills and Estates.* New York: Times Books, 1995. Written in plain language with practical situations and problems that most people are likely to encounter.

Bove, Alexander A., Jr. *The Complete Book of Wills and Estates.* New York: Henry Holt, 1989. Deals with wills and estates from every aspect; includes information on living trusts and ways to avoid probate.

Burris, Donald J. *Protecting Your Assets: Wills, Trusts, and Other Estate Planning Options.* Philadelphia: Chelsea House, 1994. Written in simple language, this book explores various estate-planning alternatives and options.

Esperti, Robert A., and Renno L. Peterson. *The Handbook of Estate Planning.* 2d ed. New York: McGraw-Hill, 1988. This book, written for the layperson, contains helpful information on ownership of property, wills, trusts, and probate.

Lynn, Robert J. *An Introduction to Estate Planning.* St. Paul, Minn.: West, 1975. Lynn's book is for lawyers and students with basic knowledge of property law.

Maple, Stephen M. *The Complete Idiot's Guide to Wills and Estates.* New York: Alpha Books, 1997. Written in a humorous manner with charts and cartoons, this book contains helpful and easily understood information.

## WISDOM

**RELEVANT ISSUES:** Culture, psychology, religion, values

**SIGNIFICANCE:** Wisdom—the capacity to give meaning to one's experience—plays an important role for the elderly as they are challenged to consolidate a sense of meaning with which to face the future, the deaths of loved ones, and their own deaths

Erik Erikson proposed a series of eight stages through which all individuals pass during their life span. Each stage represents a particular challenge that must be met for the individual to adequately manage the demands of the specific period in development. The successful completion of each stage is accomplished through achieving a balance between two opposing forces.

The infant must balance a sense of trust and a sense of mistrust, the very young child must contend with the forces of autonomy and doubt, and the school-age child is faced with balancing initiative and guilt. The preadolescent is charged with coming to terms with the competing forces of industry and inferiority; the adolescent must contend with the pull of identity and identity diffusion; the young adult must find a way to navigate the draw of isolation and intimacy; and the middle-age person is challenged with balancing generativity and stagnation. The development task of old age, according to Erikson, is defined by the need to contend with forces of integrity and despair.

Successful completion of each stage not only readies the individual for the next stage but also produces, through the integration of opposing forces, a more adaptive approach toward life. Infants who pass successfully through the first stage of development are invested with an underlying sense of hope; toddlers are ideally equipped with a basic sense of their own will; and school-age children who have successfully balanced the opposing forces of industry and inferiority can face adolescence with a sense of competence. Adolescents who have successfully met the demands of their development stage are left with a sense of fidelity to certain values. Young adults who have found a way to manage the opposing pull of isolation and intimacy develop the capacity to love in a mature way. Middle-aged adults who have successfully integrated the desire to be productive and the pull of self-involvement are imbued with a fundamental sense of purpose. Successful completion of life's final stage requires coming to terms with feelings of despair and integrity. The integration of these two opposing forces in old age, according to Erikson, produces wisdom.

*While researchers debate whether intelligence decreases or increases with age, most agree that wisdom—the ability to learn from and apply one's experiences—does develop over the years.* (Jim Whitmer)

The culminating accomplishment of human development in this model of the life span is, therefore, wisdom. The achievement of wisdom, in the view of Erikson, requires not only the completion of a single, final developmental stage but also the reworking of all seven previous stages. The various physiological changes, which mark a general and often dramatic decline in physical and sometimes cognitive functioning, require the elderly to renegotiate all of life's developmental challenges, from the dialectic of trust-mistrust to the opposition of generativity-stagnation. In addition to this, the elderly are faced with accepting the imminence of their own deaths. Wisdom is thus a backward- and forward-looking developmental accomplishment entrusting the aged with a sense of meaning that situates them in the perspective of their own lives and the lives of others past, present, and future. As Erikson writes:

> The elderly are challenged to draw on a life cycle that is far more nearly completed than yet to be lived, to consolidate a sense of wisdom with which to live out the future, to place him- or herself in perspective among those generations now living, and to accept his or her place in an infinite historical progression.

### WISDOM, ACTIVE INVOLVEMENT, AND DISENGAGEMENT

Wisdom, as the culminating achievement of the life span, imparts upon the individual a capacity to live productively with the tension of integrity and despair. Wisdom also serves to allow the aged a way of managing the competing forces of active involvement and disengagement. As with all the previous stages of development, individuals must invest themselves fully in the particular developmental challenge before them if they are to move forward. However, the aged are faced with the seemingly paradoxical task of actively involving themselves with life while at the same time disengaging from it. This happens because the waning physiological capacities of the aged make active involvement less possible and because the reality of death demands that they prepare for a future of total disengagement. "Wisdom," writes Erikson, is "truly involved disinvolvement."

The disengagement that wisdom makes possible in old age does not represent a form of apathy or nihilism. Instead, it involves the recognition that one's capacity to control the world, as well as one's ability to comprehend it, are fundamentally limited. Adaptation throughout life requires an acceptance of the potentialities and the limitations inherent in one's position along the developmental continuum. The elderly are faced with the task of accepting a greater level of reliance and dependence upon others while at the same time valuing their capacity to contribute greatly to their family and society at large. Wisdom imparts upon the elderly a dual awareness of how much is known and how much is still unknown and even unknowable. It imbues both a sense of deep trust and meaning and a playful curiosity and mystery.

### WISDOM AND RELIGION

Life span studies of the aged have found a uniform tendency among the elderly toward an increased appreciation of the importance of spirituality and religion. One theme that arises when speaking to seniors, irrespective of denominational affiliation, is the emphasis that they place on the importance of religious practice and faith for the next generation. In fact, even those in the older population who classify themselves as nonreligious often stress the value of spiritual and religious involvement for the world at large.

Among the classical Greeks, wisdom was understood to be the type of knowledge needed to discern the good and live the good life. It is a belief in the connection between wisdom and the good life, both for the society and for the individual, which appears to underlie the value that the elderly place upon religion. Psychologists have long appreciated the way in which religion functions as an adaptive force capable of reconnecting human fragmentation and providing the individual with a sense of wholeness and meaning. Religion also serves to restrain problematic drives and impulses. In facing the inevitability of death, religion may be seen by the aging as a confirmation of hope, a conservation of values, and a source of comfort.

The functional and adaptive role of spirituality and wisdom in the context of death and dying has been well researched by life span theorists. The concept of eternity has been found to be particularly salient to many older adults. Belief in an afterlife provides both the dying and those that survive them a shared frame of reference with which to give meaning to death. Loss of additional time on earth is seen as being compensated for by the promise of life everlasting. Similarly, the deterioration in quality of life experienced by the dying appears less unfair when juxtaposed with the higher quality of existence in the life to come. Religion thus supplies the elderly and those who care for them with a sense that the limitations and suffering associated with death and dying are merely a prelude to a less restricted state of being.

Beyond its capacity to comfort the elderly as they approach their physical end, wisdom has traditionally provided the aged with a sense of importance and recognition as the bearers of tradition and culture. Religion has also served to strengthen bonds linking the elderly with those who will survive them. The intergenerational transmission of wisdom functions to preserve the "mind" of culture in the same way that the transmission of rituals, art forms, cuisine, and dress ensures the conservation of a culture's "body." By passing on wisdom, the elderly act as the linchpin of cultural continuity. In doing so, they may experience a sense of immortality, of transcending their own death through their generative contribution to future generations. Awareness of both the privilege and the profound responsibility inherent in this critical cultural role may lead the elderly to reevaluate their own constructions of wisdom. Erikson, in discussing the final task of the life cycle, writes:

> For perhaps the first time, the elder is a member of the omega generation, the oldest living generation in his or her family. There are no living elders to whom to look for guidance through the next stage. Members of the omega generation must be guided by ideological heroes and by their own wisdom and memories, as they themselves serve as guides for the generations that follow.

Although theorists have increasingly recognized the psychologically adaptive quality of religion, it should be noted that wisdom and spirituality are not identical or even necessarily congruent. The compensatory quality of religion, its capacity to provide hope and comfort in the face of suffering, renders it highly vulnerable to manipulation by those interested in the marginalization or exploitation of the elderly. Unscrupulous religious organizations have been known to prey upon the intense spiritual longings of the aged and the terminally ill. Religion may be used to divert older adults away from active participation in communal political institutions and causes. Spiritual veneration for the sagacity and wisdom of the elderly may go hand in hand with the removal of their decision-making power. Idealization of the moral and spiritual greatness of the aged can be used to deflect attention away from their need for social and economic resources.

## CULMINATION OF A LIFE STORY

Some life span theorists consider the need to see one's life as a continuously evolving story bound together by a sense of connection, purpose, and direction to be a central and vital psychological need throughout development. However, it is believed that the impetus to draw together the events of a life history into a coherent whole has particular importance and salience for the aged. This perspective suggests that the fundamental tension of old age is not defined by the opposing forces of integrity and despair but is instead characterized by the dialectic of continuity and discontinuity. Wisdom, in this view, represents the threads of meaning and knowledge that weave together the various themes and events of a person's life into the tapestry of a narrative.

D. P. McAdams has argued that, from late adolescence, men and women in modern societies attempt to build a meaningful and coherent narrative of the self to provide them with a sense of direction and purpose. What seems to distinguish the creation of life stories in later life from narrative building during earlier stages of development is that older adults devote more space in their stories for generative and transcendent concerns. Unlike adolescents and younger adults who spend much of their time and energy accruing and developing "internalized" skills, talents, and knowledge, older adults tend to devote more of their life stories to "externalized" practices through which they invest their resources in wider, societal projects, causes, and movements.

During older adulthood, or mature adulthood, individuals tend to manifest their desire for generativity in the form of concrete assistance, whether this is accomplished through working within the existing power structure or by attempting to alter it. The elderly, because of their withdrawal from the public domain, tend to express their generative concerns less concretely. As the aged find themselves increasingly removed from participation in professional and political arenas, their life stories often begin to revolve around the passing on of knowledge and wisdom. Wisdom may therefore be understood as the final generative resource for the elderly as they find themselves concerned about the next generation but largely unable to act on this concern. In this way, wisdom helps the aged to continue to write a life story in which the need to maintain a prosocial identity is threatened by the loss of numerous capacities.

If wisdom helps to maintain a generative life narrative in the face of physical deterioration and societal marginalization, it also serves to make less painful the acceptance of death. That is, wisdom appears to be a basic ingredient both in lending vitality and purpose to the final chapter of a generative life story and in accepting the finality of life's end. Erikson proposed that the acceptance of death is only possible with the acquisition of wisdom. Wisdom makes possible this acceptance because it acknowledges the way in which one's own experience has been shaped by the intersection of an individual life cycle with cultural and political processes. Wisdom thus allows for an understanding of one's own life story as deeply embedded in a broader historical narrative and, in doing so, purportedly reduces the sting of death. As the final and culminating theme of a life story, wisdom makes possible what Erikson has characterized as a "post-narcissistic love of the human ego—not of the self—as an experience which conveys some world order and spiritual sense, no matter how dearly paid for."

*—Samuel Liebman and Steven Abell*

**See also** Creativity; Cultural views of aging; Death and dying; Erikson, Erik H.; Maturity; Mentoring; Middle age; Old age; Religion; Successful aging.

## FOR FURTHER INFORMATION:

Erikson, Erik H., Joan M. Erikson, and Helen Q. Kivnick. *Vital Involvement in Old Age.* New York: W. W. Norton, 1986. Based upon the interviews of twenty-nine octogenarians, this book examines the final stage of Erikson's stage theory. Continual emphasis is given to the value of vital involvement throughout each stage of development, including the last one.

McAdams, D. P., and E. St. Aubin. *Generativity and Adult Development: How and Why We Care for the Next Generation.* Washington, D.C.: American Psychological Association, 1998. This book takes the life history perspective of McAdams as a way of examining the often overlooked influence of generativity in adulthood. Using Erikson's stage theory as its starting point, the contributors explore a variety of topics related to generativity as it expresses itself in culture, history, and the development of individual personality.

Manheimer, R. P. "Wisdom and Method: Philosophical Contributions to Gerontology." In *Handbook of the Humanities and Aging,* edited by Thomas R. Cole et al. New York: Springer, 1992. This chapter examines the way in which diverse topics in philosophy—including epistemology, logic, ethics, and hermeneutics—converge in the study of aging. Studies examining both the deficits and strengths of the elderly are reviewed and compared with one another.

Oates, Wayne E. "Reconciling with Unfulfilled Dreams at the End of Life." In *The Aging Family: New Visions in Theory, Practice, and Reality,* edited by Terry D. Hargrave et al. New York: Brunner, 1997. This chapter focuses upon the theme of how the elderly cope with the limited amount of time they have to accept the death of their dreams. The author suggests the implementation of strict parameters in dealing with the particular form of grief experienced by the population's distinct circumstances.

Simonton, D. "Creativity and Wisdom in Aging." In *Handbook of the Psychology of Aging,* edited by James E. Birren et al. San Diego: Academic Press, 1990. This chapter reviews the empirical findings of life span changes in both aging and creativity. Theoretical material and empirical data are reviewed, and an attempt is made at integration.

## WOMAN'S TALE, A

**DIRECTOR:** Paul Cox

**CAST:** Sheila Florance, Gosia Dobrowolska, Norman Kaye, Chris Haywood

**DATE:** Released in 1991

**RELEVANT ISSUES:** Death, family, health and medicine, media

**SIGNIFICANCE:** This haunting Australian film depicts a woman's efforts to celebrate life despite her failing health and to live her last days fully

In *A Woman's Tale,* seventy-two year old Martha (Sheila Florance) lives alone in a walk-up apartment with her cat, canary, and mementos of a full life. The film follows her daily routine as she interacts with her home-care nurse, son, friends, and neighbors. She is dying of cancer but tries to live every day to the fullest.

Martha is visited daily by Anna (Gosia Dobrowolska), the young home-care nurse. They have developed a close, affectionate relationship. Martha loves life and romance. She supports Anna's affair with a married man by making her bedroom available for their lovemaking. When Anna reports that Martha's friend Billy (Norman Kaye), who is also Anna's patient, tried to fondle her breast, Martha suggests, "Why didn't you let him? He'll be dead soon. What's the difference?"

Billy provides a contrasting perspective on life and death. Whereas Martha celebrates the present and enjoys life, Billy lives in the past and slowly dies. His daughter is too busy to visit him. Martha helps him with toileting and other basics. In the end, Anna finds him alone in the darkness, dead in his chair.

Martha's son Jonathan (Chris Haywood) worries and checks up on her. The parent-child roles have reversed. When Martha is hospitalized after a fall and told that she has only one month to live, Jonathan tries to put her in a nursing home. She fights, with Anna's help, to return to her own home and maximize the quality of her last days of life. In the end, she tells Anna, "Life is so beautiful. . . ."

Sheila Florance won the Australian Film Institute's Best Actress award for her portrayal of Martha. She died of cancer soon afterward.

*—John W. Engel*

**See also** Cancer; Death and dying; Films; Family relationships; Friendship; Home services; Hospice; Independent living; Nursing and convalescent homes; Sexuality; Women and aging.

## WOMEN AND AGING

**RELEVANT ISSUES:** Biology, culture, demographics, health and medicine, psychology, sociology, values

*Some women do not feel the need to cover the signs of aging, despite societal pressures to do so.* (Jim Whitmer)

**SIGNIFICANCE:** The rapid increase in the number of elderly persons in the United States, with women greatly outnumbering men, raises many social and economic issues that need to be addressed

The unprecedented growth of the elderly as a proportion of the populations of all industrialized countries has political, economic, and social ramifications that require serious attention. The dimensions of the problem in the United States can be grasped by comparing statistics from the beginning of the twentieth century with those at its close.

In 1900, an informal social structure existed to care for the small number of elderly requiring care. In a generally rural economy, the elderly tended to be integrated into all aspects of family and social life and usually lived with relatives. Three million U.S. citizens, less than 4 percent of the population, were more than sixty-five years old; 44 percent were nineteen years of age or younger. The average life expectancy for women was about forty-eight years, or until about the time of the meno-

pause. The lower life expectancy was largely a result of the high incidence of deaths in infancy and early adulthood; a woman who survived her childbearing years had a good chance of living into her sixties and beyond. Nevertheless, many women died in childbirth or from its complications, and so it was less common in the first decade of the twentieth century than in the 1990's for women to live to see their grandchildren reach adulthood.

By contrast, the 1990 U.S. Census showed the following breakdown of older Americans: 18,218,481 persons sixty-five to seventy-four years of age, of whom 10,225,733 (about 56 percent) were women; and 12,976,794 persons seventy-five years and older, of whom 8,455,474 (about 65 percent) were women. Thus, more than 31 million persons were sixty-five years of age or older, or one-eighth the total U.S. population of 248.7 million; nearly 60 percent were female. Women also constituted 80 percent of the elderly living alone in the United States at that time. In 1991, 12 percent of Canada's population was more than sixty-five years of age, and women sixty years or older constituted the majority of Canadians living alone.

In the 1990's, it was estimated that the aging of the so-called baby-boom generation (the result of the large number of births during and just after World War II) to create "senior boomers" early in the twenty-first century would result in one in five Americans being over the age of sixty-five. Furthermore, as a group, the oldest elderly, those over eighty-five years of age, was growing at six times the rate of the rest of the U.S. population. There has been a demographically significant rise in the median age: In 1970, it was twenty-eight years; in the 1980's, it was predicted to be thirty-six by the year 2000 and forty-two by 2050. According to Census Bureau predictions in 1986, by the middle of the twenty-first century, those nineteen years of age or younger will make up 23 percent of the population, and those over the age of sixty-five will constitute 22 percent, resulting from a decline in birthrates and a reduction in death rates. The ratio of retired persons to workers, which was one to five in 1986, is expected to reach one to three in 2020.

The proportion of elderly relatives to younger family members has increased. The cohort (a group of people who were born at about the same time and can be expected to share many common experiences) of frail elderly in the late twentieth century came of age around the time of the Great Depression and, as a group, typically had small families. In addition, there is a low birthrate of generations succeeding the elderly cohort in the 1990's, resulting in a high dependency rate, which is projected to continue climbing. The proportion of family caregivers to recipients had changed from 3:1 in 1910 to 1.2:1 by 1973.

By the mid-1990's, elderly women had the lowest median income of any age or sex grouping in the United States and were the fastest-growing segment among the poor. The Canadian government does not compile statistics identifying a poverty line; those in the lowest economic status are defined as having "low income," the level at which a person or family spends at least 56.2 percent of its income on food, shelter, and clothing. By that measure, unattached women sixty-five years of age or older had almost the lowest income in 1991 (47.4 percent); those with the lowest income were unattached persons up to twenty-five years (55.5 percent). For the total population of Canadian elderly, 20 percent fell into the category of "low income."

## SOCIAL ISSUES

Aging can be viewed from many perspectives: chronological, biological, psychological, and social. Old age as a category is partly a function of the relative age of the surrounding population and the vitality of the persons categorized as older. What was considered to be late middle age at the end of the twentieth century would have been considered elderly in primitive societies. Even in the 1970's, gerontologists typically referred to those fifty-five to seventy-five years old as the young-old and those over seventy-five as the old-old. By the 1980's, in recognition of the growth of the elderly population, some gerontologists began using the term "young-old" to refer to those sixty-five to seventy-four years old, labeling persons seventy-five to eighty-five years old as the "old-old" and those over eighty-five as the "oldest-old."

The elderly, however defined, have been accorded different levels of status in different societies, ranging from reverence to hostility and abandonment. It appears that the status of a group advances and declines in a society as the ratio between the costs of maintaining it and the benefits it can provide changes. Thus, in societies in which the elderly control many resources or are seen as possessing special wisdom, their status is higher. Even in societies in which the elderly are revered, however, aging women often are at a disadvantage because, in most societies, they seldom control a large number of resources. When a woman's value is based on physical attractiveness or the ability to bear and care for children, the end of youth and reproductive ability leaves her with little power. In the late twentieth century, activities open to the elderly, especially in work and community leadership, were limited in industrial societies.

In rural societies—even rural communities in industrialized nations—older citizens tend to be more integrated into the life of the community than in urbanized areas. *The Aging Experience: Diversity and Commonality Across Cultures* (1994), by Jennie Keith et al., provides a fascinating study of the different experiences of the aged and of how they are viewed by others in seven towns on four continents. The authors assert that "the attributes of social and cultural settings were not simply contexts that affected aging; they were part of the very meaning of age itself." For example, in the small town of Clifden, on the rugged, isolated west coast of Ireland, few people identified one another by relative age; rather, they noted traits such as the fact that a man was unable to shop without help or that a woman was being cared for by a niece.

As more women reach old age and continue to slip into poverty, several issues arise. Although the vast majority of elderly persons remain in the community and generally are cared for by family members when ill or infirm, more than three-quarters of the residents of nursing homes are women, often with no living relatives. Several demographic trends related to this issue are expected to complicate it further, primarily the trend toward later childbearing and smaller families in the baby-boom generation, combined with the longer life expectancy of the same cohort. Another troubling demographic trend is the increase of childless women, which will result in an increasing number of isolated elderly women needing formal (that is, government-funded) help.

The picture for women is clouded by the fact that women, generally wives and daughters or daughters-in-law, have historically been expected to be the caregivers for elderly family members. Despite the increased participation of women in the workforce, this expectation seems stubbornly resistant to change. Women make up about three-quarters of the primary caregivers. In 1986, more than 60 percent of primary caregivers of the elderly were the wives of disabled, often-older hus-bands; 73 percent of these caregivers were over sixty-five years of age. At the same time, the average age of all such caregivers in the United States was fifty-seven years; more than 30 percent rated their health as fair or poor, and approximately 30 percent were classified as low income. As the population ages, the average age of these primary caregivers is likely to increase also, with the result that the oldest-old will increasingly be cared for by the merely elderly. Except in the case of spouses, both parties are likely to be women. Some women who have children in their thirties or later find themselves caring for toddlers and aging parents at the same time. Some women in their fifties and sixties must simultaneously cope with frail elderly parents and economically dependent adult children. In the 1990's, it was expected that members of this so-called sandwich generation would be legion in the twenty-first century.

A related issue of growing concern in the United States is the problem of elder abuse. In the 1990's, the typical abused elderly person was a woman over seventy-five years of age, in poor health, and dependent on her abusive caregiver. It is ironic that the average abuser was a woman approaching old age herself—between forty-five and sixty-five years of age.

In most European countries, as well as Canada, old age pensions and medical care throughout life, not merely in old age, are considered to be appropriate functions of government. In the United States, however, such social supports are reserved for the unemployed poor and the elderly. These services have, in effect, institutionalized age and made the aged a class apart. Being thus marginalized, the elderly are thought of as a separate and distinct category of people. Critics of the U.S. system believe that treating the elderly as a distinct, homogeneous, dependent group creates a welfare program that increases isolation, dependency, and state control. Furthermore, when certain roles are restricted to certain ages, these age norms result in the increasing loss of roles the older one gets. Because senior citizens lack role models, they often try to main-

*After the menopause, women have the same risk for heart disease, and heart attacks, as men do.* (Digital Stock)

tain the standards of behavior and activity they had in middle age, thus hindering not only their socialization to old age but also that of society.

One sociological model used to describe the lowered status of elderly people posits that the decline in status results from a confluence of several factors. First, advances in health technology have resulted in longer lives, causing intergenerational competition for jobs; retirement was developed to force the older generation to move aside. A second factor, the greater use of advanced technology in jobs, contributes to obsolescence of the skills of elderly people. The third factor—urbanization— caused younger family members to leave farms and rural areas for the greater opportunities of cities, which has led to generational isolation. Finally, literacy and mass education for the young meant that they had higher educational and professional status than did their elders in most cases. In the late twentieth century, elderly women were generally less educated, had less mastery of high-tech skills, and yet lived longer than men, adding an even greater degree of marginalization to their lives.

The experience of the elderly in the United States has been shaped by forces specific to the expansive nature of American society. The historical emphasis on individualism and independence and the advertising-driven emphasis on money, beauty, and sex appeal as important components of social success have created a society in which youth and vitality are prized more highly than age and wisdom. The cosmetic industry, pharmaceutical companies, and the medical specialty of cosmetic surgery profit from and reinforce the message that age will be honored mainly to the extent that one can achieve it without appearing to have been affected by it. Although men are not exempt from these appeals to vanity, the main targets and consumers of such products and services are women.

A society's social, political, and economic conditions affect how social issues, including aging, are treated and viewed. Unfortunately, many in society view the elderly as their least-able members. The variable and fluctuating nature of federal, state, and local governmental programs for the elderly have left many unmet needs. To fill these gaps, a vast web of private interests has grown up, often referred to as the "aging enterprise." Components of the aging enterprise include residen-

tial and health care facilities, including nursing homes, insurance providers that specialize in policies that cover the gap in health care payments left by Medicare, and manufacturers of products targeted toward the elderly. The aging enterprise has created a bureaucracy that further marginalizes the elderly to maintain the jobs and status of the members of the bureaucracy.

The United States pays a significantly higher percentage of its income maintenance programs to the elderly than do other countries. This does not mean, however, that the U.S. elderly receive more generous old-age pensions than other countries—only that the U.S. government provides little assistance to the nonelderly. Thus, some critics have referred to the United States as a Social Security welfare state. Because programs and policies related to old age support are based on preretirement income and work history, elderly women, the oldest-old, and elderly minorities are at the biggest financial disadvantage. In addition, far fewer women than men receive public or private pension benefits: In 1984, only 20 percent of women over the age of sixty-five received any income from such pensions, either as a spouse or as a retired worker. Many pension plans end benefits to the surviving spouse when the worker dies; thus, a woman who relies on pension income from her husband's job will lose a major portion of her income if she loses her husband. Only limited government assistance is available for persons who cannot qualify for Social Security. All these factors contribute greatly to the low economic status of elderly women as a group.

Retirement as a life stage with distinctive behaviors and expectations is a function of the creation of such social security programs. In earlier times, a person did not experience formal retirement. One farmed, baked, or sewed as long as one was able to do so, often in concert with family members. When frailty or disability precluded full participation in productive activities, one was cared for and supported by members of the extended family. Establishing retirement as a life stage in which certain roles and behaviors are predefined shapes people's ideas of what constitutes well-being. Categorizing seniors as a distinct group lessens the importance of seniority as the basis for prestige and community influence. Another factor is mobility: Younger family members move away from their aging parents, and seniors move away from established communities to be nearer to younger family members. When an elderly person moves to be near a child or other family member, he or she often moves into a community with a smaller elderly population and fewer resources for seniors to replace the social support systems he or she left behind. Research has demonstrated that communities in which residents are on the upper end of the social scale and in which there is a high level of residential mobility correlate with lower status and less social support for the elderly.

A happy marriage has been shown to provide both men and women with life-enhancing benefits of intimacy, interdependence, and a sense of belonging, although studies have shown men to be more satisfied with their marriages and the degree to which their needs are being met than are women. Women are less likely to die shortly after the death of a spouse than are men; however, after the death of a spouse, more than 25 percent of men over sixty-five years of age remarry, compared with less than 5 percent of women in that age group. Couples typically have twenty to forty years together after the last child leaves home, and retirement creates new challenges for both parties. Such long relationships are a new phenomenon: In 1900, the average length of marriage when the first partner died was twenty-eight years; in the 1990's, it had risen to more than forty-three years. As more women engage in professional careers, issues of two-person retirement arise, providing new quandaries for which there are few role models.

Most men over the age of sixty-five are married, for several reasons: Men generally marry younger women; older men are more likely to remarry than are older women; and women have a longer life expectancy than men. Elderly women, conversely, are more likely to live alone. Women also have, on average, smaller Social Security checks and less income from private pensions. Therefore, women are already living in circumstances more disadvantaged than men and thus are at greater risk of impoverishment than are men.

## HEALTH AND MEDICAL ISSUES

Women suffer more often from acute and chronic medical conditions than do men, although men have higher rates of cancer and heart disease. Despite the larger number of women in the population, women have been severely underrepresented in medical research as well as in studies of diseases in general; in addition, fewer funds are allotted for the study of diseases that are most common in women. The illnesses that most frequently strike women—arthritis, high blood pressure, strokes, diverticulitis, incontinence, and osteoporosis—are less likely to cause death and more likely to cause a woman to be bedridden for some time.

In the United States, the system of income maintenance for elderly citizens is newer, less comprehensive, and more bureaucratic than are related systems in European social democracies, partly because of different approaches to health care in different countries. The system in the United States is shaped by the U.S. medical orientation toward high-tech care for curable, acute conditions. In countries such as Ireland, however, where family care is emphasized, the state pays for medical care to old people in their homes. In fact, in the 1990's, the United States was the only industrial society without a caregiver allowance as part of its social security system. This is a particular disadvantage for older women, given that the diseases with which they are most commonly afflicted are debilitating and long-term rather than acute but curable. Women thus suffer both from the lack of financial support when they are in the caregiver role and from being more prone to conditions requiring the long-term services of a caregiver.

As technological advances have compensated for physical decline, they have also undermined the social support and personal contact that were common in earlier times and that are more readily available in less advanced societies. The technology that makes aging a more positive experience does not create the true social security of continuing social participation. In the United States, the longer life expectancy brought about by high-tech medical treatments has little payoff for the woman doomed to spend her final years alone in a nursing home. As part of the work that must be done to deal with the aging population, society must ensure that cultural age barriers do not replace physical barriers in the future.

## FEMINISM AND AGING

The women's movement in the United States that began in the 1960's often has been criticized for concentrating on the concerns of white, young and middle-aged, middle-class women. Increasingly, the movement is being urged to focus more closely on the needs of elderly women. One regular critic has been Barbara Macdonald, who, in her mid-seventies, wrote "Politics of Aging: I'm *Not* Your Mother" (*Ms.*, July/August, 1990), accusing feminists of seeing older women as mothers who should take care of them. Macdonald argued that ageism is a form of disempowerment for all women and that feminists should deal with it as such. As the movement's early leaders have aged, their concerns, mirroring their own experiences, have turned to issues such as the menopause and older women's health needs. Betty Friedan, generally considered to have ignited the late twentieth century women's movement with *The Feminine Mystique* (1963), began in her sixties to study aging, which culminated in *The Fountain of Age* (1993), a well-researched and provocative study of the aging in the late twentieth century.

—*Irene Struthers-Rush*

**See also** Ageism; *Aging Experience: Diversity and Commonality Across Cultures, The*; *All About Eve*; Beauty; Breast cancer; Breast changes and disorders; Caregiving; Cosmetic surgery; Cultural views of aging; Demographics; Divorce; Dual-income couples; Employment; Empty nest syndrome; Estrogen replacement therapy; Face lifts; Family relationships; *Fountain of Age, The*; *Golden Girls, The*; *In Full Flower: Aging Women, Power, and Sexuality*; "Jilting of Granny Weatherall, The"; Kübler-Ross, Elisabeth; Kuhn, Maggie; Kyphosis; Life expectancy; *Look Me in the Eye: Old Women, Aging, and Ageism*; Marriage; Menopause; *Murder, She Wrote*; Neugarten, Bernice; *No Stone Unturned: The Life and Times of Maggie Kuhn*; Older Women's League (OWL); Osteoporosis; *Ourselves, Growing Older: A Book for Women over Forty*; Poverty; Reproductive changes, disabilities, and dysfunctions; Retirement; Sandwich generation; Sarton, May; Sexuality; Sheehy, Gail; Single parenthood; *Sunset Boulevard*; *Tell Me a Riddle*; *Trip to Bountiful, The*; *When I Am an Old Woman I Shall Wear Purple*; Widows and widowers; *Woman's Tale, A*; "Worn Path, A."

**FOR FURTHER INFORMATION:**

Banner, Lois W. *In Full Flower: Aging Women, Power, and Sexuality.* New York: Alfred A. Knopf, 1992. Examines the position of older women in various societies throughout the ages, primarily through an exploration of literary sources. Extensive notes; index.

Copper, Baba. *Over the Hill: Reflections on Ageism Between Women.* Freedom, Calif.: Crossing Press, 1988. Essays by a well-known senior feminist. Some essays address a lesbian audience, but Copper is equally critical of negative, dismissive attitudes toward age of both young and elderly women in the heterosexual community.

Doress-Worters, Paula Brown, and Diana Laskin Siegal. *The New Ourselves, Growing Older: Women Aging with Knowledge and Power.* New York: Simon & Schuster, 1994. Comprehensive sourcebook, written in cooperation with the Boston Woman's Health Collective (the authors of *Our Bodies, Ourselves*). Covers topics including diet, exercise, sexuality, housing, retirement, and economics. Index; lengthy list of resources for help on numerous topics.

Friedan, Betty. *The Fountain of Age.* New York: Simon & Schuster, 1993. A positive exploration of aging as a natural process, not a disease or pathology. Posits that social institutions and expectations negatively skew attitudes toward the aged, and that new social structures and attitudes can lead to a great improvement in the lives of older persons.

Keith, Jennie, et al. *The Aging Experience: Diversity and Commonality Across Cultures.* Thousand Oaks, Calif.: Sage Publications, 1994. Presents results of field studies on aging and attitudes toward aging in Hong Kong; two towns in Botswana, Africa; a rural Irish town and a Dublin suburb; and a Midwestern farming community and an East Coast suburb in the United States. Accessible and informative.

Macdonald, Barbara, with Cynthia Rich. *Look Me in the Eye: Old Women, Aging, and Ageism.* San Francisco: Spinsters Ink, 1983. Brief book of essays by a U.S. feminist, lesbian, writer, and activist in her seventies, and her younger companion. Addresses ageism in society in general and in the feminist movement in particular.

Porcino, Jane. *Growing Older, Getting Better: A Handbook for Women in the Second Half of Life.* Reading, Mass.: Addison-Wesley, 1983. Comprehensive, readable information on social and health issues. Each chapter lists publications and organizations relevant to its topic, though some information may be outdated.

**WORK.** *See* **EMPLOYMENT.**

## "WORN PATH, A"

**AUTHOR:** Eudora Welty

**DATE:** Published in 1941

**RELEVANT ISSUES:** Family, health and medicine, race and ethnicity, values

**SIGNIFICANCE:** This short story exposes the cultural values and behavior of black and white folk in the rural South as an old black grandmother moves along a familiar path, struggling to adjust to the infirmities of aging

Eudora Welty's short story opens in winter against a sterile landscape which mirrors the fears of the main character, Phoenix Jackson. Phoenix is an impoverished African American grandmother completing a regular walking journey to a distant town to secure medical assistance for a family member. As she moves through wooded areas of the rural South, her vulnerability is exposed along with her fears of becoming dependent on others at this time in her life.

Phoenix represents the frail elderly who must continually readjust to changes in their aging condition. Mental and physical losses offer new challenges for an older person. When aging decreases

*Eudora Welty, the author of the short story "A Worn Path."* (Richard O. Moore)

sensory sharpness, the body cannot be trusted to complete routine tasks successfully. There is a growing need for support from others as well as more time and energy to complete simple activities.

Like the mythical bird that rose from ashes to begin a new life, however, Phoenix manages to find strength within herself to keep going. She finds satisfaction in reaching her destination and regains confidence after finding good fortune along the path.

In old age, each success can bring a renewed sense of well-being to an individual. Through a focus on both small and large accomplishments, the meaning of life is brought into focus as well. As Phoenix faces images of death, she realizes that, like life's journey, progress is made remembering past strengths and moving one step at a time. Phoenix's journey is imbued with a sense of endurance. Its completion becomes a celebration of life along one's aging course.          —*Enid J. Portnoy*

**See also** African Americans; Aging process; Cultural views of aging; Death and dying; Literature; Old age; Wisdom.

## WRINKLES

**RELEVANT ISSUES:** Biology, health and medicine

**SIGNIFICANCE:** Wrinkling is directly related to aging, as skin undergoes structural changes over time; the rate of the change can be reduced via dermatological processes

All human body fibers are formed by specialized cells in the tissues and can be classified as inelastic or elastic. Inelastic fibers are rigid and provide support to the surrounding tissue, while elastic fibers are more malleable. With the passage of time, inelastic fibers tend to become even tougher because of structural changes that occur in collagen, the major protein found in skin, bones, and ligaments. The dermis, the inner layer of the skin, contains large amounts of collagen, which is responsible for the skin's mechanical characteristics, such as strength and texture. The skin cells that make and reproduce damaged collagen are called fibroblasts.

As a person ages, collagen tends to form cross-links between different parts of the molecule or between similar molecules that are near each other, thus creating a rigidity

*The amount of pigment is a factor in the degree of wrinkling; darker skin shows less damage from the sun with age.* (James L. Shaffer)

that leads to skin sagging and wrinkling. Moreover, the recoiling ability of elastic fibers appears to be reduced, a condition that is often enhanced by calcification. Skin wrinkling is much more pronounced with prolonged exposure to wind and ultraviolet light. The effect appears to be cumulative along with collagen degeneration and epidermis thinning, as seen with people of outdoor professions. Other studies suggest that heavy cigarette smoking contributes to the risk of wrinkling.

Application of collagen-containing creams does not seem to create a desired change because the applied collagen molecules are too large to penetrate the dermis. Such applications only temporarily cover wrinkles. Injecting collagen under the wrinkles in a way that pushes the groove up, causing it to become smooth, has some positive cosmetic effect but also serious drawbacks. The main problem comes from the animal source of the collagen, which may lead to serious allergic reactions by the immune system and may, in rare cases, trigger a long-lasting autoimmune disease. Moreover, the smoothing effect of the injections appears to be brief because of the inability of the animal collagen to integrate itself into the skin's collagen mesh. Better results are observed when biotechnology-synthesized collagen is used or when the patient's own fibroblasts are removed, grown in a laboratory, and reinjected into the body. The careful administration of vitamin C, collagen amino acids, or very small quantities of copper peptides appears to stimulate the skin to produce more collagen. In addition, the topical application of growth factors and hormones that enhance the collagen-forming process of cells seems to give favorable results.

Chemical peels have been used to correct facial wrinkling in face-lift or eyelid surgeries. A mixture of chemicals is applied to the skin, leading to extreme swelling and consequent peeling of the old skin, thus providing a fresh skin in two weeks. Carbon dioxide lasers were first developed in 1964, but experiments that combined them with computer technology did not begin until the 1990's. This resurfacing technique, which affects an area of skin no more than one hair in thickness for no more than one thousandth of a second, works in a way similar to chemical peel. It is considered best for patients of fair to medium complexion who have good healing qualities and who have not used acutane in the previous year.

—*Soraya Ghayourmanesh*

***See also*** Antiaging treatments; Beauty; Cosmetic surgery; Face lifts; Skin changes and disorders; Women and aging.

*Theodor Geisel (otherwise known as Dr. Seuss), the author of* You're Only Old Once!, *at home in 1957.* (Library of Congress)

## YOU'RE ONLY OLD ONCE!

**AUTHOR:** Dr. Seuss (Theodor Seuss Geisel)

**DATE:** Published in 1986

**RELEVANT ISSUES:** Health and medicine, psychology

**SIGNIFICANCE:** In this Dr. Seuss book for "obsolete children," the central character, Everyman, who represents the aging population, presents a delightful defense against aging

Everyman has not been feeling his best. He checks into the Golden Years Clinic for a thorough checkup, even though he longs to be in the mountains with fresh air and no doctors. The book follows Everyman through a battery of tests, beginning with an eye test with a chart that reads, "Have you any idea how much money these tests are costing you?" The medical history includes questions about the ailments of parents, grandparents, and cousins. Did they have Bus Driver's Blight or Prune Picker's Plight? Did an uncle collapse from too much alphabet soup, or martinis perhaps?

The scenes are all true to life. The patient is stripped and his clothes promptly lost. He is subjected to an ear test, an internal organs test, an allergy test, a stress test, and a "pill drill." Between tests, Everyman is seated in the hallway in an embarrassingly inadequate gown with a large back door that keeps flaring open. His companion in the hallway is a fish, Norvall, who at first is quite sympathetic but quickly becomes bored with Everyman's tales of woe. Norvall has heard them all before.

The doctors' names add charm to the story; Dr. Pollen is the allergy specialist. The nutrition doctor tests Everyman to be sure he gets nothing in his diet that he likes. The pill doctor gives him ten kinds of pills. Most important, the insurance forms must be filled out so Everyman can be billed—well, Everyman or his heirs. At last, Everyman finds his clothes, dresses, and bids Norvall good-bye. The final upbeat diagnosis is that Everyman is in pretty good shape for the shape he is in.

—*Billie M. Taylor*

*See also* Health care; Humor; Literature; Medical insurance; Middle age; Old age; Stereotypes.

# BIBLIOGRAPHY: NONFICTION

## General Works, Bibliographies, and Resources

*Abstracts in Social Gerontology.* Thousand Oaks, Calif.: Sage Publications. This quarterly publication provides useful gerontology-related information through one thousand abstracts and one thousand bibliographical citations every year. Material is collected from publications around the world. Areas covered include adult education, community services, demography, governmental policies and law, care of the elderly, biology and physiology, death and bereavement, economic issues, housing, leisure, and recreation.

*Ageing and Society.* Cambridge, England: Cambridge University Press. This international journal of the Center for Public Policy on Ageing and the British Society of Gerontology contains articles from the social and behavioral sciences, as well as the humanities, that promote an understanding of the processes of human aging. It also provides book reviews and reports on current research. Published six times each year.

*Ageing International.* Montreal. Published quarterly, this is the official journal of the International Federation on Ageing (IFA). Gives an interesting global perspective on research into families, trends, policies, education and lifelong learning, environments, and diversity. Also reports on the proceedings of the IFA's Global Conference. News from around the world on achievements of the elderly and on aging issues adds to the publication's interest.

Bengtson, Vern L., and K. Warner Shaie. *Handbook of Theories of Aging.* New York: Springer, 1998. Bengtson and Shaie discuss concepts and theories from the biological, biomedical, psychological, and social science fields as they relate to aging and research on aging. The book also explores strategies for successful interventions by applying theory to practice.

Comfort, Alex. *Say Yes to Old Age.* New York: Crown, 1990. While critical of attitudes toward aging in America, the author provides an informative and optimistic look at the biological, political, and social transformations experienced by the elderly. He suggests ways to face these transformations in a positive, proactive way. Encyclopedia-style entries supply information on various aspects of aging and include ways for people to "debrainwash" themselves of society's indoctrination in respect to old age. Facts and myths on a wide range of topics are covered, including ageism, health issues, emotional factors, family, religion, and diet. A discussion follows each entry.

*Gerontology and Geriatrics Education.* Binghamton, N.Y.: Haworth Press. This quarterly publication contains articles on the sociology of gerontology, health and dentistry concepts and issues, geriatrics and gerontology education, adult learning theory, and other age-related topics.

*Journal of Applied Gerontology.* Thousand Oaks, Calif.: Sage Publications. As the official journal of the Southern Gerontological Society, this quarterly publication focuses on the application of research and knowledge related to the improvement of quality of life for the elderly. Book reviews on age-related topics are also featured.

*Journal of Gerontological Social Work.* Binghamton, N.Y.: Haworth Press. This journal frequently publishes two volumes each year, with four issues per volume. Articles deal with social work theory, research, and practice in the field of aging. Examples of content include research on life after retirement, household composition, living arrangements, minority issues, social networks, sexuality, caregiving, hospitalization, emotional needs, intergenerational perspectives, education, and advocacy.

Kausler, Donald H., and Barry C. Kausler. *The Graying of America: An Encyclopedia of Aging, Health, Mind, and Behavior.* Urbana: University of Illinois Press, 1996. The authors state that aging is a natural process experienced by all organisms but that, as the graying of America increases, it is essential to better understand the nature of aging. Useful information is provided on more than three hundred topics related to aging, ranging from physical abilities to the working memory of older people.

Manheimer, Ronald J., ed. *Older Americans Almanac.* Detroit: Gale Research, 1994. Contains detailed information on the process and status of aging in the United States. A wide range of topics is covered, including diversity in aging, employment, environments, economic issues, health, lifestyles, retirement, and social, physical, and mental factors related to aging. Provides a list of resources, organization names and addresses, and phone and fax numbers.

Manheimer, Ronald J., Denise D. Snodgrass, and Diane Moskow-McKenzie. *Older Adult Education: A Guide to Research, Progress, and Policies.* Westport, Conn.: Greenwood Press, 1995. An important resource on a broad range of topics related to older adult education. Areas covered include historical perspectives, policy trends, existing research, models and approaches, current educational programming, and projected future development of older adult education in the United States. Gives helpful information on organizations and programs, including a list of states offering age-based tuition waivers and incentives.

*Modern Maturity.* Washington, D.C. Bimonthly publication of the American Association of Retired Persons (AARP). Articles and reviews cover a broad range of topics, such as health and fitness, current affairs, legislation, family life, entertainment and leisure, travel, services, and resources. Creative work by seniors is also featured. The *AARP Bulletin,* another publication of the association, provides updates and viewpoints on current affairs and legislation.

Roy, F. Hampton, and Charles Russell. *The Encyclopedia of Aging and the Elderly.* New York: Facts on File, 1992. Presents facts about medical, psychological, social, and environmental issues relevant to older people. The book is a comprehensive and readable source of information on such topics as lifestyles of the aging, myths and misconceptions about aging, assorted health issues, nursing homes, residential arrangements, retirement patterns and issues, legal concerns, estate planning, sexuality, self-image, life span and life extension, friendship, and family relationships.

Shuldiner, David P. *Folklore, Culture, and Aging: A Research Guide.* Westport, Conn.: Greenwood Press, 1997. Shuldiner provides a broad, although not comprehensive, bibliography of folklore and customs associated with aging and the aged in various cultures. Works cited range from 1970 to 1997 and are intended to provide a sample rather than an exhaustive compilation of existing research. Listed materials—which include books, journal articles, newsletters, and films—are categorized under research tools, general works, beliefs and customs, narratives, traditional arts, health and healing, applied folklore, and films.

Smolak, Linda. *Adult Development.* Englewood Cliffs, N.J.: Prentice Hall, 1993. The author provides an overview of the physiological and social aspects of adult development and aging. The section on old age presents information on physical, cognitive, personality, and social development in later life, as well as on the causes of aging. The book covers such topics as health and aging, the prescription and use of drugs, organic brain syndromes, morale, stress, mental illness, family and social relationships, living arrangements, work, friendships, abuse, leisure, and death.

*Social Issues Resources Series: Aging.* Boca Raton, Fla. Each volume of this periodical contains articles reprinted from national and international journals, magazines, newspapers, and government documents. Articles present various viewpoints and cover a multitude of topics relevant to the interests and concerns of the elderly, including health, social life and issues, financial management, government policies, and current research. Articles about older family members and the aged also appear in the *Social Issues Resources Series* volumes *Family* and *Health*.

Vitt, Lois A., Jurg K. Siegenthaler, and Neil E. Culler, eds. *Encyclopedia of Financial Gerontology*. Westport, Conn.: Greenwood Press, 1996. Provides basic general information on the financial issues that are likely to concern aging individuals and their families. Discusses such topics as assisted living, home care, Medicaid, financial planning, Social Security, veterans benefits, legislation of age-related issues, and the education of older adults. Includes suggested readings and helpful information on organizations and competent professionals.

West, Robin L., and Jan D. Sinnott, eds. *Everyday Memory and Aging*. New York: Springer-Verlag, 1992. The focus of this work would make it meaningful chiefly to those interested in researching aging in relation to memory and the mind. Presents a variety of methodological studies on the process, domains, applications, function, evaluation, and performance of memory research.

Wheeler, Helen R. *Women and Aging: A Guide to the Literature*. Boulder, Colo.: Lynne Rienner, 1997. A useful guide to resource materials on women's aging and experiences from midlife onward. Covers general topics, such as gerontological, psychological, and sociological perspectives on women's aging, as well as more specific topics, such as economic issues, ageism, sexism, creativity, and productivity. Contains interesting sections on biographies, autobiographies, diaries, journals, letters, memoirs, oral histories, personal narratives, and literature about aging women.

Williams, Mark E. *American Geriatrics Society's Complete Guide to Aging and Health*. New York: Harmony Books, 1995. A comprehensive resource and guide to the many age-related aspects of health. Williams discusses the process of aging; the prevention, care, and treatment of physical and mental conditions; and the legal, ethical, and financial aspects of growing old. Includes a list of resources on both general and specific health needs of older individuals.

## Ethnicity and Aging

Ball, Mary M., and Frank J. Whittingham. *Surviving Dependence: Voices of African American Elders*. Amityville, N.Y.: Baywood, 1995. An inter-esting and well-organized inquiry into the challenges of old age and how they affect the seven African Americans in this study. Profiles of the informants are clearly presented, along with their views of themselves as dependents and of the caregivers on whom they depend. The authors recommend that programs be built specifically around care recipients' needs, that financial support be made more available to the aged, that coordination of services be made more efficient, that protection be set up for home care clients, and that quality of care be improved.

Benton, Linda, ed. *Families and Aging*. Amityville, N.Y.: Baywood, 1993. Benton examines the varied and complex issues impacting the lives of the aging and their families. The increasing life span, the growing diversity of the American family, and changing economic and social conditions are all shaping the lives of the aging. Topics related to this concept include relationships in later years, dating and courtship among older people, the effects of divorce and reconstitution of families on older family members, elders in certain ethnic groups, families of older homosexuals, the oldest old, grandparenthood, family caregiving, and resources.

Facio, Elisa. *Understanding Older Chicanas*. Thousand Oaks, Calif.: Sage Publications, 1996. Facio analyzes the influence of culture on the experiences, expectations, relationships, attitudes, and images of self and old age among older Chicanas. She looks at the strategies developed by this group to adapt to changing situations, increasing limitations, and everyday challenges. Through interviews and observation, she also documents the impact of poverty on the lives and options of elderly Chicanas, the majority of whom immigrated to the United States as infants or young children.

Gelfland, Donald E. *Aging and Ethnicity: Knowledge and Services*. New York: Springer, 1994. After reviewing major theories on aging and ethnicity, the author examines the impact of immigration and immigration policy on the lives of the ethnic aged. Socioeconomic factors, health, sense of security, and the role of the family and religion are reviewed. Specific challenges facing the ethnic aged and their cultures in American pluralistic society are discussed.

Jackson, James S., Linda M. Chatters, and Robert J. Taylor. *Aging in Black America.* Newbury Park, Calif.: Sage Publications, 1993. This book provides a comprehensive view of the conditions, status, and lifestyles of aging African Americans. Topics include community, friends and family, religion, health, social functioning, well-being, political and group behaviors, and retirement and work. Changing patterns of familial and social support for older African Americans are discussed. The authors argue that although health care has generally improved for older black adults and although African Americans are often resilient and successful in the face of social and psychological challenges, many are at severe risk for poverty and diminished environmental, psychological, and physical health because of the framework in which their life span experiences occur. The authors emphasize the need to develop improved social care systems for older African Americans.

Markides, Kyriakos S., and Manuel R. Miranda, eds. *Minorities, Aging, and Health.* Thousand Oaks, Calif.: Sage Publications, 1997. The articles in this book examine the needs of a growing number of minorities among the aging population in the United States. Among these minority groups are Asian Americans, Latinos, Pacific Islanders, and Native Americans. Discussion occurs on access to health care, disease, disabilities, life expectancy, long-term care, mortality, and public health care policy. Provides insight into an area where much research is still needed.

Padgett, Deborah K., ed. *Handbook of Ethnicity, Aging, and Mental Health.* Westport, Conn.: Greenwood Press, 1995. As a resource for researchers, educators, and practitioners, this book attempts to fill the gap existing in knowledge of the needs of older people from different ethnic groups. It presents information on approaches to ethnicity, aging, and mental health; examines the mental health needs of the elderly in various ethnic groups; reviews service to these groups; and discusses caregiving and other issues pertaining to them. Ethnic groups discussed include African Americans, Alaskan Natives, Asians, Latinos, and Native Americans.

## Families and Aging

Ciardi, Charmaine L., Cathy N. Orme, and Carolyn Quatrano. *The Magic of Grandparenting.* New York: Henry Holt, 1995. The number of grandparents is increasing in the United States, and with this increase has come a change in attitudes toward these older family members. The altered image and roles of grandparents are discussed and celebrated in an easy-to-read format. Tips are offered on bonding with grandchildren, expressing love in novel and meaningful ways, and enriching grandparent-grandchild relationships.

Cohen, Donna, and Carl Eisdorfer. *Caring for Your Aging Parents.* New York: Jeremy P. Tarcher/Putnum, 1993. The authors examine the issues, dilemmas, commitments, conflicts, emotional stresses, and daily activities of the growing number of Americans who provide care for their aging parents. Seven specific steps to effective caregiving are presented through individual life stories and practical advice. Gives information on selected readings, community services, programs, and state and national agencies that offer help to caregivers and elderly family members.

Elkind, David. *Grandparenting: Understanding Today's Children.* Glenview, Ill.: Scott, Foresman, 1990. A child development specialist and educator, Elkind examines the world in which modern children and adolescents are growing up, the cultural changes that have occurred in child rearing, the increase in knowledge about children's development, and the stresses faced by families in a fast-changing society and world. Knowledge of these factors can help grandparents enjoy their roles better, be more prepared to help their grandchildren live to their fullest potential, and be better prepared to cope with the stresses and joys of contemporary modern life along with their grandchildren.

Fay, Jim, and Foster W. Cline. *Grandparenting with Love and Logic.* Golden, Colo.: Love and Logic, 1994. This book offers practical advice and suggestions to help modern grandparents and grandchildren cope with changing lifestyles. Topics discussed include stepgrandchildren, disagreements with parents, divorce, grandparents' rights, and discipline. Useful "love and logic" tips are scattered throughout the book.

Morris, Virginia. *How to Care for Aging Parents*. New York: Workman, 1996. A comprehensive and practical guide to an array of emotional, financial, medical, and legal issues associated with the care of aging parents. Caregivers' needs are also examined.

Pipher, Mary. *Another Country: Navigating the Emotional Terrain of Our Elders*. New York: Riverhead, 1999. Pipher reminds readers that the growing number of aging individuals in the United States are members of families—parents, grandparents, or other relations—and talks about the need for those with older loved ones to learn the "language for nurturing interdependency." She describes the many ways in which the aged are segregated from the rest of society . Reports of the experiences of several families offer hope that bridges of understanding and communication can be constructed.

Szinovácz, Maximiliane E., ed. *Handbook on Grandparenthood*. Westport, Conn.: Greenwood Press, 1998. This is a comprehensive and organized work on the different aspects of grandparenthood, including the experience of being a grandparent, the dynamics of grandparenting, and interventions in grandparenting. Topics examined include cross-cultural factors and perspectives, ethnicity, gender, environmental influences, grandparents as caregivers, public policy, grandparents' rights, and the need for further research. Case studies and lists add to the authority of this work.

Wasserman, Selma. *The Long Distance Grandmother*. Point Roberts, Wash.: Hartley & Marks, 1988. As families become more mobile, contemporary grandparents are often geographically separated from their grandchildren. This book provides numerous ways in which grandmothers (and grandfathers) can build rich and satisfying relationships with their grandchildren across vast geographical distances. Suggestions include writing stories for grandchildren, sending "playful" gifts to them at different ages, recording voices on tape for each other, supporting troubled or disabled grandchildren, and helping those who are going through difficult times. Also includes strategies for surviving family breakdown and changes.

Weiner, Marcella B., Jeanne Teresi, and Corrine Streich. *Old People Are a Burden, but Not My Parents.* Englewood Cliffs, N.J.: Prentice Hall, 1983. Provides insights into various aspects of aging in late twentieth century life. Cites research on social and family attitudes toward older people, discusses distinguishing characteristics of normal and problem aging, and offers suggestions on coping.

Zal, H. Michael. *The Sandwich Generation: Caught Between Growing Children and Aging Parents*. New York: Plenum, 1992. Written for individuals in midlife who are raising their children and caring for their aging parents, this book serves as a guide to building relationships and strengthening bonds with the young and the old by understanding human development at different stages of life. Chapters on middle-aged children and their aging parents, and on various aspects of old age, provide useful information on understanding older people. Topics include retired parents, grandparenthood, creativity in later life, recovering from a spouse's death, sex, residence patterns and arrangements, legal and ethical concerns, caregiving, and death. Interesting vignettes about different individuals and experiences are scattered throughout the book.

## Global and Cross-Cultural Perspectives on Aging

Hareven, Tamara, ed. *Aging and Generational Relations: Life-Course and Cross-Cultural Perspectives*. Hawthorne, N.Y.: Aldine de Gruyter, 1996. Contributors to this collection examine generational relationships from a life-course perspective, which emphasizes the impact of earlier experiences on an individual's later life and on care given by adult children to aging parents. Themes explored include the relationship of earlier circumstances to later interactions, factors influencing intergenerational support, generations residing together, generations residing separately, and the effect of social change on generational relations. The articles take a cross-cultural look at these issues in Europe, Japan, Sri Lanka, Taiwan, Thailand, and the United States. Referring to historical perspectives, one article projects future generational relationship structures.

Keith, Jennie, et al. *The Aging Experience: Diversity and Commonality Across Cultures*. Thousand Oaks, Calif.: Sage Publications, 1994. Based on a ten-year collaborative research project on the aging experience in seven locations in Botswana, Hong Kong, Ireland, and the United States, this book examines the effect of culture on old age and its meanings. Cross-cultural comparisons are made on age and well-being; age and the life course; political economy and age; and health, functionality, and age. While much diversity exists, the authors warn against societal age separation of populations, point to the breakdown of family and community support networks, and urge vigilance in support of the elderly. The authors further state that whole lives and whole families, rather than fragmented aspects of their lives, need to be considered in studies of the aged. See entry in *Aging*.

Litwin, Howard, ed. *The Social Network of Older People*. Westport, Conn.: Praeger, 1996. A cross-cultural, cross-national analysis of the social networks of the elderly. These networks include family, friends, neighbors, and colleagues. The author examines the relevance and impact of these networks on older people in Sweden, France, Spain, Canada, Finland, England, Wales, Holland, Israel, and the United States and concludes that social policies in all societies must keep abreast with changes in social network structures so that the care of the elderly can be adapted to such changes.

_____. *Uprooted in Old Age: Soviet Jews and Their Social Networks in Israel*. Westport, Conn.: Greenwood Press, 1995. This book provides insights into the effects of being uprooted from familiar surroundings in old age and having to cope with transitions and stresses of aging while adapting to the unknown and the unfamiliar. The author highlights challenges faced by elderly Soviet immigrants to Israel, emphasizes the importance of social networks for these elderly immigrants, and explores ways to make networks and intervention strategies more effective and supportive.

Rasmussen, Susan. *Poetics and Politics of Tuareg Aging: Life Course and Personal Destiny in Niger*. DeKalb: Northern Illinois University Press, 1997. Rasmussen provides a cultural analysis and exploration of the biological and social life transitions of the people of northern Niger, where aging is marked by these transitions rather than by chronological age. These important life transitions are marked by rituals, specific expectations of behavior, dress, use of space, music, and dance; they serve as passages into new roles, as well as into new cohort and intergenerational relationships. A very different picture of aging emerges when the Tuareg concept of life transitions is compared to Western notions of the life cycle and aging.

Thursz, Daniel, Charlotte Nusberg, and Johnnie Prather, eds. *Empowering Older People: An International Approach*. Westport, Conn.: Auburn House, 1995. The collection of studies in this volume grew out of a workshop sponsored by several organizations committed to the empowerment of older people that was part of the United Nations Conference on Aging in San Diego in 1992. The essays examine the concept and meaning of empowerment of older people in different countries and cultures, describe ways in which organizations can empower elders or help elders empower themselves, and analyze the impact of social and economic factors on empowerment. International perspectives include both developed and developing countries, such as Great Britain, Canada, Chile, Denmark, the Dominican Republic, Mexico, Pakistan, South Africa, Sri Lanka, Thailand, and the United States.

## Health, Fitness, and Well-Being

Ben-Sira, Zeev. *Regression, Stress, and Readjustment in Aging*. New York: Praeger, 1991. After reviewing existing literature on the problems of aging, the author points out that chronological age alone should not be considered the cause of decline of mental and physical health. Ben-Sira reviews and analyzes current approaches to the stress-disease relationship, examines both the capabilities and the limitations of the fields of social work and medicine when dealing with age-related regression, and urges increased collaboration between the two professions.

Billig, Nathan. *Growing Older and Wiser: Coping with Expectations, Challenges, and Change in the Later Years*. New York: Lexington, 1993. Billig examines various aspects of aging and ways of coping more efficiently in old age. Some of the factors older people need to learn to cope with as they plan for the future are family relationships, loss, loneliness, changes in sleep patterns, sexuality, and living arrangements. Provides detailed discussion on psychological problems, such as depression and certain kinds of dementia, and on problems faced by people suffering from Alzheimer's disease and those who care for them.

Carlson, Mary B. *Creative Aging: A Meaning-Making Perspective.* New York: W. W. Norton, 1991. Drawing on theories of human development and creativity, the author attempts to extend existing images of aging and searches for models of creative aging and personal growth. Aging adults can be helped to view the aging process creatively. Society and professionals working with older clients must examine prior, noncreative attitudes that were molded by biases, fears, emotions, and beliefs about old age. The author identifies barriers to creative thinking and discusses therapies that encourage creativity. That the elderly can live full, creative, and meaningful lives is validated by the presentation of stories, shared wisdom, conversations, observations, insights, and behaviors of many older adults.

Carper, Jean. *Stop Aging Now!* New York: HarperCollins, 1995. Although some controversial material is included, the author draws on a wide range of sources to suggest ways in which the aging process can be slowed down and the aging individual's general health and vitality can be maintained. Common sense information and advice is given on nutrition, including the use of vitamins, herbs, minerals, and antioxidants. Alternative measures and suggestions are also offered.

Carter, Jimmy. *The Virtues of Aging.* New York: Ballantine, 1998. A personal account by a former president of the United States about aging, as well as the blessings and virtues that should be a part of this natural process. Carter emphasizes that the potential for self-fulfillment and service to others can be achieved by accepting challenges, continuing to seek opportunities for growth, living a simple life, and having faith and love. Some remarkable older individuals are described. See entry in *Aging.*

Cassidy, Thomas M. *Elder Care.* Far Hills, N.J.: New Horizon, 1997. Cassidy, a former senior special investigator of the Attorney General's Office, wrote this book to alert readers to potential abuse and pitfalls faced by the elderly in health care, legal, and economic areas. Dependent living arrangements, whether in assisted living or nursing homes, are side effects of increasing life spans, and shrewd planning and careful decision making are essential. Advice is offered on a wide variety of situations, such as hiring a caregiver, choosing a nursing home or other caregiving facility, finding needed resources and agencies, estate planning, and ways to prevent elder care crises. A state-by-state elder care locator is provided to help readers locate state and other resources available to older Americans.

Chopra, Deepak. *Ageless Body, Timeless Mind.* New York: Harmony, 1993. Chopra stresses the mind-body relationship. When properly understood, this relationship can help people overcome traditional fears and attitudes toward aging and can also serve as a guide to a long and satisfying life.

Dollemore, Doug, and the editors of *Prevention Health for Seniors. Home Remedies for Seniors.* Emmaus, Pa.: Rodale, 1999. This reference book provides practical advice and information for elders on ways to make decisions about their own health issues. Offers sensible suggestions on healthier living and describes numerous preventive and doctor-recommended measures for common ailments of older people.

Friel, Joe. *Cycling Past Fifty.* Champaign, Ill.: Human Kinetics, 1998. As baby boomers age, participation in sports in the middle to later years is becoming increasingly popular; the media and businesses are paying more attention to the power and economic potential of various kinds of sports indulged in by those over fifty years of age. The author discusses the aging process and its impact on the human body and explains how cycling can keep aging Americans vigorous, active, and healthy. He offers advice on training principles, injury prevention, efficient fueling of the body, and attaining a sense of mental well-being through physical activity.

Gubrium, Jaber F. *Speaking of Life: Horizons of Meaning for Nursing Home Residents.* New York: Aldine de Gruyter, 1993. To counteract the image of nursing-home residents as "faces without stories," Gubrium interviewed fifty-eight residents in six Florida nursing homes. The result is a remarkable picture of selves full of meaning created out of the daily lives of the interviewees.

These meanings are closely related to the emotional state and current circumstances in which the aging residents find themselves. The author identifies these older people as "travelers," "sisters," "spouses," "disabled," or "knowledgeable," according to their orientations to life and their circumstances. This is an interesting, unusual, and readable work on an important subject.

Holahan, Carole K., Robert R. Sears, and Lee J. Cronbach. *The Gifted Group in Later Life*. Stanford, Calif.: Stanford University Press, 1995. Part of the Terman Study of the Gifted Series, this volume reports on a longitudinal study begun in 1921, when the subjects were children averaging eleven years of age. The Terman Study claims to be the longest life cycle study in social science history. This book examines the later adult life and aging experiences of the gifted individuals who have been followed throughout the study. Questions inquire into the kinds of goals and standards set by these individuals in their later years, the role of gender in their aging, their approach to aging as compared to others in their age group, their personal and marital relationships, and the strategies they use to adjust to changes. The subjects provide perspectives and reflections on their satisfaction with various aspects of their professional and personal lives.

Hudson, Frederic M. *The Adult Years: Mastering the Art of Self-Renewal*. San Francisco: Jossey-Bass, 1991. Taking a life cycle approach, the author discusses the adult experience in a rapidly changing world and explores ways in which adults can master change to become personally empowered agents for social change. Chapters on midlife and old age define ways that people in these age groups express and enjoy their life purposes, develop new strategies to attain and savor fulfillment, and face new beginnings and challenges—including approaching dependency and death.

Johnson, Colleen L. *Life Beyond Eighty-five Years: The Aura of Survivorship*. New York: Springer, 1997. Johnson provides insights into the aging process, the daily and inner lives of the very old, and the competencies and coping strategies required to survive to be the "oldest old." Several case studies document the varied life experiences, developmental factors, and adaptation processes of these oldest adults.

Knapp, Marshall B. *Geriatrics and the Law: Patient Rights and Professional Responsibilities*. 2d ed. New York: Springer, 1992. This is a comprehensive source of information on legal issues related to aging, including nursing home regulations, guardianship provisions, financial issues, and long-term care. Knapp scrutinizes ethical concerns and existing laws on such controversial topics as euthanasia, the right to die, and research on older human subjects.

Koch, Tom. *A Place in Time: Caregivers for Their Elderly*. Westport, Conn.: Praeger, 1993. A moving collection of interviews with caregivers from Canada and the United States. The interviews vividly portray multigenerational experiences, both painful and uplifting, including social, economic, and individual costs and dilemmas that can strain or strengthen personal relationships. It is emphasized that the elderly are not sufferers of pathological conditions; rather, they are survivors and endurers with families and with a legitimate place in a society that needs to initiate more family-friendly policies.

Morley, John E. "Scientific Advances in Aging." In *Birth to Death: Science and Bioethics*, edited by David C. Thomasma and Thomasine Kushner. Cambridge, England: Cambridge University Press, 1996. Morley argues that although scientific discoveries and technological advances have made old age less formidable and have potentially added to the quality of older people's lives, "high-touch" techniques are needed to make knowledge available and to help society avoid the inappropriate use of medication or technology in the care of the elderly.

Osgood, Nancy J., Barbara A. Bryant, and Aaron Lipmant. *Suicide Among the Elderly in Long-Term Care Facilities*. Westport, Conn.: Greenwood Press, 1991. This book deals with a little-researched concern about an aspect of aging in American society that is becoming more relevant as the number of aging individuals increases. Background information is provided on long-term care facilities and on the impact of the physical and psychological environment on people as they age.

Rogers, Wendy A., and Arthur D. Fisk, eds. *Aging and Skilled Performance: Advances in Theory and*

*Applications.* Mahwah, N.J.: Lawrence Erlbaum Associates, 1996. This book documents several studies on various skills, age-related learning differences, knowledge structures, intellectual life, skill acquisition and retention, and technology use among the aged. Suggests ways to use prior training, cognitive theory, and multidisciplinary approaches and training materials to maximize the skilled performance of older adults.

Siebers, Michael J., Gail Gunter-Hunt, and Jean Farrell-Holtan. *Coping with Loss of Independence.* San Diego: Singular, 1993. Part of the Coping with Aging series, this book looks at the value placed on independence in modern Western society and examines the complex challenges that arise when adaptations must be made because of the aging process. Offers a "recipe" for independence for the elderly, along with ways to remain active participants in life even when physical and mental losses occur. The work also covers health and safety issues, housing options, transportation needs, and legal and financial decision making, and provides a comprehensive list of advocacy groups and resource agencies.

Skinner, B. F., and Margaret E. Vaughan. *Enjoy Old Age.* New York: Warner, 1983. Noted behavioral psychologist Skinner joins Vaughen, an expert on aging, to examine the emotional life of the aging and some of the challenges these individuals face. Believing that people can live well by planning well, the authors give advice to older adults on ways to enjoy themselves, to keep in touch with the world and their own past, to think more clearly, to stay busy, to feel good, to enjoy good days, to get along with other people, to keep from letting the fear of death ruin present joy of living, and to reconcile themselves to the inevitable characteristics of old age. See entry in *Aging.*

Thorman, George. *Emotional Problems of Aging.* Springfield, Ill.: Charles C Thomas, 1989. Written as a guide for nurses, mental health practitioners, psychologists, and social workers, this book examines the aging process, emotional and mental disorders of old age, assessment of emotional problems, and social casework in helping older persons cope with emotional issues. The author reviews various strategies for working with the aging and treatments involved in long-term care. He also discusses ways to help families cope with elder care and the importance of helping everyone involved face the reality of approaching death.

Tideiksaar, Rein. *Falls in Older Persons: Prevention and Management.* Baltimore: Health Professions, 1998. Tideiksaar examines the effect of falls on the quality of life of older adults, on the emotional state of the family and caregivers of the patient, and on the balance that must be found between humane practices and costs to institutions and society. Also considers physical changes undergone by the older patient, medication, staffing patterns and issues in institutions, intervention strategies and approaches, restraints or alternatives to restraints as preventive measures, and environmental factors that could increase or lessen the risk of falling.

Tobin, Sheldon S. *Personhood in Advanced Old Age: Implications for Practice.* New York: Springer, 1991. Using case studies, the author describes the psychology of being old and of exhibiting a sense of personhood in old age. Reviews therapies for older adults, including those with Alzheimer's disease. Other important topics covered include ways to relieve psychological distress during hospitalization, to provide support to older people in nursing homes, to preserve selfhood through religion, and to accept the reality of death.

Weaver, Frances. *I'm Not as Old as I Used to Be.* New York: Hyperion, 1997. Weaver meditates upon the various but never-easy aspects of growing old. With both humor and pathos, she describes her personal journey into old age and offers practical advice to help the aging enjoy life, find creative outlets, be true to themselves, and remain independent while maintaining old ties and forging new ones.

Whitbourne, Susan K. *The Aging Individual: Physical and Psychological Perspectives.* New York: Springer, 1996. Whitbourne provides insights into the compensation-making power of the aging mind and body. Although older adults experience many losses as they age, the author points out that they are continuously developing their personalities and identities. In the process, older adults use both negative and positive strategies to cope with change. Whitbourne presents data on physical and psychological changes that occur as people grow older and calls for more research on the identities that older adults create for themselves in response to these changes.

## Historical Perspectives on Aging

Banner, Lois W. *In Full Flower: Aging Women, Power, and Sexuality.* New York: Alfred A. Knopf, 1992. Banner provides a history of aging women from ancient times to the late twentieth century by describing attitudes toward and stereotypes of older women at different periods of history. She weaves mythology, religion, literature, art, facts, and social contexts into a colorful and vivid tapestry about the lives of older women across generations and time. See entry in *Aging.*

Haber, Carole, and Brian Gratton. *Old Age and the Search for Security.* Bloomington: Indiana University Press, 1994. The authors explore how Americans from colonial times to the late twentieth century looked for ways to make old age secure and meaningful. The book analyzes family life, economic status, work, retirement, age-based welfare, and images of the elderly.

Katz, Stephen. *Disciplining Old Age: The Formation of Gerontological Knowledge.* Charlottesville: University Press of Virginia, 1996. This complex and scholarly work examines the emergence of the study of old age as a valid and acceptable discipline. Katz traces the historical status of the elderly and historical concepts of old age and the aging body. He also discusses society's "problematization" of old age.

Kertzer, David I., and Peter Laslett, eds. *Aging in the Past: Demography, Society, and Old Age.* Berkeley: University of California Press, 1995. The historical demography of aging is an emerging field; as populations rapidly age across many cultures, a knowledge of the history of aging becomes relevant. This book examines lifestyles, family roles, household systems, residential patterns, widowhood, and the impact of migration and other factors on old age in the past in England, Wales, Hungary, and various parts of the United States.

Morris, Desmond. *The Book of Ages.* New York: Viking Press, 1983. An unusual collection of encyclopedia-style entries highlighting the age at which various famous people achieved great-

ness; experienced success, loss, or tragedy; or began or ended their careers. Entries range from information on the Buddha at five days old to a Japanese man aged 118 years. Morris presents typical characteristics that people exhibit at different ages, as well as the traits of those who achieve longevity. Also included are facts about life expectancy in different parts of the world, as well as information about the animal world.

Terkel, Studs. *Coming of Age: The Story of Our Century by Those Who've Lived It.* New York: The New Press, 1995. By weaving together case studies and interviews of seventy people between the ages of seventy and ninety-nine, Terkel presents a vivid tapestry of American life in the twentieth century. A picture emerges of a world being transformed by new technologies in which the struggle to remain human becomes ever more difficult as scientific and technological triumphs are tempered by a sense of what has been lost. An uplifting and thought-provoking book.

## Gender-Related Issues and Aging

Aitkin, Lynda, and Gabriele Griffin. *Gender Issues in Elder Abuse.* Thousand Oaks, Calif.: Sage Publications, 1996. Using a gender-related orientation to gender abuse, the authors find evidence that most elder abuse is inflicted upon women and that this abuse, which occurs in both domestic and institutional locations, is often perpetrated by other women. However, the authors also find evidence of cross-gender abuse: sons abusing mothers, and daughters and female partners abusing older males. Finally, the authors argue that elder abuse is a human rights issue and should be treated as such.

Beard, Patricia. *Good Daughters: Loving Our Mothers as They Age.* New York: Warner, 1999. This thoughtful and thought-provoking book examines the challenges faced by adult women and women belonging to the "sandwich generation" as they struggle to understand the meaning of being good daughters to their aging mothers, especially in a rapidly transforming culture. By describing the mother-daughter relationships of numerous interviewees, the author demonstrates that with responsibility, companionship, and love, one can be a "good enough" daughter.

Brown, Helen Gurley. *The Late Show: A Semiwild but Practical Survival Plan for Women over Fifty.* New York: William Morrow, 1993. In a humorous, even defiant manner, Brown points out that accepting the reality of one's own aging is not easy but that the challenge can be met with resource, courage, energy, pride in past achievements, and the desire to continue growing. She provides information on a variety of topics, including beauty, clothes, exercise, food, health, money, and physical and emotional concerns.

Doress-Worters, Paula B., and Diana L. Siegal. *The New Ourselves Growing Older.* New York: Simon & Schuster, 1994. Written in collaboration with the Boston Women's Health Book Collective, this book is an updated edition of the popular *Ourselves Growing Older.* It examines, in the same vibrant manner, the physical, emotional, and social health and well-being of women as they age. The authors explore challenges, advice from experts, and health issues. Personal stories and reflections make this a colorful, informative, and enriching work.

Dwyer, Jeffrey W., and Raymond T. Coward, eds. *Gender, Families, and Eldercare.* Newbury Park, Calif.: Sage Publications, 1992. This collection of articles focuses on theory and research about the role of gender in providing care for older family members. Essays examine social, demographic, and structural perspectives of caregiving relationships; review the implications of social policy on men and women as caregivers; and note the relation of caregiving issues to other areas of life, such as employment, health, and welfare.

Furman, Frida K. *Facing the Mirror: Older Women and Beauty Shop Culture.* New York: Routledge, 1997. Furman looks at the lives and experiences of older women, especially older Jewish women in American culture, and examines the meaning of the older female body for women themselves and for others in a youth-oriented culture. In this study, the beauty salon serves as a symbol and setting for the ideas, friendship, support, action, and care for those who need it. The ethnographic study was conducted over a period of eighteen months in a beauty salon and in the homes of twenty salon customers fifty-five to eighty-six years of age. Through intensive interviews, the author explores the connections among women's self-understanding, aging experiences, and appearance.

Kosberg, Jordan I., and Lenard W. Kaye, eds. *Elderly Men: Special Problems and Professional Challenges.* New York: Springer, 1997. Elderly men are a frequently forgotten and neglected segment of the population of the United States. The essays in this book examine the lives and problems of older men from a variety of perspectives: social, cultural, economic, physical, and psychological. The authors argue that within specific settings—such as the workplace, the inner city, retirement communities, and prison—elderly men have specific needs that society must begin to take into consideration.

McCall, Edith. *Sometimes We Dance Alone.* Brooklyn, N.Y.: Brett Books, 1994. McCall offers an inspiring account of how life after fifty can be rich and satisfying, and can offer some of the best times in a woman's life, even when these later years are faced alone.

Mehta, Kalyani, ed. *Untapped Resources: Women in Aging Societies Across Asia.* Singapore: Times Academic Press, 1997. In Asia, as in a majority of geographical areas, aging is being "feminized" because of the longer life expectancy of women. Various articles discuss issues related to the aging of women in Indonesia, Malaysia, Singapore, South Korea, and Thailand. Among the topics discussed are demographics, education, economics, employment, urban-rural differences, family roles, support, living arrangements, health, and social policies related to these factors.

Paoletti, Isabella. *Being an Older Woman: A Study in the Social Production of Identity.* Mahwah, N.J.: Lawrence Erlbaum Associates, 1998. This book is based on studies of a group of Italian women participating in the European Older Women's Action Project. The author states that older women in Western society face both ageism and sexism, both of which have adverse affects on women's physical and mental health. Women who participated in the Action Project increased their management, organizational, and decision-making skills, thus increasing their potential for participating more actively in the affairs of their families and communities and, to some extent, changing their socially constructed identities.

Rountree, Cathleen. *On Women Turning Fifty: Celebrating Midlife Discoveries.* New York: Harper Collins, 1993. Rountree celebrates the challenges and accomplishments of women over fifty as they discover and get in touch with their creativity, sense of independence, and freedom to be themselves, and as they face loneliness, ageism, sexism, and a realization of their mortality. Among the women who share their lifestyles, work styles, and attitudes toward relationships are Isabel Allende, Ellen Burstyn, and Gloria Steinem.

_____. *On Women Turning Sixty: Embracing the Age of Fulfillment.* New York: Three Rivers, 1997. Twenty women in their sixties offer thoughts about life and aging, facing stereotypes, dissolving myths about old age, and celebrating and creating enriched lives for themselves and others. The women, who are ethnically and professionally diverse, include Jane Goodall, Ursula K. Le Guin, Ann Richards, and Mary Travers.

_____. *On Women Turning Seventy: Honoring the Voices of Wisdom.* San Francisco: Jossey-Bass, 1999. Rountree presents sixteen portraits of women in their seventies who are leading rich and fulfilling lives and who offer thoughts, feelings, advice, and words of wisdom for other women. Included are the words of Doris Lessing, Madeleine L'Engle, Betty Friedan, Anna Halprin, and others from various walks of life.

Rubinstein, Robert L. *Singular Paths: Old Men Living Alone.* New York: Columbia University Press, 1986. The author contends that the study of men over sixty-five years of age has been neglected, since this group is a minority in America. Interviews present portraits of older men living alone as individuals who enjoy life, who face numerous challenges (especially those resulting from loneliness), and who generally participate actively in programs designed for them. Rubinstein suggests activities, programs, services, and support groups that could benefit the increasing number of older men living alone in American society.

Sinclair, Carole. *When Women Retire.* New York: Crown, 1992. Sinclair discusses the unique problems faced by women when they retire: care of dependent spouses or children, boredom, limited benefits and resources, and health issues. She suggests ways in which women can take charge of their lives, plan ahead, and live their retirement years purposefully and with security.

Weaver, Frances. *The Girls with the Grandmother Faces.* New York: Hyperion, 1996. This is an optimistic and humorous celebration of aging women, the fastest-growing segment of the population in the United States. Weaver, in an effort to show that elderly women have the potential to lead fulfilling and exhilarating lives, offers advice on such concerns as widowhood and the single life, family life, friendship, love and sex, moving, travel, and support groups; she also talks about the important decision of who women choose to be in the "last act" of their lives.

**Social, Cultural, and Ethical Aspects of Aging**

Adams, Rebecca G., and Rosemary Blieszner. *Older Adult Friendship.* Newbury Park, Calif.: Sage Publications, 1989. The authors discuss aspects of friendship in general and examine issues, problems, and the impact of social status on friendships in the later years.

Ade-Ridder, Linda, and Charles B. Hennon, eds. *Lifestyles of the Elderly: Diversity in Relationships, Health, and Caregiving.* New York: Human Sciences Press, 1989. This book presents research on the diverse lifestyles of the elderly. Included are studies dealing with caregiving issues, family, friends, and the relationship between health and quality of life.

Agich, George J. "Ethics and Aging." In *Birth to Death: Science and Bioethics*, edited by David C. Thomasma and Thomasine Kushner. Cambridge, England: Cambridge University Press, 1996. The author discusses several important aspects of aging and the ethical issues related to them. He explores the personal meaning of aging, including the need for aging individuals to retain a sense of self-worth as they face loss of vitality and autonomy, and to maintain personal dignity as physical and mental faculties diminish with age. Agich also examines justice and the generational conflicts for limited resources.

Bass, Scott A., ed. *Older and Active: How Americans over Fifty-five Are Contributing to Society.* New Haven, Conn.: Yale University Press, 1995. Using research and existing data, the authors of these articles examine the productive activities of socially engaged older people in the United States and suggest ways to maximize the social, economic, and individual potential of a growing segment of the population. Participation in the labor force, volunteerism, and caring for other elderly people are all ways in which the elderly may remain engaged in society; the authors suggest that opportunities for these and other activities should be made more readily available.

Brown, Arnold. *The Social Processes of Aging and Old Age.* Englewood Cliffs, N.J.: Prentice Hall, 1990. Brown discusses age-related processes that influence social change and social behaviors.

Chudacoff, Howard P. *How Old Are You? Age Consciousness in American Culture.* Princeton, N.J.: Princeton University Press, 1989. Chudacoff examines the American obsession with youth and the resulting tendency to discriminate against and segregate people according to age. He also surveys intergenerational trends and the integration of different age groups.

Cutler, Neal E., Davis W. Gregg, and M. Powell Lawton, eds. *Aging, Money, and Life Satisfaction: Aspects of Financial Gerontology.* New York: Springer, 1992. This book is a compilation of papers dealing with aging, financial issues and resources, and the associated well-being of the aged. Articles discuss health care trends, cross-cultural patterns of aging, economic forces, financial behaviors, social support, and the characteristics, mind-sets, and behaviors that encourage a sense of well-being and lead to improved quality of life for the elderly.

Decalmer, Peter, and Frank Glendenning, eds. *The Mistreatment of Elderly People.* Newbury Park, Calif.: Sage Publications, 1993. In this book, professionals from different fields analyze diverse perspectives on and the implications of the problem of elder abuse; they also suggest strategies for prevention and intervention.

Decker, Joanne E. *Making the Moments Count: Leisure Activities for Caregiving Relationships.* Baltimore: The Johns Hopkins University Press, 1997. Focusing chiefly on caregivers, the author advocates a positive and creative approach to designing meaningful and enjoyable leisure activities for older adults. Her PIESS system takes into account the physical, intellectual, emotional, social, and spiritual components of leisure activities. Also considered are the caregivers' needs within and outside the caregiving role. Contains a fifteen-page checklist for activities of different kinds that have proved valuable to both caregivers and those they care for.

Dorfman, Rachelle A. *Aging into the Twenty-first Century.* New York: Brunner/Mazel, 1994. Dorfman takes an "inside" perspective on aging and presents the elderly as dynamic individuals who think, feel, make decisions, and transcend the difficulties and limitations that accompany aging. The author immersed herself in the life of an elderly community to observe the lives of those residing there. Negative stereotypes that are commonplace in society are defined and counteracted by real-life stories filled with the hopes, fears, and aspirations of older adults. The values and responsibilities of this group and of society are also reviewed. Includes a useful glossary and resource list of professional and consumer organizations for older people.

Dychtwald, Ken, and Joe Flower. *Age Wave.* New York: Bantam Books, 1990. The authors state that, as America ages and the number of older Americans becomes a force to contend with, myths of aging must be retired and the "gerontophobia" expressed by the media and within social institutions must be overcome. Society needs to be redesigned, and the culture of youth needs to shift to adapt to a growing older population. The book covers a wide array of subjects, including love and marriage in the second half of life, mature consumers and their growing economic relevance, intergenerational cooperation, travel, leisure, health, and retraining in old age.

Falk, Ursula A., and Gerhard Falk. *Ageism, the Aged, and Aging in America.* Springfield, Ill.: Charles C Thomas, 1997. The authors examine negative attitudes and discrimination faced by older Americans within families and social institutions, and in relation to health care and employment. They discuss the exploitation of the elderly and the image of the elderly in popular culture, the financial and political ramifications of a growing elderly population, and the future of government support for older citizens.

Friedan, Betty. *The Fountain of Age.* New York: Simon & Schuster, 1993. Friedan considers the possibilities and the liberation that can be achieved as people grow older and contrasts them with the myth of decay and decline that modern Western society associates with aging. She examines the aging, yet fulfilling, lives of people from diverse professions and backgrounds; she asserts that aging people have new choices, can make new places for themselves, and can meet challenges with excitement rather than fear. As she debunks society's image of the elderly, Friedan examines scientific evidence and gerontological research that can give hope of living a vital life to the aging. This is a profoundly readable, informative, and wise book that proposes to break through the myth of old age as a problem or disease. It does not avoid the realities of illness, loss, discrimination, or death, but it does present old age as a time of triumph, fulfillment, and continuing achievement. Friedan also speaks of the need to transcend the battle of the sexes, since the challenges and adventures of aging must be faced by everyone. See entry in *Aging*.

Gallagher, Sally K. *Older People Giving Care*. Westport, Conn.: Auburn House, 1994. The author views caregiving from an unusual perspective: She focuses on older adults who are caregivers rather than recipients of care. Gallagher describes the types of care given and the characteristics and relationships of those involved. Through a special network analysis technique, she assesses the kind of help given and received, as well as the motivations and attitudes of helpers and caregivers. One idea that emerges is that although women's helping behaviors change or are organized differently as they age, few women disengage themselves from helping behaviors in later life.

Hansson, Robert O., and Bruce N. Carpenter. *Relationships in Old Age: Coping with the Challenge of Transition*. New York: Guilford Press, 1994. This book examines the role of older adults in initiating and constructing meaningful and supportive relationships. Hansson and Carpenter describe ways in which older people cope and adapt to transitions in their lives, propose intervention strategies and a model to facilitate relational competence, and review special problems of the elderly that affect relationships.

Kenyon, Gary M., James E. Birren, and Johannes J. F. Schroots, eds. *Metaphors of Aging in Science and the Humanities*. New York: Springer, 1991. Various writers study metaphors related to aging—drawn from literature, cultural history, mythology, gerontology, psychology, and other areas of social and cultural life—that portray the elderly as nonproductive and that often lead to stereotyping and become self-fulfilling prophecies.

Kotre, John, and Elizabeth Hall. *Seasons of Life: Our Dramatic Journey from Birth to Death*. Boston: Little, Brown, 1990. A companion to the Public Broadcasting Service (PBS) television series *Seasons of Life*, this book explores five stages of human life, including late adulthood. Each stage of an individual's life relates to a biological, social, and psychological clock. The late adulthood section discusses diversity, the impact of increased life spans, and the physical, social, and psychological changes that occur as people age. Includes vibrant stories of older adults as they experience the last "season" of life.

Moody, Harry R. *Aging: Concepts and Controversies*. 2d ed. Thousand Oaks, Calif.: Sage Publications, 1998. Moody examines demographic, economic, health, and political factors associated with the aging process from biological, psychological, and social perspectives. Controversial topics include rationing health care for older people and the meaning of old age. Conflicting viewpoints from experts, as well as questions for debate and reflection, provide much material for critical thought and analysis. Includes appendices on research, resources, and Internet usage.

Pampel, Fred C. *Aging, Social Inequality, and Public Policy*. Thousand Oaks, Calif.: Pine Forge Press/Sage Publications, 1998. This book focuses on common images of old age and on inequalities older people experience because of factors related to class, ethnicity, gender, generational issues, and government and public policies. A study of Japanese, European, and North American societies provides a comparative perspective, with narratives and vignettes documenting inequities in these societies.

Peterson, Steven A., and Robert J. Maiden. *The Public Lives of Rural Older Americans*. Lanham, Md.: University Press of America, 1993. The authors believe that there is a great need to foster feelings of self-sufficiency and empowerment among the large population of elderly people who live in rural areas in the United States. To demonstrate this need, they describe a comprehensive case study of the lives of older people in a rural county in western New York, examine the characteristics and the conditions of these elders (especially women and the oldest of the old), and analyze the programs and services provided for them.

Posner, Richard A. *Aging and Old Age.* Chicago: University of Chicago Press, 1995. Posner analyzes economic, social, and health-related factors that influenced the process of aging in the late twentieth century. He argues that, despite many contemporary problems, older Americans are, on the whole, experiencing improvements in their situations and status.

Pratt, Michael W., and Joan E. Norris. *The Social Psychology of Aging: A Cognitive Approach.* Oxford, England: Blackwell, 1994. The authors review psychological theory and research on the social experiences of adults as they age. An important focus of the book is how older adults construct the meaning of their world as it and they change. Chapters explore social cognition in relation to self, to others, to relationships, to societal involvement, to decision making, to moral reasoning, and to communication.

Price, Matthew C. *Justice Between Generations: The Growing Power of the Elderly in America.* Westport, Conn.: Praeger, 1997. Price contends that, for a growing number of people in the United States, being old means being wealthy, powerful, and entitled to increased benefits, such as health care. This has resulted in generational conflicts about sharing limited economic and other resources. The author examines historical and political events and transitions that led to changing concepts of the aged and discusses choices society must make in its search for justice between generations.

Rich, Diane W., Thomas A. Rich, and Larry C. Mullins, eds. *Old and Homeless: Double Jeopardy.* Westport, Conn.: Auburn House, 1995. The material in this book is the result of a project initiated in 1991 by the Retirement Research Foundation to develop a model training program for people working with homeless older adults. Homelessness was researched in Florida, where a growing number of aged homeless live. The

articles examine causes of homelessness from a historical viewpoint and survey government programs and workable solutions to alleviate the problem. Authors consider drug and alcohol abuse by homeless elders, along with its effects on aging minds and bodies. Other topics include health, medical treatment, community resources, and housing policies. Provides a helpful insight into a complex social issue.

Riley, Matilda W., and John W. Riley, eds. *The Quality of Aging: Strategies for Intervention.* Newbury Park, Calif.: Sage Publications, 1989. This special issue of the Annals of the American Academy of Political and Social Science contends that, although society has both the knowledge and the ability to improve the quality of life for older people, such interventions have not yet taken place on a large scale for a majority of the aging population. Articles discuss social care, mental and physical health, employment, financial issues, policies, programs, and the potential of technology to improve the lives of older people.

Sheehy, Gail. *New Passages: Mapping Your Life Across Time.* New York: Random House, 1995. In some ways a sequel to her book *Passages* (1984), Sheehy's *New Passages* explores the "second adulthood" of modern individuals—an adulthood that begins after the age of forty-five and continues into old age. Lengthened life spans have presented men and women with new territories of adult life to chart and explore. Utilizing case studies, interviews, surveys, generational comparisons, and U.S. Census reports, Sheehy illustrates and examines the new and developing life stages experienced by modern individuals.

Swisher, Karin, ed. *The Elderly: Opposing Viewpoints.* San Diego: Greenhaven Press, 1990. As part of the Opposing Viewpoint series, this volume presents a variety of perspectives on society's attitudes toward older people, on the economic status of aging people, and on the need for socially guaranteed health care for the aged. Essays include views of older adults as burdens or benefits to society, arguments about the role of nursing homes, and discussions about the influence of older voters on elections and policy making. Critical thinking activities include distinguishing between bias and reason, and between fact and fiction; recognizing stereotypes; and evaluating sources of information.

Vincent, John A. *Inequality and Old Age*. New York: St. Martin's Press, 1995. Using a life course perspective, the author analyzes social processes and changes in Western societies that adversely affect the aged and make old age a source of inequality. Social structures, moral values, and the cultural meaning of being old are examined. The author argues that linguistic and symbolic manifestations of old age within cultures are linked to the social position allotted to older people and insists that ageism, sexism, and racism must all be considered together when a society struggles to tackle the problem of inequality.

Wacker, Robbyn, Karen A. Robert, and Linda E. Piper. *Community Resources for Older Adults: Programs and Services in an Era of Change*. Thousand Oaks, Calif.: Pine Forge Press, 1998. The authors analyze legislation that has influenced networks for the aging and discuss theories and research related to the delivery and use of services for this population. The book contains examples of excellent programs nationwide and includes several case studies to encourage critical thinking about community resources. Updates on services for older adults at both federal and state levels may be obtained through links to the authors' Web site.

Willis, Sherry L., K. Warner Shaie, and Mark Hayward, eds. *Societal Mechanism for Maintaining Competence in Old Age*. New York: Springer, 1997. Part of a series dedicated to the study of aging processes in relation to social structure and social change, this volume discusses the everyday competence needed and displayed by older adults. Topics covered include active life expectancy, definition and assessment of competence, competence in institutional settings, social support, and physical environment. Commentaries by gerontologists extend and enrich each chapter and its related topic.

—*Nillofur Zobairi*

# MEDIAGRAPHY: FICTION, FILMS, MUSIC, TELEVISION

The following list is intended to direct students to books, short stories, plays, poems, films, popular songs, and television shows that touch upon the theme of aging. Some of these works delve into aging as just another normal process of life, while others focus on how elders see themselves or are seen by society in both positive and negative lights. Overall, critical aspects and themes related to aging are explored in the context of relationships—whether between spouses, parents and children, or grandparents and children—and of memories. Some of these materials also explore key roles for elders in society. This list is by no means comprehensive but rather meant to be representative of the many portrayals of elders in popular media.

## Written Works and Drama

*Autobiography of Miss Jane Pittman, The* (1971), by Ernest J. Gaines. In this novel, a black woman who is more than one century old shares her lifetime recollections, both as an individual who has grown old and as an elderly black woman. Her life experiences include firsthand observation of such disturbing historical trends as slavery and other social and racial tensions. The narrative reveals this character to have a complex understanding of human relations, and it provides a good example of the wisdom and value of elderly people's perspectives on history. See entry in *Aging*.

*Bless Me, Ultima* (1972), by Rudolfo A. Anaya. Set in the period immediately following World War II, this story focuses on the awakening process that a young boy goes through in his relationship with a woman named Ultima. Ultima is a *curandera*, or woman who uses herbs, magic, and the wisdom of ancestors for healing and guidance in spiritual and other matters. The boy matures throughout the course of the story, calling into question traditional beliefs, his guides and elders, and God. The rich relationship between the boy and the *curandera* emphasizes the value of mentorship, guidance from elders, and self-discovery. It also provides a stirring example of how a person can live on through others in lessons and memories, even after death. See entry in *Aging*.

"Dr. Heidegger's Experiment" (1837), by Nathaniel Hawthorne. This short story focuses on four elderly friends who gather at the laboratory of their friend, Dr. Heidegger, in order to participate in an experiment. They all agree to drink a special liquid, rumored to come from the fountain of youth. What ensues is a mix of expectations and wishes, as well as a temporary willing-ness to let go of the perception of oneself as being old. The story amplifies both the wish that many people have to return to their youth and the power of the mind to accomplish such a task. See entry in *Aging*.

*Driving Miss Daisy* (1988), by Alfred Uhry. This play, also developed into a feature-length film, shows the complex relationship that evolves over time between a woman and her chauffeur in the southern United States. The value of this long-term relationship overrides the obvious cultural and ethnic tensions that define the context of the story. See entry in *Aging*.

*Fried Green Tomatoes at the Whistle Stop Cafe* (1987), by Fannie Flagg. This story focuses on four women in a small town in Alabama in the 1930's who reminisce about their life experiences at the Whistle Stop Cafe fifty years earlier. Touches on relationships between women, between individuals of different racial backgrounds, and between rich and poor. The main theme of the novel, however, is the value of friendships for women in later life. The novel was the basis for the film *Fried Green Tomatoes* (1991), directed by Jon Avnet and starring Kathy Bates, Mary Stuart Masterson, Mary-Louise Parker, Jessica Tandy, and Cicely Tyson.

*Full Measure: Modern Short Stories on Aging* (1988), by Dorothy Sennett. This collection of short stories features a variety of elders as main characters, explores many of the concerns that elders deal with on a daily basis, and provides a unique elderly perspective on these issues. Though each story is unique, the overriding theme of the collection is that elders come in all forms and dispositions, have all the same desires and wants that younger people have, and definitely are not to be taken for granted. Physical and mental ailments do affect many of the characters, but each deals with them in a different way. Fears of aging, of being feeble-minded, of being unwanted, of being left alone, and of being taken advantage of are addressed in several stories. See entry in *Aging*.

*Gin Game, The* (1977), by D. L. Coburn. This novel tells the story of the kinds of relationships that can develop in retirement homes among the elderly people who live there. While the story does tackle the issues of the loneliness, physical challenges, and fears of social isolation that can accompany growing old, it also shows the power of human bonding and of knowing one is not alone. By playing the card game gin rummy, the main characters are able to develop a relationship that offers them comfort, challenges, and insights into themselves and each other. See entry in *Aging*.

*Golden Years Golden Words* (1993), by Michael Ryan. This is a collection of quotes, phrases, and stories of life lessons and of the wisdom offered by elders.

*I Never Sang for My Father* (1968), by Robert Anderson. This play tells the story of a son who commits his life to winning the love of his father. This is not an easy task, however, as the father is set in his ways and is highly opinionated. Through perseverance, the son is able to break through his father's hostility and rejection and establish an emotional, father-son connection. A screenplay of this story was made into a film in 1969. See entry in *Aging*.

"Jilting of Granny Weatherall, The" (1930), by Katherine Anne Porter. This short story is about an older woman who is on her death bed, recounting her life and the people in her life. What is most profound about this story is its message of how losses, disappointments, and the emotional trauma attached to unexpected events in life can stay with a person to the end of life and even into the process of dying. See entry in *Aging*.

*King Lear* (pr. c. 1605-1606, pb. 1608), by William Shakespeare. This is the tragic story of a king in his later years who decides to divide his kingdom among his three daughters. However, the two eldest daughters create problems by trying to manipulate the situation and wind up estranging the king from his most loyal daughter. See entry in *Aging*.

*Memento Mori* (1959), by Muriel Spark. The phrase *memento mori* is Latin for "reminder of death." Along these lines, this novel is a dark story about old age that offers both seriousness and humor. See entry in *Aging*.

*Old Man and the Sea, The* (1952), by Ernest Hemingway. This novel is about an old Cuban fisherman who encounters a huge marlin and goes on a journey of discovery as he pursues the catch of a lifetime. As with many fishing tales, what goes on in the mind of the fisherman influences what he catches. The fisherman learns the lessons of persistence in the face of loss; another major theme is the sense of courage necessary to go into battle with the unknown and to face oneself later in life. The novel was made into a film in 1958. See entry in *Aging*.

*On Golden Pond* (1979), by Ernest Thompson. This play shows how the experience of a family retreat can quell long-standing disagreements and friction among different generations of family members. It also shows the value of not letting such disagreements get in the way of having a relationship, as well as the value of developing and nurturing family relationships, even in later life. The play was made into a film in 1981. See entry in *Aging*.

*Picture of Dorian Gray, The* (serial 1890, expanded 1891), by Oscar Wilde. This classic novel tells the story of a man named Dorian Gray who desires eternal youth and is willing to pay for it with his soul. In its time, the book was criticized for its hedonic content and seeming support of intemperance. The common desire to search out eternal youth is an important theme, as is the life lesson that no mentor should be followed blindly.

"Rabbi Ben Ezra" (1864), by Robert Browning. This poem, which begins with the line, "Grow old along with me," tells the story of how old age is a time of appreciation for life. Old age, rather than being feared, is seen as a time of great wealth.

"Roman Fever" (1933), by Edith Wharton. This story follows a conversation between two elderly, lifelong acquaintances who loved the same man (who has long since passed away). It focuses on issues of self-exploration and social restrictions both in general and among the elderly. The passing of a day is used as a backdrop to symbolize the passing of a lifetime and to show how delicate social issues may present themselves in unexpected ways throughout life. See entry in *Aging*.

*Stone Angel, The* (1964), by Margaret Laurence. In this novel, ninety-year-old Hagar Shipley tells her life story. Her complex narrative focuses on the double nature of most things in life, particularly one's way of handing people and situations. The story does well to show how elders work hard to maintain a cohesive, competent social facade and how most people of age struggle to compose coherent narratives of their experiences. Key life events that occur around the beginnings and ends of relationships are also central to this work, once again emphasizing the importance of memories to everyone, but particularly to the elderly.

*Tell Me a Riddle* (1976), by Tillie Olsen. This novella, set in the early twentieth century, is about a Jewish woman who reaches old age and decides that it is time for her to assert her wishes. As a grandmother, many of her assertions challenge traditions and social behaviors that are important to her husband and family. See entry in *Aging*.

*When I Am an Old Woman I Shall Wear Purple* (1987), by Sandra K. Martz. This book is a collection of poems, stories, and photographs created by more than sixty individuals. As a whole, the book honors the process of aging and reveals the daring and power that the process can inspire. Wisdom, life experiences, and the many colors and textures of what it means to be old, particularly an older woman, are described in rich detail. The same title is also connected to a poem, written by Jenny Joseph, that is included in this book and that exemplifies the wisdom of daring to live fully throughout life. See entry in *Aging*.

"When You Are Old" (1893), by William Butler Yeats. This beautiful poem from the collection *The Rose* tells of how to cope with the last years of life. Yeats compares life to a book and reminds the reader to reread the pages written and to remember connections with those closest to the heart who were there to see the changes over the course of one's life.

"Worn Path, A" (1941), by Eudora Welty. This short story is about an elderly black woman named Phoenix Jackson. Like her first name, she is not kept down for long and seems to be able to find the good in just about any situation. An analogy for life, "A Worn Path" tells the story of a walk that Phoenix takes and the frightening, annoying, and helpful encounters she has along the way. Her journey culminates in a self-realization that prompts her to make a gift to the youth in her life. Welty touches upon the themes of being ignored, of coping with physical limitations, and of being perceived as a sick elder. See entry in *Aging*.

*You're Only Old Once!* (1986), by Dr. Seuss. In this humorous and lighthearted book, Dr. Seuss takes on some difficult topics in a non-threatening way. Such issues as the process of growing old and coping with doctors are presented sensitively and with humor. See entry in *Aging*.

"Youth and Age" (1834), by Samuel Taylor Coleridge. This poem focuses on seeing life experiences as growth experiences, even to the end of life. It also emphasizes the importance of maintaining hope and a positive perspective in order to continue enjoying life.

## Films

*Age of Miracles* (1996), directed by Peter Chan. This Chinese film tells the story of a devoted mother who decides to sacrifice her life to save one of her sons from an early death. However, her effort is not totally appreciated by the son, causing the family to experience a complex tragedy that forces them all into a better understanding of their familial bonds. Originally in Chinese and Cantonese, the film is available with English subtitles. Performers include Alan Tam, Anita Yuen, Eric Tsang, Jordan Chan, Teresa Carpio, Christina Ng, and Roy Chiao.

*Age Old Friends* (1989), directed by Allan Kroeker. This film, starring Hume Cronyn, Vincent Gardenia, Esther Rolle, and Tandy Cronyn, is about a man who turns down a chance to live with his daughter in favor of residing at a retirement home. Once at the home, he enjoys a close friendship with another resident, only to find that his friend is beginning to experience senility. The main character's struggle to decide whether to stay in the home to help his friend or to go to his daughter's home becomes the crux of this film whose primary themes are loyalty, friendship, personal meaning, and the decisions elders make later in life.

*All About Eve* (1950), directed by Joseph L. Mankiewicz. Bette Davis plays an aging actress who faces unexpected competition from a younger, ambitious actress, played by Anne Baxter, who dupes Davis's character into taking her under her wing. See entry in *Aging*.

*All of Me* (1984), directed by Carl Reiner. This comedy is about a dying woman who gets a second chance at life. However, her soul takes over only one-half of another person, who just happens to be a rather odd lawyer. Steve Martin stars in this film, along with Lily Tomlin, Madolyn Smith, Victoria Tennant, and Basil Hoffman.

*Arsenic and Old Lace* (1944), directed by Frank Capra. Starring Cary Grant, Priscilla Lane, Raymond Massey, and Peter Lorre, this film focuses on how looks can be deceiving. Two little old ladies who, on the surface, seem as gentle as can be to their young nephew are actually poisoning older gentlemen who come to visit and burying them in the cellar.

*Battling for Baby* (1992), directed by Art Wolff. Suzanne Pleshette and Debbie Reynolds each play a grandmother who competes with the other for time to baby-sit their grandchild. The film uses humor to show how important it is for grandparents to have time with a grandchild and how simple chores can take on great meaning and purpose in the life of an elder.

*Captiva Island* (1995), directed by John Biffar. This comedic and poignant film portrays the life of retirees in Florida as perceived by a teenager who becomes friends with some senior citizens. Ernest Borgnine, Arte Johnson, Bill Cobbs, George Blair, Jesse Zeigler, and Amy Bush star.

*Cemetery Club, The* (1992), directed by Bill Duke. This comedy, which stars Ellen Burstyn, Danny Aiello, Olympia Dukakis, and Diane Ladd, focuses on the weekly meetings of three friends. As each is widowed, they share their difficulties in trying to date as senior citizens, bonding together as they learn what it is like to look for a new husband.

*Cocoon* (1985), directed by Ron Howard. This inspiring film, starring Don Ameche, is about a group of elders whose quiet life in a senior citizens' home is disrupted when they are given a chance at eternal youth by extraterrestrial visitors. A 1988 sequel, *Cocoon 2: The Return*, was directed by Daniel Petrie and featured the return of the seniors to Earth to see their families. See entry in *Aging*.

*Cold Comfort Farm* (1995), directed by John Schlesinger. This comedic film stars Kate Beckinsale, Joanna Lumley, Rufus Sewell, Ian McKellen, Eileen Atkins, Sheila Burrell, Stephen Fry, Freddie Jones, and Miriam Margolyes. In it, a young, orphaned woman must live with a group of odd relatives on a farm in the country. The strong wishes of the matriarchal grandmother regarding how the house should be run clash with the desires of the young orphan.

*Country Life* (1984), directed by Michael Blakemore. This film celebrates the age-old theme of an older man finding love with a younger woman. In bringing his young love to his small town, however, the older man experiences not only social tension from the townspeople but also competition from younger men. Sam Neill, Greta Scacchi, Michael Blakemore, John Hargreaves, Kerry Fox, and Robyn Cruze star.

*Dad* (1989), directed by Gary David Goldberg. This film tells the story of a son who comes home to be reunited with his aging father. As they struggle through a family illness together, the son tries to connect with his father after a distant, two-year separation. The film emphasizes the value of parent-child relationships in later life. Jack Lemmon and Ted Danson star.

*Death of a Salesman* (1985), directed by Volker Schlondorff. This American-made production of Arthur Miller's play by the same name stars Dustin Hoffman as Willy Loman, and Kate Reid, John Malkovich, and Stephen Lang as his family members. Loman is featured as a old man so obsessed with his career and with being liked by others throughout his life that, in old age, he has become alienated from his family. The difficulties involved with being older and being emotionally estranged from one's family are central to the plot.

*Dennis the Menace* (1993), directed by Nick Castle. This classic story of a young boy who innocently drives his grouchy old neighbor crazy stars Walter Matthau and Mason Gamble. Although the film exemplifies how young people often try to cause mischief for the unsuspecting, it also shows how elders, even when duped, are never too far from appreciating the spirit of youth.

*Don Juan de Marco* (1995), directed by Jeremy Leven. In this film, an older psychologist (Marlon Brando) who is nearing retirement becomes involved in the unusual case of a young man who believes he is the fabled romancer Don Juan de Marco. Through his study of the young man, the psychologist is forced to reexamine his own ideas of what it means to love throughout life, especially during the later years. The film also features performances by Johnny Depp, Faye Dunaway, Rachel Ticotin, Bob Dishy, and Geraldine Pailhas.

*Dream a Little Dream* (1989), directed by Marc Rocco. One of many films that allow the old to become young again, *Dream a Little Dream* shows the pros and cons of such a situation when the souls of an elderly couple are placed into the bodies of two teenagers. Jason Robards and Corey Feldman star.

*Driving Miss Daisy* (1989), directed by Bruce Beresford. This film, based on the play by Alfred Uhry, shows the complex relationship that develops between an elderly southern woman and the African American chauffeur that the woman's son demands that she use to make her way around town. The film excels in highlighting issues not only about race relations among the elderly in the southern United States but also about the struggles that can occur between older parents and their children. Actors include Jessica Tandy, Morgan Freeman, Dan Aykroyd, Patti Lupone, and Esther Rolle. See entry in *Aging*.

*Eighteen Again!* (1988), directed by Paul Flaherty. In this comedy—which stars George Burns, Charlie Schlatter, Tony Roberts, Red Buttons, and Jennifer Runyon—an accident causes a lively eighty-year-old bachelor to switch souls with his grandson for a period of time.

*End, The* (1978), directed by Burt Reynolds. This comedy focuses on a middle-aged man's desire to end his life and his inability to do so. The film captures moments during which the man gets close to death, reflects on his life, and finally goes through the common process of bargaining with God to stay alive. Burt Reynolds, Sally

Field, Dom DeLuise, and Joanne Woodward star.

*Family Business* (1989), directed by Sidney Lumet. Sean Connery, Matthew Broderick, Dustin Hoffman, and Rosana De Soto star in this film about three generations of men in a family. The family traits of cleverness, a desire for excitement, pride, and criminal skill combine to bring these three men together to face a difficult choice when a risky robbery runs into trouble. Though subtle, the film portrays the important cultural theme of elders sacrificing for their children and the costs and benefits of such gestures of love between generations.

*Family Reunion* (1981), directed by Fielder Cook. This film stars Bette Davis as an old schoolteacher who feels displaced after retiring. In her efforts to reconnect with her roots and with her family, she becomes aware of some untidy business and must decide how to intervene.

*Family Reunion* (1987), directed by Vic Sarin. A grandfather's birthday celebration draws a family together for a reunion and spawns a humorous situation based on misunderstandings about a grandson's love life. This film stars David Eisner, Rebecca Jenkins, and Linda Sorensen.

*Father of the Bride* (1950), directed by Vincente Minnelli; (1991) directed by Charles Shyer. This film concerns events that parents and the rest of their family experience as their daughter prepares for marriage. The original version, made in 1950, stars Spencer Tracy, Joan Bennett, Elizabeth Taylor, Billie Burke, and Don Taylor. The film was remade in 1991 and was followed by a comedic sequel.

*Father of the Bride II* (1995), directed by Charles Shyer. Shyer revisits the story of *Father of the Bride* in a film that announces the coming of a grandchild. Steve Martin and Diane Keaton star as expectant grandparents who are struggling with what it means to have a grandchild. Martin Short, Kimberly Williams, George Newbern, and Kieran Culkin also star.

*Four Seasons, The* (1981), directed by Alan Alda. This film focuses on three couples of different ages whose lives come together in complex relationships. The story shows how maturity does not always come with age and how wisdom can sometimes be found in unexpected places. The film stars Alan Alda, Carol Burnett, Rita Moreno, Sandy Dennis, Len Cariou, and Jack Weston.

*Ghost and Mrs. Muir, The* (1947), directed by Joseph L. Mankiewicz. This film tells the story of a widow who is romanced through her loneliness by the ghost of a mariner who visits her home. The ghost helps her write a novel that brings a potential husband to her life, forcing her to choose between the ghost of the captain and the new friend. Though the film is not specifically about aging, it does deal with the difficult and complex feelings that come when one loses a spouse to death at a later age in life. Gene Tierney, Rex Harrison, George Sanders, Edna Best, Anna Lee, Robert Coote, and Natalie Wood appear.

*Going in Style* (1979), directed by Martin Brest. This comedy, starring George Burns, Art Carney, and Lee Strasberg, features three retirees who decide to rob a bank to make their retirement a little more lucrative and a little less boring. However, the robbery involves some unexpected turns of events. The film does well to highlight the issue of boredom during retirement in a humorous way.

*Goodbye People, The* (1986), directed by Herb Gardner. An elderly gentleman decides to revisit his past by reopening a hot dog stand he once had on the beach. A daughter with whom he has had a distant relationship and an artist friend help him as he embarks on his effort to recapture the past and enliven the present. The film stars Judd Hirsch, Martin Balsam, Pamela Reed, and Ron Silver.

*Grumpy Old Men* (1993), directed by Donald Petrie. This film—which stars Walter Matthau, Jack Lemmon, Ann-Margret, Burgess Meredith, Daryl Hannah, Ossie Davis, Buck Henry, and Kevin Pollack—focuses on the feud that develops between two elderly men who vie for the attentions of a young female neighbor. A sequel, *Grumpier Old Men* (1995), was directed by Howard Deutch and continues the theme of the two men feuding over yet another woman, despite her probable deleterious effect on their neighborhood. See entry in *Aging*.

*Guarding Tess* (1994), directed by Hugh Wilson. Nicolas Cage, Shirley MacLaine, Austin Pendleton, Edward Albert, James Rebhorn, and Rich-

ard Griffiths star in this film about a spirited former First Lady and her relationship with her younger, male body guard. This film portrays the off-balance, odd friendship that the two share, sometimes showing the unexpected weakness of the younger man and strengths of the older woman.

*Harold and Maude* (1971), directed by Hal Ashby. This dark comedy—starring Ruth Gordon, Bud Cort, Vivian Pickles, and Cyril Cusack—follows a fond relationship that blossoms between two unlikely people: a young man named Harold who is obsessed with death, and Maude, a woman sixty years his senior who loves to attend funerals in her celebration of life. See entry in *Aging*.

*Harry and Son* (1984), directed by Paul Newman. Newman wrote, directed, and starred in this film about a father and son who face numerous interpersonal battles as they confront their different views of life. Robby Benson, Joanne Woodward, and Ellen Barkin also star.

*Heaven Can Wait* (1943), directed by Ernst Lubitsch. This film stars Don Ameche, Laird Cregar, Charles Coburn, Marjorie Main, Lewis Calhern, and Gene Tierney. The struggle of dying, final judgment, and atoning for the mistakes of a lifetime are the themes of this film about a man who, after his death, recounts his relationships with his wife and other women.

*Heaven Can Wait* (1978), directed by Buck Henry. Though this film shares the name of an earlier motion picture, the story is a bit different. In this remake of *Here Comes Mr. Jordan* (1941), Warren Beatty plays a pro football player who dies before his time and struggles to reclaim his life and his love (played by Julie Christie). The film deals with the topic of dying before one's time and the feelings that this possibility conjures personally, in one's friends, and in loved ones. *Heaven Can Wait* also does well to portray several elders as enormously playful and clever. Other featured actors include James Mason, Jack Warden, and Dyan Cannon.

*I Remember Mama* (1948), directed by George Stevens. This film, an adaptation of John Van Druten's play of the same name, tells the story of a close-knit Norwegian family living in San Francisco at the end of the nineteenth century. A strong matriarch provides the backbone of the narrative, which touches upon the place of older women in families.

*I'm Not Rappaport* (1996), directed by Herb Gardner. In this humorous film, two elders (portrayed by Walter Matthau and Ossie Davis) become friends in Central Park in New York City, despite obvious differences in their backgrounds and lifestyles.

*It's a Wonderful Life* (1946), directed by Frank Capra. This classic black-and-white film stars Jimmy Stewart, Donna Reed, Lionel Barrymore, Thomas Mitchell, Henry Travers, Beulah Bondi, Frank Faylen, Ward Bond, and Gloria Grahame. The story features a small-town businessman who would rather face death than be ruined by a business error made by an elderly relative. The businessman is led on a review of his life that makes him appreciate his value to the world, to his community, and to his family and friends. Though often overlooked because of the broader message of the film, the fact that the error was caused by an elderly relative offers interesting social commentary. Other characters also provide interesting portrayals of elderly people as reasonable, cooperative, and generous individuals. The film is also important in the context of aging as it demonstrates the value of the life review process as a way of tapping into the meaning and value of one's life.

*Joy Luck Club, The* (1993), directed by Wayne Wang. Based on the novel by the same name, written by Amy Tan, this film tells the story of four women who gather and share their life experiences to help and support one another. Actors include Rosalind Chao, Joan Chen, France Nuyen, Tamlyn Tomita, Kieu Chinh, Lisa Lu, Tsai Chin, Ming-Na Wen, and Lauren Tom.

*Karate Kid, The* (1984), directed by John G. Avildsen. A teenager finds a mentor in a local handyman who teaches him the value of martial arts, self-discipline, and self-defense. Starring Ralph Macchio, Noriyuki Morita, Martin Kove, Elisabeth Shue, and William Zabka, this film shows the depth of the connection that can develop in mentoring relationships between young students and older teachers, as well as how learning can come even from simple tasks. Avildsen directed two sequels—*Karate Kid, Part II* (1986) and *Karate Kid, Part III* (1989)—that follow simi-

lar themes about rights of passage and life lessons from elders.

*Last Angry Man, The* (1959), directed by Daniel Mann. This film stars Paul Muni, Cicely Tyson, Billy Dee Williams, Claudia McNeil, Godfrey Cambridge, Betsy Palmer, Luther Adler, and David Wayne. An elderly doctor who has dedicated his life to tending to patients in a lower-income community is disgruntled over having spent his life this way, while colleagues have gone on to gain significant material wealth. The doctor's nephew arranges a television event to honor his uncle, despite the wishes of the doctor that no special attention be given to him. The film balances the themes of choosing certain life paths, counting one's blessings, and making peace over long-standing resentments.

*Last Home Run, The* (1996), directed by Bob Gosse. Seymour Cassel and Thomas Guiry star in this story about a retired physician who is able to reflect back on the things in his life that have brought him joy, causing him to revisit the pleasure he gained from playing baseball in his youth.

*Marvin's Room* (1996), directed by Jerry Zaks. Two estranged sisters are reunited when one of them, who has been caring for their elderly father, becomes terminally ill. The film not only deals with illness and death as transitional events for families but also raises the complex issues underlying the responsibilities of caring for an elderly parent who has health problems. Diane Keaton, Meryl Streep, and Leonardo DiCaprio star.

*Middle Age Crazy* (1980), directed by John Trent. Bruce Dern portrays a man who is going through a midlife crisis and who must stop acting childish and frivolous when his father suddenly dies. Though this is a comedy, the film struggles with the complex transition that occurs when an elderly person dies and a new person must take on the role of family patriarch.

*Moll Flanders* (1996), directed by Pen Densham. Based on the novel by Daniel Defoe, this story focuses on hope that continues throughout a lifetime, despite difficult times and stark challenges. The life experiences of the main character emphasize the value of perseverance, even in one's later years. Among the performers are Jeremy Brett, Robin Wright, Stockard Channing, Morgan Freeman, Brenda Fricker, John Lynch,

Geraldine James, Jim Sheridan, and Aisling Corcoran.

*Moonstruck* (1987), directed by Norman Jewison. This film stars Cher, Nicolas Cage, Vincent Gardenia, Olympia Dukakis, and Danny Aiello. On the surface, this romantic comedy is about the discovery of an unexpected and inconvenient love affair within a family that tests family expectations. The film also shows, however, how the home of one's parents always remains a sanctuary no matter how old children become. Many older characters have enough wit and verve to compete with any youth.

*Mrs. Doubtfire* (1993), directed by Chris Columbus. Robin Williams plays a father who has recently gone through a marital separation and has lost regular visitation with his children because of his childlike, theatrical antics. In order to spend time with them, he pretends to be an elderly British nanny who can care for them. Starring Sally Field, Pierce Brosnan, Harvey Fierstein, Robert Prosky, and Mara Wilson, this film provides a projection of all the attributes most desired in the perfect grandmother or older nanny or aunt.

*Murphy's Romance* (1985), directed by Martin Ritt. James Garner, Sally Field, Brian Kerwin, and Corey Haim star in this comedic love story about a younger woman who moves to a small town to start a horse training business and meets an intriguing older man.

*Oh, God!* (1977), directed by Carl Reiner. With the role of God being played by comedian George Burns, this film satirizes the popular notion of God as old and male and underscores the habitual association of wisdom with age. The story takes things a step further, however, by equating humor with wisdom. Sequels include *Oh, God! Book II* (1980) and *Oh, God! You Devil* (1984).

*Old Man and the Sea, The* (1958), directed by John Sturges. This film, starring Spencer Tracy and Felipe Pazos, is based on a book by Ernest Hemingway. An elderly Cuban fisherman struggles to capture a Marlin in a battle that brings up many issues about the purpose and meaning of life. See entry in *Aging*.

*Oldest Living Graduate, The* (1983), directed by Jack Hofsiss. This dramatic film stars Henry Fonda, George Grizzard, Harry Dean Stanton, and Cloris Leachman. The story tells of the battle of wills that takes place between a retired World War I veteran and his son as they determine what to do with a piece of land owned by the veteran.

*On Golden Pond* (1981), directed by Mark Rydell. This film, based on Ernest Thompson's play of the same name, focuses on the interpersonal and intrapersonal discoveries that come about as an elderly couple spends the summer with their children at a country home they have been visiting for more than forty years. Katharine Hepburn, Henry Fonda, Jane Fonda, Dabney Coleman, Christopher Rydell, and William Lanteau star. See entry in *Aging*.

*Over the Hill* (1992), directed by George Miller. Olympia Dukakis stars in this comedy about a woman who wants to live life fully and who is determined to break all the stereotypes that come with being an elderly woman.

*Paternity* (1981), directed by David Steinberg. Burt Reynolds and Beverly D'Angelo star in this comedy about an older man who has come to recognize his fading youth. As he desires an heir to whom he can pass along his possessions and legacy, he decides that he must find a surrogate mother to have his child.

*Practical Magic* (1998), directed by Griffin Dunne. This film, starring Sandra Bullock, Nicole Kidman, Dianne Wiest, and Stockard Channing, tells the story of two orphaned girls who live with their aunts and learn witchcraft from them. Though the film is primarily a romantic comedy, the idea that the older aunts possess special wisdom that the girls must learn is prominent.

*Robin and Marian* (1976), directed by Richard Lester. This film is about Robin Hood and a battle he fights later in life with the sheriff of Nottingham. Following his return home after years of adventures and a reunion with Maid Marian, Robin works to defend his father's name and legacy by defeating the sheriff of Nottingham once and for all. This film speaks to the value of defending one's legacy. Stars Sean Connery and Audrey Hepburn. See entry in *Aging*.

*Shootist, The* (1976), directed by Don Siegel. John Wayne plays a rugged, gunfighting man who must cope with a terminal illness. The film captures the challenges endured in such a situation and shows how reaching out to others is a sign of strength that can be an important part of coping with illness and death. It also shows the difficulty that can accompany imminent death in terms of making peace with others and oneself about one's own life. See entry in *Aging*.

*Simple Men* (1992), directed by Hal Hartley. This film tells the saga of two adult brothers who reunite with their father after several years of estrangement. Each son must confront his own fantasies and fears about the father's complex and contradictory life. Martin Donovan, Karen Sillas, William Sage, and Robert John Burke star.

*Steel Magnolias* (1989), directed by Herbert Ross. Set in the southern United States, this film is ultimately about women and the bonds they share. It is noteworthy in terms of the topic of aging, however, in that the older female characters are portrayed as being powerful, influential, and strong. The film stars Sally Field, Shirley MacLaine, Dolly Parton, Olympia Dukakis, Julia Roberts, Daryl Hannah, Tom Skerritt, and Sam Shepard.

*Sunset Boulevard* (1950), directed by Billy Wilder. This black-and-white film stars Gloria Swanson, William Holden, Erich Von Stroheim, Nancy Olson, and Buster Keaton. An elderly, silent film-era actress who refuses to give up on her glamorous past seeks assistance from a young writer to help revive her career. The film poignantly shows how many elderly people struggle to hold onto or retain their youth. See entry in *Aging*.

*Sunshine Boys, The* (1975), directed by Herbert Ross. Walter Matthau and George Burns play retired vaudeville stars who, despite years of hatred, agree to work together on a television reunion special. The film shows not only how resentments can run deep and last a lifetime but also how anger can become a way of bonding and how resolution of such conflicts in the face of illness can be important.

*Sweet Bird of Youth* (1962), directed by Richard Brooks. Starring Ed Begley, Mildred Dunnock, Shirley Knight, Paul Newman, Geraldine Page, and Rip Torn, this film tells the story of what happens when a couple with a large age difference between them returns to see hometown acquaintances.

*Tatie Danielle* (1990), directed by Etienne Chatiliez. Long-standing tensions and family difficulties are exposed and challenged when an elderly woman lets her feelings be known. Starring Tsilla Chelton and Catherine Jacob, this emotional foreign film is subtitled in English.

*Throw Momma from the Train* (1987), directed by Danny DeVito. This comedy—starring DeVito, Billy Crystal, Anne Ramsey, and Kim Griest—features Owen, a dysfunctional adult who can no longer tolerate his abrasive and overpowering elder mother, for whom he must care. In his desire to rid himself of his mother by any means possible, he gets involved in a crime scheme that has unintended consequences. Aside from the dark humor of this film, it also gives voice to the frustration that can come with the task of caring for older parents and the mixed feelings that may accompany the experience.

*To Grandmother's House We Go* (1995), directed by Jeff Franklin. Mary-Kate and Ashley Olsen star in this comedic film about a smart set of twin girls on their way to visit their grandmother. While the film focuses mostly on the encounters they have during their unsupervised trip, it also serves to emphasize the sweetness of the destination for all grandchildren.

*To Sleep with Anger* (1990), directed by Charles Burnett. Danny Glover plays Harry Mention, an old, mischievous storyteller who resurfaces at the house of an old friend and winds up causing trouble for his friend's family. The film presents a good example of the role of elder as storyteller.

*Trip to Bountiful, The* (1985), directed by Peter Masterson. This film, based on a play written by Horton Foote, stars Geraldine Page, John Heard, Carlin Glynn, and Rebecca De Mornay. The story focuses on an elderly woman's emotional return to the town where she raised her family. The value of family roots to elders is a primary theme. See entry in *Aging*.

*Two Thousand Year Old Man, The* (1978), directed by Leo Salkin. This animated film starring Mel Brooks and Carl Reiner is about wisdom, aging, and the meaning of life.

*Very Old Man with Enormous Wings, A* (1988), directed by Fernando Birri. Originally in Spanish but available with English subtitles, this fantasy stars Marcia Barreto, Fernando Birri, Daisy

Granados, and Asdrúbal Meléndez. It shows how older people are often seen as angels in people's lives.

*Wide Awake* (1998), directed by M. Night Shyamalan. This serious film focuses on the thoughts and feelings of a young boy and his struggle to make sense of life after the death of his grandfather. Joseph Cross and Timothy Reifsnyder star.

*Wild Strawberries* (1957), directed by Ingmar Bergman. This film, originally in Swedish and available with English subtitles, follows an older professor as he sorrowfully recounts his life as he travels to a celebration being held to honor his work. It highlights how, even in the highest moments of one's life, one can be filled with regret and sadness as one reflects on the bigger picture of life. Stars Victor Sjöström. See entry in *Aging*.

*Wizards of the Lost Kingdom* (1986), directed by Hector Olivera. Bo Svenson and Vidal Peterson star in this fantasy film that portrays the classic story of youth gaining power and skill through reliance on the wisdom of an older mentor. In a magical setting, this is accomplished through a battle between evil and good, where the latter is represented by a prince who is helped by an aging warrior mentor.

*Woman's Tale, A* (1991), directed by Paul Cox. This Australian film is about an eighty-year-old woman who desires a chance to share the wisdom of her life. Starring Sheila Florance, Gosia Dobrowolska, Norman Kaye, and Chris Haywood, the film emphasizes the value that one can feel by passing along the wisdom of experience. See entry in *Aging*.

**Popular Music**

Allan Parsons Project, The. "Time" (1980). From the album *Turn of a Friendly Card*, this song about aging captures in tempo, tone, and words the gentle and endless flow of time and the process of aging.

Beatles, The. "When I'm Sixty-Four" (1967). Written by John Lennon and Paul McCartney, this humorous, classic song from the album *Sgt. Pepper's Lonely Hearts Club Band* playfully asks whether there is any need or love for a person later in life, after the body and mind start to break down during the process of aging.

Blood, Sweat, and Tears. "When I Die" (1972). Despite the ominous title, this song is upbeat and features the band singing about a natural, unencumbered death that leaves a legacy to the next generation of people. The song is available on the remastered compact disc *Blood, Sweat, and Tears: Greatest Hits* (1999).

Chapman, Tracy. "At This Point in My Life" (1995). This song, from the album *New Beginning*, is about the process of reflecting on one's life.

Denver, John. "Grandma's Feather Bed" (1974). From the album *John Denver, Home Again*, this song captures the youthful sense of adventure that comes from being at a grandmother's home with other young family members.

Durante, Jimmy. "Look Ahead Little Girl" (1963). From the album *September Song*, this song features an older man singing some bedtime advice to a little girl about what is to come in life as she grows older.

_____. "September Song" (1963). Originally written in 1938 for the play *Knickerbocker Holiday*, this song from Durante's album *September Song* conveys the preciousness of time, particularly in relationships, as one ages. The last months of the year are used to represent the latter years of life.

_____. "Young at Heart" (1963). This song tells of the magic and importance of always keeping youth within one's mind no matter how old one gets. From the album *September Song*, "Young at Heart" maintains that a youthful outlook is more valuable than any material possession.

Eberhardt, Cliff. "My Father's Shoes" (1989). Taken from the album *Legacy: A Collection of New Folk Music*, this poignant and cutting song gives voice to a son's turmoil as he struggles with what he has inherited from his father, both materially and as a person.

Fogelberg, Dan. "In the Passage" (1980). From the album *The Age of Innocence*, this rather solemn song tells of the process of looking back on life through the eyes of wisdom and noticing decisions made, paths taken or not taken, and how, in reflection, there can be only acceptance for how one has lived.

Grateful Dead, The. "Attics of My Life" (1970). This somewhat somber song uses many metaphors to reflect on memories from a rich life and relationship. The lyrics compare memories to articles one might find in an attic, and compares the days of life to pages in a book. This song is from the album *American Beauty*.

_____. "Touch of Grey" (1987). This playful song from *In the Dark* features Jerry Garcia singing about surviving as time passes and how his touch of grey, or wisdom from life lessons and experiences, helps him on a daily basis.

Haggard, Merle, and Willie Nelson. "My Life's Been a Pleasure" (1982). In this song from *Poncho and Lefty*, Haggard and Nelson sing about how a man has had a good life because of his lasting relationship with his wife. The lyrics go on to compare the month of May to youth, a time when the relationship began and when outer beauty was noticeable in the woman for whom the song is sung.

Jennings, Waylon, Willie Nelson, Jessi Colter, and Tompall Glaser. "Yesterday's Wine" (1977). These four artists perform a stirring rendition of this song, from the album *The Outlaws*, in which each sip of wine is a metaphor for a memory. The song suggests that some memories become finer with age and are nearly intoxicating.

Kane, Daniel. "Remember When" (1982). This earlier instrumental piece from *On the Street Where You Live* (1992) was written to commemorate the value of exploring and reminiscing about memories of close personal relationships.

Mitchell, Joni. "The Circle Game" (1966). In her soulful voice, Mitchell sings of how time passes quickly for all, of teaching people to become more realistic, and of recognizing the seasons of life. The song is from the album *Ladies of the Canyon*.

Morrison, Van. "A Sense of Wonder" (1984). Morrison sings of the seasons of life, of the value of gaining experience through life, and of how the same things can take on different meaning through the eyes of wisdom and aging in this rich and hearty song from the album *A Sense of Wonder*.

Nelson, Willie. "Funny How Time Slips Away" (1976). In this reflective and light song from *The Sound in Your Mind*, Nelson sings about how quickly time passes when one does not attend to it and how this can surprise people later when they finally do stop to observe their surroundings.

Nelson, Willie, and Waylon Jennings. "Old Friends" (1983). This country-western song, from the album *Take It to the Limit*, is about recollecting the experiences that old friends share after many years of knowing each other and the special value of such relationships across a lifetime.

_____. "Would You Lay with Me (In a Field of Stone)" (1983). This ballad from *Take It to the Limit* is about a love that lasts a lifetime, through thick and thin, and through all eternity.

Nelson, Willie, and Leon Russell. "Danny Boy" (1979). From the album *One for the Road*, this song is about the love felt for a friend remembered.

Old and in the Way. "Old and in the Way" (1975). From the signature album *Old and in the Way*, this bluegrass song explores the fear that when one ages and youth fades, one may be left alone, uncared for, ignored, and unnoticed.

Pettis, Pierce. "Legacy" (1989). This song from *Legacy: A Collection of New Folk Music* captures the complex feelings that come with all the thoughts, feelings, physical attributes, relationships, and possessions that one can inherit through one's family legacy.

Pink Floyd. "Time" (1973). This song from the classic album *Dark Side of the Moon* captures, in its words and tempo, how time is elusive, is always one step ahead, can be full of surprises, and is leading everyone through the journey of life to the grave.

Presley, Elvis. "Memories" (1990). Available on the compact disc *Elvis: The Great Performances*, this song features Presley singing poignantly about the ability of memories to evoke strong feelings, no matter how brief. As in other songs, memories are said to age like fine wine and to be like pages in the book of one's life.

Ryan, Irene. "No Time at All" (1972). From the musical *Pippin*, this song advises people to live to the fullest and to stay young.

Shocked, Michelle. "When I Grow Up" (1986). This humorous song from the album *Short, Sharp, Shocked* is about a woman who wants to grow up to be very old, find an old man, and live a simple life.

Simon, Paul, and Art Garfunkel. "Bookends Theme" (1967). The importance of preserving memories is poignantly conveyed in this song from the album *Bookends*.

_____. "A Hazy Shade of Winter" (1967). The sadder side of being old is conveyed in this song of advice offered by an old man who tells the tales of being old and lonely, filled with despair, and in need. The song also touches on the themes of the importance of memory to elders and the value of being remembered by others.

_____. "Voices of Old People" (1967). In this song from *Bookends*, Simon and Garfunkel attempt to capture what it sounds like to listen to the voices of the old from a distance. It artfully captures some interesting snippets of elderly concerns in voice samples of older people recorded in New York City and Los Angeles.

Sinatra, Frank. "You Make Me Feel So Young" (1956). This song, available on the compact disc *Songs for Swingin' Lovers* (1987), features Sinatra singing about how love makes one feel good and how feeling good means feeling young.

Sonia Dada. "The River Runs Slow" (1995). *A Day at the Beach*, a relaxing and reflective album, offers this song that has the singer comparing life to a slow-running river. Transitions in life are also compared to bends in a long, winding road as a singer thinks about his growing child.

Stern, Isaac. "Sunrise, Sunset" (1971). The lyrics of this song describe how the passing of a lifetime is like the passing of a day and how elders, with a sense of both joy and sadness, watch their children grow and assume the role of adulthood. Sung by the entire cast, this soulful song comes from the musical and album *Fiddler on the Roof.*

Stevens, Cat. "Father and Son" (1970). This song of life advice from a father to a son from the album *Tea for the Tillerman* focuses on the importance of patience, judicious decision making, self-expression, valuing one's dreams, finding satisfying relationships, and accepting the impermanence of life.

Streisand, Barbra. "Way We Were" (1974). From the album *Way We Were*, this song dramatically conveys the power of memories and photographs to evoke strong feelings and how, even when strong, memories can be called into question as one struggles to make sense out of how events did or did not happen in life.

Vereen, Ben. "Simple Joys" (1972). From the 1970's musical and album *Pippin*, this song proclaims that the best things in life are the simple things, that life is to be lived in the present, and that this kind of freedom is best learned before one reaches the end of life.

Young, Neil. "Comes a Time" (1978). In this song from the album *Comes a Time*, Young sings about how recognizing that time is passing can cause a person to make changes in his or her life.

_____. "My Boy" (1985). This song from the album *Old Ways* features a father who notices his son growing up fast and who makes efforts to give advice to his son about how time passes quickly. As with other songs touching on the theme of aging, the metaphor of summer is used to represent the prime of life.

_____. "Old Man" (1972). In this song from the album *Harvest*, Young provides the voice of a son singing about his recognition of how he is like his father, about the process of growing older, and about gaining wisdom and insight during the course of aging.

_____. "Old Ways" (1985). Found on the album *Old Ways*, Young sings this self-reflective, humorous song about how it is hard to change the habits that one has acquired over a lifetime, even when one recognizes them and wants to change.

**Television Programs**

*Beverly Hillbillies, The* (1962-1971). This comedy series featured two elder characters, Granny (played by Irene Ryan) and Jed Clampett (played by Buddy Ebsen), along with their younger relatives Elly May and Jethro. The series provided a comedic and fresh portrayal of elders as clever, mischievous, persevering, and capable of defending themselves even in an environment (the big city) that differs so greatly from the one in which they were originally raised (the country).

*Golden Girls, The* (1985-1992). This television comedy series featured the day-to-day lives of four women—Blanche (Rue McClanahan), Rose (Betty White), Dorothy (Bea Arthur), and Dorothy's mother Sophia (Estelle Getty)—who were all over the age of forty. The show portrayed the caring, strong, and complex relationships among these four women and dealt with such issues as jealousy, teamwork, dating, dealing with children, and coping with decisions and fears about health. See entry in *Aging*.

*Frasier* (1993-      ). This comedy series, primarily about middle-aged radio psychologist Frasier Crane, has the unique feature of showing an elder parent living with his son. Played by John Mahoney, the character of Martin Crane regularly pushes the envelop of what it means to be an old, widowed man. He strives for time alone from his son and regularly puts an end to any notion that he is lonely, useless, or unable to have fun.

*Last of Summer Wine, The* (1972-      ). This long-running British television show is set in the small town of Yorkshire and tells many stories about the characters who live there. The focus is on three old friends—Compo, Clegg, and Foggy—and the adventures they have with neighbors and with one another. The characters are lively and shatter many elderly stereotypes.

*Matlock* (1986-1995). This television series starred Andy Griffith as Ben Matlock, an older, clever, small-town lawyer. The character was also featured in a series of television films. See entry in *Aging*.

*Murder, She Wrote* (1984-1996). Angela Lansbury portrayed the older, amateur supersleuth Jessica Fletcher, who was skilled at solving mysteries and intervening in crimes. See entry in *Aging*.

*Waiting for God* (1990-1994). This British comedy series showed the daily absurdities and humor involved in the lives of a group of slightly off-kilter elders living in the Day View Retirement Home. Power of attorney, physical operations, and dealing with relatives were some of the topics of this series.

—*Nancy A. Piotrowski*

# RESOURCES: ORGANIZATIONS AND PROGRAMS

**Administration on Aging (AoA)**
330 Independence Avenue, SW
Washington, D.C. 20201
Ph.: (800) 677-1116 (Eldercare Locator)
    (202) 619-7501 (National Aging
      Information Center)
    (202) 401-4541 (Assistant Secretary for
      Aging)
TDD: (202) 401-7575
Fax: (202) 260-1012
E-mail: *aoainfo@aoa.gov*
Web site: *http://www.aoa.gov*
The Administration on Aging (AoA) is a large governmental agency that provides a wealth of information on numerous aging topics and services. Among the programs and resources that the organization has implemented are the Older Americans Act of 1965, the Aging Network, the Administration on Aging Accomplishments, the Disaster Assistance Resources for the Aging Network, the Aging Network Resource Page, and the White House Conference on Aging. AoA fact sheets are available on a variety of topics, including age discrimination, Alzheimer's disease, American Indians, Alaskan Native and Native Hawaiian programs, elder abuse, employment, housing options, nutrition programs, ombudsman programs, senior centers, transportation, and volunteer opportunities. The AoA also sponsors the on-line National Aging Information Center, which offers information on numerous aging-related topics.

**Alzheimer's Association**
919 North Michigan Avenue
Suite 1000
Chicago, IL 60611-1676
Ph.: (800) 272-3900
    (312) 335-8700
Fax: (312) 335-1110
E-mail: *info@alz.org*
Web site: *http://www.alz.org/*
Founded in 1980, the Alzheimer's Association is the only national volunteer organization dedicated to researching the prevention, cure, and treatment of Alzheimer's disease and related disorders, and to providing support and assistance to afflicted patients and their families. With a network of more than two hundred chapters in the United States, the association helps those with the disease and their families learn about the disease and what to expect; gain understanding and emotional support; find help for legal, financial, and lifestyle needs; obtain information on care options; and gain access to clinical drug trials. The Alzheimer's Association sponsors a variety of training programs throughout the year, including "Activity-Based Alzheimer Care" and "Key Elements of Dementia Care." Local chapters also sponsor a variety of training programs in their communities. One extremely helpful resource offered by the association is the Benjamin B. Green-Field Library and Resource Center. The center collects a wide range of materials related to Alzheimer's disease and related disorders and provides service to family members, educators and students, health professionals, social service agencies, and the general public. See entry in *Aging*.

**American Association of Homes and Services for the Aging (AAHSA)**
901 E Street, NW
Suite 500
Washington, D.C. 20004-2011
Ph.: (202) 783-2242
Fax: (202) 783-2255
Web site: *http://www.aahsa.org*
The American Association of Homes and Services for the Aging (AAHSA) represents nonprofit organizations dedicated to providing high-quality health care, housing, and services to the nation's elderly. Its membership consists of more than five thousand nonprofit nursing homes, continuing care retirement communities, senior housing facilities, assisted-living services, and community services. The Web site for the association contains a wealth of information for consumers, advocates, and practitioners. For consumers and family caregivers, tips on choosing facilities and services are available with a directory. Upcoming AAHSA events—such as conferences, seminars, and state association meetings—are advertised. A job mart is available with listings and career information. The AAHSA on-line pressroom offers news releases, fact sheets, and news links, while the on-line bookstore contains a complete catalog of AAHSA publications. Member savings programs are available

from aging service providers on group purchasing, insurance, financing, and technology.

## American Association of Retired Persons (AARP)

601 E Street, NW
Washington, D.C. 20049
Ph.: (202) 434-2000
Fax: (202) 434-2320
Web site: *http://www.aarp.org/*

The American Association of Retired Persons (AARP) is a nonprofit, nonpartisan organization dedicated to helping older Americans achieve lives of independence, dignity, and purpose. Membership is restricted to adults fifty years of age or older, though they need not be retired. The AARP publishes the journal *Modern Maturity* and offers numerous membership benefits and discounts. Members are given easy access to information on such topics as community and volunteer programs, computers and the Internet, health and wellness, legislative issues, leisure activities, life transitions, independent living, and personal finances. Benefits include group health insurance, travel benefits, investment programs, credit cards, AARP pharmacy services, and auto and homeowner insurance. The AARP has four thousand local chapters across the United States. The location of a particular chapter can be obtained from the national office. See entry in *Aging.*

## American Bar Association Commission on Legal Problems of the Elderly

740 15th Street, NW
Washington, D.C. 20005-1022
Ph.: (202) 662-8690
Fax: (202) 662-8698
E-mail: *abaelderly@abanet.org*
Web site: *http://www.abanet.org:80/elderly/about.html*

The American Bar Association (ABA) Commission on Legal Problems of the Elderly was established in 1978 with the purpose of examining and responding to the legal needs of older persons in the United States. In carrying out this purpose, the commission has examined legal services to older persons, Social Security and other public benefit programs, planning for incapacity, housing needs, elder abuse, age discrimination, health and long-term care, ethical issues, dispute resolution, and problems faced by people with disabilities. The organization is composed of fifteen members, ap-

pointed annually by the president of the ABA, who represent not only ABA members but also non-lawyer experts in aging issues, including physicians, social workers, aging advocates, public officials, and gerontologists. The staff, which is composed of a director and five attorneys, conducts more than one hundred major presentations each year before professional organizations and at state, national, and international conferences. The commission also works with public and private attorneys, state and local bar associations, agencies on aging, and others to evaluate and improve the delivery of legal services to older persons through technical assistance.

## American Council of the Blind (ACB)

1155 15th Street, NW
Suite 720
Washington, D.C. 20005
Ph.: (202) 467-5081
(800) 424-8666
Fax: (202) 467-5085

The American Council of the Blind (ACB) is a national membership organization of blind and visually impaired people. It was founded in 1961 and incorporated in the District of Columbia. The council's membership numbers in the tens of thousands. The majority of its members belong to one or more of its seventy-one affiliated organizations, although there are also members-at-large. Membership is not limited to blind or visually impaired individuals. The ACB has fifty-one state and regional affiliates and twenty national special interest and professional affiliates.

The council strives to improve the well-being of all blind and visually impaired people by serving as a representative national organization of blind people; elevating the social, economic, and cultural levels of blind people; improving educational and rehabilitation facilities and opportunities; cooperating with public and private institutions and organizations concerned with blind services; encouraging and assisting all blind persons to develop their abilities; and conducting a public education program to promote greater understanding of blindness and the capabilities of blind people. *The Braille Forum*, a free monthly national magazine, has a readership of approximately twenty-six thousand. It is produced in braille, large print, cassette, and IBM-compatible computer disc and contains articles on employment, legislation, sports and leisure activities, new products and services, human interest, and other information of interest to blind and visually impaired people. The council produces a monthly half-hour radio information program called *ACB Reports* and distributes public service announcements for television and radio highlighting the capabilities of blind people.

ACB services include toll-free information and referral on all aspects of blindness, scholarship assistance to blind and visually impaired post-secondary students, public education and awareness training, support to consumer advocates and legal assistance on matters relating to blindness, leadership and legislative training, consulting with industry regarding employment of blind and visually impaired individuals, governmental monitoring, and advocacy, including the Washington Connection, a telephone service that provides information on national legislation.

### American Federation of the Blind (AFB)

11 Penn Plaza
Suite 300
New York, NY 10001
Ph.: (212) 502-7600
　　(800) 232-5463
Fax: (212) 502-7774 (publication and video orders)
E-mail: *afbinfo@afb.net*
Web site: *http://www.igc.apc.org/afb/*

A nonprofit organization founded in 1921 and recognized as Helen Keller's cause in the United States, the American Federation of the Blind (AFB) is a leading national resource for people who are blind or visually impaired, for the organizations that serve them, and for the general public. The mission of the AFB is to enable people who are blind or visually impaired to achieve equality of access and opportunity that will ensure freedom of choice in their lives. The AFB fulfills this mission through four primary areas of activity regarding the nonmedical aspects of blindness and visual impairment. The organization responds to more than 150,000 inquiries annually from people who are blind or visually impaired, their families and friends, professionals in the blindness field, and the general public requesting information about programs, services, and other topics related to blindness and visual impairment. The AFB pub-

lishes books, pamphlets, videos, and periodicals about blindness for professionals and consumers through AFB Press, including the *Journal of Visual Impairment Blindness*, the leading professional journal of its kind.

The foundation maintains and preserves the Helen Keller Archives, an invaluable collection of personal material donated by Helen Keller, who worked at AFB for more than forty years. The collection is housed at the M. C. Migel Memorial Library, one of the world's largest collections of print materials on blindness. The AFB also maintains the Careers Technology Information Bank (CTIB), a network of blind individuals from all fifty states and from Canada who use assistive technology at home, at work, or at school and who are able and willing to serve as mentors to others.

The goals of the AFB include educating the public and policymakers about the needs and capabilities of people who are blind or visually impaired, consulting on legislative issues and representing the interests of blind and visually impaired people before Congress and government agencies, increasing corporate and public awareness of the capabilities of people who are blind or visually impaired through publications, providing audiovisual presentations and exhibits, and creating public service announcements. The AFB also produces and distributes talking books and other audio materials and is under contract to the Library of Congress.

### American Geriatrics Society (AGS)

770 Lexington Avenue
Suite 300
New York, NY 10021
Ph.: (212) 308-1414
Fax: (212) 832-8648
E-mail: *info.amger@americangeriatrics.org*
Web site: *http://www.americangeriatrics.org/*

The American Geriatrics Society (AGS) is a professional organization of health care providers dedicated to improving the health and well-being of all older adults. With an active membership of more than six thousand health care professionals, the AGS has a long history of shaping attitudes, policies, and practices regarding health care for older people. AGS publications include *Geriatrics at Your Fingertips, Geriatrics Review Syllabus, AGS Clinical Practice Guidelines: The Management of Chronic Pain in Older Persons, Directory of Geriatrics Health Care Ser-*

*vices in Managed Care*, and *AGS/Pfizer Managed Care Report*.

## American Music Therapy Association (AMTA)

8455 Colesville Road
Suite 1000
Silver Spring, Maryland 20910
Ph.: (301) 589-3300
Fax: (301) 589-5175
E-mail: *info@musictherapy.org*
Web site: *http://www.namt.com/index.html*

The American Music Therapy Association (AMTA) was founded in 1998 to promote the progressive development of the therapeutic use of music in rehabilitation, special education, and community settings. Predecessors to the AMTA included the National Association for Music Therapy (founded in 1950) and the American Association for Music Therapy (founded in 1971). The AMTA is committed to the advancement of education, training, professional standards, credentials, and research in support of the music therapy profession. The organization's publications include the *Journal of Music Therapy*, a quarterly research-oriented journal; *Music Therapy Perspectives*, a semiannual, practice-oriented journal; and *Music Therapy Matters*, a quarterly newsletter.

## American Society on Aging (ASA)

833 Market Street
Suite 511
San Francisco, CA 94103-1824
Ph.: (415) 974-9600
Fax: (415) 974-0300
E-mail: *info@asa.asaging.org*
Web site: *http://www.asaging.org/*

The American Society on Aging (ASA) is a leading provider of professional information in the field of aging through its annual meeting, its Summer Series on Aging, and other conferences held throughout the United States. In addition, the ASA publishes the highly respected periodicals *Aging Today* and *Generations*, and eight specialized newsletters. Membership constituent units have been developed in the areas of mental health and aging; older adult education; managed care and aging; business and aging; gay and lesbian aging issues; retirement planning; disability and rehabilitation; and religion, spirituality, and aging.

The ASA has played an important role in broad-

ening the concerns of professionals and the public with respect to the well-being of older persons and their families. It has encouraged the development of new products and technologies to assist older persons in the activities of daily living, produced a video educating the public to the need for "elder-friendly" neighborhoods, and developed a CD-ROM to inform people about late-life depression and suicide.

## Asociacion Nacional por Personas Mayores (ANPPM)

3325 Wilshire Boulevard
Suite 800
Los Angeles, CA 90010-1724
Ph.: (213) 487-1922
Fax: (213) 385-2014

The Asociacion Nacional por Personas Mayores (ANPPM) was founded to inform policymakers and the general public regarding the status, needs, and capabilities of elderly Latinos and other low-income elderly persons. The organization provides direct social services to the Latino community, such as helping people find employment, conducting marketing studies, and offering training and technical assistance to community groups and professionals in the field of aging. The ANPPM's National Hispanic Research Center conducts national gerontological studies on the Latino community. The organization also produces and distributes bilingual information on the Latino elderly through its national Hispanic Media Center and sponsors the Fleming Hispanic Scholarship Fund.

## Association for Gerontology and Human Development in Historically Black Colleges and Universities (AGHD/HBCU)

c/o Institute of Gerontology, University of the District of Columbia
4200 Connecticut Avenue, NW
M.B. 5103
Washington, D.C. 20008
Ph.: (202) 274-6687
Fax: (202) 274-6605

The Association for Gerontology and Human Development in Historically Black Colleges and Universities (AGHD/HBCU) was founded in 1980 to represent approximately 409 historically black colleges and universities throughout the United States. The association provides education, training, and research programs in gerontology for two- and four-year colleges and universities through meetings, conferences, workshops, and publications.

### Association for Gerontology in Higher Education (AGHE)

1030 15th Street, NW
Suite 240
Washington, D.C. 20005-1503
Ph.: (202) 289-9806
Fax: (202) 289-9824
E-mail: *aghetemp@aghe.org*
Web site: *http://www.aghe.org/*

The Association for Gerontology in Higher Education (AGHE) was established in 1974 to advance gerontology as a field of study in institutions of higher learning. The objectives are to foster research, instructional, and service programs to enhance the capacities of institutions of higher education in the field of aging and to help make their resources available to benefit the wider community and society. On January 1, 1999, the AGHE became a unit of the Gerontological Society of America (GSA), whose goal is "to promote the scientific study of aging . . . and to foster growth and diffusion of knowledge related to problems of aging and of the sciences contributing to understanding." The AGHE's Web site includes information on contacting individuals in positions of leadership, on membership, on publications, on careers in aging, on annual meetings, on consultation programs, and on scholarship programs.

### Association of Jewish Aging Services (AJAS)

316 Pennsylvania Avenue, SE
Suite 402
Washington, D.C. 20003-1175
Ph.: (202) 543-7500
Fax: (202) 543-4090
E-mail: *ajas@ajas.com*

Founded in 1960, the AJAS (formerly the North American Association of Jewish Homes and Hospitals for Aging) serves as an information clearinghouse, as well as an advocacy and educational organization, for 230 community-sponsored, long-term health care facilities and housing units.

### Beverly Foundation

44 South Mentor Avenue
Pasadena, CA 91106

Ph.: (626) 792-2292
Fax: (626) 792-6117
E-mail: *bfix@netcom.com*
Web site:
*http://www.aoa.dhhs.gov/AOA/dir/67.html*

The Beverly Foundation is a nonprofit organization dedicated to optimum utilization of individual ability and function regardless of age, condition, or situation. The foundation builds public awareness of issues concerning the autonomy and well-being of older adults, and it spurs progress in health and social services for older adults by developing leading-edge educational and training materials for geriatric health providers. The organization also engages in research and demonstration projects to help extend knowledge in gerontology and geriatrics. Publications include *Choice, Challenge and Companionship: Homesharing for Older Adults, Healing People: Using Behavioral Approaches to Improve Wound Care Effectiveness,* and *Rehabilitating for Continence in Long-Term Care.*

### B'nai B'rith Center for Senior Housing and Services

1640 Rhode Island Avenue, NW
Washington, D.C. 20036
Ph.: (202) 857-6581
Fax: (202) 857-0980
E-mail: *senior@bnaibrith.com*
Web site: *http://www.bnaibrith.org/*

B'nai B'rith is a Jewish service organization that engages in community service, Jewish education, programs for youth, and public affairs advocacy. The B'nai B'rith Center for Senior Housing and Services provides opportunities for seniors and their families to enrich their quality of life through participation in a comprehensive program that includes four primary areas: federally subsidized housing and assisted living for the elderly; advocacy on behalf of issues important to seniors; continuing education, recreation, and travel programs; and the Caring Network, an information and referral service for older persons and their families.

### Center for the Study of Aging and Human Development

Duke University Medical Center
P.O. Box 3003
Durham, NC 27710

Ph.: (919) 660-7502
Fax: (919) 684-8569
E-mail: *webmaster@geri.duke.edu*
Web site: *http://www.geri.duke.edu/aging/aging.html*
In 1955, Duke University's administration chartered a university council to promote and coordinate multidisciplinary research, training, and service in the area of aging. Two years later, the U.S. Public Health Service designated the Duke Center for the Study of Aging and Human Development as one of five regional resource centers on aging. It is the oldest continually funded member of the original group.

The center's first initiatives included the Duke Longitudinal Studies, a twenty-year project begun in 1956 that monitored the physical, mental, social, and economic status of approximately eight hundred older adults. These studies, which received the 1983 Sandoz International Prize for multidisciplinary research in aging, documented the capacity of most older adults to age well, thereby helping to revolutionize thinking about human aging.

In 1975, the center's Older Americans Resources and Services (OARS) program developed the first comprehensive technique for assessing functional impairment in the elderly. OARS methods, updated to reflect changes in the aging population, continue to be used in hundreds of research studies and geriatric clinics across the United States. Duke University's Geriatric Evaluation and Treatment (GET) clinic, opened in 1967, serves older adults throughout the southeastern United States. Since 1988, the center's Long-Term Care Resources program has assisted North Carolina in developing and implementing sound public policies for serving older adults and their families in the long term. See entry in *Aging*.

### Children of Aging Parents (CAPS)

1609 Woodbourne Road
Suite 302-A
Levittown, PA 19057
Ph.: (215) 945-6900
      (800) 227-7294
Fax: (215) 945-8720
Web site: *http://www.careguide.net/*
Children of Aging Parents (CAPS) is a nonprofit organization that provides information and emotional support to caregivers of older people. Care-

givers throughout the United States can contact the information and referral service to learn about local resources. To help the public understand the special needs of older people, CAPS provides "instant aging" workshops for community groups. Training programs are available for nurses and social workers in hospitals, nursing homes, and rehabilitation centers. The organization also produces and distributes literature for caregivers. See entry in *Aging*.

### Gerontological Society of America (GSA)

1030 15th Street, NW
Suite 250
Washington, D.C. 20005-4006
Ph.: (202) 842-1275
Fax: (202) 842-1150
E-mail: *geron@geron.org*
Web site: *http://www.geron.org/*
The Gerontological Society of America (GSA) was established in 1945 to promote the scientific study of aging, to encourage exchanges among researchers and practitioners from various disciplines related to gerontology, and to foster the use of gerontological research in forming public policy. The society publishes multidisciplinary journals of research, policy analysis, and practice concepts; holds the largest annual scientific meeting concerning gerontology in the United States; and coordinates an information program that links research, policy, and practice.

The GSA is divided into sections that focus on the biological sciences, behavioral and social sciences, clinical medicine, and social research policy and practice. Student members also join a student organization, in addition to the GSA and an appropriate section. Each section has its own bylaws, officers, committees, and activities, and each organizes its own track of presentations at the annual meeting. The society also facilitates multidisciplinary networking through informal and formal interest groups organized around specific concerns of aging, such as elder abuse, Alzheimer's disease, death and dying, grandparents as caregivers, nutrition, and oral health. In 1999, there were twenty-two interest groups, and another six had been proposed.

According to the Journal Citation Reports of the Institute for Scientific Information, the GSA's journals rank in the top five of the more than twenty geriatric and gerontology science and social science journals. The GSA's Web site offers information about the annual meeting, membership, career development, employment opportunities, legislative and policy decisions, and grants, fellowships, and awards. The site also includes a complete listing of publications, a newsletter, news releases, and other valuable resources in gerontology. See entry in *Aging*.

**Gray Panthers**
733 15th Street, NW
Suite 437
Washington, D.C. 20005
Ph.: (800) 280-5362
      (202) 737-6637
Fax: (202) 737-1160
E-mail: *info@graypanthers.org*
Web site: *http://graypanthers.org/home.htm*

The Gray Panthers is a national organization of intergenerational activists—young, old, and everyone in between—dedicated to social change. Founded in 1970 by social activist Maggie Kuhn, the organization consists of more than fifty local networks that work for peace, employment, housing, antidiscrimination legislation, greater rights for the disabled, family security, environmental issues, and campaign reform. The Gray Panthers has helped fight forced retirement at age sixty-five, has exposed nursing home abuse, and has worked for the adoption of universal health care. Members of the Gray Panthers mobilize voters on a variety of issues; testify before legislative bodies, at utility board hearings, and in various forums; and take part in demonstrations, either alone or in coalitions, in order to bring certain problems to the attention of the public and the media. See entry in *Aging*.

**Green Thumb**
2000 North 14th Street
Suite 800
Arlington, VA 22201
Ph.: (703) 522-7272
Fax: (703) 522-0141
E-mail: *andrea_wooten@greenthumb.org*
Web site: *http://greenthumb.org/*

Green Thumb is a national nonprofit organization whose mission is to make a positive difference in local communities by empowering mature individuals to use their talents and abilities. Through the Senior Community Service Employment Program (SCSEP), administered by the U.S. Department of Labor and founded by Green Thumb in 1965, the organization provides low-income individuals age fifty-five and older with job training, community service employment, and placement assistance. Local communities benefit from essential services performed by program participants, including child and elder care, emergency assistance, crime prevention, health care, and disaster relief.

**Health Care Financing Administration (HCFA)**
7500 Security Boulevard
Baltimore, MD 21244
Ph.: (410) 786-3000
Web site: *http://www.hcfa.gov/about.htm*

Through its work in administering the Medicare, Medicaid, and Child Health insurance programs, the Health Care Financing Administration (HCFA) helps pay the medical bills for more than 75 million beneficiaries. Medicare is the largest health insurance program in the United States, covering more than thirty-eight million Americans at a cost of just under two hundred billion dollars. Medicare provides health insurance to people who are at least sixty-five years old; people who are disabled; and people with permanent kidney failure.

The agency's goals are to protect and improve beneficiary health and satisfaction; to promote the fiscal integrity of HCFA programs; to purchase the health care of best value for beneficiaries; to promote beneficiary and public understanding of the HCFA and its programs; to foster excellence in the design and administration of HCFA programs; and to provide leadership in the broader public interest to improve health.

Working with other federal departments and state and local governments, the HCFA takes strong enforcement action against those who commit fraud and abuse, protects taxpayer dollars, and guarantees security for the Medicare, Medicaid, and Child Health programs. The organization is also working to improve the quality of health care provided to beneficiaries. Quality improvement is based on developing and enforcing standards through surveillance, measuring and improving outcomes of care, educating health care providers about quality improvement opportunities, and educating beneficiaries to make good health care choices.

**Hospice Association of America (HAA)**
228 Seventh Street, SE
Washington, D.C. 20003
Ph.: (202) 546-4759
Fax: (202) 547-9559
Web site: *http://www.nahc.org/HAA/*
The Hospice Association of America (HAA) represents more than 2,800 hospices and thousands of caregivers and volunteers who serve terminally ill patients and their families. Ranked the most effective health care trade organization on Capitol Hill by congressional offices, the HAA is the largest lobbying group for hospice care; it advocates the industry's interests before Congress, regulatory agencies, other national organizations, the courts, the media, and the public. The association serves hospices that are freestanding and community-based, as well as those affiliated with home care agencies and hospitals.

The HAA was organized to heighten the public visibility of hospice services; to affect legislative and regulatory processes impinging on hospice services; to gather and disseminate data pertinent to the hospice industry; to promote hospice care as a viable component of the health care delivery system; to foster, develop, and promote high standards of patient care in hospice services; to provide an organized and unified voice for hospice providers; to collaborate with state organizations representing hospice interests and other organizations at the national, state, and local levels; to initiate, sponsor, and promote educational programs for and with providers and consumers of hospice services, government bodies, and other professional individuals and associations interested in hospice care; and to initiate, sponsor, and promote research directly related to hospice services.

The HAA distributes a number of general information publications about hospice to consumers. Many of these publications are available in brochure format and can be ordered by contacting the publications department. The HAA has also placed a great emphasis on expanding its educational opportunities. In collaboration with its parent organization, the National Association for Home Care, as well as other affiliates, the HAA co-sponsors five national conferences, one international conference, and ten regional conferences. The largest of these is the annual meeting and HOMECARExpo held each fall.

**Little Brothers-Friends of the Elderly**
954 W. Washington Blvd.
5th Floor
Chicago, IL 60607
Ph.: (312) 829-3055
Fax: (312) 829-3077
E-mail: *national@little-brothers.org*
Web site: *http://www.little-brothers.org/*
Little Brothers-Friends of the Elderly is a national, nonprofit organization committed to relieving isolation and loneliness among the elderly. They offer to people of good will the opportunity to join the elderly in friendship and the celebration of life. The organization was founded in 1946 by French nobleman Armand Marquiset, who devoted himself to alleviating what he termed "the greatest poverty of all—the poverty of love." After witnessing the suffering and hardships of the elderly after World War II, Marquiset began visiting and delivering hot meals with flowers to the elderly poor in Paris. Chartered in 1959 in the United States (one of eight member countries, including Canada, France, Germany, Ireland, Mexico, Morocco, and Spain), Little Brothers is a founding member of the Fédération Internationale des petits frères des Pauvres (International Federation of Little Brothers of the Poor). The U.S. national headquarters of Little Brothers is located in Chicago, and sites within the United States are located in Boston, Chicago, Cincinnati, Minneapolis-St. Paul, Philadelphia, San Francisco, and the Upper Peninsula of Michigan. Specific addresses for local sites can be obtained from the Web site or through the national office. See entry in *Aging*.

**Macular Degeneration Foundation (MDF)**
P.O. Box 9752
San Jose, CA 95157
Ph.: (888) 633-3937
    (408) 260-1335
Web site: *http://www.eyesight.org/index.html*
The Macular Degeneration Foundation (MDF) is a charitable educational and research foundation dedicated to discovering the cause of and developing cures for macular degeneration, the most common cause of blindness in the United States. The organization promotes the development of improved vision enhancement and rehabilitation aids and also provides training and support in the use of such aids to needy individuals, libraries, non-

profit organizations, elder care centers, and other community centers. Through its Web site, toll-free telephones lines, and free newsletter, the foundation is the foremost source of information, counseling, and support for patients and their families.

The MDF Research for Real Solutions program is dedicated to planning and conducting result-oriented, focused research utilizing the skills of top macular degeneration experts both in the United States and internationally. The foundation's newsletter, the *Magnifier*, is printed with extra-large type and is provided free of charge to those who request it. The *Magnifier* features reports on the latest information on macular degeneration research from the foundation's work as well as from various eye research institutes throughout the world. In addition, the publication includes articles that help people deal with the impact of the disease on their lives.

### National Asian Pacific Center on Aging (NAPCA)

Melbourne Tower
1511 Third Avenue
Suite 914
Seattle, WA 98101-1626
Ph.: (206) 624-1221
Fax: (206) 624-1023

The National Asian Pacific Center on Aging (NAPCA) is the leading national advocacy organization committed to the well-being of elderly Asians and Pacific Islanders. It develops demonstration projects and ongoing direct service programs. For example, it runs ongoing employment and training programs in several states, as well as a demonstration project for outreach, case finding, and case management in Seattle. NAPCA also identifies community-based resources for the Asian and Pacific Island elderly and disseminates information throughout the United States via resource directories and a fax-on-demand system. Finally, the organization publishes *Pacific Asian Affairs*, a bimonthly newsletter with a circulation of approximately ten thousand that is available upon request. See entry in *Aging*.

### National Association for Home Care (NAHC)

228 7th Street, SE
Washington, D.C. 20003
Ph.: (202) 547-7427
Fax: (202) 547-9559

E-mail: *webmaster@nahc.org*
Web site: *http:// www.nahc.org/*

The National Association for Home Care (NAHC) is a nonprofit organization representing the nation's home care providers and the individuals they serve. In addition to providing direct needed services to members, the NAHC works to sponsor research, influence legislation, and promote high standards of patient care in home care and hospice services.

### National Association of Area Agencies on Aging (NAAAA)

927 15th Street, NW
6th Floor
Washington, D.C. 20005
Ph.: (202) 296-8130
    (800) 677-1116 (Eldercare Locator)
Fax: (202) 296-8134
Web site: *http://www.n4a.org/*

The National Association of Area Agencies on Aging (NAAAA) represents the interests of a network of local agencies dedicated to helping all older Americans remain healthy and independent residents in their own homes and communities for as long as possible. Area agencies on aging, established under the federal Older Americans Act, address the needs of all Americans aged sixty and over within every local community. They allocate almost three billion dollars annually to such services as home-delivered meals, senior centers, transportation, home care, respite and adult day care, and legal assistance. Area agencies also provide information to older Americans and their caregivers about the availability of local aging services, handling over fifteen million requests each year.

Established by the network of area agencies in 1974, the NAAAA is a nonprofit corporation that provides assistance to the area agency network and advocates for programs benefiting older Americans and their caregivers. The NAAAA publishes the *National Directory for Eldercare Information and Referral* and operates the Eldercare Locator, a nationwide telephone service that helps caregivers locate services for older adults in their own communities. This service is supported by a cooperative agreement with the U.S. Administration on Aging. The NAAAA Web site includes the "Network News" and the "Legislative Update" for members, both of which provide current news on aging policies in Washington, D.C.

**National Association of Foster Grandparent Program Directors (NAFGPD)**

Union/Snyder Foster Grandparent Program
Laurelton Center
Box 300
Laurelton, PA 17835
Ph.: (717) 922-1130 or 5190
Fax: (717) 922-4799
E-mail: *marys@postoffice.ptd.ne*

The National Association of Foster Grandparent Program Directors (NAFGPD) was established in 1971 to provide visibility and advocacy for the Foster Grandparent Program, to provide a network of communications among Foster Grandparent Program directors and projects, and to serve as a vehicle for expression of majority opinion on behalf of the Foster Grandparent program and older Americans to Congress. The organization acts as a resource for and offers technical assistance to Foster Grandparent Program directors, program sponsors, and other community groups.

**National Association of Meal Programs (NAMP)**

1414 Prince Street
Suite 202
Alexandria, VA 22314
Ph.: (703) 548-5558
Fax: (703) 548-8024
E-mail: *namp@tbg.dgsys.com*
Web site: *http://www.projectmeal.org/*

The National Association of Meal Programs (NAMP) is the oldest and largest organization in the United States representing those who provide meal services to senior citizens and people in need. The organization was formed in 1974 in order to work toward the social, physical, nutritional, and economic betterment of older Americans. The mission of the NAMP is to provide education, training, and development opportunities that will enable its members to provide quality nutrition services and programs to people in need.

**National Association of Nutrition and Aging Services Programs (NANASP)**

2675 44th Street, SW
Suite 305
Grand Rapids, MI 49509

Ph.: (616) 513-9909
       (800) 999-6262
Fax: (616) 531-3103

The National Association of Nutrition and Aging Services Programs (NANASP) is a professional membership organization providing leadership on policy, planning, and management issues for home and community care providers. The NANASP was incorporated in 1973 and has grown from a small steering committee to an influential body of more than one thousand members from every region of the United States.

**National Association of Retired Federal Employees (NARFE)**

1533 New Hampshire Avenue, NW
Washington, D.C. 20036-1279
Ph.: (202) 234-0832
Fax: (202) 797-9697

The National Association of Retired Federal Employees (NARFE) has 1,740 chapters located throughout the United States, Puerto Rico, Guam, the Virgin Islands, Panama, and the Philippines. More than one hundred service centers, staffed by NARFE volunteers, offer preretirement counseling and provide information and assistance to members who need help dealing with government agencies regarding their retirement benefits, taxes, Social Security, and Medicare.

**National Association of Retired Senior Volunteer Program Directors (NARSVPD)**

1650 West Second Street
Owensboro, KY 42310
Ph.: (502) 683-1589
Fax: (502) 683-1580

The National Association of Retired Senior Volunteer Program Directors (NARSVPD) was created in Chicago, Illinois, in 1976 with the purpose of providing, through a national focus, visibility and advocacy for the Retired Senior Volunteer Program (RSVP) and older Americans to Congress, the administration, and other appropriate governmental and national units. The agenda of NARSVPD includes professional development of RSVP directors through workshops, training programs, and technical assistance; resource development; advocacy for older Americans as a national resource; communication on issues and ideas relevant to the RSVP; and representation and management of the RSVP through the development of surveys and databases.

### National Association of Senior Companion Program Directors (NASCPD)

Senior Companion Program
Lutheran Social Service of Minnesota
2414 Park Avenue
Minneapolis, MN 55404
Ph.: (612) 872-1719
Fax: (612) 879-5220
E-mail: *jpribyl@lss-mpls.usa.com*

The National Association of Senior Companion Program Directors (NASCPD) was created in 1978 to provide a national focus for Senior Companion Program directors. The organization is active in providing workshops and training programs for Senior Companion Program directors in areas of professional development, in advocating for older Americans as a national resource, in developing resources by networking with private and public agencies and groups, and in providing representation for those served by Senior Companion Programs by speaking on their behalf before national government bodies.

### National Association of State Units on Aging (NASUA)

1225 I Street, NW
Suite 725
Washington, D.C. 20005
Ph.: (202) 898-2578
Fax: (202) 898-2583

Founded in 1964, the National Association of State Units on Aging (NASUA) is a national public interest organization dedicated to providing general and specialized information, technical assistance, and professional development support to the fifty-seven state agencies on aging in the United States. These state and territorial government agencies are charged by the Older Americans Act and directed by governors and state legislatures to advance the social and economic agenda of older persons in their respective states. NASUA is the articulating force at the national level through which the state agencies on aging join together to promote social policies responsive to the needs of an aging America; particular attention is paid to the needs and preferences of low-income, minority, frail, and isolated older persons.

### National Caucus and Center on Black Aged (NCBA)

1424 K Street, NW
Suite 500
Washington, D.C. 20005
Ph.: (202) 637-8400
E-mail: *ncba@aol.com*
Web site: *http://www.ncba-blackaged.org/*

The National Caucus and Center on Black Aged (NCBA) is the only national organization whose major focus is improving life for African American and low-income elderly. The organization was founded by Hobart C. Jackson, a nursing home professional and advocate for African American elderly, and a group of concerned citizens to ensure that the 1971 White House Conference on Aging would address the particular needs of the African American elderly. The caucus existed as an advocacy group until 1973, when it received a grant from the Administration on Aging to conduct research, train personnel, and serve as a technical resource. In 1978, the NCBA received a major grant from the U.S. Labor Department to operate the Senior Community Service Employment Program in five states. In 1983, the NCBA expanded its programs to include senior housing.

The NCBA is one of the largest minority-focused organizations in the United States, with thirty-two chapters, employment offices in nine states and the District of Columbia, and six owned and managed housing projects. The NCBA Web site provides links to a mission and goal statement, a capability statement, membership information, announcements of conferences and meetings, chapter locations with contacts, and historical information about the organization. The NCBA also publishes a newsletter entitled *Golden Page*. Programs include the Senior Employment Program, the Senior Environmental Employment Program, and the Wellness Promotion and Disease Prevention Program. See entry in *Aging*.

### National Committee to Preserve Social Security and Medicare

2000 K Street, NW
Suite 800
Washington, D.C. 20006
Ph.: (202) 822-9459
Fax: (202) 822-9612

The National Committee to Preserve Social Security and Medicare has evolved from an intense advocacy organization to a grassroots education and advocacy organization. Its primary mission is to keep its members and supporters well informed on issues involving Social Security, Medicare, and related issues, and to represent the membership with "one voice" as the organization speaks to the Congress and the administration. The National Committee to Preserve Social Security and Medicare's grassroots operations and its advisors represent the organization across the United States by their presence and their ability to bring legislative issues to the attention of individuals, organizations, and the media. The organization believes that establishing a network of local activists is essential to achieving the goal of ensuring that congressional representatives are aware of their constituents' opinions.

**National Council of Senior Citizens (NCSC)**
8403 Colesville Road
Suite 1200
Silver Spring, MD 20910-3314
Ph.: (301) 578-8800
Fax: (301) 578-8999
E-mail: *dstone@ncscerc.org*
Web site:
  *http://www.ncscinc.org/members/naaaa.htm*
The National Council of Senior Citizens (NCSC) is an advocacy organization dedicated to the belief that America's elderly, like America's youth, are worthy of the best that the United States can give. Toward that end, the NCSC was founded in 1961, born during the struggle for Medicare, its first successful legislative achievement on behalf of seniors. The NCSC, which comprises more than two thousand senior citizens clubs, continues to speak out on behalf of the elderly.

The NCSC fights to protect Medicare, Medicaid, and Social Security and also provides housing, volunteer work, social opportunities, and jobs for the low-income elderly. The strength of the NCSC comes, in large part, from its members and supporters. The organization forms the backbone of the "Senior Power" movement in the United States.

The NCSC is one of the largest sponsors of housing for low-income elderly and handicapped people under the Department of Housing and Urban Development's Section 202 housing program, with projects in fourteen states, the District of Columbia, and Puerto Rico. In addition, the NCSC's affiliate, the National Senior Citizens Education and Research Center (NSCERC), operates a jobs program for the U.S. Department of Labor under the Senior Community Service Employment Program, Title V of the Older Americans Act. The NSCERC's program—Senior Aides—is the second-largest of its type in the United States, with 147 projects in twenty-seven states and the District of Columbia providing jobs for more than ten thousand low-income senior citizens. See entry in *Aging*.

**National Council on the Aging (NCOA)**
409 Third Street, SW
Washington, D.C. 20024
Ph.: (202) 479-1200
Fax: (202) 479-0735
E-mail: *info@ncoa.org*
Web site: *http://www.ncoa.org/*
Founded in 1950, the National Council on the Aging (NCOA) is an association of organizations and individuals dedicated to promoting the dignity, self-determination, well-being, and continuing contributions of older persons through leadership and service, education, and advocacy. The organization's members include professionals and volunteers, service providers, consumer and labor groups, businesses, government agencies, religious groups, and volunteer organizations. The NCOA accomplishes its mission through leadership, education and training, publications, research and development, community services, employment programs, coalition building, and advocacy efforts.

The NCOA has a long history of innovation, including the Meals on Wheels and Foster Grandparents programs, the first national guidelines for geriatric care managers, and the only accreditation program for adult day service providers. The organization has spoken with vigor and authority on behalf of aging Americans and their families, a constituency in which all Americans can claim membership. The NCOA actively seeks improvement in both public and private sector policies affecting older persons. To this end, the council conducts fact-finding and policy analysis, public education, and advocacy. The NCOA's advocacy often takes the form of invited testimony before

Congress and consultation with government agencies, as well as private organizations.

The NCOA is a founding member of the Leadership Council of Aging Organizations. It is represented among the nongovernmental organizations at the United Nations and is in touch with developments worldwide. The NCOA offers a wide variety of programs and services to its constituent units, including the Health Promotion Institute (HPI); the National Adult Day Services Association (NADSA); the National Association of Older Worker Employment Services (NAOWES); the National Center on Rural Aging (NCRA); the National Coalition of Consumer Organizations (NCCO); the National Institute on Community-Based Long-Term Care (NICLC); the National Institute on Financial Issues and Services for Elders (NIFSE); the National Institute on Senior Centers (NISC); the National Institute on Senior Housing (NISH); the National Interfaith Coalition on Aging (NICA); 100,000 Jobs; the Consumer Information Network; Family Friends; Maturity Works; and the Seniors Research Group. See entry in *Aging*.

### National Federation of the Blind (NFB)

1800 Johnson Street
Baltimore, MD 21230
Ph.: (410) 659-9314
E-mail: *epc@roudley.com*
Web site: *http://www.nfb.org/*
Founded in 1940, the National Federation of the Blind (NFB) is one of the nation's largest membership organizations of blind persons. With fifty thousand members, the NFB has more than seven hundred local chapters and affiliates in all fifty states, plus Washington, D.C., and Puerto Rico. As a consumer and advocacy organization, the NFB is considered a leading force in the blindness field. The purpose of the NFB is twofold: to help blind persons achieve self-confidence and self-respect, and to act as a vehicle for collective self-expression by the blind. The NFB provides public education about blindness; information and referral services; scholarships; literature and publications about blindness; aids, appliances, and other adaptive equipment for the blind; advocacy services and protection of civil rights; job opportunities; development and evaluation of technology; and support for blind persons and their families.

Special services of the NFB include Job Opportunities for the Blind (JOB), a free service to blind persons seeking competitive employment; and a materials center that contains more than eleven hundred pieces of literature about blindness and four hundred different aids and appliances used by the blind. In addition, the International Braille and Technology Center for the Blind is the world's largest and most complete evaluation and demonstration center for all speech and Braille technology used by the blind from around the world. Newsline for the Blind, the world's first free talking newspaper service, offers the blind the complete text of leading national and local newspapers with the use of a touch-tone telephone. Jobline offers national employment listings and job openings through a telephone menu system to anyone, free of charge.

NFB publications include the *Braille Monitor*, which provides a positive philosophy about blindness and discusses events and activities of the federation and in the blindness field, and *Future Reflections*, a publication of the National Organization of Parents of Blind Children, a division of the NFB. *Voice of the Diabetic*, which focuses on the special interests and needs of diabetics, is a publication of the Diabetes Action Network, also a division of the NFB.

### National Hispanic Council on Aging (NHCOA)

2713 Ontario Road, NW
Suite 200
Washington, D.C. 20009
Ph.: (202) 745-2521
Fax: (202) 745-2522
E-mail: *nhcoa@worldnet.att.net*
Web site: *http://www.nhcoa.org/right.html*
The National Hispanic Council on Aging (NHCOA) is a nationwide network of individuals, chapters, affiliates, and member organizations with members in nearly every state of the United States, as well as Puerto Rico. The NHCOA sponsors training and educational enrichment programs in collaboration with community-based organizations, state and national organizations, and education institutions. Its Management Internship program places Latinos in administrative positions in agencies located in various cities of the United States. Technical assistance and continuing education programs are provided for its chapters and af-

filiates, as well as for individual members. During the 1990's, the council focused on increasing the pool of Latino gerontologists, on leadership development, on building collaborative relationships with the aging network, and on increasing educational materials through research, needs assessment, and program evaluation. See entry in *Aging*.

**National Hospice Organization (NHO)**
1901 North Moore Street
Suite 901
Arlington, VA 22209-1714
Ph.: (703) 243-5900
Fax: (703) 525-5762
Web site: *http://www.nho.org/*
Founded in 1978, the National Hospice Organization (NHO) is the oldest and largest nonprofit public benefit organization devoted exclusively to hospice care. It is dedicated to promoting and maintaining quality care for terminally ill persons and their families, to making hospice an integral part of the health care system in the United States, and to being the nation's leader in improving end-of-life care. The NHO's mission statement includes educating about and advocating for the fundamental philosophy and principles of hospice care to meet the unique needs of each terminally ill person and his or her family, as well as serving as a voice and resources for its members.

A twenty-one-member board of directors governs the NHO. Members elect ten regional representatives and three at-large members to the board. In addition, the board membership includes representation from the National Council of Hospice Professionals, the Council of States, and the National Hospice Foundation. Among the six appointed members are the president of NHO and an international observer.

More than 2,400 hospices are provider members of the NHO. As a member, each hospice program receives technical assistance, publications (including *NHO NewsLine*, *Hospice Professional*, *Medicare Updates*, the *Guide to the Nation's Hospices*, committee publications, and monographs), savings on conference registrations and NHO store purchases, and voting privileges. In addition, more than five thousand hospice professionals and volunteers have joined the NHO as members of the National Council of Hospice Professionals (NCHP). Each NCHP member receives the peri-

odicals *Hospice Professional* and the *Hospice Journal*, significant discounts on NHO educational programs and NHO store purchases, technical assistance from staff and colleagues, and free access to the NHO Job Bank Hotline. The Job Bank can be accessed via telephone and through the Web site.

The NCHP provides individuals an opportunity to participate in the NHO and in the hospice community through the development of programs, publications, and activities that focus on the individual hospice professional within the hospice disciplinary team. Membership in the NCHP provides an opportunity to network and communicate with others in a specific field.

The NHO has developed a comprehensive library of books, directories, audio tapes, and video tapes related to hospice. This resource center, located in Arlington, Virginia, is available for use by NHO members by appointment. The NHO hosts two conferences each year: the Management and Leadership Conference, and the Annual Symposium and Exposition. While all members of the hospice team often attend the symposium, the majority of the sessions are aimed at the clinical team members, those who work directly with patients and families. With more than one hundred educational sessions, a growing exposition, and countless networking opportunities, this is the definitive conference for hospice professionals.

**National Osteoporosis Foundation (NOF)**
1150 17th Street, NW
Suite 500
Washington, D.C. 20036
Ph.: (202) 223-2226
Fax: (202) 223-2237
The National Osteoporosis Foundation (NOF) is the nation's leading authority on the diagnosis, prevention, and treatment of osteoporosis. Established in 1986 as the only nonprofit voluntary health organization dedicated to reducing the widespread prevalence of osteoporosis in the United States, the foundation has developed programs, policies, and strategies designed to comprehensively address this major public health problem.

**National Senior Citizens Law Center (NSCLC)**
1101 14th Street, NW
Suite 400

Washington, D.C. 20005
Ph.: (202) 289-6976
Fax: (202) 289-7224
E-mail: *nsclc@nsclc.org*
Web site: *http://www.nsclc.org*
The National Senior Citizens Law Center (NSCLC) provides technical assistance, research information, litigation support, and administrative and legislative advocacy services to senior citizens. The organization promotes the independence and well-being of low-income elderly individuals, as well as of persons with disabilities, with particular emphasis on women and racial and ethnic minorities. As a national support center, the NSCLC advocates through litigation, legislative and agency representation, and assistance to attorneys and paralegals in field programs. The NSCLC is a member of America's Charities, a coalition of nearly one hundred charitable organizations that provide direct services in thousands of local communities.

### National Senior Service Corps Directors Association (NSSCDA)

4958 Butterworth Place, NW
Washington, D.C. 20016
Ph.: (202) 244-2244
Fax: (202) 244-2322
The National Senior Service Corps Directors Association (NSSCDA) is composed of three private, nonprofit membership organizations of project directors from each of the three National Senior Service Corps (NSSC) programs, as well as their sponsors and supporters, who work together to enhance and build the Retired Senior Volunteer Program (RSVP), the Foster Grandparents Programs, and the Senior Companion Program and to advocate for older people. By working collaboratively, the National Association of Retired Senior Volunteer Program Directors (NARSVPD), the National Association of Foster Grandparent Program Directors (NAFGPD), and the National Association of Senior Companion Program Directors (NASCPD) are better able to amplify their message of productive aging to policymakers and to the public.

### Older Women's League (OWL)

666 11th Street, NW
Suite 700
Washington, D.C. 20001
Ph.: (202) 783-6686
Fax: (202) 638-2356
The Older Women's League (OWL) is a national grassroots membership organization that works to achieve economic and social equity for women, improve the image and status of midlife and older women, and to provide mutual support for its members. Membership is open to people of all ages who share these concerns. OWL is active in education, advocacy, research, and special programs to celebrate the contributions of older women to society. See entry in *Aging*.

### United Auto Workers (UAW) Retired and Older Workers Department

8731 E. Jefferson Avenue
Detroit, MI 48214
Ph.: (313) 926-5231
Fax: (313) 926-5666
The United Auto Workers (UAW) Retired and Older Workers Department was established in 1957 to develop programs and provide services to UAW retirees. The UAW constitution mandates each local union with twenty-five or more retirees to establish a retiree chapter. In 1999, there were 791 chartered chapters. The constitution also requires the establishment of regional councils, as well as area and international area councils. A retiree regional council has been set up in each UAW region. The regional director establishes area councils where there are too few local unions or too few retired members to organize chapters. International area councils are established by the Retired and Older Workers Department to provide services to retirees who live in those parts of the country where there are no local unions but where retirees now live. In 1999, there were a total of thirty-three international area councils. The organization also provides UAW retirees with counseling services and other problem-solving matters at drop-in centers located throughout the United States.

—*Mary E. Allen*

# NOTABLE PEOPLE IN THE STUDY OR IMAGE OF AGING

**Arthur, Beatrice** (1923?-    ; b. Bernice Frankel). American television actress. Arthur exemplified the independent middle-aged or older woman in situation comedies, first on the *All in the Family* spinoff *Maude* (1972-1978), and then as Dorothy on *The Golden Girls* (1985-1992).

**Atchley, Robert C.** (1939-    ). American sociologist. Atchley taught at Miami University in Ohio and at Naropa University. He played leadership roles in the American Society on Aging, the Gerontological Society of America, the Association for Gerontology in Higher Education, and the Conscious Aging Task Force of the Omega Institute. His book *The Social Forces in Later Life* (1972), revised as *Social Forces and Aging* (9th ed.; 1999), is a standard.

**Ball, Lucille** (1911-1989). American television and film actress. She starred in the beloved series *I Love Lucy* (1951-1957), with husband Desi Arnaz, as a middle-aged wife and mother trying to enter show business. After their divorce, Ball played an independent older woman in the series *The Lucy Show* (1962-1968) and *Here's Lucy* (1968-1974).

**Baltes, Paul B.** (1939-    ). German-American psychologist. Baltes built upon the work of Erik H. Erikson in the study of wisdom and successful aging from a cognitive prospective. Baltes taught and conducted research in both the United States and Germany. His work in life span developmental psychology and gerontology produced important books and papers, such as *Successful Aging* (1990), edited with wife Margret.

**Bengtson, Vern L.** (1941-    ). American sociologist. Bengtson conducted research on the family as head of the University of Southern California Gerontology Program. The focus of much of his studies was on intergenerational relations. One of his longitudinal studies began in 1971.

**Bismarck, Otto von** (1815-1898). German chancellor (1871-1890). In 1880, Bismarck instituted the first program of old-age pensions, which were made available at sixty-five. This became the official age for retirement, and a marker for old age, in most Western countries.

**Brennan, William J., Jr.** (1906-1997). U.S. Supreme Court justice. Appointed to the Court in 1956, Brennan continued to hear cases until 1990, when he retired at the age of eighty-four.

**Burns, George** (1896-1996; b. Nathan Birnbaum). American vaudevillian and film actor. Burns gained fame for his act with wife Gracie Allen, who died in 1964. He made a comeback at the age of seventy-nine with the film *The Sunshine Boys* (1975) and went on to star in *Oh, God!* (1977), *Going in Style* (1979), and *Eighteen Again!* (1988). Burns became a symbol for successful aging. He performed stand-up comedy routines, usually about old age, until his death at one hundred.

**Butler, Robert N.** (1927-    ). American physician. As director of the National Institute on Aging, Butler wrote *Why Survive? Being Old in America* (1975) to examine "ageism," a term coined in that Pulitzer Prize-winning work. *Why Survive?* launched many areas of social gerontology and senior rights groups such as the Gray Panthers. Butler also studied mental health and aging. He was associated with the American Association of Retired Persons (AARP) and served as president of the International Longevity Center in New York City.

**Calment, Jeanne** (1875-1997). Frenchwoman. For many years, Calment was officially the world's oldest person. She took up fencing at eighty-five and continued to ride a bicycle at one hundred. She attributed her longevity to port wine, olive oil, and chocolate. She gave up smoking in 1995 only because she could no longer light her own cigarettes. Calment gave many interviews and became a popular media figure.

**Camp, Cameron J.** (1952-    ). American psychologist. Camp became known for his studies on memory training, especially for patients with Alzheimer's disease. He worked for the Myers Research Institute, Menorah Park Center for the Aging, and at the University of Akron. Camp is one of the authors of *Adult Development and Aging* (1996).

**Coleman, Paul D.** (1927-    ). American neuroscientist. With Steve Buell, Coleman demonstrated that the dendrites of neurons grow in normal aging brains. Until this work, it was assumed that no brain development occurs in later years. Coleman taught in the neurobiology and anatomy department at the University of Rochester.

**Costa, Paul T., Jr.** (1942-    ) and **Robert R. McCrae** (1949-    ). American psychologists. Costa and McCrae both worked at the Laboratory of Personality and Cognition at the National Institute on Aging. They developed the NEO Personality Inventory-Revised and wrote *Personality in Adulthood* (1990). Costa and McCrae found that personality is quite stable in adulthood, findings that challenge the idea of a midlife crisis.

**Cotman, Carl W.** (1940-    ). American neuroscientist. As director of the Institute for Brain Aging and Dementia at the University of California, Irvine, Cotman became known for his work on the role of neurotransmitters in the aging brain. He advanced the understanding of Alzheimer's disease.

**Cronyn, Hume** (1911-    ). American film and theater actor. Cronyn often worked with his wife, Jessica Tandy. In their later years, they starred in plays and films addressing aging, such as *The Gin Game* (1984) and *Cocoon* (1985). Cronyn cowrote the play *Foxfire* (1982), for which Tandy won a Tony Award.

**Dalí, Salvador** (1904-1989). Spanish surrealist painter and writer. The eccentric Dalí was known for his distinctive moustache and his dream imagery, such as melting clocks. His prolific career spanned six decades.

**Delany, Sadie** (1889-1999; b. Sarah Louise) and **Bessie Delany** (1891-1995; b. Annie Elizabeth). African American sisters. Sadie was a teacher, and Bessie was a dentist. In 1993, they wrote *Having Our Say: The Delany Sisters' First One Hundred Years*, which described their extraordinary lives and made them celebrities.

**Dole, Bob** (1923-    ). U.S. senator from Kansas. Dole won the Republican Party's presidential nomination in 1996, at seventy-three. Some critics and humorists focused on his age as a liability. After losing the election to Bill Clinton, Dole stayed in the public eye by speaking out, from personal experience, about prostate cancer screening and treatments for erectile dysfunction, such as the drug Viagra.

**Elder, Glen H., Jr.** (1934-    ). American sociologist. Elder became known for studies on the effects of the Great Depression on adults. He found risk factors for stress during social upheaval as well as variables that made the Depression a positive experience for others; for example, certain women had positive outcomes lasting into their seventies. Elder's work is cited by those studying the effects of social change on a particular generation.

**Elizabeth, the Queen Mother** (1900-    ; b. Elizabeth Bowes-Lyon). British royal. Queen of Great Britain as the wife of George VI, she became known as the Queen Mother after the accession of her daughter Queen Elizabeth II to the throne. Immensely popular with the public, in her advanced years she remained active in the traditions of her prominent but troubled family.

**Erikson, Erik H.** (1902-1994). German psychologist. Erikson was famous for his eight stages of psychosocial development, which included three stages in adulthood. His stages of generativity (in middle age) and ego integrity (in old age) are included in every aging textbook and are cited in most works on understanding the self and relationships in adulthood. See entry in *Aging*.

**Fonda, Henry** (1905-1982). American film actor. After a long and celebrated career, Fonda won his first Academy Award as Best Actor at age seventy-seven for his role as an aging father in *On Golden Pond* (1981). Because he was too ill to take the stage, daughter and costar Jane Fonda accepted for him.

**Franklin, Benjamin** (1706-1790). American diplomat, inventor, scientist, businessman, and writer. Franklin spent his seventies as a diplomat at the court of Louis XVI in France and served as an important member of the Constitutional Convention of 1787. He was active in politics and social issues until his death at age eighty-four.

**Friedan, Betty** (1921-    ; b. Betty Goldstein). American feminist. Friedan gained fame for her book *The Feminine Mystique* (1963), which addressed the lack of fulfillment among white, middle-class housewives. She tackled the social perceptions of older people in *The Fountain of Age* (1993).

**Fry, Christine L.** *See* **Keith, Jennie**

**Glenn, John** (1921-    ). American astronaut and U.S. senator from Ohio. In 1962, as one of the original NASA astronauts, he became the first

American to orbit the earth. Glenn was elected to the U.S. Senate from Ohio in 1975. In 1998, at the age of seventy-seven, he returned to space as a member of a shuttle crew, this time to test the effects of zero gravity on the aged body. He became the oldest person to travel into space.

**Gordon, Ruth** (1896-1985). American film and theater actress, playwright, and screenwriter. Gordon won an Academy Award as Best Supporting Actress for *Rosemary's Baby* (1968). She earned a cultlike following for her starring role as a vivacious, eccentric woman turning eighty in *Harold and Maude* (1971).

**Graham, Martha** (1893-1991). American dancer, choreographer, and teacher. Graham had the greatest influence on modern dance in the twentieth century. She retired from dancing in 1970, at seventy-seven. Graham continued to choreograph, arranging Igor Stravinsky's *Rite of Spring* at the age of ninety.

**Griffith, Andy** (1926-    ). American film and television actor. Eighteen years after *The Andy Griffith Show* (1960-1968) ended, Griffith returned to television as a folksy detective in *Matlock* (1986-1995). NBC canceled the series in 1992, despite its continuing popularity among seniors, but ABC picked up the show for another three seasons.

**Hayflick, Leonard** (1928-    ). American biologist. Hayflick became known for his work on the causes of aging, primarily his theory about programmed cell death. He showed that cells can replicate only a certain number of times, known as the Hayflick limit. He is the author of *How and Why We Age* (1996).

**Hepburn, Katharine** (1909-    ). American film actress. Hepburn won four Academy Awards as Best Actress, three of them in her later years for her roles in *Guess Who's Coming to Dinner?* (1967), *The Lion in Winter* (1968), and *On Golden Pond* (1981). She remained active and outspoken throughout her life.

**Hope, Bob** (1903-    ; b. Leslie Townes Hope). American entertainer and humanitarian. A film actor, USO performer, and host of annual television specials, Hope had a contract with NBC for sixty years. He and wife Dolores contributed time and money to numerous charities and received many honors: The U.S. Congress named him an honorary veteran, Queen Elizabeth II

bestowed on him an honorary knighthood, and Pope John Paul II awarded him the papal knighthood and Dolores the title Dame of St. Gregory.

**Hopper, Grace Murray** (1906-1992). American mathematician and computer pioneer. In the 1950's, as a member of the U.S. Navy, she worked on such computer languages as FLOW-MATIC and COBOL. Rear Admiral Hopper retired in 1986, at age eighty, as the oldest active Navy officer.

**Jackson, James S.** (1944-    ). American sociologist. Jackson is known for his psychological work on the African American family, particularly the elderly. He is the author of *Life in Black America* (1991).

**Kahn, Robert L.** *See* **Rowe, John W.**

**Kalish, Richard A.** (1930-    ). American sociologist. A behavioral scientist in the field of death and dying, Kalish coined the term "new ageism." He theorized that at least three factors contribute to diminished death anxiety in the old. Kalish is the author of *The Psychology of Human Behavior* (1969) and *Death, Grief, and Caring Relationships* (1981).

**Keith, Jennie** (1942-    ) and **Christine L. Fry** (1943-    ). American anthropologists. Keith and Fry studied the aging process in very diverse societies. With other authors, they wrote *New Methods for Old-Age Research* (1986) and *The Aging Experience: Diversity and Commonality Across Cultures* (1994).

**Kennedy, Rose Fitzgerald** (1890-1995). American matriarch. As the wife of Joseph Kennedy, Sr., U.S. ambassador to Great Britain, and the mother of President John F. Kennedy and Senators Robert F. and Edward (Ted) Kennedy, Rose Kennedy helped shape the foremost political dynasty in the United States until her death at 105.

**Kevorkian, Jack** (1928-    ). American physician. Kevorkian provided the medical means for over a hundred people to end their lives. He used a suicide machine, an apparatus that dispensed lethal drugs when the patient pushed a button. The majority of his patients were middle-aged and older women, despite the fact that the suicide rate is highest for elderly men. The publicity surrounding his cases helped focus the national debate about physician-assisted suicide.

**Kleemeier, Robert W.** (1915-    ). American sociologist. Kleemeier, a former president of the Gerontological Society of America, made exemplary contributions to the quality of life through research in aging.

**Kübler-Ross, Elizabeth** (1926-    ). Swiss-American psychiatrist. Kübler-Ross described five distinct stages through which many terminally ill patients pass: denial, anger, bargaining, depression, and acceptance. She wrote in *On Death and Dying* (1969) that each stage acts as a defense mechanism against the fear of death. See entry in *Aging*.

**Kuhn, Maggie** (1905-1995). American social activist. In 1971, Kuhn founded the Consultation of Older and Younger Adults for Social Change, which was soon renamed the Gray Panthers. She worked for nursing home reform, fought ageism, and claimed that "old people constitute America's biggest untapped and undervalued human energy source." See entry in *Aging*.

**Kurosawa, Akira** (1910-1998). Japanese director. Kurosawa continued to make critically acclaimed films in his eighties, even after he became blind.

**La Lanne, Jack** (1914-    ). American fitness guru. Known as the Godfather of Physical Fitness, La Lanne began in the fitness business in 1936 and was still going strong in his eighties thanks to a vegetarian diet and an intense exercise regimen. Throughout his career, he encouraged seniors to become more active in order to lead healthier, longer lives.

**Lansbury, Angela** (1925-    ). American film, theater, and television actress. After a long career on stage and screen, Lansbury played the role of older mystery writer and amateur detective Jessica Fletcher on the popular series *Murder, She Wrote* (1984-1996).

**Lawton, M. Powell** (1923-    ). American sociologist. Lawton became known for his studies on the fit between person and environment and how that fit affects competence in the elderly. His work shows that, as with other groups, the optimal environment for the elderly involves challenge.

**Lemmon, Jack** (1925-    ). American film actor. Lemmon's later roles, often opposite Walter Matthau, appealed to older audiences. They starred in *Grumpy Old Men* (1993), *Grumpier Old Men* (1995), *Out to Sea* (1997), and *The Odd Couple II* (1998). Lemmon also starred in *My Fellow Americans* (1996) as a former U.S. president.

**Levinson, Daniel** (1920-    ). American psychologist. Levinson is known for *The Seasons of a Man's Life* (1978), the first book to address the concept of midlife crisis. He outlined the stages that men may go through in adulthood, and his later research provided information on women's stages as well.

**Lopata, Helena** (1925-    ). American sociologist. Lopata became known for her work on styles of widowhood, begun when she worked with Bernice Neugarten on the Kansas City Studies. She is the author of *Widows and Dependent Wives* (1985) and *Current Widowhood: Myths and Realities* (1996).

**McCrae, Robert R.** *See* **Costa, Paul T., Jr.**

**Marshall, Thurgood** (1908-1993). U.S. Supreme Court justice. Marshall became the first African American to sit on the Court. He fought for the rights of many groups, including the elderly, and voted against forced retirement. Marshall continued to hear cases until 1991, when he retired at the age of eighty-three.

**Matisse, Henri** (1869-1954). French painter. During the early 1930's, Matisse traveled in Europe and the United States. From 1949 to 1951, in his eighties, he decorated a Dominican chapel near Nice, France.

**Matthau, Walter** (1920-    ; b. Walter Matuschanskayasky). American film actor. Matthau's later roles, often opposite Jack Lemmon, appealed to older audiences. They starred in *Grumpy Old Men* (1993), *Grumpier Old Men* (1995), *Out to Sea* (1997), and *The Odd Couple II* (1998). Matthau also starred in *I'm Not Rappaport* (1996) and as Albert Einstein in *I.Q.* (1994).

**Michelangelo** (1475-1564). Italian painter, sculptor, and architect. A prominent figure of the Renaissance, Michelangelo was named the chief architect of Saint Peter's in Rome at the age of seventy-one. He continued to produce artworks until his death at eighty-eight.

**Moses, Grandma** (1860-1961; b. Anna Mary Robertson). American folk artist. Moses took up painting in her seventies after the death of her husband. She became known for primitive paintings depicting rural life in the nineteenth and twentieth century United States.

**Myerhoff, Barbara G.** (1936?-1985). American anthropologist. Myerhoff became known for her work with the urban elderly, especially the elderly Jews of Los Angeles, as depicted in the book and Academy Award-winning documentary *Number Our Days*. With Myerhoff's work, the anthropological study of the urban elderly grew tremendously.

**Neugarten, Bernice** (1916-    ). American sociologist. Neugarten started work on adult development and aging in the Kansas City Studies of Adult Life in the 1950's. Out of those studies emerged such important research topics as grandparenting styles, age expectations and stereotypes, perceptions of the menopause, widowhood, and the effect of personality on the aging process. See entry in *Aging*.

**Newman, Paul** (1925-    ). American film actor and businessman. A longtime favorite with critics and audiences, Newman won his first Academy Award at age sixty-one for *The Color of Money* (1986) for a reprisal of his character Fast Eddie Felson from *The Hustler* (1961). In the 1980's, he started a successful nonprofit food company called Newman's Own, and he continued his hobby of car racing into his seventies.

**O'Keeffe, Georgia** (1887-1986). American painter. By 1971, O'Keeffe's eyesight had begun to fail, and she gradually gave up painting. In 1973, Juan Hamilton, a young potter who became her companion and business manager, encouraged her to start painting again. In 1976, they wrote a book about her art, and a film crew shot a documentary at O'Keeffe's Ghost Ranch. She remained active into her nineties.

**Palmer, Arnold** (1929-    ). American golfer. Palmer won four Master championships in the 1950's and 1960's. In the 1980's, he became a popular fixture on the Senior PGA Tour, winning ten tournaments. In 1998, he played in his forty-fourth Masters but was sidelined briefly for treatment of prostate cancer.

**Pauling, Linus** (1901-1994). American chemist and pacifist. Pauling won Nobel Prizes in Chemistry (1954) and in Peace (1962). By the time of his death at age ninety-three, however, he was probably better known for his work on nutrition. He made talk-show appearances, published papers, and made presentations about a nutritional healing specialty he named "ortho-

molecular medicine." Pauling wrote best-selling books on vitamin C, the common cold, and cancer.

**Pepper, Claude** (1900-1989). U.S. representative from Florida. Pepper became known nationwide for his advocacy of the rights of older Americans. He was first elected to the House of Representatives in 1962 and served until his death at age eighty-nine. As the oldest member of Congress in his last years, he defended Social Security and opposed retirement restrictions.

**Picasso, Pablo** (1881-1973). Spanish painter and sculptor. Picasso gained fame for his cubist works and bullfighting scenes, among numerous styles and subjects. He continued to be a prolific and influential artist until his death at age ninety-one.

**Poon, Leonard** (1942-    ). American psychologist. Poon became known for his work on memory and aging. He headed the Georgia Centenarian Study, one of the largest studies on centenarians in the United States.

**Randall, Tony** (1920-    ; b. Leonard Rosenberg). American film and television actor. Randall became best known as the fussy Felix Unger on the series *The Odd Couple* (1970-1975). He founded the National Actors Theatre in 1992 and made headlines in 1997 by becoming a first-time father at the age of seventy-seven.

**Reagan, Ronald** (1911-    ). U.S. president (1981-1989). Reagan was first elected president at the age of seventy. When he left office, at seventy-eight, he was the oldest person to serve as president. In 1994, Reagan announced that he was suffering from Alzheimer's disease, thus raising awareness of this debilitating condition.

**Rowe, John W.** (1944-    ) and **Robert L. Kahn** (1918-    ). American researchers. Rowe, a gerontologist, and Kahn, a psychologist, wrote the popular book *Successful Aging* (1998), a study funded by the MacArthur Foundation. This work argues that, as people age, social and physical habits become more important to maintaining health than genetic predispositions to certain diseases.

**Salthouse, Timothy** (1947-    ). American psychologist. Salthouse became well known for his work on cognition. In a famous study, he found that while young typists have quicker keystrokes, experienced elderly typists get their work done as fast by reading further ahead in the material and thus not stopping as often. His work has been used in the fight against age discrimination in employment.

**Sanders, Harland** (1890-1980). American businessman. Known as Colonel Sanders, he opened his first restaurant in 1939. In 1952, at the age of sixty-two, he granted the first franchise in what became the international chain Kentucky Fried Chicken. In 1964, Sanders sold the company for two million dollars but stayed on as spokesperson.

**Sarton, May** (1912-1995). Belgian-American writer. Sarton examined the experience of aging in her poetry and novels and in her journals, including *At Seventy: A Journal* (1984), *Endgame: A Journal of the Seventy-ninth Year* (1992), *Encore: A Journal of the Eightieth Year* (1993), and *At Eighty-two: A Journal* (1996). See entry in *Aging*.

**Schaie, K. Warner** (1928-    ). American psychologist. Schaie became best known for his work on intelligence and aging. His longitudinal study of intelligence began in the early 1970's. Schaie's work showed that intelligence does not decline much in the healthy elderly. He taught at Pennsylvania State University.

**Sheehy, Gail** (1937-    ). American writer. Sheehy wrote the popular books *Passages: Predictable Crises of Adult Life* (1976) and *The Silent Passage: Menopause* (1992). Some claim that Sheehy stole Daniel Levinson's theories to serve as the backbone for *Passages*. See entry in *Aging*.

**Shock, Nathan** (1906-1989). American sociologist. Shock was a pioneer in gerontological research at the National Institutes of Health and a founding member of the Gerontological Society of America. The society's Nathan Shock New Investigator Award is given for outstanding contributions to knowledge about aging through basic biological research.

**Skinner, B. F.** (1904-1990). American behavioral psychologist. Skinner was the foremost authority in his field for several decades. An incredibly productive scholar, he published hundreds of books and articles during his career as professor at Harvard University. As he aged, Skinner developed lifestyle strategies in order to continue doing the work that he loved, a process he described in *Enjoy Old Age* (1983).

**Stuart, Gloria** (1910-    ). American film actress. Stuart returned to the screen after a fifty-three-year absence to play the 101-year-old Rose in *Titanic* (1997). At the age of eighty-seven, she received an Academy Award nomination as Best Supporting Actress for that performance.

**Tandy, Jessica** (1909-1994). American film and theater actress. Tandy often worked with her husband, Hume Cronyn. In their later years, they starred in plays and films about the experience of aging, such as *The Gin Game* (1984) and *Cocoon* (1985). Tandy won a Tony for the play *Foxfire* (1982), cowritten by Cronyn, and an Academy Award as Best Actress for *Driving Miss Daisy* (1989) at the age of eighty.

**Teresa, Mother** (1910-1997; b. Agnes Gonxha Bejaxhiu). Albanian nun. Mother Teresa founded the Missionaries of Charity in 1950 in Calcutta, India. She spent the rest of her life tending to the "poorest of the poor" and was awarded the 1979 Nobel Peace Prize for her work. Soon after death at age eighty-seven, the Catholic Church began an investigation into naming her a saint.

**Thurmond, Strom** (1902-    ). U.S. senator from South Carolina. Thurmond began his first term in 1954, and his reelection in 1996 at the age of ninety-four made him the oldest person ever to serve in Congress.

**Townsend, Francis Everett** (1867-1960). American physician. His campaign for federally funded old-age pensions became known as the Townsend movement.

**Walford, Roy** (1924-    ). American physician. Walford gained fame for his work on life extension through low-calorie, nutrient-rich diet and exercise. He became particularly known for his work with the experiments Biosphere 1 and 2.

**Wood, Beatrice** (1893-1998). American potter, ceramist, artist, and photographer. Known as the "Mama of Dada" for her association with painter Marcel Duchamp during World War I, Wood continued to work until her death at age 105. The inspiration for the 101-year-old character of Rose in the film *Titanic* (1997), she cited "chocolate and young men" as the keys to her longevity.

# AGING

# LIST OF ENTRIES BY CATEGORY

## CULTURAL ISSUES

Advertising
African Americans
Ageism
American Indians
Asian Americans
Baby boomers
Beauty
Communication
Cultural views of aging
Films
Gay men and lesbians
Grandparenthood
Great-grandparenthood
Greeting cards
Internet
Jewish services for the elderly
Latinos
Leisure activities
Maturity
Men and aging
Middle age
National Asian Pacific Center on Aging
National Caucus and Center on Black Aged
National Hispanic Council on Aging
Old age
Over the hill
Parenthood
Religion
Stereotypes
Television
Women and aging

## DEATH AND DYING

Acquired immunodeficiency syndrome (AIDS)
Breast cancer
Cancer
*Cocoon*
Death and dying
Death anxiety
Death of a child
Death of parents
Depression
Durable power of attorney
Estates and inheritance
Euthanasia
Funerals
Grief

*Harold and Maude*
Heart attacks
Hospice
*I Never Sang for My Father*
"Jilting of Granny Weatherall, The"
Kübler-Ross, Elisabeth
Life expectancy
Living wills
*Memento Mori*
Pets
Prostate cancer
Psychiatry, geriatric
Remarriage
*Robin and Marian*
*Shootist, The*
Stress and coping skills
Strokes
Suicide
*Tell Me a Riddle*
Terminal illness
Trusts
Widows and widowers
Wills and bequests
*Woman's Tale, A*

## EMPLOYMENT ISSUES

Absenteeism
Adult education
Age discrimination
Age Discrimination Act of 1975
Age Discrimination in Employment Act of 1967
Americans with Disabilities Act
Dual-income couples
Early retirement
Employment
Executive Order 11141
Forced retirement
Job loss
*Johnson v. Mayor and City Council of Baltimore*
*Massachusetts Board of Retirement v. Murgia*
*Matlock*
Mentoring
*Murder, She Wrote*
Older Americans Act of 1965
Older Workers Benefit Protection Act
Retired Senior Volunteer Program (RSVP)
Retirement
Retirement planning

# INDEX